YOU JUST GAINED ACCESS TO

ATLAS™

YOUR ONLINE LEARNING PLATFORM!

Atlas will take you through this book and give you access to a host of additional resources, including:

- A free, full-length official practice exam with exclusive data analysis to pinpoint you strengths and weaknesses as well as thorough explanations for every problem

- Bonus lessons to build your mastery of LSAT content and extra drills to hone your newfound skills

HOW TO ACCESS ATLAS

Go to manhattanprep.com/lsat/access and follow the instructions on the screen.

Online resource access can only be granted for a single account; the guide cannot be registered a second time for a different account.

You have one year from the date of purchase to complete your registration.

MANHATTAN
PREP

Acknowledgements

A great number of people were involved in the creation of the book you are holding.

Our Manhattan Prep resources are based on the continuing experiences of our instructors and students. The overall vision for this edition was rooted in the content expertise of Brian Birdwell, Laura Damone, Dmitry Farber, Scott Miller, Matt Sherman, Matt Shinners, and Noah Teitelbaum, who determined what strategies to cover and how to weave them into a cohesive whole.

Misti Duvall and Dmitry Farber updated this edition for the new digital format of the LSAT, and Stacey Koprince served as a sounding board during this process.

Derek Frankhouser lent his deft hand to the layout of this edition. Matthew Callan coordinated the production work. Once the manuscript was done, Laura Damone edited and Nomi Beesen proofread the guide. Carly Schnur designed the covers.

LSAT Logic Games: Strategy Guide + Online Resources, 6th Edition

Retail ISBN: 978-1-5062-6562-9
Course ISBN: 978-1-5062-6564-3
Retail eISBN: 978-1-5062-6563-6
Course eISBN: 978-1-5062-6565-0

Layout Design: Derek Frankhouser

MANHATTAN PREP

LSAT Logic Games

Strategy Guide

This comprehensive guide breaks down the Logic Games section and arms you with the tools to tackle any game. Written to be a teacher-in-a-book, this guide also includes numerous drills and solutions to push you to your top form.

Strategy Guide Series

LSAT Logic Games
(ISBN: 978-1-5062-6562-9)

LSAT Reading Comprehension
(ISBN: 978-1-5062-6570-4)

LSAT Logical Reasoning
(ISBN: 978-1-5062-6566-7)

February 4, 2020

Dear Student,

Thank you for picking up a copy *LSAT Logic Games*. I hope this book provides just the guidance you need to get the most out of your LSAT studies.

At Manhattan Prep, we continually aspire to provide the best instructors and resources possible. If you have any questions or feedback, please do not hesitate to contact us.

Email our Student Services team at lsat@manhattanprep.com or give us a shout at 212-721-7400 (or 800-576-4628 in the United States or Canada). We try to keep all our books free of errors, but if you think we've goofed, please visit manhattanprep.com/LSAT/errata.

Our Manhattan Prep Strategy Guides are based on the continuing experiences of both our instructors and our students. The authorship of the 6th Edition LSAT Logic Games guide was a collaborative effort by instructors Brian Birdwell, Laura Damone, Scott Miller, Matt Sherman, Matt Shinners, and Noah Teitelbaum. Project management was led by Matthew Callan.

Finally, we are indebted to all of the Manhattan Prep students who have given us excellent feedback over the years. This book wouldn't be half of what it is without their voice.

And now that *you* are one of our students too, please chime in! I look forward to hearing from you. Thanks again and best of luck preparing for the LSAT!

Sincerely,

Chris Ryan
Executive Director, Product Strategy

HOW TO ACCESS YOUR ONLINE RESOURCES

Go to **www.manhattanprep.com/lsat/access** and follow the instructions on the screen.

Online resource access can only be granted for a single account; the guide cannot be registered a second time for a different account.

You have one year from the date of purchase to complete your registration.

TABLE *of* CONTENTS

Chapter 1

Introduction

In This Chapter...

Logic Games

The Logic Games section of the LSAT is designed to test your ability to organize lots of pieces of information and then to make inferences—to figure out what must be true based on the given facts. When you get past the often ridiculous details—patients in a waiting room, dogs at the groomers, clowns in cars—it's not too hard to see how this section is testing skills used by law students. In law school, you'll be asked to organize lots of information, and you'll be asked to draw many inferences. And, if you are working during law school, you might even be putting dogs in order.

In order to do well on the Logic Games section, you need to be organized and consistent. You also need to be creative and flexible. These characteristics might seem like polar opposites, but, in fact, being organized is what will allow you to be creative, just as being consistent will allow you to be flexible.

The Logic Games (LG) section of the LSAT is often more intimidating to students than Reading Comprehension (RC) and Logical Reasoning (LR). Few of us have played more than the occasional Sudoku puzzle, but all of us have read passages and answered questions about them. And it's safe to say that all of us have had to reason logically. This intimidation factor actually works in your favor. With the proper preparation, you will be confident during a section that leaves many people cowering on test day. Dramatic improvements on this section are definitely possible, but it's hard to do this alone! So commit to mastering this crazy section; we're right beside you.

By the way, it's not smart to start our relationship with a lie, so we must confess that the Logic Games section of the LSAT is really called "Analytical Reasoning." But that's the last time we'll ever refer to Logic Games by the official name.

Where Logic Games Fit in the Big Picture

As of September 2019, the LSAT is administered digitally in North America. When you arrive at the testing center, you'll be given a tablet, a stylus that doubles as a pen, and some scratch paper. The tablet will allow you to make certain annotations: underlining, highlighting, eliminating answers, selecting answers, and flagging questions to come back to later. Any freehand writing or drawing must be done on scratch paper.

The Logic Games section is composed of four games, each of which has 5–7 associated questions. Overall, the section usually has 22–23 questions. The games tend to be arranged in ascending order of difficulty. However, it's unusual that you will experience the four games of a section in exactly that way. Don't be surprised, for example, if the second game is tougher for you than the third.

1

The entire LSAT exam contains five sections and an essay:

Section	Questions	Scored?	Time
Logic Games	22–23	yes	35 minutes
Reading Comprehension	26–28	yes	35 minutes
Logical Reasoning (1)	24–26	yes	35 minutes
Logical Reasoning (2)	24–26	yes	35 minutes
Experimental	22–28	no	35 minutes
Essay	1 essay	no	35 minutes

The five sections can come in any order. In previous years, the essay, formally known as the LSAT Writing Sample, was given on test day, at the testing center, and was always the last section of the exam. The Writing Sample is now administered online, can be completed from home, and does *not* have to be completed on test day. It is also not factored into your overall score.

The other piece of the LSAT puzzle that isn't factored into your overall score is the experimental section. The experimental section is used by the LSAT wizards (test writers) to test-drive questions and sections, and to calibrate their difficulty. You won't know which section is experimental, but it will be an additional Logical Reasoning, Reading Comprehension, or Logic Games section. Thus, you might receive two Logic Games sections on your LSAT.

Every question outside of those in the experimental section is worth exactly one point. Guessing is not penalized, so it's to your advantage to select an answer for every question! It's also to your advantage to move on quickly from questions that seem impossibly difficult in order to invest your time in questions that seem within reach.

In total, you'll see approximately 100 scored questions. The number of questions you answer correctly is your raw score, which is then converted into a scaled score from 120–180, and a percentile. That scaled score and percentile ranking tells law school admissions officers how you rank compared to other test-takers. The calculations done by the Law School Admission Council (LSAC, the organization that writes and administers the LSAT) are perhaps fascinating, but they're generally irrelevant to your preparation. One thing to know is that because each test is slightly different in difficulty, the conversion scale (used to convert raw scores to scaled scores) varies slightly from test to test. However, the variation is not large.

MANHATTAN
PREP

Here's a sample conversion scale:

Raw Score (minimum correct out of 100 total questions)	Scaled Score	Percentile Rank (the percentage of test-takers you outperformed)
99	180	99.9
95	175	99.5
89	170	97.5
82	165	91.5
74	160	80.1
65	155	63.1
57	150	44.1

Since your score depends on how many questions you get correct, it's actually helpful to think about how many you can get wrong and still reach your target score. Is your target score a 180? Probably not! If you don't have a target score in mind, go ahead and do some research on the schools that interest you and what GPA and LSAT score will give you a good chance of getting in. If you poke around on the LSAC website, you'll find a calculator that can help you do that. Set an initial target score for yourself based on the "easiest" school you'd be happy to attend, and once you reach that score, raise the bar.

One more note about the scores: Some people spend a lot of energy worrying about whether a particular LSAT is going to be harder than other ones. But since the scores are scaled, the difficulty of a particular test is generally of no importance to your performance. If you get an "easy" LSAT, so will everyone else, and thus the "curve" will be a bit less generous. Instead of focusing on issues that you can't control and that don't really affect your score, let's start learning about logic games!

A Quick Vocabulary Lesson

So that you know what we're talking about, let's define the terms we'll use to discuss logic games:

1. The **scenario** introduces the **elements**—usually people's names or letters representing objects—and provides the context in which those elements are to be organized:

> On Monday, seven trains—F, G, H, J, K, M, and N—leave Rivertown Station consecutively and one at a time. No other trains leave the station on Monday.

We sometimes refer to the set of elements as the **roster.**

2. The **rules** (also called **constraints**) impose limitations on the relationships between the elements and the **positions** in which they are to be placed (in this case, the positions are ordered):

> Train J is the first or seventh train to leave the station.
> Train H leaves the station before train M, and exactly two trains leave the station between H
> and M.

1

Train N leaves the station either immediately before or immediately after train M.

Train K leaves the station third.

3. The **questions** ask you to make inferences based on the scenario, the rules, and perhaps an additional limitation introduced by the question. We sometimes refer to the question itself as the **question stem.** Here's an example of a question stem and the answer choices:

If Train H leaves the station first, then which one of the following must be true?

(A) Train F leaves the station second.

(B) Train F leaves the station fifth.

(C) Train M leaves the station fifth.

✓ (D) Train N leaves the station fifth.

(E) Train G leaves the station second.

Did you attempt to solve that? The answer is (D). We'll talk about games like this soon enough.

Logic Games and the Digital LSAT

In some ways, the Logic Games section was the section most impacted by digitization. In other ways, it was the least impacted. Because the digital testing tablet doesn't support freehand drawing, most of the work that you do in Logic Games will now be done on your scratch paper. But the work *itself* will remain the same. The only thing that's changing is the location of the work.

The testing tablet will only allow you to underline and highlight text, select and eliminate answers, and flag questions that you want to come back to later. To get used to doing logic games in this way, limit yourself to those annotations, both on the pages of this book and on any paper practice tests that you complete. Do the rest of your work on scratch paper—keep a blank notebook handy as you read!

Game Types

While at this point it may seem to you that every game is unique, soon you'll see that there are only a few basic structures that are used to build all recent LSAT Logic Games.

All recent games ask you to assign elements to positions. This means your first thoughts should be: What are the elements? What are the positions? What is the relationship between the two? That might seem confusing, but it's not that complex since there are only two basic relationships:

1. **Elements can be ordered.** This is what you saw in the train game above. This is the most common task a logic game will ask of you.

2. **Elements can be placed into groups.** You might see a game that looks like this:

> Each of eight students—Mary, Noel, Orpheus, Perla, Quinn, Rheanna, Simone, and Tyrrell—is to be seated in one of two rows.

We have eight elements, and each of these has to be placed in one of two different rows. Note that we are not given information that establishes how many students are in each of the two rows.

Along with games that simply do one or the other, some games ask you to order positions *and* put them in groups. We can tweak the example above to have it include both:

> Eight students—Mary, Noel, Orpheus, Perla, Quinn, Rheanna, Simone, and Tyrrell—are to be seated in two rows. In each row there are four chairs, numbered consecutively 1 through 4.

Game Twists

There's got to be more to it than that, you say? On a basic level, there isn't. However, the Logic Games section will add some twists to these basic game types to shake things up. Some of the more common ones include the following:

1. **Subgroups.** There are occasionally different categories of elements. For example, the sample game we're using could have told us whether each student is a boy or girl in the scenario. In that case, a possible rule could have excluded a boy from sitting in the third chair.

2. **Mismatch.** Some games have more (or fewer) elements than positions. In such games, we may need to leave some positions empty or assign more than one element to a single position.

3. **Special Positions.** A less common twist involves assigning a special characteristic to one of the positions. This person may be the chairperson of a four member committee or the driver of carpooling employees. Regardless, Special Positions typically require that we defer on such assignments until after completing a hypothetical for a question.

We'll explore all those twists, and some others, in later chapters. Certain twists are so commonly paired with a major game type that we'll simply treat that pairing as a game type in itself. For example, Relative Ordering games are the focus of Chapter 4. It may seem like a lot of work to keep track of all of this, but the good news is that a single game won't have all (or even most!) of the above variations going on. Also, we're going to arm you with the tools to deal with each of the above. Finally, while the crew of geeks that wrote this book think deeply about how to categorize every nook and cranny of every game, and occasionally end up in fisticuffs over whether it's best to say that a certain game has subgroups or special positions, your job is simpler. You just need to figure out how to incorporate a twist into your diagram and get the questions right! Various approaches and diagrams to a given game can each work just fine.

Here is the general breakdown of games in recent years:

Ordering	50%
Basic Ordering	24%
Relative Ordering	11%
3D Ordering	15%
Grouping	39%
In/Out Grouping	11%
Basic Grouping	7%
Open Grouping	14%
3D Grouping	7%
Hybrids	6%
Misc.	5%

No doubt those categories don't mean much to you yet, but even when they do, the goal isn't to become a master categorizer or a strict executor. Instead, your goal is to be able to adapt to twists and make even a poorly constructed diagram work.

From Here to 170+

Every quest must have a hero, and on the Logic Games road to 170+ it's MacGyver, the man who could use a light-bulb, a pipe, and a chunk of ice to break out of a meat locker (look up the show if you don't know it). MacGyver was able to evaluate his situation and creatively adapt whatever he had at hand to solve the problem (and, usually, save someone). So how do we mortals develop our inner MacGyver?

The recipe is one we heard earlier: Be organized and consistent in order to be creative and flexible.

What will this look like in practice? Let's consider some of the differences between a typical test-taker and a phenomenal one.

Flexibility is just one of the characteristics that separate high scorers from the average test-taker. Let's consider some of the others:

Most LSAT Test-Takers	**170+ Test-Takers**
Recognize only the most basic game structures.	Quickly recognize the game types and use this recognition to inform their approach.
Lack consistent and effective diagramming methods.	Develop and maintain consistent diagramming methods.
Spend too little (or too much) time on the setup.	Use instincts and experience to help them allocate time wisely.
Use trial and error as a primary approach.	Use key inferences to save time and work.
Get confused when a game or constraint strays from the norm.	Are able to adapt their methods to work on the "curveball" game or constraint.
Struggle to apply their learned strategies in a real test environment.	Practice enough to achieve flexibility and proficiency.
Lack confidence in their approach.	Enjoy logic games!

Bridging the Gap

So how do you move from the left column to the right? There are three keys:

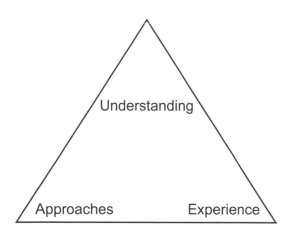

1. **Understanding.** You must learn about the tendencies and nature of the Logic Games section.

2. **Approaches.** You must develop an approach that aligns with the exam and that you feel comfortable employing.

1

3. **Experience.** In order to make your approach smoother, and in order to gain a thorough understanding of this test, you must practice a lot. This doesn't mean that you must do every logic game ever—though you should do many of them—but it does mean that you should replay tough games multiple times in order to deepen your understanding and hone your approach.

How to Read This Book if You're Already Really Good at Logic Games

Most people who buy a book on logic games are not already good at them, but we tend to see a lot of high-caliber students (it's one of our specialties). So if you're already scoring in the high 160s on timed practice LSATs, you may want to adjust how you use this book.

So that we can have high-level discussions about game playing with every student, we devote some time to exploring basic topics. It's tempting to skip parts that seem too basic for you, and we invite you to do so. However, be careful that you don't skip the sections where we discuss how to solve logic games better than you already do! Skip too much and you will finish this book simply relying on the same skills and knowledge that you entered this book with. One way to check your understanding on a section that you're skipping is to try out the drills for that section. If you can solve them the way we do, then bravo!

To get the most out of this book, make sure you're aligning your approach with ours. If you have experienced success with a different approach on a specific game type, be sure to check out how we do it and consider whether there are any aspects of our approach that would be beneficial to adopt.

Enough talk about what we will do; let's do it!

MANHATTAN
PREP

Chapter 2

Basic Ordering

In This Chapter...

Getting Familiar

You're probably wondering why we're throwing a game at you when we haven't taught you much of anything. Here's why: No matter how much you prepare for the LSAT, there are going to be some unexpected curves on your test. One way we'll train you is by throwing curveballs at you from time to time—like a timed trial you're not ready for! Do your best to complete the following game in **10 minutes** or less. Use whatever approaches you see fit.

Exactly seven swimmers—Hewitt, James, Kopov, Luis, Markson, Nu, and Price—will race in the 50-meter freestyle event. Each swimmer will swim in exactly one of seven lanes, numbered 1 through 7. No two swimmers share the same lane. Lane assignments comply with the following conditions:

> James swims in a lower-numbered lane than Kopov.
> Nu swims in either the first lane or the seventh lane.
> Markson swims in a lane numbered two lower than Price's.
> Hewitt swims in lane 4.

1. Which of the following could be an accurate list of swimmers, listed in order from lane 1 through lane 7?

   (A) Nu, Luis, James, Kopov, Markson, Hewitt, Price
   (B) James, Luis, Markson, Hewitt, Price, Kopov, Nu
   (C) Nu, Kopov, Markson, Hewitt, Price, James, Luis
   (D) Luis, Markson, James, Hewitt, Price, Kopov, Nu
   (E) Markson, Nu, Price, Hewitt, James, Luis, Kopov

2. Which one of the following must be false?

   (A) Price swims in lane 5.
   (B) Price swims in lane 7.
   (C) Markson swims in lane 2.
   (D) Kopov swims in lane 3.
   (E) James swims in lane 6.

3. If James swims in lane 1, then each of the following could be true EXCEPT:

   (A) Kopov swims in a lower-numbered lane than Hewitt.
   (B) Luis swims in a lower-numbered lane than Hewitt.
   (C) Markson swims in a higher-numbered lane than Hewitt.
   (D) Kopov swims in a lower-numbered lane than Price.
   (E) Luis swims in a lower-numbered lane than Markson.

4. If Price swims in lane 3, which one of the following could be true?

   (A) Kopov swims in lane 2.
   (B) James swims in lane 6.
   (C) Luis swims in lane 2.
   (D) Nu swims in lane 1.
   (E) Kopov swims in lane 7.

5. Which of the following could be a partial and accurate list of swimmers matched with the lanes in which they swim?

   (A) lane 1: Nu; lane 2: Markson; lane 6: Luis
   (B) lane 5: James; lane 6: Kopov; lane 7: Luis
   (C) lane 3: Luis; lane 4: Hewitt; lane 5: James
   (D) lane 4: Hewitt; lane 5: Luis; lane 7: Kopov
   (E) lane 2: James; lane 5: Markson; lane 6: Kopov

We will revisit this game later in the chapter. We promise.

Ordering

The most common task asked of you in Logic Games is to put elements in order. More than half of LSAT games require you to order elements. This is a big topic!

Ordering games come in several flavors. In the following chapters, we will go into great detail about each of these variations and suggest specific strategies for each of them. In this chapter, we will lay the groundwork for the entire **Ordering Family** of games by discussing Basic Ordering games. We're also going to discuss the two most common question types you're going to face.

Basic Ordering

A Basic Ordering game in its simplest form will ask you to take a set of elements and order them from first to last. Common twists include presenting the elements in subgroups or presenting more (or fewer) elements than positions. Each twist increases the complexity from the most basic form. So to begin our discussion of Basic Ordering games, let's begin by limiting our discussion of Basic Ordering to the simplest form. Later, in Chapter 6, we'll review how adding twists will change our approach.

While you can think of Basic Ordering games as "simple" games, by no means do we mean to suggest that all Basic Ordering games are *easy*. Admittedly, Basic Ordering games do tend to fall on the lower end of the difficulty scale, but there have been a few Basic Ordering games that have been quite difficult. If you run into a Basic Ordering game as your fourth game, it's much more likely that you'll find it to be on the higher end of the difficulty scale.

Basic Ordering games are extremely common. They show up about once in every four games; you're very likely to see one on test day. Let's get friendly with these games!

Picturing Basic Ordering Games

Basic Ordering games are simple to picture. For the purposes of discussion, let's use the following hypothetical game scenario:

> Seven runners—K, L, M, N, O, P, and S—finish a race in a certain order. There are no other runners, and there are no ties. The following conditions apply:
>
>> S finishes before O.
>> N finishes fourth.
>> L finishes two spots ahead of P.
>> K is either first or seventh.
>> If L finishes third, M finishes before K.

Start all games by reading the scenario and quickly scanning the rules. Don't start diagramming on your scratch paper until you've taken a peek at the rules, as they will often tell you what sort of diagram to use. Once you recognize that you're dealing with a Basic Ordering game, write down the elements to be placed and draw numbered slots for positions:

___ ___ ___ ___ ___ ___ ___   K L M N O P S
 1   2   3   4   5   6   7

This is probably what you would do naturally, but maybe it seems more natural to you to put the first position to the far right, and to go from right to left. That can work, but we recommend that you stick with left to right, since that's how the elements in a game will be ordered in answer choices and that's how we tend to read in English. But we admire rebels; just be a consistent rebel. Develop a system and stick with it.

Keep an eye out for situations where slot 1 could be the lowest or highest value (e.g., "most popular to least popular" or "tallest to shortest"). Check which side of the spectrum gets assigned to 1. And, while we're talking about tricky setups, there also have been some ordering games that are naturally easier to imagine in a vertical organization. Imagine you were assigning businesses to different floors of a building—floors 1 through 7—and all of the rules were about above and below; in that case, it would likely be to your benefit to visualize the game this way:

7 ___

6 ___

5 ___

4 ___

3 ___

2 ___

1 ___

Or, perhaps you'll soon be so used to Ordering games that you will feel perfectly comfortable thinking about the order of floors as going from left to right. With these types of minor decisions, go with whatever feels most comfortable for you. (By the way, that's not some "let's all get along" sort of broad advice. It is *critical* that you are comfortable with your diagram, because you need to be able to manipulate it in order to answer questions.)

Now, let's move on to thinking about the rules in greater detail.

Basic Ordering Rules

The rules that accompany Basic Ordering games will give you information that falls into two general categories. They will give you details about either **assignment** or **order.**

Rules of Assignment

As we discussed in the introductory chapter, all LSAT games are about assigning elements to positions. Therefore, all games are likely to have some **rules of assignment,** and rules of assignment are the simplest rules that we will encounter.

Assignment rules give us one of two types of details:

1. **An element will be assigned to a position.** In our hypothetical game, we had the assignment rule "N finishes fourth." We can notate this by placing N in the fourth position, like so:

$$\underset{1}{\rule{1cm}{0.4pt}} \quad \underset{2}{\rule{1cm}{0.4pt}} \quad \underset{3}{\rule{1cm}{0.4pt}} \quad \underset{4}{\overset{N}{\rule{1cm}{0.4pt}}} \quad \underset{5}{\rule{1cm}{0.4pt}} \quad \underset{6}{\rule{1cm}{0.4pt}} \quad \underset{7}{\rule{1cm}{0.4pt}}$$

(We know, this is pretty straightforward so far!)

2. **An element will be excluded from a position.** Imagine that instead we were told, "N does not finish fourth." We could notate this information like so:

$$\underset{1}{\rule{1cm}{0.4pt}} \quad \underset{2}{\rule{1cm}{0.4pt}} \quad \underset{3}{\rule{1cm}{0.4pt}} \quad \underset{4}{\rule{1cm}{0.4pt}} \quad \underset{5}{\rule{1cm}{0.4pt}} \quad \underset{6}{\rule{1cm}{0.4pt}} \quad \underset{7}{\rule{1cm}{0.4pt}}$$
$$\cancel{N}$$

Rules about Order

Naturally, Ordering games will also have rules about order. Let's consider the range of Ordering rules that are possible.

Ordering rules can relate elements to other elements (i.e., "S finishes before O") or to positions (i.e., "M finishes no later than third"). Most Ordering rules that appear on the LSAT relate elements to other elements. They can do so in a few different ways:

1. **Ordering rules can relate elements without giving us any specific information about how many spaces are between them.** These rules are very common, and we call these **Relative Ordering** rules.

The rule "S finishes before O" is an example of a Relative Ordering rule, and we can represent it this way:

S — O

We can draw this on the side of our Number Line or below it.

From this rule, we know S must be before O, but we don't know much else. They can finish right next to one another, or they can be further spread apart.

Note that we could be given the same rule with slightly trickier wording: "O does not finish before S."

MANHATTAN
PREP

If this rule were part of a game in which elements could tie, it would mean something different (it would mean that O could tie with S or finish after it). However, since elements can't tie in this game, "O does not finish before S" means S finishes before O.

Relative Ordering rules can sometimes involve three and (rarely) even four elements. For example:

L finishes before M but after P.

or

S finishes after both L and N.

$$P < L < M$$

$$\begin{matrix} L \\ N \end{matrix} < S$$

We can diagram these rules, respectively, as follows:

$$P - L - M \qquad \begin{matrix} L \\ \\ N \end{matrix} \!\!\! > S$$

The dash (—) will be a significant symbol in our notation system, and it will always mean the same thing: We know of a *relative* relationship between elements, but nothing more specific than that.

2. **Ordering rules can tell us the exact number of positions between elements.** In our Getting Familiar game, we had the rule "L finishes two spots ahead of P." We can diagram this as follows:

$$\boxed{L \_ P} \qquad\qquad L\_P \qquad L = P - 2$$

This rule seems simple enough, but it's very easy to misinterpret as:

$$\boxed{L \_ \_ P}$$

You must be vigilant about, and practiced at, interpreting and diagramming these common rules accurately.

You probably already figured out that we're using an underscore "_" to indicate a known space between elements. Just to clarify the difference, "J–S" means that J comes sometime before S, while "J_S" means that J comes exactly two spots before S.

When elements have a known number of slots in between them, they form what we call a **chunk.** While the name is sort of gross, as you start to solve ordering games, you'll quickly see that chunks are crucial.

3. **Ordering rules can give us a somewhat specific, but not exact, relationship between elements.**

Imagine that in our initial example we had the rule "L finishes at least two spots ahead of P."

In this case, we'd know something specific—L can't finish right before P—but the information is also somewhat diffuse; we don't know more beyond that. By the way, terms like "at least" might be small, but they can have a huge impact on how a game works.

This type of rule is less common than the previous two types, but it is challenging and thus important to be prepared for. We can represent this rule as follows:

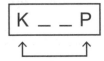

" __ +" indicates that there is at least one space, and possibly more, between L and P. (Some people prefer "L __ ... P.") While the exact number of spaces isn't known, we'll still often refer to this as a chunk.

4. Ordering rules can specify the distance between elements, without indicating order.

Imagine we had the following rule: "Exactly two people finish between K and P."

In this case, we would know that there are two spots between K and P, but we wouldn't know whether K went before P, or vice versa. We could represent this situation in the following manner:

K _ _ P
↑_____↑

The double-sided arrow might be a bit awkward at first, but if you are consistent in your notation, it should be intuitive soon enough. Some students have found it helpful to use this alternative notation:

K _ _ P   or   P _ _ K

Similarly, the rule "G and R finish consecutively" could be represented in one of these two ways:

We think it's faster to use the one on the left, but follow your heart on decisions like this, and then stay consistent within a given game.

Keep in mind that many of these Ordering rules could be given to us in terms of "nots." For example, we could have a rule that states, "L does not finish exactly two spots ahead of P." If such a rule appears, we can just adjust our common notation with a exclusion, like this:

MANHATTAN
PREP

As mentioned above, almost all Ordering rules relate elements to one another, but if we do happen to get an Ordering rule that relates an element to a position, we can handle it easily enough.

If we take the example "M finishes no later than third," we can represent this in one of two ways:

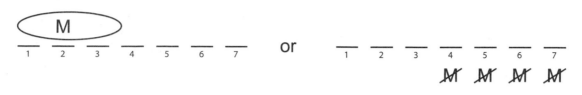

Either method would be fine, although, depending on the particular game, one might be a smidge more useful than the other.

The oval notation on the left, which we call a **cloud,** is frequently used for situations in which we know elements must fit in a certain range, but we don't know the exact positions of these elements. For example, we might know that K, L, and M have to go in the first three positions, but we do not know their relative order. In this case, we can put them in a cloud.

Here's a table that includes all of our diagramming suggestions thus far:

Rules of…	
Assignment	
N finishes fourth.	$\underline{}\ \underline{}\ \underline{}\ \underset{4}{\overset{N}{\underline{}}}\ \underline{}\ \underline{}\ \underline{}$
N does not finish fourth.	$\underline{}\ \underline{}\ \underline{}\ \underset{4}{\underline{}}\ \underline{}\ \underline{}\ \underline{}$ with N̶ under position 4
Order	
S finishes before O.	S − O
L finishes two spots ahead of P.	L _ P (boxed)
L finishes at least two spots ahead of P.	L _ + P (boxed)
Exactly two people finish between K and P.	K _ _ P (boxed, with arrows)
M finishes no later than third.	M in cloud over positions 1 2 3 4 5 6 7

In addition to the type of information that they can give, rules are further defined by the manner in which they give that information.

Most commonly, rules give us information in a simple way:

> S finishes before O.
> N finishes fourth.
> Q finishes immediately before T.
> L finishes two spots ahead of P.

However, rules can also give us information in two other ways:

1. **Rules can present *either/or (but not both)* scenarios.** We've actually already dealt with a "hidden" either/or (but not both) scenario above: "Exactly two people finish between K and P" means either:

$$\boxed{\text{K \_ \_ P}} \quad \text{or} \quad \boxed{\text{P \_ \_ K}}$$

Additionally, the test writers are apt to take many of the other types of rules given above and convert them into either/or (but not both) scenarios. Here are some examples of common rules, as they would apply to the runner game above, along with suggestions for how to diagram these rules:

> K is either first or seventh.

$$\underset{1}{\overset{\text{K/}}{\rule{1.5em}{0.4pt}}} \quad \underset{2}{\rule{1.5em}{0.4pt}} \quad \underset{3}{\rule{1.5em}{0.4pt}} \quad \underset{4}{\rule{1.5em}{0.4pt}} \quad \underset{5}{\rule{1.5em}{0.4pt}} \quad \underset{6}{\rule{1.5em}{0.4pt}} \quad \underset{7}{\overset{\text{/K}}{\rule{1.5em}{0.4pt}}}$$

> Either L or P finishes third.

$$\underset{1}{\rule{1.5em}{0.4pt}} \quad \underset{2}{\rule{1.5em}{0.4pt}} \quad \underset{3}{\overset{\text{L/P}}{\rule{1.5em}{0.4pt}}} \quad \underset{4}{\rule{1.5em}{0.4pt}} \quad \underset{5}{\rule{1.5em}{0.4pt}} \quad \underset{6}{\rule{1.5em}{0.4pt}} \quad \underset{7}{\rule{1.5em}{0.4pt}}$$

> L finishes before S or N, but not both.

The last rule is certainly the most challenging of the set above to diagram. Before you read on, take a moment to sketch how you might diagram that one.

Many test-takers would stop at this:

> L – S
>   or
> L – N

MANHATTAN
PREP

However, keep in mind that if L finishes before S, it can't finish before N, and, since they can't tie, that must mean that N finishes before L. If L finishes before N, it must finish after S. Basically, L is in the middle. We should actually write this:

$$N - L - S$$

Also, keep in mind that unless the design of a game prevents it, or unless it is explicitly stated, the phrase "either/or" does not exclude the possibility of both. The reason we know that the rule "K is in either 1 or 7" means K is in 1 or 7, but not both, is that we know, based on the parameters of the game, that K won't finish twice. For the rule "L finishes before S or N, but not both," if instead we had simply been told, "L finishes before S or N," without the "but not both," then three options would be valid:

$$S - L - N \qquad\qquad N - L - S \qquad\qquad L\!<\!\begin{matrix}N\\S\end{matrix}$$

Again, unless explicitly stated or prohibited by the nature of the game, the either/or phrase does not exclude both. This is a tricky concept, but fortunately one that is not particularly significant for the vast majority of Ordering games. We'll cover this concept in greater detail in the chapters for which it's more relevant.

2. **Rules can be _conditional_.** Conditional logic is central to the construction of the LSAT, and we'll discuss it at length in other parts of this book (and also in even greater depth in our _LSAT Logical Reasoning_ Strategy Guide), but one easy way to think about conditional rules is that they are triggers that set off a certain outcome or guarantee.

The most common marker of a conditional rule is the word "if." We had one conditional rule in our original hypothetical game:

   If L finishes third, M finishes before K.

We recommend that you diagram this type of rule below or off to the side of the diagram, and we recommend that you diagram it like this:

$$L_3 \rightarrow M - K$$

Note that we do not want to put L into the third slot in our main diagram, because L may or may not be in that slot. We can use subscript for this situation. We could just as easily represent it in either of the following ways:

$$L_3 \quad \text{or} \quad \underset{3}{\underline{L}}$$

Use whatever feels best for you.

Let's think for a moment about the specific significance of a conditional statement. So that we can stay focused on the reasoning involved, let's use a simple conditional:

> If K finishes fifth, N will finish third.

We can represent this rule as follows:

$$K_5 \rightarrow N_3$$

Let's look at various scenarios to see what this rule does and does not mean: *What do we know if K finishes fifth?*

We know for sure that N *must* finish third. Pretty straightforward, right?

Take a moment to consider what we could infer (i.e., know with certainty) in each of these situations:

a. K doesn't finish fifth.	b. N finishes third.	c. N doesn't finish third.

Figured those out? Let's take a look:

a. What if K doesn't finish fifth?	*b. What if N finishes third?*	*c. What if N does not finish third?*
Does that mean N won't finish third? Not necessarily. If K doesn't finish fifth, this rule doesn't apply, and **we can't infer anything.**	Do we know for sure that K finished fifth? No. It could have, but we don't know that for sure. **We can't infer anything.**	Do we know anything about K? Yes! We know that K did not finish fifth (otherwise, N would have finished third). We know K **must not** have finished fifth.

We know that if N does not finish third, K does not finish fifth. If we wanted to, we could notate this as follows:

$$-N_3 \rightarrow -K_5$$

Notice the relationship between the original conditional statement and this valid inference—the elements have been *reversed* and *negated*. We can *always* derive inferences from conditional statements by reversing and negating both sides of the statement, and these inferences have a special name: **contrapositives.**

Generally, students choose to deal with contrapositives in one of two ways:

1. **By diagramming them along with the original conditional statements.**

This is simple enough, and it's a habit you will quickly become comfortable with.

MANHATTAN
PREP

2. By being mindful of them.

For certain game types that we will explore in depth later in the book, conditional statements are the heart and soul of the game, and for those games, we'll strongly recommend writing out all contrapositives. However, for other game types, such as Basic Ordering, we're also fine with you not writing out contrapositives, and instead being mindful of their significance. If you feel more comfortable writing out the contrapositives, especially while you're still new to games, go for it. Figure out what works for you.

For Logic Games, the concept of trigger and consequence can be useful in wrapping your head around the contrapositive. Put simply, the contrapositive simply means that **if the consequence didn't happen, the trigger didn't happen.**

Here are a few examples of conditional rules, along with suggestions for how to notate them:

Statement	Notation	Contrapositive
If S finishes second, O will finish sixth.	$S_2 \rightarrow O_6$	If O doesn't finish sixth, S doesn't finish second.
If L finishes before S, P will finish before O.	$L - S \rightarrow P - O$	If P doesn't finish before O, L doesn't finish before S.
If L and O finish next to one another, though not necessarily in that order, M will finish second.	$\boxed{LO} \rightarrow M_2$	If M doesn't finish second, L and O don't finish next to one another.

2

Smart Tip: Combine Rules as You Go

It is fairly common that you will find the same element mentioned in more than one rule, and when that happens you can often combine the two rules. Combining rules will pay off nicely by helping you fill in the Number Line and reducing the amount of uncertainty in the game.

For example, imagine we had the following two rules for a game:

> K finishes before S.
> S finishes immediately before T.

We can combine these two rules in the following notation:

$$K - \boxed{ST}$$

Keep in mind that the test writers will not always conveniently place rules sharing the same element next to one another. Some test-takers aggressively look to combine rules as they first notate them. For example, when they've dealt with a rule about G and P, instead of simply moving to notate the next rule, these folks will scan the other rules looking for a reference to G or P. For some games, "reordering" rules is essential, so it's not a bad habit to employ all the time. At a minimum, try to combine related rules as you notate them.

MANHATTAN
PREP

Here are five other pairings of rules that can be notated together. See if you can figure out a way to bring the two rules together and sketch out the combined notation before looking at the solutions. Keep in mind that we're still working with the same basic scenario with runners finishing a race:

1. S finishes immediately before or immediately after L.
    K finishes before L.

2. S finishes before O.
    K finishes after O.

3. P finishes after N but before L.
    M finishes immediately before or immediately after P.

4. N finishes fourth.
    K finishes before N.

5. O finishes at least two spots ahead of or behind M.
    Exactly one runner finishes between L and O.

Solutions

1. S finishes immediately before or immediately after L.
K finishes before L.

$$K - \boxed{SL}$$
$\hookleftarrow \hookrightarrow$

2. S finishes before O.
K finishes after O.

$$S - O - K$$

3. P finishes after N but before L.
M finishes immediately before or immediately after P.

$$N - \boxed{PM} - L$$
$\hookleftarrow \hookrightarrow$

4. N finishes fourth.
K finishes before N.

$$\overset{\bigcirc\!\!\!K}{\_} \ \_ \ \_ \ \overset{N}{\_} \ \_ \ \_ \ \_$$

or

$$K - N_4$$

5. O finishes at least two spots ahead of or behind M.
Exactly one runner finishes between L and O.

Did you struggle with this one? Curveball! While you could write out a pretty complex notation for this combination of rules, since there are so many options, it's fine to not combine their notations but simply to know that you'll have to keep an eye on how they interact. If you were brave, perhaps you came up with something like this:

$$L \_ O \ \text{ or } \ O \_ L$$
$$\boxed{M \_ + O}$$

or

$$L \_ O \ \text{ or } \ O \_ L$$
$$\boxed{O \_ + M}$$

MANHATTAN
PREP

Drill It: Basic Ordering Diagrams

Now that we've discussed the full spectrum of rules that you are likely to see in a Basic Ordering game, let's practice setting up our diagrams.

In this drill, we've got four stripped-down mini versions of Basic Ordering games. For each one, practice creating your diagram and notating rules. As you are doing so, you may notice and uncover additional truths about the game—inferences—by bringing the rules together. Notate these inferences as you'd like.

Two last tips before you start:

1. **When you're done notating all the rules and listing all the elements, circle any elements that are not obviously affected by any rules.** (One of our nerdier teachers calls them "free radicals.") This will tighten your grasp on how a game works, and once in a while, the move pays off handsomely in the questions.

2. **As much as possible, put the rules on the Number Line instead of off to the side.** The more that your rules are on the Number Line (or whatever diagram a game requires), the more they'll be front and center in your mind. That said, some rules are too complex to be immediately included, and others, like conditional rules, can't be placed in the diagram because they may (or may not) be triggered in a given question.

1. Seven circus clowns—Roy, Stew, Tony, Urma, Xi, Yang, and Zip—are to emerge one at a time from a suitcase. No other clowns are to emerge from the suitcase. The following conditions apply:

    Urma emerges either first or last.
    Stew emerges immediately after Xi.
    Yang emerges at least two spots before Roy.
    Tony emerges at some point after Xi.

2. A scientist is testing each of seven experimental medicines—N, P, Q, R, S, T, U. No medicine can be tested at the same time as another, and the scientist will test only those medicines. The testing of the medicines must be conducted according to these rules:

> If R is tested third, N cannot be tested first.
> If S is tested first, T is tested immediately after P.
> P is tested either fifth or seventh.
> If U is tested before S, Q is tested after N.

3. Six race cars—F, G, H, I, J, K—will be lined up in starting positions 1–6, going from left to right. The following conditions apply:

> J is not in position five.
> H is positioned to the left of K.
> Either G or K is in position four.
> F is after G or J, but not both.

4. Six office departments—legal, management, operations, personnel, shipping, and tech—are to be assigned to floors 1–6 in a new office building. Each department will occupy its own entire floor and no other departments will be in the building. The assignment of departments to floors must follow the following rules:

> Tech cannot occupy the top or bottom floor.
> Management must occupy either the fifth or sixth floor.
> Shipping must be placed directly above or below operations.
> Personnel must be placed either on a floor higher than tech or on one higher than shipping, but not both.

Solutions: Basic Ordering Diagrams

Here are solutions to the diagramming drill. Note that in some places you may have put in additional inferences that we did not, and perhaps in other places we notated inferences that you did not. This is fine. We'll discuss inferences in greater detail in just a bit. For now, the most critical thing to review is that you notated each rule correctly.

1. $\dfrac{U/}{1}$ $\overline{2}$ $\overline{3}$ $\overline{4}$ $\overline{5}$ $\overline{6}$ $\dfrac{/U}{7}$ R S T U X Y Ⓩ

    $\boxed{XS}$ - T

    $\boxed{Y\_ \ \bullet R}$

2. $\overline{1}$ $\overline{2}$ $\overline{3}$ $\overline{4}$ $\dfrac{P/}{5}$ $\overline{6}$ $\dfrac{/P}{7}$ N P Q R S T U

    $R_3 \rightarrow \cancel{N}_1$

    $S_1 \rightarrow \boxed{PT}$

    $U - S \rightarrow N - Q$

3. $\overline{1}$ $\overline{2}$ $\overline{3}$ $\dfrac{G/K}{4}$ $\overline{5}$ $\overline{6}$ F G H Ⓘ J K
    $\underset{\cancel{J}}{}$ H - K

    G - F - J

4. 6 $\underline{M/}$ $\cancel{L}$

    5 $\underline{/M}$ Ⓛ M O P S T

    4 $\underline{}$

    3 $\underline{}$ $\boxed{\begin{array}{c}S\\O\end{array}}$ $\boxed{\begin{array}{c}S\\P\\I\\T\end{array}}$

    2 $\underline{}$

    1 $\underline{}$ $\cancel{L}$

Inferences

If an LSAT question asks, "Which of the following must be true?" the right answer will *not* be something that must be true directly from the rules that we are given.

Huh?

Here's what we mean. If we're given a rule that specifically tells us that T must go in the fourth position, we'll never be asked, "Which of the following must be true?" and have "T is fourth" as an answer choice.

The correct answer to that problem will be one that we can **infer,** or deduce, by bringing together the various things we know about the game. When it comes to logic games, inferences are our best friends. We love inferences because they frequently allow us to answer a question in 10 seconds rather than 100 or to solve a complete game in 6 minutes rather than 12. We're going to be making inferences at every point in our game-solving process: as we initially picture games, as we absorb the rules, and as we answer the questions.

Inferences are the key to solving logic games quickly, but before we talk about what to do, let's lay out some common misunderstandings on either side of the inference spectrum.

At one end are test-takers who do not understand the significance of inferences. These students often fail to make up-front inferences and, even more commonly, fail to make inferences when questions include a new rule (such as "If G is fourth, which of the following…"). Failing to make inferences forces these students to use more deliberate, error-prone, and time-consuming methods, such as trial and error.

At the other end of the spectrum are test-takers who are overly eager to make all inferences—to "solve" games—during the initial setup of a game. This mentality can lead to false inferences, and it can also lead to a lot of extra work that ultimately proves to be of little worth. Finally, this mentality can lead to panic when games are invariably *not* solved during the setup.

The reality is, certain games are "front-end" games, designed to yield key up-front inferences, while others are "back-end," designed with few inferences up front and more work in the questions. We want you to be able to recognize and be comfortable with both of these tendencies. As we discuss individual game types, we'll talk about the front-end/back-end tendencies of each one. More importantly, you'll develop your own ability to see which category a game falls into.

Let's discuss inferences in more specific detail. It can be helpful to organize our thinking in terms of inferences made during the setup and inferences made during the questions themselves.

Inferences in Our Setup

As we just mentioned, **front-end** games yield significant inferences during the setup stage of a game, and **back-end** games do not. In general, Basic Ordering games are back-end games. We may be able to uncover a few truths up front, but it's likely we will do most of our inferring in the questions themselves.

MANHATTAN
PREP

Still, there are usually a few front-end inferences we can make that we definitely want to put down on our papers, and often there are even more that we can make that we simply want to keep in mind. (Since you're just starting out with Basic Ordering games, err on the side of over-diagramming inferences until you figure out for yourself which inferences you don't need to write out.)

Remember that inferences are based on bringing information together, and, when it comes to Basic Ordering games, we are simply bringing together information about order and assignment. Let's use the hypothetical Ordering rule "K is two positions ahead of N" to illustrate all the ways one Ordering rule might come together in holy inference matrimony with another piece of information in the game.

We can diagram the rule like this:

K _ N

Using that, here are three types of combinations you'll encounter:

1. Ordering Rules + Other Ordering Rules

We already worked on this a bit—when two Ordering rules share a common element, they can often be combined.

For example, what do we know if "L is immediately before K" and "K is two positions ahead of N"? We can infer that L is three positions before N, and we can diagram the combination like this:

LK _ N

While some rules easily fuse together like that, sometimes we can make inferences by thinking about how Ordering rules link up, even if they don't share a common element.

For example, imagine that we have a game involving six slots, and along with the rule "K is two positions ahead of N" is the rule "There are three people who finish after L but before P."

This second rule we could diagram like this:

L _ _ _ P

Now, before you read on, think for a minute about how these two rules interact with one another.

Is it possible for the two chunks not to overlap? No. We'd need a minimum of eight spaces for them not to overlap. In how many different ways could they overlap? Not too many. Here they are:

```
K L N _ _ P
_ L K _ N P
L K _ N P _
L _ _ K P N
```

2. Ordering Rules + Rules of Assignment

Very commonly, Basic Ordering games are defined by the interaction between a chunk and the assignment of an element to some position in the middle of our order.

Imagine that, in addition to our "K is two positions ahead of N" rule, we had one that stated, "F is fourth." What could we infer in our six-slot game? Take a moment to think about it before reading on.

If K is exactly two positions ahead of N, and if F is fourth, K cannot be second. Furthermore, N cannot be sixth. Did you figure out where the K _ N chunk can go? It can go only in slots 1 _ 3 or 3 _ 5. Notice a commonality between those options? Wherever that chunk goes, part of it is going in slot 3, so we can write "K/N" there.

This sort of inference is not too easy to spot, and it will surely be useful during the questions, so we definitely want to note it on our diagram:

$$
\underset{1}{\underline{}} \quad \underset{2}{\underline{}} \quad \underset{3}{\underline{\text{K/N}}} \quad \underset{4}{\underline{\text{F}}} \quad \underset{5}{\underline{}} \quad \underset{6}{\underline{}}
$$

$$
\cancel{K}\cancel{N}
$$

Far less commonly, we may also make inferences based on "not" assignment rules. If, in addition to knowing "K is two positions ahead of N," we knew "N is not fifth," we would know that K could not be third.

3. Ordering Rules + the Construction of the Game

Almost all Ordering rules will allow us to make at least some inferences about where elements can't go, based on the construction of the game—more specifically, based on the fact that there is a beginning and an end to the Number Lines we're using!

Again, imagine that our rule "K is two positions ahead of N" came in a game involving six positions. What would we know about where K and N could and, perhaps more importantly, could not go?

N cannot be in positions one or two, because then there would be no place for K. Similarly, K cannot be in positions five or six, because then there would be no place for N.

We *could* notate these inferences as follows:

$$
\underset{1}{\underline{}} \quad \underset{2}{\underline{}} \quad \underset{3}{\underline{}} \quad \underset{4}{\underline{}} \quad \underset{5}{\underline{}} \quad \underset{6}{\underline{}}
$$

$$
\cancel{N} \quad\quad \cancel{N} \cancel{K} \quad\quad \cancel{K}
$$

To Note or Not to Note, That Is the Question

Did you notice we just said that you *could* notate those inferences? For some test-takers, perhaps you, those inferences are so obvious that they aren't worth writing out, especially if there are not multiple restrictions for the slots in question. In terms of what you do actually diagram on your paper and what you don't, there is no perfect diagram, and the "right" amount of inference-notating is based in large part on your personal preferences, strengths, and style. In general, we suggest that you start off by overdoing it; diagram more rather than less, especially when you are not confident that you will remember a particular inference.

However, inferences that involve Ordering rules coming into conflict with particular slots—we'll call them exclusion inferences—are so common that after serious prep, many people end up not needing to notate them on their diagrams. There are also certain game types for which there are so many such inferences that, if you were to carefully diagram each one, it would be a waste of time and energy. That said, on other games, a slot might have so *many* exclusions that you can infer something really helpful. Say, for example, a game has six elements, four of which can't occupy the last slot. You can infer that the last slot must be occupied by one of the remaining two elements. That type of inference is really valuable. As you experiment with the extent to which you want to notate exclusion inferences, keep an eye out for these situations. As exclusions build up under a slot, always ask yourself which elements are left that *could* go there.

Again, you want to be on the lookout for inferences in all parts of your setup. We also strongly recommend pausing after you've diagrammed all the rules and inferences you found to take one last look for inferences. We call this step in the game solving process **The Big Pause.**

The Big Pause

Imagine that you are a participant on a game show that somehow has managed to combine the quiet challenge of solving crossword puzzles with the frenetic ordeal of grocery shopping. Here's how the show works: First, you have to use a series of crossword puzzle–like clues to uncover eight items that exist on a grocery store shopping list. Second, you have to run through a supermarket finding the elements on that list. The contestant who finds all items first wins.

The game is on! You've just had a hell of a time figuring out the word clues. Finally, you figure out the list of elements: ice cream, toothpaste, milk, cheese, sugar cookies, frozen peas, orange juice, and earwax remover.

It took you longer than you'd like, and your competition finished figuring out the same list about 10 seconds before you did. So, as soon as you are done with figuring out the last item, you rush into the aisles, looking for the first element on your list: ice cream.

2

If we were coaching you for this competition, we would *not* suggest that you rush in looking for that ice cream.

Why not?

Because we recognize that a few seconds spent organizing what you know can prevent you from wasting a ton of time and energy going about your task in an inefficient manner.

It would take hardly any time at all to consider the fact that ice cream and frozen peas are likely very close to one another. The milk, cheese, and orange juice are similarly likely to be adjacent, and both the toothpaste and earwax remover are likely to be found in the "non-foods" section. Perhaps in this pause you consider which elements are easiest to find, and you start with those. Or, you see that earwax remover may be the toughest element to find (you've never had to look for it before!), and you come up with a plan of attack focusing on that.

Whatever the strategy, a few seconds of organization and reflection can save a lot of time on the back end.

This is consistently true of LSAT games as well.

The LSAT is a time-pressured test, and it's easy to get in a mind-set where we think we have to rush, or go as fast as possible, through each part of the process. However, this reaction to the time pressure can be detrimental.

It can be helpful to think about the time pressure not as something that forces you to go faster in your general thinking, but rather as something that forces you to make decisions about where and how to invest your time. Solving a game well is somewhat like dancing well—you need *rhythm*. You have to understand when you should be swift and clean, and when you should be slow and deliberate.

One of the critical points at which it's super helpful to remember to pause is between setting up your diagram and jumping into the questions. At this critical moment, you are often going to feel like the person in our game show example—like you are already behind and you've got to get going. However, the way you spend the few seconds during the transition is likely going to have a key impact on how easy or how difficult the questions feel to you.

We want you to use this pause to get comfortable with your diagram and to get ready for the questions. Specifically, we want you to get in the habit of using this pause to think about three critical aspects of game solving:

1. Get comfortable with your notations.

Go one notation at a time, and make sure you've correctly understood and represented each rule. For each rule you diagrammed off the board (i.e., not on the slots), think quickly about how that rule would play out on the board.

Note which elements have no rules attached to them, and circle them.

MANHATTAN
PREP

2. Take one last look for significant inferences or possible frames.

While they're usually back-end games, Basic Ordering games do often have one or two significant inferences. You will generally be able to catch them as you diagram, but it's good to be in the habit of double-checking. Some up-front inferences for Basic Ordering games are so important that missing them will cause you significant delays when you get to the questions.

We'll talk about frames later, but in short, they are diagrams to represent every direction in which a highly restricted game could go. Instead of one diagram to rule them all, you'll have two or three. Together, they'll represent every way the game could possibly pan out.

3. Pick your key rules.

As we go through the process of solving questions, we are going to have to think about how the various rules come together with one another, and with the layout of the slots. The order in which you think about these rules can have a significant impact on your pace and overall success.

Put simply, there are certain rules that are more important than others. It can be very helpful to identify and prioritize these key rules.

On a general level, we can think of the most useful rules as those that help us understand the most about a game.

For Basic Ordering games, the most significant rules are generally those that give us a chunk. A two-element chunk is great. A three- (or four-) element chunk—a "super chunk"—is even better. And, of course, the more specific the relationship between the elements, the better. Often, games will have two chunks, and the key to success will involve thinking about the limited ways in which these chunks fit together. Other times, games will involve a limiting relationship between a chunk and an assignment somewhere in the middle of the board, and the key to success will be to think of the limited ways in which the chunk interacts with that assignment.

Drill It: Basic Ordering Inferences and The Big Pause

In this drill, we've got another four stripped-down mini versions of Basic Ordering games. For each one, practice creating your diagram and notating rules. As much as possible, get those rules *into* the diagram, not on the side. As you are doing so, you should be able to make more inferences about the game by bringing the rules together. When you're done diagramming the rules, take a moment to consider the game in general—The Big Pause! There isn't always some large inference to figure out, but you want to be in the habit of creating some space for that discovery to occur, and it's also useful to notice which elements are "rule-less" and which rules you want to prioritize.

1. Six high school marching bands—Kearny, Linden, Manchester, Newark, Orange, and Patterson—will parade in front of a grandstand consecutively, one at a time. No other bands will be in the parade. The following conditions will apply:

   > Kearny will parade either first or fifth.
   >
   > Newark will parade third.
   >
   > Manchester will parade immediately after Kearny.
   >
   > Patterson will parade two spots after Linden.

2. Six different surgeries—N, O, P, Q, R, and S—are to take place in one operating room and one at a time over the course of 24 hours. No other surgeries will be performed in that operating room. The scheduling of the surgeries must adhere to the following conditions:

   > R is scheduled at some point after both N and O.
   >
   > Q cannot be scheduled third.
   >
   > If N is scheduled first, P is scheduled last.
   >
   > O is scheduled immediately after S.

3. A rock band will make exactly seven consecutive stops during its next tour. The stops are Pasadena, Rialto, Sonoma, Tustin, Vallejo, Woodside, and Yucaipa. The following rules apply to the tour schedule:

> Woodside is the stop immediately after Sonoma or Vallejo.
>
> The Rialto stop is scheduled for some time after Pasadena or Yucaipa, but not both.
>
> Sonoma is exactly two stops before the Vallejo stop.
>
> Tustin and Vallejo are consecutive stops.

4. A secret society is planning to meet annually from the year 2020 to the year 2025 using six different locations—K, L, M, N, O, and P. Each location will be used exactly once. The meetings will take place only at those locations, and no more than one meeting can take place in any given year. The schedule of meetings must adhere to the following requirements:

> P must be used for a meeting in 2022.
>
> K and M must be used two years apart.
>
> N and O must be used in consecutive years.
>
> M cannot be used until L has been used.

Solutions: Basic Ordering Inferences and The Big Pause

1.

The L/P in slot 4 inference was tough to figure out! It's clear that this game will hinge on the placement of the two chunks. (We didn't write in all the exclusions here, as we probably wouldn't spend more time on the setup in order to do so, relying on our understanding of the chunks to carry us through the questions.)

2.

The most important issue in this game will be the N, R, SO group.

We could have noted that R is "floating" above slots 4–6 since it cannot go in slots 1–3.

3.

MANHATTAN
PREP

Bravo if you figured out how to combine the SW or VW chunk rule with the S_V and VT rules! These super chunks will determine four of the assignments in the Number Line, with the P–R–Y rule taking up the other three.

4.

Did you figure out the K/M inference? We saw the same sort of thing in game 1 (L/P in slot 4).

This game, like most Basic Ordering games, will be ruled by the placement of its chunks. In this case, the placement of one chunk will determine the placement of the other. In fact, we could sketch out each of these *frames* (we'll discuss framing in much detail in a future chapter).

Here's the frame for when the NO chunk is in the first two slots:

And here is the frame for when the NO chunk is in the last two slots:

Inferences in the Questions

Because Basic Ordering games are generally back-end games, we will typically be making most of our inferences as we solve the questions themselves.

We will make these inferences at two different points—mostly, we'll make them at the point of the question stem, but sometimes we will make them in the answer choices themselves. In some ways, where you should be spending your thinking time is built into the design of each question. While certain questions require you to spend considerable thought time in the answer choices, we want you to develop a habit of doing as much work in the question stem as you can *before* considering the answers—this is another pause that ultimately saves time.

Some question stems provide no new information; we call these **unconditional questions.** These will ask you to consider something specific about the game as a whole—say, which elements can go in the final three spots, or, quite broadly, what must be true. Other unconditional questions will ask something specific about a position or an element such as "Who can go third?" or "Where can F go?" If the question limits itself to a certain element or part of the Number Line, make sure to run through these considerations before evaluating the answers. If the question asks something broad such as "What could be true?" you'll have to spend more time considering the answer choices, although a well-developed diagram and approach will help you quickly tackle these questions.

Conditional questions contain new information that we need to incorporate into what we know about a game. The new piece of information is applicable only to that question. That's why you should leave your original diagram alone and create a new one for most every conditional question. It will be helpful to organize your scratch paper with a clear set of work for each question. Label the work with the question number. If you're testing an answer choice, label that, too. Often, especially for back-end games, it will feel like the new piece of information in the condition is that central jigsaw piece that allows you to assemble a bunch of different rules that weren't coming together before. The new question-specific diagram that you create will frequently provide one or more satisfying inferences. It may even start a chain reaction that puts all the elements in slots. Knowing that, you want to be in the habit of fleshing out these inferences—"following the inference chain"—before moving on to the answer choices. Simply reading the new condition and then testing out the answer choices is inefficient. There won't always be a big chain of inferences, but when there is, the few moments you spend looking for it will pay big dividends. In fact, in every section of the exam, one of the main things the LSAT is designed to test is your ability to make inferences. If you're going to score your best, you need to use the mental muscles the LSAT is evaluating: your inference-making muscles.

While the new condition in a conditional question might trigger a breathtaking cascade of inferences, some are just not so impressive. It's rare that the condition will totally determine each element's position; at least a couple of elements are usually left "floating." If you try to force the inferences, you might end up making false ones. Instead, be comfortable noting which elements are left to take the remaining positions and noting which rules are attached to them that might further restrict their placement. Asking yourself "Who's left?" in this way is crucial to quickly solving many questions. If you're tempted to get an LSAT tattoo (don't), consider having it read: "Know what you know; know what you don't."

MANHATTAN
PREP

Drill It: Inferences in the Questions

Inferences are better learned through experience than through reading, so let's do a drill that exercises the inference-making muscles that you will rely on to solve questions. You will be given three Basic Ordering examples. After diagramming these examples and making any front-end inferences you can, you will be provided with a series of statements to evaluate. Some of them will be *unconditional,* in that the statements will not provide you with further information. Some of them will be *conditional,* in that they will ask you to evaluate the situation in light of additional information. For conditional statements, make sure to infer from the new condition the best you can before evaluating the statement. In all cases, your task is to figure out whether the statement must be true, must be false, or neither (i.e., could be true or false).

The two key skills we want you to work on are:

1. Being able to distinguish between what you know and what you don't
2. Inferring fully, but not over-inferring, when given conditional information in the statement

We suggest that you do your work and note your answers on a piece of scratch paper to better approximate your process on the digital test. This will also allow you to redo this exercise later if needed. Check your answers after each game to make sure you're on the right track.

1. Six movies—*Justice, Karina, Liberation, Martians, Naples,* and *Originals*—are to be played during a film festival, one at a time and consecutively. No other movies are to be shown, and each movie is shown only once. The schedule of movies must adhere to the following conditions:

    Naples is shown third.
    Liberation and *Originals* must be shown consecutively.
    Exactly one movie is shown between *Martians* and *Justice.*
    Karina is not shown second.

Statement	Must be true	Could be true or false	Must be false
1. *Martians* is shown first.			
2. *Liberation* is shown second.			
3. *Originals* is shown fourth.			
4. *Justice* is shown last.			
5. If *Karina* is shown first, *Justice* is shown last.			
6. If *Justice* is shown last, *Karina* is shown fifth.			
7. If *Liberation* is shown first, *Martians* is shown fourth.			
8. If *Naples* is shown after *Justice*, *Originals* is shown next to *Martian*.			

Remember to check your answers after each game.

2

2. Seven singers—S, T, V, W, X, Y, and Z—will perform on a variety show, one at a time and in order. The following conditions apply:

> Both T and W perform before Z.
> Exactly two singers perform after S but before V.
> Either V or X performs last.
> W does not perform immediately before or immediately after T.

Statement	Must be true	Could be true or false	Must be false
1. S performs first.			
2. W performs sixth.			
3. Z performs fourth.			
4. V does not perform third.			
5. If S is third, Z is fourth.			
6. If V is fifth, Z is sixth.			
7. If Z is fourth, Y is sixth.			
8. If W is fifth, Y is first.			

MANHATTAN
PREP

3. Seven different appetizers—P, Q, R, S, T, V, and W—are to be brought out during a cocktail party one at a time and in order. No other appetizers are to be served. The order in which the appetizers are served must adhere to the following conditions:

> Exactly two appetizers are served both before T and after R.
> V is served before W, with exactly one appetizer served in between them.
> Q is served fourth.
> If V is served before R, P must be served immediately before or after T.

Statement	Must be true	Could be true or false	Must be false
1. R is served third.			
2. V is served fifth.			
3. V is served first and P is served last.			
4. T is served immediately before V.			
5. If P is served second, W is served last.			
6. V is served third.			
7. P is served last.			
8. S is served immediately before R.			

Solutions: Inferences in the Questions

Note that your diagram might have more inferences than ours. We limited our inferences to the first and second levels of inferences that a test-taker would probably make in real time. Also note that you might later find writing out all the inferences for Basic Ordering games to be overkill. As we've mentioned before, for now, err on the side of overdoing it.

1.

Statement	Must be true	Could be true or false	Must be false
1. *Martians* is shown first.			X
2. *Liberation* is shown second.		X	
3. *Originals* is shown fourth.			X
4. *Justice* is shown last.		X	
5. If *Karina* is shown first, *Justice* is shown last.			X
6. If *Justice* is shown last, *Karina* is shown fifth.	X		
7. If *Liberation* is shown first, *Martians* is shown fourth.		X	
8. If *Naples* is shown after *Justice*, *Originals* is shown next to *Martians*.		X	

1. **Must be false.** If M were first, J would have to be third. Since N must be third, this is impossible.

2. **Could be true or false.** If L is second, then O must be first. Then the MJ chunk must go in 4–6, leaving K to go in 5:

   O   L   N   M/J   K   J/M

3. **Must be false.** This would leave nowhere for the MJ chunk:

(It's a good idea to strike through any invalid hypothetical you create as you work through a game—you don't want to mistake it later for a valid one and use it to answer a question incorrectly.)

MANHATTAN
PREP

4. **Could be true or false.** If J is last, M must be in 4. This leaves room for the OL chunk in 1 and 2:

<u>O/L</u>   <u>O/L</u>   <u>N</u>   <u>M</u>   <u>   </u>   <u>J</u>

5. **Must be false.** With K in 1, the only way to properly arrange our chunks is to place the OL chunk in 5 and 6, leaving space for the MJ chunk to straddle N:

<u>K</u>   <u>M/J</u>   <u>N</u>   <u>J/M</u>   <u>O/L</u>   <u>L/O</u>

6. **Must be true.** J in 6 puts M in 4, and the OL chunk in 1 and 2. The only space left for K is 5:

<u>O/L</u>   <u>L/O</u>   <u>N</u>   <u>M</u>   <u>K</u>   <u>J</u>

7. **Could be true or false.** L first puts O second, and the MJ chunk in 4 and 6. It's acceptable for M to be in either slot:

<u>L</u>   <u>O</u>   <u>N</u>   <u>M/J</u>   <u>K</u>   <u>J/M</u>

8. **Could be true or false.** The only way for J to go before N is for J to be in 2. If J were in 1, M would have to be in 3:

<u>   </u>   <u>J</u>   <u>N</u>   <u>M</u>   <u>   </u>   <u>   </u>

This leaves only the last two slots for O and L, and while O could go in 5, it could also go in 6.

2.

By the way, you could have combined the rules about T, W, and Z into something like this:

Statement	Must be true	Could be true or false	Must be false
1. S performs first.		X	
2. W performs sixth.			X
3. Z performs fourth.		X	
4. V does not perform third.	X		
5. If S is third, Z is fourth.			X
6. If V is fifth, Z is sixth.		X	
7. If Z is fourth, Y is sixth.	X		
8. If W is fifth, Y is first.		X	

1. **Could be true or false.** If S performs first, we have this framework:

$$\underline{\text{S}} \quad \underline{} \quad \underline{} \quad \underline{\text{V}} \quad \underline{} \quad \underline{} \quad \underline{\text{X}}$$

And here's one possibility:

$$\underline{\text{S}} \quad \underline{\text{T}} \quad \underline{\text{Y}} \quad \underline{\text{V}} \quad \underline{\text{W}} \quad \underline{\text{Z}} \quad \underline{\text{X}}$$

However, S certainly doesn't have to go first, as we will see below.

Note that in the hypothetical we created above, T and W could switch places. This will always be true in this game—we will stop noting it—unless we see a condition that states the placement of one or the other.

2. **Must be false.** Z must follow W, and this breaks the rule that V or X must be last.

3. **Could be true or false.**

$$\underline{\text{T}} \quad \underline{} \quad \underline{\text{W}} \quad \underline{\text{Z}} \quad \underline{} \quad \underline{} \quad \underline{}$$

This leaves only one place for our SV chunk:

$$\underline{\text{T}} \quad \underline{\text{S}} \quad \underline{\text{W}} \quad \underline{\text{Z}} \quad \underline{\text{V}} \quad \underline{} \quad \underline{}$$

We can place X last and Y right before it.

But we also have seen examples in which Z is not fourth.

4. **Must be true.** If we were to place V third, where would S go?

5. **Must be false.**

$$\underline{} \quad \underline{} \quad \underline{\text{S}} \quad \underline{} \quad \underline{} \quad \underline{\text{V}} \quad \underline{}$$

MANHATTAN
PREP

To fill in Z, we need the TW chunk to come before it. Since we only have two spaces available before slot 4 and they are consecutive, we can't place Z fourth.

6. **Could be true or false.**

   ___   S   ___   ___   V   ___   X

At this point, do we have to put Z sixth? We know we need T and W before Z, perhaps like this:

   W   S   T   ___   V   ___   X

Z and Y are the only elements left, and there's a space for each of them. Z might go sixth, but it could also go fourth.

7. **Must be true.** If Z is fourth, there is only one spot for our SV chunk:

   T   S   W   Z   V   ___   ___

We'll have to place X last, and Y must go sixth.

Note that placing Z fourth determines the placement of every element except T and W.

8. **Could be true or false.**

   ___   ___   ___   ___   W   Z   V/X

If we place X in 7, we will need the SV chunk in 1–4:

   S   ___   ___   V   W   Z   X

However, if we place V in 7, we *can* place Y first:

   Y   ___   ___   S   W   Z   V

2

3.

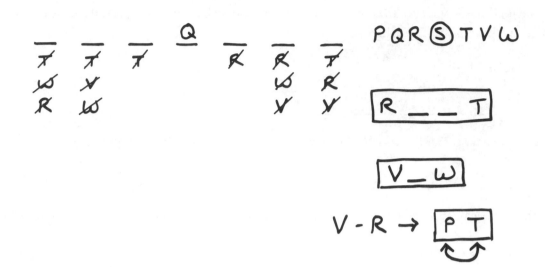

Statement	Must be true	Could be true (or false)	Must be false
1. R is served third.		X	
2. V is served fifth.		X	
3. V is served first and P is served last.			X
4. T is served immediately before V.			X
5. If P is served second, W is served last.	X		
6. V is served third.			X
7. P is served last.			X
8. S is served immediately before R.		X	

1. **Could be true or false.** We have no written inferences indicating that this is prohibited. We could do a quick mental hypothetical:

   __ __ R Q __ T __

   There's still space for the VW chunk, and the V–R rule is not triggered. It's totally fine for R to go third.

2. **Could be true or false.** The last question set us up for this. This definitely can work:

   P/S   P/S   R   Q   V   T   W

   But, we also could place V somewhere else:

   V   R   W   Q   T   P   S

3. **Must be false.** From the last question, we see that P doesn't have to be last in this situation. But could it be? If V is first, it must come before R, meaning T and P must be consecutive. That gives us:

MANHATTAN
PREP

V __ W Q S T P

But we can't correctly place the R three spots before T.

4. **Must be false.** This would create an R___ ___ TV ___W super chunk. Wow—that spans all seven slots and pushes Q out of slot 4! This is a common issue with two chunks: they often have trouble coexisting without causing trouble.

5. **Must be true.** With P in 2, where can we fit R___ ___T? Only in 3–6:

__ P R Q __ T __

The VW chunk must go in slots 5–7.

6. **Must be false.** If V is in 3, W is in slot 5:

__ __ V Q W __ __

The RT chunk can't fit anywhere. We should add to the original diagram that V can't go third and W can't go fifth.

7. **Must be false.** If P is last, it seems we have plenty of room to place everyone. We can place the RT chunk in 3–6:

__ __ R Q __ T P

But we can't fit our VW chunk anywhere. If we place the RT chunk in 2–5, we bypass that problem:

__ R __ Q T __ P

We can put V in 1–3, but now V is before R, which requires TP.

Regardless of where we put the RT chunk, P last doesn't work.

8. **Could be true or false.** We saw in question 2 that S could go right before R—and we saw that it could not!

Did you notice how restricted this game is? We could actually break up the diagram (frame it) according to where we place the RT chunk:

V R W Q T P S

With S and P perhaps switching places in the second frame, there are only three different arrangements in total. Consider how much easier it would have been to answer all the questions with those frames. Let's talk about that later!

Question Type Spotlight: Orientation and Standard Questions

Mastery over Logic Games isn't just about being able to set up clever diagrams. It's necessary to be strong at each part of the process. One critical component of this mastery is the ability to attack questions in an efficient manner.

Throughout these first few chapters, we will break down the various types of questions that appear in Logic Games. For some of them, hopefully for many of them, the processes we recommend will be completely intuitive—processes you would have used anyway—and they will require no work for you to implement effectively.

However, for other types of questions, it is very likely that the most efficient approach might seem at first a bit counterintuitive or twisted to you. It's understandable why—some of the most challenging Logic Games questions are just like tongue twisters for your mind. It's going to take work and commitment to improve in these areas, because improvement not only requires learning concepts, it requires turning this understanding into good habits.

Let's start by taking a close look at the two most common types of questions you will see in Logic Games: what we call *Orientation questions* and *Standard questions*. These question types together make up more than 80% of all questions that you will see in the games section.

Orientation Questions

Nearly every game that appears on the LSAT will begin with what we call an **Orientation question.** Orientation questions ask us to identify one arrangement of elements that is possible based on the game's rules. Every Orientation question we've seen asks us to identify one possible arrangement that *could* be valid, given the rules; the four wrong answer choices are arrangements that, per the rules, *cannot* work.

We've talked a lot about how important it is to make inferences, but for many Orientation questions, you can work directly from the rules without making any inferences. Each of the wrong choices will directly violate a given rule. This is different from all other question types.

Furthermore, for most games, Orientation questions are generally designed so that individual rules allow you to eliminate exactly one of the answer choices. If you have four rules in a game, it's likely that each of them will allow you to get rid of exactly one of the four wrong answer choices. If you have fewer than four rules relating to the arrangement of elements, you should expect rules to eliminate more than one answer each. However, sometimes there's a rule embedded in the scenario. For example, a scenario might tell you that "every student performs exactly once," and one of the incorrect answers to the Orientation question might leave out a student and illegally list another twice.

Based on all of these characteristics, the general process that we recommend for Orientation questions is for you to use the rules, one at a time, to eliminate answer choices. You want to develop a good sense of when it might be possible for rules to eliminate more than one answer (such as when you have fewer than four rules about the arrangement of elements), but in general expect that if a rule eliminates an answer choice, it won't eliminate others, and you can save a little time by moving on to the next rule after eliminating one answer.

Let's return to the Orientation question from our Getting Familiar game on page 23 to discuss this further.

> James swims in a lower-numbered lane than Kopov.
> Nu swims in either the first lane or the seventh lane.
> Markson swims in a lane numbered two lower than Price's.
> Hewitt swims in lane 4.

1. Which of the following could be an accurate list of swimmers, listed in order from lane 1 through lane 7?

   (A) Nu, Luis, James, Kopov, Markson, Hewitt, Price
   (B) James, Luis, Markson, Hewitt, Price, Kopov, Nu
   (C) Nu, Kopov, Markson, Hewitt, Price, James, Luis
   (D) Luis, Markson, James, Hewitt, Price, Kopov, Nu
   (E) Markson, Nu, Price, Hewitt, James, Luis, Kopov

All we need to do is read one rule at a time and scan the answer choices for one that violates the rule.

The first rule tells us that J comes before K.

We scan the answers quickly for the one answer we can eliminate based on this rule. We see that in answer (C), J comes after K, so eliminate that choice. It's unlikely that the LSAT will have two answers that violate this rule, so we can save time by "restarting" with a new rule instead of seeing if J comes before K in answers (D) and (E)—most likely it does.

Now we're looking for N to be in 1 or 7.

Which of the remaining choices doesn't have N in either spot?

We can eliminate answer (E) and move on.

Now we're looking for M to be two lower than P (M___P). Answer (D) violates this. (By the way, if you misunderstood this rule to mean M___ ___P, it should have been a red flag that *so many* of the answer choices violate that interpretation.)

Easy so far?

Now we're down to one rule and two answers. H is in 4. We can eliminate (A). **Answer (B) is correct.**

Do we need to verify it? It'd be nice to do so, but we don't have the time.

The correct answer for an Orientation question could turn out to be a valuable tool to be used for other questions—it is one order that you know for sure works. Especially when you are stuck on other problems, having one possible order can turn out to be very useful.

You may intuitively feel that it would be easier to evaluate the answer choices one at a time, comparing them against your diagram or against the rules. That's completely understandable, but it tends to be more efficient to focus clearly on one issue at a time than to check each answer choice for all possible issues at once. However, feel free to experiment and see what works fastest.

Smart Tip: Rule Reordering and Using Your Diagram

One approach that you might want to try with Orientation questions is using the "simpler" rules first to evaluate answer choices. For example, imagine that a game includes these two rules:

> H is either two floors below J or two floors above K.
> K is fifth.

Which one of those do you want to use first to scan five answer choices? Clearly, it will be a lot faster to start with the second rule!

Try reordering the rules to see if it makes things easier. If it adds unnecessary complexity to your life, forget about it!

Another alternative strategy you might want to test out is to use your diagram to eliminate answers to an Orientation question. Each of the rules should be represented in your diagram! This can serve as a good check of your diagram and help you "own" the game more thoroughly. It's generally best to simply look at the rules, not the inferences you drew from those rules, although very occasionally you'll face an Orientation question for which working from the inferences you've made will speed up your work. In these cases, your comfort with working from the diagram will help you adjust to looking at the inferences when you realize that the original rules aren't doing the trick.

By the way, certain types of games will at times allow for alternative methods for solving Orientation questions. We'll discuss these methods in the respective chapters.

MANHATTAN
PREP

Standard Questions

We use the term **Standard questions** for a set of questions that are all very closely related to one another.

Standard questions ask us to evaluate five answer choices based on the information we've been given and to determine what must be true, could be true or false, or must be false.

Certain Standard questions begin by giving us new, additional information that applies to that question only; for example, "If X is third ..." or "If Y is before S ..." We discussed these in the inferences section, and we call these **conditional questions.**

Here are some examples of unconditional and conditional question stems for Standard questions:

Unconditional
Which of the following must be true?
Which of the following cannot be false?
Which of the following could be true?
Each of the following must be false EXCEPT:

Conditional
If X is third, which of the following could be false?
If K is before N, each of the following must be true EXCEPT:
If G is on the same team as H, which of the following must be false?
If M is not selected, which of the following cannot be true?

Perhaps you noticed that some of these question stems represent different ways of asking the same question. When you encounter question stems that involve EXCEPT or CANNOT and you find yourself a bit turned around, it can be helpful to think about the more basic equivalent question stem. Here's a chart of different ways of asking the same thing:

This...	Is equivalent to...	And...
Which of the following must be true?	Each of the following could be false EXCEPT:	Which of the following cannot be false? (rare)
Which of the following could be true?	Each of the following must be false EXCEPT:	
Which of the following could be false? (rare)	Each of the following must be true EXCEPT:	
Which of the following must be false?	Each of the following could be true EXCEPT:	Which of the following cannot be true? (rare)

Keep in mind that question stems in the second and third columns are generally far less common than those in the first. However, you certainly want to be prepared for anything that can come up, and if you understand the equivalents, it's easy enough.

The manner in which a particular Standard question is asked should intuitively impact how you are going to approach and think about the five answer choices. Let's lay out a few key principles:

Evaluating answers is less about proving statements true or false and more about recognizing what you know and what you don't.

Let's think about the most basic question stem possible:

"Which of the following must be true?"

On a different type of exam, if we were given five answer choices and told that exactly one of them must be true, we might expect that the other four answers must be false.

However, on the LSAT, except for a few rogue situations, the wrong answers to a "must be true" question will *not* be answers that must be false. The wrong answers will be ones that could be true or that could be false. In other words, **wrong answers to a must be true question will be answers about which we do not have enough information to be certain.**

Here's a chart of the four different ways Standard questions can be asked, along with what you should typically expect from the correct and incorrect answer choices:

If the question stem is…	The right answer…	The wrong answers…
Which of the following must be true?	must be true	almost always could be true or false (though a few rare ones must be false)
Which of the following could be true?	could be true	must be false
Which of the following could be false? (rare)	could be false	must be true
Which of the following must be false?	must be false	are almost always ones that could be true or false (though a few rare ones must be true)

Focus on what you know, and worry less about what you don't.

As we mentioned earlier, the ability to differentiate between what "could be" and what "must be" is absolutely critical to your success—you simply will not be successful with these games unless you are able to organize information in this way.

Faced with this reality, many of us are inclined to try to keep track of both sides of the fence—all of those things that must be true or false and all of those variations that could be true. And we can make things even more complex by trying to keep them separate in our minds. Trying to accomplish all of this can make the games harder than they need to be, and we don't suggest this, particularly when you're early in your LSAT prep.

Instead, focus on correctly understanding that which *must* be—either must be true or must be false, depending on the situation—and pay less attention (and time) to ways that rules or games *could* play out. That's not to say that you won't ever need to figure out what could be, but it's common for students to spend too much time on that side of the fence. You *always* need to understand what must be true, while you only *sometimes* need to know what could be true. Finally, what's particularly dangerous is figuring out something that could be true and mistaking it for something that must be. Keep yourself focused on the "must be" side of the fence, and when you need to peek over to the other side, do it.

Conveniently, it is far easier to keep track of what must be, and to recognize when inferences and answers don't fit into that bucket. It is much more difficult to keep track of what must be *and* what could be as you make your inferences and evaluate answer choices.

Eliminate wrong answers OR search for a right answer.

For Reading Comprehension and Logical Reasoning, we recommend that you answer most every question by using a process of elimination. This is not what we recommend for Logic Games.

Rather, for Logic Games, we recommend that your process be driven by whether it will be easier to identify the correct answer or to knock out the wrong ones. You generally want to stick with one strategy on each pass through the answer choices. For instance, you might first do an elimination pass and then consider which of the remaining answers is correct.

Let's break down a couple of different question stems to see what this might look like:

Stem 1: *"Which of the following must be true?"* For a question like this, we know that one answer, the correct answer, will be something that must be true. Ideally, the right answer for this type of question will be something we *already* know to be true, based on an inference we made in the setup or based on a new condition in the question stem. Knowing this, how should we attack such a question? By searching for the right answer!

Of course, the ideal situation isn't always the real situation. Perhaps you missed an inference. Or, perhaps the way the question is designed, the right answer is one that you just can't anticipate before looking at the answers. That's fine; you can most definitely still get these questions correct, and we'll discuss secondary strategies for these situations in just a bit. However, do keep in mind that for "must be true" questions, your baseline strategy should be to look to your inferences for the answer. For conditional "must be true" questions, this means following the inference chain until you don't see any more inferences, asking "who's left" to see if you missed any, and *then* doing your first pass through the answers.

Let's take a look at another question stem:

Stem 2: *"Which of the following could be true?"* For this type of question, we know that the right answer could be true, and the four wrong answers must be false.

Will it be easy to spot what could be true?

Sometimes you'll know for certain that an answer could be true, but more often you won't. Most of the time, knowing for sure that an answer could be true will require you to invest some time and energy.

For a question that asks what could be true, it makes more sense to use a process of elimination. You know that four of the answer choices **must be false,** and it's easier to make quick decisions about what must be. So, in general, for a "could be true" question, you want to arrive at the correct answer by eliminating incorrect answers.

Stem 3: *"Which of the following could be false?"* Here, the four wrong answers will be things that must be true and should be the easier ones to spot. Start by eliminating those.

Stem 4: *"Which of the following must be false?"* For these, the correct answer will generally be easier to find than the four incorrect (could be true) answers.

To summarize, we want you to develop flexibility, tailoring your approach to the answers to the specific task the question asks you.

Here's a chart listing the approaches:

Question Stem	Primary Strategy
Which of the following must be true?	**Find** the "must be true" right answer.
Which of the following could be true?	**Eliminate** the "must be false" wrong answers.
Which of the following could be false?	**Eliminate** the "must be true" wrong answers.
Which of the following must be false?	**Find** the "must be false" right answer.

When testing answers, break the "must be trues" and prove the "could be trues."

Imagine you're looking to find the answer that must be true and it isn't jumping out. This doesn't mean you skip the question! It's time to go to plan B: **testing answers.**

You're down to answers (D) and (E):

    (D) J finishes no later than fourth.
    (E) F finishes no earlier than third.

Both look good on first glance, so it's time to dig deeper and test them. What do you do?

How does the following strategy sound? You test out (D) by placing J third and seeing if it works. It does! You pick (D) and move on.

Sound good? No! You have not tested out whether J *must* finish earlier than fourth, you've simply confirmed that it *can*. When you want to test an answer choice for a "must be" question, you should try to "break it." You should see if J can be placed later than fourth. If answer (D) is correct, you'll be unable to place J anywhere but in slots 1–4.

Confused? Imagine a mischievous farmer tells you that all carrots, tangerines, and melons must be orange, and your job is to figure out which one of those three "rules" is true. What would you do? Would you go looking for orange carrots? No! You would search for carrots (and tangerines and melons) that were not orange. You'd try to "break" these alleged rules. Finding an orange melon would not prove that melons must be orange (since some could be orange and others not), but finding a yellow melon would definitely prove something. **To test a "must be," see if you can "break it"!**

The rule of breaking "must be" questions applies to both must be true and must be false questions. With must be true questions, you try to prove that answers can be false. With must be false questions, you aim to show that answers could be true.

Quick quiz: How would you check answer choice (E)? (F finishes no earlier than third.)

You would see if you can have F finish earlier than third.

Quick quiz 2: If you eliminated answer (D) in the scenario above, what should you do?

If you're short on time, select answer (E), flag the question, and come back and confirm it if you have time. If you're on pace to complete the section comfortably, confirm it right then and there.

Now we have our rule about how to test "must be" questions, but what about "could be" questions? Consider it for a moment; how would you confirm that, for example, G could come before L? The way to test could be answers is probably more straightforward to you: Simply see if it works! For could be false questions, you are working to prove that an answer could be false, which, a bit confusingly, means you are testing the opposite of the answer choice (e.g., if you're testing whether "K finishes fourth" could be false, you see if K could finish in another spot).

At this point, we have our testing strategies—break "must be" questions, prove "could be" questions—but we shouldn't forget that testing answers is not necessarily the most efficient strategy. In fact, trial and error is a slow strategy and one that we should only use when the other tools in our arsenal are not working. That said, a MacGyver game player knows that there will be times when we need to test out answers. Sometimes we will need to test the final two choices after more efficient tools have eliminated the other three, and sometimes we will have to test four answers in a row, either because the question is designed to require that level of work or because we've missed an inference in our diagram.

Here's our chart again, this time with our backup strategies:

Question Stem	Primary Strategy	Backup
Which of the following must be true?	Find the "must be true" right answer.	Test answers by trying to prove they could be false.
Which of the following could be true?	Eliminate the "must be false" wrong answers.	Test answers by trying to prove they could be true.
Which of the following could be false?	Eliminate the "must be true" wrong answers.	Test answers by trying to prove they could be false.
Which of the following must be false?	Find the "must be false" right answer.	Test answers by trying to prove if they could be true.

If you're the type of student that is trying to memorize that chart, stop! You can't memorize your way to a great LSAT score; instead, make sure you *understand* the ideas, and then *practice* them on your way to a great LSAT score! Soon you'll find yourself naturally using the primary strategy and switching midstream to the backup strategy when needed. Great. This exam isn't about following fixed strategies—the LSAT rewards flexibility.

All of the question-specific advice can seem overly regimented if we get too lost in the details, but hopefully these processes will soon (or already) feel intuitive for you. In summary, when thinking about the answer choices, our first option is to use what we know to either quickly identify the right answer or to eliminate wrong answers (and we want to avoid trying to do both of these things at once). If that isn't viable, then we want to evaluate answer choices efficiently, running through hypothetical scenarios in a way that allows us to know with certainty that each answer is correct or incorrect. You should soon find yourself switching strategies to match the specifics of each question.

When in doubt, defer.

One of the easiest ways to run out of time on the Logic Games section is to spend too much time investigating answers—particularly those that we end up eliminating. To avoid this, we want to work from what must be true whenever possible. We also want to be savvy, or what ordinary people refer to as "lazy."

Anyone who has played a few games has experienced what we'll call the "d'oh!" moment. It can look like this: it's the second question of a game, and you're asked to find what must be true. You are facing four "could be true" answers and one must be true. You look at answer (A) and can't quickly decide, so you start to test it. 10 seconds later, you've proven it's not a must be true. Answer (B) also looks good, and it's only after 15 seconds of testing that it turns out to be a dud. Answer (C) takes another 15 seconds to eliminate, and when you get to answer (D), it takes you only 5 seconds to realize that it's the correct answer—d'oh!

Wouldn't it have been lovely if you had looked at answer (A), **deferred judgment,** thinking, "Geez, I don't know, let me see if there's an easy answer," again deferred judgment on answers (B) and (C), and then quickly seen that answer (D) was correct? That sequence could take about 20 seconds as compared to the 45 the original sequence took. The key was to defer judgment, and that is one of the hallmark moves of high-level game players/MacGyvers.

Many Logic Games questions are designed so that the right answer will be easy to spot by anyone who has done his or her homework during the diagramming phase or after considering the new condition that an "If" question provides. The wrong answers, as we discussed above, can take a lot of time to confirm as incorrect, and thus deferring judgment can save you significant time.

But what if you end up deferring judgment on all five answer choices? That definitely happens, even to strong game players, but let's do the math and see how bad the damage is. Imagine there are five questions on which you whip out the deferring judgment tactic. For one of those questions, you end up not finding a "d'oh!" answer on the first pass. How much time have you wasted? It might be only 30 seconds. How much time do you save on the four other questions? Easily more than 30 seconds.

The key to deferring judgment is keeping your cool. It will happen at times that you cannot defer your way to an obvious answer, and in those situations, you'll have to restart and use your other strategies. Probably, you'll need to dig deeper into answer choices.

Use your gut.

At times, you'll have no choice but to start testing out answer choices, and then the issue becomes which choices to test first. It definitely doesn't matter if you start with (A) or (E), but if you happen to have seen an answer that somehow strikes you as more tempting, start with that one! If it turns out to be the answer and this is a practice test, flag the question and when you go back to review the question, figure out what about that answer might have made it more tempting. Perhaps it involved an element in a chunk (often helpful in "must be false" questions), or perhaps it involved an element that had no rules attached to it (often in correct "could be true" answers).

It's impossible to say what would make an answer choice more tempting in general, but there are small issues that your deep LSAT brain might understand before the rest of you does! It might seem like we're suggesting you "use the Force," and if you do have some Jedi mind trick abilities, definitely use them, but what we're actually saying is to let all the patterns and understandings you gain through your study and practice inform your choices.

Smart Tip: The LSAT Likes Math

If you're not sure where to start looking at answer choices, and if two or three answers involve math (e.g., "G is assigned to no more than three groups") and the other two are more straightforward (e.g., "G is assigned to the Bluegrass group"), there's a slightly higher chance that the answer will be one of the "math" choices. Why? Because those answers are often harder to figure out, and the LSAT needs to put some tough questions in each LSAT to help make it easier to tell the difference between a 174 and a 178 game player.

We'll talk in later chapters about how to stay on top of the mathematical issues that arise in games, but for now, when in doubt, head towards the math answers. Are we saying that you can count on this and simply choose based on how the answers look? No. But a lot of timing strategies on the LSAT are about knowing where to start working, and when you're lost, this is a better place than others.

Use hypotheticals.

At times, you might find that you'll need to draw out a scenario to test an answer choice. We call these **hypotheticals** (and we'll use this term to refer to valid hypotheticals only). While using hypotheticals is sometimes a sign that you're missing an inference in your diagram, or not approaching a question correctly, there may be times when there's not much else you can do. Even in those times when you are missing an inference, it's often faster to start drawing out a hypothetical than to sit there hoping for a flash of inspiration. Even if it's not ideal, we want to make this approach as efficient as possible.

Be very careful not to get turned around when using hypotheticals with "must be true" questions. It's not really possible for one hypothetical to prove that a situation must be true. That would be like looking at the sky, seeing a cloud directly above, and stating that clouds are always directly above you!

When you are facing a "must be" question, you more often use a hypothetical scenario to *disprove* answers. If you do need to confirm that something must be true with a hypothetical, you'll need to use multiple hypotheticals. If something must be true, it will be true in every hypothetical you can create. Clearly, this is not a very efficient strategy.

MANHATTAN
PREP

That doesn't mean you shouldn't understand how to use it, but you'll also want to note any question on which you find yourself scrambling so dramatically, and later review that game and question to see how you could have avoided such a situation.

When you are facing a "could be" question, hypotheticals are more obviously useful. If you want to determine whether it could be true that Z comes before X, and you can make a hypothetical in which it is true, then that's the answer! However, what if you write out a hypothetical and X comes before Z? Should you eliminate the answer that states that Z can come before X? No! Just because your one hypothetical didn't work, that doesn't mean another one wouldn't. So again, you're forced to use multiple hypotheticals to work through the answer choices, and again, this is inefficient.

Make your previous work count.

Smart game players know that once they've answered a few questions, they're already armed with some hypotheticals. Let's imagine that the answer to an Orientation question for a Basic Ordering game was the following:

(D)   R, M, O, F, T

Let's also imagine that we were subsequently asked the following:

3. Each of the following could be true EXCEPT:

    (A) M comes exactly two spaces before F.
    (B) M comes exactly one space before F.
    (C) R comes at some time before T.
    (D) O comes exactly two spaces before R.
    (E) O comes exactly two spaces after R.

Which answers can we immediately eliminate? Because we know that the correct answer to that earlier Orientation question is a possible scenario, we can eliminate answer choices (A), (C), and (E), each of which describes that scenario, and therefore could be true.

Similarly, in the question below, which answers can we eliminate based on the answer to the Orientation question?

4. Which of the following must be true?

    (A) R comes at some point after O.
    (B) M and F are separated by at least two other elements.
    (C) Either F or O comes last.
    (D) F and R come consecutively.
    (E) M comes third.

We're messing with you—they can *all* be eliminated, which only occurs in LSAT nightmares. They can all be eliminated because we see that none of the answer choices describe what is true in the scenario we compared them against. While you hopefully won't use this strategy to eliminate all five answer choices, you should look for opportunities to

MANHATTAN
PREP

use previous work to eliminate and choose answers. If during your work on a question you draw out a scenario that is invalid, **be sure to cross it out** so that you don't later misguidedly use it as an example of a valid scenario.

The strategy behind using previous work is no different from what we discussed above. For "must be" questions, look for past examples that disprove answers, and for "could be" questions, look for examples that show them to be possible.

Move along or heed the warning!

If you are able to answer each and every question in every games section with enough finesse and speed to finish the section with a few minutes to spare, bravo! You can put this book down and relax. But if you're a regular person, you're going to find that some questions are stumping you. When should you move on and when should you not?

In general, if you're struggling with the first two questions of a game, it's an indication that either you made a careless error when representing a rule—perhaps misreading the word "before" as "after"?—or you've missed a big inference in your diagram. The questions in a game are *very* roughly organized in order of difficulty, so you should be able to figure out the first two questions quickly. If you do find yourself spinning your wheels on question 2, for example, take one more look at the question stem and choices, and if you don't see that you've made a slip-up, take a slow turn through your rules and then each choice. Most likely, you've missed an inference, and this question is kindly telling you so. Hopefully, you've just misread the question, and when you return to it later, you will see the errors of your ways.

If you're struggling on a question later on in a game, it's more likely that it's simply a tougher question and you're not seeing the inference that's being tested. Luckily, these questions aren't worth any more than the easier questions.

Get the right ones wrong.

Huh?

Yes, you will be more successful on the LSAT if you allow yourself to get a certain number incorrect. The key is to get the harder, time-consuming questions wrong, and the easier ones right. Ideally, by working speedily through the easy questions, and moving on when you encounter impossible questions, you will save time for the tough-but-not-impossible questions.

If you go into a test with this mind-set, you will be much more likely to finish a section on time and get a score that accurately reflects your ability to reason the way the LSAT demands. If you lose three minutes on each of three impossible questions—probably still getting them wrong—and end up having to guess on five questions that would have been simple for you if you had simply had a bit more time, your score will reflect your inability to manage your time on the test, not your impressive brain power vis-à-vis logic and reasoning.

If you end up with extra time, go back and work on those impossible questions.

Become familiar with how many questions you generally can get wrong and still get your goal score, and go ahead and get that number incorrect.

Each time you get a higher score on a practice test, simply set your goal score two points higher than the last time, and reduce the number of questions you can get wrong by two. You may be surprised at the results…

MANHATTAN
PREP

Getting Familiar (Take 2!)

Now that we've laid out the primary strategies for setting up Basic Ordering games, let's return to the game we tried at the beginning of the chapter. We'll use it as an opportunity to practice what you've just learned, and we'll reinforce those ideas in the solution write-up. Try solving it again on your own before reading through our solution. (By the way, we suggest that you replay games regularly—it's a great way to master them.)

One last tip: keep an eye on how often the chunk is crucial!

Exactly seven swimmers—Hewitt, James, Kopov, Luis, Markson, Nu, and Price—will race in the 50-meter freestyle event. Each swimmer will swim in exactly one of seven lanes, numbered 1 through 7. No two swimmers share the same lane. Lane assignments comply with the following conditions:

> James swims in a lower-numbered lane than Kopov.
> Nu swims in either the first lane or the seventh lane.
> Markson swims in a lane numbered two lower than Price's.
> Hewitt swims in lane 4.

1. Which of the following could be an accurate list of swimmers, listed in order from lane 1 through lane 7?

    (A) Nu, Luis, James, Kopov, Markson, Hewitt, Price
    (B) James, Luis, Markson, Hewitt, Price, Kopov, Nu
    (C) Nu, Kopov, Markson, Hewitt, Price, James, Luis
    (D) Luis, Markson, James, Hewitt, Price, Kopov, Nu
    (E) Markson, Nu, Price, Hewitt, James, Luis, Kopov

2. Which one of the following must be false?

    (A) Price swims in lane 5.
    (B) Price swims in lane 7.
    (C) Markson swims in lane 2.
    (D) Kopov swims in lane 3.
    (E) James swims in lane 6.

3. If James swims in lane 1, then each of the following could be true EXCEPT:

    (A) Kopov swims in a lower-numbered lane than Hewitt.
    (B) Luis swims in a lower-numbered lane than Hewitt.
    (C) Markson swims in a higher-numbered lane than Hewitt.
    (D) Kopov swims in a lower-numbered lane than Price.
    (E) Luis swims in a lower-numbered lane than Markson.

4. If Price swims in lane 3, which one of the following could be true?

    (A) Kopov swims in lane 2.
    (B) James swims in lane 6.
    (C) Luis swims in lane 2.
    (D) Nu swims in lane 1.
    (E) Kopov swims in lane 7.

5. Which of the following could be a partial and accurate list of swimmers matched with the lanes in which they swim?

    (A) lane 1: Nu; lane 2: Markson; lane 6: Luis
    (B) lane 5: James; lane 6: Kopov; lane 7: Luis
    (C) lane 3: Luis; lane 4: Hewitt; lane 5: James
    (D) lane 4: Hewitt; lane 5: Luis; lane 7: Kopov
    (E) lane 2: James; lane 5: Markson; lane 6: Kopov

MANHATTAN
PREP

2

How to Review Your Work

You've just done a game (again) and you're ready to check your answers. Before you do that, let's discuss how to use the explanations to check your *work,* which is much more important than checking just the answers.

Let's start by outlining the typical (and less-than-ideal) approach. Imagine that you've just finished a really tough game. You dutifully start reading the explanations, and with their help, the clouds of confusion part. "Ah!" you say. "I now see how I should have done that." You feel good.

The problem with this is that you've now let the explanation do all the work and you've passively received it. That good feeling is a trap because we tend to fool ourselves into thinking that we've learned something when reading explanations. The goal of practice is to actively develop your skills, not simply to admire someone else's!

To wring the most learning out of your work, do as much of the figuring out on your own as you can, using the explanations as confirmation. Here's how:

1. **Solve a game.** Flag any questions that take you too long or are particularly difficult.

2. **If you crashed and burned,** take a break and then come back and give it another try. If you're still stumped, take a quick glance at the first part of the explanation provided. Is there a general idea that you didn't have when playing the game? An inference you missed? If so, jump back into the game and try to solve it yourself. In short, use as much of the explanation as you need, but no more, to kick-start your own work on the game.

3. **If you do okay** (i.e., you don't crash and burn), check your answers with the answer key. Don't look at the solutions yet. Instead, go back and re-solve any that you flagged, including those that you ultimately got right. If you flagged them on your first pass, clearly you were unsure about something or moving too slowly. Go back through each question a second time and look for a cleaner, more efficient way to solve the problem.

4. **Once you've finished the game and checked your answers,** compare your process to what is described in our solutions. If your approach is different than ours, get a general sense of our approach, stop reading, and see if you can re-solve the game using that approach. When you're done, use the solutions to evaluate your work. Look for ways that you could have solved the game more efficiently.

5. Finally, **if you struggled with a game** (this includes games that you were successful on but which took too long), note it in a special list and re-solve the game in a few days, and then a week or two after that. While it might be counterintuitive, replaying games until you've mastered them is just as valuable as, and sometimes more valuable than, doing a new game for the first time.

Answer Key

1. B   4. C
2. C   5. E
3. C

Step 1: Picture the Game

We recommend that you start every game by reading the scenario *and* skimming the rules before you start drawing in order to gain a big-picture understanding of the parameters. This game began with the following scenario and rules:

> Exactly seven swimmers—Hewitt, James, Kopov, Luis, Markson, Nu, and Price—will race in the 50-meter freestyle event. Each swimmer will swim in exactly one of seven lanes, numbered 1 through 7. No two swimmers share the same lane. Lane assignments comply with the following conditions:
>
>> James swims in a lower-numbered lane than Kopov.
>> Nu swims in either the first lane or the seventh lane.
>> Markson swims in a lane numbered two lower than Price's.
>> Hewitt swims in lane 4.

The first thing we recognize when we read this is that we are placing elements in order. We have seven elements for seven positions, we don't have anything else other than their names—such as whether the swimmers wear red or purple Speedos—and we don't see any strange issues, such as a mismatch between the number of elements and positions. The rules are all about order, with one about assignment. This has all the characteristics of a Basic Ordering game. We can start by setting up a board like this:

H J K L M N P

| 1 | 2 | 3 | 4 | 5 | 6 | 7 |

Now that we've got the lay of the land, let's take a careful look at each of the rules.

Step 2: Notate the Rules and Make Inferences

We'll go one rule at a time and discuss our real-time processes:

> James swims in a lower-numbered lane than Kopov.

We can notate this next to the diagram like so:

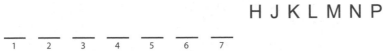

H J K L M N P

| 1 | 2 | 3 | 4 | 5 | 6 | 7 | J – K

2

We can infer at this point that J cannot go in lane 7 and K cannot go in lane 1. We'll add this to our diagram, but since this a pretty basic inference, advanced students might choose not to do so.

Next, we get the following rule:

> Nu swims in either the first lane or the seventh lane.

This we can notate much more directly. We suggest that you elevate it just a bit from the slot, so that you don't mistakenly assume that the slot is filled.

```
N/   __  __  __  __  __  /N    H J K L M N P
  1    2   3   4   5   6   7
 K̶                      J̶      J — K
```

Let's move on to the third rule:

> Markson swims in a lane numbered two lower than Price's.

This is a rule that is very easy to misunderstand. It is often helpful to play out different hypothetical situations in order to correctly understand the meaning of rules. If P is in 4, M must be in…2? Well, if the cost of M was $2 lower than the cost of P, and P was $4, then M would be $2. Yes, if P is in 4, M must be in 2. This rule means that we have M, one other swimmer, then P. We can represent the rule this way:

```
N/   __  __  __  __  __  /N    H J K L M N P
  1    2   3   4   5   6   7
 K̶   P̶              M̶  J̶      J — K
 P̶                  M̶          ┌─────────┐
                               │ M _ P   │
                               └─────────┘
```

And we know this is an important rule—a chunk! Similar to our exclusions for J and K, our chunk allows us to exclude M and P from certain lanes. Check our work above to make sure you follow along.

Finally:

> Hewitt swims in lane 4.

At this point, perhaps we notice the significance of how the final rule relates to our chunk—M can't go in lane 2, and P can't go in lane 6. Because that might be difficult to see during the process of solving problems, it makes sense for us to notate that inference:

$$\underset{1}{\underline{\text{N/}}} \quad \underset{2}{\underline{}} \quad \underset{3}{\underline{}} \quad \underset{4}{\underline{\text{H}}} \quad \underset{5}{\underline{}} \quad \underset{6}{\underline{}} \quad \underset{7}{\underline{\text{/N}}}$$

H J K L M N P

K̶　P̶　　　　　　M̶　J̶　　　J — K

P̶　M̶　　　　　　P̶　M̶　　　☐ M _ P ☐

It seems there are no other major inferences to extract.

Step 3: The Big Pause

Let's start by circling L, since it has no rules attached to it. Next, we'll check that we've understood and notated the rules correctly. We did, so now we'll prioritize the rules.

In this case, our instinct should be to prioritize the MP chunk. There are a limited number of places it could go—three to be exact—and placing it dictates and limits the possibilities for other elements. With that in mind, we know we're in great shape, and we can move on to the questions.

Step 4: Attack the Questions

Let's discuss the real-time processes we could use to solve these questions not just effectively but *efficiently*. We've split this process up into the thoughts we'd have while reading the question stem and the thoughts we'd have as we walk through the answer choices.

1. Which of the following could be an accurate list of swimmers, listed in order from lane 1 through lane 7?

As we discussed earlier, the first question of the game is almost always an Orientation question. The approach: Go through the rules one at a time, eliminating answers that violate that rule.

Remember, what we are suggesting is very different from going through each answer choice one at a time and comparing it against the rules. The method we suggest will generally prove to be much faster.

In this case, we are given four rules:

Rule 1, "James swims in a lower-numbered lane than Kopov," eliminates (C).
Rule 2, "Nu swims in either the first lane or the seventh lane," eliminates (E).
Rule 3, "Markson swims in a lane numbered two lower than Price's," eliminates (D).
Rule 4, "Hewitt swims in lane 4," eliminates (A).

MANHATTAN
PREP

(A) Nu, Luis, James, Kopov, Markson, Hewitt, Price

(B) James, Luis, Markson, Hewitt, Price, Kopov, Nu

(C) Nu, Kopov, Markson, Hewitt, Price, James, Luis

(D) Luis, Markson, James, Hewitt, Price, Kopov, Nu

(E) Markson, Nu, Price, Hewitt, James, Luis, Kopov

We're left with (B), the correct answer. While you could invest time in confirming (B), we recommend you trust your work at this point and move on.

2. Which one of the following must be false?

Aha! We know this sort of question. Four answers will be "could be true" answers, and the right one will be always false. Do you remember what to do? Let's find what must be false, and if we need to, confirm that some answers could be true. Since it's the second question of the game, we can expect that the answer will probably be based on a simple inference or it will directly violate a rule. It might be something we figured out while diagramming. Let's look:

(A) Price swims in lane 5.

(B) Price swims in lane 7.

(C) Markson swims in lane 2.

(D) Kopov swims in lane 3.

(E) James swims in lane 6.

We know Markson can't swim in lane 2, so **answer choice (C) is correct.**

Second questions are often on the easier side, so feel free to be particularly "lazy," deferring judgment to see if an easy answer "jumps out."

3. If James swims in lane 1, then each of the following could be true EXCEPT:

This is a **conditional question,** and when they give us new information in the question stem, as they have done here, it's expected that we do our homework, making additional inferences from the new condition. Let's try doing that by placing J in the first position in a new diagram we draw for this question (and, by the way, we don't need to copy over every original front-end inference we made—we can always refer to our original diagram for those):

If J is in 1, one thing we know directly is that N must be in 7. As usual, it's now helpful to think of our beloved chunk. M and P must go in 3 and 5 respectively. That leaves us with two open spaces—2 and 6—and we have two elements, L and K, that can fill either of those spaces.

$$
\begin{array}{ccccccc}
\text{J} & \text{K/L} & \text{M} & \text{H} & \text{P} & \text{L/K} & \text{N} \\
\hline
1 & 2 & 3 & 4 & 5 & 6 & 7
\end{array}
$$

K̶ P̶   M̶ K̶

P̶ M̶   P̶ M̶

H J K Ⓛ M N P

J — K

[M _ P]

With our inferences laid out, we can attack the answer choices. Since we are asked for the one answer that can't be true, we are looking for an answer that must be false:

(A) Kopov swims in a lower-numbered lane than Hewitt.

(B) Luis swims in a lower-numbered lane than Hewitt.

(C) Markson swims in a higher-numbered lane than Hewitt.

(D) Kopov swims in a lower-numbered lane than Price.

(E) Luis swims in a lower-numbered lane than Markson.

Answer choice (C) is correct.

Markson must swim in lane 3 and therefore cannot swim in a higher-numbered lane than Hewitt. Because of the uncertainty we have about Luis and Kopov, all other answers could be true or false. Notice that the wrong answers all include L and K, the two elements that were still uncertain.

4. If Price swims in lane 3, which one of the following could be true?

This is another conditional question, but in this case we're asked to identify an answer that *could* be true. In general, the easiest way to separate out a "could be true" answer is to recognize the four answers that must be false.

But first things first—let's start by seeing what we can infer if we place P in position 3.

If P is in the third slot, M must be in the first slot, and N must be in the seventh slot. That leaves us with three elements for the three remaining slots. Though we know a bit about where these elements can go, there's a lot of uncertainty, so we'll just write them above in a cloud to remind us of who's left:

$$\boxed{J - K, L}$$

$$\underset{1}{M} \quad \underset{2}{} \quad \underset{3}{P} \quad \underset{4}{H} \quad \underset{5}{} \quad \underset{6}{} \quad \underset{7}{N}$$

Here are the answer choices:

(A) Kopov swims in lane 2.

(B) James swims in lane 6.

(C) Luis swims in lane 2.

(D) Nu swims in lane 1.

(E) Kopov swims in lane 7.

If we remember the J–K rule, then we know (A) can't be true.

By the same rule, answer choice (B) can't be true.

Answer choice (C) looks likely, so now either we defer judgment and see if answers (D) and (E) are indeed false, or we spend a moment to confirm that answer (C) is correct. Let's play out the first strategy—our diagram quickly tells us that answers (D) and (E) are impossible.

That leaves (C), the correct answer. As a free radical, L could definitely go in lane 2. We could put J in 5 and K in 6.

5. Which of the following could be a partial and accurate list of swimmers matched with the lanes in which they swim?

This is very similar to the Orientation question we began with—we're looking for a set of assignments that could satisfy the conditions. The big difference here is that the answer choices give us partial information instead of a complete and accurate list.

The design of this question requires us to do some work to evaluate each answer choice—it's not easy to see why an answer is wrong with just a glance. However, we do know that four of the answer choices will violate our rules in one way or another. Let's go through each answer choice:

   (A) lane 1: Nu; lane 2: Markson; lane 6: Luis

We know M can't be in lane 2, and so we can eliminate this answer.

   (B) lane 5: James; lane 6: Kopov; lane 7: Luis

This is a tougher answer to eliminate, and perhaps one you wisely deferred judgment on, but if all these assignments were true, that would force N into position 1, and there would be no place for the MP chunk. Therefore, we can eliminate answer choice (B).

   (C) lane 3: Luis; lane 4: Hewitt; lane 5: James

If positions 3, 4, and 5 are all occupied, there is no place for the MP chunk. We can eliminate (C).

   (D) lane 4: Hewitt; lane 5: Luis; lane 7: Kopov

If positions 4, 5, and 7 are all occupied, N must go in 1, and there is no place for the MP chunk. We can eliminate (D).

   (E) lane 2: James; lane 5: Markson; lane 6: Kopov

At this point, depending on how confident you are in your eliminations, you can either move on to the next question, quickly check this answer against the rules, or, if you have any doubt, quickly prove that this answer can work with the rules:

$$\underline{N} \quad \underline{J} \quad \underline{L} \quad \underline{H} \quad \underline{M} \quad \underline{K} \quad \underline{P}$$

Answer choice (E) is correct.

Smart Tip: Reviewing Practice Games

Now that you've had a chance to take another look at the game, and to read how another person might approach solving the questions, how do you feel?

As you review games you've completed, it can be helpful to compartmentalize the challenges you've faced, and it's always easier to address concrete concerns than it is to address vague ones, so you want to get to know yourself as a test-taker the best you can.

Here are some questions you can ask yourself in order to evaluate your understanding of a logic game:

1. Could I picture the game easily? Did I understand the general situation?

In this game, this step may not have been particularly challenging, but in other games, this will be a very important consideration.

2. Did I understand the rules correctly? Did I notate them in a way that allowed me to think about them easily?

For many students, this is the primary issue that prevents consistent success. However, this is an issue that is easily fixed. Almost all rules fall into very understandable and intuitive categories, and with the right practice, you can get very comfortable at understanding and notating just about anything.

3. Did I make the key inferences at the right times? Did I understand which rules to prioritize?

We discussed this just before we re-solved this game. For this game, the key was to prioritize the MP chunk. Chunk rules always take up a lot of space, so we always need to make sure to leave room for them.

4. Did I attack each question wisely?

In large part, this is about knowing when to look for the right answer, and when to eliminate wrong answers. It's also about knowing when to defer work, which is a critical component of high-level success.

MANHATTAN
PREP

Conclusion

You've learned your first game type, and along the way you've gotten some practice using the four-step process to tackle some common question types. That's a lot! What you've learned here is the bedrock of everything else you're going to do.

Here's a quick review:

1. **General process**

   • Read the scenario and scan the rules before you start diagramming—that will help you determine what sort of game you're facing and how to set up the basic framework of your diagram.

   • When you work with the rules, notate them in a way that makes sense to you, and as much as possible, put the rules *into* the diagram, not on the side. Make inferences as you go along, look for connections between the rules, and…

   • Pause before you start into the questions so that you can consider what the game's major issues are. And never forget to look for stray elements, the ones that have no rules attached.

2. **Orientation questions**

   • For most Orientation questions, work from the rules, eliminating answer choices.

   • It's common for each rule to be violated in one answer choice, so it may be efficient to move on to a new rule if you've found one offending choice.

3. **Standard questions**

   • If you're given a new condition, make inferences before you evaluate the answer choices.

   • If you're not given a new condition, you should be able to answer based on your initial diagram, the rules, and any inferences you made.

   • When you use hypothetical scenarios, build them so that they can allow you to make eliminations, either proving or breaking answers as needed.

4. **Basic Ordering games**

   • Basic Ordering games are Ordering games with no bells or whistles. The rules will be about either the assignment of elements to positions, or about the relative order of the elements.

   • These games tend to be back-end game. Pausing and identifying the game's big issues before you move into the answers is crucial.

   • Chunks are important! Super chunks are super important!

Practice Game 1: PT32, S3, G3

Use this difficult game to polish your complete four-step process for Basic Ordering games (and don't forget The Big Pause). Except where noted, we suggest that you do the games in this book untimed, leaving the timer for the practice sets that you do in addition to your work in this book. Be extra conscious of making the correct moves, even if that means going a little slower at first. When you make the right moves, you often find that you can go slower and still finish games much faster! Before you begin, let's talk about scratch paper.

Scratch Paper

To prepare for test day, organize your scratch paper with a space for your main diagram (e.g., in the upper left corner) and plenty of space for each question. Doing the games in this book on scratch paper also means you can use the games again! If this appeals to you, consider taking a moment to draw out each question number and a column with the letters A through E for each question before you begin the game. This gives you a place to make eliminations and flag questions for review without polluting the game on the page.

At a concert, exactly eight compositions—F, H, L, O, P, R, S, and T—are to be performed exactly once each, consecutively and one composition at a time. The order of their performance must satisfy the following conditions:

> T is performed either immediately before F or immediately after R.
> At least two compositions are performed either after F and before R, or after R and before F.
> O is performed either first or fifth.
> The eighth composition performed is either L or H.
> P is performed at some time before S.
> At least one composition is performed either after O and before S, or after S and before O.

12. Which one of the following lists the compositions in an order in which they could be performed during the concert, from first through eighth?

    (A) L, P, S, R, O, T, F, H
    (B) O, T, P, F, S, H, R, L
    (C) P, T, F, S, L, R, O, H
    (D) P, T, F, S, O, R, L, H
    (E) T, F, P, R, O, L, S, H

13. P CANNOT be performed

    (A) second
    (B) third
    (C) fourth
    (D) sixth
    (E) seventh

14. If T is performed fifth and F is performed sixth, then S must be performed either

    (A) fourth or seventh
    (B) third or sixth
    (C) third or fourth
    (D) second or seventh
    (E) first or fourth

15. If O is performed immediately after T, then F must be performed either

    (A) first or second
    (B) second or third
    (C) fourth or sixth
    (D) fourth or seventh
    (E) sixth or seventh

16. If S is performed fourth, which one of the following could be an accurate list of the compositions performed first, second, and third, respectively?

    (A) F, H, P
    (B) H, P, L
    (C) O, P, R
    (D) O, P, T
    (E) P, R, T

17. If P is performed third and S is performed sixth, the composition performed fifth must be either

    (A) F or H
    (B) F or O
    (C) F or T
    (D) H or L
    (E) O or R

18. If exactly two compositions are performed after F but before O, then R must be performed

    (A) first
    (B) third
    (C) fourth
    (D) sixth
    (E) seventh

2

Solutions: PT32, S3, G3

> Remember, you should be reviewing all games using the method described on page 73. If you've forgotten what we suggested, check back now.

Answer Key

12. A	16. C
13. E	17. C
14. A	18. D
15. E	

Step 1: Picture the Game

At a concert, exactly eight compositions—F, H, L, O, P, R, S, and T—are to be performed exactly once each, consecutively and one composition at a time. The order of their performance must satisfy the following conditions:

> T is performed either immediately before F or immediately after R.
> At least two compositions are performed either after F and before R, or after R and before F.
> O is performed either first or fifth.
> The eighth composition performed is either L or H.
> P is performed at some time before S.
> At least one composition is performed either after O and before S, or after S and before O.

We can recognize that this is an ordering game, and we don't have any subsets or mismatches between the number of positions and the number of elements. Therefore, we can think of this as a Basic Ordering game, and start by setting up the following base for our diagram:

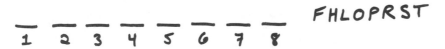

MANHATTAN
PREP

Step 2: Notate the Rules and Make Inferences

Here is our diagram with the rules notated. Check your work against it:

Keep in mind that the first rule, an "or" rule, does not exclude the possibility of both events happening at the same time—as far as we know at this point, T can be both immediately before F and immediately after R. However, the second rule does make it impossible for both to occur in this game.

The other "or" rules do exclude the possibility of both, simply because it's not possible for both possibilities to occur at once—for example, O cannot be performed both first *and* fifth.

Overall, this is a complicated Basic Ordering game with a lot of rules and a lot of positions to be filled. However, as we notate the rules and think about how the game comes together, perhaps the most defining characteristic of this particular game is that there are very few up-front inferences. We can infer that S can't go first, and P can't go last. Other than that, there is very little else that we can figure out.

As mentioned before, Basic Ordering games tend to be more back-end games than they are front-end games. We can think of this example as an extreme back-end game, because there are hardly any inferences up front and that we can tell that we are going to have to do a lot of work within the individual questions.

With back-end games, it is critical that we clearly and correctly understand the exact meaning of each of our notations, and that we are able to prioritize the rules in terms of which will be most useful. This is exactly what we should do during…

Step 3: The Big Pause

For this game, the two rules to prioritize are the second rule—*At least two compositions are performed either after F and before R, or after R and before F*—and the last—*At least one composition is performed either after O and before S, or after S and before O*. These rules give us two chunks that both need to fit into the diagram, and that will, together, fill up four of the eight spots. They would be more useful to us if they were more exact (e.g., if we knew that there were *exactly* two compositions between F and R), but they are still the most useful rules we've got. One could also think of those rules as defining what can't be true. For the second rule, for example, we can write that S and O cannot be next to each other, giving us a prohibited chunk.

The most challenging rule to deal with while answering questions is probably the first one—*T is performed either immediately before F or immediately after R*. Imagine that at some point we place T, F, or R on the diagram—it's not easy to see the exact ramifications of this rule.

Scanning the rules and the roster, we can see that every element is mentioned in a rule.

So here's what we know: This is an extreme back-end game with a lot of rules to keep track of, and we have two chunks that are going to help fill in our board. With that in mind, we take one quick look through each of our notations, and we get to work on the questions. Making the decision to go into the questions without inferences can be hard, but don't waste time looking for something you don't know exists. You can always go back and make inferences, but you can't get time back once you spend it looking for an inference that isn't there.

Step 4: Attack the Questions

12. Which one of the following lists the compositions in an order in which they could be performed during the concert, from first through eighth?

    (A) L, P, S, R, O, T, F, H
    (B) O, T, P, F, S, H, R, L
    (C) P, T, F, S, L, R, O, H
    (D) P, T, F, S, O, R, L, H
    (E) T, F, P, R, O, L, S, H

Answer choice (A) is correct.

This is an Orientation question, and as we mentioned before, it is generally fastest to answer Orientation questions by going one rule at a time, eliminating answer choices that violate that rule:

> "T is performed either immediately before F or immediately after R" eliminates answer (B).
> "At least two compositions are performed either after F and before R, or after R and before F" eliminates (E).
> "O is performed either first or fifth" eliminates answer (C).
> "At least one composition is performed either after O and before S, or after S and before O" eliminates answer (D).

(A), the lone answer remaining, is our correct answer.

If you like to reorder which rules you use first based on how "easy" they are, you might start with the third rule, then perhaps the first, and finish off the remaining answer choices with the second and sixth rules.

MANHATTAN
PREP

13. P CANNOT be performed

   (A) second
   (B) third
   (C) fourth
   (D) sixth
   (E) seventh

Answer choice (E) is correct.

We want to figure out where P can't perform before evaluating the answer choices.

If we look at our diagram, there is only one rule involving P: P must be before S. We also know that either L or H has to go in the eighth spot. Putting these two things together, we can see that P cannot go second to last (because we'd have no space for S). There doesn't seem to be a reason why P cannot go in any of the other positions.

14. If T is performed fifth and F is performed sixth, then S must be performed either

   (A) fourth or seventh
   (B) third or sixth
   (C) third or fourth
   (D) second or seventh
   (E) first or fourth

Answer choice (A) is correct.

This is a conditional question, so we want to play out the information given in the question stem before evaluating the answer choices. We can draw a separate diagram next to this question.

We can make a couple of basic inferences once we place T and F. O must go first, since it's not going fifth.

Also, placing F in the sixth position limits where the R can go; in fact, R can go only in the second or third slot. There is little else that we can infer quickly:

The question asks specifically about the slots in which S can go, and makes it clear that S can only go in one of two slots. Let's go through the remaining open slots carefully.

Can S go in slot 1? Of course not, O is there.

Can S go in slot 2? No, because we know P must be before S, and we also need at least one slot between O and S.

Can S go in slot 3? No. This is a bit trickier, but we know R must occupy 2 or 3, and we know P must go before S. Therefore, there is no way S can go in 3.

We've effectively eliminated answer choices (B) through (E) since we've proven that S can't go in at least one slot mentioned in each choice, and if we're short on time, we'll choose (A) and move on, perhaps flagging the question to remind ourselves to come back and confirm if we have some extra time at the end of the section.

Can S go in slot 4? There doesn't seem to be a reason why not.

Can S go in slot 7? There doesn't seem to be a reason why not.

15. If O is performed immediately after T, then F must be performed either

    (A) first or second
    (B) second or third
    (C) fourth or sixth
    (D) fourth or seventh
    (E) sixth or seventh

Answer choice (E) is correct.

Again, since this is a conditional question, we want to do our inferring homework before evaluating the answers. As in the last problem, it can be helpful to scan the answer choices to know, going in, that F will end up having just two possible positions.

Here's the diagram with the new condition and the inferences it brings about:

$$\underset{1}{\_\_}\ \underset{2}{\_\_}\ \underset{3}{\overset{R}{\_\_}}\ \underset{4}{\overset{T}{\_\_}}\ \underset{5}{\overset{O}{\_\_}}\ \underset{6}{\overset{\boxed{F}}{\_\_}}\ \underset{7}{\_\_}\ \underset{8}{\overset{L/H}{\_\_}}$$

If O is after T, we know that O must be fifth. Similarly, since this prevents a TF chunk, we are required to put R into the third position.

Once R is in the third position, we can see that F must go in either 6 or 7.

MANHATTAN
PREP

16. If S is performed fourth, which one of the following could be an accurate list of the compositions performed first, second, and third, respectively?

    (A) F, H, P
    (B) H, P, L
    (C) O, P, R
    (D) O, P, T
    (E) P, R, T

Answer choice (C) is correct.

This is another conditional question, so we need to draw out a new diagram and place S in the fourth position. Checking our rules, two talk about S: P is before it and O can't be next to it. Since O also has to be in either the first or fifth slot, and the fifth slot is next to S, we must place O in the first slot.

Next, we know that P must be before S, so it must occupy slot 2 or 3.

Finally, we know we have to fit the FR chunk in somewhere. Since we can't fit the entire chunk after S, either F or R has to occupy one of the first three positions.

Here's our diagram with the inferences laid out:

With these inferences made, (C) stands out as the correct answer.

17. If P is performed third and S is performed sixth, the composition performed fifth must be either

    (A) F or H
    (B) F or O
    (C) F or T
    (D) H or L
    (E) O or R

Answer choice (C) is correct.

If S is sixth, O must be first. Notice at this point that we are now extremely limited in terms of where we can place either the TF or the RT chunk—these pairings can only go in the 4/5 slots. Since TF or RT must go in 4 and 5, either F or T must go in slot 5.

Your diagram might look like this:

$$\boxed{\begin{array}{c} \text{RT} \\ \hline \text{TF} \end{array}}$$

$$\underset{1}{\underline{O}} \quad \underset{2}{\underline{}} \quad \underset{3}{\underline{P}} \quad \underset{4}{\underline{}} \quad \underset{5}{\underline{}} \quad \underset{6}{\underline{S}} \quad \underset{7}{\underline{}} \quad \underset{8}{\underline{^L/_H}}$$

18. If exactly two compositions are performed after F but before O, then R must be performed

(A) first

(B) third

(C) fourth

(D) sixth

(E) seventh

Answer choice (D) is correct.

First step? Make sure you represent this new chunk from the question correctly. We need to have two slots *between* F and O; this is different than the rule that says O is two slots later than F. If O is not first, then O must go in the fifth position, and F in the second position. Once we make this inference, we know that R must go in the sixth or seventh position.

At this point, it would be efficient to simply try out one of these—if it works, then that's the answer! If it doesn't, the other one is correct. Can R go in the sixth position? Seems very possible, and here's one way it could work: P F S L O R T H.

Did you start by asking whether R can go in the seventh position? Let's play that out. Since there is now no room for an RT chunk, we need the TF chunk in positions one and two:

$$\underset{1}{\underline{T}} \quad \underset{2}{\underline{F}} \quad \underset{3}{\underline{}} \quad \underset{4}{\underline{}} \quad \underset{5}{\underline{O}} \quad \underset{6}{\underline{}} \quad \underset{7}{\underline{R}} \quad \underset{8}{\underline{^L/_H}} \qquad \boxed{F\,\_\,\_\,O}$$

We have a problem at this point—there is no way to put S at least two spaces away from O, while also allowing for P to finish before S. We can't have R in the seventh position. At this point, you could pick (D) since you've ruled out all the other answers. If you do that on test day, you might also want to flag the question so that you can come back around and check (D) if you have time.

MANHATTAN
PREP

Practice Game 2: PT19, S1, G1

Here is one final game for the chapter. This was a first game when it originally appeared on the LSAT, but it was fairly challenging nonetheless. Keep your focus on implementing the four-step process.

During a period of six consecutive days—day 1 through day 6—each of exactly six factories—F, G, H, J, Q, and R—will be inspected. During this period, each of the factories will be inspected exactly once, one factory per day. The schedule for the inspections must conform to the following conditions:

> F is inspected on either day 1 or day 6.
> J is inspected on an earlier day than Q is inspected.
> Q is inspected on the day immediately before R is inspected.
> If G is inspected on day 3, Q is inspected on day 5.

1. Which one of the following could be a list of the factories in the order of their scheduled inspections, from day 1 through day 6?

   (A) F, Q, R, H, J, G
   (B) G, H, J, Q, R, F
   (C) G, J, Q, H, R, F
   (D) G, J, Q, R, F, H
   (E) J, H, G, Q, R, F

2. Which one of the following must be false?

   (A) The inspection of G is scheduled for day 4.
   (B) The inspection of H is scheduled for day 6.
   (C) The inspection of J is scheduled for day 4.
   (D) The inspection of Q is scheduled for day 3.
   (E) The inspection of R is scheduled for day 2.

3. The inspection of which one of the following CANNOT be scheduled for day 5?

   (A) G
   (B) H
   (C) J
   (D) Q
   (E) R

4. The inspections scheduled for day 3 and day 5, respectively, could be those of

   (A) G and H
   (B) G and R
   (C) H and G
   (D) R and J
   (E) R and H

5. If the inspection of R is scheduled for the day immediately before the inspection of F, which one of the following must be true about the schedule?

   (A) The inspection of either G or H is scheduled for day 1.
   (B) The inspection of either G or J is scheduled for day 1.
   (C) The inspection of either G or J is scheduled for day 2.
   (D) The inspection of either H or J is scheduled for day 3.
   (E) The inspection of either H or J is scheduled for day 4.

6. If the inspections of G and of H are scheduled, not necessarily in that order, for days as far apart as possible, which one of the following is a complete and accurate list of the factories any one of which could be scheduled for inspection for day 1?

   (A) F, J
   (B) G, H
   (C) G, H, J
   (D) F, G, H
   (E) F, G, H, J

7. If the inspection of G is scheduled for the day immediately before the inspection of Q, which one of the following could be true?

   (A) The inspection of G is scheduled for day 5.
   (B) The inspection of H is scheduled for day 6.
   (C) The inspection of J is scheduled for day 2.
   (D) The inspection of Q is scheduled for day 4.
   (E) The inspection of R is scheduled for day 3.

Solutions: PT19, S1, G1

Answer Key

1. B   5. D
2. E   6. D
3. C   7. C
4. E

Step 1: Picture the Game

During a period of six consecutive days—day 1 through day 6—each of exactly six factories—F, G, H, J, Q, and R—will be inspected. During this period, each of the factories will be inspected exactly once, one factory per day. The schedule for the inspections must conform to the following conditions:

> F is inspected on either day 1 or day 6.
> J is inspected on an earlier day than Q is inspected.
> Q is inspected on the day immediately before R is inspected.
> If G is inspected on day 3, Q is inspected on day 5.

Simple enough—we've got six elements for six slots. We can start off like this:

$$\overline{\underset{1}{}\quad \overline{\underset{2}{}}\quad \overline{\underset{3}{}}\quad \overline{\underset{4}{}}\quad \overline{\underset{5}{}}\quad \overline{\underset{6}{}}} \qquad FGHJQR$$

Step 2: Notate the Rules and Make Inferences

All of these rules should feel fairly comfortable to you by this point. One key is recognizing that the second and third rules can be brought together.

Here is the diagram with the rules notated. Feel free to write out the contrapositive of the last rule if you find it to be helpful. There are some things we know to be true about the order—for example, we know that neither Q nor R can be first—but there are no significant and difficult-to-recognize inferences that we *need* to mark.

Here is a completed diagram for this game:

MANHATTAN
PREP

Step 3: The Big Pause

There isn't too much to think about in this game. The J–QR chunk (chunk on a leash?) is going to be a key for us—it's going to fill in half of the available positions.

The F options will be important, too. We can expect to rely on the conditional rule from time to time, but only when it's triggered.

We should also note that H has no rules attached to it by circling it.

Step 4: Attack the Questions

1. Which one of the following could be a list of the factories in the order of their scheduled inspections, from day 1 through day 6?

   (A) F, Q, R, H, J, G
   (B) G, H, J, Q, R, F
   (C) G, J, Q, H, R, F
   (D) G, J, Q, R, F, H
   (E) J, H, G, Q, R, F

Answer choice (B) is correct.

This is an Orientation question, and we can use the rules one at a time to eliminate the answer choices. The first rule eliminates answer (D). The second rule eliminates answer (A). The third rule eliminates answer (C). The fourth rule eliminates answer (E).

2. Which one of the following must be false?

   (A) The inspection of G is scheduled for day 4.
   (B) The inspection of H is scheduled for day 6.
   (C) The inspection of J is scheduled for day 4.
   (D) The inspection of Q is scheduled for day 3.
   (E) The inspection of R is scheduled for day 2.

Answer choice (E) is correct.

We know that four of these answers could be true and one must be false. We want to delay doing work on answers that feel uncertain—that could be true—and focus on identifying the answer that must be false.

With answers (A) through (D), there's no obvious reason why these placements can't be made.

With answer choice (E), we know of two elements that must go before R. Therefore, R cannot go second.

3. The inspection of which one of the following CANNOT be scheduled for day 5?

    (A) G
    (B) H
    (C) J
    (D) Q
    (E) R

Answer choice (C) is correct.

If we look at the fifth position and think about the rules we've been given, the only element we know for sure can't go in position 5 is J, which has at least two elements that go after it. Therefore, we can look for J in the answer choices.

4. The inspections scheduled for day 3 and day 5, respectively, could be those of

    (A) G and H
    (B) G and R
    (C) H and G
    (D) R and J
    (E) R and H

Answer choice (E) is correct.

This is a question that requires a little bit of work with each of the answer choices. We know four of them must be false, and we can identify those four by comparing the answers against the four rules we have diagrammed.

If G is third, then we know Q must be fifth. That allows us to eliminate answers (A) and (B).

If H is third and G is fifth, there is no place for the J–QR chunk. We can eliminate answer (C).

If J is fifth, there is no place for the QR chunk. We can eliminate answer (D). In fact, one of our inferences already let us know that J can't be fifth!

We're left with answer choice (E). Depending on your confidence in your eliminations and the amount of time you have left, at this point you might choose to move on, or, if you were less certain, play it out. Answer choice (E) can work out with the following order: J Q R G H F.

5. If the inspection of R is scheduled for the day immediately before the inspection of F, which one of the following must be true about the schedule?

    (A) The inspection of either G or H is scheduled for day 1.
    (B) The inspection of either G or J is scheduled for day 1.
    (C) The inspection of either G or J is scheduled for day 2.
    (D) The inspection of either H or J is scheduled for day 3.
    (E) The inspection of either H or J is scheduled for day 4.

Answer choice (D) is correct.

The condition in this question allows us to add F to our chunk, and since in this situation we know that F must finish sixth, we could draw the following next to this question:

We are unsure where J, G, and H will go, so we'll put them in a cloud above slots 1–3.

(Perhaps you notice something about G—more on this in just a bit.)

Let's go through the answer choices:

(A) doesn't seem like it must be true, because there doesn't seem to be a reason why J can't be in 1.

(B) doesn't seem like it must be true, because there doesn't seem to be a reason why H can't go in 1.

(C) doesn't seem like it must be true, because there doesn't seem to be a reason why H can't go in 2.

(D) is easy to lump in with the previous three answers, but when we try to put G into 3, we notice there is a consequence. If G is in the third position, Q must be in the fifth position, and we don't have that. Therefore, G can't go in the third position, and answer choice (D) is correct. This question highlights why it's sometimes useful to have the contrapositive written out. As soon as we saw that Q *isn't* in 5, the contrapositive would let us infer that G isn't in 3.

Perhaps you made the inference about G and the third spot up front. If so, terrific; that, of course, makes the problem much easier to solve.

You may also have noticed that these answer choices have a lot in common—they are all about the three elements we have remaining for the three slots, and they seem to be hinting at the fact that one of those slots is restricted to just two of the three elements. If, at that point, you had gone back to see if J, G, or H had some reason they couldn't go in 1, 2, or 3, that would have been a great strategy as well.

6. If the inspections of G and of H are scheduled, not necessarily in that order, for days as far apart as possible, which one of the following is a complete and accurate list of the factories any one of which could be scheduled for inspection for day 1?

    (A) F, J
    (B) G, H
    (C) G, H, J
    (D) F, G, H
    (E) F, G, H, J

Answer choice (D) is correct.

Here we've got a conditional question in which the condition given requires quite a bit of work from us. Still, it would be a mistake to move on to the answers before we go through our inference chain.

We want to think about how G and H can be as far apart on our Number Line as possible—they can't go in 1 and 6, because F has to go in one of those two spaces. Therefore, it makes sense to think of G and H going in either 1 and 5 or 2 and 6.

Can G go in 1 and H in 5? Sure, and you can run through a quick hypothetical in your head to confirm: G J Q R H F. In fact, as long as we're not talking about the third slot, G and H are interchangeable.

Can H go in 1 and G in 5? Sure—we can use the same hypothetical and just switch G and H around to confirm: H J Q R G F.

Can F go in 1 and G and H in 2 and 6? Sure. We can think of a hypothetical if we want, but you can also just imagine taking some of the work we've just done and flipping the F over from the back of the line to the front. Shifting everyone over one space to the right wouldn't violate any of the rules; one version that would work would be F G J Q R H.

Note that if we put another element into slot 1, then we'd have to put F in 6, and we would not have the maximum space between G and H.

Therefore, F, G, and H are the three elements that can go in slot 1.

7. If the inspection of G is scheduled for the day immediately before the inspection of Q, which one of the following could be true?

    (A) The inspection of G is scheduled for day 5.
    (B) The inspection of H is scheduled for day 6.
    (C) The inspection of J is scheduled for day 2.
    (D) The inspection of Q is scheduled for day 4.
    (E) The inspection of R is scheduled for day 3.

Answer choice (C) is correct.

Like question 5, this question requires us to add on to our chunk. We can do so as follows:

$$J - \boxed{G\ Q\ R}\ H$$

$$\frac{F/}{1} \quad \frac{}{2} \quad \frac{}{3} \quad \frac{}{4} \quad \frac{}{5} \quad \frac{/F}{6}$$

We know that F is going to go at the beginning or the end and that H is a stray. We also have to avoid triggering our conditional rule. We can't have G in 3, or Q would have to go in 5 instead of following right after G.

Using our diagram and our one conditional, we can get rid of answers (A), (D), and (E) immediately because they must be false.

Answer choice (B) requires a bit more work—if H is on day 6, then the order would be set as: F J G Q R H. This would violate the conditional rule that if G is third, Q must be fifth. Generally, when you're down to two remaining answers, if something doesn't leap out at you in the first couple seconds, it's better to just start testing one of the answers than to sit and puzzle too long.

Conditional Logic 101

In This Chapter...

(Re)Introduction to Conditional Statements

What Is a Conditional Statement?

The most basic type of conditional statement is triggered by IF/THEN phrasing:

IF Jeremy eats a big lunch, **THEN** he won't be hungry for dinner.

IF Raj lives in San Francisco, **THEN** Raj lives in California.

IF Susan attends the concert, **THEN** Jamal will stay home with their children.

IF Hiromi wins the election, **THEN** she had the most organized campaign.

Sufficient vs. Necessary Conditions

The "if" part of the conditional statement is called the **sufficient condition,** because it is *sufficient* to guarantee the truth of the "then" part of the statement. The "then" part of the statement is called the **necessary condition** because, when the sufficient condition is true, it is required, or *necessary,* that the "then" portion be true as well. To summarize:

Sufficient condition: The "if" part of the statement. When satisfied, it guarantees the truth of the necessary condition.

Necessary condition: The "then" part of the statement. It is required if the sufficient condition is true.

Note that while the sufficient condition is *sufficient* to guarantee the truth of the necessary condition, it is not *required* to arrive at the truth of the necessary condition. Let's look at a very simple example to illustrate:

IF you give me a gift, **THEN** I will be happy.

In this case, the condition, "you give me a gift," is *sufficient* to guarantee the truth of the necessary condition, "I will be happy." However, there could be other conditions that are also sufficient to guarantee the truth of the necessary condition:

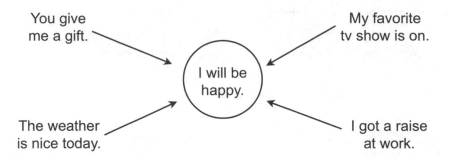

So, what can we conclude? Two things for now:

1. Your giving me a gift is *sufficient* to guarantee that I will be happy.
2. If I am happy, this does *not* guarantee that you have given me a gift (maybe I'm happy for a different reason). In other words, the relationship doesn't necessarily work the other way around.

This will be very important to keep in mind later on when we consider the types of inferences that can be made from conditional statements.

Conditional Statements in Logic Games

In/Out Grouping games rely heavily on conditional statements. We'll cover that game type in the second half of this book. Conditional statements can, however, show up in any game type, including Ordering games. While they most commonly appear within the rules of a game, occasionally you may confront them in the answer choices as well. Applying a conditional rule is hard enough, but proving whether a conditional answer could be true, must be true, or must be false can be very challenging.

Conditional Inferences

Valid vs. Invalid

Before we get back to our "happiness" example, let's consider a simpler conditional statement:

    IF Sally lives in Boston, **THEN** Sally lives in Massachusetts.

Now consider the following related inferences that might be made given the statement above:

1. **Is the negative true?** If Sally does not live in Boston, then Sally does not live in Massachusetts.
2. **Is the reverse true?** If Sally lives in Massachusetts, then Sally lives in Boston.
3. **Is the negative AND the reverse true?** If Sally does not live in Massachusetts, then Sally does not live in Boston.

Which of these inferences, if any, are valid? This is a simpler case because you already know that Boston is not the only city or town in Massachusetts. You can probably see already that the first and second inferences are *not* valid. Even so, let's use our picture to illustrate:

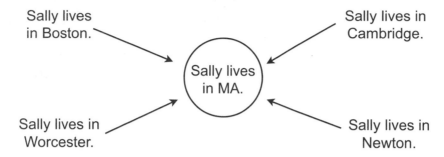

1. If Sally does not live in Boston, then Sally does not live in Massachusetts.

This, of course, is not necessarily true. After all, Sally could live in Newton, which would still put her in Massachusetts.

2. If Sally lives in Massachusetts, then Sally lives in Boston.

This isn't necessarily true, either. There are many places Sally could live, including Cambridge, Worcester, and Newton, that are in Massachusetts but outside of Boston.

3. If Sally does not live in Massachusetts, then Sally does not live in Boston.

This, of course, *must* be true. This is the only inference of the bunch that is valid.

Let's now apply the same logic to the "happiness" example, which is a bit tougher:

IF you give me a gift, **THEN** I will be happy.

Now consider the following related inferences that might be made given the statement above:

1. **Is the negative true?** If you do not give me a gift, then I will not be happy.
2. **Is the reverse true?** If I am happy, then you have given me a gift.
3. **Is the negative AND the reverse true?** If I am not happy, then you have not given me a gift.

Which of these inferences, if any, are valid? To evaluate our potential inferences, let's consider our picture again, remembering that there may be other sufficient conditions that would guarantee my happiness.

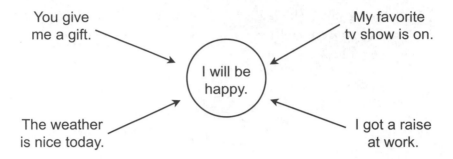

3

1. If you do not give me a gift, then I will not be happy.

This, of course, is not necessarily true. Remember, while giving me a gift is *sufficient* to make me happy, it is not *required.* Maybe you haven't given me a gift, but perhaps I am happy because I got a raise at work today. Thus, this is an invalid inference.

2. If I am happy, then you have given me a gift.

Remember, there could be other reasons why I am happy. This is an invalid inference.

3. If I am not happy, then you have not given me a gift.

This *must* be true. If you give me a gift, it is guaranteed that I will be happy. So, if I am not happy, you could not possibly have given me a gift. This is the only valid inference of the bunch.

By now you may be noticing that the only correct inference, regardless of the original conditional statement, is the one that reverses and negates the original.

We can reduce this complex train of thought down to a reliable rule. To do so, let's start by organizing our thinking through the use of symbols. Let's use a G to symbolize "You give me a gift" and an H to symbolize "I will be happy." The arrow indicates the IF/THEN relationship:

Statement	Symbols	Valid/Invalid	Description
If you give me a gift, then I will be happy.	**G → H**	**Given**	**Given**
1. If you do not give me a gift, then I will not be happy.	–G → –H	Invalid	Negate
2. If I am happy, then you have given me a gift.	H → G	Invalid	Reverse
3. If I am not happy, then you have not given me a gift.	**–H → –G**	**Valid**	**Reverse & Negate**

MANHATTAN
PREP

You can see by looking at the symbols that the first inference simply negates the components of the original given statement. The second inference simply reverses the original components. The third inference both reverses and negates the components of the original statement. Thus, the only valid inference is one that reverses and negates the form of the original given statement. This inference is so useful that it has its own fancy name. It's called the **contrapositive,** and we will use contrapositives a lot when dealing with conditional statements.

Contrapositive: The valid inference derived by reversing and negating the components of a given conditional statement.

Let's generalize:

Statement	Symbols	Valid/Invalid	Description
If X, then Y.	$X \rightarrow Y$	**Given**	**Given**
1. If not X, then not Y.	$-X \rightarrow -Y$	Invalid	Negate
2. If Y, then X.	$Y \rightarrow X$	Invalid	Reverse
3. If not Y, then not X.	$-Y \rightarrow -X$	**Valid**	**Reverse & Negate**

Take some time now to practice making inferences from conditional statements.

Drill It: The Contrapositive

Diagram each of the conditional statements below, then diagram the contrapositive relationship by reversing and negating the components of the original. Finally, use the contrapositive diagram to write a statement that expresses the valid inference made. Be sure to check your responses against the solutions after each mini-exercise.

Example: **Given:** If X is selected, then Y is selected.

Given Diagram: $X \longrightarrow Y$

Contrapositive Diagram: $-Y \longrightarrow -X$

Valid Inference: If Y is not selected, then X is not selected.

1. **Given:** If Sid is on the committee, then Jana is on the committee.

Given Diagram:

Contrapositive Diagram:

Valid Inference:

2. **Given:** If Raul is invited to the party, then Shaina is not invited to the party.

Given Diagram:

Contrapositive Diagram:

Valid Inference:

3. **Given:** If Brooks is not on the bus, then Traiger is not on the bus.

Given Diagram:

Contrapositive Diagram:

Valid Inference:

4. **Given:** If the tiger is not in the cage, then the lion is in the cage.

Given Diagram:

Contrapositive Diagram:

Valid Inference:

5. **Given:** I will not go jogging if it is raining outside.

Given Diagram:

Contrapositive Diagram:

Valid Inference:

6. **Given:** If Tamika gives the speech, then she won the speech competition.

Given Diagram:

Contrapositive Diagram:

Valid Inference:

7. **Given:** Yohei plays guitar if Juan plays drums.

Given Diagram:

Contrapositive Diagram:

Valid Inference:

8. **Given:** If T is not chosen for the team, then N is not chosen for the team.

Given Diagram:

Contrapositive Diagram:

Valid Inference:

9. **Given:** G is not selected for the club if F is selected for the club.

Given Diagram:

Contrapositive Diagram:

Valid Inference:

10. **Given:** If Beethoven is played, then Mozart is also played.

Given Diagram:

Contrapositive Diagram:

Valid Inference:

Solutions: The Contrapositive

1. **Given:** If Sid is on the committee, then Jana is on the committee.

Given Diagram:　$S \longrightarrow J$

Contrapositive Diagram:　$-J \longrightarrow -S$

Valid Inference: If Jana is not on the committee, then Sid is not on the committee.

2. **Given:** If Raul is invited to the party, then Shaina is not invited to the party.

Given Diagram:　$R \longrightarrow -S$

Contrapositive Diagram:　$S \longrightarrow -R$

Valid Inference: If Shaina is invited to the party, then Raul is not invited to the party.

3. **Given:** If Brooks is not on the bus, then Traiger is not on the bus.

Given Diagram:　$-B \longrightarrow -T$

Contrapositive Diagram:　$T \longrightarrow B$

Valid Inference: If Traiger is on the bus, then Brooks is on the bus.

4. **Given:** If the tiger is not in the cage, then the lion is in the cage.

Given Diagram:　$-T \longrightarrow L$

Contrapositive Diagram:　$-L \longrightarrow T$

Valid Inference: If the lion is not in the cage, then the tiger is in the cage.

5. **Given:** I will not go jogging if it is raining outside. = **If it is raining outside, then I will not go jogging.**

Be careful with this one! Notice that the original statement puts the "if" part second. This doesn't change the conditional relationship.

MANHATTAN
PREP

Given Diagram: R → -J

Contrapositive Diagram: J → -R

Valid Inference: If I go jogging, then it is not raining outside.

6. **Given:** If Tamika gives the speech, then she won the speech competition.

Given Diagram: T → W

Contrapositive Diagram: -W → -T

Valid Inference: If Tamika did not win the speech competition, then she will not give the speech.

7. **Given:** Yohei plays guitar if Juan plays drums. = **If Juan plays drums, then Yohei plays guitar.**

Given Diagram: J → Y

Contrapositive Diagram: -Y → -J

Valid Inference: If Yohei does not play guitar, then Juan does not play drums.

8. **Given:** If T is not chosen for the team, then N is not chosen for the team.

Given Diagram: -T → -N

Contrapositive Diagram: N → T

Valid Inference: If N is chosen for the team, then T is chosen for the team.

9. **Given:** G is not selected for the club if F is selected for the club. = **If F is selected for the club, then G is not selected for the club.**

Given Diagram: F → -G

Contrapositive Diagram: G → -F

Valid Inference: If G is selected for the club, then F is not selected for the club.

10. **Given:** If Beethoven is played, then Mozart is also played.

Given Diagram: B → M

Contrapositive Diagram: -M → -B

Valid Inference: If Mozart is not played, then Beethoven is not played.

Only/Only If

Translate this statement into formal notation: **Carlos eats fish only on Fridays.**

Based on that statement, which of the following is true?

      (A)   If it's Friday, Carlos is eating fish.

      (B)   If Carlos is not eating fish, it is not Friday.

      (C)   If Carlos is eating fish, it is Friday.

      (D)   If it is not Friday, Carlos is not eating fish.

The first two cannot be inferred from the given statement. Even though Carlos only eats fish on Fridays, he doesn't *have* to eat fish on Fridays. He might eat nothing! If he does indeed eat nothing on Friday, we have not violated the given rule, and thus we have disproven (B).

(C) is inferable since Friday is the only day he eats fish! Similarly, (D) must be true. Thus, the translation of the given statement is CF $\longrightarrow$ Fri, and the contrapositive is –Fri $\longrightarrow$ –CF.

"Only" and "only if" usually indicate the necessary part of a conditional statement. However, be careful not to apply this rule robotically. Translate this statement: **The only way to win the lottery is to have a ticket.**

If you placed "win the lottery" in the necessary position, you missed the point of the statement (and you created a world where everyone wins!). What is guaranteed by the statement is that if someone wins the lottery, they must have had a ticket. Thus, the translation is Win $\longrightarrow$ Ticket. This is a rare twist on an "only" statement; the vast majority of the time, "only" does come right before the necessary condition. Accordingly, we could rewrite the statement to read, "You can win the lottery only if you have a ticket." (If you're looking for a quick tip, "the only" introduces the sufficient condition. It's an annoying exception to an already tricky concept!)

The point is that while some repetitive exercise will help you hone your ability to recognize and symbolize conditional statements, do not aim to become rigid and robotic about it! Yes, language cues are extremely important, but the test writers exploit nuanced forms of expression to utilize key words and imbue them with another meaning (e.g., "only if" introduces necessity, while "if only" introduces sufficiency).

Biconditionals

Consider these two statements and take a moment to translate them into formal notation before reading on:

   1. Ramona will eat if you bring her macaroni and cheese.

   2. Ramona will eat only if you bring her macaroni and cheese.

They translate to the following:

   1. Mac ⟶ Eat

   2. Eat ⟶ Mac

And how would you combine the two statements into one sentence?

One way is to simply write a long sentence: Ramona will eat if you bring her macaroni and cheese, and Ramona will eat only if you bring her macaroni and cheese.

That's correct, but not very elegant! How can we shorten it? One way is this: Ramona will eat *if, and only if,* you bring her macaroni and cheese. Take a moment to confirm that the statement includes both rules established by the original two statements.

Now, how would we write that "if and only if" statement in formal notation? Since it communicates the same rules as the original pair, we could cheat and simply copy what we wrote before:

     Mac ⟶ Eat   Eat ⟶ Mac

But there's a fancier way. Probably you noticed that each statement is the reverse of the other. When that's true, we have a **biconditional.** We can—but don't have to—represent it like this:

     Mac ⟷ Eat

Of course, we also have the contrapositives of the two original statements:

     –Eat ⟶ –Mac   –Mac ⟶ –Eat

And those, too, can be combined into one statement: –Eat ⟷ –Mac. Both sides of the statement are triggers! Each one guarantees the other, and each one is guaranteed by the other.

For a tiny bit of practice, go ahead and write out in formal notation all the conditional statements you can draw from this rule:

     K will be fourth if and only if J is third.

You could have written out four statements, but you also could have combined them into two:

     K_4 ⟷ J_3 –K_4 ⟷ –J_3

Connecting Conditional Statements

In Chapter 9, you'll learn a couple of fancy moves you can use when working with conditional statements. You already know the most important move—creating contrapositives. Another that you want to know right now—and probably could figure out on your own—is how to connect statements. Consider these rules:

1. Trains only come to town on Wednesdays.

2. If Leo is not working, it is not Wednesday.

Go ahead and write those in formal notation, along with the contrapositives before reading on.

1. Train → Wed

   −Wed → −Train

2. −Work → −Wed

   Wed → Work

So, what can you infer if a train comes to town?

From the first rule you know that it's Wednesday. But you also know, per the second rule's contrapositive, that if it is Wednesday, Leo is working. The end of one rule links to the beginning of another:

Train → Wed → Work

Furthermore, we can apply the contrapositive rule to that entire chain, reversing and negating the whole thing, starting with −Work:

−Work → −Wed → −Train

Linking conditional statements is an important move, and one you'll use often. For In/Out Grouping games, we will teach you a way to incorporate those links into a diagram, but when you see linkable conditional statements in other games, go ahead and link them as we've done here.

You've finished Conditional Logic 101! Let's apply what you've learned to the next game type.

MANHATTAN
PREP

Chapter 4

Relative Ordering

In This Chapter...

Getting Familiar

Spend at most **10 minutes** on the following game. If you finish before then, great! If you don't, that's fine, too. It's a tricky new game type, and we don't want you getting too bogged down before going over our approach. That said, a little frustration is good for the learning process.

Exactly eight rock bands—M, N, O, P, R, S, T, and V—perform consecutively at a showcase on Friday night. No band performs more than once, and no two bands perform simultaneously. The following conditions apply:

T and P both perform at some time before O.
S performs at some time before R.
T performs at some time before N.
V performs at some time after S.
M performs at some time before V and at some time after O.

1. Which of the following could be the order of the performances from first to last?

   (A) P, T, O, M, R, S, V, N
   (B) T, N, M, P, S, O, V, R
   (C) P, T, N, O, M, V, S, R
   (D) T, P, N, O, S, M, V, R
   (E) T, N, O, S, P, R, M, V

2. Which of the following must be true?

   (A) At least four bands perform at some time after P.
   (B) At least four bands perform at some time after T.
   (C) At least two bands perform at some time after M.
   (D) At least two bands perform at some time before N.
   (E) At least two bands perform at some time before R.

3. If P performs fifth, then each of the following could be true EXCEPT:

   (A) R is the sixth band to perform.
   (B) N is the fourth band to perform.
   (C) S is the second band to perform.
   (D) T is the third band to perform.
   (E) R performs at some time before N but at some time after T.

4. If S performs at some time after N, and P performs at some time before T, which of the following could be true?

   (A) N performs earlier than P but later than O.
   (B) R performs earlier than M but later than N.
   (C) O performs earlier than N but later than S.
   (D) R performs later than S but earlier than T.
   (E) P performs earlier than O but later than R.

5. Each of the following could be true EXCEPT:

   (A) V performs earlier than N.
   (B) R performs earlier than T.
   (C) N performs earlier than P.
   (D) S performs later than O.
   (E) M performs earlier than P.

6. If T performs third and V performs sixth, then exactly how many different orders are there in which the bands can perform?

   (A) 1
   (B) 2
   (C) 3
   (D) 4
   (E) 5

7. There can be at most how many bands that perform after N but before S?

   (A) 1
   (B) 2
   (C) 3
   (D) 4
   (E) 5

Relative Ordering

About one in every nine games that appear on the LSAT is what we call a **Relative Ordering** game.

Hopefully, even if you found the Getting Familiar game to be a challenge, you didn't find it to be too unusual or unexpected. It should have seemed related to the games we played in the previous chapter. Indeed, Relative Ordering games are a subset of Ordering games; however, because they are so common, and because they present a particular set of recognizable characteristics, it's useful for us to separate them out and discuss them specifically. Relative Ordering games are to general Ordering games as jeans are to pants—jeans are a type of pants, but so common that we also define them as a unique clothing category.

What Defines a Relative Ordering Game?

It's not the scenario given before the rules. To illustrate, let's take a look at the scenario for the Getting Familiar game you just played:

> Exactly eight rock bands—M, N, O, P, R, S, T, and V—perform consecutively at a showcase on Friday night. No band performs more than once, and no two bands perform simultaneously. The following conditions apply:

This introduction is not very different from the ones we saw for Basic Ordering games, and in fact, it could very well be the introduction to a Basic Ordering game.

> What defines a Relative Ordering game are the rules themselves.

Let's take a look at the rules from the same game to illustrate:

> T and P both perform **at some time before** O.
> S performs **at some time before** R.
> T performs **at some time before** N.
> V performs **at some time after** S.
> M performs **at some time before** V and at **some time after** O.

Notice the similarity among all of the rules. They are all what we call Relative Ordering rules—rules that inform us of a general ordering relationship between elements. None of these rules tell us exactly how many positions are between elements, and none of these rules tell us about specific assignments of elements to positions.

A Relative Ordering game is an Ordering game for which all, or almost all, of the rules are about relative ordering. Relative Ordering games are one of the two types of games in which you'll always see all or almost all the rules conform to just one type. (The other type is In/Out Grouping, which we'll cover in a later chapter.)

MANHATTAN
PREP

Picturing Relative Ordering Games and Notating Rules

When you first tried the Getting Familiar game, it's very possible that you drew a Number Line to get started. That's perfectly fine—there is no negative to drawing it, and it may serve as a useful reference later on.

However, notice that none of the rules are such that any elements can be placed on the Number Line. Other than some exclusions that you may or may not choose to notate, for this type of game, the Number Line is not particularly helpful in organizing the information given to us in the rules.

For Relative Ordering games, we recommend that you use another type of diagram that better represents the type of information these rules contain—we call this diagram the **Tree.**

To create a Tree diagram, we don't need to start with a "base" of slots. Once you've recognized that a game is a Relative Ordering game, you can start creating your diagram with the first rule that you read. This game type demonstrates why it's generally a good idea to do a quick scan of the rules before settling on a diagram—you don't truly know if you're in a Basic or Relative Ordering game until then!

Creating a Tree diagram is actually quite simple, and it plays off skills that you already worked on in the previous chapter. Let's use the Getting Familiar game to illustrate how to set up a Tree diagram, step by step.

Here are the scenario and rules again:

> Exactly eight rock bands—M, N, O, P, R, S, T, and V—perform consecutively at a showcase on Friday night. No band performs more than once, and no two bands perform simultaneously. The following conditions apply:
>
> T and P both perform at some time before O.
> S performs at some time before R.
> T performs at some time before N.
> V performs at some time after S.
> M performs at some time before V and at some time after O.

Step 1: Start with the first rule and draw lines between any two letters for which the relative position is known.

This form of notation should be familiar to you from the previous chapter. The line in between elements will always mean the same thing in our diagrams—we know of a relative relationship between elements, but not a specific one. Note that this rule doesn't tell us the relationship between T and P, so we don't connect these elements to one another.

Also notice that though we chose to draw T above P, we could just as well have drawn it below P. When we construct a Tree diagram, the vertical organization of elements is irrelevant—all we care about is the horizontal relationship between elements. Again, this notation allows us to see that both T and P are before O, but also that we do not know, specifically, the relationship between T and P.

Step 2: Move on to the next rule that can be connected to any part of the existing diagram.

You want to develop a habit, from early on and for any game, of handling the rules in an order that is most convenient for you.

For Relative Ordering games, that means looking out for rules that share a common element. In this case, once we've diagrammed the first rule, we want to skip the second rule, because it shares no elements in common with the first.

The third rule has a T, which also appeared in our first rule. So we want to add that third rule, like this:

Let's pause for a minute and think about what we know at this point, having brought these two rules together.

We know that T is before N, and that T is before O, but what about the relationship between N and O? Note that the way we drew in the second rule was somewhat arbitrary. We could have placed N a bit to the left of O or a bit to the right, and either would have been fine. We don't know about the relationship between N and O. We know both come after T, but that's it.

What about the relationship between N and P? We never knew the relationship between T and P to begin with, so we certainly don't know the relationship between N and P.

Let's keep going.

Step 3: Repeat until all rules have been used.

It's a good idea to keep track of the rules we've already notated, and one way we can do so is to put check marks next to these rules. It might look something like this:

  ✓T and P both perform at some time before O.
   S performs at some time before R.
  ✓T performs at some time before N.
   V performs at some time after S.
   M performs at some time before V and at some time after O.

We want to look for the next rule that shares a common element with what we've got in our diagram so far, and in this case it is the fifth one, which tells us that we can place an M after the O we already have, and a V after our M, like so:

```
T — N
  ⟩
      O — M — V
P
```

If you were confused by that last rule, consider that it contains two pieces of information about M: M comes before V, and M comes after O. Dealing with compound rules one piece at a time is a good habit to get into so you don't misinterpret it by moving too quickly.

Now let's pause again for a moment and think a bit about what we know of the relationship between P and V. It appears that P must be before V, but do we know that for certain?

Yes, we do, because we have a link of inferences that we can follow: P is before O, which we know is before M, which we know is before V. Therefore, P must be before V.

What about the relationship between N and V? N is positioned on the page to the left of V, but do we know that N comes before V?

No, we don't. All we know about N, actually, is that it is after T. So it could be right after T and well before V, or it could be well after T and even after V.

Why can we infer something about the relationship between P and V, but not about N and V? At this point, it may be that you get why this is so, but perhaps not in a clear, definable way. Knowing when a relationship can be inferred is an important concept to understand, and one we'll revisit in just a bit. For now, let us plant this seed in your mind: We can stretch or shrink the T–N connection so that N appears to come before or after V. But no matter how you shrink or stretch the P–O–M–V connections, P will always be before V. Hmmm.

For now, let's get back to creating our diagram. We can move on to the fourth rule, which involves S, and add that rule to what we already have:

```
T — N
  ⟩
      O — M — V
P         ⟩
          S
```

Finally, we have a place to attach the second rule. We can finish up our diagram like so:

```
T — N
  ⟩
      O — M — V
P         ⟩
          S — R
```

Note that our final diagram could have ended up looking quite different while giving us exactly the same information. Remember that vertical orientation, as well as the length of the lines used to connect elements, is not relevant to the inferences that this diagram yields. All we care about are the horizontal (left to right or right to left) relationships between elements. These three somewhat different looking diagrams all give us exactly the same horizontal relationships:

The Tree diagram consolidates the information from all the rules and gives us a clear picture of the relationships between the elements. The Tree does not give us the order of elements, nor is it meant to; we do not have enough information to make such a determination. The Tree does give us every single inference regarding relative relationships, and as you'll see shortly, these inferences are the key to success on Relative Ordering games. We will unlock the full power of the Tree momentarily when we discuss how to draw inferences from the diagram in order to answer questions. First, let's get more comfortable with the setup process by drilling the mechanics.

MANHATTAN
PREP

Drill It: Relative Ordering Setups

Each setup will contain one or more rules. Your task is to construct a Tree diagram for each one. Be sure to check your diagram against the solution on the next page **after each and every setup.** Make sure you understand each setup before moving on to the next one.

Example:

S departs at some point after R.
O departs at some time before P but at some point after Q.
P departs at some point after R.

Q — O — P
        /
R — S

1. X plays earlier than W but later than T.
    Y plays later than Z.
    Z plays earlier than X.

4. M arrives at some time after O.
    L arrives earlier than N.
    J arrives at some time after L but before P.
    S arrives at some time after J.
    N arrives later than O.

2. Both M and H are written later than N.
    O is written at some time before H but after J.
    J is written earlier than K.
    K is written earlier than N.

5. Both S and Y finish at some time before R.
    T finishes at some time after X.
    S finishes at some time after W but before V.
    X finishes earlier than Z.

3. Both T and V call at some time before M.
    N calls at some time after R.
    O calls at some time before N but after M.
    P calls at some time before M.
    T calls at some time before S.

6. K is produced at some time after N but before O.
    Both L and J are produced at some time before N.
    M is produced at some time after P.
    R is produced at some time before O.
    J is produced at some time before M.

Solutions: Relative Ordering Setups

1. X plays earlier than W but later than T.
   Y plays later than Z.
   Z plays earlier than X.

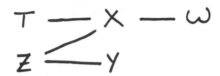

2. Both M and H are written later than N.
   O is written at some time before H but after J.
   J is written earlier than K.
   K is written earlier than N.

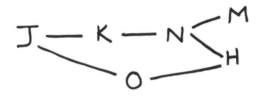

3. Both T and V call at some time before M.
   N calls at some time after R.
   O calls at some time before N but after M.
   P calls at some time before M.
   T calls at some time before S.

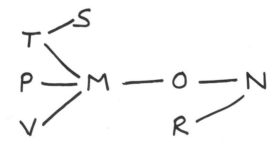

4. M arrives at some time after O.
   L arrives earlier than N.
   J arrives at some time after L but before P.
   S arrives at some time after J.
   N arrives later than O.

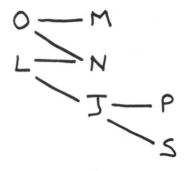

5. Both S and Y finish at some time before R.
   T finishes at some time after X.
   S finishes at some time after W but before V.
   X finishes earlier than Z.

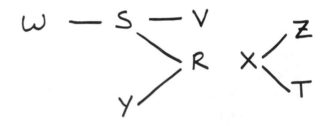

(Yes, you might end up with two Trees! Don't try to force them together.)

6. K is produced at some time after N but before O.
   Both L and J are produced at some time before N.
   M is produced at some time after P.
   R is produced at some time before O.
   J is produced at some time before M.

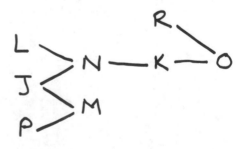

MANHATTAN
PREP

Using the Tree to Make Inferences

Now you know how to draw these fancy Trees, but how can you use them to answer the questions? Let's figure out how to use this powerful diagramming system.

If you have properly set up your Tree diagram, you have essentially uncovered *all* of the key relative ordering inferences required to answer the questions. Your ability to utilize these inferences, however, depends on your ability to correctly read the Tree. There are just two important rules that you must keep in mind. We'll discuss these rules one at a time using our completed Tree diagram from our rock band example:

```
T — N
     \
P  >  O — M — V
              \
          S — R
```

Rule 1: The relative position between two elements, or letters, *can* be determined if we can trace a continuous path between these two elements without changing the horizontal direction of our path.

It should make sense why this is so. If T is before O, and O is before M, and M is before V, we can say for certain that T must be before V. As long as we are linking our understanding in "one direction," we can make such valid inferences.

Example: P to V

Starting at P, we can follow a solid line to the right towards O, continue to the right towards M, and again trace to the right to arrive at V. Note that we have traced a *continuous* path from P to V, and we did not have to change horizontal directions to do so. We moved to the right the entire time. Thus, the position of P relative to V is known. Even though the rules never referenced a direct relationship between the two, we can infer that P sits somewhere before V (with at least O and M between them).

Example: M to T

From M, we can follow a solid line to the left towards O, then continue on a solid line to the left arriving at T. Thus, we can conclude that T sits somewhere before M.

Rule 2: The relative position between two elements *cannot* be determined if the path between them includes one or more changes in horizontal direction. In other words, if there's a zigzag connection between two elements, we don't know which one comes before the other.

Example: N to O

From N, we can follow a solid line to the left towards T, but then we must change horizontal directions, moving back to the right to arrive at O. Thus, the position of N relative to O *cannot* be determined. N could come somewhere before O, but it could also come somewhere after O.

Example: P to R

This is a tough one. It *looks* like P comes before R, but the relationship between them is actually unknown. Remember, the Tree is a map of relative position, *not* a physical picture of order. From P, we can follow continuous, solid lines to the right towards V, but then we must change horizontal directions back to the left towards S, and then change again to move right towards R. Thus, the position of P relative to R *cannot* be determined. P could come somewhere before R, but it could also come somewhere after R. This is tough for some folks at first since R is so far to the right of S in the diagram. But remember that since the connections between elements simply show that one precedes the other, we can make our lines as short or as long as we like. All you would need to do is stretch the S–V connection and your diagram could look like this (and still be correct):

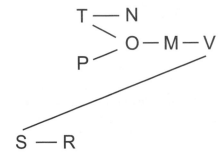

That's it! The Tree diagram presents a visual representation of all that we know about the relative relationships between elements, and as long as you understand how to utilize the above two rules, the Tree can be a powerful tool for helping you get through a Relative Ordering game quickly and effectively.

Here are some additional tips for utilizing the Tree effectively:

1. **Be mindful of strays.** We define strays a little differently in these games. Normally, elements with no rules are strays (and that will continue to be true here). However, we extend the definition to include elements that have a known relationship with just one other element.

If we take a look at our sample diagram:

The two strays for this game are N and R. We know that N comes after T, but we know nothing else about N. We know R comes after S, but we know nothing else about R.

Before you read on, identify all the various positions in the Number Line, one through seven, that N can occupy, and all the positions that R can occupy.

N can occupy any position from two to eight, as can R. Because these elements have a lot of flexibility in terms of where they can be placed, they can often be the key "wrinkle" in a particular problem. Furthermore, because of the way we tend to represent these strays, it can be easy to forget them or misunderstand them. For our image above, for example, it can be very easy to forget that N could be the last element. (Some students find it helpful to circle these strays.)

2. **Become practiced at placing elements into positions during questions.** Note that in setting up our diagram, we focused on the relationships between elements, rather than on where those elements can and cannot go. With most Relative Ordering games, we don't recommend spending time making additional inferences onto a Number Line during your setup. However, when we get to the point of answering questions, we'll often need to transfer what we know about relative relationships to a set of concrete positions.

Let's think for a moment about the diagram we have set up. What positions in the order could M occupy? Think about it on your own before reading on.

Here's what we know about M: There are three elements—T, O, and P—that all *must* go before M, and there is one element—V—that *must* go after M. Therefore, M can't go in one of the first three positions, and M can't go in the last position. M could go in positions 4, 5, 6, or 7.

Let's think about the diagram from another perspective. Which elements could go first? Again, think about it on your own before reading on.

To answer this, it's helpful to know what prevents an element from going first. An element can't go first if there are other elements that have to go before (or to the left) of it. If we look at our diagram, there are three elements that have no other elements to the left of them—that is, no elements that must go before them. These three elements—T, P, and S—all could go first.

3. **Know when to draw a new Tree.** For conditional questions that provide an *assignment* (e.g., R is third), drawing out a Number Line makes a lot of sense. But for those times when we're provided with a new *relationship*—F comes before Q—drawing a new Tree for that question generally is more appropriate.

Just as with conditional questions that provide an assignment, with these relationship conditionals you might find that you can do the inference work in your head. Great. As you start your prep, default to writing out your work, and later, as you develop a strong grasp on your approach and an understanding of what your brain can actually handle under pressure, you can start to pull away from the paper for easier questions.

Using the Cloud to Represent Limited Uncertainty

Now, let's imagine that in a different question, we are told that T occupies the fourth position. We would start thinking about the situation by drawing a Number Line beside the question, and placing T fourth, like so:

$$\underline{\quad}\ \underline{\quad}\ \underline{\quad}\ \overset{\textstyle T}{\underline{\quad}}\ \underline{\quad}\ \underline{\quad}\ \underline{\quad}\ \underline{\quad}$$

What do we know about T? We know that N, O, M, and V must all come after T. If T is fourth, there are four spaces after it—5, 6, 7, and 8—in which to place these four elements. However, we can't be sure exactly which position each element goes in. We do know something that severely limits our options—O must be before M which must be before V—but we don't want to waste time thinking about and representing every possibility for every position. Instead, we can do something like this:

$$\underline{\quad}\ \underline{\quad}\ \underline{\quad}\ \overset{\textstyle T}{\underline{\quad}}\ \overset{\textstyle \boxed{N,O-M-V}}{\underline{\quad}\ \underline{\quad}\ \underline{\quad}}\ \underline{\quad}$$

The cloud tells us generally where elements go, while also noting that there are still various options. It makes it easy to see that we have four elements to occupy four spots, and because the cloud preserves the known relationships between the elements, it's easy to do more specific deductive work about the specific positions elements can go in if the answer choices require that from us.

Note that we do not know anything directly about T's relationship with P, S, or R, and one way we know that we don't know anything is that we can't connect T to any of these elements without changing our horizontal direction. But since N, O, M, and V are taking up all the slots after T, we can infer that the rest of the elements fall before T.

We can finish off our diagram by placing the remaining three elements in a cloud in front of the T:

$$\overset{\textstyle \boxed{P,S-R}}{\underline{\quad}\ \underline{\quad}\ \underline{\quad}}\ \overset{\textstyle T}{\underline{\quad}}\ \overset{\textstyle \boxed{N,O-M-V}}{\underline{\quad}\ \underline{\quad}\ \underline{\quad}}\ \underline{\quad}$$

Drill It: Tree Inferences

Each exercise will contain a completed Tree diagram. Your task is to answer the associated questions based on your understanding of the diagram. Be sure to check your answers against the solutions **after each set of questions.** Make sure you understand before moving on to the next exercise.

Game 1:

1. Does V come somewhere before O? Yes, no, or maybe?

2. Does T come somewhere before R? Yes, no, or maybe?

3. How many letters must come after P?

4. Of the eight letters, which ones could occupy the eighth position?

5. Of the eight letters, which ones could occupy the first position?

6. What is the earliest position that O could occupy?

Game 2:

1. Does M come somewhere before R? Yes, no, or maybe?

2. Does K come somewhere before J? Yes, no, or maybe?

3. How many letters must come before O?

4. Of the eight letters, which ones could occupy the eighth position?

5. Of the eight letters, which ones could occupy the first position?

6. If N occupies the third position, what is the earliest position that M could occupy?

Game 3:

```
O — M
L   N
  J — P
    S
```

1. Of the seven letters, which ones could occupy the first position?

2. Of the seven letters, which ones could occupy the last position?

3. How many letters must come before J?

4. How many letters must come after L?

5. What is the latest position that O could occupy?

6. If J occupies the third position, list all of the possible positions that N could occupy.

Game 4:

```
        X — T
W — S   V
        R
  Y
```

1. What is the earliest position that R could occupy?

2. What is the earliest position that T could occupy?

3. If V occupies the third position, what is the earliest position that R could occupy?

4. What is the latest position that S could occupy?

5. If Y occupies the second position and V occupies the fourth position, how many different possibilities are there for the ordering of the seven letters? Write them out.

6. If T occupies the fourth position, which letters could occupy the seventh position?

MANHATTAN
PREP

Solutions: Tree Inferences

Game 1:

1. Does V come somewhere before O? Yes, no, or maybe? **Yes**

We can trace a solid line from V to M to O without changing horizontal directions.

2. Does T come somewhere before R? Yes, no, or maybe? **Maybe**

From T, we can trace a solid line all the way to N without changing directions, but then we must move back to the left in order to arrive at R. Thus, we *cannot* determine the position of T relative to R. T could come before R or after R.

3. How many letters must come after P? **Three**

Moving to the right, we can trace a continuous connection between P and M, P and O, and P and N. Thus, M, N, and O must all come after P. Remember, R is a stray! It could potentially come before P.

4. Of the eight letters, which ones could occupy the eighth position? **N, S**

Remember that S is a stray! The only thing we know about S is that it must come after T. Other than that, S is free to occupy any position, including the eighth position.

5. Of the eight letters, which ones could occupy the first position? **T, P, V, R**

Remember that R is a stray! The only thing we know about R is that it must precede N. Other than that, R is free to occupy any position, including the first position.

6. What is the earliest position that O could occupy? **Fifth**

Notice that T, P, V, and M must all come before O. If these four letters must precede O, then the fifth position is the earliest position that O could occupy.

Game 2:

```
        R
L         
 \      /
  N — K — O
 /        
J      
 \    M
  \  /
P
```

1. Does M come somewhere before R? Yes, no, or maybe? **Maybe**

Tracing the path from M to R involves changing directions twice. Thus, the position of M relative to R *cannot* be determined. M could come before or after R.

2. Does K come somewhere before J? Yes, no, or maybe? **No**

From J, we can trace a continuous path to the right to arrive at K. Thus, K comes *after* J, not before.

3. How many letters must come before O? **Five**

R, K, N, L, and J can all be traced back to O on a continuous, one-directional path.

4. Of the eight letters, which ones could occupy the eighth position? **O, M**

We know that M must be preceded by both J and P. Other than that, however, M is free to occupy any position, including the last position.

5. Of the eight letters, which ones could occupy the first position? **L, J, P, R**

Don't forget about the stray R! We know that R must come before O. Other than that, however, R is free to occupy any position, including the first.

6. If N occupies the third position, what is the earliest position that M could occupy? **Fifth**

If N occupies the third position, L and J must occupy the first and second positions (not necessarily in that order). We know that P must come before M. With the first three positions filled, the earliest that P could come is fourth. Thus, the fifth position is the earliest position that M could occupy.

Game 3:

```
O ——— M
  L ———  N
      ⟍ J ——— P
          ⟍ S
```

1. Of the seven letters, which ones could occupy the first position? **O, L**

Every other letter has at least one letter that must precede it.

2. Of the seven letters, which ones could occupy the last position? **P, S, M, N**

Watch out for the stray M! Also, we know that O and L must precede N. Other than that, however, N is free to occupy any position, including the last.

3. How many letters must come before J? **One**

L must come before J, and P and S must come after J. J's relationship with O, N, and M is uncertain because we cannot trace a one-directional line between J and O, J and N, or J and M.

4. How many letters must come after L? **Four**

N, J, P, and S must all come after L. L's relationship with O and M is uncertain because we cannot trace a one-directional line between L and O or L and M.

5. What is the latest possible position that O could occupy? **Fifth**

All we know about O is that both M and N must come after it. Thus, O cannot occupy the sixth or seventh positions, but it could occupy the fifth position.

6. If J occupies the third position, list all of the possible positions that N could occupy. **Fourth, fifth, sixth, seventh**

If J occupies the third position, L and O must occupy the first and second positions (not necessarily in that order). This leaves the fourth, fifth, sixth, and seventh positions for M, N, P, and S. Since there is no one-directional connection between any of these four letters, their relative positioning is uncertain. Thus, N could occupy any one of the last four positions.

Game 4:

1. What is the earliest position that R could occupy? **Fourth**

S, Y, and W must all come before R.

2. What is the earliest position that T could occupy? **Fourth**

X, S, and W must all come before T.

3. If V occupies the third position, what is the earliest position that R could occupy? **Fifth**

If V occupies the third position, W and S must occupy the first and second positions, respectively. Y must come before R. With the first three positions filled, the fourth position is the earliest that Y could occupy. R could occupy the fifth position immediately after Y.

4. What is the latest possible position that S could occupy? **Third**

X, T, V, and R must all come after S. Thus, the latest position that S could occupy is the third.

5. If Y occupies the second position and V occupies the fourth position, how many different possibilities are there for the ordering of the seven letters? Write them out.

W Y S V R X T

W Y S V X R T

W Y S V X T R

If Y occupies the second position and V occupies the fourth position, W must occupy the first position and S must occupy the third position.

6. If T occupies the fourth position, which letters could occupy the seventh position? **V, R**

If T occupies the fourth position, W, S, and X must occupy the first, second, and third positions, respectively. This leaves V, R, and Y for the last three positions. Y must come before R, so Y can't occupy the last position.

MANHATTAN
PREP

Try It Again

Now that you've learned how to draw inferences from the Tree diagram, it's time to put your skills to good use. Let's revisit the rock band game introduced at the start of the chapter. Try developing your Tree from scratch, and then use it to tackle the questions. This time, try the game without a time limitation. We'll work through the solutions together on the pages to come.

Exactly eight rock bands—M, N, O, P, R, S, T, and V—perform consecutively at a showcase on Friday night. No band performs more than once, and no two bands perform simultaneously. The following conditions apply:

T and P both perform at some time before O.
S performs at some time before R.
T performs at some time before N.
V performs at some time after S.
M performs at some time before V and at some time after O.

1. Which of the following could be the order of the performances from first to last?

   (A) P, T, O, M, R, S, V, N
   (B) T, N, M, P, S, O, V, R
   (C) P, T, N, O, M, V, S, R
   (D) T, P, N, O, S, M, V, R
   (E) T, N, O, S, P, R, M, V

2. Which of the following must be true?

   (A) At least four bands perform at some time after P.
   (B) At least four bands perform at some time after T.
   (C) At least two bands perform at some time after M.
   (D) At least two bands perform at some time before N.
   (E) At least two bands perform at some time before R.

3. If P performs fifth, then each of the following could be true EXCEPT:

   (A) R is the sixth band to perform.
   (B) N is the fourth band to perform.
   (C) S is the second band to perform.
   (D) T is the third band to perform.
   (E) R performs at some time before N but at some time after T.

4. If S performs at some time after N, and P performs at some time before T, which of the following could be true?

   (A) N performs earlier than P but later than O.
   (B) R performs earlier than M but later than N.
   (C) O performs earlier than N but later than S.
   (D) R performs later than S but earlier than T.
   (E) P performs earlier than O but later than R.

5. Each of the following could be true EXCEPT:

   (A) V performs earlier than N.
   (B) R performs earlier than T.
   (C) N performs earlier than P.
   (D) S performs later than O.
   (E) M performs earlier than P.

6. If T performs third and V performs sixth, then exactly how many different orders are there in which the bands can perform?

   (A) 1
   (B) 2
   (C) 3
   (D) 4
   (E) 5

7. There can be at most how many bands that perform after N but before S?

   (A) 1
   (B) 2
   (C) 3
   (D) 4
   (E) 5

How Did You Do?

Answer Key

1. D   5. E
2. B   6. D
3. A   7. C
4. B

Steps 1 and 2: Picture the Game, Notate the Rules, and Make Inferences

Since we discussed the setup of this game earlier, we're going to just transfer our diagram and focus on the questions themselves. Please refer back a few pages if you need help with any part of the setup.

```
T — N
  >       O — M — V
P           S — R
```

Step 3: The Big Pause

In Relative Ordering games, the Tree diagram serves as a thorough representation of all the inferences, so there's no need for any deep consideration of the game or prioritization of the rules. However, it's definitely worth checking that you've notated each rule correctly. At some point, you'll see how time-consuming it is when you jump into the questions with a diagram based on *F is after G* when the rule actually says *F is before G*!

Step 4: Attack the Questions

1. Which of the following could be the order of the performances from first to last?

   (A) P, T, O, M, R, S, V, N
   (B) T, N, M, P, S, O, V, R
   (C) P, T, N, O, M, V, S, R
   (D) T, P, N, O, S, M, V, R
   (E) T, N, O, S, P, R, M, V

   Answer choice (D) is correct.

MANHATTAN
PREP

This is an Orientation question and we can use the rules to eliminate answers:

The first rule allows us to eliminate (E).
The second rule allows us to eliminate (A).
The fourth rule allows us to eliminate (C).
The fifth rule allows us to eliminate (B).

Alternatively, if you are comfortable with your Tree diagram, you can use an approach that we call the **String Technique.** Here's how it works:

Looking at our Tree, we see a P–O–M–V string. These four letters must come in that order (not necessarily consecutively, but certainly in that order). So let's start by eliminating any answer choices that do *not* contain the P–O–M–V string. Answer (B) has M–P–O–V. Eliminate it. Answer (E) has O–P–M–V. Eliminate it. Now let's take another string: S–V. Let's eliminate any choice that does *not* contain the S–V string. Eliminate answer choice (C). Lastly, we'll evaluate the S–R string. Eliminate answer (A). We're left with answer choice (D).

Note that the String Technique is just a different way of using rules to eliminate wrong answers, but it can be a bit faster since you're testing more than one rule at a time.

2. Which of the following must be true?

    (A) At least four bands perform at some time after P.
    (B) At least four bands perform at some time after T.
    (C) At least two bands perform at some time after M.
    (D) At least two bands perform at some time before N.
    (E) At least two bands perform at some time before R.

Answer choice (B) is correct.

N, O, M, and V must all perform after T.

Remember that a big key to questions such as this one is to not spend too much time on incorrect answers. If you are asked to identify an answer that must be true, or must be false, you want to focus on just finding the right answer, rather than on eliminating incorrect answers.

3. If P performs fifth, then each of the following could be true EXCEPT:

    (A) R is the sixth band to perform.
    (B) N is the fourth band to perform.
    (C) S is the second band to perform.
    (D) T is the third band to perform.
    (E) R performs at some time before N but at some time after T.

Answer choice (A) is correct.

If P performs fifth, we know O, M, and V must follow it (in that order), and so O must be sixth, M seventh, and V eighth. That leaves T, N, S, and R for the first four slots. We can represent the information we know as follows:

(T – N, S – R)   P   O   M   V
___ ___ ___ ___   ___ ___ ___ ___

We are looking for an answer that must be false, and that's (A).

4. If S performs at some time after N, and P performs at some time before T, which of the following could be true?

   (A) N performs earlier than P but later than O.
   (B) R performs earlier than M but later than N.
   (C) O performs earlier than N but later than S.
   (D) R performs later than S but earlier than T.
   (E) P performs earlier than O but later than R.

Answer choice (B) is correct.

Here's our second conditional question. Unlike the previous one, this question provides a *relationship* instead of a *position*. Therefore, instead of drawing a Number Line to make inferences, we'll want to draw a new Tree.

We can start by simply noting the two relationships, roughly placing them in a position that might work in terms of where all the elements will eventually be placed:

N ——— S

P ——— T

Now, we want to build the rest of the diagram around these relationships. No need to be fancy; simply take a rule and add it in. See if you can finish that off before reading on.

You could start by adding in that T must come before N, and then add that O must follow T:

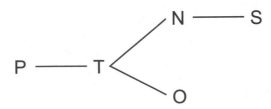

The final diagram for this question should look something like this:

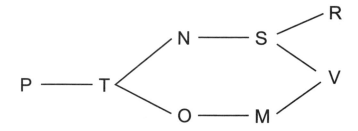

It may seem odd to build a new diagram for a question, but it shouldn't take long, and it will set us up nicely to move through the answer choices quickly.

We want something that could be true, so the four wrong answers must all be false.

Answer (A) is wrong—N can't perform earlier than P.

Answer (B) is correct. R and M are connected by a zigzag, so R could definitely come before M, and R must come after N.

You wouldn't keep moving through the choices, but go ahead now and confirm for yourself why answers (C) through (E) must be false.

5. Each of the following could be true EXCEPT:

    (A) V performs earlier than N.
    (B) R performs earlier than T.
    (C) N performs earlier than P.
    (D) S performs later than O.
    (E) M performs earlier than P.

Answer choice (E) is correct.

This is another question that requires us to identify one answer that must be false. M cannot perform before P, because we know P performs before O and O performs before M.

The other four answers represent relations about which we are not certain. For practice, you may want to think about how connecting each of the elements in the respective answer choices—V and N for (A), R and T for (B), etc.— requires you to change horizontal directions. Remember that a zigzag is the physical sign that allows us to see that we do *not* know the relationship between two particular elements.

6. If T performs third and V performs sixth, then exactly how many different orders are there in which the bands can perform?

   (A) 1
   (B) 2
   (C) 3
   (D) 4
   (E) 5

Answer choice (D) is correct.

We will discuss this type of question in fuller detail a bit later in this chapter.

7. There can be at most how many bands that perform after N but before S?

   (A) 1
   (B) 2
   (C) 3
   (D) 4
   (E) 5

Answer choice (C) is correct.

We will discuss this type of question in fuller detail later in this chapter as well!

Review Questions

Now that you've had a chance to take another look at the game, and to read how another person might approach solving the questions, how do you feel?

Here are some of the review questions we discussed in the previous chapter. Let's apply them to this game and then use them to think about other Relative Ordering games.

1. Could I picture the game easily? Did I understand the general situation?

Do you understand what characteristics make this a Relative Ordering game? Will you able to recognize Relative Ordering games when you see them on the exam?

2. Did I understand the rules correctly? Did I notate them in a way that allowed me to think about them easily?

Were you able to correctly put together your Tree or did you make an error somewhere? Do you feel confident that you can construct similar diagrams without error or do you feel you need practice to get more comfortable?

3. Did I make the key inferences at the right times? Did I understand which rules to prioritize?

For Relative Ordering games, the Tree diagram gives us every up-front inference we need going into the questions. It will show us every link between relative relationships, and it will make it easy to see which positions elements can and cannot go into (and we need not and should not notate all of these possibilities up front). The Big Pause is simply a diagram check. The questions themselves will require us to make additional inferences, often by applying what we know to specific positions on a Number Line. Make sure you have a good understanding of how to think about inferences for Relative Ordering games.

4. Did I attack each question wisely?

In reading the solutions for this game, hopefully you were able to notice similarities and differences between your own thought process and the one we've outlined. If any questions took you more time than they should have, think carefully about the "unnecessary" steps you may have taken or the moment at which your thought process may have gotten stuck. Perhaps just as importantly, think carefully about the questions that you answered very quickly and effectively. Walk through your thought process and consider what the keys that led to such success were.

Spotlight on Question Types: Options Questions

In the previous chapter, we discussed the two most common types of questions, Orientation questions and Standard questions. On a typical exam, the majority of the questions that you will see in the Logic Games section will fit into one of those two categories (with Standard questions being, by far, the most frequent category). In this chapter and the next, we will discuss the two "families" of minor question types—we'll discuss **Options** questions in this chapter and **Rule** questions in the next.

Options questions require you to use what you know about a game to consider various possibilities for how to arrange the elements. Options questions come in five main types:

1. Possible Arrangements
2. Min/Max
3. Possible Elements
4. Possible Positions
5. Determine Positions

1. Possible Arrangements

We had an example of this type of question in our Getting Familiar game:

> *If T performs third and V performs sixth, then exactly how many different orders are there in which the bands can perform?*

Almost all such questions that ask us to calculate total possibilities are conditional in nature; that is, they give us new information that will help us to further limit options before we have to count them. It makes sense why this is so: Without new rules, there would generally be so many possibilities that it would be unreasonable to expect us to count them all in the course of a minute or so.

Therefore, you can expect conditions for these questions, and you should expect to be able to whittle down the uncertainty to just a few unset positions and a few unassigned elements.

Let's return to the question mentioned above to discuss these concepts further:

6. If T performs third and V performs sixth, then exactly how many different orders are there in which the bands can perform?

    (A) 1
    (B) 2
    (C) 3
    (D) 4
    (E) 5

We want to start by placing T third and V sixth. Initially, it might appear that those are the only assignments we know for certain, but it would be a mistake, at this point, to move into thinking about the number of possibilities for each remaining position. With six positions open, the math is simply too much. We *know* we can uncover other assignments that are certain.

And if we think about it, there is more to uncover. Since there are two positions between third and sixth, and two elements—O and M—that must go between T and V, in that particular order, O must go in the fourth position and M must go in the fifth position.

That leaves P, S, N, and R for the remaining open positions—1, 2, 7, and 8.

We know we're going to get further limitations—if we just have four elements for four positions, with no other restrictions, that would yield 24 possible orders (we won't list them here), which is too many for the test writers to realistically expect us to calculate in the limited time frame. (It's also not an answer choice.)

We can figure out that P must go in one of the first two positions and N in one of the final two positions. Since S must perform before R, that means S must also go in one of the first two positions and R in one of the final two positions. As we mentioned in the solution before, we end up with the following hypothetical:

There are certain mathematical formulas that we can use to think about our possibilities. However, in general, we don't recommend that you use such formulas. The situations presented are always limited enough that it makes more sense to manually count out the possibilities.

One tip we have is to focus on the positions that are uncertain. Once we've filled 3–6, we don't have to think about them anymore, and, mentally at least, the issue looks something like this:

Now, it's a bit easier, perhaps, to walk through all four possible permutations:

P, S	N, R
P, S	R, N
S, P	N, R
S, P	R, N

Drill It: **Possible Arrangements**

Here is a mini drill to practice Possible Arrangements questions. Use the provided diagrams to solve each question.

1.

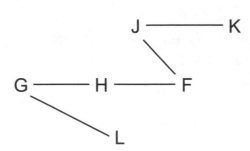

If H is third and L is fifth, how many possible sequences of letters are there?

(A) 2

(B) 3

(C) 4

(D) 5

(E) 6

2.

$$\frac{H/}{1} \quad \frac{}{2} \quad \frac{J/F}{3} \quad \frac{}{4} \quad \frac{}{5} \quad \frac{}{6} \quad \frac{/H}{7}$$

H J F T Ⓝ O P

P — O — T

If N comes immediately before H, how many orderings of letters are possible?

(A) 5

(B) 6

(C) 7

(D) 8

(E) 9

3.

$$\underline{}_{1} \ \underline{}_{2} \ \underline{}_{3} \ \underline{}_{4} \ \underline{}_{5} \ \underline{}_{6}$$

G F R S T W

S — T — R

W — F

W — G → S — R

If T is third and F is fourth, how many different arrangements are possible?

(A) 1
(B) 2
(C) 3
(D) 4
(E) 5

4.

$$\underline{}_{1} \ \underline{}_{2} \ \underline{}_{3} \ \underline{}_{4} \ \underline{}_{5} \ \underline{}_{6}$$

N P Ⓡ S T W

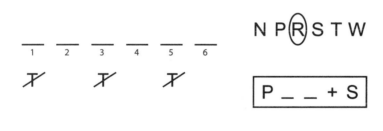

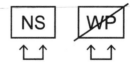

If R comes fourth, how many different assignments are possible?

(A) 2
(B) 3
(C) 4
(D) 5
(E) 6

Solutions: Possible Arrangements

1. **Answer choice (C) is correct.** H must come after G and before F. So we know G is in either slot 1 or 2, and F is in either slot 4 or 6. J must come before F and K, so we know J is in either slot 1 or 2, and K is in either 4 or 6:

$$\boxed{G \quad J} \quad \underline{H} \quad \underline{F/K} \quad \underline{L} \quad \underline{F/K}$$
$$ \quad 1 \qquad 2 \qquad 3 \qquad 4 \qquad 5 \qquad 6$$

Thus, four scenarios are possible:

$$G \ J \ H \ F \ L \ K$$
$$G \ J \ H \ K \ L \ F$$
$$J \ G \ H \ F \ L \ K$$
$$J \ G \ H \ K \ L \ F$$

2. **Answer choice (D) is correct.** N must be in slot 6 to come immediately before H. We still have to determine the positions for P, O, T, and J/F:

$$\boxed{P-O-T, \quad J/F}$$

$$\underline{} \quad \underline{} \quad \overset{J/F}{\underline{}} \quad \underline{} \quad \underline{} \quad \overset{N}{\underline{}} \quad \overset{H}{\underline{}}$$
$$1 \qquad 2 \qquad 3 \qquad 4 \qquad 5 \qquad 6 \qquad 7$$

Assuming that J goes third, there would be four places F could go: slots 1, 2, 4, or 5. Since it also could be F going third instead of J (and J going in slots 1, 2, 4, or 5), that gives us a total of eight arrangements.

3. **Answer choice (D) is correct.** We have to place W in either slot 1 or 2. Because of the S, T, R rule, we'll have to place either R or S before T as well. That leaves the other (R or S) to slot 5 or 6, along with G. We have this so far:

$$\boxed{W \quad S/R} \quad \underline{T} \quad \underline{F} \quad \boxed{G \quad S/R}$$
$$ \quad 1 \qquad 2 \qquad 3 \qquad 4 \qquad 5 \qquad 6$$

However, we've ignored the W – G → S – R rule! Since W will definitely come before G in this case, S must come before R. Thus, we actually have this situation:

$$\boxed{W \quad S} \quad \underline{T} \quad \underline{F} \quad \boxed{G \quad R}$$
$$ \quad 1 \qquad 2 \qquad 3 \qquad 4 \qquad 5 \qquad 6$$

And from here we can see that there are four possible arrangements:

$$W \quad S \quad T \quad F \quad G \quad R$$
$$W \quad S \quad T \quad F \quad R \quad G$$
$$S \quad W \quad T \quad F \quad G \quad R$$
$$S \quad W \quad T \quad F \quad R \quad G$$

4. Answer choice (B) is correct. Since R is in slot 4, T can only be in 2 or 6. However, T in 6 would leave only slots 1–3 for the NS chunk, and since P must come at least three spaces before S, that will not work. Thus, T must go in slot 2. There's now only one place to put the NS chunk—slots 5 and 6. If S is in 6, P can go in either 1 or 3, with W in the other. That's two arrangements so far. If S is in 5, P cannot go in 3, so P must go in 1 and W in 3. Thus, there are three possible arrangements:

$$W \quad T \quad P \quad R \quad N \quad S$$
$$P \quad T \quad W \quad R \quad N \quad S$$
$$P \quad T \quad W \quad R \quad S \quad N$$

The Possible Arrangements Flip Side

Like many questions on the LSAT, Possible Arrangements questions have a "flip-side" equivalent. While this *doppelgänger* is far less common, it is still worth discussing.

Here is the question we were looking at:

If T performs third and V performs sixth, then exactly how many different orders are there in which the bands can perform?

Imagine if the same question were written in the following manner:

If T performs third and V performs sixth, then for exactly how many of the bands is their position in the order known?

Note that both of these questions require the same type of work from us—we must take the given information and make inferences from it. The difference in the questions is that the answer choices are meant to test different aspects of our thought process.

For either type of question, the work we do gives us the following information:

If we get the question in the first form, we find our answer in the positions still left uncertain. If we get the second, less common form of the question, we look at the positions that are now certain (the correct answer would be four—T, O, M, and V).

2. Min/Max

Another common form of the Options question involves consideration of minimums and maximums. These minimums and maximums can be about a few different types of issues. We can be asked about the maximum number of positions between two elements in an Ordering question, or, in some other game that doesn't have anything to do with ordering, we can be asked the about the maximum number of elements in a particular group.

The final question from the previous game was an example of a Max/Min question. Let's break it down and evaluate it further:

MANHATTAN
PREP

7. There can be at most how many bands that perform after N but
   before S?

   (A) 1
   (B) 2
   (C) 3
   (D) 4
   (E) 5

When confronted with a Min/Max question during an Ordering game, we want to think about three possible issues:

1. What is the *earliest* that (in this case) N can perform?
2. What is the *latest* that (in this case) S can perform?
3. How many bands *must* (in this case) perform *between* the two?

Go ahead and think about these issues one at a time before reading on:

1. The earliest N can perform is second, because it must perform after T.
2. The latest S can perform is sixth, because it must perform before R and V.
3. Since there is zigzag between N and S, there are no requirements for how many bands must perform between them.

Therefore, there can be at most three elements after N and before S (P, O, and M in positions 3, 4, and 5, respectively).

3. Possible Elements for a Particular Position

> *Example: Which of the following is a complete list of bands, any one of which could perform third?*

This is a more limited type of Options question—one that requires you to consider the options for just one particular slot.

When you're asked this question about a particular slot, take a second or two to consider what other elements *can't* go in the space. Armed with what you've figured out, you typically can eliminate several answer choices.

Now you want to test the remaining elements strategically, and the elements that are most attractive to test are the ones that differentiate the answers.

For example, let's imagine we have been given the question below, along with five answers. Let's also imagine that our well-honed powers of deduction have allowed us to eliminate two of the answer choices:

Note: The following question is not based on the Relative Ordering Tree we've worked with for other questions. There is no associated diagram.

Which of the following is a complete list of bands, any one of which could perform third?

    (A) M, N, O
    (B) M, N, O, P, Q
    (C) M, N, P
    (D) M, N, Q
    (E) M, N, O, P

If we are uncertain about which of the remaining answers is correct, it would make sense to try out O and P in the third slot, since the differences between the remaining answers involve O and P. As a counterpoint, trying out M or N in the third position would do us no good.

4. Possible Positions for a Particular Element

> *Example: Which of the following is a complete list of positions, any one of which can be occupied by O?*

For most games, we probably won't already have thought out where O *can* go, but rather, we'll have considered where it *cannot* go. So, we'll start by thinking about where O can't go and then eliminate wrong answers. This will typically allow us to eliminate several answers.

When we're down to a few answer choices, we'll want to try out positions, and like on the previous type of question, we want to be strategic about the positions we try out—look for those that differentiate the answer choices from one another.

Note that this is the flip side of the question "O can go in each of the following positions EXCEPT:"

5. Determines the Positions of All Elements

> *Example: Which of the following, if true, would determine the complete order of performances?*

You can always ensure you get the right answer to these questions by trying out each answer choice, but that would be time-consuming. Get ready to spend a bit of extra time if you run into this type of question.

Why is this question time-consuming? By its nature, this is a question that requires us to consider the answer choices. This is not a question where we can easily find an answer, or even eliminate wrong answers, based on our initial understanding of the game or the question stem.

We'll look at one of these questions in just a bit, but in general, the most important thing to keep in mind is that four answers will *not* lead to a complete assignment of elements to positions. That is, four answers will eventually result in uncertainty about where elements can go. Uncertainty can lead to doubt and panic in the typical test-taker. A key to your success is that you understand the uncertainty for what it is and manage it.

MANHATTAN
PREP

For these types of questions, do not waste time on wrong choices. If you can't make complete inferences from an answer, the answer is probably wrong and you should move on. Try to find the one right answer that is "sticky"—that has multiple ramifications for the other elements—and that leads you on a chain of inferences. Even if you are a little uncertain of your path, if you find an answer that allows you to make three or four deductions, most likely that is going to be the right answer. Also, paradoxically, answers that set the position for strays tend to be correct. After all, you can't fully determine the order without placing the stray, and you won't be able to do that using the given rules since none reference it!

A more high-level addition to your approach to this question type is to take a moment to consider the issues at play before you dive into the answer choices. Your understanding of the game's mechanics—an understanding you gained through The Big Pause and through your work on earlier questions—can help you speed up your work on this question type. For example, if you know that the answer must deal with the choice between F and G for the first position, as well as the ambiguous ordering of H, I, and J, keep that in the back of your mind as you evaluate answer choices. If an answer clearly leaves the relevant issues unresolved, then move on to the next one.

4

Practice Game 1: PT38, S2, G1

Note that on the next page we've added seven bonus questions for this game. These are questions you can use to practice the minor question type processes we've just discussed. Note that these additional questions are NOT official LSAT questions, so don't go yelling at the nice folks over there if the questions are particularly hard.

A car drives into the center ring of a circus and exactly eight clowns—Q, R, S, T, V, W, Y, and Z—get out of the car, one clown at a time. The order in which the clowns get out of the car is consistent with the following conditions:

> V gets out at some time before both Y and Q.
> Q gets out at some time after Z.
> T gets out at some time before V but at some time after R.
> S gets out at some time after V.
> R gets out at some time before W.

1. Which one of the following could be the order, from first to last, in which the clowns get out of the car?

   (A) T, Z, V, R, W, Y, S, Q
   (B) Z, R, W, Q, T, V, Y, S
   (C) R, W, T, V, Q, Z, S, Y
   (D) Z, W, R, T, V, Y, Q, S
   (E) R, W, T, V, Z, S, Y, Q

2. Which one of the following could be true?

   (A) Y is the second clown to get out of the car.
   (B) R is the third clown to get out of the car.
   (C) Q is the fourth clown to get out of the car.
   (D) S is the fifth clown to get out of the car.
   (E) V is the sixth clown to get out of the car.

3. If Z is the seventh clown to get out of the car, then which one of the following could be true?

   (A) R is the second clown to get out of the car.
   (B) T is the fourth clown to get out of the car.
   (C) W is the fifth clown to get out of the car.
   (D) V is the sixth clown to get out of the car.
   (E) Y is the eighth clown to get out of the car.

4. If T is the fourth clown to get out of the car, then which one of the following must be true?

   (A) R is the first clown to get out of the car.
   (B) Z is the second clown to get out of the car.
   (C) W is the third clown to get out of the car.
   (D) V is the fifth clown to get out of the car.
   (E) Y is the seventh clown to get out of the car.

5. If Q is the fifth clown to get out of the car, then each of the following could be true EXCEPT:

   (A) Z is the first clown to get out of the car.
   (B) T is the second clown to get out of the car.
   (C) V is the third clown to get out of the car.
   (D) W is the fourth clown to get out of the car.
   (E) Y is the sixth clown to get out of the car.

6. If R is the second clown to get out of the car, which one of the following must be true?

   (A) S gets out of the car at some time before T does.
   (B) T gets out of the car at some time before W does.
   (C) W gets out of the car at some time before V does.
   (D) Y gets out of the car at some time before Q does.
   (E) Z gets out of the car at some time before W does.

7. If V gets out of the car at some time before Z does, then which one of the following could be true?

   (A) R is the second clown to get out of the car.
   (B) T is the fourth clown to get out of the car.
   (C) Q is the fourth clown to get out of the car.
   (D) V is the fifth clown to get out of the car.
   (E) Z is the sixth clown to get out of the car.

MANHATTAN
PREP

Bonus Questions

B1. How many different positions in the order are there at which T could get out?

(A) 2
(B) 3
(C) 4
(D) 5
(E) 6

B2. Which of the following is a complete and accurate list of clowns, any one of which could exit the car third?

(A) R, T, V
(B) W, T, V
(C) W, T, Z
(D) W, T, V, Z
(E) W, T, V, Y, Z

B3. If Y exits fourth and Q exits sixth, for how many clowns do we know the position in which they exited?

(A) 4
(B) 5
(C) 6
(D) 7
(E) 8

B4. What is the maximum number of clowns that can exit after Z but before V?

(A) 1
(B) 2
(C) 3
(D) 4
(E) 5

B5. Which of the following trio of clowns, exiting fourth, fifth, and sixth, respectively, would determine the complete order of exits for all clowns?

(A) W, Y, Z
(B) V, Z, Q
(C) W, Y, S
(D) W, S, Z
(E) V, Y, S

B6. If V exits fifth, which of the following is a complete and accurate list of all clowns who could exit fourth?

(A) T, Z
(B) W, T
(C) W, T, Z
(D) R, W, T
(E) R, W, T, Z

B7. If S exits fifth, which of the following could be a complete and accurate list of the clowns that exit before S but after R, though not necessarily in the order listed?

(A) T, V
(B) T, W, Z
(C) T, V, Q
(D) T, W, Z
(E) T, V, W, Y, Z

Solutions: PT38, S2, G1

Answer Key

1. E	5. D	B1. B	B5. C
2. D	6. E	B2. D	B6. C
3. C	7. E	B3. C	B7. A
4. D		B4. C	

Step 1: Picture the Game

We're asked to find the order in which these clowns exit the car and we're given only Relative Ordering rules. Yep, it's a Relative Ordering game. Get ready to build a Tree.

We want to think about the order in which the clowns get out of the car and since it's our default, we'll use left for earlier and right for later.

Step 2: Notate the Rules and Make Inferences

Apart from irrelevant issues like whether you placed W above or below the main R–T–V–Q branch, your diagram should look like this:

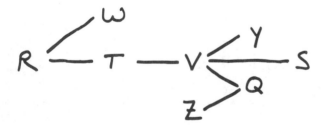

Keep in mind that in this instance we were able to handle the rules in the order in which they were given, but this won't always be the case. Make sure you are in the habit of taking the rules in an order that is best for *you*.

Step 3: The Big Pause

At this point, perhaps we double-check our rules against our diagram to make sure we've got a strong handle on the rules. With a Tree diagram, the inferences are baked in, so let's move on to the questions.

MANHATTAN
PREP

Step 4: Attack the Questions

1. Which one of the following could be the order, from first to last, in which the clowns get out of the car?

   (A) T, Z, V, R, W, Y, S, Q
   (B) Z, R, W, Q, T, V, Y, S
   (C) R, W, T, V, Q, Z, S, Y
   (D) Z, W, R, T, V, Y, Q, S
   (E) R, W, T, V, Z, S, Y, Q

Answer choice (E) is correct.

This is an Orientation question, so we have a few options for how we can answer this. Let's go ahead and answer it by using the rules to eliminate answers:

> The first rule eliminates (B).
> The second rule eliminates (C).
> The third rule eliminates (A).
> The fifth rule eliminates (D).

That leaves us with answer (E).

2. Which one of the following could be true?

   (A) Y is the second clown to get out of the car.
   (B) R is the third clown to get out of the car.
   (C) Q is the fourth clown to get out of the car.
   (D) S is the fifth clown to get out of the car.
   (E) V is the sixth clown to get out of the car.

Answer choice (D) is correct.

For this type of question, you are typically going to have an easier time eliminating the incorrect answers (because they violate a rule) than finding the correct answer:

> (A) must be false because at least three clowns must get out before Y.
> (B) must be false because only one clown can get out before R.
> (C) must be false because at least four clowns get out before Q.
> (E) must be false because at least three clowns get out after V.

3. If Z is the seventh clown to get out of the car, then which one of the following could be true?

   (A) R is the second clown to get out of the car.
   (B) T is the fourth clown to get out of the car.
   (C) W is the fifth clown to get out of the car.
   (D) V is the sixth clown to get out of the car.
   (E) Y is the eighth clown to get out of the car.

Answer choice (C) is correct.

If Z is seventh, Q must be eighth, and we can see that the other clowns are mostly put in order. You can choose to keep these inferences in your head or to write them out like so:

We can see that answers (A), (B), (D), and (E) are all not possible, leaving us with only answer choice (C). Looking at our diagram for this question, we can see that W is free as a bird (within the cloud), making it a likely candidate for a correct answer.

4. If T is the fourth clown to get out of the car, then which one of the following must be true?

   (A) R is the first clown to get out of the car.
   (B) Z is the second clown to get out of the car.
   (C) W is the third clown to get out of the car.
   (D) V is the fifth clown to get out of the car.
   (E) Y is the seventh clown to get out of the car.

Answer choice (D) is correct.

Start by drawing a Number Line and placing T fourth. There are four clowns that must get out after T: V, Y, S, and Q. Since V must come before Y, S, and Q, it must be fifth. The remaining three clowns, R, W, and Z, must all get out before T. You can note these inferences like so:

Answer choice (D) must be true, while all the other answers only could be true.

5. If Q is the fifth clown to get out of the car, then each of the following could be true EXCEPT:

   (A) Z is the first clown to get out of the car.

   (B) T is the second clown to get out of the car.

   (C) V is the third clown to get out of the car.

   (D) W is the fourth clown to get out of the car.

   (E) Y is the sixth clown to get out of the car.

Answer choice (D) is correct.

If Q is fifth, we know the four clowns that must precede it: R, T, V, and Z. The remaining clowns must then get out after Q. We can note these inferences like so:

Since we are looking for an answer that must be false, (D) is correct. W, because it must get out after Q, cannot get out of the car fourth.

6. If R is the second clown to get out of the car, which one of the following must be true?

   (A) S gets out of the car at some time before T does.

   (B) T gets out of the car at some time before W does.

   (C) W gets out of the car at some time before V does.

   (D) Y gets out of the car at some time before Q does.

   (E) Z gets out of the car at some time before W does.

Answer choice (E) is correct.

Z is the only element that can go before R, so with R in the second slot, Z goes first. We can create a cloud with the other elements and our Number Line will look like this:

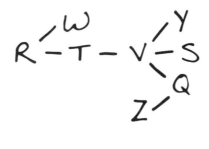

Since this is a "must be true" question, we should look for an answer with Z, since that's the only clown we've filled in with certainty. (E) tells us that Z gets out before W and, since Z is first, this must be true.

(R–T–V, Z) Q (W, Y, S) proves that W doesn't have to come before V and that Y doesn't have to come before Q.

Only (E) is true in all possible arrangements of both hypotheticals.

Alternatively, we could create a new hypothetical for this question ignoring our previous work. If R gets out of the car second, Z must get out first, since no one other than R and Z can ever exit first. We can use our original diagram to consider how the other elements can go in positions 3–8, but it's clear that there's a lot of uncertainty. Since it must be true that Z is first, and this is a "must be true" question, it's very likely that Z will be a part of the correct answer. Why? Because Z exiting first is the only certain inference we were able to make. If we scan the answer choices for Z, we can save time and choose (E)—since Z is first, it must be before W.

7. If V gets out of the car at some time before Z does, then which one of the following could be true?

   (A) R is the second clown to get out of the car.
   (B) T is the fourth clown to get out of the car.
   (C) Q is the fourth clown to get out of the car.
   (D) V is the fifth clown to get out of the car.
   (E) Z is the sixth clown to get out of the car.

Answer choice (E) is correct.

While you might have been able to mentally track this new rule using your original diagram, some of these questions will more drastically alter the Tree, so you want to develop the ability to quickly draw an adjusted diagram. In this case, if V is before Z, and we already know Z is before Q, we can adjust our diagram like this:

If Z is after V, (E) is the only one of the answer choices that could be true.

Bonus Questions

B1. How many different positions in the order are there at which T could get out?

  (A) 2

  (B) 3

  (C) 4

  (D) 5

  (E) 6

Answer choice (B) is correct.

There is one element that must exit before T, so T can't go first. There are four elements that must follow T, so T can't be in one of the final four spots. That means T can exit second, third, or fourth.

B2. Which of the following is a complete and accurate list of clowns, any one of which could exit the car third?

  (A) R, T, V

  (B) W, T, V

  (C) W, T, Z

  (D) W, T, V, Z

  (E) W, T, V, Y, Z

Answer choice (D) is correct.

Here is a place where using previous work can be the most elegant way to get to the right answer quickly. Who have we previously placed third in a diagram? Z and W in question 4 and Z and V in question 5. Since the list needs to be complete, we're already able to knock out any answer choices that do not include V, W, and Z. (A), (B), and (C) are thus out. The difference between (D) and (E) is Y, but we know that Y can't finish third because at least three clowns must exit before Y. Eliminate (E)!

B3. If Y exits fourth and Q exits sixth, for how many clowns do we know the position in which they exited?

  (A) 4

  (B) 5

  (C) 6

  (D) 7

  (E) 8

Answer choice (C) is correct.

If Y exits fourth, we know R, T, and V must exit before it in positions 1, 2, and 3. If Q is sixth, Z must go before it in position 5. That leaves S and W for the final two positions.

Pop quiz! How many possible arrangements are there in this scenario?

Since S and W are the only elements that can switch, there are just two.

B4. What is the maximum number of clowns that can exit after Z but before V?

    (A) 1
    (B) 2
    (C) 3
    (D) 4
    (E) 5

Answer choice (C) is correct.

The earliest Z can go is first, and if Z is first, the latest V can go is fifth. Three elements (R, T, and W) can go in slots 2, 3, and 4 between them.

B5. Which of the following trio of clowns, exiting fourth, fifth, and sixth, respectively, would determine the complete order of exits for all clowns?

    (A) W, Y, Z
    (B) V, Z, Q
    (C) W, Y, S
    (D) W, S, Z
    (E) V, Y, S

Answer choice (C) is correct.

This type of question requires us to evaluate each answer choice. With so many moving parts, how could we answer the question otherwise?

    (A) W, Y, Z in positions 4, 5, 6 give us the order of the first three elements (R–T–V) but leave uncertainty about S and Q in positions 7 and 8.

    (B) V, Z, Q in positions 4, 5, 6 tells us Y and S must follow, but doesn't give us an order for them.

    (C) W, Y, S in positions 4, 5, 6 tells us that Z and Q must go in the final two positions, with Z before Q. R, T, V have to go in positions 1, 2, 3, in that order. (C) gives us an exact order and is therefore correct.

    In real time, you wouldn't continue to evaluate answers, but in case you're wondering today:

    (D) W, S, Z in positions 4, 5, 6 leaves R, T, and V in positions 1, 2, and 3, respectively, but we are left uncertain about the order of Y and Q in positions 7 and 8.

    (E) V, Y, S in positions 4, 5, 6 leaves us with many possibilities for the order, in large part because both W and Z can be either in the first three positions or in the final two.

MANHATTAN
PREP

B6. If V exits fifth, which of the following is a complete and accurate list of all clowns who could exit fourth?

    (A) T, Z

    (B) W, T

    (C) W, T, Z

    (D) R, W, T

    (E) R, W, T, Z

Answer choice (C) is correct.

If V exits the car fifth, we know that Y, S, and Q must all exit after V. The four clowns that exit before V would be R, W, T, and Z. All of these can be fourth except for R, which must precede T and W.

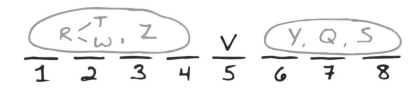

B7. If S exits fifth, which of the following could be a complete and accurate list of the clowns that exit before S but after R, though not necessarily in the order listed?

    (A) T, V

    (B) T, W, Z

    (C) T, V, Q

    (D) T, W, Z

    (E) T, V, W, Y, Z

Answer choice (A) is correct.

Notice the difference between the wording of this question and the previous one? Here, we're asked for *which could be a list*, while in the previous question we were asked for *a list of those that could work*. It's the same difference between a shopping list—a list of items you will buy—and a catalog—a list of all the items you could possibly buy!

If S exits the car fifth, we know that R–T–V must come before it, along with one other clown. The only possibilities for that one are W, Z, and Y. T and V must always come between R and S, so we can eliminate any answers without those two, leaving us with answers (A), (C), and (E). We can eliminate answer (C) since Q exiting before S would require Z to exit before S as well, and there isn't enough room before S for that.

Answer (A) is a list that could work (i.e., a viable scenario), while answer (E) is the list of *all those* that could work. There isn't room for all of them at once! Since we're asked for what could be a list (not the list of what could be), answer choice (A) is correct.

In case you're wondering, one scenario in which (A) would work is Z R T V S W Y Q.

How Did You Do?

Again, you want to ask yourself the four basic questions:

1. Could I picture the game easily? Did I understand the general situation?
2. Did I understand the rules correctly? Did I notate them in a way that allowed me to think about them easily? Did I make the key inferences at the right times?
3. Did I understand which rules to prioritize? Did I have a solid sense of how the game works before starting the questions?
4. Did I attack each question wisely?

In particular, if some of the Options questions caused you more trouble than you'd like, it's worth your while to take note of them now. We're just getting started and we've got plenty of games in front of us. If you are aware of habits you need to develop, or question types you need to improve on, there will be plenty of time to practice and get those things taken care of.

Either/Or

The majority of Relative Ordering games that have appeared on modern LSATs have functioned very similarly to the two examples we've already discussed. However, the LSAT tends to throw in some curveballs, and so we should expect for games to stray from their basic templates. A common way in which test writers complicate otherwise standard Relative Ordering games is to introduce a relative rule that works in an *either/or* fashion.

To illustrate, let's use a standard game scenario. Imagine we have six appointments—M, N, O, P, Q, and R—to schedule, in order. No two appointments can happen at once and in addition, we get the following rules:

> M is at some point before O.
> Q and S are at some point after P.
> N is after P but before M.

Hopefully, by this point, you feel fairly comfortable diagramming the above situation.

We can start with M before O:

> M — O

Connect the third rule:

> P — N — M — O

MANHATTAN
PREP

And, finally, add the second rule:

$$P \overset{\nearrow Q}{\underset{\searrow S}{-}} N - M - O$$

Not too bad, right? Now let's complicate this by making the final rule into an either/or situation. Imagine the same scenario, but with the following three rules instead:

> M is at some point before O.
> Q and S are at some point after P.
> N is either after P but before M, or after M but before P.

Perhaps we think of starting our diagram the same way we did before, by notating the first rule, but when we go to connect the third rule, things become complicated. This third rule essentially means that N must go between P and M, but either P or M could go earliest among the three. In general, we recommend that you represent this type of situation as follows:

P — N — M
or
M — N — P

It's a bit of a challenge to figure out how to connect this to our first rule, and perhaps a bigger challenge to consider how we would add on the second rule.

What we suggest is that during the Picture the Game phase, you take note of any either/or rules and, when it comes time to diagram, start with the either/or statement and use it to create two separate Trees.

We can start with something like this:

P — N — M   M — N — P

Now, what we are going to do is build two separate diagrams that represent the two ways the game can play out, splitting at the either/or.

At this point, we can add the first and second rule to both diagrams, and end up with something like this:

```
      S                              Q
     /                              /
P — N — M — O      M — N — P
     \                              \
      Q                    O         S
```

For this game, we would go into the questions with these two diagrams, which collectively represent the ways in which this game can play out.

When we use multiple diagrams, rather than just one, to represent a game situation, we call this **framing.** Framing is not a tool you will use on every game, but it can be a very effective way to take control of certain types of unwieldy games. By creating frames around the either/or, we can clearly lay out the various links and inferences that follow from the separate scenarios. If we kept it as one diagram, it would be tougher to consider various possibilities, especially when it comes to answering the questions.

We'll talk about framing in general more in just a bit, but for now, let's get practiced at framing Relative Ordering games that have an either/or rule.

Drill It: Relative Ordering Frames

Here is a mini drill involving stripped-down Relative Ordering situations similar to the one we just discussed. For each one, practice working from the either/or statement to create frames for the game. Assume there are no other letters to include in the diagram, that every letter mentioned is included, and that there are no ties.

As usual, check your work after each one.

1. S arrives at some point before W.
    V arrives at some point after T.
    R arrives at some point before Q.
    Either T arrives before both R and S, or else
      T arrives before neither of them.

2. Both L and J are examined after G.
    L is examined after F or after M, but not
      both.
    K is examined after F.

3. Y is interviewed prior to S.
    Z is interviewed prior to T.
    X is interviewed after both T and Y.
    W is interviewed after Y, or else before S,
      but not both.

4. N is placed immediately to the left of O.
    S is placed to the right of N.
    If O is placed to the left of P, L is placed to
      the right of R.
    If P is placed to the left of O, R is placed to
      the right of L.
    R is placed to the left of S.

5. K performs before G and I.
    H performs after F.
    I performs after H.
    M performs after G, or else before K,
      but not both.
    M performs before J, or else before L,
      but not both.

6. R must sit immediately behind or immediately
      ahead of V.
    T must sit immediately behind or immediately
      ahead of W.
    V sits ahead of T, or else V sits behind S, but
      not both.

Solutions: Relative Ordering Frames

1.

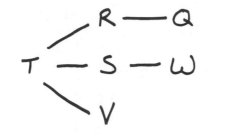

4

2.

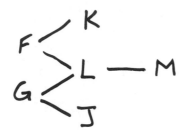

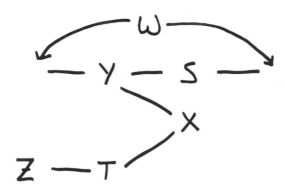

3.

You could have written out a frame for each position of W, but if you notice that the majority of the Tree is the same, you can get everything into a single diagram with W having two options.

MANHATTAN
PREP

4.

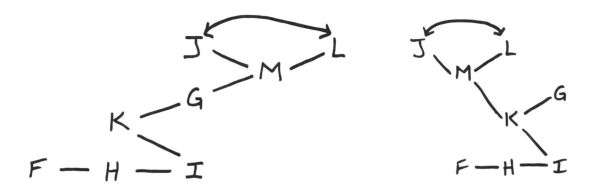

5.

Tough one! You could have framed the issue of whether the order is J–M–L or L–M–J, creating four frames, but this would be a great situation to create just two frames with the J/L options represented this way.

6. This was a very difficult one! Furthermore, it's rare to have two chunks in a Relative Ordering game. But we can still use a Tree, especially since the chunks are all related to other elements with Relative Ordering rules:

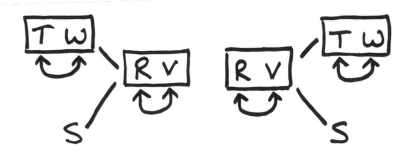

Basic Framing Concepts

As we just discussed, framing is a strategy of utilizing a set of diagrams to represent all the possibilities in a logic game. We'll discuss general framing strategies in some detail here, and we'll also revisit the topic at various points throughout this book after you've gotten some more games under your belt.

We'll always design frames around some characteristic of a game that funnels the possibilities of that game into limited channels—what we will call a **division with consequences.** Either/or statements are by their nature *divisions,* and are thus some of the most likely restrictions we'll use to design our frames.

Earlier, we were given the statement *N is either after P but before M, or after M but before P.* For many test-takers, this type of rule can inspire anxiety. However, for the veteran test-taker, these rules are often the key to handling a game quickly and easily.

We know that this rule limits us to two possible orders for M, N, and P:

> P–N–M or M–N–P

Just as importantly, this rule prevents us from arranging the elements in any other fashion. (For example, the three elements will never go P–M–N or M–P–N.) Thus, these two options represent an exhaustive set of possibilities. This is very important for framing. These wouldn't actually be frames if they were just two of many possible arrangements of P, N, and M. In fact, it's dangerous to mistake a nonexhaustive selection of possibilities for frames.

Looking at how different the two frames are, it's clear that this choice between P–N–M and M–N–P has *consequences.* The two diagrams are significantly different because there is a lot to infer based on which way the order of M, N, and P goes. For example, Q and S are forced toward the back of the Tree in one frame, but have almost complete freedom of position in the other:

Other divisions we will encounter do not have consequences and are not worth framing. For example, on the next page is the diagram for the first game we played, back in Chapter 2.

MANHATTAN
PREP

N/ __ __ H __ /N __   H J K L M N P
1 2 3 4 5 6 7

K̶ P̶   M̶ J̶   J — K
P̶ M̶   P̶ M̶

M _ P

N's placement does provide a division, but there are no significant consequences to that division.

It seems like the decision to frame a game can be a tough one, and it definitely is. However, there are some guidelines we can give you:

1. *Definitely use* frames when a division prevents you from creating a normal diagram.

Relative to the LSAT definition of the word, we are using the term "definitely" somewhat loosely—it is certainly possible to nail these games without framing, and countless test-takers have done so. However, frames can save a lot of time in certain games, so it's important to build them when you can.

The P–N–M scenario we started with is an example of this type of game. The last rule was such that we could not create a Tree in the way we normally do, and any attempt at modifying the Tree to represent both possible worlds at once would have slowed us down.

2. *Consider* frames when a division stands in the way of making inferences.

In an ideal world, we want be able to think about a game and organize rules and inferences in a linear mental order. That is, we want one certainty to lead to another certainty to lead to another certainty and so on. For example, for a game in which six elements must be ordered, maybe we learn that R must go in position 2, then, because of another rule, S must go in position 3, and that forces T into position 6, then V into position 1, then W into position 4. Finally the remaining element, Z, is left to go into the one open position, good ol' number 5.

Oh, if only the LSAT were designed so! Alas, LSAT games are not Sudoku puzzles (which, by the way, aren't the worst extracurricular activities you could do as part of LSAT prep). On the LSAT, the inferences are likely to be far less definite. And it makes sense that the LSAT would choose to do this. After all, LSAT games are designed to challenge your ability to organize information. Frames can be a very useful tool for making concrete much of the uncertainty that games can present.

Let's imagine we had the following simple game scenario. Go ahead and try diagramming it, if you'd like, before reading further:

Seven people—G, H, I, J, K, L, and M—will be interviewed, one at a time. No other candidates will be interviewed. The following conditions apply:

M will be interviewed second.
H will be interviewed after I but before J.
Exactly one person will be interviewed after G but before L.
Either I or J will be interviewed fourth.

If we simply draw a Number Line, and notate the elements as we've done in the past, we should end up with something like this (your diagram may have more inferences written in):

If this were a real LSAT game, at this point you might feel pretty darn good about the game. The information given to us poses some clear and significant restrictions on where we can place elements, and as we juggle information in the process of solving questions, we can imagine that this information wouldn't be terribly difficult to manage.

Still, let's consider what our diagram might look like if we set up frames. Of the four rules given, the final rule provides the clearest division for our frames.

If you didn't think to frame based on the fourth rule initially, try it now before reading on. Create two different diagrams, one with I fourth and one with J fourth, and try to apply the other rules to these frames.

Take a look at all you can infer in each frame:

Wow, is that satisfying!

With these two possible frames in hand, the questions will be markedly less difficult to solve.

As is often the case, one frame is more complete than the other. At this point, we could frame the two options for the GL chunk, or, more likely, just recognize that there are not many options left for that frame and trust that we can figure those out when and if needed.

3. There is no right answer to the framing question.

Hopefully, we've convinced you of the value of frames. But it is easy for students to freak out about the framing decision.

One of our curriculum developers was asked to make a video that included a logic games solution. It turns out that the game had been chosen as part of a lesson about framing, but the instructor *didn't frame it*. And look, we all survived! Clearly, it didn't matter *that* much. PS: We still showed the video because it reinforced an important message about how a flexible game player can make various approaches work.

Here are just a couple questions we'd like you to consider at this point:

1. Do all games present divisions?

Yes! Every game presents numerous either/or scenarios. Let's take a look at this super-simple scenario to illustrate:

Four students—M, N, O, and P—compete in a race. They finish one at a time.

> M finishes before P.
> O does not finish third.

Here are some options sets this game presents:

> O could be first or O could not be first.
> M can be either first, second, or third.
> O can finish first, second, or fourth.
> Either M must finish after N or M must finish before N.
> Either N must finish second or N must not finish second.

And so on. You get the picture. The much more important question is…

2. How will I know whether to frame a division?

There is no easy answer for this, and to frame or not to frame is definitely a subjective decision; different students draw the line in the sand at different positions.

Wherever you draw that line, here are the two primary questions you should be considering:

1. **Do I see the division as having a direct consequence on the other rules?** This is the first question to ask yourself when deciding whether framing around a particular division will be useful. Sometimes these consequences are a bit more obvious because you see the same elements in multiple rules (though this is almost always the case for Relative Ordering games, so here we're talking about other game types). This repetition might indicate that there are cascades of inferences waiting to be triggered.

2. **Do I feel uncomfortable with the level of uncertainty in this game?** All games have uncertainty, but sometimes we feel that we can easily manage this uncertainty, and other times we feel less in-control. Framing can be an especially helpful tool for the games that we find more difficult to conceptualize and control.

Here are some final points before we return to our normal program:

- While it's rare, occasionally you'll encounter a game that is worth breaking off into more than two or three frames.
- As we've already discussed, some conditional questions will warrant a strategy similar to framing! As a reminder, we call these question-specific frames, and we'll continue to use them as we work through the book.

Conclusion

Another power-packed chapter! Let's quickly look back at what we've learned:

1. Relative Ordering games

- With such front-end games, one of the biggest dangers is incorrectly diagramming a rule. Slow down and get it right, and double-check your diagram against the rules.
- Remember, you can only make inferences if you don't have to change horizontal directions to trace a line between elements!
- For conditional questions, draw a Number Line if you're given a specific position; redraw a Tree if you're given a new Relative Ordering rule.

2. Options questions

- Avoid the math; just draw it out.
- Focus on the positions that are uncertain.
- For Min/Max questions, start with the extremes.
- For Determines Positions questions, work from wrong to right.

3. Framing

- Frame if there is a divide with consequences.
- In Relative Ordering games, be prepared to frame either/or situations.
- Look for opportunities to frame, but don't assume they are in every game. Frames are great, but they're never necessary.

MANHATTAN
PREP

Practice Game 2: PT51, S4, G2

Here is one final Relative Ordering game to finish the chapter. This is one of the more unusual Relative Ordering games, so feel free to give yourself some extra time, especially during the Picture the Game phase.

Six hotel suites—F, G, H, J, K, and L—are ranked from most expensive (first) to least expensive (sixth). There are no ties. The ranking must be consistent with the following conditions:

> H is more expensive than L.
> If G is more expensive than H, then neither K nor L is more expensive than J.
> If H is more expensive than G, then neither J nor L is more expensive than K.
> F is more expensive than G, or else F is more expensive than H, but not both.

6. Which one of the following could be the ranking of the suites, from most expensive to least expensive?

   (A) G, F, H, L, J, K
   (B) H, K, F, J, G, L
   (C) J, H, F, K, G, L
   (D) J, K, G, H, L, F
   (E) K, J, L, H, F, G

7. If G is the second most expensive suite, then which one of the following could be true?

   (A) H is more expensive than F.
   (B) H is more expensive than G.
   (C) K is more expensive than F.
   (D) K is more expensive than J.
   (E) L is more expensive than F.

8. Which one of the following CANNOT be the most expensive suite?

   (A) F
   (B) G
   (C) H
   (D) J
   (E) K

9. If L is more expensive than F, then which one of the following could be true?

   (A) F is more expensive than H.
   (B) F is more expensive than K.
   (C) G is more expensive than H.
   (D) G is more expensive than J.
   (E) G is more expensive than L.

10. If H is more expensive than J and less expensive than K, then which one of the following could be true?

   (A) F is more expensive than H.
   (B) G is more expensive than F.
   (C) G is more expensive than H.
   (D) J is more expensive than L.
   (E) L is more expensive than K.

Solutions: PT51, S4, G2

Answer Key

6. B   9. D
7. C   10. D
8. A

Steps 1, 2, and 3: Picture the Game, Notate the Rules, and Make Inferences (Sometimes it's all smooshed together like that.)

Six hotel suites—F, G, H, J, K, and L—are ranked from most expensive (first) to least expensive (sixth). There are no ties. The ranking must be consistent with the following conditions:

> H is more expensive than L.
> If G is more expensive than H, then neither K nor L is more expensive than J.
> If H is more expensive than G, then neither J nor L is more expensive than K.
> F is more expensive than G, or else F is more expensive than H, but not both.

This is a Relative Ordering game in which it pays to take a moment to establish what first and last place represent. While we can imagine a game in which the last slot is the most expensive, in this game the first slot is. A quick first read-through lets us see that there are conditional rules, as well as *two* division rules. The second and third rules together create a division, and the fourth rule by itself is an either/or rule. Our decisions on how to deal with these options will definitely shape how successful we are on this game.

The second and third rules are certainly the most difficult to understand completely, so let's take a moment to discuss them now before we delve fully into our diagramming process.

In most cases, conditional rules are only relevant when the sufficient condition is triggered. In other words, there are hypothetical situations where the rule doesn't apply. However, take a look at the relationship between the second and third rules. Because there are no ties, the combination of *G is more expensive than H* and *H is more expensive than G* represents the complete range of possibilities for the relationship between G and H. Since we have a division based on the order of G and H, and that division has consequences, we should consider framing around this rule!

But hold up a minute! The last rule is also presenting an either/or situation: F is more expensive than G *or* H, but not both. We've seen this type of rule before and it means that F is between G and H, but we don't know which is before and which is after.

Step 3: The Big Pause

As we discussed before, when there's a clear division, and that division has consequences, frames are going to be a good strategy. The question here, then, is which division should we build our frames around: the second/third rule or the fourth rule?

We decided to use the fourth rule. Why? Well, it includes both of the elements from the other division. It's also less to keep track of, since we don't have to worry about the conditional part of the other two rules when we're just getting our bearings. So, we can start with these two frames:

After that, let's add in our first rule since it's more straightforward. (Here's another example of why it's smart not to simply start diagramming rules the minute you get to them—a moment to consider your plan of attack pays off handsomely.) Sure enough, these frames make it much easier for us to think about the second and third rules—the second rule applies to the second of our frames and the third rule applies to the first of our frames. We can add this information into our frames:

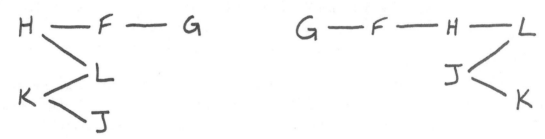

And now we are ready to go into the questions! Though the rules presented information in a challenging fashion, this information ended up coming together to create a fairly simple understanding of the game. As is often the case with Relative Ordering games, The Big Pause is short and sweet—a quick check for strays and a double check on the rules to make sure we didn't mess up.

Step 4: Attack the Questions

6. Which one of the following could be the ranking of the suites, from most expensive to least expensive?

    (A) G, F, H, L, J, K
    (B) H, K, F, J, G, L
    (C) J, H, F, K, G, L
    (D) J, K, G, H, L, F
    (E) K, J, L, H, F, G

Answer choice (B) is correct.

MANHATTAN
PREP

This is an Orientation question, so we can use the rules to eliminate answers. These rules are a bit more challenging than normal, so if the process took you a bit longer, that's understandable (and expected). If you tried the String Technique, you were in for a painful surprise. Because of the two frames, you need to use the old-fashioned approach for this Orientation question.

The first rule is much easier to understand than the rest, so let's start there; it allows us to eliminate (E).

The final rule might be the easiest of the remaining three to use next. In short, we're looking for an instance when F is *not* between H and G, so we can eliminate (D).

The second rule, which applies when G is more expensive than H, allows us to eliminate (A).

The third rule, which applies when H is more expensive than G, allows us to eliminate (C).

That leaves (B).

7. If G is the second most expensive suite, then which one of the following could be true?

    (A) H is more expensive than F.
    (B) H is more expensive than G.
    (C) K is more expensive than F.
    (D) K is more expensive than J.
    (E) L is more expensive than F.

Answer choice (C) is correct.

If G is the second most expensive suite, then we know we are dealing with the second frame since G cannot go second in the first frame.

For the second frame, if G goes second, the only element that can go first is J.

That leaves the F–H–L chain, along with K, for the remaining four positions:

$$\frac{J}{1} \quad \frac{G}{2} \quad \overbrace{\frac{}{3} \quad \frac{}{4} \quad \frac{}{5} \quad \frac{}{6}}^{F-H-L,\ K}$$

Now, let's take a look at the answer choices. Keep in mind that for "could be true" questions, it's usually easier to eliminate wrong answers than search for the correct answer.

Alternatively, we can keep an eye out for our stray, K, since it has the most options:

(A) must be false—in the second frame, F is always more expensive than H.

(B) must be false—in the second frame, G is always more expensive than H.

(C) could be true, and is thus the correct answer. We do not know the relationship between K and F.

(D) must be false—in the second frame, K cannot be more expensive than J.

(E) must be false—in the second frame, F is always more expensive than L.

8. Which one of the following CANNOT be the most expensive suite?

(A) F

(B) G

(C) H

(D) J

(E) K

Answer choice (A) is correct.

This is an unconditional question, so we should consider the possibilities presented in both frames. We're looking for one element that can't be first in either frame.

Because F can't be first in either of the frames, it is therefore the correct answer.

On the test, it would be wise to select answer (A) and move on. However, for the sake of discussion, let's quickly consider the other answer choices:

(B) G can be first in frame 2.

(C) H can be first in frame 1.

(D) J can be first in frame 2.

(E) K can be first in frame 1.

9. If L is more expensive than F, then which one of the following could be true?

(A) F is more expensive than H.

(B) F is more expensive than K.

(C) G is more expensive than H.

(D) G is more expensive than J.

(E) G is more expensive than L.

Answer choice (D) is correct.

MANHATTAN
PREP

We know that L can only be more expensive than F in frame 1, so we know that for this question we only need to consider that frame. While you might have felt comfortable enough to hold the new arrangement in your head, we're going to draw it out so we don't accidentally invert something:

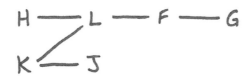

Since we're asked what could be true, it's likely that the answer will involve J's placement, since it is the stray element, able to go in any slot from the second onward.

Let's evaluate the answer choices and knock off those that must be false:

(A) must be false in frame 1—H is more expensive than F.

(B) must be false when we consider that L is more expensive than F (the new condition) and that K is more expensive than L.

(C) must be false in frame 1—H is more expensive than G.

(D) could be true and is therefore correct. We know nothing about the relationship between G and J, and the new condition has no impact on that uncertainty.

(E) must be false per the new condition—if L is more expensive than F, and we already know F is more expensive than G, then it must be true that L is more expensive than G.

10. If H is more expensive than J and less expensive than K, then which one of the following could be true?

    (A) F is more expensive than H.
    (B) G is more expensive than F.
    (C) G is more expensive than H.
    (D) J is more expensive than L.
    (E) L is more expensive than K.

Answer Choice (D) is correct.

This question is a bit tougher to conceptualize than the last, so even pros may want to draw it out. Taking a look at our frames, this new condition doesn't work in the second frame since J is more expensive there than K. Thus, we know that this question is giving us additional information about our first frame—H must come after K and before J. We can reimagine the Tree like this:

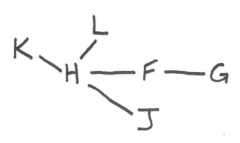

J and L are both strays, so we could prioritize answers with those elements, and (D) has both. Since we don't know the relative position of L and J, this is our answer.

    (A) must be false.
    (B) must be false.
    (C) must be false.
    (D) must be false.

Note that in this case we were able to eliminate all four wrong choices simply by understanding which frame the condition put us in. We never actually needed to use the information about K–H–J! Solving this question boiled down to knowing which frame we were supposed to look at.

LG

Chapter 5

3D Ordering

In This Chapter...

Getting Familiar

Do your best to complete the following game. Use whatever approach you see fit. Give yourself **10 minutes** to complete this game. As always, doing your work on scratch paper will better prepare you for test day, and will keep this game pristine for a replay down the road!

A publishing company published exactly six novels—*Forgiven, Grain, Highwire, June, Lampoon,* and *Melted*—in the years from 1991 to 1996. Exactly one novel was published in each of the six years. Three authors—Robinson, Stewart, and Tamiko—each wrote exactly two of the novels. The following conditions apply:

Exactly one of Robinson's novels was published before the first of Stewart's novels was published.

Neither of Robinson's novels was published in 1991 or 1994.

None of the authors had novels published in consecutive years.

June was published in 1994.

Highwire was published exactly two years after *Melted*.

1. Which of the following could be an accurate representation of the authors and the novels they wrote, listed in order of publication?

   (A) Tamiko: *Lampoon*; Robinson: *Grain*; Tamiko: *Forgiven*; Stewart: *Melted*; Robinson: *June*; Stewart: *Highwire*

   (B) Tamiko: *Lampoon*; Robinson: *Forgiven*; Stewart: *Melted*; Tamiko: *June*; Robinson: *Highwire*; Stewart: *Grain*

   (C) Stewart: *Melted*; Robinson: *Lampoon*; Stewart: *Highwire*; Tamiko: *June*; Robinson: *Forgiven*; Tamiko: *Grain*

   (D) Tamiko: *Melted*; Robinson: *Grain*; Stewart: *Highwire*; Stewart: *June*; Tamiko: *Forgiven*; Robinson: *Lampoon*

   (E) Robinson: *Forgiven*; Tamiko: *Grain*; Stewart: *Melted*; Robinson: *June*; Tamiko: *Highwire*; Stewart: *Lampoon*

2. Which one of the following must be true?

   (A) One of Stewart's novels was published in 1993.
   (B) One of Tamiko's novels was published in 1994.
   (C) One of Robinson's novels was published in 1992.
   (D) One of Robinson's novels was published in 1995.
   (E) One of Stewart's novels was published in 1996.

3. If *Forgiven* was published in 1995, each of the following could be true EXCEPT:

   (A) Stewart wrote *Grain*.

   (B) Tamiko wrote *June*.

   (C) Tamiko wrote *Highwire*.

   (D) Robinson wrote *Lampoon*.

   (E) Robinson wrote *Highwire*.

4. If Tamiko wrote *June*, then which one of the following must be false?

   (A) Tamiko wrote *Melted*.

   (B) Tamiko wrote *Highwire*.

   (C) Stewart wrote *Melted*.

   (D) Stewart wrote *Highwire*.

   (E) Stewart wrote *Forgiven*.

5. If *Lampoon* was published in the year immediately preceding the publication of *Melted*, which one of the following must be true?

   (A) Tamiko wrote *Forgiven*.

   (B) Tamiko wrote *Grain*.

   (C) Robinson wrote *Lampoon*.

   (D) Robinson wrote *Highwire*.

   (E) Stewart wrote *Melted*.

6. Each of the following could be true EXCEPT:

   (A) Tamiko wrote a novel that was published in 1995.

   (B) *Melted* was published exactly three years before *Grain*.

   (C) Stewart wrote *June*.

   (D) *Lampoon* was published before *Highwire* but after *Melted*.

   (E) Both of Tamiko's novels were published before either of Stewart's novels were published.

7. Which of the following, if substituted for the condition that exactly one of Robinson's novels was published before the first of Stewart's novels was published, would have the same effect in determining the years in which the novels were published and the authors who wrote the novels?

   (A) Neither of Robinson's novels was published in 1996.

   (B) Neither of Stewart's novels was published in 1992.

   (C) The earliest that either one of Stewart's novels could have been published is 1993.

   (D) The earliest that either one of Robinson's novels could have been published is 1992.

   (E) The earliest that either one of Robinson's novels could have been published is 1993.

3D Ordering

About 10% of all games that appear on the LSAT are what we call **3D Ordering** games.

You probably found that you were already familiar with most of the elements in the Getting Familiar game. Indeed, 3D Ordering games are firmly planted in the Ordering family of games. But, as you surely noticed, there's a twist.

What Defines a 3D Ordering Game?

In short, a 3D Ordering game is a Basic Ordering game with an extra dimension. (While it sounds fun, in this case, we're not talking about quantum physics or anything deep like that.)

Imagine you are one of the devilishly brilliant folks who write the LSAT, and you are told to write a 3D Ordering game. If you are lazy, you could commit borderline plagiarism by simply taking a Basic Ordering game and adding on another dimension. Let's do it!

Below is the game you saw in the Basic Ordering chapter. Take a quick moment to read it over:

> Exactly seven swimmers—Hewitt, James, Kopov, Luis, Markson, Nu, and Price—will race in the 50-meter freestyle event. Each swimmer will swim in exactly one of seven lanes, numbered 1 through 7. No two swimmers share the same lane. Lane assignments comply with the following conditions:
>
> > James swims in a lower-numbered lane than Kopov.
> > Nu swims in either the first lane or the seventh lane.
> > Markson swims in a lane numbered two lower than Price's.
> > Hewitt swims in lane 4.

Now, let's see it in 3D:

> Exactly seven swimmers—Hewitt, James, Kopov, Luis, Markson, Nu, and Price—will race in the 50-meter freestyle event. **Three swimmers will wear red caps, three will wear white caps, and one will wear a yellow cap.** Each swimmer will swim in exactly one of seven lanes, numbered 1 through 7. No two swimmers share the same lane and **no swimmer wears more than one cap.** Lane assignments comply with the following conditions:
>
> > James swims in a lower-numbered lane than Kopov.
> > **The swimmer in the sixth lane must wear a red cap.**
> > Nu swims in either the first lane or the seventh lane.
> > Markson swims in a lane numbered two lower than Price's.
> > **Hewitt wears a red cap** and swims in lane 4.
> > **Luis wears a white cap.**
> > **No two swimmers wearing red caps can swim in consecutively numbered lanes.**

It's clear (from the bold lettering, perhaps?) that we added the cap dimension to both the scenario and rules. Welcome to the third dimension!

Remember that in creating logic games, the test writers have many ways to pull their levers, but they only have a few levers to pull! At the most basic level, the games can ask you either to order elements or to place them in groups (or, as we'll see later, both). 3D Ordering games clearly are based on ordering elements.

The next set of levers is about further defining elements or positions—adding in characteristics. And here's where we meet the 3D twist: the scenario introduces these characteristics. For example, a certain position will be held by either a French, Russian, or Polish speaker, or perhaps by a live or recorded performance, or, as we saw in the above game, by either a red-, white-, or yellow-capped swimmer. Regardless of the actual categories, what is happening is that along with ordering elements into positions, we now also must track the characteristics.

Looking at the game above, we have several relationships to consider:

1. **Swimmer and lane (element and position)**
   Which swimmer goes in which lane?

2. **Swimmer and color (element and characteristic)**
   Which color cap is each swimmer wearing?

3. **Color and lane (characteristic and position)**
   Which cap color does each lane correspond to?

That probably seems like a lot to keep tabs on, but this is where your diagram will come in handy. We'll get to that in a moment. In terms of recognizing when you're facing a 3D Ordering game, keep in mind two ideas:

1. **Keep the order.** If there's no ordering, it's not 3D Ordering!

2. **Add another dimension.** If it feels like Basic Ordering, but you're struggling to manage another dimension of the game, it's likely 3D Ordering.

Picturing 3D Ordering Games and Notating Rules

When you played the Getting Familiar game, you probably started with a Number Line. Perfect! As we just stated, a game is not 3D Ordering if there isn't ordering! But while we'll always start with a Number Line to anchor the ordering aspect of the game, that line is clearly not enough to represent the entirety of the game's structure. (Ideally, you would have realized that *before* you drew it, in the Picture the Game phase.) We need a second line for our additional dimension. This forms what we call a **3D Number Line.**

We suggest that the elements go on the bottom row and the characteristics, for which there are usually only two or three options, go on the top row. However you do it, definitely keep the ordering on the bottom of the whole diagram. (If you'd like to further distinguish between the elements and characteristics, you can use lowercase for the characteristics.)

Let's build one for the 3D swimmers game from above. To start, write your rosters of elements next to the corresponding rows:

— — — — — — —   R W Y

— — — — — — —   H J K L M N P
1 2 3 4 5 6 7

If you might get confused, label the rows; in this case it would be *caps* and *swimmers*.

Before we go on, we should make one tweak to the team roster. Do you remember what the game says about the caps? Go back and reread the scenario if not.

It says that three caps are red, three are white, and one is yellow. Don't forget that some rules are embedded in the scenario!

When you know how many of each characteristic are in a game, represent that in your diagram like so:

— — — — — — —   R R R W W W Y

— — — — — — —   H J K L M N P
1   2   3   4   5   6   7

Let's move to the rules. As we mentioned above, there are three different relationships in play in 3D Ordering games, and all three can show up in the rules. Sometimes two relationships will show up in one rule, as we see in the fifth rule of this game. Let's categorize the rules:

1. **Swimmer and lane (element and position)**

James swims in a lower-numbered lane than Kopov.

Nu swims in either the first lane or the seventh lane.

Markson swims in a lane numbered two lower than Price's.

You already know how to notate these rules.

2. **Swimmer and cap color (element and characteristic)**

Luis wears a white cap.

With these sorts of rules, you want to notate them in a way that is consistent with how your diagram is laid out. Since the caps are on the top row and the swimmers are on the bottom one, notate accordingly:

3. **Cap color and lane (characteristic and position)**

The swimmer in the sixth lane must wear a red cap.

No two swimmers wearing red caps can swim in consecutively numbered lanes.

As with the rules connecting the swimmers and the caps, represent these rules in a way that is easy to transfer into the diagram. The first rule above should go straight into the diagram, while the second one should go to the side:

Notice we crossed out the items that were "used"—it's an easy way to keep track of who is left.

The fifth rule of the game references two types of relationships:

Hewitt wears a red cap and swims in lane 4.

While a rule that references multiple relationships might sound complex in theory, this one can go straight onto our Number Line.

Go ahead and create a completed diagram (with inferences) before reading on. As you infer various restrictions, put them either above or below the 3D Number Line, depending on whether the restriction involves the teams or the swimmers. Here are the rules once again and a template to fill in:

MANHATTAN
PREP

James swims in a lower-numbered lane than Kopov.

The swimmer in the sixth lane must wear a red cap.

Nu swims in either the first lane or the seventh lane.

Markson swims in a lane numbered two lower than Price's.

Hewitt wears a red cap and swims in lane 4.

Luis wears a white cap.

No two swimmers wearing red caps can swim in consecutively numbered lanes.

__ __ __ __ __ __ __   R R R W W W Y

__ __ __ __ __ __ __   H J K L M N P
1   2   3   4   5   6   7

Below is what we came up with—notice how we arranged things:

With so many relationships to keep track of, notating this way can help keep things clear.

As usual, your diagram might look a little different. Perhaps you wrote in "W/Y" in the top row of slots 3, 5, and 7. That's fine. A smart move you might not have done is crossing out the two R's that were placed. This helps you see who's left.

Talking about smart, if you started thinking about the remaining colors and where they can go, bravo! That last R can go only in either slot 1 or 2. You can add that to your diagram using a cloud:

R̶   R̶   R̶

(R) _ R _ R _   R̶ R̶ R W W W Y   [R̶ R̶]   [W]
                                              [L]

N/ _ _ H _ /N   H J K L M N P
 1 2 3 4 5 6 7
                                      J — K   [M _ P]
K̶ P̶   M̶ J̶

P̶ M̶   L̶ M̶

P̶

5

We'll do some more work on diagramming 3D Ordering games in a bit, but let's take a quick detour and look at some of the subtler issues of this game type.

Insider Overview of 3D Ordering

Historically, 3D Ordering games have been front-end games. They've called for a lot of up-front inference work. Lately, though, the LSAT has been delivering more back-end versions.

As you practice, you'll come across more examples of front-end 3D Ordering games (and this makes sense, since with 20+ years of LSATs behind us, there are a lot more historical LSATs than recent ones). What does this mean for you? In short, be ready for either. Just because many of your practice 3D Ordering games can unfold with a dazzling sequence of inferences before you even look at the first question, don't force it. Some games simply are not designed to work that way.

If you sense that a 3D Ordering game is a front-end game, dive in! You know how to do this: Work from the rules, look for restrictions, identify any divisions with consequences, etc.

If you quickly hit a brick wall, don't force it by writing out lots of hypotheticals or by making frames where you shouldn't. Instead, know that you'll probably have more work to do in the questions and, therefore, be sure you have a firm grip on the rules. One way to see if you have a firm grip is to look at each of your notations, say to yourself what it means, and then check your interpretation against the written rule.

If you're unsure whether the game is a front- or back-end game, cover both bases: Make sure you are in control of the rules *and* consider how the game works during The Big Pause. The LSAT generously provides an early warning system: If the second (or first) question of the game stumps you—meaning you're not even sure how to approach it—you probably should go back to work on understanding the game.

Drill It: 3D Ordering Setups

Let's go back to working on diagramming 3D Ordering games. Work through the 3D Number Line setup for each of the games below. Be sure to check your work against the solutions after each game.

1. Exactly six items—F, G, H, J, K, and L—are sold at a yard sale. The items are sold one at a time and consecutively, and each item is sold for either $10 or $20. The following rules govern the sale of the items:

   J is sold either first or sixth.
   No two $10 items are sold consecutively.
   The item sold third is sold for $10.
   L is sold for $20.

2. Exactly seven students—Moore, Nelson, Polanski, Oh, Sullivan, Tang, and Webb—sit in the seats numbered sequentially 1 through 7 in the first row of a classroom. Exactly one student sits in each of the seven seats. Each student is either right-handed or left-handed, but not both. The seating arrangement adheres to the following conditions:

   No right-handed student can sit in a seat numbered one lower than the seat of a left-handed student.
   Moore sits in a seat numbered two lower than the seat in which Polanski sits.
   A left-handed student sits in seat 3.
   Tang is a right-handed student.
   Oh sits in seat 6.

3. On Monday, exactly five flights—P, Q, R, S, and T—depart from the same airport. The flights depart one at a time, and each flight departs exactly once. Two of the flights are bound for Japan, two are bound for Germany, and the remaining flight is bound for France. The following conditions apply:

   No flight bound for Germany can depart until at least one flight bound for Japan has departed.
   Flight Q departs at some time before flight S and at some time after flight R.
   The flight that departs first is not bound for Japan.
   Flight P is bound for Germany.

4. One evening, a television station broadcasts exactly six programs: M, N, O, P, R, and S. No two programs are broadcast simultaneously, and no other programs are broadcast. Each program is either 30 minutes in length or 60 minutes in length. The following must be true:

   N is 60 minutes in length.
   The broadcast of S immediately precedes the broadcast of O.
   Each 30-minute program is immediately followed by a 60-minute program.
   P is broadcast at some time before O.
   A 30-minute program is broadcast fourth.

5

Solutions: 3D Ordering Setups

1.

~~10 10~~										

$$: ___ 20 10 20 ___ ___   10 20

20 L

item: J̶/ ___ ___ ___ ___ /J

   1   2   3   4   5   6   Ⓕ G Ⓗ J K̶ⓁL̶

         X̶

2.

Note that an R must go in slot 7. If an L went in slot 7, the whole top row would be L's (since an R cannot immediately precede any L), and we know that we must have at least one R (Tang is right-handed).

R̶L		R
		T

M _ P

hand: L L L ___ ___ ___ R   R L

student: ___ ___ ___ ___ ___ 0̶ ___   M N P O S T W

         1   2   3   4   5   6   7

         P̶ P̶ T̶ M̶   M̶

         T̶ T̶

3.

   ´J
J̶–G–G | G |
         | P |
R–Q–S

where: G̶ G̶
        X̶ G̶
        F J ___ ___ ___   X̶ J G G F̶

flight: ___ ___ ___ ___ ___   P Q R S Ⓣ

        1   2   3   4   5

        Q̶ S̶   R̶ Q̶

        S̶ P̶   R̶

        P̶

Japan can't go first (as the third constraint tells us), and since G can't go until after at least one J, G can't go in slot 1 or 2! This means P can't go in 1 or 2 either (since P is bound for Germany).

4.

If 30, then | 30 60 | | 60 |
            | P – 50 | | N |

length: ___ ___ 60 30 60 60   30 60

show: ___ ___ ___ ___ ___ ___   Ⓜ N O P Ⓡ S

      1   2   3   4   5   6

      O̶ O̶   N̶ P̶ S̶

      S̶   P̶

MANHATTAN
PREP

Using Previous Work

We're about to throw you back into that first game about the six novels and three authors—nobody could ever forget the raw emotional power of Tamiko's novel *Forgiven*—but it's important to step back from 3D Ordering games specifically to look at a crucial strategy for the entire Logic Games section: using previous work. We've already used this method for explanations in several questions, so let's have an actual discussion of the strategy.

Before we start, we want to clear up a myth that many LSAT students have: expert gamers will not scramble. In fact, most expert gamers are experts *because* they can scramble! While testing answers and using previous work can feel clumsy, these can be powerful and efficient tools when used correctly.

So what is it? Using previous work means that after you have drawn out a hypothetical as part of your work solving a question (often for a conditional question), you can, and often should, use that work to speed up your work on a subsequent unconditional question. For that reason, it's important to organize your scratch paper so that it's easy to find and use your work from previous questions. If you're making a diagram for a conditional question, label it with the question number so you can refer back to the rule that triggered that diagram if necessary. If you're making a diagram to test an answer choice, cross it off if it turns out to be invalid so you don't accidentally use it later.

To see this in action, we'll use a diagram that we built earlier. Here's the game again, along with a question. (Work those speed and accuracy muscles and re-diagram this game!)

> Exactly seven swimmers—Hewitt, James, Kopov, Luis, Markson, Nu, and Price—will race in the 50-meter freestyle event. Three swimmers will wear red caps, three will wear white caps, and one will wear a yellow cap. Each swimmer will swim in exactly one of seven lanes, numbered 1 through 7. No two swimmers share the same lane and no swimmer wears more than one cap. Lane assignments comply with the following conditions:
>
> > James swims in a lower-numbered lane than Kopov.
> > The swimmer in the sixth lane must wear a red cap.
> > Nu swims in either the first lane or the seventh lane.
> > Markson swims in a lane numbered two lower than Price's.
> > Hewitt wears a red cap and swims in lane 4.
> > Luis wears a white cap.
> > No two swimmers wearing red caps can swim in consecutively numbered lanes.
>
> If P wears a yellow cap and swims in lane three, which of the following must be false?
>
> (A) K and M both wear red caps.
> (B) L and M both wear white caps.
> (C) J and K both wear white caps.
> (D) J and K swim in adjacent lanes.
> (E) H and L swim in adjacent lanes.

Your diagram for this question should have looked something like this:

RRR/WWW/Y (R,W) Y R W R W
HJK LMNP   M J/L P H L/J K N
           1   2   3 4 5   6 7

With that work in-hand, we can see that (C) must be false: while J can wear a white cap, K must wear a red one.

Imagine later in the game a question asks, "Each of the following could be true EXCEPT:"

This sort of question could easily eat up a lot of time. Four of the answers are scenarios that could be true; writing out each one to confirm this would take more time than we have. Your first line of attack is to quickly look at each one, hoping that one will jump out as something that must be false. But what do you do when that isn't the case? You could methodically work through each answer or you could use previous work. This is the sort of scenario where using previous work can be the most helpful: when the alternative is going answer by answer. If you can use your work on earlier questions to eliminate even a couple of answers, the number of answers that you're left testing is far more manageable.

Imagine an answer choice offers, "M wears a white cap and swims in lane 1." Our diagram above illustrates quite clearly that this could be true. Eliminate! Go ahead and see what other answers you can eliminate using our previous work above:

Each of the following could be true EXCEPT:

(A) J swims in the fifth lane wearing a white cap.

(B) L swims in the fifth lane wearing a white cap.

(C) J swims in the second lane wearing a red cap.

(D) Both K and L swim in lanes lower-numbered than the one in which H swims.

(E) Both K and L swim in lanes higher-numbered than the one in which H swims.

Hopefully you eliminated every answer except (D) using our previous work. While it might have felt a bit awkward this time, with practice, using previous work almost surely will prove to be the faster way to solve at least a few questions you face on test day. It usually won't work out as conveniently as it did above: Eliminating all four wrong answers using a single previous hypothetical is not that common. However, when you have multiple hypotheticals on your page, eliminating all four wrong answers becomes a possibility, and eliminating three answers is fairly common.

MANHATTAN
PREP

Here are some tips on using previous work:

1. When writing out scenarios for conditional questions:

- Keep your work neat and organized by question number so that you can refer to it later in the game if needed.
- Write out the potential variations by using clouds so that that your previous work shows multiple possibilities.
- Cross out any work that you realize depicts an impossible situation (so that you don't accidentally use it thinking it shows a true hypothetical).
- Don't forget that the correct answer to the Orientation question is a valid hypothetical! If you find that using previous work is especially helpful for you, you may want to jot that free hypothetical down on your scratch paper. Because you can see only one question at a time on the LSAT digital testing platform, you'll have to write it down if you hope to use it later.

2. Feel free to tinker with your previous work a bit, but be careful to check that you haven't violated any rules. (E.g., in the above, P in lane four could also have worn a white cap, but not a red one.)

3. Previous work shows one hypothetical that could be true, which makes it great for finding the right answer in "could be true" questions. But what about using previous work to answer other types of questions?

Question Type	Use of Previous Work
Could Be True	**Find the right answer.** If an answer shows up in even one valid hypothetical, select it.
Could Be False	**Find the right answer.** If an answer is false in even one valid hypothetical, it's your answer.
Must Be True	**Eliminate wrong answers.** Even if an answer shows up in every hypothetical, it might not be the right answer (since there might be more hypotheticals out there in which it is false). However, if we have even one hypothetical that goes against the answer, it's not something that must be true and that allows us to eliminate it.
Must Be False	**Eliminate wrong answers.** Even if an answer doesn't show up in any hypothetical, it isn't necessarily false (since there might be more hypotheticals out there in which it could be true). However, if an answer does show up in even one valid hypothetical, that proves that it's not something that must be false and can therefore be eliminated.

Practice this strategy! Like everything else in this book, if you don't use it during your practice, you won't be able to use it on test day. When reviewing your work, see if any questions would have gone faster through the use of previous work.

That's your introduction to using previous work. To get you started on actually using this strategy, on the next game, there is a tough question where you can eliminate each incorrect answer through the use of previous work—be on the lookout for it!

Try It Again

Now that you've learned how to identify and diagram 3D Ordering games, let's return to the initial game you played. We'll work through the solutions together on the pages to come.

A publishing company published exactly six novels—*Forgiven, Grain, Highwire, June, Lampoon,* and *Melted*—in the years from 1991 to 1996. Exactly one novel was published in each of the six years. Three authors—Robinson, Stewart, and Tamiko—each wrote exactly two of the novels. The following conditions apply:

> Exactly one of Robinson's novels was published before the first of Stewart's novels was published.
> Neither of Robinson's novels was published in 1991 or 1994.
> None of the authors had novels published in consecutive years.
> *June* was published in 1994.
> *Highwire* was published exactly two years after *Melted*.

1. Which of the following could be an accurate representation of the authors and the novels they wrote, listed in order of publication?

   (A) Tamiko: *Lampoon*; Robinson: *Grain*;
       Tamiko: *Forgiven*; Stewart: *Melted*;
       Robinson: *June*; Stewart: *Highwire*

   (B) Tamiko: *Lampoon*; Robinson: *Forgiven*;
       Stewart: *Melted*; Tamiko: *June*;
       Robinson: *Highwire*; Stewart: *Grain*

   (C) Stewart: *Melted*; Robinson: *Lampoon*;
       Stewart: *Highwire*; Tamiko: *June*;
       Robinson: *Forgiven*; Tamiko: *Grain*

   (D) Tamiko: *Melted*; Robinson: *Grain*;
       Stewart: *Highwire*; Stewart: *June*;
       Tamiko: *Forgiven*; Robinson: *Lampoon*

   (E) Robinson: *Forgiven*; Tamiko: *Grain*;
       Stewart: *Melted*; Robinson: *June*;
       Tamiko: *Highwire*; Stewart: *Lampoon*

2. Which one of the following must be true?

   (A) One of Stewart's novels was published in 1993.
   (B) One of Tamiko's novels was published in 1994.
   (C) One of Robinson's novels was published in 1992.
   (D) One of Robinson's novels was published in 1995.
   (E) One of Stewart's novels was published in 1996.

MANHATTAN
PREP

3. If *Forgiven* was published in 1995, each of the following could be true EXCEPT:

   (A) Stewart wrote *Grain.*

   (B) Tamiko wrote *June.*

   (C) Tamiko wrote *Highwire.*

   (D) Robinson wrote *Lampoon.*

   (E) Robinson wrote *Highwire.*

4. If Tamiko wrote *June,* then which one of the following must be false?

   (A) Tamiko wrote *Melted.*

   (B) Tamiko wrote *Highwire.*

   (C) Stewart wrote *Melted.*

   (D) Stewart wrote *Highwire.*

   (E) Stewart wrote *Forgiven.*

5. If *Lampoon* was published in the year immediately preceding the publication of *Melted,* which one of the following must be true?

   (A) Tamiko wrote *Forgiven.*

   (B) Tamiko wrote *Grain.*

   (C) Robinson wrote *Lampoon.*

   (D) Robinson wrote *Highwire.*

   (E) Stewart wrote *Melted.*

6. Each of the following could be true EXCEPT:

   (A) Tamiko wrote a novel that was published in 1995.

   (B) *Melted* was published exactly three years before *Grain.*

   (C) Stewart wrote *June.*

   (D) *Lampoon* was published before *Highwire* but after *Melted.*

   (E) Both of Tamiko's novels were published before either of Stewart's novels were published.

7. Which of the following, if substituted for the condition that exactly one of Robinson's novels was published before the first of Stewart's novels was published, would have the same effect in determining the years in which the novels were published and the authors who wrote the novels?

   (A) Neither of Robinson's novels was published in 1996.

   (B) Neither of Stewart's novels was published in 1992.

   (C) The earliest that either one of Stewart's novels could have been published is 1993.

   (D) The earliest that either one of Robinson's novels could have been published is 1992.

   (E) The earliest that either one of Robinson's novels could have been published is 1993.

5

How Did You Do?

Answer Key

1. B   5. C
2. C   6. A
3. E   7. C
4. B

Step 1: Picture the Game

We can be pretty sure we're facing an Ordering game from these clues in the scenario: "1991 to 1996" and "exactly one novel was published in each of the six years." We know this is a 3D Ordering game because we're dealing with three distinct variables: novels, authors, and years of publication.

We'll start with our 3D Ordering Number Line and notate the two rosters:

author: __ __ __ __ __ __   R R S S T T

novel: __ __ __ __ __ __   F G H J L M

  1   2   3   4   5   6

Step 2: Notate the Rules and Make Inferences

If you're pretty confident that you nailed this diagram, and would like to skip over the discussion of the setup, take a peek a few pages ahead and see if your diagram matches ours. If not, or if you'd like to get a guided tour regardless, let's go through the setup together:

Exactly one of Robinson's novels was published before the first of Stewart's novels was published.

Since this rule references relative positions, we can express this relationship using a mini Tree. One R, and one R only, must come before the first S. The second R and the second S, therefore, must come after the first S (though we don't know in which order). Also note that this rule allows us to infer that S cannot be in 1991. If exactly one R must precede the first S, then an S cannot possibly occupy the first slot (otherwise, the R would fall off the left end of the diagram). We'll note this by using a exclusion:

R — S < R / S   author: ⅋
                                __ __ __ __ __ __   R R S S T T

                       novel:
                                __ __ __ __ __ __   F G H J L M

                                 1   2   3   4   5   6

MANHATTAN
PREP

Neither of Robinson's novels was published in 1991 or 1994.

Once we've notated that R can't be in author slots 1 or 4, we should notice that neither R nor S can occupy slot 1. Thus, T must go in slot 1. Finally, if R cannot go in slot 1, then S cannot go in slot 2 (since exactly one R must come before the first S):

author:
novel:

R — S < R
        S

    R̶
    S̶ S̶   R̶
    T _ _ _ _ _   R R S S T̶ T
    _ _ _ _ _ _   F G H J L M

    1 2 3 4 5 6

5

None of the authors had novels published in consecutive years.

This rule tells us that we cannot place like letters adjacent to each other in the author row. Also, this means that T cannot go in slot 2 (since T occupies slot 1). Thus, R must go in slot 2! Lastly, if R is in slot 2, R cannot go in slot 3 (we can't have two R's next to each other):

R — S < R
        S

    R̶ T̶
    S̶ S̶ R̶ R̶   X̶X̶
    T R _ _ _ _   R̶ R S S T̶ T
    _ _ _ _ _ _   F G H J L M

    1 2 3 4 5 6

June was published in 1994.

This is an easy one! That said, be sure to keep your elements straight. *June* is a novel; we must be sure to place the J in the correct row.

   Highwire was published exactly two years after Melted.

A chunk! You should immediately recognize this as a crucial relationship. We can notate it to the side of the diagram, but we can (and should) also recognize some inferences that this chunk creates. If *Highwire* was published two years after *Melted*, *Highwire* cannot occupy the first or second slots and *Melted* cannot occupy the fifth or sixth slots. Furthermore, the J in slot 4 means that H cannot occupy slot 6 (because that would put M in slot 4) and M cannot occupy slot 2 (because that would put H in slot 4):

R — S < R / S   author: (col1: ~~R~~ ~~S~~ T) (col2: ~~T~~ ~~S~~ R)   ~~R~~   ~~R~~   ___   ___

novel: ___ ___ ___ J ___ ___

1 2 3 4 5 6

(col1: ~~H~~ ~~M~~) (col2: ~~H~~)   ~~M~~   ~~H~~ ~~M~~

Legend:
[XX]
~~R~~ R S S ~~T~~ T
F G H ~~J~~ L M
[M _ H]

Step 3: The Big Pause

We should swing through our rules again, make sure we've understood them correctly, and see if there are any inferences we can add to our diagram. We should also circle F, G, and L as strays.

One issue that should jump out is that the mini Tree of R's and S's is pretty limited in terms of where those authors could go. Also, for the novels row, the MH chunk is similarly limited. Indeed, there are only two places M could go.

Is this game worth framing? It's doable—you'd want to create a list of possible orders of authors and novels—but rather complex and unwieldy. And framing around the placement of M won't have many consequences since we have so many stray elements in the novel row and very few connections between the novel and author rows. The important takeaway from The Big Pause is to identify the two important limitations on the game.

Step 4: Attack the Questions

1. Which of the following could be an accurate representation of the authors and the novels they wrote, listed in order of publication?

   (A) Tamiko: *Lampoon*; Robinson: *Grain*;
       Tamiko: *Forgiven*; Stewart: *Melted*;
       Robinson: *June*; Stewart: *Highwire*

   (B) Tamiko: *Lampoon*; Robinson: *Forgiven*;
       Stewart: *Melted*; Tamiko: *June*;
       Robinson: *Highwire*; Stewart: *Grain*

   (C) Stewart: *Melted*; Robinson: *Lampoon*;
       Stewart: *Highwire*; Tamiko: *June*;
       Robinson: *Forgiven*; Tamiko: *Grain*

   (D) Tamiko: *Melted*; Robinson: *Grain*;
       Stewart: *Highwire*; Stewart: *June*;
       Tamiko: *Forgiven*; Robinson: *Lampoon*

   (E) Robinson: *Forgiven*; Tamiko: *Grain*;
       Stewart: *Melted*; Robinson: *June*;
       Tamiko: *Highwire*; Stewart: *Lampoon*

MANHATTAN
PREP

Answer choice (B) is correct.

If a game has characteristics, often the first question is not a standard Orientation question because only one of our two groups of elements will be referenced in the answers (with our Swimmers game, imagine answers that didn't talk about cap color). Since many of our rules might reference the missing information, we couldn't simply work from the rules. Rather, we'd have to work from the diagram and the inferences we made there. We'll see plenty of these situations soon enough. Here, however, we're facing a standard Orientation question since the answers reference both element sets, so we know the drill!

> The first rule allows us to eliminate (C).
> The second rule allows us to eliminate (E).
> The third rule allows us to eliminate (D).
> The fourth rule allows us to eliminate (A).

Answer choice (B) is the last one standing. Let's move on!

2. Which one of the following must be true?

(A) One of Stewart's novels was published in 1993.

(B) One of Tamiko's novels was published in 1994.

(C) One of Robinson's novels was published in 1992.

(D) One of Robinson's novels was published in 1995.

(E) One of Stewart's novels was published in 1996.

Answer choice (C) is correct.

Our hard work diagramming pays off—we can immediately see that (C) is the answer. There must be an R in author slot 2.

Consider how tough this question would have been if we had not made our inferences earlier. If we had skipped that step, this question would have been a wake-up call to go and do some more work on the diagram.

Again, during the exam, there would be no need to check the other answer choices. For the sake of practice, however, it would be a good idea to take a moment now to convince yourself that the four remaining choices need not be true.

3. If *Forgiven* was published in 1995, each of the following could be true EXCEPT:

(A) Stewart wrote *Grain*.

(B) Tamiko wrote *June*.

(C) Tamiko wrote *Highwire*.

(D) Robinson wrote *Lampoon*.

(E) Robinson wrote *Highwire*.

Answer choice (E) is correct.

Note that this is an EXCEPT question. We can translate "Each of the following could be true EXCEPT" to "Which one must be false?" Also note that this is a conditional question. We'll draw an abbreviated, temporary diagram that puts F in novel slot 5.

As we learned in previous chapters, chunks are the key to ordering. Once we put F in novel slot 5, we can see that the MH chunk must be placed in slots 1–3:

Now, as we look at the answer choices, we should *not* try to verify the answers that could be true. Rather, we should look for the answer that is obviously false. If an answer is not obviously false, defer judgment. It might be tempting, for example, to start with answer (A) and try to prove its validity, but we don't want to spend time on trial and error unless we need to. It's likely that the correct answer, once we get to it, will be obviously false. Nothing jumps out in answers (A) through (D). However, answer (E) clearly cannot be true. H is in slot 3, and R can never be there since we cannot have two consecutive R's.

4. If Tamiko wrote *June*, then which one of the following must be false?

   (A) Tamiko wrote *Melted.*
   (B) Tamiko wrote *Highwire.*
   (C) Stewart wrote *Melted.*
   (D) Stewart wrote *Highwire.*
   (E) Stewart wrote *Forgiven.*

Answer choice (B) is correct.

This is also a conditional question, so we'll start by drawing out a hypothetical that puts a T with J:

There must be some inferences that we can draw based on this new information. With R in slot 2 and T in slot 4, neither R nor T can go in slot 3. (Remember, authors cannot publish books in consecutive years.) Thus, S must go in author slot 3.

MANHATTAN
PREP

Again, we'll work our way through the choices, deferring judgment on any answer that is not obviously false. Answer (A) would put an M in slot 1, under the T. There's no obvious rule against this, so we'll defer judgment on (A).

Answer (B) would put an H in slot 1, underneath the T, since it's the only remaining T now that *June* is in slot 4. There *is* a problem with this. Our original diagram tells us that H cannot go in slot 1. Thus, (B) must be false.

Notice that our inference (S must go in slot 3) didn't really help us here. That's okay. It's important to note these inferences whenever you see them. Most of the time they will come into play. In fact, this question is unusual in that the answer does not depend on the new condition.

5. If *Lampoon* was published in the year immediately preceding the publication of *Melted*, which one of the following must be true?

    (A) Tamiko wrote *Forgiven.*
    (B) Tamiko wrote *Grain.*
    (C) Robinson wrote *Lampoon.*
    (D) Robinson wrote *Highwire.*
    (E) Stewart wrote *Melted.*

Answer choice (C) is correct.

Another conditional question. This additional information adds to our MH chunk. If *Lampoon* is published immediately before *Melted*, we have: L M _ H. There is only one place this chunk can go. We'll draw a hypothetical:

$$\begin{array}{ccccccc}
\underline{\text{T}} & \underline{\text{R}} & \underline{} & \underline{} & \underline{} & \underline{} \\
\underline{} & \underline{\text{L}} & \underline{\text{M}} & \underline{\text{J}} & \underline{\text{H}} & \underline{} \\
{\scriptstyle 1} & {\scriptstyle 2} & {\scriptstyle 3} & {\scriptstyle 4} & {\scriptstyle 5} & {\scriptstyle 6}
\end{array}$$

There doesn't seem to be anything else to easily infer, so let's move to the answer choices. Again, we'll defer judgment on the answer choices until we find an answer that looks good.

Answer (A) doesn't jump off the page. It would probably take some trial and error to prove or disprove it. So we'll defer judgment for now.

Same story with answer (B). We could probably prove it or disprove it, but this would require some time and energy. Let's bet that there will be a more obvious answer down the line. Defer judgment on (B).

Aha! We see that answer (C) must be true (assuming we were able to draw our hypothetical). R and L appear in slot 2.

6. Each of the following could be true EXCEPT:

(A) Tamiko wrote a novel that was published in 1995.

(B) *Melted* was published exactly three years before Grain.

(C) Stewart wrote *June.*

(D) *Lampoon* was published before *Highwire* but after *Melted.*

(E) Both of Tamiko's novels were published before either of Stewart's novels were published.

Answer choice (A) is correct.

This EXCEPT question can be rephrased to "Which one must be false?" We should try deferring judgment on answers that are not obviously false, but a quick scan of the answer choices gets us nowhere. None of the answers are obviously false given our diagram. This is quite common on one of the last questions of a game. We must be prepared to spend some time on this question. Using previous work might be useful, but in this case, all that is clear is that the answer to question 1 eliminates (B).

Let's look at (A). We'll have to use a trial and error approach to see if Tamiko could have a novel in 1995. Let's try diagramming it. If T is in author slot 5, then S must go in author slot 3 (the two T's are used up and we can't put an R in slot 3 next to the R in slot 2). Thus, the second S must go in slot 6 (we can't put an S in slot 4 next to the S in slot 3). Therefore, the second R must go in slot 4.

Wait! Our original diagram tells us that R can't go in author slot 4. Thus, (A) must be false. While on the exam we wouldn't do this, take the time now to verify the possibility of the remaining four answer choices. And thank the writer of this question for putting the correct answer first!

7. Which of the following, if substituted for the condition that exactly one of Robinson's novels was published before the first of Stewart's novels was published, would have the same effect in determining the years in which the novels were published and the authors who wrote the novels?

(A) Neither of Robinson's novels was published in 1996.

(B) Neither of Stewart's novels was published in 1992.

(C) The earliest that either one of Stewart's novels could have been published is 1993.

(D) The earliest that either one of Robinson's novels could have been published is 1992.

(E) The earliest that either one of Robinson's novels could have been published is 1993.

Answer choice (C) is correct.

This is an Equivalent Rule question. We will look more closely at this question type in the next section of this chapter, but let's take a quick look at this one.

Our task for this type of question is to choose an answer choice that has the same effect on the diagram as the rule being replaced. In other words, after the substitution, our diagram should provide the same exact information as the original—no more, no less.

The rule being substituted in this case (*Exactly one of Robinson's novels was published before the first of Stewart's novels was published*) gave us a bunch of information in the top row of our diagram. Most importantly, we inferred from the rule that S can't go first. Later, based on the fact that R couldn't go in slot 1, we were able to infer that S couldn't go in slot 2. As seems to happen a lot on the LSAT, there was more to infer! With both S and R restricted from slot 1, T had to go there, forcing R into slot 2. Without that first rule, we are left with this:

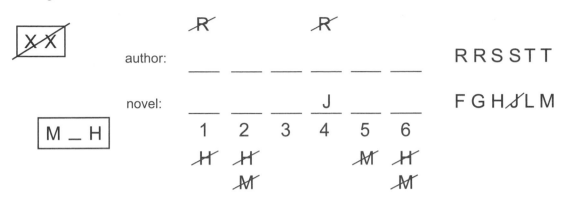

So which of the answer choices will give us back our T in 1 and R in 2 without adding any new information?

Answer (A) would prohibit an R from being placed in slot 6. This is information that *doesn't* exist in the original diagram. Eliminate (A).

Answer (B) would prohibit an S from being placed in slot 2, but this leaves open the possibility of an S or a T in slot 1 and an R or a T in slot 2. Thus, (B) does not have the same effect as the original rule. Eliminate (B).

Answer (C) would prohibit an S from being placed in slot 1 or 2. If S can't go in 1, and we already know that R can't go in 1, slot 1 must be filled with a T. Since no author can have books published in consecutive years, slot 2 could not get a T. Well, now we know that 2 can't get a T or an S, so slot 2 must get an R. This means R can't go in 3. This is starting to look like the original!

In fact, (C) gives us exactly what the original rule got us. You may be wondering, "What about the mini Tree notation involving the R's and S's? Does this new rule provide the same ordering rules?" Note that the new rule forces an R before either one of the S's (just like the original rule did) and, since R can't go in slot 3 or 4, we know that at least one S must come before the second R (just what we knew from the original rule). This is an equivalent rule, so (C) is the correct answer.

Go ahead and try (D) and (E) just for practice. You will find that neither leads to the same diagram as the original.

Spotlight on Question Types: Rule Questions

The last question of the game we just discussed was an example of one of the two types of **Rule questions** you will face on the LSAT:

1. Equivalent Rule questions

2. Rule Substitution questions

The first one has become increasingly common while the second one has become increasingly rare. While we'll focus more on the first one, let's take a look at both.

Equivalent Rule Questions

As we just saw, Equivalent Rule questions ask us to identify a replacement for a given rule that would result in the same possibilities and restrictions as the original. The four wrong answers affect the game in some other way; either they don't do everything the original rule does, or they tell us something new, or both.

If you understand the original rule, some of the wrong answers shouldn't take much effort to spot. In fact, don't be surprised if the correct answer is simply a rewording of the rule. Some answers are tougher to decode, but these will hinge on inferences that you could draw from that original rule. Thus, your best weapons for an Equivalent Rule question will be understanding the original rule and eliminating wrong answers.

To get a bit deeper into this question type, go ahead and diagram this game (and the major inferences):

Five people—Q, R, S, T, and U—finish a race in a certain order with no ties.

S finishes third.
T finishes immediately before or immediately after S.
Q finishes at some point before R.

Pretty straightforward, right? Here's the diagram with the basic inferences you should have drawn:

$$Q - R$$

Now, let's give you a temporary job writing LSAT questions. Go ahead and write two (or more) possible correct answers to this question:

> Which of the following, if substituted for the rule that T finishes immediately before or immediately after S, would have the same consequence on determining the order in which the five people finish the race?

Done? If so, *how* do you come up with the right answer?

For many, the first idea would be to reword the same exact information in a different way. We'll consider this as our first option:

Option 1: Reword It

Here are three equivalent rules for the original rule—*T finishes immediately before or immediately after S*—that are all simply rewordings of the rule:

> *No one finishes between T and S.*

> *Either S finishes immediately before T, or T finishes immediately before S.*

> *Neither Q, nor R, nor U can finish between S and T.*

Be ready for such simple answers. They show up more often than you might expect.

Option 2: Match the Direct Consequences

What do we know about the spots that T can occupy? Because S must be in the third spot, and T must be next to S, T must be in the second or fourth spot. Imagine we were told one of the following:

> *T must finish in the second or fourth spot.*

> *T does not finish first or last.*

A direct consequence of either would be that T would have to be immediately before or after S. Thus, these are valid matches for the given rule. They appear to give us different information from that presented in the original rule, but when applied to the game, they produce the same results.

This is generally as tricky as the LSAT gets. But every once in a while, the LSAT throws in an exceptionally hard answer.

Option 3: Match the Indirect Consequences

In this option, the test writer creates an answer that doesn't relate directly to the original rule, but, in some incredibly clever way, ends up yielding the same consequences.

Instead of directly confining T to slots 2 and 4, as we did in Options 1 and 2, we could add complexity to our answer by limiting those who could finish first and last. It turns out there are only a few orders for this game:

QTSRU   UTSQR   QUSTR

QTSUR   QRSTU   UQSTR

So, we could write an answer like these:

> *Either Q or U is first, and either U or R is last.*

> *If U is not first or last, then only Q or R can be first or last.*

These rules look very little like the original rule that we were given, and they center on very different information, yet they ultimately have exactly the same impact on the game. Either of these rules would force T into slot 2 or 4, and would thus force T next to S. These rules would also not have any other unintended, or mismatching, consequences.

It's rare that the LSAT will create such involved answers.

So now we know how the test writers can approach this question. What does this mean for *our* approach? Here are the keys:

1. **Understand the original rule.** Since most correct answers to Equivalent Rule questions have a relatively straightforward construction (they're based on Option 1 or 2), simply understanding the rule goes a long way. Especially if the rule is multifaceted, understanding the rule and its consequences will likely be all you need to eliminate several, if not all, of the wrong choices. Don't rush this step.

2. **Know when and where to spend your time.** A big key here is to limit yourself. Do spend some time considering what the original rule means, but don't waste time looking for *all* possible secondary inferences when considering the meaning of the original rule. Per our understanding of how these problems work, that work will be unnecessary at best, and a distraction at worst.

3. **Work from wrong to right.** Eliminate choices that seem to have very different ramifications from those of the original rule. This may seem obvious, but if you are focused on advanced inferences, these answers can be some of the most tempting. It's useful to know that if an answer sounds way off, chances are it is.

MANHATTAN
PREP

However, as always, be cautious. Be mindful of the fact that you could have missed some initial inferences. Don't be afraid to slow down and confirm that certain answers are wrong. Depending on the difficulty level of the question, deferring judgment may leave you with most or all of the answer choices un-eliminated and glaring at you!

Assuming you have some time to spare, confirm that the right answer has the same consequences as the original rule—no more and no less.

Rule Substitution Questions

As we mentioned earlier, Rule Substitution questions are becoming passé. We're seeing them infrequently these days, while we're seeing a lot more Equivalent Rule questions. While we believe in focusing on recent trends, it's worth spending a bit of time looking at Rule Substitution questions. After all, they do still show up on occasion, and they're a great way to work on developing a flexible approach to questions.

Rule Substitution questions can take three forms:

1. A rule is suspended, but all other rules remain in effect.

2. A rule is replaced with a different rule, and all other rules remain in effect.

3. A rule is added to the game, and all other rules remain in effect.

To be honest, the first and third versions aren't technically "substitutions," but the approaches are similar, so we'll discuss them here. In fact, the third version is basically a fancy conditional question, and we talked about these before in the context of Relative Ordering games! Instead of a question introducing a simple condition such as *T is third*, we are told something like *If T is third, it is not given a deluxe treatment*. The difference is that we cannot apply this new rule until we get to the answer choices since we don't actually know if T is third! With a typical conditional question, we should follow the inference chain *before* looking at the answer choices.

What all three options have in common is that, regardless of the change or addition, all the other rules remain in effect.

What might seem daunting to some test-takers is that they spend a significant amount of time mastering a game and then suddenly are forced to adjust the game. Success on LSAT logic games depends on knowing what we know and what we don't, and Rule Substitution questions force us to change both! Fortunately, when these questions show up, they're usually the last question of a game, so we're not expected to learn a game, change our understanding for a Rule Substitution question, and then change back to our original understanding for another question. Even for the LSAT, that would be too cruel! Also, since this sort of question is usually the last one of a set, if we want to adjust our main diagram, we don't have to worry about having to "undo" our adjustments for the next question.

However, even though we're free to do so, we don't always want to adjust our original diagram. Sometimes a Rule Substitution question is better approached by *redrawing the entire diagram*. Indeed, there are two approaches to considering the new rule in Rule Substitution questions, each with their pros and cons:

1. **Adjust your diagram to incorporate the change.** This *tends* to be faster, but may lead you to miss important inferences. More specifically, you might miss that you should *undo* some of the original inferences. When you create a diagram, you don't simply notate each rule; you also notate the inferences that come from the interactions of the rules. With one rule removed or changed, we can expect some rule interactions to change as well.

2. **Draw a new diagram from scratch.** This *tends* to be slower and more accurate, but can be overkill; if you can avoid redrawing, do so. But sometimes the situation calls for it: Perhaps you have time in the bank, and perhaps the change is connected to a chain of inferences.

Note that when we compare the relative strengths of each approach, we are speaking about *tendencies*. Exceptions abound: in part because of the particulars of this or that question, in part because of your timing on a particular Logic Games section, and in part because of your style and strengths. Each approach is useful and each one can be used successfully in any situation. However, since one is sometimes more efficient than the other, you should be armed with both.

It would be unwise to have a hard and fast rule for when to redraw and when to amend, since the choice depends on several factors. Here are the main considerations:

1. **The complexity of the diagram.** This issue cuts both ways. If the diagram is very complex, it may be too time-consuming to redraw, but the complexity might also make it hard for you to figure out the consequences of the new rule without redrawing.

2. **The complexity of the substitution's impact.** The more consequences the rule substitution has, the more likely it is that you'll want to redraw.

3. **Your ability to reverse engineer the diagram.** How easily can you undo the inferences you made originally? This depends on the issues above, as well as on your comfort with the game you're facing.

4. **How much time you have in the bank.** This is pretty straightforward. For example, if you're on the last question of the last game of the entire section, and you have four minutes to spare, the decision to do a possibly time-intensive redrawing is an easier one to make. On the other hand, if you've got one minute left on the section, you can't afford to do an involved redrawing.

Once you've done your work and either redrawn the diagram or amended the one you have, it's time to attack the answer choices. Your approach at this point depends in part on whether you're facing a "could be true" or a "must be true" or "must be false" question.

If you're asked to identify what could be true (or, less frequently, could be false), then it's likely that you'll have to spend more time considering each answer choice. Along with figuring out how the diagram has changed from the rule substitution, you're also faced with putting that diagram to work.

If you're looking for an answer that must be true (or must be false), it's possible that your new or amended diagram already notes the answer. Deferring judgment in search of the correct answer is a smart approach here, though at times you will be forced to do a second pass and dig a bit deeper into each choice.

Since you did all that work of changing your diagram to incorporate the new rule regime, the answer will more than likely require you to apply the new rule. Thus, be wary of answers that clearly don't involve the elements or positions that you had to adjust because of the rule substitution.

Drill It: Rule Questions

Here's a devilish game designed to work your Rule question muscles. We suggest that you play through to completion, and then go back and slowly check your work, making sure to test any answers you deferred judgment on.

A tour company offers six tours each day, and each tour is led by one of six guides—Jack, Kaley, Lyle, Moquetta, Naru, and Olley. Each guide is assigned to lead one tour. In addition, each guide is either experienced or inexperienced. When scheduling the day's tours, the following rules apply:

> No two consecutive tours can be led by inexperienced guides.
>
> There are exactly two tours between the tour that Lyle leads and the tour that Moquetta leads.
>
> The tour that Kaley leads is either immediately before or immediately after the tour that Olley leads.
>
> Jack leads the fourth tour.
>
> The third tour is led by an inexperienced guide.
>
> Both Kaley and Olley are experienced.

1. Which of the following, if substituted for the rule that no two consecutive tours can be led by inexperienced guides, would have the same effect?

   (A) No two consecutive tours can be led by experienced guides.

   (B) An inexperienced tour guide can lead neither the second nor the fourth tour.

   (C) Each tour led by an inexperienced guide must follow and be followed by a tour led by an experienced guide.

   (D) Naru and exactly one other guide are inexperienced.

   (E) Jack is an experienced guide, as are two of the guides who precede him and at least one of the guides who follow him.

2. Which of the following would have the same consequence on the order of the tours if substituted for the rule that there are exactly two tours between the tour that Lyle leads and the tour that Moquetta leads?

   (A) Either Moquetta or Lyle leads the third tour.

   (B) Either Moquetta or Lyle leads the last tour.

   (C) Either Kaley or Olley leads the first tour and Naru leads the fifth tour.

   (D) Either Kaley or Olley leads the first tour and either Lyle or Moquetta leads the third tour.

   (E) The tour led by Naru precedes the tour led by Moquetta or the tour led by Lyle, but not both.

3. If substituted for the rule that Kaley and Olley must lead consecutive tours, which one of the following would have the same effect in determining the order of the tours?

    (A) Moquetta is inexperienced.

    (B) Lyle is inexperienced.

    (C) Either Kaley or Olley must lead the first tour.

    (D) Naru leads the fifth tour.

    (E) Neither Kaley nor Olley leads the sixth tour.

4. If the rule that the tour that Kaley leads is either immediately before or immediately after the tour that Olley leads is replaced with a rule that says there must be exactly two tours between the tours that Kaley and Olley lead, which of the following must be true?

    (A) Olley must lead the second tour.

    (B) Naru must lead the fifth tour.

    (C) Moquetta must lead the sixth tour.

    (D) Naru's tour can neither directly precede nor directly follow any tour led by Moquetta.

    (E) Jack's tour can neither directly precede nor directly follow any tour led by Lyle.

5. If the rule that there are exactly two tours between the tour that Lyle leads and the tour that Moquetta leads is replaced with the rule that there is exactly one tour between the tours that Lyle and Moquetta lead, how many different tours could Naru lead as an experienced guide?

    (A) 1

    (B) 2

    (C) 3

    (D) 4

    (E) 5

Solutions: Rule Questions

Answer Key

1. E   4. D
2. C   5. B
3. D

Steps 1, 2, and 3: Picture the Game, Notate the Rules, Make Inferences, and The Big Pause

We will do only a brief discussion of the diagram for this game so that we can focus on the questions, the real emphasis in this devilish practice game.

The diagram for this 3D Ordering game is as follows:

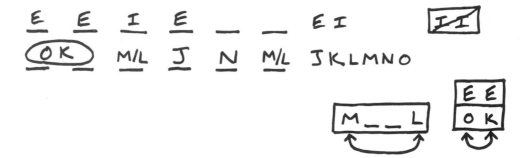

Step 4: Attack the Questions

If your diagram was different—and we mean something other than cosmetically—take some time to work through the game again until you can understand all the inferences we drew, and then try your hand at the questions one more time. An incomplete diagram would make the questions significantly more difficult.

1. Which of the following, if substituted for the rule that no two consecutive tours can be led by inexperienced guides, would have the same effect?

   (A) No two consecutive tours can be led by experienced guides.

   (B) An inexperienced tour guide can lead neither the second nor the fourth tour.

   (C) Each tour led by an inexperienced guide must follow and be followed by a tour led by an experienced guide.

   (D) Naru and exactly one other guide are inexperienced.

   (E) Jack is an experienced guide, as are two of the guides who precede him and at least one of the guides who follow him.

Answer choice (E) is correct.

There are few inferences that we drew from the original rule prohibiting consecutive I's other than that slots 2 and 4 must have E's.

> (A) This rule allows for consecutive I's!
>
> (B) Both of those restrictions are in our diagram, but we need to prevent I in slots 5 and 6, which this rule allows.
>
> (C) This answer seems like a wordy way of saying the original rule! If you have an I, it must be sandwiched between two E's. If you fell for this answer, consider what inferences you would draw from this notation: I $\longrightarrow$ EIE. You would surely infer that I cannot go in the first or last slots. But in the original diagram, we can have an I in slot 6.
>
> (D) While it's true that the original rule requires that at most two guides are inexperienced, there's no reason that Naru must be inexperienced.
>
> (E) If two of these guides that precede J are experienced, these must be in slots 1 and 2, as we already have an I in 3. After J, we can have E I, I E, or E E. This matches the restrictions in our original diagram.

2. Which of the following would have the same consequence on the order of the tours if substituted for the rule that there are exactly two tours between the tour that Lyle leads and the tour that Moquetta leads?

(A) Either Moquetta or Lyle leads the third tour.

(B) Either Moquetta or Lyle leads the last tour.

(C) Either Kaley or Olley leads the first tour and Naru leads the fifth tour.

(D) Either Kaley or Olley leads the first tour and either Lyle or Moquetta leads the third tour.

(E) The tour led by Naru precedes the tour led by Moquetta or the tour led by Lyle, but not both.

Answer choice (C) is correct.

The LM chunk, in connection with the other rules, required that M and L occupy slots 3 and 6:

> (A) This provides only half of what we want!
>
> (B) This provides only the other half of what we want.
>
> (C) This rule forces K and O to occupy the first two slots—since they're a chunk—and with N occupying the fifth slot, the only places left for the remaining elements, M and L, are the third and sixth slots. Thus, this rule has the same effect as the original rule.
>
> (D) This tempting answer allows either M or L to go in slot 5, followed by N.
>
> (E) If we already know that K and O are in slots 1 and 2, this rule forces part of what we want—M and L on opposite sides of N. However, with only N between L and M, we could reach the following arrangement: L N M J K O.

3. If substituted for the rule that Kaley and Olley must lead consecutive tours, which one of the following would have the same effect in determining the order of the tours?

    (A) Moquetta is inexperienced.

    (B) Lyle is inexperienced.

    (C) Either Kaley or Olley must lead the first tour.

    (D) Naru leads the fifth tour.

    (E) Neither Kaley nor Olley leads the sixth tour.

Answer choice (D) is correct.

This rule, in combination with the other rules, restricted the KO chunk to the first two slots.

(A) This rule means that M cannot go in slot 2, but L still could! This would allow O L N J M K. Also note that in our diagram, one of L or M must be inexperienced (because slot 3 has an I), but we don't know which one, so this rule adds an extra restriction.

(B) This answer is logically equivalent to the rule in answer (A), except that it switches L and M! We can eliminate for the same reasons.

(C) This rule doesn't restrict the elements enough. There's nothing keeping K and O together! For instance, we might arrange the elements like this: K L N J M O.

(D) If N is in slot 5, there's only one way to place the LM chunk—in slots 3 and 6—leaving K and O to the first two slots. That's what we want!

(E) This rule restricts K and O quite a bit. They can't go in slot 3, because they are both experienced, and now they can't go in slot 6. However, this rule would allow one of them to go in slot 5, as in the following: K N L J O M.

4. If the rule that the tour that Kaley leads is either immediately before or immediately after the tour that Olley leads is replaced with a rule that says there must be exactly two tours between the tours that Kaley and Olley lead, which of the following must be true?

    (A) Olley must lead the second tour.

    (B) Naru must lead the fifth tour.

    (C) Moquetta must lead the sixth tour.

    (D) Naru's tour can neither directly precede nor directly follow any tour led by Moquetta.

    (E) Jack's tour can neither directly precede nor directly follow any tour led by Lyle.

Answer choice (D) is correct.

MANHATTAN
PREP

In this Rule Substitution question, we now have a K _ _ O or O _ _ K chunk. Since that chunk and the L_ _ M / M _ _ L chunk will have to overlap, it's wise to consider where they could go. With J in slot 4, there are only two slots—5 and 6—for the second element of each chunk. It seems that we have two options:

$$\underline{N} \quad \underline{L/M} \quad \underline{K/O} \quad \underline{J} \quad \underline{L/M} \quad \underline{K/O} \qquad\qquad \underline{N} \quad \underline{K/O} \quad \underline{L/M} \quad \underline{J} \quad \underline{K/O} \quad \underline{L/M}$$

But be careful! One of those frames is not valid. Can you see which one and why?

It's important to remember that this is a 3D Ordering game! The guide in slot 3 must be inexperienced, and since both K and O must be experienced, neither can go in slot 3. Thus, only the second frame is valid. With that in hand, let's look at the answer choices:

> (A) This answer is incorrect, because either K or O could be second.
> (B) This answer would be correct if it said "first" instead of "fifth."
> (C) M might come last, but so might L.
> (D) This answer translates to an anti-chunk: N and M cannot be consecutive. Since N is forced into slot 1, and M is in either slot 3 or slot 6, this is definitely true, so (D) is correct.
> (E) L and J could be in slots 3 and 4, respectively.

5. If the rule that there are exactly two tours between the tour that Lyle leads and the tour that Moquetta leads is replaced with the rule that there is exactly one tour between the tours that Lyle and Moquetta lead, how many different tours could Naru lead as an experienced guide?

> (A) 1
> (B) 2
> (C) 3
> (D) 4
> (E) 5

Answer choice (B) is correct.

Finally, a problem in which one of the first two answer choices is correct! (It's almost as if whoever wrote this drill wanted you to have to wrestle with a lot of wrong answers…)

If the L _ _ M/M _ _ L chunk is replaced with L _ M/M _ L, what can we infer? There are now two places that chunk could go: slots 1–3 or slots 3–5. These both work out fine (K and O stay clear of slot 3):

N can go in slot 2 or slot 6, and could be experienced in either case.

Conclusion

Even to the well-prepared test-taker, 3D Ordering games can be intimidating at first glance. And while some of these games are much more bark than bite, some provide a good serving of both. This is exactly the sort of game that separates the average test-taker from the more prepared one, and is thus *exactly the sort of game on which you can distinguish yourself.* Let's look at the three hurdles:

1. **Identifying the game type**

   - It's easy to confuse these games with others that we'll learn about later *if you ignore the ordering.* The ordering aspect of these games is their anchor.

2. **Front-end or back-end game**

   - While we're seeing more back-end 3D Ordering games lately, you have to stay vigilant. The true danger is that you might not notice when a game is a front-end game. But thankfully, your experience on the first two questions will generally give you a not-so-gentle warning if you've done that.

3. **Rule questions**

   - While not specific to 3D Ordering games, Rule questions can certainly be intimidating! They're often designed to take more time, so if you want to get to them, you better develop an efficient approach to the Standard questions. Since the majority of the questions you face will be Standard questions, gaining time on these will leave you the extra room you need to think through the occasional Rule question. But if you are struggling to make it through the Standard questions in time, it may be wise to just guess and move on if you encounter a tough Equivalent Rule question.

   - That said, there are definitely some moves to speed up the process. For Equivalent Rule questions, spend a moment considering what the original rule means. For Rule Substitution, consciously decide whether the question warrants a new diagram, and look for answers that relate to the new rule's impact.

Practice Game 1: PT53, S2, G3

Let's put your new skills to work with this 3D Ordering game. We've added a tough question on the next page.

Detectives investigating a citywide increase in burglaries questioned exactly seven suspects—S, T, V, W, X, Y, and Z—each on a different one of seven consecutive days. Each suspect was questioned exactly once. Any suspect who confessed did so while being questioned. The investigation conformed to the following:

> T was questioned on day three.
> The suspect questioned on day four did not confess.
> S was questioned after W was questioned.
> Both X and V were questioned after Z was questioned.
> No suspects confessed after W was questioned.
> Exactly two suspects confessed after T was questioned.

12. Which one of the following could be true?

   (A) X was questioned on day one.
   (B) V was questioned on day two.
   (C) Z was questioned on day four.
   (D) W was questioned on day five.
   (E) S was questioned on day six.

13. If Z was the second suspect to confess, then each of the following statements could be true EXCEPT:

   (A) T confessed.
   (B) T did not confess.
   (C) V did not confess.
   (D) X confessed.
   (E) Y did not confess.

14. If Y was questioned after V but before X, then which one of the following could be true?

   (A) V did not confess.
   (B) Y confessed.
   (C) X did not confess.
   (D) X was questioned on day four.
   (E) Z was questioned on day two.

MANHATTAN
PREP

15. Which one of the following suspects must have been questioned before T was questioned?

    (A) V
    (B) W
    (C) X
    (D) Y
    (E) Z

16. If X and Y both confessed, then each of the following could be true EXCEPT:

    (A) V confessed.
    (B) X was questioned on day five.
    (C) Y was questioned on day one.
    (D) Z was questioned on day one.
    (E) Z did not confess.

17. If neither X nor V confessed, then which one of the following must be true?

    (A) T confessed.
    (B) V was questioned on day two.
    (C) X was questioned on day four.
    (D) Y confessed.
    (E) Z did not confess.

18. Which of the following, if substituted for the rule that exactly two suspects confessed after T was questioned, would have the same effect both in determining the order in which suspects were questioned and in identifying which suspects confessed during questioning?

    (A) The final suspect to confess was the sixth suspect questioned.
    (B) W and the suspect questioned immediately before W were the last two suspects to confess.
    (C) W was the last suspect to confess.
    (D) The suspects questioned fifth and sixth both confessed.
    (E) S was questioned last and immediately after W.

Solutions: PT53, S2, G3

Answer Key

12. B   16. A
13. E   17. D
14. A   18. D
15. E

Step 1: Picture the Game

Wow! What a tough game! We can get this, though, if we diagram effectively and use the diagram to make wise inferences. This is clearly an Ordering game. The suspects will be interviewed in some order, 1 through 7. But there's an extra dimension here. Each suspect will either confess or not confess during the interview. So we have to put suspects in positions (day interviewed), and the positions have two characteristic options: confession or no confession. The 3D Number Line is the most appropriate diagram for this job. We'll use a "C" for confession and an "N" for no confession:

```
Confession:  __ __ __ __ __ __ __   CN

Suspect:     __ __ __ __ __ __ __   STVWXYZ
              1  2  3  4  5  6  7
```

Step 2: Notate the Rules and Make Inferences

Here's where the tough work really begins. Making and tracking inferences during the setup is crucial. If we passively notate the rules without thinking about what the implications are, we won't have a chance to uncover the key inferences. Think as you diagram. Actively search for inferences. Let's walk through the rules slowly. The first two are fairly easy to deal with:

> T was questioned on day three.
> The suspect questioned on day four did not confess.

The next two rules are Relative Ordering rules. As always, we'll use connecting lines to indicate the relative ordering of the letters. We can make some standard inferences from them:

> S was questioned after W was questioned.
> Both X and V were questioned after Z was questioned.

MANHATTAN
PREP

Confession: _ _ _ N _ _ _   CN

W—S

Suspect: _ _ T _ _ _ _   STVWXYZ

Z ⟨ X
      V

1 2 3 4 5 6 7
8   Z̶ 8̶
X̶   Z̶
X̶

And now for the last two rules. Here's where we really need to do some thinking:

> No suspects confessed after W was questioned.
> Exactly two suspects confessed after T was questioned.

We already know that S comes after W, so S must *not* confess if no one after W confesses. Note that this says nothing about whether W himself confesses. We know that no one *after* W confesses, but we're unsure of W himself.

If exactly two suspects confess after T, then W must come after T, right? Remember, no one can confess after W. So if T is in the third slot, we must have exactly two confessions after the third slot. Slot 4 is already a no confession slot (from a previous rule), so we must have exactly two confessions in slots 5, 6, or 7. But remember that we must leave room for S, a no confession suspect, after W. Thus, we must get confessions in slots 5 and 6, with W in 6 and S in 7:

Confession: _ _ _ N C C N   CN

W—S

Suspect: _ _ T _ _ W S   STVWXYZ

Z ∕ X
      V

1 2 3 4 5 6 7
8   Z̶ 8̶
X̶   Z̶
X̶

That's a lot of work just to get this rule on the page, but don't be afraid to follow the inference chain if it seems like it's going somewhere good!

Step 3: The Big Pause

Now that we've got W and S in slots 6 and 7, we can go back and see that Z can't go in slots 4 or 5. Remember, X and V must come after Z. We could put exclusions under 4 and 5 to represent this or, as we've done here, we can put Z in a cloud over slots 1 and 2:

Confession: _ _ _ N C C N CN

Suspect: (Z) T _ _ W S STVWXYZ
1 2 3 4 5 6 7
8   8
X
Y

W — S

Z < X
    V

About half of the elements and subsets are left undetermined. However, there are a lot of limitations on the remaining suspects. Because Z must come before both X and V, the order of the suspects is fairly limited.

Notice that when Z is in slot 2, Y must be in slot 1, because it's the only remaining element that can precede Z. A quick scan tells us that every element is part of some rule. At this point, we're ready for the questions.

Step 4: Attack the Questions

Confession: _ _ _ N C C N CN

Suspect: (Z) T _ _ W S STVWXYZ
1 2 3 4 5 6 7
8   8
X
Y

W — S

Z < X
    V

12. Which one of the following could be true?

(A) X was questioned on day one.

(B) V was questioned on day two.

(C) Z was questioned on day four.

(D) W was questioned on day five.

(E) S was questioned on day six.

Answer choice (B) is correct.

(A) No! We've got an X exclusion under slot 1. Z has to come before X, so X can't be first.

(B) Nothing seems to prohibit this, but let's defer judgment for now instead of trying to prove that it would work. Plus, since this is the first question, it's reassuring to confirm that our diagram allows us to eliminate all the other answer choices.

(C) No! Z can't be in slot 4.

(D) No! W must be in slot 6.

(E) No! S must be in slot 7.

This question is much easier if we've done the hard, careful work of setting up the diagram and making inferences. Did you notice that this first question of the set is not an Orientation question? It's rare for this to happen, but we still checked our understanding of the rules by eliminating all the wrong answer choices.

13. If Z was the second suspect to confess, then each of the following statements could be true EXCEPT:

    (A) T confessed.

    (B) T did not confess.

    (C) V did not confess.

    (D) X confessed.

    (E) Y did not confess.

Answer choice (E) is correct.

Because it's conditional, we'll draw a hypothetical for this question. We know that there are only two possibilities for Z: slot 1 or slot 2. If Z is the second to confess, then Z can't go in slot 1, so it must go in slot 2. This also means that whoever goes in slot 1 also confessed. Since X and V must come after Z, they've got to be in slots 4 and 5, though we don't know what order they'll go in. That leaves Y to occupy slot 1.

$$\underline{C}\ \ \underline{C}\ \ \underline{}\ \ \underline{N}\ \ \underline{C}\ \ \underline{C}\ \ \underline{N}$$

$$\underline{Y}\ \ \underline{Z}\ \ \underline{T}\ \ \underline{\widehat{X,V}}\ \ \underline{W}\ \ \underline{S}$$
$$\ \ 1\ \ \ \ 2\ \ \ \ 3\ \ \ \ 4\ \ \ \ 5\ \ \ 6\ \ \ 7$$

Like any "could be true EXCEPT" question, this one can be translated to "Which one must be false?" That means we'll have one correct answer that must be false and four incorrect ones that could (or must) be true.

    (A) This could be true, since we have no information about T's confession. Eliminate.

    (B) Eliminate! We still have no information about T's confession slot.

    (C) We know that V will go in slot 4 or 5. Slot 4 is a no confession slot, and slot 5 is a confession slot. So this could be true.

    (D) The same is true for X. It could go in slot 4 or 5, so this could be true.

    (E) Our diagram tells us that Y must confess. Answer (E) must be false and is therefore correct. Note that because the new condition forced Y and Z into certain slots and forced them both to confess, we could have expected that the correct answer would reference one of those two elements.

14. If Y was questioned after V but before X, then which one of the following could be true?

    (A) V did not confess.

    (B) Y confessed.

    (C) X did not confess.

    (D) X was questioned on day four.

    (E) Z was questioned on day two.

Answer choice (A) is correct.

If Y was questioned after V but before X, Z must be in the first slot (since Y is the only suspect that can go ahead of Z). We'll sketch out a hypothetical next to the question. If Y is after V but before X, Y must go in slot 4, V must go in slot 2, and X must go in slot 5. Since this is a "could be true" question, we can expect the answer to refer to Z, V, or T, the only three suspects for whom there is still something undetermined.

$$
\begin{array}{ccccccc}
\rule{1.5em}{0.5pt} & \rule{1.5em}{0.5pt} & \rule{1.5em}{0.5pt} & N & C & C & N \\
Z & V & T & Y & X & W & S \\
\hline
1 & 2 & 3 & 4 & 5 & 6 & 7
\end{array}
$$

(A) This choice involves V, and nothing seems to prohibit V from confessing. Since it's the first answer, we'd probably spend an extra moment to confirm that it could be true instead of eliminating all the other answers. But we could also defer judgment for now.

(B) No! Y is in slot 4, which is a no confession slot.

(C) No! X is in slot 5, which is a confession slot.

(D) No! X must be questioned on day five in this scenario.

(E) No! Even though this refers to Z, and we don't know if Z confessed, we do know that Z must be questioned on day one.

15. Which one of the following suspects must have been questioned before T was questioned?

    (A) V

    (B) W

    (C) X

    (D) Y

    (E) Z

Answer choice (E) is correct.

This is a free point if we've got the correct diagram.

MANHATTAN
PREP

16. If X and Y both confessed, then each of the following could be true EXCEPT:

   (A) V confessed.
   (B) X was questioned on day five.
   (C) Y was questioned on day one.
   (D) Z was questioned on day one.
   (E) Z did not confess.

Answer choice (A) is correct.

This "could be true EXCEPT" question can be translated to "Which of the following must be false?"

If X and Y both confessed, then neither X nor Y can go in slot 4 (since slot 4 is a no confession slot). We already know that Z can't go in 4, so this leaves V in slot 4. So V does not confess. Therefore, (A) must be false.

17. If neither X nor V confessed, then which one of the following must be true?

   (A) T confessed.
   (B) V was questioned on day two.
   (C) X was questioned on day four.
   (D) Y confessed.
   (E) Z did not confess.

Answer choice (D) is correct.

If neither X nor V confessed, then we can't have either in slot 5, since it is a confession slot. Thus, Y must be in slot 5, Z in slot 1, and X and V in slots 2 and 4, not necessarily in that order:

$$
\begin{array}{ccccccc}
\_ & N & \_ & N & C & C & N \\
Z & V/X & T & X/V & Y & W & S \\
1 & 2 & 3 & 4 & 5 & 6 & 7
\end{array}
$$

We're looking for something that must be true, so we should be quick to defer on any answer that refers to the confession slots for Z, V, T, or X. We might want to go hunting for an answer that refers to Y, since its position and confession status are set.

   (A) We don't have any information on T's confession slot, so this certainly could be true, but it doesn't have to be.
   (B) Again, could be true, but doesn't have to be true. X could also go in slot 2.
   (C) Could be true but doesn't have to be true. V could also go in slot 4.
   (D) Yes! Y is in slot 5, which is a confession slot.
   (E) We know nothing about Z's confession slot in this case. Could be true but doesn't have to be true.

18. Which of the following, if substituted for the rule that exactly two suspects confessed after T was questioned, would have the same effect both in determining the order in which suspects were questioned and in identifying which suspects confessed during questioning?

   (A) The final suspect to confess was the sixth suspect questioned.

   (B) W and the suspect questioned immediately before W were the last two suspects to confess.

   (C) W was the last suspect to confess.

   (D) The suspects questioned fifth and sixth both confessed.

   (E) S was questioned last and immediately after W.

Answer choice (D) is correct.

We added this Equivalent Rule question to keep you on your toes (the LSAT didn't yet dish out this question type when this game came out).

The first step is to understand the original rule. What is the effect of exactly two suspects confessing after T is questioned? Since T is questioned third, this gives us two N's and two C's in slots 4–7. Another rule tells us that the suspect in slot 4 does not confess, so we're left with two Cs and an N to place in slots 5–7. From the fact that all suspects questioned after W must not confess, we can then infer that the order of these must be C C N.

The chain of inferences from the original rule looks like this:

2 C's after T ➔ 5–7 have 2 C's and 1 N ➔ C, C, N in 5, 6, and 7, respectively ➔ W and S in 6 and 7, respectively.

The three links correspond roughly to the three options that we discussed in creating Equivalent Rule answers. And the correct answer could provide us an equivalent for any part of that chain.

Let's dive into the answer choices, looking to eliminate but ready to defer judgement:

(A) This answer puts a C in slot 6, but what about slot 5? Eliminate.

(B) It would be very reasonable to defer judgment on this very tempting answer. It seems that if W confesses along with the suspect questioned before him, we can infer that W must go in slot 6. However, there's no reason that W couldn't go in slot 2, putting an N in each of slots 3–7. That's not allowed in the original diagram. Eliminate.

(C) As with (B), according to this rule we could have W in slot 2 (or, in this case, even slot 1) and have every subsequent suspect not confess. And, as with (A), we definitely have not determined from this rule that a C must go in the fifth slot. Adios.

(D) This might have been a tough answer to spot, but armed with a solid grip on the meaning of the original rule, we can see that this rule is an equivalent to the given rule. If the sixth suspect confesses, we know that W and S are in slots 6 and 7, because after W, no one else can confess. So now we have C C N in slots 5–7, with W and S in slots 6 and 7. This rule gives us the exact same consequences as the original rule.

(E) This answer doesn't establish that slot 5 has an N or that W confessed.

MANHATTAN
PREP

Practice Game 2: PT30, S1, G3

Exactly five cars—Frank's, Marquitta's, Orlando's, Taishah's, and Vinquetta's—are washed, each exactly once. The cars are washed one at a time, with each receiving exactly one kind of wash: regular, super, or premium. The following conditions must apply:

The first car washed does not receive a super wash, though at least one car does.

Exactly one car receives a premium wash.

The second and third cars washed receive the same kind of wash as each other.

Neither Orlando's nor Taishah's is washed before Vinquetta's.

Marquitta's is washed before Frank's, but after Orlando's.

Marquitta's and the car washed immediately before Marquitta's receive regular washes.

11. Which one of the following could be an accurate list of the cars in the order in which they are washed, matched with type of wash received?

(A) Orlando's: premium; Vinquetta's: regular; Taishah's: regular; Marquitta's: regular; Frank's: super

(B) Vinquetta's: premium; Orlando's: regular; Taishah's: regular; Marquitta's: regular; Frank's: super

(C) Vinquetta's: regular; Marquitta's: regular; Taishah's: regular; Orlando's: super; Frank's: super

(D) Vinquetta's: super; Orlando's: regular; Marquitta's: regular; Frank's: regular; Taishah's: super

(E) Vinquetta's: premium; Orlando's: regular; Marquitta's: regular; Frank's: regular; Taishah's: regular

12. If Vinquetta's car does not receive a premium wash, which one of the following must be true?

(A) Orlando's and Vinquetta's cars receive the same kind of wash as each other.

(B) Marquitta's and Taishah's cars receive the same kind of wash as each other.

(C) The fourth car washed receives a premium wash.

(D) Orlando's car is washed third.

(E) Marquitta's car is washed fourth.

13. If the last two cars washed receive the same kind of wash as each other, then which one of the following could be true?

   (A) Orlando's car is washed third.
   (B) Taishah's car is washed fifth.
   (C) Taishah's car is washed before Marquitta's car.
   (D) Vinquetta's car receives a regular wash.
   (E) Exactly one car receives a super wash.

14. Which one of the following must be true?

   (A) Vinquetta's car receives a premium wash.
   (B) Exactly two cars receive a super wash.
   (C) The fifth car washed receives a super wash.
   (D) The fourth car washed receives a super wash.
   (E) The second car washed receives a regular wash.

15. Which one of the following is a complete and accurate list of the cars that must receive a regular wash?

   (A) Frank's, Marquitta's
   (B) Marquitta's, Orlando's
   (C) Marquitta's, Orlando's, Taishah's
   (D) Marquitta's, Taishah's
   (E) Marquitta's, Vinquetta's

16. Suppose that in addition to the original five cars Jabrohn's car is also washed. If all the other conditions hold as given, which one of the following CANNOT be true?

   (A) Orlando's car receives a premium wash.
   (B) Vinquetta's car receives a super wash.
   (C) Four cars receive a regular wash.
   (D) Only the second and third cars washed receive a regular wash.
   (E) Jabrohn's car is washed after Frank's car.

Try a question that we wrote for this game (assume that the rule change in question 16 is not applicable):

17. Which of the following, if substituted for the rule that the first car washed does not receive a super wash, though at least one car does, would have the same effect in determining the order of car washes and the type of each?

   (A) Vinquetta's car can receive only a regular or premium wash.
   (B) No more than three cars receive a regular wash.
   (C) Frank's car receives a super wash if, and only if, Taishah's car receives a regular or premium wash.
   (D) All cars except Frank's and Taishah's must receive either a regular or premium wash.
   (E) Either Frank's or Taishah's car receives a super wash, and no other car can receive that type of wash.

Solutions: PT30, S1, G3

Answer Key

11.	B	15.	B
12.	A	16.	A
13.	B	17.	E
14.	E		

Step 1: Picture the Game

Another tough game, with lots of rules and lots of inferences to make! The cars will be washed in some order, 1 through 5, and each car will receive one of three types of wash. So the cars are put in positions, and the positions have three characteristic possibilities. Clearly, the 3D Number Line is what we need for this job:

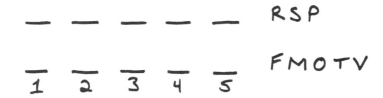

Step 2: Notate the Rules and Make Inferences

With a lot of rules, and some rules having two parts, it's important to take our time. Take a look at how we notated each rule and the basic inferences we drew (there's a bit more to infer—we'll get to that in a moment). If you have something radically different, take some time to figure out where your process went wrong. If you have a cosmetic difference—for example, perhaps you didn't note R/P in slot 1 or perhaps you didn't note the numerical limitations the same way—don't worry, those are basically issues of style. (Though feel free to steal our style!)

$$\cancel{S}$$

S - 1$^+$
P - 1

$$\underline{P/R} \quad \underline{\quad} = \underline{\quad} \quad \underline{\quad} \quad \underline{\quad}$$

RSP

$$\underline{V} \quad \overset{R}{\underbrace{O-M-F, T}}$$

FMOTV

$$\underset{1}{\underline{\quad}} \quad \underset{2}{\underline{\quad}} \quad \underset{3}{\underline{\quad}} \quad \underset{4}{\underline{\quad}} \quad \underset{5}{\underline{\quad}}$$

```
        ┌─R   R─┐
    O   │     M │ - F
  V     └───────┘
    T
```

Did you catch the odd-looking way we combined the Relative Ordering rule and the rule about the type of wash M's car receives? If that doesn't work for you, discard it.

Step 3: The Big Pause

We intentionally left out one major inference from the diagram above. This one is easy to overlook, so if you don't see anything missing in the work so far, take one more moment to look over the diagram again, considering the rules that have a strong connection with each other.

There are still inferences to mine from the intersection of the rule defining M's wash type (and that of the preceding car) and the rule that requires that the second and third cars receive the same wash type. From this intersection, we can determine the wash types for slots 2 and 3.

Because M is between O and F, it can go only in slot 3 or 4. If M goes in slot 3, both slots 2 and 3 receive an R, since we know that M and the car before it must receive an R. If M goes in slot 4, again, because of the rule about M's wash type, we know that slot 3 must also receive an R. And, since slots 2 and 3 receive the same type of wash, slot 2 receives an R as well. Thus, regardless of whether M is in slot 3 or 4, slots 2 and 3 receive R's.

Another inference we can make is about S. Since it can't go in slots 1–3, and we must have at least one S, we know we have to place an S in slot 4, slot 5, or both.

Did you miss all of those inferences the first time you played the game? If so, it's probably a sign that you didn't take enough time to complete your diagram and consider the game as a whole.

Our final diagram looks like this:

Did you frame this game? It's one approach you can use, but not a necessary one. There are some frameable divisions in this game, though probably the most promising is the two positions for M:

Frame 1   Frame 2

If you used frames, replay the game without them. If you didn't, replay the game with them. You'll see that the frames help with several questions, but you can also efficiently solve the game without them.

Step 4: Attack the Questions

11. Which one of the following could be an accurate list of the cars in the order in which they are washed, matched with type of wash received?

   (A) Orlando's: premium; Vinquetta's: regular; Taishah's: regular; Marquitta's: regular; Frank's: super

   (B) Vinquetta's: premium; Orlando's: regular; Taishah's: regular; Marquitta's: regular; Frank's: super

   (C) Vinquetta's: regular; Marquitta's: regular; Taishah's: regular; Orlando's: super; Frank's: premium

   (D) Vinquetta's: super; Orlando's: regular; Marquitta's: regular; Frank's: regular; Taishah's: super

   (E) Vinquetta's: premium; Orlando's: regular; Marquitta's: regular; Frank's: regular; Taishah's: regular

Answer choice (B) is correct.

With so many rules, expect that some will not yield any eliminations:

> The first rule eliminates answer (D).
>
> The second rule doesn't eliminate anything remaining (but would have eliminated (D) also).
>
> The third rule eliminates nothing.
>
> The fourth rule eliminates answer (A).
>
> The fifth rule eliminates answer (C). Down to (B) and (E).
>
> The sixth rule eliminates nothing!

Keep your calm, and swing through the rules one more time with answers (B) and (E). It turns out that the first rule eliminates (E) as well. If we had broken the first rule into its two components—no S in the first slot, and there must be at least one S—we could have avoided doing a second pass.

12. If Vinquetta's car does not receive a premium wash, which one of the following must be true?

(A) Orlando's and Vinquetta's cars receive the same kind of wash as each other.

(B) Marquitta's and Taishah's cars receive the same kind of wash as each other.

(C) The fourth car washed receives a premium wash.

(D) Orlando's car is washed third.

(E) Marquitta's car is washed fourth.

Answer choice (A) is correct.

We know that V must receive a regular wash. So what can we infer? Since we must have one premium wash, we know that slots 4 and 5 have an S and P, though not necessarily in that order. Since this is the second question, which is usually on the simpler side of the spectrum, we probably can get away without drawing out a hypothetical. (If we use the frames we discussed, we can infer that we are dealing with the first one; therefore, we have O and M in slots 2 and 3.)

> (A) Must be true. Since O must be in slot 2 or 3, it receives a regular wash. Pull the trigger and move on.

We wouldn't check, but of course, all the other answers could be false, or are false:

> (B) Could be false. T is in slot 4 or 5, and so might receive a P or an S wash.
>
> (C) Could be false. Slot 4 might have an S wash.
>
> (D) False! O is second.
>
> (E) False! M is third.

13. If the last two cars washed receive the same kind of wash as each other, then which one of the following could be true?

    (A) Orlando's car is washed third.

    (B) Taishah's car is washed fifth.

    (C) Taishah's car is washed before Marquitta's car.

    (D) Vinquetta's car receives a regular wash.

    (E) Exactly one car receives a super wash.

Answer choice (B) is correct.

What could those last two washes be? They must be both S's, since we need at least one S, and slots 1–3 can't have an S. Since we need one P, we put that in the first slot. But don't forget that this is a 3D game. What can we infer about the bottom row? Since M and the preceding car must receive an R wash, M must go in slot 3. Thus, we have the following:

We're looking for something that could be true, so let's scan our answers for something involving F or T, the two elements that are not completely determined. Answer (B) is something that could be true—T is in slot 4 or 5. Of course, the other answers all must be false.

14. Which one of the following must be true?

    (A) Vinquetta's car receives a premium wash.

    (B) Exactly two cars receive a super wash.

    (C) The fifth car washed receives a super wash.

    (D) The fourth car washed receives a super wash.

    (E) The second car washed receives a regular wash.

Answer choice (E) is correct.

Our hard work in diagramming this game pays off. We know that the second car must have an R. Every other answer could be false.

15. Which one of the following is a complete and accurate list of the cars that must receive a regular wash?

    (A) Frank's, Marquitta's

    (B) Marquitta's, Orlando's

    (C) Marquitta's, Orlando's, Taishah's

    (D) Marquitta's, Taishah's

    (E) Marquitta's, Vinquetta's

Answer choice (B) is correct.

Let's look at our diagram before we look at the answer choices. We know that M has to receive a regular wash, along with whichever cars are in slots 2 and 3. Who must go in one of those two slots? O! We might quickly consider T, but we know that it could go in slot 4 or 5 and not receive a regular wash.

Alternatively, we might have looked at the answer choices after a shorter consideration of the question stem. Since M is in every answer choice, no need to think about it. O is in two choices, so it's worth considering. Once we realize that it must receive a regular wash, we're down to answers (B) and (C). We just need to confirm that T doesn't need a regular wash, and we're done.

Of course, if you framed this game, you probably took a quick look at your frames and saw that M and O are the only cars that must always receive an R.

16. Suppose that in addition to the original five cars Jabrohn's car is also washed. If all the other conditions hold as given, which one of the following CANNOT be true?

(A) Orlando's car receives a premium wash.

(B) Vinquetta's car receives a super wash.

(C) Four cars receive a regular wash.

(D) Only the second and third cars washed receive a regular wash.

(E) Jabrohn's car is washed after Frank's car.

Answer choice (A) is correct.

A Rule Substitution question! Here we're adding a sixth car to the game. Though it's likely you redrew the diagram—a fine decision, we might add—let's take a look at how a test-taker might have done this by simply amending the diagram.

We'll start by adding another position:

Now, what do we have to change? Perhaps the most obvious change is that there is now an element other than V that could take the first position.

MANHATTAN
PREP

Another important change is that we can no longer infer that slots 2 and 3 definitely receive R's. Perhaps M is in slot 5 now, requiring R's only in slots 4 and 5.

Also notice that S is no longer restricted to the last two slots. It's possible to place S's in both slots 2 and 3.

On this question, it's probably easier to work from scratch than to amend the diagram, but either way, you should have arrived at a diagram like this:

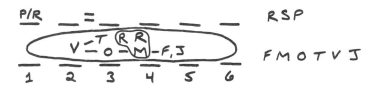

There are a lot of restrictions we could write in—all the places where M cannot go, for example—but we don't have the time to do that just for this one question. We'll figure out those restrictions as we need them.

We've done enough homework—let's look at the answer choices. We're looking for something that must be false. Ideally, it would be notated in our diagram already, but considering how few restrictions we drew in, that's unlikely. Since four of the answers will be things that could be true, that might be time-consuming to confirm. Let's look for something that must be false.

Answer choice (A) must be false. This calls for a bit of thought. Where could O go? With one element forced before it, and two forced after it, O can only go in slots 2–4. Could it receive a P in any of those positions? No. In slots 2 and 3, P is forbidden since those two slots must share a wash type and there is only one P. If O is placed in slot 4, that means M and F are in slots 5 and 6, respectively, meaning that O must receive an R, since it would be the element directly before M.

All the other answers could be true:

(B) V could go in slot 2 and receive an S, along with whatever car is in slot 3.
(C) Slots 2–5 could receive R's, leaving a P for slot 1 and an S for slot 6.
(D) M could go in slot 3, P in slot 1, and slots 4–6 could be S's.
(E) There are no restrictions on where J can go.

17. Which of the following, if substituted for the rule that the first car washed does not receive a super wash, though at least one car does, would have the same effect in determining the order of car washes and the type of each?

(A) Vinquetta's car can receive only a regular or premium wash.
(B) No more than three cars receive a regular wash.
(C) Frank's car receives a super wash if, and only if, Taishah's car receives a regular or premium wash.
(D) All cars except Frank's and Taishah's must receive either a regular or premium wash.
(E) Either Frank's or Taishah's car receives a super wash, and no other car can receive that type of wash.

Answer choice (E) is correct.

We wrote this Equivalent Rule question to give you more practice with this question type. Note that the LSAT would not ask such a question right after a Rule Substitution question! We'll ignore question 16 in solving this one.

Let's start by understanding the consequences of the original rule. If slot 1 (car V) cannot be an S, we know that it must be a P or an R. No other consequences may spring to mind, but remember that this is a two-part rule. The last part tells us that at least one car does receive an S. Since slots 1–3 can't receive an S (due to various rules and their interactions), we can infer that there must be an S in slot 4 or 5. It's important to note that S's could be placed in *both* slots 4 and 5.

Let's dive into the answer choices:

(A) We can eliminate this answer since it only deals with the first half of the rule.

(B) This answer provides an equivalent only for the second part! With (B) in place, we know that there must be at least one S, but there's nothing stopping us from placing an S in slot 1.

(C) This is a complex answer choice, but we don't see any restriction placed on S going in slot 1. Eliminate! Furthermore, there's no reason that F and T can't both have S's.

(D) This answer restricts S to F and T. But we also need to require an S. With this answer, it's possible to avoid having any S's.

(E) Here we get both parts of the original rule. The second part of this answer restricts V from receiving a super wash. It isn't a problem that it also restricts O in the same way; we learned in question 15 that O must receive a regular wash. The first part of this answer requires either F or T to receive an S, and this can only happen in slots 4 and 5. Note that the answer does not state "but not both," so it's possible that both receive an S.

MANHATTAN
PREP

Chapter 6

Ordering Twists

In This Chapter. . .

Getting Familiar

Give yourself **10 minutes to complete this game.** Use whatever approaches you see fit. However, it's important to remember that this is still an Ordering game, so adapt what you know instead of creating something new.

Doctor X will see exactly five of seven patients—K, L, M, N, O, P, and Q—that are all waiting in the lobby. She will see these patients one at a time and in order. The following conditions apply:

She will see both K and M, and she will see K before M.

If she does not see O, she will see P.

She will see Q or P, but not both.

If she sees either L or O, she will see them after M.

If she sees N, she must see N first.

1. Which of the following could be the order of patients that Doctor X sees, from first to last?

   (A) N, Q, K, M, P
   (B) N, Q, K, O, M
   (C) N, Q, K, M, L
   (D) N, Q, K, M, O
   (E) N, Q, M, K, O

2. Each of the following could be true EXCEPT:

   (A) The doctor sees Q first.
   (B) The doctor sees M second.
   (C) The doctor sees K fourth.
   (D) The doctor sees P last.
   (E) The doctor sees Q last.

3. If the doctor sees K third, which of the following must be true?

   (A) She sees N first.
   (B) She sees Q second.
   (C) She sees L last.
   (D) She sees P.
   (E) She sees O.

4. Which of the following must be true?

   (A) If the doctor does not see L, she will also not see Q.
   (B) If the doctor does not see N, she will also not see P.
   (C) If the doctor does not see Q, she will also not see P.
   (D) If the doctor does not see Q, she will also not see O.
   (E) If the doctor does not see O, she will also not see Q.

5. If the doctor sees M fourth, which of the following could be true?

   (A) The doctor sees K first.
   (B) The doctor sees K second.
   (C) The doctor sees P first.
   (D) The doctor sees Q last.
   (E) The doctor sees P last.

6. Which of the following, if true, would determine which patients the doctor will see and the order in which she will see them?

   (A) The doctor sees N first and P third.
   (B) The doctor sees N first and Q third.
   (C) The doctor sees K first and M second.
   (D) The doctor sees K first and O fourth.
   (E) The doctor sees K second and M fourth.

Ordering Twists

Now that you've mastered the major types of Ordering games, we need to look at some important variations on those fundamental themes. Up until now, things have been pretty straightforward: When there were seven positions to fill, we had seven elements to fill those positions, and the elements were generally one homogenous group (e.g., students; clowns; trucks). This is the LSAT, though, and things are not always so simple. In this chapter, we'll examine variations on the basic themes. We'll start with the two most common: Sometimes the number of positions is different than the number of elements, creating a **mismatch;** other times, the elements are divided into different sets, which we call **subgroups.** Let's take a deeper look at each of these **twists.**

Mismatch

As you just experienced, Ordering games with a mismatch contain a small but important departure from Basic Ordering games. Our elements and positions can no longer be matched up one to one!

What Defines a Mismatch?

There are two basic flavors of mismatch in Ordering games. There are either **extra elements** or **extra positions.**

Imagine you're a personal trainer trying to schedule five consecutive training sessions, but you have seven people who want appointments. You have *extra elements*. How could this be resolved in real life? You could either tell two people that they have to skip their sessions or you could turn a session into a group class and double (or even triple) up on elements.

The other mismatch flavor might involve a film festival with eight consecutive times for showings, but only five films to show. Here, we have *extra positions*. There are two solutions. Either some of those films need to be shown more than once or some showtimes need to remain empty.

That's it! There are either extra elements, extra positions, or some combination of the two flavors. (If you're wondering how there can be extra elements *and* extra positions, just you wait and see!)

MANHATTAN
PREP

Extra Elements

The most common type of ordering mismatch is one in which there are extra elements. The key to picturing these games is to draw slots where we can track excluded positions. For example, imagine there were six potential elements—P, Q, R, S, T, and U—but only four positions. Your diagram should look like this:

In the game above, we probably wouldn't come across a rule telling us that R comes before S, since we're not even sure whether R and S are in! Instead, it's more common to see a conditional rule, something like "If R and S are both performing in the show, then R performs at some time before S." The conditional nature of that rule allows R and S to end up in the excluded slots.

Less commonly, you'll face a game in which the slots are allowed to hold more than one element—we call this "doubling up." At times, the rules will define which position or positions hold more than one element; at other times, it's left unclear. If you know which slots will double (or triple) up, then notate that accordingly:

$$\underline{\quad} \quad \quad \quad \underline{\quad} \quad \text{P Q R S T U}$$
$$\underline{\quad}_1 \quad \underline{\quad}_2 \quad \underline{\quad}_3 \quad \underline{\quad}_4$$

However, if you are not sure which position or positions will double up, you can place an extra line above every position, like so:

$$\underline{\quad} \quad \underline{\quad} \quad \underline{\quad} \quad \underline{\quad} \quad \text{P Q R S T U}$$
$$\underline{\quad}_1 \quad \underline{\quad}_2 \quad \underline{\quad}_3 \quad \underline{\quad}_4$$

Alternatively, you can use a standard Number Line and remember that doubling up must occur. Often, the rules will help define where the doubling up can or does occur.

It's easy to incorrectly assume that every slot in an ordering game must be filled. Be sure to ask yourself whether that's true for each game. While it's probably unnecessary for most folks, if you like to be very thorough in your diagramming and want to make it clear that in a certain game each position receives at least one element, a way to notate that (and in a way that is consistent with how we'll handle some future game types) is to place a box over each slot on the bottom row:

Dealing with mismatches in your diagram isn't particularly difficult, but it's crucial that you clarify the mismatch issues before you reach the questions in a game.

Before we look at how to picture the other flavor of Ordering games with a mismatch, let's return to the Getting Familiar game to get some practice in with extra elements. If you struggled with the game and think that having the excluded slots in your diagram would have dramatically helped you tackle it, feel free to replay it. Otherwise, let's dive into the solutions. Keep an eye out for situations in which tracking the excluded slots is crucial.

Try It Again

Doctor X will see exactly five of seven patients—K, L, M, N, O, P, and Q—that are all waiting in the lobby. She will see these patients one at a time and in order. The following conditions apply:

> She will see both K and M, and she will see K before M.
> If she does not see O, she will see P.
> She will see Q or P, but not both.
> If she sees either L or O, she will see them after M.
> If she sees N, she must see N first.

1. Which of the following could be the order of patients that Doctor X sees, from first to last?

   (A) N, Q, K, M, P
   (B) N, Q, K, O, M
   (C) N, Q, K, M, L
   (D) N, Q, K, M, O
   (E) N, Q, M, K, O

2. Each of the following could be true EXCEPT:

   (A) The doctor sees Q first.
   (B) The doctor sees M second.
   (C) The doctor sees K fourth.
   (D) The doctor sees P last.
   (E) The doctor sees Q last.

3. If the doctor sees K third, which of the following must be true?

   (A) She sees N first.
   (B) She sees Q second.
   (C) She sees L last.
   (D) She sees P.
   (E) She sees O.

4. Which of the following must be true?

   (A) If the doctor does not see L, she will also not see Q.
   (B) If the doctor does not see N, she will also not see P.
   (C) If the doctor does not see Q, she will also not see P.
   (D) If the doctor does not see Q, she will also not see O.
   (E) If the doctor does not see O, she will also not see Q.

5. If the doctor sees M fourth, which of the following could be true?

   (A) The doctor sees K first.
   (B) The doctor sees K second.
   (C) The doctor sees P first.
   (D) The doctor sees Q last.
   (E) The doctor sees P last.

6. Which of the following, if true, would determine which patients the doctor will see and the order in which she will see them?

   (A) The doctor sees N first and P third.
   (B) The doctor sees N first and Q third.
   (C) The doctor sees K first and M second.
   (D) The doctor sees K first and O fourth.
   (E) The doctor sees K second and M fourth.

How Did You Do?

Answer Key

1. D   4. E
2. C   5. B
3. A   6. B

Step 1: Picture the Game

The scenario makes it clear that only five of the seven elements will be ordered, so we should create a Number Line with two slots for the excluded elements. We also see a lot of conditional rules, a common feature of ordering mismatches with excluded elements.

K L M N O P Q

$$\underline{\quad}\ \underline{\quad}\ \underline{\quad}\ \underline{\quad}\ \underline{\quad} \Big| \underline{\quad}\ \underline{\quad}$$
$$\quad 1 \quad\ 2 \quad\ 3 \quad\ 4 \quad\ 5$$

Step 2: Notate the Rules and Make Inferences

She will see both K and M, and she will see K before M.

The first rule tells us who two of the five patients in the numbered slots will be, as well their relative order. You can write this off to the side, but we'd prefer to write it above our numbered slots in the Number Line.

If she does not see O, she will see P.

The second rule takes a bit more thought. We'll start by writing this as a conditional statement:

–O → P and –P → O.

So can we write something into our diagram? It can be tricky to see, but we actually do have something to fill in. If O is excluded, then P is included, and vice versa. This rule means that we can't exclude both; in other words, at least one is included! Let's write an O/P option next to the KM rule. Be careful: O and P can both be included. Take a moment to think about why and then check out our diagram so far:

K – M   P/O   K L M N O P Q

$$\underline{}\quad\underline{}\quad\underline{}\quad\underline{}\quad\underline{}\ \Big|\ \underline{}\quad\underline{}$$
1   2   3   4   5

–O → P
–P → O

She will see Q or P, but not both.

This rule is similar to the second one in that it requires one of two specific elements to be included. However, unlike the second rule, this one tells us that we can't have both included. In simpler terms, one is included and one is excluded. What will this rule look like written out? Since we know we have Q or P in and the other one out, this is a biconditional:

Q ⟷ –P and P ⟷ –Q.

Feel free to write out that conditional, but we'd recommend instead writing this into your diagram. Create linked options, with Q/P included and P/Q excluded. We'll write Q/P above our Number Line and reserve one of the excluded slots for P/Q. Notice that we've filled up half of our excluded slots. If we can fill that other one during the game, then we'll know who's in (everyone else), with the exception of the Q/P choice.

If she sees either L or O, she will see them after M.

Be careful: this rule doesn't tell us that the doctor definitely sees either L or O (we already know she sees M). But *if* the doctor sees L, then L is after M; same with O. Since either L or O would trigger this rule, we can split the rule in two:

L → M –L and O → M –O.

On to our last rule: If N is in, N is first. It's easy enough to write the rule to the side, but let's see if we can put the rule into the diagram. We can't put an N in slot 1, since we don't know if N is included or excluded. But we know for sure where N *won't* go, namely slots 2–5!

At this point, our diagram looks as follows:

K – M   P/O   P/Q   K L M N O P Q

P/Q ___

___	___	___	___	___
1	2	3	4	5

N̸ (2) N̸ (3) N̸ (4) N̸ (5)

N → N̲
       1

–O → P
–P → O

Q ↔ –P
P ↔ –Q

L → M — L
O → M — O

Step 3: The Big Pause

As usual, let's take a breath before diving into the questions. A quick check shows us we have no stray elements. Do we have any connections between the rules? O and P are not only connected by the second rule, but they're also connected to other elements in the third and fourth rules, making them key elements to consider as we play this game.

Is this a game worth framing? Probably not. We *could* frame the Q/P option, the O/P option, or even N (N first; N not seen). (While we don't recommend framing a conditional situation like the N rule generally, a conditional rule that creates a binary situation is an exception. The N rule leaves only two placement options for N. One of them—N not seen—would trigger a bunch of rules by forcing the inclusion of several other elements.) Feel free to play around with those frames to decide on their value for yourself. If you frame around O/P, be sure to get all *three* frames (O in, P out; O out, P in; O and P in).

Step 4: Attack the Questions

1. Which of the following could be the order of patients that Doctor X sees, from first to last?

    (A) N, Q, K, M, P
    (B) N, Q, K, O, M
    (C) N, Q, K, M, L
    (D) N, Q, K, M, O
    (E) N, Q, M, K, O

    Answer choice (D) is correct.

The first rule (*She will see both K and M, and she will see K before M*) eliminates (E).

The second rule (*If she does not see O, she will see P*) eliminates (C).

The third rule (*She will see Q or P, but not both*) eliminates (A).

The fourth rule (*If she sees L or O, she will see them after M*) eliminates (B).

2. Each of the following could be true EXCEPT:

    (A) The doctor sees Q first.

    (B) The doctor sees M second.

    (C) The doctor sees K fourth.

    (D) The doctor sees P last.

    (E) The doctor sees Q last.

Answer choice (C) is correct.

(A) triggers several rules, which often leads to a situation that doesn't work. We should test this out. With Q first, both P and N are excluded (Q and P can't both be included; N has to be first if it's included). Everything else must be in, and there doesn't seem to be a problem with, say, Q K M O L.

(B) forces K first, which excludes N. However, it leaves open plenty of space for O and L, which we know to look out for generally, so let's defer.

(C) forces M into slot 5. Since we know M shows up in the fourth rule, we should check this answer. From the fourth rule, L and O, if included, must be later than M, which is impossible with M in the last slot. L and O are both excluded, but, with P or Q also excluded, they don't all fit. This can't be true, so it's our answer!

There is no need to confirm that the other answers could be true, but it's something you should do when reviewing the game to build your skills at creating (and working through) hypotheticals.

3. If the doctor sees K third, which of the following must be true?

    (A) She sees N first.

    (B) She sees Q second.

    (C) She sees L last.

    (D) She sees P.

    (E) She sees O.

Answer choice (A) is correct.

Let's put K third and see what we see. With K third, M must be either fourth or fifth. But, as we learned in the last question, we can't have M last (since it would force both L and O out), so M must be fourth, with either L or O last. What else? Since we can put only one of the L/O options last, we know that the other will be out. That means we're left with this:

$$\underline{}_1 \quad \underline{}_2 \quad \underline{\text{K}}_3 \quad \underline{\text{M}}_4 \quad \underline{\text{L/O}}_5 \quad \bigg| \quad \text{Q/P} \quad \text{L/O}$$

At this point, we could start looking at the answer choices, but a quick check will show us that we don't have the answer yet. Heading back to the diagram, we see that the excluded slots are filled, so everyone else is included! N must be first, with Q or P going second (whichever isn't excluded). And with that, we know the answer is (A).

4. Which of the following must be true?

    (A) If the doctor does not see L, she will also not see Q.

    (B) If the doctor does not see N, she will also not see P.

    (C) If the doctor does not see Q, she will also not see P.

    (D) If the doctor does not see Q, she will also not see O.

    (E) If the doctor does not see O, she will also not see Q.

Answer choice (E) is correct.

Glancing at the answer choices, it seems that this question will take a bit more time than others. To work wrong-to-right, we'll need to prove that the four wrong answers are not necessarily true. To prove that a conditional statement is not necessarily true, we need to show the sufficient condition can be true without the necessary condition following suit. In other words, we need a hypothetical in which the sufficient condition is true and the necessary condition is false. That sounds like a lot of work! Let's see if we can get through this without taking so much time.

(A) can be eliminated using the work from our last question. We know that L could be out and Q could be in. Eliminate.

If you didn't use previous work, it would be time-consuming to test out (A). If you run into this situation and don't have prior work to use, look over the rules to see if the elements in question are connected. Here, L and Q aren't, so let's defer judgment.

(B) doesn't raise any alarms since there's no obvious connection between N and P. Defer.

(C) is flat out false! We know we need to see either Q or P. Eliminate.

(D) raises alarms since Q and O are both related to P in our rules, so they might impact each other. However, excluding Q forces P to be included, and the conditional $-\text{O} \longrightarrow \text{P}$ isn't triggered. After raising alarms initially, this answer doesn't appear to be something that must be true.

(E) is the reverse of answer (D) and we should consider it for similar reasons. With O excluded, we know P must be included. And with P included, Q must be excluded. Here's our answer.

MANHATTAN
PREP

5. If the doctor sees M fourth, which of the following could be true?

   (A) The doctor sees K first.
   (B) The doctor sees K second.
   (C) The doctor sees P first.
   (D) The doctor sees Q last.
   (E) The doctor sees P last.

Answer choice (B) is correct.

As we worked through question 2, we noticed a new inference: at least one of L and O is included. With M fourth, L or O must go fifth and the other one is excluded. Who's left? N must be in—and first—and we have K and Q/P left. Here's our diagram:

We want something that could be true, but there's still too much up in the air to have a solid prediction.

(A) can't be true, but (B) can. Select it and move on. (Every other answer, of course, can't be true.)

6. Which of the following, if true, would determine which patients the doctor will see and the order in which she will see them?

   (A) The doctor sees N first and P third.
   (B) The doctor sees N first and Q third.
   (C) The doctor sees K first and M second.
   (D) The doctor sees K first and O fourth.
   (E) The doctor sees K second and M fourth.

Answer choice (B) is correct.

We're with you. This question is definitely the hardest of the bunch. We're looking for something that will establish which elements are included *and* in what order. It's hard to know where to get started, but it's worth 10 seconds to consider what elements will be the hardest to pin down. After all, if an answer does not determine the positions of each element, on this question it isn't correct.

In this game, every element has a rule associated with the order in which it'll appear except P and Q. We'll need to figure out their order to answer this question, so it'd be good to pick an answer that sets their location These elements each also help us decide which other elements are included and which are excluded. They're a great place to start, so we should look at (A) and (B) first.

Answer choice (A) looks promising. With N first, P third, and both K and M included, we have four of our five included elements. Who will fill the last spot? Either L or O. Since there's no reason it would have to be one or the other, we can eliminate this answer since we still have a question as to who is included.

Moving on to (B), we notice it's pretty similar. With Q in, we'd need P out. And, with P out, we'd need O in. The roster is set: Q, O, K, M, N. And, with slots 1 and 3 filled by N and Q, K–M must go in slots 2 and 4, leaving O to come after M in the final slot.

Take a moment to confirm for yourself why answers (C) through (E) would not determine the roster and order, and consider how you might have eliminated—or deferred—quickly. These questions are difficult because of time considerations. After all, you can get the right answer by testing out each answer choice, but that's definitely not the most efficient way to do so!

Extra Positions

We've looked pretty closely at the first flavor of ordering mismatches—extra elements—so let's move to the other flavor: extra positions.

As we mentioned in an earlier example, if there were only five films available to be shown at eight different showtimes, the game might require us to repeat some films. We would represent this situation in the roster with question marks representing the three unknown repeats:

F J K L M ? ? ?

```
___  ___  ___  ___  ___  ___  ___  ___
 1    2    3    4    5    6    7    8
```

Or perhaps the game calls for some positions to remain empty. Even if we weren't sure which positions were empty, we'd want to add those empty slots to our roster:

F J K L M x x x

```
___  ___  ___  ___  ___  ___  ___  ___
 1    2    3    4    5    6    7    8
```

(It may go without saying, but you can use whatever letter or symbol you want to represent the empty slots—for some, an "e" makes more sense.)

In some cases, we'll figure out which slots are empty. We'll note that as follows:

F J K L M

```
___  _\_  ___  _\_  _\_  ___  ___  ___
 1    2    3    4    5    6    7    8
```

An issue that can come up with extra positions is that empty slots impact where chunks can go. For example, in the above Number Line, if K and M had to be consecutive, where could they go? Not too many places!

If the game allows elements to be repeated, pay particular attention to rules that limit the number of times an element can be repeated. The rules won't always explicitly state these numbers—we might get a rule that says no element can go twice in a row.

Regardless of how the extra positions will be used, and regardless of the specific manner in which you make your notations, it's essential that you notice any mismatches and pay careful attention to the numbers involved. Make sure you're asking yourself the right questions: How many element repeats are needed? Can there be an empty position? How many elements need to double up—and is it possible for something to go more than twice?

Drill It: Ordering Mismatch Setups

Let's quickly practice identifying mismatches and diagramming them correctly. We suggest you check your work after each one.

1. Five political candidates—Hughes, Jones, Kampoyle, Langston, and Nordecki—will appear on a TV talk show during the course of one week, Monday through Sunday. Each candidate will appear exactly once, and no two candidates will appear on the same day. The scheduling of the candidates must adhere to the following conditions:

    > Jones must appear after Nordecki and before Kampoyle.
    >
    > Either Langston or Hughes must be the last candidate to appear.
    >
    > Kampoyle cannot appear on the day immediately following a day on which any other candidate appears.
    >
    > Nordecki cannot appear before Tuesday.

2. Exactly four emergency room doctors—Oronsky, Praya, Quayle, and Ralston—must cover all six shifts on Wednesday and Thursday. Each day is broken up into three consecutive shifts: morning, afternoon, and evening. Only one doctor will cover each shift, and each doctor must cover at least one shift. The scheduling during the two days must adhere to the following rules:

    > No doctor can cover consecutive shifts on a given day.
    >
    > The only shift that Quayle can cover is the afternoon shift on Wednesday.
    >
    > Praya will cover the morning shift on Thursday.
    >
    > Ralston will cover at least one shift before and one shift after any shift Praya takes.

3. A classical guitarist must perform five different songs from her recent album at an upcoming concert. The album contains a total of eight songs: Revolt, Stampede, Tango, Vein, Waning, Xeric, Yawn, and Zeal. The songs are played one at a time and no other songs are played during the concert. The following rules apply to the order and selection of the songs:

> If S is played, W is not.
> If T is played, it is played third.
> Either X or Y is played, but not both.
> Z is played second.
> V is played.

4. A certain banking website requires a five-digit password that must be composed entirely of the digits 0–6. The following rules apply to any one password:

> No digit may be used twice.
> Either 4 or 5 is the third digit.
> The last digit must be exactly twice the value of the first one.
> Two digits that have consecutive values cannot be used in consecutive positions in a password.

Solutions: Ordering Mismatch Setups

1.

It is easy to assume that L or H must go on Sunday, but there could be an "X" there.

2.

Often, you'll figure out the "identity" of one of the mystery repeats as you work through the game's inferences. Above, it became clear we needed at least two R's.

3.

4.

MANHATTAN
PREP

Practice Game 1: PT32, S3, G4

On each of exactly seven consecutive days (day 1 though day 7), a pet shop features exactly one of three breeds of kitten—Himalayan, Manx, Siamese—and exactly one of three breeds of puppy—Greyhound, Newfoundland, Rottweiler. The following conditions must apply:

Greyhounds are featured on day 1.
No breed is featured on any two consecutive days.
Any breed featured on day 1 is not featured on day 7.
Himalayans are featured on exactly three days, but not on day 1.
Rottweilers are not featured on day 7, nor on any day that features Himalayans.

19. Which one of the following could be the order in which the breeds of kitten are featured in the pet shop, from day 1 though day 7?

    (A) Himalayan, Manx, Siamese, Himalayan, Manx, Himalayan, Siamese

    (B) Manx, Himalayan, Siamese, Himalayan, Manx, Himalayan, Manx

    (C) Manx, Himalayan, Manx, Himalayan, Siamese, Manx, Siamese

    (D) Siamese, Himalayan, Manx, Himalayan, Siamese, Siamese, Himalayan

    (E) Siamese, Himalayan, Siamese, Himalayan, Manx, Siamese, Himalayan

20. If Himalayans are not featured on day 2, which one of the following could be true?

    (A) Manx are featured on day 3.
    (B) Siamese are featured on day 4.
    (C) Rottweilers are featured on day 5.
    (D) Himalayans are featured on day 6.
    (E) Greyhounds are featured on day 7.

21. Which one of the following could be true?

    (A) Greyhounds and Siamese are both featured on day 2.
    (B) Greyhounds and Himalayans are both featured on day 7.
    (C) Rottweilers and Himalayans are both featured on day 4.
    (D) Rottweilers and Manx are both featured on day 5.
    (E) Newfoundlands and Manx are both featured on day 6.

22. If Himalayans are not featured on day 7, then which one of the following pairs of days CANNOT feature both the same breed of kitten and the same breed of puppy?

    (A) day 1 and day 3
    (B) day 2 and day 6
    (C) day 3 and day 5
    (D) day 4 and day 6
    (E) day 5 and day 7

23. Which one of the following could be true?

    (A) There are exactly four breeds that are each featured on three days.
    (B) Greyhounds are featured on every day that Himalayans are.
    (C) Himalayans are featured on every day that Greyhounds are.
    (D) Himalayans are featured on every day that Rottweilers are not.
    (E) Rottweilers are featured on every day that Himalayans are not.

24. If Himalayans are not featured on day 7, which one of the following could be true?

    (A) Greyhounds are featured on days 3 and 5.
    (B) Newfoundlands are featured on day 3.
    (C) Rottweilers are featured on day 6.
    (D) Rottweilers are featured only on day 3.
    (E) Rottweilers are featured on exactly three days.

Solutions: PT32, S3, G4

Answer Key

19. E	22. B
20. B	23. A
21. D	24. D

Step 1: Picture the Game

From reading the scenario and scanning the rules, we quickly learn that this is not a Basic Ordering game. We have to place *both* a kitten and a puppy each day. It's a 3D Ordering game, with an equal number of options for both rows.

One issue that is hard to pin down is whether each breed must be featured. Since the scenario doesn't tell us that we need at least one of each breed, the minimum for each breed is zero.

Step 2: Notate the Rules and Make Inferences

Most of the rules should be pretty standard for you to understand at this point in your preparation, but some might have been hard to get into the diagram. Take a look at what we came up with and at some of the inferences we drew:

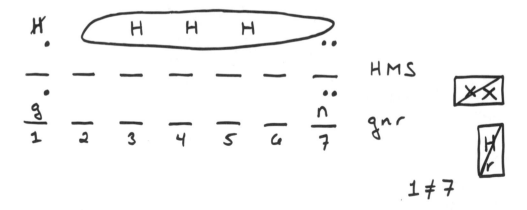

We must have an n in puppy slot 7, since the third rule cuts out g and the final rule cuts out r. We've also used an XX anti-chunk to represent that no breed can go in consecutive slots.

One notation that is new here is the use of dots. We'll use this notation more in grouping games, but in short, the way we're using it here is to indicate that if two positions on the same row have a different number of dots, they must have different breeds. It's slightly dicey using this notation here, since the two breeds in position 1 are *not* the same; but since that's a pretty fundamental fact in this game—that puppies and kitties are on different rows—we should be okay.

MANHATTAN
PREP

We're using upper and lower case to differentiate the element subsets. It was a tough decision about whether to make the kittens or puppies upper case. But since cats can be vengeful, we decided to give them top honors.

There's a bit more to infer about this game. For example, you can write "M/S" in kitty slot 1. However, most of these final inferences are the type we leave to your personal style. Still, when in doubt, write them in!

Step 3: The Big Pause

We have a pretty open diagram, and it's definitely worth a moment to consider what's going on. For starters, who is the most important element here?

Definitely H!

Where can those three H's go? There actually aren't that many options, so it wouldn't take long to sketch them out in broad fashion (go ahead and do so now if you didn't earlier).

You could have drawn something like this:

Or you could have gone a bit more into the details shown here as two frames:

We could also write out the four possibilities. Though it wouldn't take up much time, it probably isn't worth completely framing this since there aren't significant inferences flowing from each of those frames.

What *is* worth doing is noting that there are not too many ways the three H's can be arranged, and since we can't place an r anywhere we have an H, this is an important issue.

We don't have any rules attached to M or S specifically, nor do we know if we'll actually need to include both of those. However, they're technically a part of the second rule, so they're not full strays (pun intended). Let's move to the questions.

Step 4: Attack the Questions

19. Which one of the following could be the order in which the breeds of kitten are featured in the pet shop, from day 1 though day 7?

    (A) Himalayan, Manx, Siamese, Himalayan, Manx, Himalayan, Siamese
    (B) Manx, Himalayan, Siamese, Himalayan, Manx, Himalayan, Manx
    (C) Manx, Himalayan, Manx, Himalayan, Siamese, Manx, Siamese
    (D) Siamese, Himalayan, Manx, Himalayan, Siamese, Siamese, Himalayan
    (E) Siamese, Himalayan, Siamese, Himalayan, Manx, Siamese, Himalayan

Answer choice (E) is correct.

Sorry, puppies; we're focusing only on kitties here.

Let's use our diagram for this one:

> We know that H can't go first, eliminating answer (A).
> We need three H's, eliminating answer (C).
> We can't have the first and last be the same, eliminating answer (B).
> We can't have the same breed shown consecutively, eliminating answer (D).

20. If Himalayans are not featured on day 2, which one of the following could be true?

    (A) Manx are featured on day 3.
    (B) Siamese are featured on day 4.
    (C) Rottweilers are featured on day 5.
    (D) Himalayans are featured on day 6.
    (E) Greyhounds are featured on day 7.

Answer choice (B) is correct.

If there's no H in 2, we have to consider where the three H's can go. It must be slots 3, 5, and 7. There are a few inferences we can put into a quick and dirty diagram (notice that we ditched the numbering and are using just one row of lines to speed up our work):

MANHATTAN
PREP

There may be more to infer, but let's see if our first round of inferences gets us our answer:

(A) is impossible. H is there!

(B) seems fine. We'd probably confirm it, but we might move quickly through (C) through (E) instead.

(C) is the same as (A)—H is there!

(D) is wrong; there's no H there.

(E) is always impossible!

21. Which one of the following could be true?

(A) Greyhounds and Siamese are both featured on day 2.

(B) Greyhounds and Himalayans are both featured on day 7.

(C) Rottweilers and Himalayans are both featured on day 4.

(D) Rottweilers and Manx are both featured on day 5.

(E) Newfoundlands and Manx are both featured on day 6.

Answer choice (D) is correct.

Nothing to work with on this unconditional question (other than our impressive brain power and understanding of the game).

(A) is wrong since g can never go in slot 2.

We can add that to our diagram! We'll also note the similar restriction about n in slot 6.

Figuring out more about your diagram mid-game is common; be sure to add in those details to your master diagram.

(B) is a no-no—g can never go in slot 7.

(C) is another silly answer—r and H can never go together.

(D) seems okay. Let's defer, since it'll probably be faster to eliminate (E) than to confirm (D).

(E) is incorrect, since we can't have n in both slots 6 and 7.

And now we have a somewhat better master diagram:

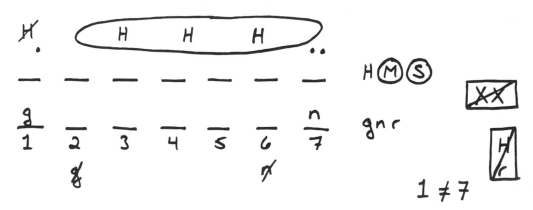

22. If Himalayans are not featured on day 7, then which one of the following pairs of days CANNOT feature both the same breed of kitten and the same breed of puppy?

  (A) day 1 and day 3
  (B) day 2 and day 6
  (C) day 3 and day 5
  (D) day 4 and day 6
  (E) day 5 and day 7

Answer choice (B) is correct.

This question stem is tricky, but let's start by making inferences from the new condition. With no H in 7, we must have H's in 2, 4, and 6. We can then draw several inferences about the bottom row based on that and the H and r restriction:

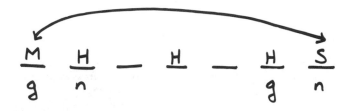

Now, it's time to understand the stem. We're asked for two slots that cannot have the same exact pair of breeds. There are a few obvious candidates in our diagram; let's see what the answers give us:

  (A) seems okay. Slot 3 is not determined, so let's defer.
  (B) is our answer! No time to confirm that the rest are wrong, but it's always fine to flag the question, and, if there's time at the end of the section, return to confirm that (C) through (E) are possible, and thus incorrect. For this question, notice that each incorrect answer refers to a slot that cannot be determined.

23. Which one of the following could be true?

  (A) There are exactly four breeds that are each featured on three days.
  (B) Greyhounds are featured on every day that Himalayans are.
  (C) Himalayans are featured on every day that Greyhounds are.
  (D) Himalayans are featured on every day that Rottweilers are not.
  (E) Rottweilers are featured on every day that Himalayans are not.

Answer choice (A) is correct.

This is definitely a much harder question than the others we've seen in this game. If you struggled a lot, hopefully you moved on and came back to it later; this question could eat up a lot of precious time. Let's look at the answer choices:

(A) is tough to confirm off the bat. It might have felt dangerous to devote the time to testing out whether, for example, we could have 3 H's, 3 M's, 1 S, 3 g's, 3 n's, and 1 r. By the way, best to not use 3 r's in creating a scenario, since that makes trouble for the 3 H's. A smart move with this answer would be to defer judgment.

(B) seems okay as well. Let's defer and try to keep our cool.

(C) is impossible! We have g in slot 1 and H can't go there. Eliminate.

(D) is a freebie elimination. Just as with (C), slot 1 proves this answer impossible.

(E) takes only a moment to eliminate, using slot 1 again. We don't have an H and we have g rather than r. Bye bye.

We're down to two answers, so now we can simply test out either one. We'll test (B), since there's a bit more to work with. Could we have a g every time we have an H?

Since we couldn't have an H and thus a g in slot 2 (there's a g in slot 1), we'll start by pushing the three H's down to 3, 5, and 7. Wait, then we'd need a g in slot 7 and we have n there already. Eliminate!

24. If Himalayans are not featured on day 7, which one of the following could be true?

   (A) Greyhounds are featured on days 3 and 5.

   (B) Newfoundlands are featured on day 3.

   (C) Rottweilers are featured on day 6.

   (D) Rottweilers are featured only on day 3.

   (E) Rottweilers are featured on exactly three days.

Answer choice (D) is correct.

We know the drill on this new condition. With no H in 7, the H's go in slots 2, 4, and 6. We have worked this out already on question 22. We'll look at the work we did there:

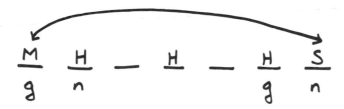

Hopefully the answers will be in this diagram already:

   (A) is impossible, since we have a g in slot 6.

   (B) is impossible, since we have an n in slot 2. (Note that we could have written out those restrictions in our diagram.)

   (C) is impossible. Slot 6 is quite full.

   (D) works—there's no problem having an r in slot 3 and then filling up the rest of the diagram with the other elements. Perhaps we'd skip that and simply check that we can eliminate (E).

   (E) is indeed incorrect. Where would we fit three r's? We have only three open slots and they're consecutive.

Subgroups

A game with subgroups will divide the elements into two (or more)…well, subgroups. For example:

> Seven books must be placed on a shelf from left to right. There are two mysteries (F, G), two novels (M, O), and three textbooks (Q, R, S).

Our first challenge is to choose a method for keeping track of who is who. When there are only two different subgroups, the simplest solution is to use capital letters for one subgroup and lower-case letters for the other (or another solution is cursive letters and print).

When there are three or more subgroups, you might consider using subscripts if you find that you're losing track of the elements. Just make sure your subscripts are clear.

$$\text{Mysteries} \quad F_m \ G_m$$
$$\text{Novels} \quad M_n \ O_n$$
$$\text{Textbooks} \quad Q_t \ R_t \ S_t$$

One way that the LSAT simplifies tracking all of this is by keeping each subgroup's elements in different "sections" of the alphabet, as you see above.

Another option is to forgo the subscripts and, instead, refer to the initial list of elements throughout the game in order to track the subgroups.

This approach won't have the convenience of closely tracking each element's subgroup within the diagram itself, but on the other hand, your diagram is less likely to get crowded and messy. However, you'll probably end up reading and rereading the list of elements, which can be time-consuming. As you practice, try out several different approaches to get a sense of which method you prefer.

Whichever method you decide on, clearly notating the elements is a huge part of success in working with subgroups, because the rules and questions will often refer to both the specific elements and the subgroups directly. The easier those connections are to see, the more fluidly you will proceed through the game.

Okay, ready to dive in? Let's try one!

Practice Game 2: PTA, S3, G3

The seven members of an academic department are each to be assigned a different room as an office. The department members are professors F and G, lecturers Q, R, and S, and instructors V and W. The available rooms are seven consecutive rooms along one side of a straight hallway numbered sequentially 101 through 107. The assignment must conform to the following conditions:

  Neither instructor is assigned a room next to a professor's room.

  Neither professor is assigned room 101 and neither professor is assigned room 107.

  G is not assigned a room next to R's room.

  W is not assigned a room next to V's room unless R is also assigned a room next to V's room.

11. If F and G are assigned rooms that have exactly one room between them, which one of the following is the list of department members each of whom could be assigned to the intervening room?

    (A) Q, R
    (B) Q, S
    (C) Q, V
    (D) R, W
    (E) S, V

12. Which one of the following is a possible assignment of rooms for members R, V, and W?

    (A) 101: V; 102: W; 103: R
    (B) 101: V; 102: W; 104: R
    (C) 101: V; 103: W; 104: R
    (D) 103: W; 104: V; 106: R
    (E) 105: R; 106: W; 107: V

13. If R is assigned room 104, which one of the following must be assigned either room 103 or else room 105?

    (A) F
    (B) G
    (C) Q
    (D) V
    (E) W

14. What is the greatest number of rooms that could be between the rooms to which F and G are assigned?

    (A) one
    (B) two
    (C) three
    (D) four
    (E) five

15. Which one of the following CANNOT be assigned room 104?

    (A) F
    (B) G
    (C) Q
    (D) S
    (E) V

16. If no two faculty members of the same rank are assigned adjacent rooms, which one of the following must be true?

    (A) F is assigned either room 103 or else room 104.
    (B) Q is assigned either room 102 or else room 106.
    (C) R is assigned either room 102 or else room 105.
    (D) S is assigned either room 104 or else room 105.
    (E) V is assigned either room 101 or else room 107.

17. If F and G are not assigned rooms that are next to each other, which one of the following CANNOT be assigned room 107?

    (A) W
    (B) V
    (C) S
    (D) R
    (E) Q

Solutions: PTA, S3, G3

Answer Key

11. B   15. E
12. C   16. E
13. A   17. D
14. A

Step 1: Picture the Game

There are no changes to our basic Number Line here, but we need to be sure to write out the elements in their proper subgroups:

Prof   Lec   Inst

FG   QRS   VW

___ ___ ___ ___ ___ ___ ___
101 102 103 104 105 106 107

Step 2: Notate the Rules and Make Inferences

The first three rules are easy enough to notate—we'll rule out F and G from 101 and 107 and throw in a couple of anti-chunks ruling out the possibility of a professor or an instructor sitting next to each other. These rules also highlight one of the primary ways the LSAT uses subgroups: to create chunks and anti-chunks. If you have subgroups in an Ordering game, expect to see rules that say certain subgroups cannot (or must) be assigned to positions next to each other.

For the third rule, we need to use our conditional logic chops. "Unless" is a conditional language cue and, as we'll see in Chapter 7, it's meaning is the same as "if not." With this substitution, we can rephrase the rule as "If R is NOT next to V, then V isn't next to W." Conditionals containing a double negative can be tricky to work with, so let's take the contrapositive: If V is next to W, then V is also next to R. That's how we wrote it out below, but if you kept the original version, that's fine, too!

MANHATTAN
PREP

Prof   Lec   Inst

FG   QRS   VW

$\overline{101}$ $\overline{102}$ $\overline{103}$ $\overline{104}$ $\overline{105}$ $\overline{106}$ $\overline{107}$

Taking a quick look at our rules, they're almost all anti-chunks and don't lead to any quick exclusions or inferences. Same with the conditional—since we don't know whether W *is* next to V, we don't know whether the rule applies. If you noted V can't be in 101 or 107 if it's next to W, there's nothing wrong with that. But be careful you don't write those exclusions under the Number Line! After all, they only apply *if* W and V are consecutive.

Step 3: The Big Pause

Let's start off where we normally do: stray elements. Here, both Q and S don't have a rule attached. Additionally, they're both lecturers. Since we have two elements that are exactly the same as far as the game is concerned—both in the same subgroup; no rules attached—we refer to them as twins. It can be helpful to notice twins as you get into the questions.

Next, we should move on to the elements that do show up in the rules to think about inferences and frames. For frames, it should be a quick decision: There are no divisions other than whether or not W is next to V, and we know that conditionals generally lead to bad frames. The rest of our rules are anti-chunks, so we don't have a clear division.

Looking for inferences, we should focus on elements that show up a lot. And F and G sure seem to be unpopular—there are two people who won't occupy an office next door to F and three who won't next to G! Add to that the rules prohibiting them from being in 101 and 107, and G is definitely the most limited element, with F a close second. Who *can* have an office next to them? Only F, Q, and S can take an office adjacent to G and only G, Q, R, and S can be adjacent to F. In short, those two have very limited options for neighbors!

In fact there are only two options when it comes to F and G. Either they're in adjacent offices or they can have at most one office between them. There simply aren't enough friendly colleagues (or offices without neighbors!) willing to sit near either of them for there to be two offices between them.

Step 4: Attack the Questions

11. If F and G are assigned rooms that have exactly one room between them, which one of the following is the list of department members each of whom could be assigned to the intervening room?

    (A) Q, R
    (B) Q, S
    (C) Q, V
    (D) R, W
    (E) S, V

Answer choice (B) is correct.

This question boils down to the following: Which elements can be next to both F and G? Consider what we figured out in our Big Pause: G can be next to F, Q, and S, while F can be next to G, Q, R, and S. The only elements that are in both sets are Q and S.

12. Which one of the following is a possible assignment of rooms for members R, V, and W?

    (A) 101: V; 102: W; 103: R
    (B) 101: V; 102: W; 104: R
    (C) 101: V; 103: W; 104: R
    (D) 103: W; 104: V; 106: R
    (E) 105: R; 106: W; 107: V

Answer choice (C) is correct.

This question is testing our understanding of the fourth rule. If W and V are adjacent, then V and R must also be adjacent. (A), (B), (D), and (E) can each be eliminated using the fourth rule. Each of the incorrect answers places V and W next to each other, triggering our rule. It seems this question was just checking to see if you understood that fourth rule!

Be careful! There is a nasty little trap here: the given positions are not always adjacent. Look closely at answer choice (C): V and W aren't actually adjacent, so the rule doesn't kick in. If you move too quickly through this one, you'll unwittingly eliminate the correct answer.

13. If R is assigned room 104, which one of the following must be assigned either room 103 or else room 105?

    (A) F
    (B) G
    (C) Q
    (D) V
    (E) W

Answer choice (A) is correct.

MANHATTAN
PREP

This is vintage LSAT: Drop an element in the middle of the Number Line and see if you can infer the consequences. Guess which element this affects? Just search the rules for R and you'll see that G can't be assigned next door in 103 or 105.

Add to that the exclusions for G in 101 and 107, and there are only two places G can go: 102 and 106.

$$\overline{\underset{101}{}} \quad \overline{\underset{102}{}} \quad \overline{\underset{103}{}} \quad \overset{R}{\overline{\underset{104}{}}} \quad \overline{\underset{105}{}} \quad \overline{\underset{106}{}} \quad \overline{\underset{107}{}}$$

If we sketch these out quickly, we can make some exclusions around G. Starting with G in 102, we can say that W and V both can't go in 101 and 103. This means they're in a cloud between 105 and 107. F can't be next to either of them, so F must be in 101 or 103, but it can't go in 101 because of our rules. It looks like, in this case, F goes in 103. (A) is looking good.

If you feel comfortable picking (A) at this point, it'll save some time. However, if we take a look at G in 106, it's possible to notice that it's a mirror image of our hypothetical with G in 102. All the same inferences apply, but you should walk yourself through them. We end up with F in 105, confirming (A) as our answer:

$$\overline{} \quad \overset{G}{\overline{}} \quad \overset{F}{\overline{}} \quad \overset{R}{\overline{}} \quad \overline{} \quad \overline{} \quad \overline{}$$

$$\overline{\underset{101}{}} \quad \overline{\underset{102}{}} \quad \overline{\underset{103}{}} \quad \overset{R}{\overline{\underset{104}{}}} \quad \overset{F}{\overline{\underset{105}{}}} \quad \overset{G}{\overline{\underset{106}{}}} \quad \overline{\underset{107}{}}$$

14. What is the greatest number of rooms that could be between the rooms to which F and G are assigned?

   (A) one
   (B) two
   (C) three
   (D) four
   (E) five

Answer choice (A) is correct.

For these questions, you should check prior work as a baseline while also checking the rules. In question 11, F and G were separated by one room, but since one is the smallest possibility given, we don't get to eliminate any other answer choices, so this wasn't too helpful.

Our rules limit F and G from going in slots 101 and 107, so the closest they could be (ignoring other rules) is in 102 and 106. This would place three slots *between* them—be sure to interpret the question correctly! Seeing this eliminates (D) and (E).

Now, check to see if this arrangement is possible within the given constraints. Checking our rules for F and G, we see that an anti-chunk prevents V and W from being in adjacent slots. This rules out 101, 103, 105, and 107 as potential slots—and leaves only 104 for both W and V! Since they can't share an office, this doesn't work, so (C) isn't our answer.

If we move F and G one space closer and repeat these steps, we see there's no way to arrange V and W such that neither of them takes a room adjacent to F or G—eliminate answer choice (B).

After eliminating everything greater than one, (A)'s the only answer left standing.

This question would have been a lot easier if we had made the inference during The Big Pause that F and G are next to each other or that they are separated by one slot. There is a way to figure it out, but it's difficult. Most people will find it more efficient to head directly into the questions. However, if you're up for a challenge, head back to the game and see if you can figure it out.

15. Which one of the following CANNOT be assigned room 104?

    (A) F
    (B) G
    (C) Q
    (D) S
    (E) V

Answer choice (E) is correct.

A quick check of our diagram shows us that we didn't infer any exclusions, so we unfortunately will have to do some work. For questions like this, we should check our prior work quickly to see if there are any eliminations. However, we have written out only one hypothetical so far, and that one had R in room 104, and R is not an answer choice. Instead, with such an open-ended question, it can be helpful to glance at the choices, keeping in mind the likely suspects. Who are the most limited elements? F and G (G slightly more so). V and W are also limited, but not to the same degree since they are not excluded from 101 and 107. Q and S are not limited at all, and, more importantly, they're twins. Since there's no difference between them, if one can't go in 104, neither can the other. That would make both (C) and (D) the answer, which can't happen. We can eliminate these two answers.

At this point, we can either think some more or we can start testing out answers. Since G is more restricted than F, (B) is more likely than (A). However, we'd probably test out (E) first. Take a second to think about why.

MANHATTAN
PREP

For us, F and G are pretty close in rules, and there doesn't seem to be many issues with R that would make much of a difference in the middle. However, in question 14, we saw that W and V often created problems when forced into the middle. Let's put V in 104 to see if it creates problems; if it does, it's our answer:

$$
\begin{array}{ccccccc}
\text{W} & & \text{W} & & \text{W} & & \text{W} \\
\underline{} & \dfrac{\text{F/G}}{} & \underline{} & \dfrac{\text{V}}{} & \underline{} & \dfrac{\text{G/F}}{} & \underline{} \\
101 & 102 & 103 & 104 & 105 & 106 & 107 \\
\cancel{\text{F}} & & \cancel{\text{F}} & & \cancel{\text{F}} & & \cancel{\text{F}} \\
\cancel{\text{G}} & & \cancel{\text{G}} & & \cancel{\text{G}} & & \cancel{\text{G}}
\end{array}
$$

With V in 104, F and G are excluded from both 103 and 105. One will go in 102 and the other in 106. We should know from the last question that they can't be this far apart; we can also see that this creates a situation where we can't get W an office. Seeing that V can't be in 104 let's us know that (E) is our answer.

Sometimes, the most efficient route to an answer is to eliminate a couple and then work through the others. Always take a couple seconds before testing out an answer to think about which one is most likely. Even if it takes you two tries, however, that's usually faster than staring at the page, hoping for inspiration to strike!

16. If no two faculty members of the same rank are assigned adjacent rooms, which one of the following must be true?

(A) F is assigned either room 103 or else room 104.

(B) Q is assigned either room 102 or else room 106.

(C) R is assigned either room 102 or else room 105.

(D) S is assigned either room 104 or else room 105.

(E) V is assigned either room 101 or else room 107.

Answer choice (E) is correct.

No elements within a subgroup can take adjacent rooms, including F and G. So now we know that F and G are assigned rooms separated by exactly one (which we learned in question 14). Knowing that F and G severely restrict the place of V and W (and G restricts R), we can start to build a chunk. Between G and F, we can't have V, W, or R, so it'll be either S or Q. Since R can't go next to G, but F can, R will have to be next to F. Between Q and S, whichever isn't between F is next to G. And since this question tells us that V and W can't be next to each other, they have to be on the ends:

On the Number Line, a lot of these elements can flip around, but there's a lot of symmetry. We should be able to analyze the answers at this point and, checking through them, (E) is the only one that pans out.

17. If F and G are not assigned rooms that are next to each other, which one of the following CANNOT be assigned room 107?

   (A) W
   (B) V
   (C) S
   (D) R
   (E) Q

Answer choice (D) is correct.

F and G not in adjacent rooms? That's where we started our last question, so let's reuse some work from there.

If F and G are separated by exactly one slot, then we need Q/S in there (this was also the answer to an earlier question). Since V and W can't be next to F or G, we have to put R and S/Q on the outside of the chunk, with R next to F:

Remember: This entire chunk is reversible.

Now we have V and W left. If they're next to each other, R also has to be next to V. If they're not next to each other, we need one on each side of the chunk. Either way, R is pushed towards the inside of the chunk, making it impossible to get it into 107.

MANHATTAN
PREP

A quick strategy note: Q and S show up again as answers. Since they're twins, we can quickly eliminate them here. Even if you didn't know how to approach this question, eliminating two answers should let you try out a couple that are left in enough time to finish the section on time. Don't make a habit of it, but don't beat yourself up if you have to try out a few answers!

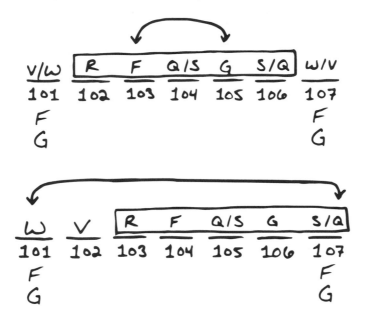

Special Positions

Sometimes one or more of the positions in a game are different than the others. Perhaps the first student in a line is the class president or maybe one juror in each jury is designated the foreman. Tracking **special positions** can be tricky. Often, they're used on only a few questions, and often, it's not feasible to build the special position into your diagram (and when you try, the ambiguity creates havoc in your work). If you find it difficult to add the special position to your diagram, feel free to defer on identifying it until after you have a hypothetical that forces your assignment.

Practice Game 3: PT54, S3, G4

A panel reviews six contract bids—H, J, K, R, S, and T. No two bids have the same cost. Exactly one of the bids is accepted. The following conditions must hold:

> The accepted bid is either K or R and is either the
>   second or the third lowest in cost.
> H is lower in cost than each of J and K.
> If J is the fourth lowest in cost, then J is lower in cost
>   than each of S and T.
> If J is not the fourth lowest in cost, then J is higher in
>   cost than each of S and T.
> Either R or S is the fifth lowest in cost.

18. Which one of the following could be an accurate list
    of the bids in order from lowest to highest in cost?

    (A) T, K, H, S, J, R
    (B) H, T, K, S, R, J
    (C) H, S, T, K, R, J
    (D) H, K, S, J, R, T
    (E) H, J, K, R, S, T

19. Which one of the following bids CANNOT be the
    fourth lowest in cost?

    (A) H
    (B) J
    (C) K
    (D) R
    (E) T

MANHATTAN
PREP

20. Which one of the following bids CANNOT be the second lowest in cost?

    (A) H
    (B) J
    (C) K
    (D) R
    (E) T

21. If R is the accepted bid, then which one of the following must be true?

    (A) T is the lowest in cost.
    (B) K is the second lowest in cost.
    (C) R is the third lowest in cost.
    (D) S is the fifth lowest in cost.
    (E) J is the highest in cost.

22. Which one of the following must be true?

    (A) H is lower in cost than S.
    (B) H is lower in cost than T.
    (C) K is lower in cost than J.
    (D) S is lower in cost than J.
    (E) S is lower in cost than K.

23. If R is the lowest in cost, then which one of the following could be false?

    (A) J is the highest in cost.
    (B) S is the fifth lowest in cost.
    (C) K is the third lowest in cost.
    (D) H is the second lowest in cost.
    (E) K is the accepted bid.

Solutions: PT54, S3, G4

Answer Key

18.	B	21.	D
19.	A	22.	C
20.	B	23.	A

Step 1: Picture the Game

Six elements, six positions. They don't tell us whether "lowest" should be the leftmost or rightmost position, so we set 1 as lowest and 6 as highest. If you inverted that, it's not a big deal, but make sure that all your rules are inverted, as well.

There's no mismatch here, but what's the deal with the "accepted bid"? We're not sure how to deal with it yet, so let's make a note of it but hold off on getting it into our diagram until the rules tell us more about it. And if it doesn't show up in the rules, it's probably not very important!

$$\text{H J K R S T} \quad \text{low} \; \underset{1}{\_} \; \underset{2}{\_} \; \underset{3}{\_} \; \underset{4}{\_} \; \underset{5}{\_} \; \underset{6}{\_} \; \text{high}$$

Step 2: Notate the Rules and Make Inferences

Rule 1 narrows both which element is our accepted bid and also where the accepted bid will be ranked. Good thing we held off on worrying about it—this rule tells us everything we need to know:

$$\text{H J K R S T} \quad \text{low} \; \underset{1}{\_} \; \underset{2}{\underset{\rule{1.5em}{0.4pt}}{\boxed{\text{K/R}}}} \; \underset{3}{\_} \; \underset{4}{\_} \; \underset{5}{\_} \; \underset{6}{\_} \; \text{high}$$

Rule 2 is a partial Tree that you should feel quite comfortable with at this stage:

$$H \begin{smallmatrix} \nearrow J \\ \searrow K \end{smallmatrix}$$

Rules 3 and 4 create a fork in the road—J is either fourth or not fourth, and we have a rule for each possibility. Might be worth exploring during The Big Pause. We can represent it this way:

MANHATTAN
PREP

$$J_4 \rightarrow J \langle{}^{S}_{T}$$

$$\not J_4 \rightarrow {}^{S}\searrow{}_{J} \nearrow{}^{J}_{T}$$

Rule 5 is simple enough—put an R/S option in slot 5:

HJKRST

$$H \langle{}^{J}_{K}$$

$$\text{low} \; \underline{}_{1} \; \underline{\boxed{K/R}}_{2 \quad 3} \; \underline{}_{4} \; \underline{R/S}_{5} \; \underline{}_{6} \; \text{high}$$

$$J_4 \rightarrow J \langle{}^{S}_{T}$$

$$\not J_4 \rightarrow {}^{S}\searrow{}_{J} {}_{T}\nearrow$$

Step 3: The Big Pause

Let's explore the fork created by rules 3 and 4. The easier task is to figure out if anything follows from J being the fourth lowest bid since we start this frame by filling in a slot. J would be lower than both S and T, and we can connect that partial Tree to our existing partial Tree created by the second rule, creating a nearly complete Tree! From there, we know S must be fifth (based on our option) and T sixth. With three slots filled in, we can create a cloud with the rest of our elements.

What happens if J isn't fourth? We can combine our trees to see that H, S, and T are all lower than J. That excludes J from slots 1, 2, and 3. Since this frame is based on J not being fourth, and slot 5 is taken up by our option, J has to be sixth!

Frame 1   Frame 2

Our special position here ended up not dictating very much about our approach, but we should still remember it's there. When this happens—a special position is established but doesn't really impact much—the LSAT tends to "forget" about it until a later question.

Step 4: Attack the Questions

18. Which one of the following could be an accurate list of the bids in order from lowest to highest in cost?

    (A) T, K, H, S, J, R
    (B) H, T, K, S, R, J
    (C) H, S, T, K, R, J
    (D) H, K, S, J, R, T
    (E) H, J, K, R, S, T

Answer choice (B) is correct.

The first rule knocks out answer choice (C), the second rule knocks out (A), the third knocks out (D), and the fourth eliminates (E).

19. Which one of the following bids CANNOT be the fourth lowest in cost?

    (A) H
    (B) J
    (C) K
    (D) R
    (E) T

Answer choice (A) is correct.

MANHATTAN PREP

Slam dunk! Our frames tell us that J, T, K, R, and S could each be the fourth lowest in cost. Rule them out and we're left with answer choice (A). Alternatively, if you didn't build frames, H must be lower in cost than J and K. With R/S in slot 5, that pushes H to slot 3 or lower.

20. Which one of the following bids CANNOT be the second lowest in cost?

    (A) H

    (B) J

    (C) K

    (D) R

    (E) T

Answer choice (B) is correct.

Another slam dunk! Reading from our frames, we can see that H, K, R, T, and S could be the second lowest in cost. That leaves J as the only possibility. Again, without frames, we'd see that J is either fourth highest in cost (or higher), thus also not second lowest.

21. If R is the accepted bid, then which one of the following must be true?

    (A) T is the lowest in cost.

    (B) K is the second lowest in cost.

    (C) R is the third lowest in cost.

    (D) S is the fifth lowest in cost.

    (E) J is the highest in cost.

Answer choice (D) is correct.

low ___ ___ (R) ___ ___ S ___ high
      1   2   3   4   5   6

If R is accepted, then it must be either second or third. The last rule let's us fill S into slot 5. Wow, these last three questions have been fast and easy! Let's not get carried away though—we should remember to tap the brakes in the event that one of the final questions is difficult.

22. Which one of the following must be true?

    (A) H is lower in cost than S.

    (B) H is lower in cost than T.

    (C) K is lower in cost than J.

    (D) S is lower in cost than J

    (E) S is lower in cost than K.

Answer choice (C) is correct.

If you have the frames, this question becomes a matter of checking each answer against them. Remember, for a game with two frames, the correct answers must show up in both.

  (A) need not be true in the second frame.
  (B) need not be true in the second frame
  (D) is not true in the first frame.
  (E) is not true in the first frame.

If you don't have the frames, this is a much harder question. You'd probably have to test a few answer choices out after deciding which were more likely to be correct. An argument for building frames here!

23. If R is the lowest in cost, then which one of the following could be false?

  (A) J is the highest in cost.
  (B) S is the fifth lowest in cost.
  (C) K is the third lowest in cost.
  (D) H is the second lowest in cost.
  (E) K is the accepted bid.

Answer choice (A) is correct.

We can infer that S must be fifth and that K must be the accepted bid in either slot 2 or 3. Plugging this in and then folding in the rest of our frames, two rankings are possible:

Frame 1   Frame 2

(B) through (E) must be true in both frames.

Special Connections

Logic Game aficionados, rejoice! This next twist is going to make your day. In games with **special connections,** there will be a relationship between different positions or between elements that falls outside of what we normally see. Sometimes, you'll find a great way to include the connection into your diagram, while in other cases you won't really get a complete handle on it until you get through the rules or even into the questions. In those situations, make a note of the connection and keep your eye on it, regularly checking back on it throughout the game. Remember that it's okay to "grow into" a logic game as you're working through it—you do *not* need to have every detail worked out before you start on the questions.

Practice Game 4: PT38, S2, G4

Musicians perform each of exactly five pieces—Nexus, Onyx, Synchrony, Tailwind, and Virtual—once, and one at a time; the pieces are performed successively (though not necessarily in that order). Each piece is performed with exactly two instruments: Nexus with fiddle and lute, Onyx with harp and mandolin, Synchrony with guitar and harp, Tailwind with fiddle and guitar, and Virtual with lute and mandolin. The following conditions must apply:

Each piece shares one instrument with the piece performed immediately before it or after it (or both). Either Nexus or Tailwind is performed second.

20. Which one of the following could be the order, from first to last, in which the pieces are performed?

    (A) Nexus, Synchrony, Onyx, Virtual, Tailwind
    (B) Synchrony, Tailwind, Onyx, Nexus, Virtual
    (C) Tailwind, Nexus, Onyx, Virtual, Synchrony
    (D) Tailwind, Nexus, Synchrony, Onyx, Virtual
    (E) Virtual, Nexus, Synchrony, Onyx, Tailwind

21. Which one of the following instruments CANNOT be shared by the third and fourth pieces performed?

    (A) fiddle
    (B) guitar
    (C) harp
    (D) lute
    (E) mandolin

22. If each piece (except the fifth) shares one instrument with the piece performed immediately after it, then which one of the following could be true?

    (A) Virtual is performed first.
    (B) Synchrony is performed second.
    (C) Onyx is performed third.
    (D) Nexus is performed fourth.
    (E) Tailwind is performed fifth.

23. Each of the following could be the piece performed first EXCEPT:

    (A) Nexus
    (B) Onyx
    (C) Synchrony
    (D) Tailwind
    (E) Virtual

24. If Synchrony is performed fifth, then which one of the following could be true?

    (A) Nexus is performed third.
    (B) Onyx is performed third.
    (C) Tailwind is performed fourth.
    (D) Virtual is performed first.
    (E) Virtual is performed second.

Solutions: PT38, S2, G4

Answer Key

20. D   23. B

21. A   24. D

22. A

Step 1: Picture the Game

At first glance, this game appears odd. The fundamental task isn't too difficult—we have five musical pieces to place in order—but things get wild when we realize that we have to track the *connections* between instruments assigned to each element.

A Number Line would allow us to place the musical pieces in order. We can add a list on the side to track the instruments used with each piece:

We could notate the remaining rules, make inferences, and run with this diagram as is, but we know that the connections between instruments are an important part of the game. It's a safe bet that some (if not all) of the questions will hinge on these connections. What have we used before to track characteristics for elements? A 3D Number Line! Let's modify our diagram accordingly:

Step 2: Notate the Rules and Make Inferences

There are only two rules to notate! That's also a bit odd. It could mean that this is a very back-end game or perhaps the two rules will somehow connect and lead to a cascade of inferences. Our job is the same either way: We'll notate the rules and make as many inferences as we can.

The first rule is definitely using chunk language, but it's hard to see how to diagram it at first. We could write an abbreviated form in English next to our diagram. Or we could get a little creative and do something like this:

$$\boxed{\text{i}\quad\text{i}} \quad or \quad \boxed{\text{i}\quad\text{i}}$$
$$\quad P \qquad\qquad\quad P$$

Either way, it's crucial to understand what the rule means. Each piece must share an instrument with the piece immediately before it *or* the one after it. It's okay to share an instrument with both, but that's not required. For example, if the piece in slot 2 shares an instrument with slot 1, that satisfies the rule. Slot 2 could also share an instrument with slot 3, but it doesn't have to. A correct understanding of this rule will keep us from making incorrect inferences.

The second rule is, thankfully, much easier to notate:

NOSTV

$$\begin{array}{ccccc} \_ & \dfrac{g/l}{} & \_ & \_ & \_ \\ \_ & \dfrac{f}{} & \_ & \_ & \_ \\ \_ & \underline{N/T} & \_ & \_ & \_ \\ 1 & 2 & 3 & 4 & 5 \end{array}$$

instruments
instruments
pieces

When adding N's and T's instruments to the diagram, we notice that they share an instrument: f. We will always have an f in slot 2.

Step 3: The Big Pause

There are some important connections between rules that we should notice. We know that each piece has two instruments assigned to it and that each piece must have an instrument in common with the piece before or after it. It might be useful to track the pieces that share an instrument. We can use our list of the instruments for each piece to create a list showing the pairs of songs that share each instrument:

$$\left. \begin{array}{l} N: f\ l \\ O: h\ m \\ S: g\ h \\ T: f\ g \\ V: l\ m \end{array} \right\} \rightarrow \begin{array}{l} f: N\ T \\ l: N\ V \\ h: O\ S \\ m: O\ V \\ g: S\ T \end{array}$$

On the LSAT, inverting a list in this manner very often makes your job tracking these connections much easier. If the scenario gives you a list of elements that share certain characteristics, or a list of possible connections, take a moment to write out the flipped version.

Also notice that the rule, *Each piece shares one instrument*, gives us a limited set of possibilities. Since the first piece is on an end, it must share an instrument with the second—there's no other piece for the first to share with! Likewise, the fifth piece must share an instrument with the fourth. The other three positions all have options. Since slots 1 and 5 are the most constrained, let's keep our eyes on them.

We should also consider frames. The second rule provides a clear division—N or T second—that will have direct consequences. Since the first piece must share an instrument with the second, the N/T option will limit the pieces that can go first:

NOSTV

Frame 1

f	f			
g	l			
T	N	___	___	___
1	2	3	4	5

Frame 2

l	f			
m	l			
V	N	___	___	___
1	2	3	4	5

Frame 3

f	f			
l	g			
N	T	___	___	___
1	2	3	4	5

Frame 4

g	f			
h	g			
S	T	___	___	___
1	2	3	4	5

There are many possible ways for the rest of the pieces to play out, so we should head to the questions. LSAT students, attack!

Step 4: Attack the Questions

20. Which one of the following could be the order, from first to last, in which the pieces are performed?

(A) Nexus, Synchrony, Onyx, Virtual, Tailwind

(B) Synchrony, Tailwind, Onyx, Nexus, Virtual

(C) Tailwind, Nexus, Onyx, Virtual, Synchrony

(D) Tailwind, Nexus, Synchrony, Onyx, Virtual

(E) Virtual, Nexus, Synchrony, Onyx, Tailwind

Answer choice (D) is correct.

MANHATTAN
PREP

Even with our normal strategy, this Orientation question is going to be rough. We don't get the instruments listed out, so we're going to have to cross-check a lot to eliminate based on the first rule. Instead, let's start with the second. That allows us to eliminate choice (A). We were hoping for more eliminations, but we have to roll with it.

We could examine all of the pieces in each remaining answer choice to see if any violate the first rule, but perhaps there is a more strategic approach. During The Big Pause, we noticed slots 1 and 5 are the most limited, so let's start there.

The first two pieces in answer choices (B) through (E) are all valid combinations, so we can't eliminate anything based on that. Shifting to the last two pieces, we see that (B) still passes the test: N and V share a lute. Choice (D) is also fine, since O and V share a mandolin. However, we can eliminate choice (C), since V and S don't share anything. Choice (E) is also out, since O and T have no instruments in common. We're making progress!

With only two answer choices left, we'll examine the third position, remembering that it must share an instrument with either the second or fourth. In choice (B), O is stranded with no connection to either T or N. Eliminate! This leaves us with choice (D) as the correct answer.

Phew! We never thought we'd have to work so hard for an Orientation question.

21. Which one of the following instruments CANNOT be shared by the third and fourth pieces performed?

    (A) fiddle

    (B) guitar

    (C) harp

    (D) lute

    (E) mandolin

Answer choice (A) is correct.

If you thought the Orientation question was hard…

It's difficult to even start. If you run into a question like this on the exam and have no idea how to tackle it, it's wise to take a guess and move on. Flag it and come back to take another look if you have time, perhaps using your work from one or more of the later questions to gain some leverage.

Let's not be hasty, though. It's an unconditional question. Our normal process is to compare each answer choice to our diagram, eliminating any choices that don't match up. Let's look at choice (A). Can the fiddle be shared by the third and fourth pieces? No! Why not? We know that each instrument will be shared by exactly two pieces, and both frames have a piece played on the fiddle in slot 2. If the fiddle is the shared instrument between slots 2 and 3, then there's no fiddle piece left for slot 4. If it isn't the shared instrument, then it's not in slot 3.

Lucky thing this was answer choice (A). However, we knew from our initial inferences that a fiddle must always be in slot 2, which would prevent it from being in two other slots. If you were able to answer the question based just on that initial inference, bravo!

22. If each piece (except the fifth) shares one instrument with the piece performed immediately after it, then which one of the following could be true?

   (A) Virtual is performed first.
   (B) Synchrony is performed second.
   (C) Onyx is performed third.
   (D) Nexus is performed fourth.
   (E) Tailwind is performed fifth.

Answer choice (A) is correct.

When you come across a conditional question with a tricky new rule, it's important to slow down and properly digest it. Here, we need slot 1 to share an instrument with slot 2, 2 with 3, and so on down the line. However, if slot 1 is sharing with slot 2 and 2 with 3, then we also know slot 3 is sharing with slot 2 and 2 with 1. The rule is really telling us that each piece shares an instrument with all of the pieces surrounding it.

With this understanding, let's draw some hypotheticals based on our frames. We know that N only shares instruments with two other pieces—T and V—so those pieces must occupy the positions on either side of N in Frame 1, leaving O and S for the last two slots. Likewise, N and S must occupy the positions on either side of T in Frame 2, leaving O and V for slots 4 and 5. Some of the possibilities represented between the cloud/option won't work (V N T O S, for example), but let's see if we have an answer just from what we have so far:

MANHATTAN
PREP

Based on the first frame, choice (A) could be true. Let's confirm that it's correct by eliminating the other choices:

(B) violates the original rules, since N or T must be second.

(C) cannot be true because only T, V, N, or S can be third.

(D) cannot be true because N must be first, second, or third.

(E) cannot be true because T is limited to the first three positions, just like N.

Alternatively, you could have worked out the four options:

$$T \; N \; V \; O \; S$$

$$V \; N \; T \; S \; O$$

$$S \; T \; N \; V \; O$$

$$N \; T \; S \; O \; V$$

This would have ensured you had the answer before heading to the questions, but it would have been a larger investment of time.

23. Each of the following could be the piece performed first EXCEPT:

(A) Nexus

(B) Onyx

(C) Synchrony

(D) Tailwind

(E) Virtual

Answer choice (B) is correct.

At last! A question we can answer by referencing our original frames. T, V, N, and S are the only pieces that could be performed first. Onyx, since it doesn't share an instrument with N or T, cannot be performed first.

Alternatively, the hypotheticals from the last question eliminate all but (B).

24. If Synchrony is performed fifth, then which one of the following could be true?

    (A) Nexus is performed third.
    (B) Onyx is performed third.
    (C) Tailwind is performed fourth.
    (D) Virtual is performed first.
    (E) Virtual is performed second.

Answer choice (D) is correct.

If S is fifth, the special connection defined in our first rule requires T or O to be fourth. As you bring this new information into your frames, you'll find that if T is performed fourth, N must be performed second. This leaves us with:

$$O/V \quad N \quad V/O \quad T \quad S$$

However, while N has a connecting instrument with V, it doesn't share one with O. This would force O to be third, but then it also wouldn't share an instrument with T. In other words, T can't be performed fourth! It must be O.

Drawing out the possibilities, we end up with:

$$T \, N \, V \, O \, S$$
$$V \, N \, T \, O \, S$$
$$N \, T \, V \, O \, S$$

(A), (B), (C), and (E) each cannot be true.

Circular

While there have only been a few Circular Ordering games ever, one might suspect that they hold sentimental value to the LSAT test writers. PT1, G1 was not only the modern LSAT's first logic game, it was also a Circular Ordering game. These games are rare, so don't over invest your valuable time preparing for something unlikely to happen. But they are a good opportunity to practice being flexible.

Circular games essentially play like those with a Number Line, but "twisted" over (pun *intended*) so that the beginning meets the end. In other words, the first slot is adjacent to the last slot, like a snake biting its tail. The game will also often talk about people who sit across from each other, which our basic Number Line can't comfortably account for. How can we make this easier on ourselves?

Linear

K L M N O P

It will help to draw the slots in a circle on your paper (people sitting around a table, for example). We recommend using the "clock face method" to keep things neat, drawing slots at 12 and 6, then 9 and 3, etc.

Clock Face

K
P   L
O   M
N

Alternatively, you could draw the "spokes" of a wheel and seat elements at the ends of each spoke:

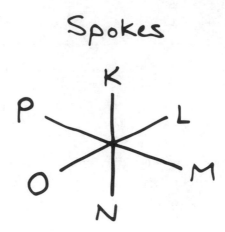

You can often use Basic Ordering tools, such as chunks, to notate the rules, but as always, be willing to improvise!

MANHATTAN
PREP

Practice Game 5: PT1, S2, G1

Exactly six trade representatives negotiate a treaty: Klosnik, Londi, Manley, Neri, Osata, Poirier. There are exactly six chairs evenly spaced around a circular table. The chairs are numbered 1 through 6, with successively numbered chairs next to each other and chair number 1 next to chair number 6. Each chair is occupied by exactly one of the representatives. The following conditions apply:

Poirier sits immediately next to Neri.
Londi sits immediately next to Manley, Neri, or both.
Klosnik does not sit immediately next to Manley.
If Osata sits immediately next to Poirier, Osata does not sit immediately next to Manley.

1. Which one of the following seating arrangements of the six representatives in chairs 1 through 6 would NOT violate the stated conditions?

    (A) Klosnik, Poirier, Neri, Manley, Osata, Londi
    (B) Klosnik, Londi, Manley, Poirier, Neri, Osata
    (C) Klosnik, Londi, Manley, Osata, Poirier, Neri
    (D) Klosnik, Osata, Poirier, Neri, Londi, Manley
    (E) Klosnik, Neri, Londi, Osata, Manley, Poirier

2. If Londi sits immediately next to Poirier, which one of the following is a pair of representatives who must sit immediately next to each other?

    (A) Klosnik and Osata
    (B) Londi and Neri
    (C) Londi and Osata
    (D) Manley and Neri
    (E) Manley and Poirier

3. If Klosnik sits directly between Londi and Poirier, then Manley must sit directly between

    (A) Londi and Neri
    (B) Londi and Osata
    (C) Neri and Osata
    (D) Neri and Poirier
    (E) Osata and Poirier

4. If Neri sits immediately next to Manley, then Klosnik can sit directly between

    (A) Londi and Manley
    (B) Londi and Poirier
    (C) Neri and Osata
    (D) Neri and Poirier
    (E) Poirier and Osata

5. If Londi sits immediately next to Manley, then which one of the following is a complete and accurate list of representatives any one of whom could also sit immediately next to Londi?

    (A) Klosnik
    (B) Klosnik, Neri
    (C) Neri, Poirier
    (D) Klosnik, Osata, Poirier
    (E) Klosnik, Neri, Osata, Poirier

6. If Londi sits immediately next to Neri, which one of the following statements must be false?

    (A) Klosnik sits immediately next to Osata.
    (B) Londi sits immediately next to Manley.
    (C) Osata sits immediately next to Poirier.
    (D) Neri sits directly between Londi and Poirier.
    (E) Osata sits directly between Klosnik and Manley.

7. If Klosnik sits immediately next to Osata, then Londi CANNOT sit directly between

    (A) Klosnik and Manley
    (B) Klosnik and Neri
    (C) Manley and Neri
    (D) Manley and Poirier
    (E) Neri and Osata

Solutions: PT1, S2, G1

Answer Key

1. B   5. E
2. A   6. C
3. B   7. E
4. E

Step 1: Picture the Game

In this game, there are six people sitting around a table that has exactly six seats, so we need a circular diagram with six slots. We can either use the clock method with slots at 12 and 6, 2 and 8, and 4 and 10. Or we can use the spoke method with three lines.

When you scanned the rules and the questions, did you notice that there are almost no seat numbers mentioned? Outside of the Orientation question, seat numbers aren't mentioned. When this happens, we shouldn't label our slots. If something brings up a specific seat, we'll worry about it then. Unless that happens, this game is going to be more about who can and can't sit next to each other than the specific seat number they're sitting in.

Here are two ways you could have successfully represented the game:

We're going to use the clock face diagram, but hopefully it's not too hard to translate if you used the spokes.

MANHATTAN
PREP

Step 2: Notate the Rules and Make Inferences

Let's fill in each diagram with our rules to compare how each one would work:

> Poirier sits immediately next to Neri.

Since there are no set positions, we simply can add those elements to our diagrams. We don't have to worry if they're in the "wrong" slots, because we haven't *labeled* the slots:

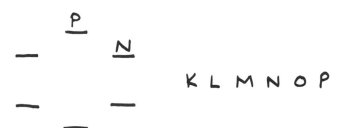

But what if N is on the other side of P? It's a valid concern! Let's draw a cloud around them to remember that N could be counterclockwise to P.

Let's move to the next rule:

> Londi sits immediately next to Manley, Neri, or both.

We've got two reversible chunks in an option. Complicated? Yes. Something we don't know how to handle? Never!

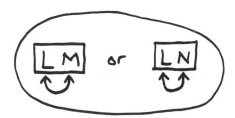

Remember, "or" statements leave open the possibility of both being true. If you find yourself forgetting that, feel free to get the "third" option in—L is between M and N.

Since we don't know which option we have or where these chunks are in relation to what we already have, it's time to move on:

> Klosnik does not sit immediately next to Manley.

Since we have created a way to indicate anti-chunks, this is easy to represent:

And this is another rule that we can't get into the diagram. Let's see what's next:

If Osata sits immediately next to Poirier, Osata does not sit immediately next to Manley.

This is a tricky conditional chunk! But, we can handle this:

To consider what this really means, see if you can devise a simpler way of notating the rule.

If you can't figure it out, consider what sort of chunk is now impossible. We could never have O next to both P and M:

We have all our rules notated:

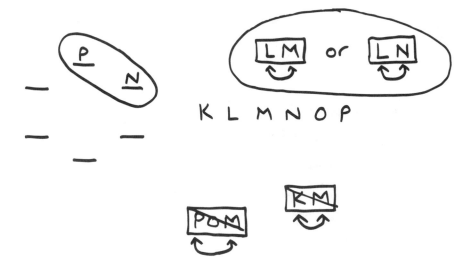

Step 3: The Big Pause

It looks like there's a lot of uncertainty in this game. Our PN chunk is nice, but the other chunk comes in the form of an option. The other rule is an anti-chunk, and those don't normally lead to big inferences.

We see that every element is part of some rule, but no inferences are jumping off the page at us. There might be something with the PN chunk and LMN option/chunk, but it seems there are too many possibilities to really nail down.

Step 4: Attack the Questions

1. Which one of the following seating arrangements of the six representatives in chairs 1 through 6 would NOT violate the stated conditions?

    (A) Klosnik, Poirier, Neri, Manley, Osata, Londi
    (B) Klosnik, Londi, Manley, Poirier, Neri, Osata
    (C) Klosnik, Londi, Manley, Osata, Poirier, Neri
    (D) Klosnik, Osata, Poirier, Neri, Londi, Manley
    (E) Klosnik, Neri, Londi, Osata, Manley, Poirier

Answer choice (B) is correct.

> The first rule eliminates answer (E).
> The second rule eliminates answer (A).
> The third rule eliminates answer (D). "Wait, what?" you might ask. Don't forget that these games wrap around!
> The final rule eliminates answer (C).

2. If Londi sits immediately next to Poirier, which one of the following is a pair of representatives who must sit immediately next to each other?

    (A) Klosnik and Osata
    (B) Londi and Neri
    (C) Londi and Osata
    (D) Manley and Neri
    (E) Manley and Poirier

Answer choice (A) is correct.

As is typical of second questions, this question provides a quick confirmation of whether we successfully understood the basics of this game:

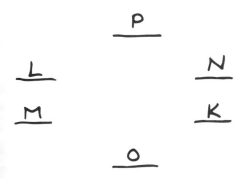

With L next to P, we know we have P between L and N. We don't know which direction LPN will sit around the table, but it won't matter since the answers don't refer to order and the two diagrams will be mirror images of each other.

Since we know L must sit next to either M or N, and L can't be next to N, M must be in that next seat. And since K can't be next to M, K is next to N. That leaves O to sit across from P. Everything is filled in, so it's time to jump into the answers.

3. If Klosnik sits directly between Londi and Poirier, then Manley must sit directly between

   (A) Londi and Neri
   (B) Londi and Osata
   (C) Neri and Osata
   (D) Neri and Poirier
   (E) Osata and Poirier

Answer choice (B) is correct.

Let's start by putting K between L and P. N still sits next to P, which means M sits next to L for the option. O's in the only remaining seat, so M sits between O and L.

Want to see something cool? Try that question again, but reverse the positioning of P and N. See if you can figure out why the directional order of the elements doesn't matter.

Notice anything about the diagrams? They're mirror images of each other! This isn't limited to circular games (in fact, our subgroups game had a similar symmetry). The reason that the direction doesn't matter in this game is that neither the rules nor the questions refer to direction—for example, clockwise or counterclockwise—and so it doesn't matter which way the circle goes.

---

4. If Neri sits immediately next to Manley, then Klosnik can sit directly between

   (A) Londi and Manley
   (B) Londi and Poirier
   (C) Neri and Osata
   (D) Neri and Poirier
   (E) Poirier and Osata

Answer choice (E) is correct.

What is the impact of the new condition? We'll have a PNM chunk, with L, K, and O left to place. We know that we need to place L next to M since LN is no longer an option. Our chunk has grown to PNML, with K and O left. K is "protected" from M, so nothing to worry about there. Our diagram for this question looks like this:

K must fall between O and L or O and P.

5. If Londi sits immediately next to Manley, then which one of the following is a complete and accurate list of representatives any one of whom could also sit immediately next to Londi?

    (A) Klosnik
    (B) Klosnik, Neri
    (C) Neri, Poirier
    (D) Klosnik, Osata, Poirier
    (E) Klosnik, Neri, Osata, Poirier

Answer choice (E) is correct.

This is a great question for using previous work. Looking back, where do we see L next to M? Every question, in fact. From those, we see L sitting next to K (1, 3, and 4), P (2), and O (4). Either (D) or (E) is correct, but we still have to see if L can sit next to N.

Let's try placing L between M and N. That would give us M L N P. K and O are left (once again), and we can separate K and M by putting O between them. This works, so (E) is correct:

If we didn't use our previous work, the question would still be doable—of course—but testing out scenarios would take much longer. Ideally, we have a firm enough grasp on the rules that we could identify some possibilities by simply thinking it out, and we wouldn't need to write out the scenarios. Try doing it now. It's not easy! This is definitely a question where looking back at earlier work pays dividends.

6. If Londi sits immediately next to Neri, which one of the following statements must be false?

    (A) Klosnik sits immediately next to Osata.

    (B) Londi sits immediately next to Manley.

    (C) Osata sits immediately next to Poirier.

    (D) Neri sits directly between Londi and Poirier.

    (E) Osata sits directly between Klosnik and Manley.

Answer choice (C) is correct.

We just created a scenario in question 5 in which L sits next to N, and now question 6 asks us for what must be false. Any answer choice that matches our question 5 diagram can therefore be eliminated, so (A) is out as is (B). (C) doesn't match our diagram, so keep it. Since (D) matches and so does (E), both are eliminated. Previous work prevails again!

7. If Klosnik sits immediately next to Osata, then Londi CANNOT sit directly between

    (A) Klosnik and Manley

    (B) Klosnik and Neri

    (C) Manley and Neri

    (D) Manley and Poirier

    (E) Neri and Osata

Answer choice (E) is correct.

Previous work has so far been useful on this game, so let's start by checking for diagrams in which K is next to O. We can use our diagram from question 5 to rule out (C) immediately. In question 4, K was also next to O, and L was between K and M, so (A) is out as well. What about in question 2? K and O were next to each other there, too, while L sat directly between P and M, so (D) is out. We're left testing only (B) and (E).

Let's test (B) first. We'll start with O next to K (from the question stem), and then place L between K and N. N is next to P, and M fills the last open slot:

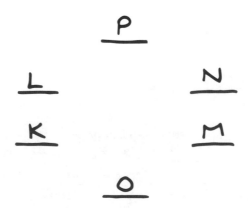

This is a valid hypothetical, so eliminate (B)!

MANHATTAN
PREP

(E) can't work. If L is between N and O, and P next to N, we will need to put K and M in the remaining two slots. Those two can't sit together!

What Can We Learn from This Challenge?

That was probably one of the stranger Logic Games you've seen so far. If you struggled, replay the game before you get up from this prep session. Then play it again in a couple of weeks.

1. **Make sure to ID what's different.** While we are still ordering, on this game we need to adjust our Number Line to help keep track of who's sitting across the table from whom, as well as the fact that the first and last positions are adjacent.

2. **Flexibility is critical—look at the MacGyver moves we made:**

- We turned our Number Line into a Number Circle.
- We left our slots unnumbered because the rules and most questions didn't reference them by number.
- We used previous work.

Conclusion

Phew! Those were some tough games. The LSAT sure likes to throw curve balls at us.

It might seem like every game has a twist after going through this lesson. In reality, you're likely to see only a couple twists on test day. They'll be in the harder games, after you've already earned some points and built some momentum on the more basic ones.

But when you run into a twist, remember that you're not in a whole new game type. We're just *adapting* our basic tools, and, in the case of ordering games, that's the Number Line.

We've seen a number of twists today, including:

- Mismatch
- Subgroups
- Special Positions
- Special Connections
- Circular

While challenging, for each game, we adapted a standard Number Line to meet the twist. And this is the main point we want you to walk away with from the chapter: These twists represent ways in which the test writer increases the difficulty of Basic Ordering.

Some games feature more than one twist, but always build off of what you already know how to do. If you come back to these (and other twisted games you come across) and replay them, you'll be ready for any combination the LSAT can throw at you on test day.

LG

Chapter 7

Conditional Logic 202

In This Chapter...

Conditional Logic for In/Out Grouping

Now that we know the basics of conditional logic, we're ready to dig a little deeper. But first, for context, let's quickly introduce the next game type we'll be learning: In/Out Grouping.

In/Out Grouping involves two types of scenarios. In one kind of scenario, there is a single group, and each element of the game must be either selected for inclusion in the group (in), or not (out). Here's an example:

> One or more of exactly seven basketball players—F, G, H, J, K, L, and M—from the Riverside
> High School basketball team will be selected for the league All-Star team.

In other scenarios, there will be two groups, and each element of the game must be assigned to one of the two groups. Here's an example:

> Seven employees—F, G, H, J, K, L, and M—will each be assigned to exactly one of the following
> two departments: sales, marketing.

Note that these two scenarios are really just variations on the same theme. In each case, your job is to divide up the elements into two groups: in the first case, those who are selected for the team vs. those who are not selected, and in the second case, those who are assigned to sales vs. those who are assigned to marketing.

The rules for these In/Out Grouping scenarios will take the form of conditional statements:

> If H is selected, then J is also selected.
> If K is selected, then L and F are not selected.
> If F is assigned to marketing, then L is assigned to sales.

Your success will depend on your ability to make valid inferences from these conditional statements. As we'll see shortly, making these inferences is tricky without the proper tools!

Alternative Wordings

We noted earlier that basic conditional statements are triggered by IF/THEN language. However, the LSAT won't always make things so simple for you. In the modern era of Logic Games (since the year 2000), the LSAT uses many different wordings in its conditional statements in order to add to the complexity of your task.

The following is a list of eight rules meant to illustrate the range of advanced conditional statements that have appeared on In/Out Grouping games since the year 2000.

1. J and K cannot both be selected.

2. If M is selected, both G and H must be selected.

3. Neither H nor K is selected if L is selected.

4. If J is selected, then G is selected but L is not.

5. F cannot be selected unless H is also selected.

6. L is selected if, and only if, M is also selected.

7. If either Q or R is selected, both must be selected.

8. N and W cannot be on the same team.

As you can see, it could be very easy to get turned around with statements such as these and either miss a critical inference or make up an inference that doesn't actually exist. Ideally, you'll have enough experience by test day that making the relevant notations and inferences will feel more like a reflex than a thought process. Toward that end, let's work on a process for converting those difficult statements into easier ones.

Converting to Simple IF/THEN Form

We know how to use simple IF/THEN statements, right? Diagram using an arrow symbol, and reverse and negate to get the contrapositive. You're already a pro at this. It makes sense, then, to tackle these advanced statements by first converting them into simple IF/THEN form. Once we convert to simple IF/THEN form, we're in the clear. The challenge comes in the conversion.

Let's start with the first of our eight examples.

1. J and K cannot both be selected.

This statement is difficult to deal with because it has no IF/THEN language. We need to convert it. To do so, let's imagine we have a box that represents selection (a letter placed inside the box has been selected while a letter placed outside the box has not been selected). In this case, we have two letters to the side that are awaiting judgment, so to speak:

J   K   [ ]

The easiest way to derive a simple IF/THEN phrase from this difficult statement is to experiment. If we start by putting J in the box, what does that mean for K? Well, since J and K cannot both be selected, putting J in the box means we have to put K outside the box:

Start by putting J inside: [J]   K

We've just created an IF/THEN statement: **IF** J is selected, **then** K is not selected. But what if we had started with K? We'll put K in the box to begin with. Since J and K cannot both be selected, we'd have to put J outside the box:

Start by putting K inside: [K]   J

So we have another simple IF/THEN: **IF** K is selected, **then** J is not selected. Now let's start with J again and see what happens if we put J *outside* the box to begin with. Putting J outside the box doesn't really give us any clues for K. We could put K outside as well, or we could put K inside. Neither of these would break the original rule (*J and K cannot both be selected*):

Start by putting J outside: [   ]   J K   OR   [K]   J

So, putting J outside doesn't lead to any reliable IF/THEN statement. The same would be true if we started with K outside. In the end, we're left with the two statements we derived above:

IF J is selected, **then** K is not selected.
IF K is selected, **then** J is not selected.

We can express these in symbol form and then we can take the contrapositives:

IF/THEN Form	Symbol Form	Contrapositive
IF J is selected, **THEN** K is not selected.	J $\longrightarrow$ –K	K $\longrightarrow$ –J
IF K is selected, **THEN** J is not selected.	K $\longrightarrow$ –J	J $\longrightarrow$ –K

If you're really sharp, you've already noticed that the two IF/THEN statements we just derived are simply the contrapositives of one another. So essentially, the original statement *J and K cannot both be selected* gives us exactly two valid inferences. In plain English, we'd say something like, "Since they cannot both be selected, this means that if J is in, K must be out," and conversely, "If K is in, J must be out." Our notation looks like this:

$$J \longrightarrow -K$$

$$K \longrightarrow -J$$

Now that you've got the hang of using "in the box thinking" to turn advanced conditional statements into standard IF/THEN form, take a look at the remaining seven advanced statements. If you were completely unsure of how to translate them earlier, flip back and give them a second shot now using the box idea from above.

2. If M is selected, both G and H must be selected.

We can break down this rule into two distinct IF/THEN statements: 1) If M is selected, then G is selected, and 2) If M is selected, then H is selected. In general, if you can split up a rule, do so:

IF/THEN Form	Symbol Form	Contrapositive
IF M is selected, **THEN** G is selected.	$M \longrightarrow G$	$-G \longrightarrow -M$
IF M is selected, **THEN** H is selected.	$M \longrightarrow H$	$-H \longrightarrow -M$

In a few pages, we'll talk more about statements with "and" and "or."

3. Neither H nor K is selected if L is selected.

Again, we can break this down into two distinct IF/THEN statements: 1) If L is selected, then H is not selected, and 2) If L is selected, then K is not selected:

IF/THEN Form	Symbol Form	Contrapositive
IF L is selected, **THEN** H is not selected.	$L \longrightarrow -H$	$H \longrightarrow -L$
IF L is selected, **THEN** K is not selected.	$L \longrightarrow -K$	$K \longrightarrow -L$

4. If J is selected, then G is selected but L is not.

This is very similar to the two previous examples. We can break it down into two distinct IF/THEN statements: 1) If J is selected, then G is selected, and 2) If J is selected, then L is not selected:

IF/THEN Form	Symbol Form	Contrapositive
IF J is selected, **THEN** G is selected.	$J \longrightarrow G$	$-G \longrightarrow -J$
IF J is selected, **THEN** L is not selected.	$J \longrightarrow -L$	$L \longrightarrow -J$

MANHATTAN
PREP

5. F cannot be selected unless H is also selected.

This is a tough one. Let's experiment with the box. We know that we can't put F in unless we put H in. So, if we start with H in, we can put F in, too. But do we have to? Can we leave F out?

Sure. So we can't build a conditional statement that begins with selecting H. In fancier terms, we could say that "H in" does not function as a sufficient condition here. Similarly, if you can't dance unless there's music, just having music on is not sufficient to guarantee that you'll be dancing.

On the other hand, if we start with F in, what do we know? To put in F, we would need to have H in. After all, we can't select F unless we select H. So, we know that if F is in, H must also be in:

Start by putting F inside: F H

IF/THEN Form	Symbol Form	Contrapositive
IF F is selected, **THEN** H is selected.	F ⟶ H	–H ⟶ –F

We could also have started by putting H *outside* of the box. When H is out, F must be out as well. Notice that this is what our contrapositive tells us.

A quick way to handle "unless" statements is to replace the word "unless" with the words "if not." For example, using the example above, *F cannot be selected **if** H is **not** also selected.* Or, reworded, *If H is not selected, F cannot be selected.* Note that this is the contrapositive of what we started with above.

6. L is selected if, and only if, M is also selected.

We've already met this sort of statement. Like some of the other statements above, we can break this down into two parts, specifically by looking at the "if" and "only if" as two separate structures: 1) L is selected if M is selected (or even better, If M is selected, then L is selected), and 2) L is selected only if M is selected.

We can even deepen our understanding by applying our box technique. We'll start by putting M in. L is selected if M is selected, so we also must put L in:

Start by putting M inside: M L

But what if we'd started by putting L inside? What does this mean for M? Well, remember that L is selected *only if* M is selected. So if L is in, M must be in as well:

Start by putting L inside:

$$\boxed{\text{L M}}$$

So, from this original statement, we get two simple IF/THEN statements:

IF/THEN Form	Symbol Form	Contrapositive
IF M is selected, THEN L is selected.	$M \longrightarrow L$	$-L \longrightarrow -M$
IF L is selected, THEN M is selected.	$L \longrightarrow M$	$-M \longrightarrow -L$

As we learned in Chapter 5, we can also represent these with double-sided arrows:

$$M \longleftrightarrow L$$
$$-L \longleftrightarrow -M$$

7. If either Q or R is selected, both must be selected.

In this case we see two different triggers. Interestingly, including either letter requires us to include the other. Thus, we can derive two statements:

IF/THEN Form	Symbol Form	Contrapositive
IF Q is selected, THEN R is selected.	$Q \longrightarrow R$	$-R \longrightarrow -Q$
IF R is selected, THEN Q is selected.	$R \longrightarrow Q$	$-Q \longrightarrow -R$

Note that this statement is different from "Either Q, R, or both is selected." In that case, neither Q nor R is a trigger, but the absence of either one would trigger the inclusion of the other. Again, we could have used double-sided arrows here:

$$Q \longleftrightarrow R$$

8. N and W cannot be on the same team.

This example is applicable to an In/Out Grouping game in which elements are put on one team or another. It is also another example in which we don't see an "If." However, as in the last example, it turns out that both letters are triggers. If either of the two elements is "in," the other must be "out." If we call our teams X and Y, for instance, we know that when N is on team X, W is on team Y. And when N is on team Y? W must be on X, as shown below:

IF/THEN Form	Symbol Form	Contrapositive
IF N is selected for team X, THEN W is selected for team Y.	$N_X \longrightarrow W_Y$	$W_X \longrightarrow N_Y$
IF N is selected for team Y, THEN W is selected for team X.	$N_Y \longrightarrow W_X$	$W_Y \longrightarrow N_X$

Note that we could just as easily have started with the contrapositives of these two statements. Whatever team W is on, N must be on the other. In any case, we have another biconditional on our hands! Our diagram covers all four possible triggers: N_X, N_Y, W_X, and W_Y. To save yourself time and space on the exam, you will probably want to get used to notating biconditionals with double arrows:

$$N_X \longleftrightarrow W_Y \qquad N_Y \longleftrightarrow W_X$$

Compound Conditional Statements

Compound conditional statements are statements that have a two-part *sufficient* condition (a two-part trigger such as "If X and Y, then…") and/or a two part *necessary* condition (a two-part outcome such as "…then Y or Z"). Earlier on, we saw a few examples of compound statements. Here's one from before. This particular example has a two-part outcome:

If M is selected, then both G and H must be selected.

We dealt with this by splitting it into two separate conditionals:

If M is selected, then G is selected. (M ⟶ G)
If M is selected, then H is selected. (M ⟶ H)

While this is the most common type of compound statement that you'll see, it's not the only type. Let's take a moment to define the four types of compound statements that are fair game on the LSAT, starting with the type discussed above:

1. **AND in the outcome:** If M is selected, then both G and H must be selected.

In this case, M, the sufficient condition, is enough to trigger *both* G and H. In other words, M alone is enough to trigger G, and M alone is enough to trigger H. Thus, we can split the compound statement into two simple statements as we've already learned to do:

If M is selected, then G is selected. (M ⟶ G)
If M is selected, then H is selected. (M ⟶ H)

Of course, from these two simple statements, we can derive two contrapositives:

If G is not selected, then M is not selected. (–G ⟶ –M)
If H is not selected, then M is not selected. (–H ⟶ –M)

It's important to note that compound statements won't always have the word "and" explicitly written in the statement. For example:

If M is selected, then G is selected but H is not.

This is a similar compound statement in disguise! Selecting M triggers two outcomes: G is selected AND H is *not* selected. We could split this up as follows:

$$M \longrightarrow G$$
$$M \longrightarrow -H$$

So, it's the same type of statement, just disguised in different phrasing.

2. **OR in the trigger:** If M or G is selected, then H must be selected.
In this case, M on its own is enough to trigger H. We can say the same for G. *Either one* is sufficient to trigger the outcome, H.

Thus, we can split this compound statement into two simple statements:

If M is selected, then H is selected. (M $\longrightarrow$ H)
If G is selected, then H is selected. (G $\longrightarrow$ H)

Again, we can generate contrapositives:

If H is not selected, then M is not selected. (–H $\longrightarrow$ –M)
If H is not selected, then G is not selected. (–H $\longrightarrow$ –G)

3. **AND in the trigger:** If M and G are selected, then H is selected.
Here, *both* M and G *together* are enough to trigger H, but neither one *alone* is enough. Thus, we *cannot* split this statement into two parts. We must keep it together:

M and G $\longrightarrow$ H

See if you can figure out the contrapositive of that statement before reading on. Consider what we know if H is not selected.

To find the contrapositive of a statement like this, reverse and negate the elements and *swap "and" for "or"* or vice versa (we'll discuss why shortly):

–H $\longrightarrow$ –M or –G

4. **OR in the outcome:** If M is selected, then G or H is selected.
Notice that M is enough to trigger G or H, but not necessarily both. In other words, the outcome is at least one of G and H, but we can't be certain which one. Thus, we *cannot* split this statement into two parts. We must keep it together:

M $\longrightarrow$ G or H

Again, to find the contrapositive, reverse, negate, and swap *"and" for "or"* or vice versa:

–G and –H $\longrightarrow$ –M

MANHATTAN
PREP

By the way, when the LSAT uses "or," as in "X or Y must be selected," you can assume that "both" would also trigger the rule. Thus, three possibilities can be derived from that statement: Either 1) X is selected and not Y, 2) Y is selected and not X, or 3) X and Y are both selected. The exception to this rule is when a phrase like "but not both" is included. "Either X or Y, but not both, must be selected." In this case, "both" is not allowed, and there only two possibilities: Either 1) X is selected and Y is not, or 2) Y is selected and X is not.

Statements with "and" in the outcome are by far the most common compound conditionals on the LSAT, and the other three kinds mentioned above are quite rare. Nevertheless, it's a good idea to be prepared to deal with them when they do crop up. Let's summarize the four types:

Type	Example	Strategy	Notation	Contrapositive	Frequency
AND as an outcome	If J, then K and L.	Split it up.	$J \longrightarrow K$ $J \longrightarrow L$	$-K \longrightarrow -J$ $-L \longrightarrow -J$	Common
OR as a trigger	If M or N, then P.	Split it up.	$M \longrightarrow P$ $N \longrightarrow P$	$-P \longrightarrow -M$ $-P \longrightarrow -N$	Rare
AND as a trigger	If R and S, then X.	Keep together.	R and S $\longrightarrow$ X	$-X \longrightarrow -R$ or $-S$	Rare
OR as an outcome	If Q, then T or V.	Keep together.	Q $\longrightarrow$ T or V	$-T$ and $-V \longrightarrow -Q$	Rare

To Memorize or to Reason?

For *standard* conditional statements, it's not only unnecessary for us to reason our way to the contrapositive, but it's also dangerous—it creates a potential for error. Reverse and negate and be done with it. If we're told $K \longrightarrow -L$, we know that $L \longrightarrow -K$ and we shouldn't have to think much about why. But a compound conditional statement might require a bit of thought.

While it's easy enough for many people to remember to swap "and" for "or," this is exactly the sort of thing that trips some of us up when we're under the gun. Therefore, it can be helpful to have a process to reason your way to the contrapositive so that your rules make sense. Plus, it's a good brain stretcher even for those who are comfortable with the automation.

To reason your way to a compound contrapositive, start by thinking of the "If" part of the conditional as the "trigger," and the "then" part as the "outcome," as we've suggested previously. Then you can reason your way to the contrapositive as follows:

> "If the outcome isn't true, then the trigger can't be true."

Let's see how this thought process can help us get the contrapositives for four more compound conditionals:

1. If Jean and Fran go, Bill will not.

This can be represented as J and F ⟶ –B.

We can think of Jean and Fran going as the trigger and Bill not going as the outcome. Let's apply our reasoning:

"If the outcome isn't true, then the trigger can't be true."

What would make the outcome not true? *If Bill went.*

What would make the trigger not true? *If either Jean or Fran didn't go.* Be careful if you thought, "If Jean and Fran didn't go"! While both of them not going would mean the trigger didn't occur, it isn't necessary, and thus it's not the logical opposite.

We can represent this contrapositive as follows:

B ⟶ –J or –F

2. If neither Ted nor Seth is selected, Raj will be.

This can be represented as –T and –S ⟶ R.

"If the outcome isn't true, then the trigger can't be true."

What would make the outcome not true? *If Raj is not selected.*

What would make the trigger not true? *If either Ted or Seth is selected.*

We can represent this contrapositive as follows:

–R ⟶ T or S

3. If Carol doesn't go, either Bruce or Erica will go.

This can be represented as –C ⟶ B or E.

"If the outcome isn't true, then the trigger can't true."

What would make the outcome not true? *If both Bruce and Erica didn't go.*

What would make the trigger not true? *If Carol went.*

We can represent this contrapositive as follows:

–B and –E ⟶ C

4. If Matt is on the finance committee, Greg or Jan will not be.

This can be represented M $\longrightarrow$ –G or –J.

> "If the outcome isn't true, then the trigger can't be true."

What would make the outcome not true? *If both Greg and Jan are on the committee.*

What would make the trigger not true? *If Matt is not on the committee.*

We can represent this contrapositive as follows:

> G and J $\longrightarrow$ –M

Let's try one more to discuss what "but not both" might do to the situation:

5. If Sam goes, either Ruth or Tim, but not both, will go.

This one is difficult to represent! We know that if Sam goes, we'll have one of the following situations: Ruth will not go but Tim will or Tim will not go but Ruth will. We can represent that as the following:

> S $\longrightarrow$ (–R + T) or (–T + R)

The "but not both" is implied in that representation, since we could never have both (–R + T) and (–T + R). That would require Ruth and Tim to both go and not go at the same time!

> "If the outcome isn't true, then the trigger can't be true."

What would make the outcome not true? *In this case, two different situations: Both Ruth and Tom don't go, or both Ruth and Tom do go.* Tricky!

What would make the trigger not true? *If Sam doesn't go.*

We can represent this contrapositive as a "compound compound" statement:

> (R + T) or (–R + –T) $\longrightarrow$ –S

We can also think of this as two separate triggers that lead to the same outcome:

> R + T $\longrightarrow$ –S
> –R + –T $\longrightarrow$ –S

Again, we want to stress that for some students, it's far easier to think about conditional logic in a more formal or mathematical fashion, and for others, it's easier to think about these situations by reasoning through them. In fact, we imagine you might know already which process feels more comfortable to you. Learn both, but then use whichever approach feels most comfortable.

We also want to stress that compound conditionals such as the ones above are rare on the exam, and, in our experience, it is not critical that you define and write down the contrapositive during your initial setup. However, it is likely that you will need to think about the contrapositive at some point to answer at least one of the questions.

It's worth mentioning again that "or" does not exclude "and." For example, based on the statement "Either Ken or Han is selected," *both* Ken and Han can be selected. This combination is only excluded when it's made explicit that "and" is not okay. It would look like this: "Either Ken or Han is selected, but not both." If this is confusing, or seems completely counterintuitive to you, think of any "or" as "and/or" (unless, again, it's explicitly stated that "and" is not allowed), or as "at least one."

Now that you've got a handle on advanced conditional statements, it's time to practice. Then, in the next chapter, you'll learn to apply your understanding of conditional statements and their contrapositives to In/Out Grouping games.

7

MANHATTAN
PREP

Drill It: Advanced Conditional Statements

Convert each of the statements into conditional diagrams, and then derive contrapositive inferences. Be sure to check your responses against the solutions **after each exercise.**

Example: If X is selected, then both Y and Z are selected.

	Conversions:	Contrapositives:
	X $\longrightarrow$ Y	–Y $\longrightarrow$ –X
	X $\longrightarrow$ Z	–Z $\longrightarrow$ –X

1. Martinez is not chosen unless Jones is chosen.

2. If H is selected, then J is selected but G is not.

3. Rolfson and Strapini cannot both be selected.

4. If K is selected, then neither M nor N is selected.

5. If Fiora is chosen, then both Lane and Newsam are chosen.

6. V is selected if, and only if, P is selected.

7. If both P and Q are selected, then R is selected.

8. L is chosen if, and only if, G is selected.

9. W and X cannot both be chosen.

10. If Paulson is selected, then Oster is selected but Vicenza is not.

11. T is not selected unless R is selected.

12. Neither X nor Y is chosen if Z is chosen.

Solutions: Advanced Conditional Statements

1. Martinez is not chosen unless Jones is chosen.

$$M \longrightarrow J \qquad -J \longrightarrow -M$$

2. If H is selected, then J is selected but G is not.

$$H \longrightarrow J \qquad -J \longrightarrow -H$$
$$H \longrightarrow -G \qquad G \longrightarrow -H$$

3. Rolfson and Strapini cannot both be selected.

$$R \longrightarrow -S \qquad S \longrightarrow -R$$

4. If K is selected, then neither M nor N is selected.

$$K \longrightarrow -M \qquad M \longrightarrow -K$$
$$K \longrightarrow -N \qquad N \longrightarrow -K$$

5. If Fiora is chosen, then both Lane and Newsam are chosen.

$$F \longrightarrow L \qquad -L \longrightarrow -F$$
$$F \longrightarrow N \qquad -N \longrightarrow -F$$

6. V is selected if, and only if, P is selected.

$$P \longleftrightarrow V \quad OR \quad -V \longleftrightarrow -P$$

$$P \longrightarrow V \qquad -V \longrightarrow -P$$
$$V \longrightarrow P \qquad -P \longrightarrow -V$$

7. If both P and Q are selected, then R is selected.

$$P \text{ and } Q \longrightarrow R \qquad -R \longrightarrow -P \text{ or } -Q$$

8. L is chosen if, and only if, G is selected.

$$L \longleftrightarrow G \quad OR \quad -G \longleftrightarrow -L$$

$$L \longrightarrow G \qquad -G \longrightarrow -L$$
$$G \longrightarrow L \qquad -L \longrightarrow -G$$

9. W and X cannot both be chosen.

$$W \longrightarrow -X \qquad X \longrightarrow -W$$

10. If Paulson is selected, then Oster is selected but Vicenza is not.

$$P \longrightarrow O \qquad -O \longrightarrow -P$$
$$P \longrightarrow -V \qquad V \longrightarrow -P$$

11. T is not selected unless R is selected.

$$T \longrightarrow R \qquad -R \longrightarrow -T$$

12. Neither X nor Y is chosen if Z is chosen.

$$Z \longrightarrow -X \qquad X \longrightarrow -Z$$
$$Z \longrightarrow -Y \qquad Y \longrightarrow -Z$$

MANHATTAN
PREP

Chapter 8

Timing

In This Chapter...

Timing

At this point, you've learned each of the game types that appear on the LSAT and you've played a large number of games. With the exception of the Getting Familiar games, we haven't asked you to limit your time strictly—the goal being to give you the space to consider various approaches and learn the process of tackling games:

> Step 1: Picture the Game
> Step 2: Notate the Rules and Make Inferences
> Step 3: The Big Pause
> Step 4: Attack the Questions

Now it's time to start working on some of the more timing-specific strategies—the icing on the timing cake. Let's start by looking at the games section as a whole.

Section Timing

35 minutes ÷ 4 games = 8:45/game. Right?

That formula would work well if every game were the same difficulty level. But, as you likely already know, there are some games that you find very simple and others that are extremely challenging. Fortunately, the test writers balance out the difficulty of the games so that the overall difficulty of the games sections is fairly consistent. On test day, most prepared test-takers find one or two games quite easy, one or two of average difficulty, and at least one game quite hard.

The difficulty of the games generally increases from the first game to the last. However, this is very much a generality. It's quite possible that you—or even most everyone taking an LSAT—will find the third game to be the hardest of the section. The difficulty of each game falls into a general range:

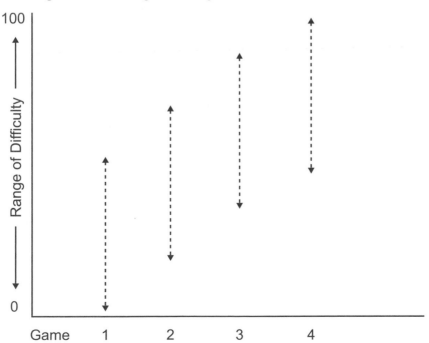

And, while the specific difficulty of each game might vary and fall "out of order," the section's difficulty will average out:

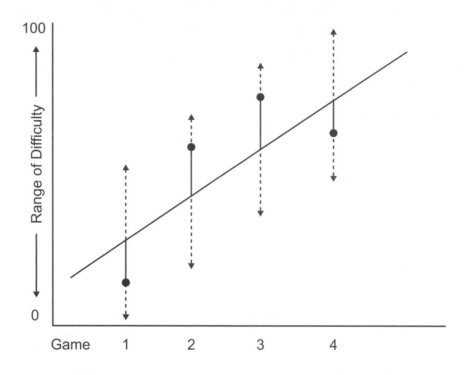

In general, you want to spend less time on the easy games and more time on the tougher ones. Perhaps your timing will be such that you spend 7 minutes on the easiest game, 8 on the next hardest, 9 on the next, and 11 on the hardest one. But it's unrealistic to expect this to happen, or, more importantly, to try to make your game playing fit into that plan. You might face two easy games and two harder ones, requiring a 6, 6, 11, 12 timing. Furthermore, you won't know the difficulty of each game until you are in the midst of it. A rigid timing strategy is one of the surest ways to implode on test day.

Instead, develop a flexible timing strategy. We suggest that you use what we referred to earlier as the **Time Bank.** The idea is to allot each game 8 minutes, leaving 3 minutes in the bank. If the first game takes only 6 minutes—and that's possible—you now have a total of 5 minutes in the bank. Then, if the second game ends up taking 9 minutes, you're now down to 4 minutes in the bank. And then if the third game…you get the idea!

Skipping Games vs. Skipping Questions

One obvious way to put more time in the bank is to skip an entire game. This is not a strategy we recommend—and we'll explain why—but let's spend a moment understanding why some might be attracted to this plan. Planning to skip a game automatically gives you an average of 11 minutes and 40 seconds per game, making it much easier to work through a game and recover from errors. If someone uses a lot of time-consuming trial and error, having 11:40 per game is useful. But the downside is obvious—you can expect to miss almost all the questions on the game you skip! Planning to skip a game is a strategy we would suggest only to those who are a week away from test day, have never been able to finish all four games, and are usually in a mad rush on the last two games. For everyone else, we recommend that you set a goal of finishing all four games. If skipping is required, *skip tough and time-consuming questions.*

To illustrate why this is a better strategy, compare these two performances by the same average (or slightly below average) hypothetical test-taker on the same hypothetical Logic Games section:

Grant "the Game Skipper"	Quinn "the Question Skipper"
Game 1: 10 minutes. 5/6 correct. One wrong because of a silly mistake.	Game 1: 9 minutes. 5/6 correct. One wrong because of a silly mistake.
Game 2: 13 minutes. 6/6. Perfect performance! That fifth question was a doozy, though!	Game 2: 9 minutes. 5/6 correct. Had to skip and guess (incorrectly) on that fifth question when it was clear that it would be too time-consuming.
Game 3: 1 minute. 1/5 correct. Skipped the game when he realized it was tough, and guessed (D) for every answer.	Game 3: 10 minutes. 3/5 correct. Last two questions skipped (guessed incorrectly) when they quickly proved very difficult.
Game 4: 11 minutes. 4/5 correct. Had to guess (incorrectly) on that really tough fourth question after spending two and a half minutes on it.	Game 4: 7 minutes. 4/5. Had to skip and guess (incorrectly) on that really tough fourth question when it was clear that time was running out.
Guesses: 6 Score: 16/22	Guesses: 4 Score: 17/22

Clearly, the point of the dramatic game-by-game comparison is that skipping questions is a better strategy than skipping games. But why did it work out better? It wasn't because Grant guessed on significantly more questions—Quinn guessed on four! Quinn did better because she didn't spend a lot of time on the hardest questions of the section. Instead, she invested that time in the easier questions of the game that Grant skipped. In short, she got the easy ones right and the hard ones wrong. Grant, on the other hand, got many easy ones right and several—in the skipped game—wrong, and he conquered only a couple more of the hard ones than Quinn. Furthermore, if Grant had actually needed three minutes to figure out that the third game was the one he wanted to skip, he might have found himself performing even worse on the final game of the section.

We've made our point, but the truth is that we've fudged the numbers—it's highly unlikely that anyone who needs to skip an entire game could actually perform as well as Grant. If you are able to correctly answer all (or close to all) of the questions for three games, you already have most of the skills tested in the Logic Games section and it's likely that by improving your approach—for instance, by learning to follow the inference chain instead of using trial and error—you can get to all four games.

If you ignore our number-fudging, Quinn did only one point better than Grant. That's not incredibly compelling. But if Quinn sticks with her strategy through months of prep, she'll develop the ability to tell when a question is too tough for her and she'll also regularly challenge herself to move faster. Grant will focus on becoming better at confirming the answers on his three games, probably using time-consuming trial and error, and he will not expose himself to the hardest games under the pressure of the clock ticking away, since he'll be skipping those.

Join Quinn's question-skipping team; commit to attacking every game and question. As you develop your abilities, you should soon find yourself skipping only two or three questions per section. And because you'll be comfortable moving on from impossible questions, you will not fall for the most deadly of logic game traps: wasting so much time on two tough questions that you have no time for four easy ones.

In summary, **if you're not expecting to get a perfect score on Logic Games, get the easy and average ones right and the hardest ones wrong.** Quickly tackling the easy questions and skipping the impossible ones will give you time in the bank to spend on the challenging-but-doable ones.

Developing Your Personal Timing Strategy

The Time Bank is designed to adapt to the reality of whatever Logic Games section you're facing. In one sense, it's impossible to plan how it will work out. However, it's useful to set some goals to push yourself to move faster. Each person's timing strategy will be different, and it's up to you to develop your own. Now that you've learned each of the game types, your practice tests will be a good source of data on which to build your timing strategy. It's likely that you've already developed a strong sense of which game types you find more intuitive and which game types you struggle with. How fast can you go on those easier games? When you spend 13 minutes on a game, do you get every question right and do you have enough time for the subsequent games? In other words, is it worth it to spend that much time? When you skip time-consuming questions, does it seem to pay off? If you're still struggling with completing a section within 35 minutes and you haven't tried skipping a question within a game, take the opportunity in your next timed section to give it a try.

Game-Specific Timing

Hitting your timing goals requires you to manage your timing within each game. Part of this is understanding when to speed up and when to slow down. The Big Pause is a great example of how slowing down can allow you to speed up later. Another piece of the puzzle is adapting your strategy to both front-end and back-end games.

As you know, front-end games require more time in their setup phase. There are important inferences to be made before tackling the questions. On the other hand, there are fewer (or no) inferences to be made during the setup of back-end games, and naturally the questions will take longer. Here is a chart showing the tendencies of the various game types we've looked at in this book:

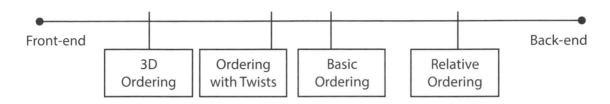

Obviously, these are broad tendencies. Can there be a Relative Ordering game that calls for a complex diagram involving frames? Of course. The idea is not that you see a Relative Ordering game, decide that you should be into the first question after 1:30, and freak out when you're not. You clearly have to adjust to the game in front of you. More important than memorizing which game type falls where on the spectrum is developing a sense of whether a specific game's diagram deserves more time. Erring on either side of that decision—not thinking enough about a front-end game, or spinning your wheels for a long time on a back-end diagram when there is nothing more to discover—will slow you down.

Reordering Questions

Clearly some questions are easier than others. Some test-takers thus reason that if their job is to get the easier ones right and the hardest ones wrong, they should start with the easier questions to make sure they get to them. We do not recommend this strategy, but, as we did with the idea of skipping a game, let's spend a moment to consider it.

To some extent, we agree: If you're in a mad dash for time on the last game, go for the easier questions. The first two questions of a game are generally much easier than the rest. Conditional questions can be a bit easier to jump into since they give you something to work with and some unconditional questions are quite time-consuming—since there's no condition setting off a chain of inferences, each answer choice may require some thinking.

However, there are some problems with turning this under-the-wire strategy into how you approach every game. Many questions do not neatly follow the "law" about difficulty levels—conditional questions can be much harder than unconditional ones. Furthermore, since the questions in a game are laid out in a generally increasing order of difficulty, moving through the game in the given order means that earlier questions serve as warm-ups for the harder ones. Each question is an opportunity to further "own" the rules and to prepare to apply them on later questions in more complex ways.

Your focus should be on understanding the game and attacking each question correctly. Picking and choosing questions is a distraction, and it takes up precious time. If you're aiming for a 170+ score, few questions, if any, should be out of your reach.

We do recommend, however, skipping the most challenging questions as you encounter them. As we discussed earlier, know how many questions you can get wrong and still achieve your target score, remember that every question is worth the same number of points, and develop your sense of when enough is enough on a given question. Finally, recognize that some question types are simply designed to take more time (Equivalent Rule, unconditional "could be true," Determines Positions, etc.). If you're in a rush, flag those questions and guess at their answers. Then, come back later and try them in earnest if you have time.

Practice Makes Perfect

As you approach test day, it's important to find a timing strategy that works for you. As you've worked through this book, you've been primarily focused on getting familiar with each game type and getting stronger at finding more efficient approaches. Outside of your work in this book, you'll also need to take practice tests and complete individual sections of Logic Games under timed conditions. Think of your timed section work as an opportunity to practice your timing strategy. Tinker with it and get comfortable making timing decisions under the pressure of a ticking clock. After you complete a section, go back and review each game. Ask yourself whether your approach was the most efficient. Could you have spent more time during the setup and found an inference or a set of frames that would have made the game much easier? Did you follow the inference chain on each conditional question or did you waste time fumbling through the answers with an incomplete picture of what the new rule implies? Initially, your decisions during a timed section reflect your instincts. Some of them you may want to reinforce, others you may want to consciously fight against.

Keep a timing device in front of you as you complete timed sections and full tests from paper practice exams. When you complete digital sections and practice tests, track your timing using the timer on the screen. Check the clock after you complete each game or if you feel you've been lingering for too long on a question. If you're unsure whether your pacing is appropriate, record how much time was spent on the setup and on each question of a game. Look for questions that you should have skipped and consider how you'll recognize them next time. And remember, timing is a reflection of understanding—as your approach strengthens, the time pressure you face will diminish.

Set 1

In This Practice Set...

Mixed Practice: Set 1

How are you going to become the best game player you can be? You will need to have more than just one angle of attack. The very best game players are comfortable with various approaches—framing, hypotheticals, previous work, etc.—and have played enough games that they know when to use which approach.

In this first set, we're going to force you to use one of the most underutilized and powerful techniques for deepening your mastery: replaying the same game. When you play a game more than once, you'll increase your comfort with making the sort of inferences the LSAT requires and spotting new opportunities to use strategies you've learned. Since you won't have to think as much about the basics of the game, you can focus more on refining your process. You might also uncover some dark corner of the game that you missed the first time. Finally, after some time, you will naturally start drawing connections between the game you're working on and others you've already completed and reviewed. When you start thinking, "Oh, this game is so much like the one where…," you're well on your way to mastery.

Your task? Complete these games twice. For your first time, treat it like an actual section: give yourself 35 minutes to finish the set of four. At the end, we've included QuickChecks—these are essentially what our work looked like when we did the games, including both the answers we eliminated on screen and the work we did on our scratch paper. Check your answers and work against ours, and make sure you understand our process. Once you've reviewed, take a day away from the games, then come back and replay them. During this replay, complete them one at a time, reviewing again using the QuickChecks. Try to ingrain good habits, and make a few inferences (or frames) you didn't catch the first time!

Practice Game 1: PT38, S2, G1

A car drives into the center ring of a circus and exactly eight clowns—Q, R, S, T, V, W, Y, and Z—get out of the car, one clown at a time. The order in which the clowns get out of the car is consistent with the following conditions:

V gets out at some time before both Y and Q.

Q gets out at some time after Z.

T gets out at some time before V but at some time after R.

S gets out at some time after V.

R gets out at some time before W.

1. Which one of the following could be the order, from first to last, in which the clowns get out of the car?

    (A) T, Z, V, R, W, Y, S, Q
    (B) Z, R, W, Q, T, V, Y, S
    (C) R, W, T, V, Q, Z, S, Y
    (D) Z, W, R, T, V, Y, Q, S
    (E) R, W, T, V, Z, S, Y, Q

2. Which one of the following could be true?

    (A) Y is the second clown to get out of the car.
    (B) R is the third clown to get out of the car.
    (C) Q is the fourth clown to get out of the car.
    (D) S is the fifth clown to get out of the car.
    (E) V is the sixth clown to get out of the car.

3. If Z is the seventh clown to get out of the car, then which one of the following could be true?

    (A) R is the second clown to get out of the car.
    (B) T is the fourth clown to get out of the car.
    (C) W is the fifth clown to get out of the car.
    (D) V is the sixth clown to get out of the car.
    (E) Y is the eighth clown to get out of the car.

4. If T is the fourth clown to get out of the car, then which one of the following must be true?

    (A) R is the first clown to get out of the car.
    (B) Z is the second clown to get out of the car.
    (C) W is the third clown to get out of the car.
    (D) V is the fifth clown to get out of the car.
    (E) Y is the seventh clown to get out of the car.

5. If Q is the fifth clown to get out of the car, then each of the following could be true EXCEPT:

    (A) Z is the first clown to get out of the car.
    (B) T is the second clown to get out of the car.
    (C) V is the third clown to get out of the car.
    (D) W is the fourth clown to get out of the car.
    (E) Y is the sixth clown to get out of the car.

6. If R is the second clown to get out of the car, which one of the following must be true?

    (A) S gets out of the car at some time before T does.
    (B) T gets out of the car at some time before W does.
    (C) W gets out of the car at some time before V does.
    (D) Y gets out of the car at some time before Q does.
    (E) Z gets out of the car at some time before W does.

7. If V gets out of the car at some time before Z does, then which one of the following could be true?

    (A) R is the second clown to get out of the car.
    (B) T is the fourth clown to get out of the car.
    (C) Q is the fourth clown to get out of the car.
    (D) V is the fifth clown to get out of the car.
    (E) Z is the sixth clown to get out of the car.

MANHATTAN
PREP

Practice Game 2: PT35, S3, G4

Exactly seven professors—Madison, Nilsson, Orozco, Paton, Robinson, Sarkis, and Togo—were hired in the years 1989 through 1995. Each professor has one or more specialities, and any two professors hired in the same year or in consecutive years do not have a specialty in common. The professors were hired according to the following conditions:

Madison was hired in 1993, Robinson in 1991.
There is at least one specialty that Madison, Orozco, and Togo have in common.
Nilsson shares a specialty with Robinson.
Paton and Sarkis were each hired at least one year before Madison and at least one year after Nilsson.
Orozco, who shares a specialty with Sarkis, was hired in 1990.

18. Which one of the following is a complete and accurate list of the professors who could have been hired in the years 1989 through 1991?

    (A) Nilsson, Orozco, Robinson
    (B) Orozco, Robinson, Sarkis
    (C) Nilsson, Orozco, Paton, Robinson
    (D) Nilsson, Orozco, Paton, Sarkis
    (E) Orozco, Paton, Robinson, Sarkis

19. If exactly one professor was hired in 1991, then which one of the following could be true?

    (A) Madison and Paton share a specialty.
    (B) Robinson and Sarkis share a specialty.
    (C) Paton was hired exactly one year after Orozco.
    (D) Exactly one professor was hired in 1994.
    (E) Exactly two professors were hired in 1993.

20. Which one of the following must be false?

    (A) Nilsson was hired in 1989.
    (B) Paton was hired in 1990.
    (C) Paton was hired in 1991.
    (D) Sarkis was hired in 1992.
    (E) Togo was hired in 1994.

21. Which one of the following must be true?

    (A) Orozco was hired before Paton.
    (B) Paton was hired before Sarkis.
    (C) Sarkis was hired before Robinson.
    (D) Robinson was hired before Sarkis.
    (E) Madison was hired before Sarkis.

22. If exactly two professors were hired in 1992, then which one of the following could be true?

    (A) Orozco, Paton, and Togo share a specialty.
    (B) Madison, Paton, and Togo share a specialty.
    (C) Exactly two professors were hired in 1991.
    (D) Exactly two professors were hired in 1993.
    (E) Paton was hired in 1991.

23. If Paton and Madison have a specialty in common, then which one of the following must be true?

    (A) Nilsson does not share a specialty with Paton.
    (B) Exactly one professor was hired in 1990.
    (C) Exactly one professor was hired in 1991.
    (D) Exactly two professors were hired in each of two years.
    (E) Paton was hired at least one year before Sarkis.

Practice Game 3: PT1, S2, G1

Exactly six trade representatives negotiate a treaty: Klosnik, Londi, Manley, Neri, Osata, Poirier. There are exactly six chairs evenly spaced around a circular table. The chairs are numbered 1 through 6, with successively numbered chairs next to each other and chair number 1 next to chair number 6. Each chair is occupied by exactly one of the representatives. The following conditions apply:

Poirier sits immediately next to Neri.
Londi sits immediately next to Manley, Neri, or both.
Klosnik does not sit immediately next to Manley.
If Osata sits immediately next to Poirier, Osata does not sit immediately next to Manley.

1. Which one of the following seating arrangements of the six representatives in chairs 1 through 6 would NOT violate the stated conditions?

   (A) Klosnik, Poirier, Neri, Manley, Osata, Londi
   (B) Klosnik, Londi, Manley, Poirier, Neri, Osata
   (C) Klosnik, Londi, Manley, Osata, Poirier, Neri
   (D) Klosnik, Osata, Poirier, Neri, Londi, Manley
   (E) Klosnik, Neri, Londi, Osata, Manley, Poirier

2. If Londi sits immediately next to Poirier, which one of the following is a pair of representatives who must sit immediately next to each other?

   (A) Klosnik and Osata
   (B) Londi and Neri
   (C) Londi and Osata
   (D) Manley and Neri
   (E) Manley and Poirier

3. If Klosnik sits directly between Londi and Poirier, then Manley must sit directly between

   (A) Londi and Neri
   (B) Londi and Osata
   (C) Neri and Osata
   (D) Neri and Poirier
   (E) Osata and Poirier

4. If Neri sits immediately next to Manley, then Klosnik can sit directly between

   (A) Londi and Manley
   (B) Londi and Poirier
   (C) Neri and Osata
   (D) Neri and Poirier
   (E) Poirier and Osata

5. If Londi sits immediately next to Manley, then which one of the following is a complete and accurate list of representatives any one of whom could also sit immediately next to Londi?

   (A) Klosnik
   (B) Klosnik, Neri
   (C) Neri, Poirier
   (D) Klosnik, Osata, Poirier
   (E) Klosnik, Neri, Osata, Poirier

6. If Londi sits immediately next to Neri, which one of the following statements must be false?

   (A) Klosnik sits immediately next to Osata.
   (B) Londi sits immediately next to Manley.
   (C) Osata sits immediately next to Poirier.
   (D) Neri sits directly between Londi and Poirier.
   (E) Osata sits directly between Klosnik and Manley.

7. If Klosnik sits immediately next to Osata, then Londi CANNOT sit directly between

   (A) Klosnik and Manley
   (B) Klosnik and Neri
   (C) Manley and Neri
   (D) Manley and Poirier
   (E) Neri and Osata

Practice Game 4: PTA, S3, G3

The seven members of an academic department are each to be assigned a different room as an office. The department members are professors F and G, lecturers Q, R, and S, and instructors V and W. The available rooms are seven consecutive rooms along one side of a straight hallway numbered sequentially 101 through 107. The assignment must conform to the following conditions:

Neither instructor is assigned a room next to a professor's room.

Neither professor is assigned room 101 and neither professor is assigned room 107.

G is not assigned a room next to R's room.

W is not assigned a room next to V's room unless R is also assigned a room next to V's room.

11. If F and G are assigned rooms that have exactly one room between them, which one of the following is the list of department members each of whom could be assigned to the intervening room?

   (A) Q, R
   (B) Q, S
   (C) Q, V
   (D) R, W
   (E) S, V

12. Which one of the following is a possible assignment of rooms for members R, V, and W?

   (A) 101: V; 102: W; 103: R
   (B) 101: V; 102: W; 104: R
   (C) 101: V; 103: W; 104: R
   (D) 103: W; 104: V; 106: R
   (E) 105: R; 106: W; 107: V

13. If R is assigned room 104, which one of the following must be assigned either room 103 or else room 105?

   (A) F
   (B) G
   (C) Q
   (D) V
   (E) W

14. What is the greatest number of rooms that could be between the rooms to which F and G are assigned?

   (A) one
   (B) two
   (C) three
   (D) four
   (E) five

15. Which one of the following CANNOT be assigned room 104?

   (A) F
   (B) G
   (C) Q
   (D) S
   (E) V

16. If no two faculty members of the same rank are assigned adjacent rooms, which one of the following must be true?

   (A) F is assigned either room 103 or else room 104.
   (B) Q is assigned either room 102 or else room 106.
   (C) R is assigned either room 102 or else room 105.
   (D) S is assigned either room 104 or else room 105.
   (E) V is assigned either room 101 or else room 107.

17. If F and G are not assigned rooms that are next to each other, which one of the following CANNOT be assigned room 107?

   (A) W
   (B) V
   (C) S
   (D) R
   (E) Q

For these mixed practice sets, we are not providing full explanations. Part of the learning process here is looking at our QuickChecks and figuring out what we did.

Here's how to read them:

Key to the Code:

Darker shade = information provided explicitly by the game's rules, by a specific question stem, or by the information in a given answer choice.

Lighter shade = inferences made on the basis of that provided information.

X = answer eliminated

(A) = correct answer

"Prev. work" = an answer choice was eliminated/selected based on a consideration of scenarios that were written for previous problems. The problem number used is listed in parentheses.

A
(B)   When only the correct answer is circled, this means that the test-taker actively looked for
C   the correct answer and found it, without pausing to specifically eliminate wrong
D   answers.
E   If a hypothetical scenario is written out to test an answer choice and the scenario turns out to
       be invalid, there will be an "X" beside it.

X
B   When the correct answer is written to the side of the answer choices, rather than just being
C (C) circled, this indicates that the correct answer was chosen because the other four answers were
D   found to be wrong. The correct answer itself was not evaluated.
E

A
B   When two or three answer choices are underlined, this indicates that some eliminations were
C   easy (the crossed out answers that are not underlined), while the underlined choices needed
D   careful consideration. Here, it would be an arbitrary choice whether we started by testing
E   (C) or (E).

MANHATTAN
PREP

Ⓐ 3
Ⓑ 2
C Ⓒ
Ⓓ 1
Ⓔ 4

On Orientation questions, the number next to the eliminated answer choice indicates which rule the answer choice breaks (some answers break more than one rule, but only one is listed).

"fyi" = the correct answer could have been obtained without evaluating these answer choices, but an explanation of why they are wrong is provided.

in   out

T / V   V / Ⓣ

The placeholder indicates that early in the deduction process, the test-taker split up these two elements. The circled letter shows that ultimately the test-taker realized that only one of those choices worked.

QuickCheck: PT38, S2, G1

Q R S T V W Y Z

R ⟨ W
  T — V ⟨ S
        Y
   Z ⟩ Q

$\frac{R/Z}{1}$ $\frac{}{2}$ $\frac{}{3}$ $\frac{}{4}$ $\frac{}{5}$ $\frac{}{6}$ $\frac{}{7}$ $\frac{}{8}$

The Big Pause

- No floaters
- R/Z must get out first.
- S/Y/Q/W must get out last.

Frames?

We don't frame Relative Ordering games too frequently. We don't have an option rule here, so no frames.

---

1. (A) 3
   (B) 1
   (C) 2
   (D) 5
   (E) **(E)**

2. (A) R, T, V before (3)
   (B) W, T, V, Y, S, Q after (6)
   (C) R, T, V, Z before (4)
   (D) R, T, V before (3)
   (E)

3. $\frac{R}{1}$ $\underbrace{\frac{W, T - V \langle {}^Y_S}{2 \quad 3 \quad 4 \quad 5 \quad 6}}$ $\frac{Z}{7}$ $\frac{Q}{8}$
   (A)
   (B)
   (C)
   (D)
   (E)

4. $\underbrace{\frac{R - W, Z}{1 \quad 2 \quad 3}}$ $\frac{T}{4}$ $\frac{V}{5}$ $\underbrace{\frac{Y, S, Q}{6 \quad 7 \quad 8}}$
   (A)
   (B)
   (C)
   (D)
   (E)

5. $\underbrace{\frac{R - T - V, Z}{1 \quad 2 \quad 3 \quad 4}}$ $\frac{Q}{5}$ $\underbrace{\frac{W, S, Y}{6 \quad 7 \quad 8}}$
   (A)
   (B)
   (C)
   (D)
   (E)

6. $\frac{Z}{1}$ $\frac{R}{2}$ $\underbrace{\frac{W, \; T - V \langle {}^S_{Y}_Q}{3 \quad 4 \quad 5 \quad 6 \quad 7 \quad 8}}$
   (A)
   (B)
   (C)
   (D)
   (E)

7. R ⟨ ^{W}
     T — V ⟨ S
            Z
            Y — Q

   $\frac{R}{1}$ $\frac{}{2}$ $\frac{}{3}$ $\frac{}{4}$ $\frac{}{5}$ $\frac{}{6}$ $\frac{}{7}$ $\frac{}{8}$
   (A)
   (B)
   (C)
   (D)
   (E)

QuickCheck: PT35, S3, G4

M N O P R S T

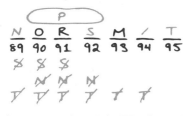

P

N   O   R   S   M   /   T
89   90   91   92   93   94   95

N〈P／S〉M

The Big Pause

- No strays
- So much filled in already!

Frames?

With this much filled in, we should head straight into the questions. Expect mainly unconditional.

---

18. N, O, R, P
 (A)
 (B)
 (C)
 (D)
 (E)

19.

~~P~~
／
N   O   R   S   M   /   T
89   90   91   92   93   94   95
 (A)
 (B)
 (C)
 (D)
 (E)

20. (A)
 (B)
 (C)
 (D)
 (E)

21. (A)
 (B)
 (C)
 (D)
 (E)

22.
P
N   O   R   S   M   /   T
89   90   91   92   93   94   95
 (A)
 (B)
 (C)
 (D)
 (E)

23.
P
N   O   R   S   M   /   T
89   90   91   92   93   94   95
 (A)
 (B)
 (C)
 (D)
 (E)

QuickCheck: PT1, S2, G1

K L M N O P

The Big Pause
- No floaters
- Questions don't care about seat numbers.

Frames?

Might be something with L/N/M option, but it looks like there would be too many possibilities.

1. (A) 2
   (B) **B**
   (C) 4
   (D) 3
   (E) 1

2.

   (A)
   (B)
   (C)
   (D)
   (E)

3.

   (A)
   (B)
   (C)
   (D)
   (E)

4.

O, P or O, L

   (A)
   (B)
   (C)
   (D)
   (E)

5.

Q1=K, Q2=P, Q4=O
Test N, works → K, P, O, N

   (A)
   (B)
   (C)
   (D)
   (E)

6.

   (A)
   (B)
   (C)
   (D)
   (E)

7.

   (A) prev work (4)
   (B) prev work (6)
   (C) prev work (6)
   (D) prev work (2 or 5)
   (E)

MANHATTAN
PREP

QuickCheck: PTA, S3, G3

P: F, G
L: Ⓠ, R, Ⓢ
I: V, W

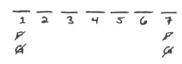

```
__ __ __ __ __ __ __
1  2  3  4  5  6  7
F̶              F̶
G̶              G̶
```

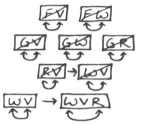

FV̶   FW̶
GV̶ GW̶ GR̶
RV̶ → LOV
WV → WVR

The Big Pause

- Subgroups twist. Mainly used to create anti-chunks.
- Q and S are strays (and both are lecturers, so they're twins).

Frames?

Since most of our rules are exclusions/anti-chunks, we probably won't have frames.
The conditional might be tempting, but it's rarely useful to frame around that type of rule.

11.

```
[ F __ G ]
Ⓠ R Ⓢ X̶ W̶
```

(A)
Ⓑ
(C)
(D)
(E)

12. (A̶) Rule 4 elim
(B̶) Rule 4 elim
(C) Ⓒ
(D̶) Rule 4 elim
(E̶) Rule 4 elim

13.
```
( V, W )  R  F  G
          G  F  R  ( V, W )
1  2  3  4  5  6  7
G̶    G̶    G̶    G̶
F̶              F̶
```
Ⓐ
(B)
(C)
(D)
(E)

14.
```
     F̶ __ __ G̶ W̶
     F̶ __ W̶ __ G̶
1  2  3  4  5  6  7
F̶  V̶  V̶  F̶
G̶  W̶  W̶  G̶
X̶        X̶
W̶        W̶
```
Ⓐ
(B̶)
(C̶)
(D̶)
(E̶)

15. (A)
(B)
(C̶) Twins
(D̶) Twins
Ⓔ
```
__ F̶ __ V __ G̶ __
1  2  3  4  5  6  7
F̶  F̶           F̶
G̶  G̶  G̶  G̶
W̶  W̶  W̶  W̶
        (W?)
```

16.
V/W	R	F	Q/S	G	S/A	W/V
1	2	3	4	5	6	7
7	6	5	4	3	2	1 (mirror)

FG   QR   QS   RS   VW
(A̶)
(B̶)
(C̶)
(D)
Ⓔ

17. (A̶) prev work (16)
(B̶) prev work (16)
(C̶) twins
Ⓓ
(E̶) twins

LG

Chapter 9

In/Out Grouping

In This Chapter...

Curves Ahead!

This chapter is unlike any other in this book: We're going to learn two different approaches to a game type. They both represent all the rules and allow you to make inferences, but there will be times when one suits you more than the other. We want you to put both in your tool belt so you're ready to tackle any of these games.

Also, we're not going to sugarcoat it: The second approach looks weird at first. We know. But it's a powerful tool that lets you quickly make inferences and answer unconditional questions, so stick with it!

Buckle up and give both approaches your full attention!

Getting Familiar

Give yourself **10 minutes** for this next game and then move on to the rest of the chapter. We don't want you to get too bogged down with this type of game before we get into the approach!

A horse breeder is deciding which of seven horses—Nimbler, Orion, Pride, Renegade, Sam, Trix, and Velvet—to sell at auction this year. The breeder will determine which horses to sell according to the following restrictions:

> If Renegade is sold at auction, Pride is not.
> Either Orion or Nimbler is sold at auction, but not both.
> If Sam is not sold at auction, neither is Renegade.
> If Trix is not sold at auction, Velvet is.

1. Which one of the following is an acceptable list of the horses sold at auction?

   (A) Orion, Renegade, Sam
   (B) Renegade, Sam, Trix, Velvet
   (C) Orion, Pride, Sam, Velvet
   (D) Nimbler, Renegade, Trix, Velvet
   (E) Nimbler, Orion, Renegade, Sam, Velvet

2. If Renegade is sold, which of the following must be true?

   (A) Sam and Orion are also sold.
   (B) Nimbler and Pride are not sold.
   (C) At least five horses are sold.
   (D) At most four horses are sold.
   (E) At least two horses are not sold.

3. What is the maximum number of horses that can be sold?

   (A) three
   (B) four
   (C) five
   (D) six
   (E) seven

4. If either Renegade or Sam is sold, but not both, which of the following could be a complete and accurate list of horses that are NOT sold?

   (A) Renegade, Trix
   (B) Nimbler, Sam, Velvet
   (C) Orion, Sam, Trix
   (D) Orion, Pride, Renegade
   (E) Orion, Pride, Renegade, Nimbler

9

In/Out Grouping

About 11% of all games are In/Out Grouping. These games tend to be very difficult for those without a solid diagram. We'll discuss one method shortly, but first let's take a look at the characteristics that define In/Out Grouping.

Scenario Cues

Remember, there are two main organizational schemes that appear in the Logic Games section: ordering and grouping. In/Out scenarios ask you to split the given elements into exactly two groups. In fact, since they're always binary, we considered calling these games "Conditional Binary Grouping," but that name seems more appropriately relegated to a tongue twister. These binary scenarios are presented in one of the following two ways:

1. **In** or **out.** In this classic type of In/Out scenario, some elements are selected to be a part of the "in" group, while the remaining elements are left to the "out" group. Here are some examples:

> One or more of exactly seven actors—Q, R, S, T, V, W, and Y—will be cast in a play at the community theater.

> A hedge fund manager will purchase shares of at least one of the following six publicly traded companies—F, G, H, J, K, and L. The manager will not purchase shares in any other company.

> A florist creates a bouquet from some of the following available flowers—daisies, gladiolas, lilacs, roses, snapdragons, and tulips.

2. **One** or the **other.** In this type of In/Out scenario, elements are divided among two distinct groups or assignments. Is it a bit of a stretch to call these In/Out? Well, the members are *in or out* of each group…yes? Yes, it's a bit of a stretch. These are relatively infrequent, though, so we picked a name that made sense for the majority of this game type. Here are some examples:

> Each of seven bus drivers—Q, R, S, T V, W, and Y—will be assigned to drive exactly one of two bus routes—the Highland route or the Grass Hill route.

> Each of six employees at the Acme corporation—Francine, George, Henry, Ian, Jennifer, and Marisa—will be assigned either to the sales team or else to the marketing team. Company policy requires that no employee is assigned to both teams.

> At Eastside University, six exchange students—Igor, Judith, Klaus, Sven, Tomás, and Wilmar—will each enroll in exactly one of two seminars offered by the economics department—one at 8am, the other at 9am.

In/Out Grouping Rules

In/Out Grouping games are characterized by an abundance of conditional rules. In fact, you should view this as a requirement to use the tools we're about to develop. Even if a game features two groups, if it doesn't have conditional rules, we should use our Grouping Board, which we'll look at in Chapter 10.

In the previous chapter, we looked at different types of conditional statements you are likely to encounter on the LSAT. When you confront a logic game that is comprised of rules that are all (or nearly all) conditional rules, you're likely facing an In/Out Grouping game. Let's review the common conditional statements we introduced in the previous chapter:

1. J and K cannot both be selected.

2. If M is selected, both G and H must be selected.

3. Neither H nor K is selected if L is selected.

4. If J is selected, then G is selected, but L is not.

5. F cannot be selected unless H is also selected.

6. L is selected if, and only if, M is also selected.

7. If either Q or R is selected, both must be selected.

8. N and W cannot be on the same team.

If these statements are uncomfortable for you to work with (specifically how to notate them using formal logic), now would be a good time to review the previous chapter; your work on In/Out Grouping depends on your ability to notate and infer from conditional statements.

9

Putting It Together

Let's revisit the horse game introduced earlier in this chapter:

A horse breeder is deciding which of seven horses—Nimbler, Orion, Pride, Renegade, Sam, Trix, and Velvet—to sell at auction this year. The breeder will determine which horses to sell according to the following restrictions:

If Renegade is sold at auction, Pride is not.
Either Orion or Nimbler is sold at auction, but not both.
If Sam is not sold at auction, neither is Renegade.
If Trix is not sold at auction, Velvet is.

In this scenario, horses are either sold or they are not. This is a classic "in" or "out" scenario. Notice that there is no explicit limitation on the number of horses that can be sold. Some In/Out Grouping games will include such a limit (e.g., "four of the seven horses will be sold"), and we'll tackle that twist and others later on. Also, notice that each of the four rules is, or can be, expressed as a conditional statement.

Now that we can identify In/Out Grouping, let's discuss one way to approach the setup.

The In/Out Rule Chart

Let's start by notating the rules in the game above in formal logic. Go ahead and write each rule in notational form (we've done the first one for you). Remember to notate the contrapositive for each as well:

	Rule	**Contrapositive**
If Renegade is sold at auction, Pride is not.	R ⟶ –P	P ⟶ –R

Either Orion or Nimbler is sold at auction, but not both.

If Sam is not sold at auction, neither is Renegade.

If Trix is not sold at auction, Velvet is.

Check your work on the next page.

Our notated rules:

	Rule	**Contrapositive**
If Renegade is sold at auction, Pride is not.	R ⟶ –P	P ⟶ –R
Either Orion or Nimbler is sold at auction, but not both.	O ⟶ –N	N ⟶ –O
	–O ⟶ N	–N ⟶ O
If Sam is not sold at auction, neither is Renegade.	–S ⟶ –R	R ⟶ S
If Trix is not sold at auction, Velvet is.	–T ⟶ V	–V ⟶ T

Did you write the second rule as O ⟷ –N and N ⟷ –O? That's great, too!

Perhaps you used a similar list of rules to answer the questions. Likely, you didn't enjoy it; that's a lot of rules to contend with! Cross-checking and jumping around isn't just slow; it's error-prone. Clearly, we need to organize our rules to make finding and using the relevant ones easier. One complexity to manage is the sheer number of triggers—there are 10 different ones above! One easy way to manage that complexity is to put the positive triggers on one side of a chart and the negative triggers on the other, making it easier to find the ones that apply to a given situation.

9

We'll start what we call a **Rule Chart** and let you finish it:

Sold	Not Sold
R → –P	–O → N
P → –R	

If Renegade is sold at auction, Pride is not.

Either Orion or Nimbler is sold at auction, but not both.

If Sam is not sold at auction, neither is Renegade.

If Trix is not sold at auction, Velvet is.

Check your work on the next page.

Our completed In/Out Rule Chart:

Sold	Not Sold
R $\rightarrow$ –P	–O $\rightarrow$ N
P $\rightarrow$ –R	–N $\rightarrow$ O
O $\rightarrow$ –N	–S $\rightarrow$ –R
N $\rightarrow$ –O	–T $\rightarrow$ V
R $\rightarrow$ S	–V $\rightarrow$ T

We didn't do any new work here; we've simply organized our rules into a chart for easy referencing. We're just about ready to replay the Getting Familiar game, but first we want to look quickly at one tool that you might find useful as you answer the two conditional questions.

Conditional T-Charts

As with every game, when we get a conditional question we want to create a new mini diagram. With In/Out Grouping, an easy way to track your work is with a **t-chart.** Begin by creating a chart, like the one below, with a side for each group (usually in and out). Then, place whatever information the question provides into the correct column (e.g., N is sold), as shown below.

Sold	Not Sold
N	

Then add to the t-chart any inferences that follow from the rules. (Hint: Look for rules containing the provided condition first and place the triggered elements. Next, look for rules that include the letters from your inferences. Continue this way until no further inferences remain.) Finally, note any elements whose placement cannot be determined below the t-chart.

In this case, if we learned that N is sold, we'd create this t-chart:

Sold	Not Sold
N	O

P R S T V

Remember, as you replay the game from the beginning of this chapter, be sure to use a t-chart on the two conditional questions.

MANHATTAN
PREP

Try It Again

Let's revisit our Getting Familiar game. As usual, at this stage, we believe it's more important for you to focus on process than timing, so put that stopwatch down.

A horse breeder is deciding which of seven horses—Nimbler, Orion, Pride, Renegade, Sam, Trix, and Velvet—to sell at auction this year. The breeder will determine which horses to sell according to the following restrictions:

If Renegade is sold at auction, Pride is not.
Either Orion or Nimbler is sold at auction, but not both.
If Sam is not sold at auction, neither is Renegade.
If Trix is not sold at auction, Velvet is.

1. Which of the following is an acceptable list of horses sold at the auction?

    (A) Orion, Renegade, Sam
    (B) Pride, Renegade, Trix, Velvet
    (C) Orion, Pride, Sam, Velvet
    (D) Nimbler, Renegade, Trix, Velvet
    (E) Nimbler, Orion, Renegade, Sam, Velvet

2. If Renegade is sold, which of the following must be true?

    (A) Sam and Orion are also sold.
    (B) Nimbler and Pride are not sold.
    (C) At least five horses are sold.
    (D) At most four horses are sold.
    (E) At least two horses are not sold.

3. What is the maximum number of horses that can be sold?

    (A) three
    (B) four
    (C) five
    (D) six
    (E) seven

4. If either Renegade or Sam is sold, but not both, which of the following could be a complete and accurate list of horses that are NOT sold?

    (A) Renegade, Trix
    (B) Nimbler, Sam, Velvet
    (C) Orion, Sam, Trix
    (D) Orion, Pride, Renegade
    (E) Orion, Pride, Renegade, Nimbler

9

How Did You Do?

Answer Key

1. C   3. C
2. E   4. D

Step 1: Picture the Game

We're trying to figure out which horses are sold and which aren't. That's an In/Out setup—some horses are in (sold), while others are out (not sold). We'll be using our Rule Chart, so get it set up. We also don't know how many horses are sold, so this is an Open In/Out Grouping game.

Step 2: Notate the Rules and Make Inferences

We've written out the rules and their contrapositives below. Then, we organized them in our Rule Chart. Check your work against ours. There are times that there could be more than one right answer; this isn't one of them. If your diagram doesn't match ours, it's wrong. Make sure you understand the conditional logic before moving on:

Sold	Not Sold
R $\rightarrow$ –P	–O $\rightarrow$ N
P $\rightarrow$ –R	–N $\rightarrow$ O
O $\rightarrow$ –N	–S $\rightarrow$ –R
N $\rightarrow$ –O	–T $\rightarrow$ V
R $\rightarrow$ S	–V $\rightarrow$ T

Step 3: The Big Pause

Let's start by looking for floaters. None to be found! It's also hard to find any hidden inferences, especially since these rules simply do not link together. However, often there are rules that will require that at least one element from within a pair to be in (or out). In this game there are three such rules:

> Rule 1 requires that at least one of R and P is not sold.
> Rule 2 requires that exactly one of N and O is sold, while the other is not sold.
> Rule 4 requires that at least one of T and V is sold.

MANHATTAN
PREP

Some of our instructors suggest displaying the above with placeholders in a t-chart:

Sold	Not Sold
	R/P
N/O ←--→	O/N
T/V	

Step 4: Attack the Questions

1. Which of the following is an acceptable list of horses sold at the auction?

   (A) Orion, Renegade, Sam

   (B) Renegade, Sam, Trix, Velvet

   (C) Orion, Pride, Sam, Velvet

   (D) Nimbler, Renegade, Trix, Velvet

   (E) Nimbler, Orion, Renegade, Sam, Velvet

Answer Choice (C) is correct.

   (A) is eliminated by Rule 4.
   (B) is eliminated by Rule 2.
   (D) is eliminated by Rule 3.
   (E) is eliminated by Rule 2.

2. If Renegade is sold, which of the following must be true?

   (A) Sam and Orion are also sold.

   (B) Nimbler and Pride are not sold.

   (C) At least five horses are sold.

   (D) At most four horses are sold.

   (E) At least two horses are not sold.

Answer choice (E) is correct.

Since we're facing a conditional question, let's track the inferences with a t-chart. We'll show the Rule Chart again for easy reference.

Rules:

Sold	Not Sold
R $\rightarrow$ –P	–O $\rightarrow$ N
P $\rightarrow$ –R	–N $\rightarrow$ O
O $\rightarrow$ –N	–S $\rightarrow$ –R
N $\rightarrow$ –O	–T $\rightarrow$ V
R $\rightarrow$ S	–V $\rightarrow$ T

If R is in, P is out while S is in.

Sold	Not Sold
R	P
S	

N O T V

Notice that we also tracked who's left (N, O, T, V) by writing them below the t-chart. We could also use the place-holders at this point to add even more detail:

Sold	Not Sold
R	P
S	O/N
N/O	
V/T	

(A) and (B) are incorrect for the same reason: We don't know where N and O go. (C) is tougher to eliminate. Can we disprove that at least five horses must be sold? Can we sell just four? Looking at our t-chart for this question, it's easy to see that R and S are sold. Adding O (or N) and V (or T), we can see that we could have just R S O V:

Sold	Not Sold
R	P
S	N
O	T
V	

While this is not the only possible hypothetical, it rules out answer choice (C).

(D) is similar to (C). Can we use our previous work? Yes! If we add T to the hypothetical from the last question, we have a hypothetical that eliminates (D):

Sold	Not Sold
R	P
S	N
O	
V	
T	

(E) better be correct! Can we have fewer than two horses not sold? P is not sold. We also know that exactly one of N and O is not sold (and one is sold). At least two horses are not sold:

Sold	Not Sold
R	P
S	O/N
T/V	
N/O	

3. What is the maximum number of horses that can be sold?

    (A) three
    (B) four
    (C) five
    (D) six
    (E) seven

Answer choice (C) is correct.

Looking at the hypothetical t-chart built for the last question, we know that five can be sold. We can eliminate (A) and (B). Next, let's look at the rules that are triggered on the side we're trying to maximize (in this case, the Sold side of our t-chart) and that trigger something moving to the other side. In other words, we're looking for rules that have a "positive" sufficient condition (indicating the rule is triggered by a horse being sold) and a "negative" necessary condition (indicating the outcome is a horse not being sold). In this case, the first and second rules are the ones to examine. (The other rules are triggered by placing elements on the Not Sold side.)

> If Renegade is sold at auction, Pride is not.
> Either Orion or Nimbler is sold at auction, but not both.

Both of these rules could be read as, "Both of these horses can't be on sale." Since one of N and O is not on sale and at least one of R and P is not on sale, at least two horses are not on sale (and at most five horses are on sale):

Sold	Not Sold
O/N	N/O
P/R	R/P
T	
V	
S	

4. If either Renegade or Sam is sold, but not both, which of the following could be a complete and accurate list of horses that are NOT sold?

(A) Renegade, Trix

(B) Nimbler, Sam, Velvet

(C) Orion, Sam, Trix

(D) Orion, Pride, Renegade

(E) Orion, Pride, Renegade, Nimbler

Answer choice (D) is correct.

If R or S is sold, but not both, then R cannot be sold while S must be. Remember, if R were sold, then S would be sold as well—not possible according to the question's condition! So S is sold and R is not. We also know that one, but not both, of N and O are sold and that at least one of T and V are sold:

Sold	Not Sold
S	R
N/O	O/N
T/V	

(A) has neither N nor O, while (E) has both.

(B) and (C) are both missing R.

Getting Unfamiliar

Solve this game with the Rule Chart. At the end, we're going to discuss why it's so difficult to do just that!

One or more of six violinists—Greene, Holiday, Liu, Mann, Underwood, and Wilson—will be selected to perform at the year-end concert. No other violinists will be selected. The following conditions apply:

> If Holiday is selected, then Mann is not selected.
> If Liu is selected, then both Mann and Wilson are selected.
> If Underwood is not selected, then Holiday is selected.
> Wilson is not selected unless Greene is selected.

1. Which of the following could be a complete and accurate list of the violinists selected for the concert?

    (A) Holiday, Liu, Wilson, Underwood
    (B) Liu, Mann, Wilson
    (C) Holiday, Liu, Mann
    (D) Liu, Mann, Wilson, Underwood
    (E) Mann, Underwood

2. Which of the following must be false?

    (A) Liu is selected but Underwood is not.
    (B) Neither Underwood nor Liu is selected.
    (C) Holiday is selected but Liu is not.
    (D) Both Greene and Underwood are selected.
    (E) Holiday is selected but Mann is not.

3. If Greene is not selected, then each of the following could be true EXCEPT:

    (A) Exactly two violinists are selected.
    (B) Exactly one violinist is selected.
    (C) Mann is selected.
    (D) Holiday is selected.
    (E) Liu is selected.

4. Which of the following could be the only violinist selected for the concert?

    (A) Liu
    (B) Mann
    (C) Greene
    (D) Wilson
    (E) Underwood

9

The Problem

We hope you were able to eventually tackle that game with your Rule Chart, but we're guessing that you found it to be a bit of a slog! Many of the rules connected, but those links weren't easily exploited with the Rule Chart since the rules don't visually connect. For example, consider these two rules:

> If Holiday is selected, then Mann is not selected.
> If Liu is selected, then both Mann and Wilson are selected.

They translate into the following:

In	Out
H $\rightarrow$ –M	–M $\rightarrow$ –L
M $\rightarrow$ –H	–W $\rightarrow$ –L
L $\rightarrow$ M	
L $\rightarrow$ W	

L and M show up a lot! Any time that L is in, M and W are too. And M in means H out. It's not impossible to follow the inference chain using the Rule Chart, but it requires a lot of looking around, and it's easy to overlook a rule that applies. Hopefully you were successful! Here are the answers so that you can check for yourself:

1. E
2. A
3. E
4. E

The Rule Chart is a great tool, and there are some games for which it's ideal. But there are other games where the conditional rules entirely (or nearly so) link up. For now, it's time for the main event of this chapter: introducing a much more efficient method of solving In/Out Grouping games, the Logic Chain!

MANHATTAN
PREP

The Logic Chain

The Logic Chain is the best approach for most In/Out Grouping games. The Logic Chain is a diagramming method that may look intimidating at first, but will be easy to use and powerful once you get comfortable with it. Let's set one up for the game we just tried with a Rule Chart:

Step 1: Create Binary Columns

After determining that we are dealing with an In/Out Grouping game, we begin by creating two columns. One will represent "in" (selected for the concert) and one will represent "out" (not selected), like below:

In   Out

Step 2: Diagram the First Rule

If Holiday is selected, then Mann is not selected.

This first rule contains an H and an M. We want to start our diagram by placing an H and an M in both the In and the out columns. Note that we place our letters about halfway down the empty space we've left under the column headers. We want to leave room above and below so that we can add in other letters later on.

Now we're ready to draw in our first conditional arrow. The rule tells us: H ⟶ –M. In other words, an H "in" triggers an M "out." We start with the H "in" trigger (left column) and draw an arrow to M "out."

Step 3: Diagram the Contrapositive of the First Rule

The given rule is: H ⟶ –M, so the contrapositive (reverse and negate) is: M ⟶ –H. In other words, M "in" triggers H "out." So, we'll start with the M "in" trigger and draw an arrow to H "out."

Step 4: Move to the Next Rule that Shares a Common Letter

Part of the challenge of the Logic Chain is keeping your diagram neat and tidy so you can read it quickly when you're attacking the questions. In order to facilitate this, we want to place connected letters as close to each other as possible. We currently have H and M on our diagram, so let's find the next rule that contains an H or an M:

- ✓ If Holiday is selected, then Mann is not selected.
     If Liu is selected, then both Mann and Wilson are selected.
     If Underwood is not selected, then Holiday is selected.
     Wilson is not selected unless Greene is selected.

In this case, the second rule shares an M:

> If Liu is selected, then both Mann and Wilson are selected.

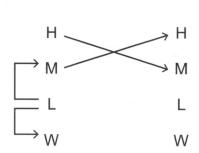

Since Liu is directly connected with Mann, we'll put our L's directly below the M's on our diagram, and then we'll place the W's below the L's.

To keep your chain neat, always write the same letters directly across from each other.

Recall from the previous chapter on conditional logic that the second rule actually gives us two distinct relationships: 1) If L is in, then M is in, and 2) If L is in, then W is in.

To diagram the first part of this, we'll start with the L "in" trigger and trace an arrow to the M "in" trigger. Notice that this creates a same-column connection. We want to draw this connection on the outside to keep things neat.

To diagram the second part of this rule, we'll start with the L "in" trigger and trace an arrow to W "in." Again, this creates a same-column connection.

Step 5: Diagram the Contrapositive

Since we had two statements from this rule, we'll have two contrapositives. If we reverse and negate part 1, we get: If M is out, then L is out. To diagram this, we'll start with the M "out" trigger and trace an arrow to L "out."

If we reverse and negate part 2, we get: If W is out, then L is out. To diagram this, we'll start with the W "out" trigger and trace an arrow to L "out."

Step 6: Repeat Steps 4 and 5 for the Rest of the Rules

Move to the next rule that shares a common letter with one already on the diagram:

> If Underwood is not selected, then Holiday is selected.

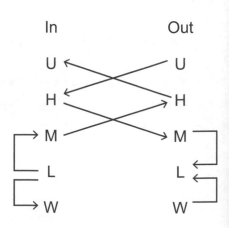

Since the U will be connected to the H, we'll draw our U's directly above our H's. Then, we'll start with U "out" and trace an arrow to H "in."

To diagram the contrapositive of this, we'll start with H "out" and trace an arrow to U "in."

Last rule:

> Wilson is not selected unless Greene is selected.

Since the G will be connected to the W, we'll place our G's immediately below the W's in the diagram.

MANHATTAN
PREP

This is an advanced rule that we studied in the previous chapter. As we learned in Chapter 7, the easiest way to deal with "unless" is to replace it with "if not." Rephrasing our rule, it becomes *If Greene is not selected, then Wilson is not selected.*

The contrapositive is: W in, then G in.

Let's double-check that we've used all six elements; sometimes there's a floater for which there are no rules:

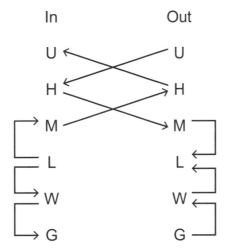

Now, we have a completed diagram that looks pretty strange! However, we haven't yet seen the real power of the Logic Chain. Let's take a look at how we can use it to our advantage.

Logic Chain Power: Second-Level Inferences

The utility of the Logic Chain is that it connects the rules automatically. This will come in handy when we go to answer the questions. Take a look at a few examples that demonstrate the power of the Logic Chain:

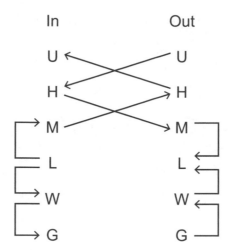

What do we know if U is out?

Well, our original rules told us that if U is out, then H is in. However, there's more to be uncovered. Follow the arrows (the Logic Chain) from U "out." If U is out, H is in, which means M is out, which means L is out! We can summarize with a t-chart:

In	Out
H	U
	M
	L

You MUST remember to read only in the direction of the arrows. A common mistake would be to start with U out, trace it across to H in, then back to M out, then down to L out, *and then down to W out.* L out does *not* lead to W out! Read only in the direction of the arrows to make your inferences.

What do we know if L is in?

Before reading on, create a t-chart and make all the possible inferences from L being in.

L in has two distinct branches coming off of it. The bottom one takes us to W in, which leads to G in. The other branch takes us to M in, which leads to H out, which leads to U in. In summary, when L is in we get:

In	Out
L	H
W	
G	
M	
U	

In a moment, we'll use our diagram to tackle the questions associated with the violinist game, but first let's practice the mechanics of the Logic Chain setup.

MANHATTAN
PREP

9

Drill It: Mini Logic Chain Setups 1

Create a Logic Chain diagram for each of the mini scenarios presented below (don't forget the contrapositives). Assume that each game is a binary situation. Be sure to check the solutions **after each exercise.** We've started the first one for you.

1. If H is in, then G is in.

In	Out
H	H
G	G

2. If L is out, then M is in.

3. R and T cannot both be in.

4. If V is in, then both P and Q are out.

5. X plays volleyball only if Y plays squash.

6. Z and W are paramedics covering the Monday and Friday shifts. Each only works one day, and they can't both work on the same day.

9

Solutions: Mini Logic Chain Setups 1

Check your Logic Chains against our solutions. You may have arranged the letters differently, but make sure that all of your connections are the same.

1. If H is in, then G is in.

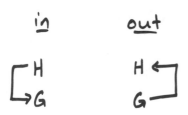

4. If V is in, then both P and Q are out.

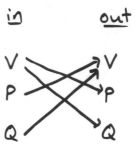

2. If L is out, then M is in.

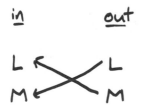

5. X plays volleyball only if Y plays squash.

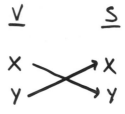

3. R and T cannot both be in.

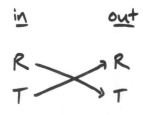

6. Z and W are paramedics covering the Monday and Friday shifts. Each only works one day, and they can't both work on the same day.

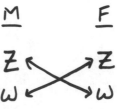

Special Situations

The Logic Chain is a powerful diagram for working though In/Out Grouping games; you will feel like a wizard as you follow a string of inferences around the chain. However, as with every game type, there are times when you'll need to adapt the diagram to accommodate some particularly tricky rules. It's worth exploring some of these rules here:

1. **Biconditionals.** Take a look at this scenario and the accompanying rules:

> Floyd, George, and Hank are each being assigned to one of only two camp activities—swimming or tennis. The assignments must adhere to the following conditions:
>
> > George and Hank cannot be assigned to the same activity.
> > Floyd will be assigned to swimming if, but only if, Hank is.

To start, we can tell this is a In/Out Grouping game because there is a choice between two groups and there are only conditional rules. We'll create the two columns and place the elements that are used in the first rule:

George and Hank cannot be assigned to the same activity.

Now, let's think about the implications of this first rule. If G is assigned to swimming, we know that H is assigned to tennis. We also know that if H is assigned to swimming, G is assigned to tennis. So far, we have the chart to the right:

Did you notice another set of relationships? Indeed, if G or H is assigned to tennis, then the other person is assigned to swimming, so we could write this:

But that's a lot of arrows. We can simplify by creating double-sided arrows, but there's one thing to be wary of: at this point, you should be well on your way to reading only "down" the arrows. However, with a double-sided arrow, you have to read in *both* directions. There's a danger that you might not realize, for example, that H in swimming means G in tennis, since it seems like you're reading illegally "up" that arrow. If you're able to stay aware of the bidirectionality, great. If you think you'll forget, consider using some other symbol at the end of double-sided arrows, like a circle or an "X."

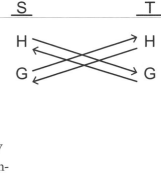

If you use something like what's shown to the right, you'll definitely remember that these arrows are not the usual ones.

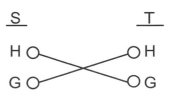

Using the diagram below, draw the arrows for the second rule:

Floyd will be assigned to swimming if, but only if, Hank is.

Since "if, but only if" indicates that the relationship is biconditional, you should have drawn something like the following:

2. Compound conditionals

Remember, in Chapter 7, we advised you to split all compound conditional statements that can be split and then to take the contrapositives of those individual statements. Also remember that the compound statements that can be split are those that include an "or" in the trigger or an "and" in the outcome.

The compound conditionals that cannot be split are those that include an "and" in the trigger or an "or" in the outcome. Because they're unsplittable, these statements cannot be drawn easily into your chain and ought to be written to the side. As we mentioned in the last chapter, these types of statements are relatively rare.

Smart Tip: Find the Contrapositive Rhythm

Have you noticed a rhythm to drawing in contrapositives? In short, it goes like this: "Whatever I end with, I start with its opposite." To demonstrate, consider the rule *If Q is out, R is in.* You'd start with Q out and draw an arrow to R in. Now, *start with the opposite* of R in, which is R out, and draw a line to the opposite of Q out. If you find yourself struggling to correctly write contrapositives, use the next drill as an opportunity to practice this rhythm.

MANHATTAN
PREP

Drill It: Mini Logic Chain Setups 2

Create a Logic Chain diagram for each of the mini scenarios presented below. Be sure to check the solutions **after each exercise.**

1. If H is in, then G is in.
   If J is out, then G is out.

4. If Q is in, then V is in, but P is not.
   If V is in, then P or R is in.

2. If K is out, then both L and M are in.
   If L is in, then K is out.

5. Everyone must have exactly one numbered locker (1–100).

   X and W cannot both have odd-numbered lockers. Neither Y nor Z can have odd-numbered lockers if W has an odd-numbered locker.

3. S cannot be out unless T is in.
   If R is in, then S is in.

6. If F and N are selected, O will not be.
   If O is selected, P and S will not be.

Solutions: Mini Logic Chain Setups 2

Check your Logic Chains against our solutions. You may have arranged the letters differently, but make sure all of your connections match ours.

1. If H is in, then G is in.
    If J is out, then G is out.

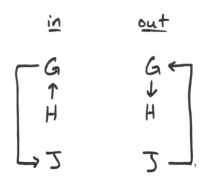

2. If K is out, then both L and M are in.
    If L is in, then K is out.

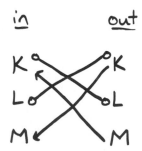

3. S cannot be out unless T is in.
    If R is in, then S is in.

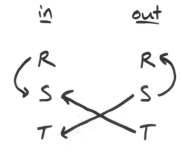

4. If Q is in, then V is in, but P is not.
    If V is in, then P or R is in.

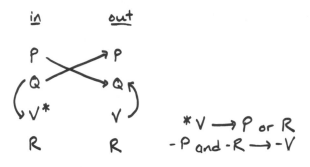

5. Everyone must have exactly one numbered locker (1–100).
    X and W cannot both have odd-numbered lockers.
    Neither Y nor Z can have odd-numbered lockers if W has an odd-numbered locker.

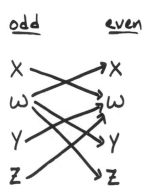

6. If F and N are selected, O will not be.
    If O is selected, P and S will not be.

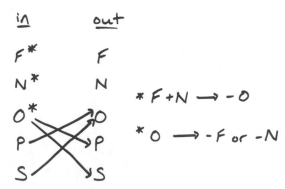

MANHATTAN
PREP

Drill It: Mini Logic Chain Setups 3

Another drill already? Yes! Let's move ahead to using our Logic Chains by creating t-charts for conditional questions. Create a Logic Chain diagram for each of the mini scenarios presented below and then answer the associated questions. Be sure to check the solutions **after each exercise.**

1. Four candidates—P, Q, R, and S—interview for jobs at Microsite, Inc. No other candidates interview for jobs at Microsite, and each candidate who interviews is either hired or not hired. The following conditions apply:

   P cannot be hired unless S is also hired.
   If R is hired, then both Q and P are hired.

(a) What do we know if R is hired?

(b) What do we know if R is *not* hired?

2. Five commuters—L, M, N, O, and P—each take exactly one of two trains to work: the Highbrook train or the Sullivan train. These commuters take no other train to work, and the following conditions apply:

> If O takes the Sullivan train, then M takes the Highbrook train.
> If P takes the Highbrook train, then L takes the Sullivan train and N takes the Highbrook train.
> M and L cannot take the same train.

(a) What do we know if P takes the Highbrook train?

(b) What do we know if M takes the Sullivan train?

3. Jenny's Juice Store will have a sale on at least one of the following five kinds of juice: grape, mango, orange, pineapple, and tomato. No other juices will be included in the sale. The following rules apply:

> If mango juice is included in the sale, then grape juice is also included but tomato juice is not.
> Pineapple juice is not included in the sale unless orange juice is included.
> If grape juice is included in the sale, then orange juice is also included.

(a) What do we know if mango juice is on sale?

(b) What do we know if grape juice is not on sale?

(c) What do we know if one and only one of either mango or grape juice is on sale?

MANHATTAN
PREP

4. Six kindergarten students—R, S, T, V, X, and Y—will each be assigned to one of two teachers: Mr. Paulson or Mrs. Hanson. None of these six students will be assigned to any other teacher, and the following conditions apply:

> If S is assigned to Mrs. Hanson, then V is assigned to Mr. Paulson.
> If X is assigned to Mr. Paulson, then T is assigned to Mr. Paulson.
> If R is assigned to Mrs. Hanson, then V is also.

(a) What do we know if S is assigned to Mrs. Hanson?

(b) What do we know if V is assigned to Mr. Paulson?

(c) What do we know if both V and X are assigned to Mr. Paulson?

Solutions: Mini Logic Chain Setups 3

Check your Logic Chains against our solutions. You may have arranged the letters differently, but make sure all of your connections match ours. If you are missing any connections, or if you misdiagrammed, check the numbered arrows in the diagram against the numbered rules to see where you may have gone wrong. The numbers also represent the order in which we drew the connecting arrows.

1. Four candidates—P, Q, R, and S—interview for jobs
    at Microsite, Inc. No other candidates interview for
    jobs at Microsite, and each candidate who interviews
    is either hired or not hired. The following conditions
    apply:

    P cannot be hired unless S is also hired.
    If R is hired, then both Q and P are hired.

    (1) P cannot be hired unless S is also hired.
        $(-S \rightarrow -P)$
    (2) Contrapositive $(P \rightarrow S)$
    (3) If R is hired, then both Q and P are hired.
        $(R \rightarrow Q, R \rightarrow P)$
    (4) Contrapositives
        $(-Q \rightarrow -R, -P \rightarrow -R)$

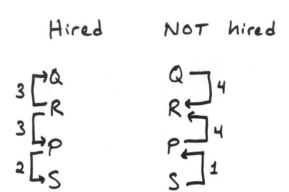

(a) What do we know if R is hired?

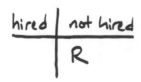

(b) What do we know if R is NOT hired?

Be careful! Read only in the direction of the arrows. R
not hired tells us nothing about P, Q, or S.

MANHATTAN
PREP

2. Five commuters—L, M, N, O, and P—each take
   exactly one of two trains to work: the Highbrook train
   or the Sullivan train. These commuters take no other
   train to work, and the following conditions apply:

   > If O takes the Sullivan train, then M takes the
   >   Highbrook train.
   > If P takes the Highbrook train, then L takes the
   >   Sullivan train and N takes the Highbrook train.
   > M and L cannot take the same train.

(1) If O takes the Sullivan train, then M takes the
    Highbrook train. (Os → Mh)
(2) Contrapositive (Ms → Oh)
(3) The second rule doesn't share any common letters
    with what we have on the diagram so far (O and M),
    so we'll skip to the last rule: M and L cannot take the
    same train.

This one is a bit tricky. If M and L can't take the same
train, then M and L are what we would call **mutually
exclusive** elements. What happens if M is on a given
train? Then L is not. The relationship holds in both
directions. If L is on a given train, then M is not. So we
have a biconditional:

$$Mh \longleftrightarrow Ls \quad Lh \longleftrightarrow Ms$$

Remember, this bidirectionality is *not* usually valid for
normal conditional statements; this is a special case that
hinges on the fact that each commuter must take one of
the two trains. Generally, in an In/Out Grouping game
with two distinct groups (like our trains here), a rule that
doesn't mention a specific group creates a biconditional.

On the Logic Chain diagram, we notate these mutually
exclusive relationships with special arrows.

(4) Now we'll double back to the second rule. If P takes
    the Highbrook train, then L takes the Sullivan train
    and N takes the Highbrook train. (Ph → Ls,
    Ph → Nh)

(5) Contrapositives (Lh → Ps, Ns → Ps)

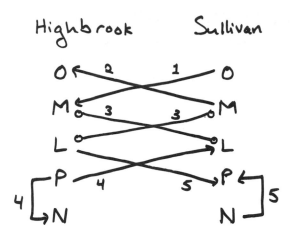

(a) What do we know if P takes the Highbrook train?

Be careful! It's easy to miss the two-sided arrow coming
off L.

(b) What do we know if M takes the Sullivan train?

Be careful! Do *not* trace from Ps against the arrow
to Ns!

9

3. Jenny's Juice Store will have a sale on at least one of the following five kinds of juice: grape, mango, orange, pineapple, and tomato. No other juices will be included in the sale. The following rules apply:

> If mango juice is included in the sale, then grape juice is also included but tomato juice is not.
> Pineapple juice is not included in the sale unless orange juice is included.
> If grape juice is included in the sale, then orange juice is also included.

(1) If mango juice is included in the sale, then grape juice is also included but tomato juice is not. (M ➔ G, M ➔ –T)

(2) Contrapositives (–G ➔ –M, T ➔ –M)

(3) The second rule doesn't contain an M, T, or G, so we'll skip down to the third rule. If grape juice is included in the sale, then orange juice is also included. (G ➔ O)

(4) Contrapositive (–O ➔ –G)

(5) Now we'll double back to the second rule. Pineapple juice is not included in the sale unless orange juice is included. (–O ➔ –P)

(6) Contrapositive (P ➔ O)

(a) What do we know if mango juice is on sale?

S	NS
M	T
G	
O	

(b) What do we know if grape juice is not on sale?

S	NS
	G
	M

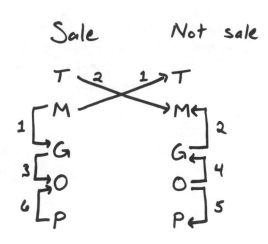

(c) What do we know if one and only one of either mango or grape juice is on sale?

S	NS
G	M
O	

We can't have mango on sale, because that would force in grape, too!

4. Six kindergarten students—R, S, T, V, X, and Y—will each be assigned to one of two teachers: Mr. Paulson or Mrs. Hanson. None of these six students will be assigned to any other teacher, and the following conditions apply:

> If S is assigned to Mrs. Hanson, then V is assigned to Mr. Paulson.
> If X is assigned to Mr. Paulson, then T is assigned to Mr. Paulson.
> If R is assigned to Mrs. Hanson, then V is also.

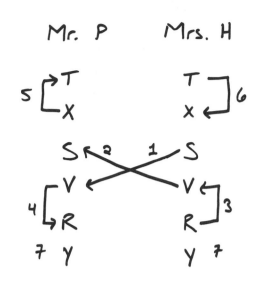

(1) If S is assigned to Mrs. Hanson, then V is assigned to Mr. Paulson. (Sh ⟶ Vp)

(2) Contrapositive (Vh ⟶ Sp)

(3) The second rule does not contain an S or a V, so we'll move to the third rule. If R is assigned to Mrs. Hanson, then V is also. (Rh ⟶ Vh)

(4) Contrapositive (Vp ⟶ Rp)

(5) If X is assigned to Mr. Paulson, then T is assigned to Mr. Paulson. (Xp ⟶ Tp)

(6) Contrapositive (Th ⟶ Xh)

(7) Since there was no rule for Y, we'll simply write it into our t-chart.

(c) What do we know if both V and X are assigned to Mr. Paulson?

```
 P | H
---+---
 V |
 X |
 R |
 T |
```

(a) What do we know if S is assigned to Mrs. Hanson?

(b) What do we know if V is assigned to Mr. Paulson?

```
 P | H
---+---
 V |
 R |
```

Try It Again

Now that you've learned how to set up the Logic Chain, it's time to put your skills to good use. Let's revisit our Getting (Un) Familiar game. Develop the Logic Chain from scratch, and then use it to tackle the questions. We'll work through the solutions together on the pages to come.

One or more of six violinists—Greene, Holiday, Liu, Mann, Underwood, and Wilson—will be selected to perform at the year-end concert. No other violinists will be selected. The following conditions apply:

> If Holiday is selected, then Mann is not selected.
> If Liu is selected, then both Mann and Wilson are
>   selected.
> If Underwood is not selected, then Holiday is selected.
> Wilson is not selected unless Greene is selected.

1. Which of the following could be a complete and
    accurate list of the violinists selected for the concert?

    (A) Holiday, Liu, Wilson, Underwood
    (B) Liu, Mann, Wilson
    (C) Holiday, Liu, Mann
    (D) Liu, Mann, Wilson, Underwood
    (E) Mann, Underwood

2. Which of the following must be false?

    (A) Liu is selected but Underwood is not.
    (B) Neither Underwood nor Liu is selected.
    (C) Holiday is selected but Liu is not.
    (D) Both Greene and Underwood are selected.
    (E) Holiday is selected but Mann is not.

3. Which of the following could be the only violinist
    selected for the concert?

    (A) Liu
    (B) Mann
    (C) Greene
    (D) Wilson
    (E) Underwood

4. If Underwood is not selected, then which of the following must be true?

   (A) Wilson is not selected.
   (B) Greene is selected.
   (C) At least two violinists are selected.
   (D) At most three violinists are selected.
   (E) Neither Liu nor Holiday is selected.

5. If Greene is not selected, then each of the following could be true EXCEPT:

   (A) Exactly two violinists are selected.
   (B) Exactly one violinist is selected.
   (C) Mann is selected.
   (D) Holiday is selected.
   (E) Liu is selected.

6. Which of the following CANNOT be a complete and accurate list of the violinists who are selected for the concert?

   (A) Greene, Liu, Mann, Underwood, Wilson
   (B) Greene, Mann, Underwood
   (C) Greene, Mann, Wilson
   (D) Greene, Underwood
   (E) Holiday

7. Which of the following, if substituted for the condition that if Liu is selected then both Mann and Wilson are selected, would have the same effect in determining the violinists who are selected to perform?

   (A) If Liu is selected, then exactly two other violinists are selected.
   (B) If Liu is selected, then both Greene and Underwood are selected but Holiday is not.
   (C) If Mann and Wilson are selected, then Liu is selected.
   (D) If Liu is selected, then Mann is one of exactly five violinists selected.
   (E) If Liu is not selected, then neither Mann nor Wilson is selected.

How Did You Do?

Answer Key

1. E   5. E
2. A   6. C
3. E   7. D
4. D

Step 1: Picture the Game

This game has In/Out Grouping written all over it! Each violinist is either in or out of the concert, and the rules are all conditionals. Other than setting up in and out columns, there's nothing to do until we start diagramming our first rule in the middle of the chart.

Step 2: Notate the Rules and Make Inferences

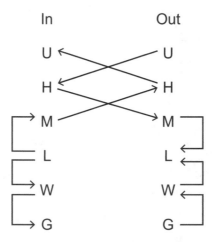

Check your diagram above and work against the following explanations. **Read through the entire explanation for each question, even if you got the question correct.** We've included many general tips and takeaways that you should find useful.

Step 3: The Big Pause

With the Logic Chain showing all the relationships, it can feel like The Big Pause for In/Out Grouping is a waste of time. However, pros are likely to explore a few subtle issues. As always, we can identify any floaters. In this case, there are none, but there could have been some, and we would want to write any floaters below our Logic Chain. Framing is rare on In/Out Grouping, since the rules are typically conditional statements. However, we can often identify the most important elements in the game. In other words, which elements are at the start of major inference chains? In this game, L in is an obvious one to keep an eye on, as is U out.

MANHATTAN
PREP

There's one more move that you could adopt during The Big Pause on In/Out Grouping, called a Placehold Chart. Pay attention to rule pairs that cross from one side of the chain to the other, such as U and H above. These pairs tell us that at least one element of the pair will show up on the side that both arrows point to. In this game, either U or H must be in, and either H or M must be out. We can create a Placehold t-chart to reference later on:

In	Out
U/H	H/M

Step 4: Attack the Questions

1. Which of the following could be a complete and accurate list of the violinists selected for the concert?

(A) Holiday, Liu, Wilson, Underwood

(B) Liu, Mann, Wilson

(C) Holiday, Liu, Mann

(D) Liu, Mann, Wilson, Underwood

(E) Mann, Underwood

Answer choice (E) is correct.

This is an Orientation question. You can either use the rules in written form, conveniently placed directly above the Orientation question, or you can "read" the rules from the diagram you've created. It's worth trying out this latter approach as it can force you to engage with your diagram, making it easier to use it for future questions. It's also a good check on your diagram—did you forget to notate a rule? It's imperative that you diagram correctly.

Let's see how this approach of reading the rules from your diagram would play out for In/Out Grouping games. We'll start at the top of our Logic Chain and identify the first rule: U and H cannot both be out. Note that this one statement actually encompasses two rules, one about U out, the other about H out. Scanning the answer choices, this eliminates answer (B).

Moving down the Logic Chain, the next thing we know is that H and M cannot both be in. This eliminates answer (C).

The next rule is that L in forces M and W in as well. Eliminate (A). We're left with answers (D) and (E).

The next rule we can use is that W in requires G to be in. Answer (D) violates this rule, leaving us with (E) as the correct answer.

2. Which of the following must be false?

    (A) Liu is selected but Underwood is not.

    (B) Neither Underwood nor Liu is selected.

    (C) Holiday is selected but Liu is not.

    (D) Both Greene and Underwood are selected.

    (E) Holiday is selected but Mann is not.

Answer choice (A) is correct.

(A) states that L is selected but U is not. What do we know when L is in?

In	Out
L	H
M	
U	
W	
G	

Thus, (A) can't be true.

As you become more adept at reading your Logic Chain, you'll probably find that you can skip the t-chart. We suggest that you always use a t-chart for conditional questions, but for questions such as this one, in which you're looking for a violation, it can be easy to simply trace connections with your finger. Try it out and see if that works for you as you prove to yourself that answers (B) through (D) could be true (though you wouldn't bother doing so during an LSAT).

3. Which of the following could be the only violinist selected for the concert?

    (A) Liu

    (B) Mann

    (C) Greene

    (D) Wilson

    (E) Underwood

Answer choice (E) is correct.

Remember our pro move from The Big Pause? We thought about our placeholders. These were pairs where at least one of them was in or at least one of them was out.

We left a placeholder for U/H on our in side, because we need at least one of them—if H is out, U is in, and vice versa.

Since one of those two *must* be in, our answer is either going to be H or U.

4. If Underwood is not selected, then which of the following must be true?

    (A) Wilson is not selected.

    (B) Greene is selected.

    (C) At least two violinists are selected.

    (D) At most three violinists are selected.

    (E) Neither Liu nor Holiday is selected.

Answer choice (D) is correct.

What do we know when U is out?

In	Out
H	U
	M
	L

We can eliminate answers (A) and (B), as we know nothing about W and G when U is out.

We can also eliminate answer (E), as we know that H must be in.

So it's down to answers (C) and (D). The only elements we're unsure of are W and G. Notice that if we put W in, then G must be in as well. So we *could* have the following:

In	Out
H	U
W	M
G	L

But notice that we can't have more than three elements in. After all, we know from our t-chart that U, M, and L must be out.

Thus, answer (D) is the answer.

5. If Greene is not selected, then each of the following could be true EXCEPT:

    (A) Exactly two violinists are selected.

    (B) Exactly one violinist is selected.

    (C) Mann is selected.

    (D) Holiday is selected.

    (E) Liu is selected.

Answer choice (E) is correct.

What do we know when G is out?

In	Out
	G
	W
	L

W and L are out. Thus, it's impossible for L to be selected.

If you found yourself testing out all the answer choices, start working more strategically. On a conditional question—particularly one that is asking what must be true or false—once you've made some inferences, go look for answer choices that involve those inferences. In this case, you'd want to seek out answers with L or W in them.

6. Which of the following CANNOT be a complete and accurate list of the violinists who are selected for the concert?

   (A) Greene, Liu, Mann, Underwood, Wilson

   (B) Greene, Mann, Underwood

   (C) Greene, Mann, Wilson

   (D) Greene, Underwood

   (E) Holiday

Answer choice (C) is correct.

This is similar to an Orientation question, except that it's asking which CANNOT be a complete and accurate list. We usually read a rule and eliminate an answer choice that violates the rule until there's only one answer remaining. However, in this case, we should do the opposite: Read a rule, and if an answer violates that rule, *select* it. In other words, this question is asking, "Which one of the following violates a rule?"

Going through our rules one at a time, we eventually see that (C) violates our third rule, since both U and H are not selected:

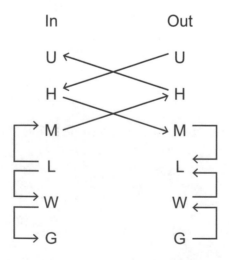

Alternatively, we could have used our Logic Chain to check the answers. In that case, our first rule (about U and H) would let us pick (C).

MANHATTAN
PREP

7. Which one of the following, if substituted for the condition that if Liu is selected then both Mann and Wilson are selected, would have the same effect in determining the violinists who are selected to perform?

(A) If Liu is selected, then exactly two other violinists are selected.

(B) If Liu is selected, then both Greene and Underwood are selected but Holiday is not.

(C) If Mann and Wilson are selected, then Liu is selected.

(D) If Liu is selected, then Mann is one of exactly five violinists selected.

(E) If Liu is not selected, then neither Mann nor Wilson is selected.

Answer choice (D) is correct.

This is an Equivalent Rule question.

The original rule gives us a bunch of arrows on our Logic Chain. It tells us that if L is in, then M and W are selected. Using the other rules, we can infer that U and G would also be in and H would be out. If we remove this rule, we're left with the following:

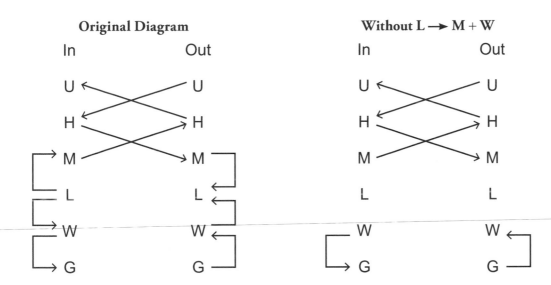

We want to choose an answer that provides the arrows that we're now missing.

Answer (A) doesn't give any indication as to which additional violinists are selected. This is not an equivalent rule to the original. Eliminate (A).

Answer (B) gives us G and U with L and forces out H, but what about M and W? The original rule forces M and W in whenever L is in. (B) does not give us an equivalent result. Eliminate.

Answer (C) gives us reversed logic. If you don't know your conditional logic, you might be tempted by this answer, but simply reversing the terms of the rule does *not* give an equivalent rule.

9

Answer (D) tells us that if L is selected then M is selected as well (this gives us our missing arrow from L in to M in), and five violinists are selected in total. Well, if M is in, we already know that H is out and U is in (follow the arrows from M in). To get to five total, we'd need W and G in as well. This gives us our missing arrow from L in to W in. So, when L is in, this rule forces in M and W. In the end, we arrive at the same place we started: L in means M, U, W, and G in and H out.

Answer (E) is the negation of our original rule. Again, this is a conditional logic trap. The negation of a conditional does not provide the same information as the original!

Practice Game: PT41, S2, G3

Here's your first chance to put all the pieces together on a new game. We'll work through the setup and solutions together on the pages to come.

Each of the seven members of the board of directors— Guzman, Hawking, Lepp, Miyauchi, Upchurch, Wharton, and Zhu—serves on exactly one of two committees—the finance committee or the incentives committee. Only board members serve on these committees. Committee membership is consistent with the following conditions:

> If Guzman serves on the finance committee, then
>   Hawking serves on the incentives committee.
> If Lepp serves on the finance committee, then
>   Miyauchi and Upchurch both serve on the
>   incentives committee.
> Wharton serves on a different committee from the
>   one on which Zhu serves.
> Upchurch serves on a different committee from the
>   one on which Guzman serves.
> If Zhu serves on the finance committee, so does
>   Hawking.

13. Which one of the following could be a complete and accurate list of the members of the finance committee?

    (A) Guzman, Hawking, Miyauchi, Wharton
    (B) Guzman, Lepp, Zhu
    (C) Hawking, Miyauchi, Zhu
    (D) Hawking, Upchurch, Wharton, Zhu
    (E) Miyauchi, Upchurch, Wharton

14. Which of the following pairs of board members CANNOT both serve on the incentives committee?

   (A) Guzman and Hawking
   (B) Guzman and Wharton
   (C) Hawking and Wharton
   (D) Miyauchi and Upchurch
   (E) Miyauchi and Wharton

15. What is the maximum number of members on the finance committee?

   (A) two
   (B) three
   (C) four
   (D) five
   (E) six

16. If Miyauchi and Wharton both serve on the finance committee, which one of the following could be true?

   (A) Guzman and Lepp both serve on the finance committee.
   (B) Guzman and Upchurch both serve on the incentives committee.
   (C) Hawking and Zhu both serve on the finance committee.
   (D) Lepp and Upchurch both serve on the incentives committee.
   (E) Zhu and Upchurch both serve on the finance committee.

17. If Guzman serves on the incentives committee, then which one of the following must be true?

   (A) Hawking serves on the finance committee.
   (B) Lepp serves on the incentives committee.
   (C) Miyauchi serves on the finance committee.
   (D) Wharton serves on the incentives committee.
   (E) Zhu serves on the finance committee.

Solutions: PT41, S2, G3

Answer Key

13. E   16. D
14. C   17. B
15. C

Step 1: Picture the Game

While this game doesn't present the usual in vs. out situation, this is a binary situation. There are only two committees, and everyone serves on one or the other (as opposed to a situation in which there is a third category: those who don't serve on either). Once we see all the conditional rules, we can quickly conclude that this is an In/Out Grouping game.

We'll carefully note which side of the diagram corresponds to which committee, and dive into our first rule.

Step 2: Notate the Rules and Make Inferences

This is a tough diagram, so we'll take it step by step. However, if you're feeling confident, flip to the completed diagram and see if your confidence is deserved!

The first rule is:

If Guzman serves on the finance committee, then Hawking serves on the incentives committee.
(Gf → Hi, contrapositive Hf → Gi)

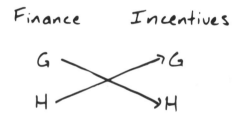

We'll start by placing our G's and H's about halfway down, and then we'll draw in the conditional arrows for both the original rule and the contrapositive.

Neither the second nor the third rule contains a G or an H, so we'll skip down to the fourth rule:

Upchurch serves on a different committee from the one on which Guzman serves.

Since the U will be connected with the G, we'll place our U's directly above our G's in the diagram. Did you notice that this is a biconditional rule? Since U and G must be on different committees, Uf means Gi (and vice versa), and Gf means Ui (and vice versa). (Uf ⟷ Gi and Gf ⟷ Ui.) This is a great time to use the special arrows with circles at each end. In general, if you're in an In/Out Grouping game with two groups, rules that don't mention a specific group will be biconditionals.

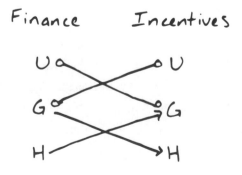

MANHATTAN
PREP

The last rule contains an H, so we can use this one now:

If Zhu serves on the finance committee, so does Hawking.
(Zf ⟶ Hf, contrapositive Hi ⟶ Zi)

Since the Z is connected with the H, we'll place the Z's directly beneath the H's in the diagram.

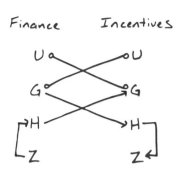

Now that we have a U on our diagram, we can double back to the second rule:

If Lepp serves on the finance committee, then Miyauchi and Upchurch both serve on the incentives committee.

This gives us two separate relationships:
Lf ⟶ Mi and Lf ⟶ Ui.

The contrapositives are:
Mf ⟶ Li and Uf ⟶ Li.

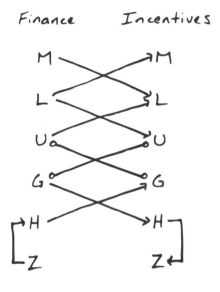

The only rule remaining is the third rule:

Wharton serves on a different committee from the one on which Zhu serves.

This is another rule that doesn't mention a specific group, so it's biconditional:
Wf ⟵⟶ Zi and Zf ⟵⟶ Wi.

If you really struggled with this diagram, start again from scratch. Do it as many times as required to make the process flawless.

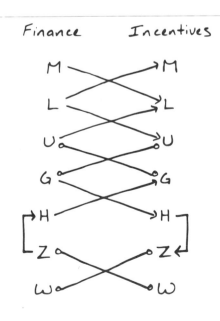

Step 3: The Big Pause

In this game, there are far more elements that force others into incentives than into finance. We should be ready for more situations to be affected by placing elements on the left side, but with two biconditional arrow pairs, there's a large variety of "moves" happening. In terms of "big players," W out is probably our largest. Take a quick look at how many elements are affected by W in incentives: all but M!

We also should notice the two mutually exclusive pairs: UG and ZW. We know that each of these pairs will be split between the two groups. Not only does this help us when working through scenarios, but it also provides important information about the numbers: we know that at least two elements are in finance and two are in incentives. With seven in total, that leaves only three left to consider numerically. Given the number of relationships that force at least one of a pair to incentives, we can guess that we will generally (if not always) have more elements on the incentives side.

Some Manhattan Prep instructors suggest that students actually note these relationships in a t-chart during The Big Pause, like shown below:

Finance	Incentives
U/G	G/U
W/Z	Z/W

Step 4: Attack the Questions

13. Which one of the following could be a complete and accurate list of the members of the finance committee?

    (A) Guzman, Hawking, Miyauchi, Wharton
    (B) Guzman, Lepp, Zhu
    (C) Hawking, Miyauchi, Zhu
    (D) Hawking, Upchurch, Wharton, Zhu
    (E) Miyauchi, Upchurch, Wharton

Answer choice (E) is correct.

This is an Orientation question, so we'll use the rules to eliminate. While we could effectively use the rules in their written form, let's "read" the rules from our diagram. We want to keep in mind that the question asks for a complete and accurate list of members for the *finance* committee.

The first rule pair is that M and L cannot be together on finance. No answer choice violates this rule, so we'll look at the next rule pair: L and U cannot be on finance together. Again, no answer violates this rule, but we have a lot of rules, so it's not time to panic—let's keep moving along!

MANHATTAN
PREP

The next rule pair we encounter is that U and G cannot be on the same committee. At first glance, it appears that no answers violate this rule. However, the rule here applies to both groups. While we don't get a list of those on incentives, we can make one for each answer choice—whoever's not on the list must be in incentives. In (C), we don't see either U or G, so they both must be on incentives. This violates the rule, so we can eliminate it.

This misdirect—having an answer choice that violates a rule by putting people together in the unlisted group—is common for In/Out Grouping games when dealing with two different groups.

Alternatively, we could have used our placeholder to note that this rule tells us that one of U/G is on finance, and the other is on incentives. (C) has neither U nor G, so we could eliminate it.

Moving down the Logic Chain, we see that G and H cannot be on finance together—let's eliminate (A).

Next, we can apply the rule that Z will serve on finance only if H does. (B) violates this rule.

To choose between answers (D) and (E), let's use the final rule that Z and W must serve on different committees. We see both Z and W in answer (D), so we can eliminate it.

14. Which of the following pairs of board members CANNOT both serve on the incentives committee?

    (A) Guzman and Hawking
    (B) Guzman and Wharton
    (C) Hawking and Wharton
    (D) Miyauchi and Upchurch
    (E) Miyauchi and Wharton

Answer choice (C) is correct.

This type of question is pretty common on In/Out Grouping games, and it can be tough to figure out what it's asking for. We like to rephrase it as, "For which one of the following pairs is it true that, if one is in, the other is out?" In this case, we need to find an answer where putting one of the paired elements in incentives forces the other one to finance.

We start tracing the line with H on incentives, Z must be on incentives, and if Z is on incentives, W must be on finance. Watch out for the double arrow! This means H and W cannot both be on incentives.

15. What is the maximum number of members on the finance committee?

    (A) two
    (B) three
    (C) four
    (D) five
    (E) six

Finance	Incentives
U/G	G/U
W/Z	Z/W

Answer choice (C) is correct.

This is the toughest of the questions we've seen for this game so far, and the only one that requires a level of logic that goes beyond what is on the Logic Chain diagram itself. You will occasionally run into questions like this one, so it is important to have a strategy and some extra time.

On these Maximum questions, we want to start with the total number of elements and work our way down. Here, we have seven elements, but they can't all be in finance. Looking at our placeholders, we can see that at least two elements have to be on incentives! Additionally, checking our Logic Chain, we see that L and M are also a pair at least one of which must be on incentives, and this pair doesn't overlap with either of our other placeholders. (We could have written this in during The Big Pause, but it's not an inference we'd expect to make on game day.) G and H are also such a pair, but, since G is already in a placeholder rule, this introduces complications. However, between U/G, Z/W, and L/M, at least three elements have to be on incentives! That brings our maximum on finance down to four.

There's one final step: confirming that we can actually get four people on finance. The placeholder chart is a good place to start, but we want to make sure that there aren't additional interactions we're missing.

So, can we have four on the finance committee? Yes! We can have U, H, Z, and M on finance and everyone else on incentives.

Finance	Incentives
Z	G
H	L
U	W
M	

16. If Miyauchi and Wharton both serve on the finance committee, which one of the following could be true?

    (A) Guzman and Lepp both serve on the finance committee.

    (B) Guzman and Upchurch both serve on the incentives committee.

    (C) Hawking and Zhu both serve on the finance committee.

    (D) Lepp and Upchurch both serve on the incentives committee.

    (E) Zhu and Upchurch both serve on the finance committee.

Answer choice (D) is correct.

A quick t-chart. Don't forget to write in the placeholders!

    (A) No. L serves on incentives in this case.
    (B) No. G and U are always on different committees.
    (C) No. Z serves on incentives here.
    (D) There's no reason to eliminate.
    (E) No. Z serves on incentives.

Finance	Incentives
M	L
W	Z
U/G	G/U
	H

MANHATTAN
PREP

17. If Guzman serves on the incentives committee, then which one of the following must be true?

    (A) Hawking serves on the finance committee.

    (B) Lepp serves on the incentives committee.

    (C) Miyauchi serves on the finance committee.

    (D) Wharton serves on the incentives committee.

    (E) Zhu serves on the finance committee.

Answer choice (B) is correct.

With the Logic Chain, this question should be quick. If G is on incentives, U is on finance, and L must be on incentives.

Chaining the Rule Chart

Hopefully, at this point, you can see the power of the Logic Chain. As we said earlier, of all the approaches we've learned so far, the Logic Chain takes the most practice to learn, but it's the most powerful. However, there is good reason we started this chapter with the Rule Chart: You might need to fall back on it. Why? Two possible reasons:

1. You are facing a game that doesn't fit into the Logic Chain.

    A few games in LSAT history do not lend themselves to the Logic Chain. You'll know it quickly if you meet one of these: they either have many unsplittable compound conditionals and/or have rules that don't chain together.

2. You simply cannot stand the Logic Chain.

    There are some students for whom the Logic Chain simply does not click. We don't take it personally! Be careful to not put yourself into this category too quickly, though. The Logic Chain does take some time to master.

Because you should feel comfortable using the Rule Chart if one of these situations occurs, be sure to practice using the Rule Chart. Take the In/Out Grouping games that you solved with the Logic Chain and replay them with the Rule Chart. But, before you do that, take a moment now to learn how you might link up the rules in the Rule Chart.

As we mentioned at the end of the Rule Chart section of this chapter, one challenge of the approach is that the chart does not help us to link up rules. The Logic Chain is a really powerful tool for linking rules, but it's possible to do it while using the Rule Chart as well. Let's take a look at the steps we'll need to go through after completing our Rule Chart:

1. Look for elements that show up in multiple rules.
2. Write one of the rules towards the middle of your scratch paper (so you have room to attach rules to either side).
3. Cross out that rule in the Rule Chart (so that you have it listed only once on your paper).

9

4. Look for a rule that you can attach to either the "front" or "back" of the rule you've written, add it to your chain, and cross it out in your rule chart.

5. Repeat step 4 until you've exhausted all the connectable rules.

6. Examine the rules that you haven't crossed out, looking for another element that shows up in multiple rules. If you find one, repeat steps 1–5.

7. Write out the contrapositive chain (if you find that useful).

Try building a Rule Chart and a chain of the rules for the Violins game we worked on earlier:

One or more of six violinists—Greene, Holiday, Liu, Mann, Underwood, and Wilson—will be selected to perform at the year-end concert. No other violinists will be selected. The following conditions apply:

If Holiday is selected, then Mann is not selected.
If Liu is selected, then both Mann and Wilson are selected.
If Underwood is not selected, then Holiday is selected.
Wilson is not selected unless Greene is selected.

You should have ended up with something like this:

In	Out
H → –M	–M → –L
M → –H	–W → –L
L → M	–U → H
L → W	–H → U
W → G	–G → –W

$$L \nearrow M \to -H \to U$$
$$\searrow W \to G$$

Chained Rule Chart

$$-U \to H \to -M \searrow$$
$$-L$$
$$-G \to -W \nearrow$$

Contrapositives

Try It Again, Once More!

Now try to play that game again using the diagram that you just built. Don't be lazy—do it!

1. Which of the following could be a complete and accurate list of the violinists selected for the concert?

   (A) Holiday, Liu, Wilson, Underwood

   (B) Liu, Mann, Wilson

   (C) Holiday, Liu, Mann

   (D) Liu, Mann, Wilson, Underwood

   (E) Mann, Underwood

2. Which of the following must be false?

   (A) Liu is selected but Underwood is not.

   (B) Neither Underwood nor Liu is selected.

   (C) Holiday is selected but Liu is not.

   (D) Both Greene and Underwood are selected.

   (E) Holiday is selected but Mann is not.

3. Which of the following could be the only violinist selected for the concert?

   (A) Liu

   (B) Mann

   (C) Greene

   (D) Wilson

   (E) Underwood

4. If Underwood is not selected, then which of the following must be true?

   (A) Wilson is not selected.

   (B) Greene is selected.

   (C) At least two violinists are selected.

   (D) At most three violinists are selected.

   (E) Neither Liu nor Holiday is selected.

5. If Greene is not selected, then each of the following could be true EXCEPT:

   (A) Exactly two violinists are selected.

   (B) Exactly one violinist is selected.

   (C) Mann is selected.

   (D) Holiday is selected.

   (E) Liu is selected.

6. Which of the following CANNOT be a complete and accurate list of the violinists who are selected for the concert?

   (A) Greene, Liu, Mann, Underwood, Wilson

   (B) Greene, Mann, Underwood

   (C) Greene, Mann, Wilson

   (D) Greene, Underwood

   (E) Holiday

7. Which of the following, if substituted for the condition that if Liu is selected then both Mann and Wilson are selected, would have the same effect in determining the violinists who are selected to perform?

   (A) If Liu is selected, then exactly two other violinists are selected.

   (B) If Liu is selected, then both Greene and Underwood are selected but Holiday is not.

   (C) If Mann and Wilson are selected, then Liu is selected.

   (D) If Liu is selected, then Mann is one of exactly five violinists selected.

   (E) If Liu is not selected, then neither Mann nor Wilson is selected.

9

Before we give you the answer key: how did that go? Probably it was a bit choppy. That's not because it's not doable, it's because you need to practice it more. Go ahead and stretch your abilities by solving In/Out Grouping games with both methods. Note that later on we'll tackle some twisted versions of In/Out Grouping games (with selection limits and subgroups)—those twisted In/Out Grouping games are, for reasons that will be clear later, typically better attacked with the Logic Chain.

QuickCheck: Violin Concert

GHLMUW

+	−
H →· -M	-M →· -L
M →· -H	-W →· -L
L → M	-U → H
L → W	-H → U
W → G	-G →· -W

K↙ M ← H ← U̶
K↙ W̶ ← G̶

The Big Pause

L, −U, and −G have the biggest impacts:

In	Out
U/H	H/M

Frames?

In/Out Grouping games typically won't be framed.

9

1. (A̶) R2
   (B̶) R3
   (C̶) R1
   (D̶) R4
   (Ⓔ)

2. (Ⓐ) L → M → H̶ → U
   (B)
   (C)
   (D)
   (E)

3. (A) placeholder chart
   (B) notes that we must
   (C) have either U or H
   (D) in. U is only option
   (Ⓔ)

4. (A)
   (B)

In	Out
H	U
	M
	L

   (C)
   (Ⓓ)
   (E)

5. (A̶)
   (B̶)

In	Out
U/H	H/M
	G
	W
	L

   (C̶)
   (D̶)
   (Ⓔ)

6. (A̶)
   (B̶)
   (Ⓒ) M → H̶ → U
   (D)
   (E)

7.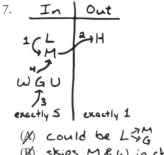

In	Out
¹↙L ²→H
↳M
WGU
↓³
exactly 5	exactly 1

   (A̶) could be L→G^M
   (B̶) skips M&W in chain
   (C̶) reversal
   (Ⓓ)
   (E̶) negation

Conclusion

1. **Practice, practice, practice.**

- The Logic Chain takes time to learn. First you need to be very comfortable with your conditional logic basics. If you are still a bit unsure of your ability to read and interpret conditional statements, now's the time to revisit Chapters 3 and 7.

- At this point, you are probably beginning to see the power of the Logic Chain, even if you aren't completely comfortable implementing it. Take the time now to redo the games in this chapter. Do them multiple times. Come back to them in a few days and try them again. The only way you'll get comfortable working with this tool is through repetition.

2. **Stay flexible.**

- As you encounter In/Out Grouping games in your practice, you'll see some twists. How well will you adapt? Learn and practice the fundamentals of the Logic Chain, and then work to apply it flexibly and with confidence. But also be willing to use the Rule Chart if the Logic Chain isn't helping on a game. This is rare, but there are games with many compound conditionals that can't be split and the Logic Chain has trouble with them.

3. **Pay attention to double-sided arrows.**

- The most common mistake that people make when reading the Logic Chain is failing to see double-sided arrows. Replace the arrowheads with a different mark, like an "X" or a small circle, to remind yourself that the arrow is biconditional. Pay attention to mutually exclusive pairs; they will often help you uncover important inferences during the questions.

9

Set 2

In This Practice Set . . .

Mixed Practice: Set 2

Now that we've crossed the divide into the world of grouping, our mixed sets are going to become even more challenging. While there are games in this practice set you've already played, you'll also find at least one new game, and it will be a little different than what you've already seen.

For the games in this set it will be important to make inferences up front. Linger on your setup and extend The Big Pause. If framing is something you don't feel comfortable with yet, this is an opportunity for you to practice it. In fact, if you don't frame at least one of these games, you'll likely find it unbearably hard to answer the questions. Unlike the first practice set, don't time yourself here. Instead, give yourself the freedom and space to see these games in all their complexity. Take the extra time to find a better approach. Then, replay them as a section, giving yourself 35 minutes to finish the set!

Practice Game 1: PT51, S4, G2

Six hotel suites—F, G, H, J, K, L—are ranked from most expensive (first) to least expensive (sixth). There are no ties. The ranking must be consistent with the following conditions:

> H is more expensive than L.
>
> If G is more expensive than H, then neither K nor L is more expensive than J.
>
> If H is more expensive than G, then neither J nor L is more expensive than K.
>
> F is more expensive than G, or else F is more expensive than H, but not both.

6. Which one of the following could be the ranking of the suites, from most expensive to least expensive?

   (A) G, F, H, L, J, K
   (B) H, K, F, J, G, L
   (C) J, H, F, K, G, L
   (D) J, K, G, H, L, F
   (E) K, J, L, H, F, G

7. If G is the second most expensive suite, then which one of the following could be true?

   (A) H is more expensive than F.
   (B) H is more expensive than G.
   (C) K is more expensive than F.
   (D) K is more expensive than J.
   (E) L is more expensive than F.

8. Which one of the following CANNOT be the most expensive suite?

   (A) F
   (B) G
   (C) H
   (D) J
   (E) K

9. If L is more expensive than F, then which one of the following could be true?

   (A) F is more expensive than H.
   (B) F is more expensive than K.
   (C) G is more expensive than H.
   (D) G is more expensive than J.
   (E) G is more expensive than L.

10. If H is more expensive than J and less expensive than K, then which one of the following could be true?

    (A) F is more expensive than H.
    (B) G is more expensive than F.
    (C) G is more expensive than H.
    (D) J is more expensive than L.
    (E) L is more expensive than K.

MANHATTAN
PREP

Practice Game 2: PT7, S2, G2

Doctor Yamata works only on Mondays, Tuesdays, Wednesdays, Fridays, and Saturdays. She performs four different activities—lecturing, operating, treating patients, and conducting research. Each working day she performs exactly one activity in the morning and exactly one activity in the afternoon. During each week her work schedule must satisfy the following restrictions:

She performs operations on exactly three mornings.
If she operates on Monday, she does not operate on Tuesday.
She lectures in the afternoon on exactly two consecutive calendar days.
She treats patients on exactly one morning and exactly three afternoons.
She conducts research on exactly one morning.
On Saturday she neither lectures nor performs operations.

8. Which one of the following must be a day on which Doctor Yamata lectures?

(A) Monday
(B) Tuesday
(C) Wednesday
(D) Friday
(E) Saturday

9. On Wednesday Doctor Yamata could be scheduled to

(A) conduct research in the morning and operate in the afternoon
(B) lecture in the morning and treat patients in the afternoon
(C) operate in the morning and lecture in the afternoon
(D) operate in the morning and conduct research in the afternoon
(E) treat patients in the morning and treat patients in the afternoon

10. Which one of the following statements must be true?

(A) There is one day on which the doctor treats patients both in the morning and in the afternoon.
(B) The doctor conducts research on one of the days on which she lectures.
(C) The doctor conducts research on one of the days on which she treats patients.
(D) The doctor lectures on one of the days on which she treats patients.
(E) The doctor lectures on one of the days on which she operates.

11. If Doctor Yamata operates on Tuesday, then her schedule for treating patients could be

(A) Monday morning, Monday afternoon, Friday morning, Friday afternoon
(B) Monday morning, Friday afternoon, Saturday morning, Saturday afternoon
(C) Monday afternoon, Wednesday morning, Wednesday afternoon, Saturday afternoon
(D) Wednesday morning, Wednesday afternoon, Friday afternoon, Saturday afternoon
(E) Wednesday afternoon, Friday afternoon, Saturday morning, Saturday afternoon

12. Which one of the following is a pair of days on both of which Doctor Yamata must treat patients?

(A) Monday and Tuesday
(B) Monday and Saturday
(C) Tuesday and Friday
(D) Tuesday and Saturday
(E) Friday and Saturday

Practice Game 3: PT41, S2, G3

Each of the seven members of the board of directors—Guzman, Hawking, Lepp, Miyauchi, Upchurch, Wharton, and Zhu—serves on exactly one of two committees—the finance committee or the incentives committee. Only board members serve on these committees. Committee membership is consistent with the following conditions:

If Guzman serves on the finance committee, then Hawking serves on the incentives committee.

If Lepp serves on the finance committee, then Miyauchi and Upchurch both serve on the incentives committee.

Wharton serves on a different committee from the one on which Zhu serves.

Upchurch serves on a different committee from the one on which Guzman serves.

If Zhu serves on the finance committee, so does Hawking.

13. Which one of the following could be a complete and accurate list of the members of the finance committee?

   (A) Guzman, Hawking, Miyauchi, Wharton
   (B) Guzman, Lepp, Zhu
   (C) Hawking, Miyauchi, Zhu
   (D) Hawking, Upchurch, Wharton, Zhu
   (E) Miyauchi, Upchurch, Wharton

14. Which one of the following pairs of board members CANNOT both serve on the incentives committee?

   (A) Guzman and Hawking
   (B) Guzman and Wharton
   (C) Hawking and Wharton
   (D) Miyauchi and Upchurch
   (E) Miyauchi and Wharton

15. What is the maximum number of members on the finance committee?

   (A) two
   (B) three
   (C) four
   (D) five
   (E) six

16. If Miyauchi and Wharton both serve on the finance committee, then which one of the following could be true?

   (A) Guzman and Lepp both serve on the finance committee.
   (B) Guzman and Upchurch both serve on the incentives committee.
   (C) Hawking and Zhu both serve on the finance committee.
   (D) Lepp and Upchurch both serve on the incentives committee.
   (E) Zhu and Upchurch both serve on the finance committee.

17. If Guzman serves on the incentives committee, then which one of the following must be true?

   (A) Hawking serves on the finance committee.
   (B) Lepp serves on the incentives committee.
   (C) Miyauchi serves on the finance committee.
   (D) Wharton serves on the incentives committee.
   (E) Zhu serves on the finance committee.

MANHATTAN PREP

Practice Game 4: PT30, S1, G2

The six messages on an answering machine were each left by one of Fleure, Greta, Hildy, Liam, Pasquale, or Theodore, consistent with the following:

At most one person left more than one message.
No person left more than three messages.
If the first message is Hildy's, the last is Pasquale's.
If Greta left any message, Fleure and Pasquale did also.
If Fleure left any message, Pasquale and Theodore did also, all of Pasquale's preceding any of Theodore's.
If Pasquale left any message, Hildy and Liam did also, all of Hildy's preceding any of Liam's.

6. Which one of the following could be a complete and accurate list of the messages left on the answering machine, from first to last?

(A) Fleure's, Pasquale's, Theodore's, Hildy's, Pasquale's, Liam's
(B) Greta's, Pasquale's, Theodore's, Theodore's, Hildy's, Liam's
(C) Hildy's, Hildy's, Hildy's, Liam's, Pasquale's, Theodore's
(D) Pasquale's, Hildy's, Fleure's, Liam's, Theodore's, Theodore's
(E) Pasquale's, Hildy's, Theodore's, Hildy's, Liam's, Liam's

7. The first and last messages on the answering machine could be the first and second messages left by which one of the following?

(A) Fleure
(B) Hildy
(C) Liam
(D) Pasquale
(E) Theodore

8. If Greta left the fifth message, then which one of the following messages CANNOT have been left by Theodore?

(A) the first message
(B) the second message
(C) the third message
(D) the fourth message
(E) the sixth message

9. Each of the following must be true EXCEPT:

(A) Liam left at least one message.
(B) Theodore left at least one message.
(C) Hildy left at least one message.
(D) Exactly one person left at least two messages.
(E) At least four people left messages.

10. If the only message Pasquale left is the fifth message, then which one of the following could be true?

(A) Hildy left the first message.
(B) Theodore left exactly two messages.
(C) Liam left exactly two messages.
(D) Liam left the second message.
(E) Fleure left the third and fourth messages.

QuickCheck: PT51, S4, G2

F G H J K L

$\stackrel{\$\$}{\underline{1}}\ \underline{2}\ \underline{3}\ \underline{4}\ \underline{5}\ \underline{6}^{\$}$

H – L

G – H → J $\langle^K_L$

H – G → K $\langle^J_L$

F – G or F – H, not both

H – F – G or G – F – H

The Big Pause

- Relative Ordering game made complicated by conditional and option rules.

Frames?

Yes! We should definitely build two Trees based on the option rule. If you decided to build frames around the second and third rules, that also would have worked.

Frame 1

H – F — G

  ⟩ L

K $\langle$

    J

Frame 2

G – F – H – L

      J ⟩

        K

6. (A) 2
   (B) Ⓑ
   (C) 3
   (D) 4
   (E) 1

7. $\underline{\overset{J}{1}}\ \underline{\overset{G}{2}}\ \overset{\overparen{K,\ F-H-L}}{\underline{3}\ \underline{4}\ \underline{5}\ \underline{6}}$

   Frame 2: G – F – H – L
              J ⟩
                K

   (A)
   (B)
   Ⓒ
   (D)
   (E)

8.   <u>can be</u>
   Frame 1: H K
   Frame 2: G J

   Ⓐ
   (B)
   (C)
   (D)
   (E)

9.   Frame 1
   H – L – F – G
   K $\langle$
       J

   (A)
   (B)
   (C)
   Ⓓ
   (E)

10.   Frame 1
              L
   K – H – J
              ⟍ F – G

   (A)
   (B)
   (C)
   Ⓓ
   (E)

MANHATTAN
PREP

QuickCheck: PT7, S2, G2

L O T R

am (O R/T) O / O T/R OOOTR
pm (T LL) / T T [L] TTT
     M T W Thu F Sa

$O_M \rightarrow \cancel{O}_T$ L
$O_T \rightarrow \cancel{O}_M$ Ø

The Big Pause

- Mismatch
- Make sure you get your letters straight.
- Easy to miss that she skips Thursday.

Frames?

Nope! Our diagram is already very filled, so no need to make frames.

---

8. $\frac{T}{M}$ $\frac{L}{T}$ $\frac{L}{W}$

(A)
(B)
(C)
(D)
(E)

9. am $\frac{O}{}$
    pm $\frac{T/L}{W}$

(A)
(B)
(C)
(D)
(E)

10. (A)
    (B)
    (C)
    (D)
    (E)

11. am R/T O O / O T/R
    pm (T LL) / T T
         M T W Thu F Sa

(A) F am
(B) M or W pm   fyi - There
(C) W am   are other reasons
(D) W am   some of these
(E)   are wrong, but you
                     shouldn't waste time
                     after coming across
                     one reason.

12. Fri + Sat
(A)
(B)
(C)
(D)
(E)

QuickCheck: PT41, S2, G3

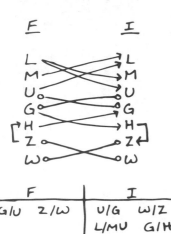

G H L M U W Z

The Big Pause

- Lots of connections
- A couple biconditionals
- Placeholders will be important!

Frames?

In/Out games rarely get framed, and this is no exception. While you could frame around the biconditionals, you'd have to pick one. Both look like at least one of the frames would be relatively empty.

13. (A) 1
    (B) 5
    (C) 4
    (D) 3
    (E) (E)

14. (A)
    (B)
    (C) C
    (D)
    (E)

15.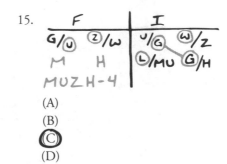

    MUZH-4

    (A)
    (B)
    (C) C
    (D)
    (E)

16.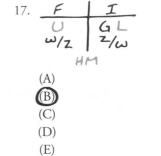

    (A)
    (B)
    (C)
    (D) D
    (E)

17.

F	I
U	G L
W/Z	Z/W

HM

(A)
(B) B
(C)
(D)
(E)

MANHATTAN
PREP

QuickCheck: PT30, S1, G2

F G H L P T – can repeat

$$\overline{1} \; \overline{2} \; \overline{3} \; \overline{4} \; \overline{5} \; \overline{6} \; \Big| \; \overline{\text{out}}$$

⌈ at most, 1 repeater
⌊ max: 3 msgs

$H_1 \rightarrow P_6$

⌈ G → F + P
⌈ F → P + T (P – T)
⌈ P → H + L (H – L)

⌊ G → F + P
     ↳ P + T (P – T)
         ↳ H + L (H – L)

The Big Pause

- Crazy Ordering mixed with In/Out, mismatched, with repeating elements!
- Long conditional chain that all starts with G.
- Should figure out distributions with repeater and others leaving messages.

Frames?

Our distributions inferences will have to serve here, as there aren't any strong divisions.

Distributions

In	Out
1 - 1 - 1 - 1 - 1 - 1	—
2 - 1 - 1 - 1 - 1 - 0	G
3 - 1 - 1 - 1 - 0 - 0	G F

HLPT always In!

6. (A) 5
    (B) 4
    (C) 3
    (D) **(D)**
    (E) 1

7. Gmax = 1
    H-L, P-T
    F – no ordering constraints

    F ⟨ H-L, P-T ⟩ F

    (A)
    (B)
    (C)
    (D)
    (E)

---

8. 1 - 1 - 1 - 1 - 1 - 1
    ⟨ P-T, H·L, F ⟩

$$\overline{1} \; \overline{2} \; \overline{3} \; \overline{4} \; \overline{\underset{G}{5}} \; \overline{6}$$

    (A)
    (B)
    (C)
    (D)
    (E)

9. (A)
    (B)
    (C)
    (D)
    (E)

    P = 1

    ⟨ H-L, T, ?, ? ⟩

$$\overline{1} \; \overline{2} \; \overline{3} \; \overline{4} \; \overline{\underset{P}{5}} \; \overline{6}$$

    6̸

10. (A)
    (B)
    (C) **C**
    (D)
    (E)

    Both trigger 2·1-1-1-1-0
    which means G Out + rest In.
    For (B), F In forces both T
    into 6th.

    (H) $\underline{L} \; \underline{F} \; \underline{F} \; \underline{P} \; \underline{T} \; \Big| \; \underline{G}$

LG

Chapter 10

Basic Grouping

In This Chapter...

Getting Familiar

Do your best to complete the following game in **10 minutes**. Use whatever approach you see fit.

Six doctors—Haddad, Johnson, Kwong, Lester, Murray, and Nelson—are assigned to the following three training rotations: orthopedics, pediatrics, surgery. Each doctor is assigned to exactly one rotation, and each rotation is assigned exactly two doctors. No other doctors are assigned.

The following conditions must be met:

    Kwong is not assigned to the same rotation as Lester.
    Murray is not assigned to surgery.
    If Lester is assigned to orthopedics, then Haddad is
      assigned to surgery.
    Johnson is assigned to surgery.

1. Which one of the following could be an accurate assignment of doctors to rotations?

    (A) orthopedics: Kwong, Haddad
        pediatrics: Lester, Nelson
        surgery: Johnson, Murray

    (B) orthopedics: Lester, Nelson
        pediatrics: Johnson, Murray
        surgery: Haddad, Kwong

    (C) orthopedics: Kwong, Nelson
        pediatrics: Lester, Murray
        surgery: Haddad, Johnson

    (D) orthopedics: Murray, Nelson
        pediatrics: Kwong, Lester
        surgery: Haddad, Johnson

    (E) orthopedics: Lester, Murray
        pediatrics: Haddad, Kwong
        surgery: Johnson, Nelson

2. If Kwong is assigned to surgery, each of the following could be true EXCEPT:

    (A) Murray is assigned to pediatrics.

    (B) Haddad is assigned to orthopedics.

    (C) Lester is assigned to orthopedics.

    (D) Nelson is assigned to pediatrics.

    (E) Nelson is assigned to orthopedics.

3. It can be determined to which rotation each of the six doctors is assigned if which one of the following statements is true?

    (A) Both Murray and Kwong are assigned to orthopedics.

    (B) Both Kwong and Nelson are assigned to pediatrics.

    (C) Both Haddad and Johnson are assigned to surgery.

    (D) Both Johnson and Lester are assigned to surgery.

    (E) Both Haddad and Nelson are assigned to pediatrics.

4. If Murray and Lester are assigned to the same rotation, for how many of the six doctors is it known to which rotation each is assigned?

    (A) one

    (B) two

    (C) three

    (D) four

    (E) six

5. If Nelson is assigned to surgery, which of the following is a complete and accurate list of doctors who could be assigned to the same rotation as Murray?

    (A) Kwong

    (B) Kwong, Lester

    (C) Haddad, Lester

    (D) Haddad, Kwong, Lester

    (E) Haddad, Johnson, Kwong, Lester

10

Basic Grouping

While about half of the games you'll face on the LSAT involve putting elements into groups, in the modern era of Logic Games, only about 7% are Basic Grouping games. Basic Grouping games are similar to Basic Ordering games in that they are relatively free of complications in comparison to other members of their family. However, while there are no bells and whistles, these games often fall on the more challenging side of the spectrum. The reason? Generally speaking, very few inferences can be made during the setup.

When you're expected to put elements into groups, and you are not facing an In/Out Grouping game (i.e., two groups and all conditional rules), or uncertainty about the number in each group, or a third dimension such as ordering, you're dealing with a Basic Grouping game. Often, you will see references to "assignment" in the scenario, as that is an easy way for the test writers to describe the task of putting elements into groups.

We generally represent ordering horizontally using a Number Line. We will generally represent grouping vertically (which we saw, to some degree, with In/Out Grouping games). We call the diagram for Basic Grouping a Closed Board because the number of elements in each group is known. The different groups form the base of the board, with the elements filled into slots above. Even if this isn't what you did in the Getting Familiar game, we hope that it sounds intuitive! Most diagrams we've seen students draw on their own are functionally equivalent to the Closed Board.

How Did You Do?

The challenge of Basic Grouping is generally not in recognizing what sort of game you're dealing with nor in flawlessly executing a complex diagram. Instead, the challenge is usually in the questions. There are no fancy diagramming techniques to teach you, so let's just work through the Getting Familiar game and start tackling these challenges:

> Six doctors—Haddad, Johnson, Kwong, Lester, Murray, and Nelson—are assigned to the following three training rotations: orthopedics, pediatrics, surgery. Each doctor is assigned to exactly one rotation, and each rotation is assigned exactly two doctors. No other doctors are assigned. The following conditions must be met:
>
> > Kwong is not assigned to the same rotation as Lester.
> > Murray is not assigned to surgery.
> > If Lester is assigned to orthopedics, then Haddad is assigned to surgery.
> > Johnson is assigned to surgery.

Step 1: Picture the Game

This is a classic Basic Grouping situation. We are placing doctors in groups. We could twist this game to say that we're assigning rotations to doctors, using the six doctors as the base of the diagram, but this would make it hard to form groups! Each doctor "group" would have only one element assigned to it, which is a good sign that you've picked the wrong base. We should train ourselves to see that, in a grouping game, we want to arrange a diagram that highlights the groups. With that in mind, we'll place the three rotations as our base, and since each one has two doctors assigned to it, we'll place two lines above each one. Our Closed Board looks like this:

$$\underline{\quad}\ \ \underline{\quad}\ \ \underline{\quad}\qquad \text{H J K L M N}$$
$$\overline{O}\ \ \ \ \overline{P}\ \ \ \ \overline{S}$$

We can see that we'll use each doctor only once, and there are no mismatch issues to worry about since every slot will be filled.

Step 2: Notate the Rules and Make Inferences

At this point in your LSAT prep, the rules and our representations should all feel somewhat familiar—take a look:

Notice that the Closed Board setup process in this case doesn't really lead to any inferences. This is fairly common on Basic Grouping games. The important thing is that we create a visual image of what the grouping structure will be and that we gather all of the rules, in symbol form, in one place.

Step 3: The Big Pause

There isn't much to notice, but it's worth noting that there's a lot left undetermined with the five elements left to group. On the other hand, M is limited to two groups, and if the L rule is triggered, we'll have at least half of the elements placed.

Checking for strays, we see N doesn't show up in any rules. Circle the good doctor and, at this point, we're ready to attack the questions.

Step 4: Attack the Questions

1. Which one of the following could be an accurate assignment of doctors to rotations?

    (A) orthopedics: Kwong, Haddad
        pediatrics: Lester, Nelson
        surgery: Johnson, Murray

    (B) orthopedics: Lester, Nelson
        pediatrics: Johnson, Murray
        surgery: Haddad, Kwong

    (C) orthopedics: Kwong, Nelson
        pediatrics: Lester, Murray
        surgery: Haddad, Johnson

    (D) orthopedics: Murray, Nelson
        pediatrics: Kwong, Lester
        surgery: Haddad, Johnson

    (E) orthopedics: Lester, Murray
        pediatrics: Haddad, Kwong
        surgery: Johnson, Nelson

Answer (C) is correct.

We know the deal with this question!

> Rule 1 eliminates answer (D).
> Rule 2 eliminates answer (A).
> We'll skip the Rule 3, as it's wordy, and use Rule 4 to eliminate answer (B).
> Rule 3 eliminates answer (E).

2. If Kwong is assigned to surgery, each of the following could be true EXCEPT:

    (A) Murray is assigned to pediatrics.

    (B) Haddad is assigned to orthopedics.

    (C) Lester is assigned to orthopedics.

    (D) Nelson is assigned to pediatrics.

    (E) Nelson is assigned to orthopedics.

Answer choice (C) is correct.

By this point in the book, you should be comfortable rephrasing EXCEPT questions. We can rephrase this question as: "Which one must be false?"

If we're not careful, it's easy to overlook the big inference we can draw from the new condition. If J and K are filling up the S group, we cannot have L in the O group—where would H go? Thus, we know the answer is (C).

MANHATTAN
PREP

3. It can be determined to which rotation each of the six doctors is assigned if which one of the following statements is true?

    (A) Both Murray and Kwong are assigned to orthopedics.

    (B) Both Kwong and Nelson are assigned to pediatrics.

    (C) Both Haddad and Johnson are assigned to surgery.

    (D) Both Johnson and Lester are assigned to surgery.

    (E) Both Haddad and Nelson are assigned to pediatrics.

Answer choice (E) is correct.

On a Determines Positions question, most test-takers will start with (A), plug in the information, and work through until they find the answer that forces everything else into place. Another approach, however, involves targeting answer choices with desired characteristics.

The correct answer to these questions generally does two things: 1) it determines the position of a stray (or "slippery" element, like a reversible chunk), and 2) it triggers a rule. Since N is our stray, we should start by looking at answers (B) and (E).

Outside of N, (B) talks about K, which is in an anti-chunk with L. However, there are still two positions for L, so let's defer on this answer.

(E) brings up H and N. With H in pediatrics, our conditional is triggered and L can't be in orthopedics. With pediatrics filled up by the new information in this answer, there's only one place for L to go—surgery. Now that surgery and pediatrics are filled in, the rest of the doctors must go to orthopedics. Reviewing the rules confirms this hypothetical.

$$\frac{\text{M}}{\underset{\text{O}}{\text{K}}} \quad \frac{\text{H}}{\underset{\text{P}}{\text{N}}} \quad \frac{\text{J}}{\underset{\text{S}}{\text{L}}}$$

4. If Murray and Lester are assigned to the same rotation, for how many of the six doctors is it known to which rotation each is assigned?

    (A) one

    (B) two

    (C) three

    (D) four

    (E) six

Answer choice (A) is correct.

Murray and Lester both could be assigned to orthopedics or pediatrics. With only six positions to fill, creating hypotheticals can be done quickly.

We'll start with M and L assigned to O. Remember that if L is assigned to O, then H must be assigned to S. This leaves K and N for P!

So this means we know where each doctor is assigned without a doubt, right? Not quite. Keep in mind that Murray and Lester could also be assigned to pediatrics. From there, none of the remaining doctors assignments are known. We could put H in orthopedics, K in orthopedics, and N in surgery, for example.

So if Murray and Lester are assigned to the same rotation, there are at least two viable scenarios:

$$\begin{array}{ccc|ccc} \underline{M} & \underline{K} & \underline{J} & \underline{H} & \underline{M} & \underline{J} \\ \underline{L} & \underline{N} & \underline{H} & \underline{K} & \underline{L} & \underline{N} \\ O & P & S & O & P & S \end{array}$$

The only doctor assigned to the same rotation in each scenario is Johnson. Johnson must be in surgery. Thus, if Murray and Lester are assigned to the same rotation, we can be certain about only one doctor's assignment. Answer (A) is correct. Tricky, LSAT! We've known this from the beginning.

5. If Nelson is assigned to surgery, which of the following is a complete and accurate list of doctors who could be assigned to the same rotation as Murray?

    (A) Kwong

    (B) Kwong, Lester

    (C) Haddad, Lester

    (D) Haddad, Kwong, Lester

    (E) Haddad, Johnson, Kwong, Lester

Answer choice (B) is correct.

Since surgery is now filled up, we can't assign L to orthopedics (that would force H into surgery). So, L must be assigned to pediatrics. Since K and L can't be assigned to the same rotation, K must then be assigned to orthopedics. This leaves M for orthopedics and H for pediatrics, or vice versa.

$$\begin{array}{ccc} \overline{\underline{H \quad M}} & \underline{J} \\ \underline{K} & \underline{L} & \underline{N} \\ O & P & S \end{array}$$

Thus, M can be paired with either K or L, but nothing else. Thus, (B) is correct.

Be careful! If we had changed the question slightly, (A) would have been the correct answer. Can you rephrase the question in a way that would make answer (A) correct?

If the question read, "If Nelson is assigned to surgery, which of the following could be a complete and accurate list of doctors who are assigned to the same rotation as Murray?" answer choice (A) would be correct. Moving the word "could" in front of "complete and accurate list," the question shifts from one about all hypothetical pairings, to one about a single hypothetical pairing. The LSAT asks both and likes switching between them (even in the same game!), so take an extra second when answering one of these questions to make sure you know which one you're facing.

MANHATTAN
PREP

Drill It: Rule Juggling

Since the key to many Basic Grouping games is to have a firm grasp on the rules, let's practice quickly handling rules in the questions. Skip the usual steps of the initial diagramming process and instead push yourself to solve these questions as fast as you can, while still maintaining accuracy.

Game 1:

```
____   ____   ____    L M N O P R
____   ____   ____
 1      2      3
```

M and P must ride in the same car.
L and O cannot ride in the same car.
R rides in car 1.

1. If O rides in car 3, which of the following must be true?

   (A) M rides in car 1.
   (B) L rides in car 2.
   (C) N rides in a car with R.
   (D) L rides in a car with R.
   (E) N rides in a car with P.

2. Which of the following could be true?

   (A) N rides in a car with R.
   (B) O rides in a car with P.
   (C) O rides in a car with R.
   (D) L rides in car 2 and O rides in car 3.
   (E) N rides in car 2 and L rides in car 3.

Game 2:

```
____            F G H I J K
____   ____
____   ____   ____
 X      Y      Z
```

J is kept in Region Y.
K is kept in Region X if, and only if, H is kept in Region Y.
I and G cannot be kept in the same region.
If F is kept in Region Z, then I is kept in Region X.

1. If H is kept in Region Y, which of the following must be false?

   (A) F and I are kept in the same region.
   (B) F and K are kept in the same region.
   (C) F and G are kept in the same region.
   (D) F and K are kept in different regions.
   (E) G and H are kept in different regions.

2. Which of the following could be true?

   (A) K is kept in Region Y and F is kept in Region Z.
   (B) I is kept in Region Y and K is kept in Region X.
   (C) H is kept in Region X and F is kept in Region Z.
   (D) G is kept in Region X and F is kept in Region Z.
   (E) K is kept in Region X and I is kept in Region Z.

Solutions: Rule Juggling

Note that our solutions to these games skip parts of the setup process. Some of these games can be framed, but to focus the drill on rule juggling, we've skipped that.

Game 1:

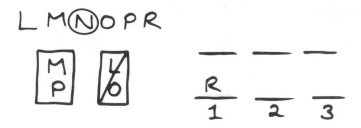

1. If O rides in car 3, which of the following must be true?

    (A) M rides in car 1.
    (B) L rides in car 2.
    (C) N rides in a car with R.
    (D) L rides in a car with R.
    (E) N rides in a car with P.

Answer choice (D) is correct.

If O rides in car 3, the MP chunk must be in 2. This leaves only car 1 for L. Once we place N in the remaining spot in car 3, we have determined all of the placements. Only answer (D) must be true (and, in this case, the rest must be false).

2. Which of the following could be true?

    (A) N rides in a car with R.
    (B) O rides in a car with P.
    (C) O rides in a car with R.
    (D) L rides in car 2 and O rides in car 3.
    (E) N rides in car 2 and L rides in car 3.

Answer choice (C) is correct.

MANHATTAN
PREP

$$\underline{L/O} \quad \underline{M} \quad \underline{N} \qquad\qquad \underline{L/O} \quad \underline{N} \quad \underline{M}$$

$$\frac{R}{1} \quad \frac{P}{2} \quad \frac{O/L}{3} \qquad\qquad \frac{R}{1} \quad \frac{O/L}{2} \quad \frac{P}{3}$$

Answer (A) cannot be true since that would require L and O to form a group. Answer (B) is impossible since M and P are a chunk. Answer (C) is possible! Both answers (D) and (E) leave no room for the MP chunk.

Game 2:

F G H I J K

I/G

$K_x \longleftrightarrow H_y$

$F_z \longrightarrow I_x$

$$\frac{\quad}{X} \quad \frac{\underline{\quad}\ \underline{\quad}}{\underset{Y}{J}} \quad \frac{\quad}{Z}$$

1. If H is kept in Region Y, which of the following must be false?

   (A) F and I are kept in the same region.
   (B) F and K are kept in the same region.
   (C) F and G are kept in the same region.
   (D) F and K are kept in different regions.
   (E) G and H are kept in different regions.

Answer choice (D) is correct.

$$\underline{F}$$
$$\underline{I/G} \quad \underline{H}$$
$$\frac{K}{X} \quad \frac{J}{Y} \quad \frac{G/I}{Z}$$

If H is in Region Y, then K must be in X. We're left with F, I, and G to place in the two remaining slots in X and the one slot in Z. Since I and G cannot go together, one must be in Z and the other in X, forcing F to X. Thus, F and K must be in the same region. Answers (B) and (E) must be true and (D) must be false. Answers (A) and (C) could be true, depending on the placement of I and G.

2. Which of the following could be true?

   (A) K is kept in Region Y and F is kept in Region Z.

   (B) I is kept in Region Y and K is kept in Region X.

   (C) H is kept in Region X and F is kept in Region Z.

   (D) G is kept in Region X and F is kept in Region Z.

   (E) K is kept in Region X and I is kept in Region Z.

Answer choice (E) is correct.

F G H I J K

I / G $K_x \longleftrightarrow H_y$
          $F_z \longrightarrow I_x$

          ___

          ___   ___

                  J
          ___   ___   ___
          X   Y   Z

Answer choice (A)'s two placements force I and G to be together in X. (B) doesn't work because K in X forces H in Y, and there's no room. In answer (C), our conditional rules force I into X and K *out* of X. Since I is in X, G is also excluded there. With Z full, we now have three elements—J, K, and G—trying to squeeze into the two spots in Y. (D) forces I into X with G. Our work from question 1 shows that (E) could be true.

Smart Tip: Turn Your Anti-Chunks into Groups

Many Basic Grouping games involve chunks and anti-chunks, and it's important to capitalize on them. One way to do so, when the number of elements and groups is quite limited, is to write anti-chunks as two partially filled chunks. For example, if we have six elements—W, Q, R, S, T, and U—that we will place in three groups of two, and we know that T and W must be together but R and Q cannot be, we could draw the chunks and anti-chunks like this:

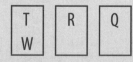

Since we have only S and U left, we could add those in like so:

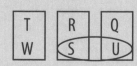

Try replaying the first game of the drill you just did using that technique.

MANHATTAN
PREP

Conclusion

Before we jump into our practice games, let's review the main points from the chapter:

1. **Basic Grouping**

   - In Basic Grouping games, the number of positions in each group is fixed. That means we'll see less variation in our diagram from one hypothetical to the next.

2. **Short setup**

   - The Closed Board setup is generally simple and quick, leading to very few extra inferences. The bulk of the work on Basic Grouping games comes when answering the questions.

3. **Rule control**

   - Basic Grouping games require accurate and quick application of the rules. Slow down initially and make sure that you understand each rule, and that your notations are correct. Consider using your diagram to answer the Orientation question in order to strengthen your grasp on the diagram.

4. **Inference chain**

   - On conditional questions, you will save yourself lots of time if you use the new information given in the question to start an inference chain. Follow this chain to its conclusion before you implement a trial-and-error approach. Often, the inference chain will end with the correct answer.

Practice Game 1: PT52, S2, G2

Here's a chance to apply the approaches we've discussed.

On a field trip to the Museum of Natural History, each of six children—Juana, Kyle, Lucita, Salim, Thanh, and Veronica—is accompanied by one of three adults— Ms. Margoles, Mr. O'Connell, and Ms. Podorski. Each adult accompanies exactly two of the children, consistent with the following conditions:

> If Ms. Margoles accompanies Juana, then Ms. Podorski accompanies Lucita.
>
> If Kyle is not accompanied by Ms. Margoles, then Veronica is accompanied by Mr. O'Connell.
>
> Either Ms. Margoles or Mr. O'Connell accompanies Thanh.
>
> Juana is not accompanied by the same adult as Kyle; nor is Lucita accompanied by the same adult as Salim; nor is Thanh accompanied by the same adult as Veronica.

8. Which one of the following could be an accurate matching of the adults to the children they accompany?

   (A) Ms. Margoles: Juana, Thanh; Mr. O'Connell: Lucita, Veronica; Ms. Podorski: Kyle, Salim

   (B) Ms. Margoles: Kyle, Thanh; Mr. O'Connell: Juana, Salim; Ms. Podorski: Lucita, Veronica

   (C) Ms. Margoles: Lucita, Thanh; Mr. O'Connell: Juana, Salim; Ms. Podorski: Kyle, Veronica

   (D) Ms. Margoles: Kyle, Veronica; Mr. O'Connell: Juana, Thanh; Ms. Podorski: Lucita, Salim

   (E) Ms. Margoles: Salim, Veronica; Mr. O'Connell: Kyle, Lucita; Ms. Podorski: Juana, Thanh

9. If Ms. Margoles accompanies Lucita and Thanh, then
    which one of the following must be true?

    (A) Juana is accompanied by the same adult as
        Veronica.
    (B) Kyle is accompanied by the same adult as
        Salim.
    (C) Juana is accompanied by Mr. O'Connell.
    (D) Kyle is accompanied by Ms. Podorski.
    (E) Salim is accompanied by Ms. Podorski.

10. If Ms. Podorski accompanies Juana and Veronica,
    then Ms. Margoles could accompany which one of
    the following pairs of children?

    (A) Kyle and Salim
    (B) Kyle and Thanh
    (C) Lucita and Salim
    (D) Lucita and Thanh
    (E) Salim and Thanh

11. Ms. Podorski CANNOT accompany which one of the
    following pairs of children?

    (A) Juana and Lucita
    (B) Juana and Salim
    (C) Kyle and Salim
    (D) Salim and Thanh
    (E) Salim and Veronica

10

12. Mr. O'Connell CANNOT accompany which one of
    the following pairs of children?

    (A) Juana and Lucita
    (B) Juana and Veronica
    (C) Kyle and Thanh
    (D) Lucita and Thanh
    (E) Salim and Veronica

Solutions: PT52, S2, G2

Answer Key

8.	B	11.	D
9.	E	12.	C
10.	A		

Step 1: Picture the Game

We see that we're putting the kids into groups and there are no fancy bells, whistles, or mismatches; we're facing a Basic Grouping game. We want to start by creating our board, and since we're grouping the children, we'll put the adults along the bottom with two slots above each:

$$J K L S T V \qquad \underline{}\ \underline{}\ \underline{}$$
$$\underline{}\ \underline{}\ \underline{}$$
$$M \quad O \quad P$$

Step 2: Notate the Rules and Make Inferences

The first two rules are conditionals, which you should be getting good at. We've used subscripts to represent the groups, but feel free to use your own system. Just be careful not to invert it—if you use the subscripts to represent the groups, don't flip it and use them to represent the elements halfway through the game!

> If Ms. Margoles accompanies Juana, then Ms. Podorski accompanies Lucita.
> If Kyle is not accompanied by Ms. Margoles, then Veronica is accompanied by Mr. O'Connell.

$$J K L S T V \qquad \underline{}\ \underline{}\ \underline{} \qquad J_M \longrightarrow L_P \qquad -K_M \longrightarrow V_O$$
$$\underline{}\ \underline{}\ \underline{}$$
$$M \quad O \quad P \qquad -L_P \longrightarrow -J_M \qquad -V_O \longrightarrow K_M$$

> Either Ms. Margoles or Mr. O'Connell accompanies Thanh.
> Juana is not accompanied by the same adult as Kyle; nor is Lucita accompanied by the same adult as Salim; nor is Thanh accompanied by the same adult as Veronica.

MANHATTAN
PREP

The first of these two remaining rules tells us that Thanh cannot be assigned to Ms. Podorski, so we'll notate this with a exclusion below the P. The second of the two gives us a bunch of illegal pairings. Because we've set up our diagram with the slots in vertical columns above each adult, we'll use anti-chunks to represent the rules, but they'll be vertical. This way, we get a visual match with the orientation of the diagram.

As is typical with Basic Grouping games, there aren't any obvious inferences so far.

Step 3: The Big Pause

Once again we see a Basic Grouping game that seems rather back-ended. There are essentially two types of rules to keep in mind. There are rules about who can and can't go with whom (mostly the last rule) and there are conditional rules that are triggered by certain assignments.

We haven't figured out much, so we can expect to do more work during the questions. Before moving on, we check for strays—there are none.

Step 4: Attack the Questions

8. Which one of the following could be an accurate matching of the adults to the children they accompany?

(A) Ms. Margoles: Juana, Thanh; Mr. O'Connell: Lucita, Veronica; Ms. Podorski: Kyle, Salim

(B) Ms. Margoles: Kyle, Thanh; Mr. O'Connell: Juana, Salim; Ms. Podorski: Lucita, Veronica

(C) Ms. Margoles: Lucita, Thanh; Mr. O'Connell: Juana, Salim; Ms. Podorski: Kyle, Veronica

(D) Ms. Margoles: Kyle, Veronica; Mr. O'Connell: Juana, Thanh; Ms. Podorski: Lucita, Salim

(E) Ms. Margoles: Salim, Veronica; Mr. O'Connell: Kyle, Lucita; Ms. Podorski: Juana, Thanh

Answer choice (B) is correct.

At this point, it's unlikely that you need us to walk you through an Orientation question.

> Rule 1 eliminates (A).
> Rule 2 eliminates (C).
> Rule 3 eliminates (E).
> Rule 4 eliminates (D).

9. If Ms. Margoles accompanies Lucita and Thanh, then which one of the following must be true?

(A) Juana is accompanied by the same adult as Veronica.

(B) Kyle is accompanied by the same adult as Salim.

(C) Juana is accompanied by Mr. O'Connell.

(D) Kyle is accompanied by Ms. Podorski.

(E) Salim is accompanied by Ms. Podorski.

Answer choice (E) is correct.

Before we start testing the answers, we want to follow the inference chain as far as it will take us.

If L and T occupy M's column, then K is *not* assigned to M. This triggers one of our conditional statements—V must be assigned to O. So we have J, S, and K remaining. We know that J and K can't be paired together, so J and K must be split between O and P. Thus, S must be assigned to P:

That leads us directly to answer (E). The chain of inferences took us all the way there.

10. If Ms. Podorski accompanies Juana and Veronica, then Ms. Margoles could accompany which one of the following pairs of children?

(A) Kyle and Salim

(B) Kyle and Thanh

(C) Lucita and Salim

(D) Lucita and Thanh

(E) Salim and Thanh

Answer choice (A) is correct.

If J and V occupy P's column, we're left with K, L, S, and T. We know that L and S can't be paired together, so L and S must be split between M and O. We also know that if V is not in O's column, K must be assigned to M. This leaves T for the remaining slot in O's column:

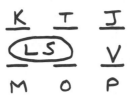

Thus, Ms. Margoles could be assigned K and L or K and S.

11. Ms. Podorski CANNOT accompany which one of the following pairs of children?

   (A) Juana and Lucita
   (B) Juana and Salim
   (C) Kyle and Salim
   (D) Salim and Thanh
   (E) Salim and Veronica

Answer choice (D) is correct.

Before you start trying things, check the diagram! We've already made the inference that T can't go in P's column.

12. Mr. O'Connell CANNOT accompany which one of the following pairs of children?

   (A) Juana and Lucita
   (B) Juana and Veronica
   (C) Kyle and Thanh
   (D) Lucita and Thanh
   (E) Salim and Veronica

Answer choice (C) is correct.

Four of these answers represent pairs that *can* be assigned to O and one answer represents a pair that *cannot*. Because this question asks us about assignments to O's column, it's very likely that the answer will hinge on our rule that deals with O: $-V_O \rightarrow K_M$. So let's look for answer choices that do not contain V, because this will trigger the rule. We'll start with (A). If we put J and L with O, can we place the other letters without any violations? There doesn't seem to be anything stopping us from obeying the conditional and placing K in the M group. J and L are safely paired up, so we just need to separate T and V and we're in the clear.

Answer choice (C) also does not contain V, so we'll look at this next. We know that when V is not assigned to O, K must be assigned to M. So if V is not assigned to O, K can't be either. Answer (C) violates this rule. Thus, (C) is the correct answer, as it represents a pair that *cannot* be assigned to O.

10

Practice Game 2: PT16, S1, G1

Eight new students—R, S, T, V, W, X, Y, Z—are being divided among exactly three classes—class 1, class 2, and class 3. Classes 1 and 2 will gain three new students each; class 3 will gain two new students. The following restrictions apply:

> R must be added to class 1.
> S must be added to class 3.
> Neither S nor W can be added to the same class as Y.
> V cannot be added to the same class as Z.
> If T is added to class 1, Z must also be added to class 1.

1. Which one of the following is an acceptable assignment of students to the three classes?

	1	2	3
(A)	R, T, Y	V, W, X	S, Z
(B)	R, T, Z	S, V, Y	W, X
(C)	R, W, X	V, Y, Z	S, T
(D)	R, X, Z	T, V, Y	S, W
(E)	R, X, Z	V, W, Y	S, T

2. Which one of the following is a complete and accurate list of classes any one of which could be the class to which V is added?

(A) class 1

(B) class 3

(C) class 1, class 3

(D) class 2, class 3

(E) class 1, class 2, class 3

3. If X is added to class 1, which one of the following is a student who must be added to class 2?

(A) T

(B) V

(C) W

(D) Y

(E) Z

4. If X is added to class 3, each of the following is a pair of students who can be added to class 1 EXCEPT:

   (A) Y and Z
   (B) W and Z
   (C) V and Y
   (D) V and W
   (E) T and Z

5. If T is added to class 3, which one of the following is a student who must be added to class 2?

   (A) V
   (B) W
   (C) X
   (D) Y
   (E) Z

6. Which one of the following must be true?

   (A) If T and X are added to class 2, V is added to class 3.
   (B) If V and W are added to class 1, T is added to class 3.
   (C) If V and W are added to class 1, Z is added to class 3.
   (D) If V and X are added to class 1, W is added to class 3.
   (E) If Y and Z are added to class 2, X is added to class 2.

10

Solutions: PT16, S1, G1

Answer Key

1. D   4. E
2. E   5. C
3. A   6. D

Step 1: Picture the Game

We see three groups with various numbers of elements assigned to each. With three in two of those classes and two in the other, we have a total of eight positions, which exactly matches our eight elements. The rules are about assignment and the relationship between the assignments of elements. This is a Basic Grouping game. Let's set up our Closed Board:

Step 2: Notate the Rules and Make Inferences

We've seen rules similar to all of these before. Compare your diagram to ours. You might notice one rule "missing" from ours. See if you can figure out why we left it out:

Your diagram probably included a more formal notation noting that Y and S can't be in the same group (similar to the restriction on YW). However, since we already know which group S is in, we need only note that Y can't be in group 3.

There's a lot of uncertainty in the game at this point, as well as a lot of rules. Unfortunately, no inferences are coming to mind.

MANHATTAN
PREP

Step 3: The Big Pause

In terms of prioritizing the rules, the two anti-chunks—YW and VZ—seem most relevant since they'll always apply (as opposed to the conditional). It's tough to see exactly how those two pairs will intersect. Y, for example, could be with either V or Z, or with neither. The TZ rule, if triggered, would fill group 1, forcing Y to group 2, W to group 3, and V and X to the remaining spots in group 2. This one rule thus has a large effect, but it is not worth framing per se, since the possibilities when T is not in group 1 are too varied.

Before diving into the questions, circle X, as it has no rules attached to it.

Step 4: Attack the Questions

1. Which one of the following is an acceptable assignment of students to the three classes?

	1	2	3
(A)	R, T, Y	V, W, X	S, Z
(B)	R, T, Z	S, V, Y	W, X
(C)	R, W, X	V, Y, Z	S, T
(D)	R, X, Z	T, V, Y	S, W
(E)	R, X, Z	V, W, Y	S, T

Answer choice (D) is correct.

Rule 1 does not eliminate an answer choice.
Rule 2 eliminates (B).
Rule 3 eliminates (E).
Rule 4 eliminates (C).
Rule 5 eliminates (A).

2. Which one of the following is a complete and accurate list of classes any one of which could be the class to which V is added?

(A) class 1

(B) class 3

(C) class 1, class 3

(D) class 2, class 3

(E) class 1, class 2, class 3

Answer choice (E) is correct.

Tough question—especially if you didn't use the answer to the Orientation question! We know that answer (D) in the last question works, so we know that V can be part of class 2. That eliminates answers (A) through (C)! All that's left to do is compare answers (D) and (E) and test out any difference, which in this case is whether V can be in class 1. Why not just sketch out a possibility? To keep things simple, we'll try to avoid triggering the TZ rule:

$$
\begin{array}{ccc}
\underline{Y} & \underline{W} & \\
\underline{V} & \underline{Z} & \underline{X} \\
\underline{R} & \underline{T} & \underline{S} \\
1 & 2 & 3
\end{array}
$$

It works, so (E) is the correct answer.

One way to make that sort of work pay off for more than one question is to note which elements can switch places without affecting anything else in the game. In this case, we could have Y and W switch, and we could also have V and Z switch. We'll note that by using clouds, in case these hypotheticals come up later. Note that this modified diagram does not represent all possible arrangements. For instance, we might swap V and X or Z and X, but it would be tough to capture all that. We can leverage our existing diagram to prove possibilities, but not to establish what must be true:

$$
\begin{array}{ccc}
\overline{(Y} & \overline{W)} & \\
\overline{(V} & \overline{Z)} & \underline{X} \\
\underline{R} & \underline{T} & \underline{S} \\
1 & 2 & 3
\end{array}
$$

3. If X is added to class 1, which one of the following is a student who must be added to class 2?

(A) T

(B) V

(C) W

(D) Y

(E) Z

Answer choice (A) is correct.

MANHATTAN
PREP

What effect does X in class 1 have? It's not really clear at first glance. To help us think this through, let's write out who's left, noting the mutually exclusive pairs:

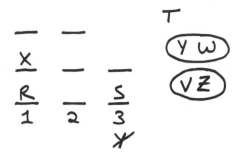

It all seems up in the air, but clearly someone has to be in class 2—look at the question! What about those mutually exclusive pairs? Where could they go? And where can we put T, the one element that isn't in one of those pairs? We know we can't put T in class 1 because of the TZ rule. Let's skip considering class 2 and instead see if T's also restricted from class 3, the other class with only one open slot.

With T in class 3, where would the mutually exclusive pairs go? Y and W could span classes 1 and 2, but where would V and Z go? We need to be able to put one of them in class 3, which is filled by T and S in this case. Aha! T must go in class 2. In short, if it's not in class 2, there's no room to spread out those mutually exclusive pairs.

4. If X is added to class 3, each of the following is a pair of students who can be added to class 1 EXCEPT:

    (A) Y and Z
    (B) W and Z
    (C) V and Y
    (D) V and W
    (E) T and Z

Answer choice (E) is correct.

With X taking up the second and final slot in class 3, we know we'll need to separate our two mutually exclusive pairs between classes 1 and 2. As in the last problem, the only place to put T is in class 2.

While some people might be able to hold this in their heads, the rest of us should write it out:

$$
\begin{array}{ccc}
\boxed{Y \quad W} \\
\underline{} \quad \underline{} \\
\boxed{V \quad Z} \quad X \\
\underline{V} \quad \underline{Z} \quad \underline{X} \\
\underline{R} \quad \underline{T} \quad \underline{S} \\
1 \quad 2 \quad 3
\end{array}
$$

10

We're looking for a group that can't be in class 1. We know that the LSAT won't give us an answer with S or X in it. That would be too easy and wouldn't be testing whether we drew inferences from the new condition. Thus, we can expect the correct answer to involve T. (E) it is! Note that answers (A) through (D) are simply the four ways we can combine one element each from our two pairs.

By the way, did you notice that we've re-created our diagram from the second question of the game? We could have saved some time by just referring to that!

5. If T is added to class 3, which one of the following is a student who must be added to class 2?

   (A) V
   (B) W
   (C) X
   (D) Y
   (E) Z

Answer choice (C) is correct.

This question is similar to the last one, except that all we need to do is switch the positions of T and X. In this case, X must be in class 2.

6. Which one of the following must be true?

   (A) If T and X are added to class 2, V is added to class 3.
   (B) If V and W are added to class 1, T is added to class 3.
   (C) If V and W are added to class 1, Z is added to class 3.
   (D) If V and X are added to class 1, W is added to class 3.
   (E) If Y and Z are added to class 2, X is added to class 2.

Answer choice (D) is correct.

It's been a while since we've had an unconditional question in this game! One obvious approach to this question is to simply consider each choice, perhaps testing out some of them, but that will take quite some time. Let's look at how to work the question with a minimum of writing.

Each answer choice "uses up" two elements in the conditional trigger. Instead of writing them into a diagram, cover up those elements in the roster with a finger or two to help you focus on who is left.

For example, with (A), you would cover up T and X in your master diagram:

We see that we have the two mutually exclusive pairs left. There's only one open slot left in class 2, but with two slots left to fill in class 1, and one more in class 3, we should be able to spread out those pairs. And, most importantly, there's no apparent reason we can't fit V into class 1 or 2. Since we were able to "break" answer (A), we can eliminate it.

Go ahead now and work your way through the other answer choices and see if you can do the maneuvers in your head, with a bit of help from your fingers.

Another approach to this question is to use previous work. Here are two hypotheticals we have already developed for this game:

Before reading on, see which answers you can eliminate using these two diagrams. Let's compare each answer choice to these two hypotheticals to see if we can "break" them, and thus eliminate the answer. These aren't a complete set of frames, though, so if we don't see the condition, we'll need to defer judgment.

The first part of answer (A)—the sufficient condition—doesn't occur in either scenario, so let's defer judgment.

The sufficient condition of answer choice (B) can occur in the second scenario, and T is clearly not in class 3. Eliminate.

The sufficient condition of (C) can happen in the hypothetical from question 2, and Z isn't in 3, so we can also rule this answer out.

The sufficient condition of answer choice (D) doesn't occur in either scenario, so we'll defer judgment.

The sufficient condition of answer choice (E) can occur in the first scenario, where X is in class 3. Eliminate.

We're down to answers (A) and (D), and the obvious strategy here is to choose one answer, re-create the sufficient condition, and try to avoid the supposedly necessary one. Looking at answer (A), we'd start by placing T and X in class 2, without placing V in class 3. If V goes in class 2, for example, we then have to place Z elsewhere, leaving us with Y and W to place in classes 1 and 3 respectively:

$$
\begin{array}{ccc}
Y & V & \\
Z & X & W \\
R & T & S \\
\hline
1 & 2 & 3
\end{array}
$$

We were able to "break" the necessary condition of answer (A), so answer (D) must be correct. If we had tried answer (D), we would have found it impossible to avoid placing W in class 3 with V and X in class 1.

Chapter 11

Open Grouping

In This Chapter. . .

Getting Familiar

Do your best to complete the following game. Use whatever approach you see fit. Give yourself **10 minutes.**

The Mizotron Corporation has exactly six managers: Holmes, Jin, Kaufman, Lu, Orr, and Pearson. Each manager has expertise in one or more of the following three areas: finance, marketing, technology. None of the managers has expertise in any other area. The following conditions apply:

Jin does not share any area of expertise with Orr.
Holmes has fewer areas of expertise than Lu.
Jin, Kaufman, and Pearson all have expertise in finance.
Holmes and Pearson have exactly two areas of expertise in common.
Orr does not have expertise in marketing.

1. Which one of the following pairs of managers must have at least one area of expertise in common?

    (A) Holmes and Kaufman
    (B) Kaufman and Orr
    (C) Lu and Orr
    (D) Holmes and Jin
    (E) Jin and Orr

2. For how many of the six managers is it possible to determine exactly which of the three areas of expertise they have?

    (A) one
    (B) two
    (C) three
    (D) four
    (E) five

3. Which of the following must be false?

    (A) Exactly four of the six managers have exactly two areas of expertise.
    (B) Exactly one of the six managers has exactly two areas of expertise.
    (C) Exactly one of the six managers has exactly one area of expertise.
    (D) Exactly three of the six managers have exactly one area of expertise.
    (E) Exactly four of the six managers have exactly one area of expertise.

4. Which one of the following is a complete and accurate list of the managers who could have exactly three areas of expertise?

    (A) Holmes, Kaufman, Lu, Pearson
    (B) Kaufman, Lu, Pearson
    (C) Holmes, Lu
    (D) Kaufman, Lu
    (E) Pearson

5. Which of the following must be false?

    (A) Both Jin and Pearson have expertise in marketing.
    (B) Both Lu and Orr have expertise in technology.
    (C) Both Holmes and Lu have expertise in marketing.
    (D) Both Holmes and Orr have expertise in finance.
    (E) Both Kaufman and Pearson have expertise in technology.

6. Exactly how many of the managers could have expertise in both marketing and technology?

    (A) two
    (B) three
    (C) four
    (D) five
    (E) six

Open Grouping

Open Grouping games, like In/Out Grouping games, tend to be very difficult for those who do not have a repeatable method with which to attack the setup. We'll discuss this method shortly, but first let's take a look at the characteristics that define Open Grouping.

Putting the "Open" in Open Grouping

Open Grouping games are games in which elements are assigned to groups and the number of elements that are assigned to each group is unknown.

Compare these two scenarios:

Six students—Harry, Jack, Kylie, Lin, Maxwell, and Nan—will be tutored by exactly three teachers: Mr. Peters, Mrs. Raul, and Mr. Singh. Each teacher will tutor exactly two students, and no student will be tutored by more than one teacher.

Exactly six performers—Q, R, T, V, W, and X—will perform at the county fair. Each performer will perform one or more of the following three acts: juggling, sword swallowing, unicycle riding.

The first example is a familiar Basic Grouping setup. Each of the three teachers will be assigned exactly two students. We can create two slots for each teacher, and every valid arrangement in this game will use all six slots:

$$\frac{\rule{1cm}{0.4pt}\quad\rule{1cm}{0.4pt}\quad\rule{1cm}{0.4pt}}{P\quad R\quad S}$$

Now, let's look at the second example. Notice that each performer will be assigned one or more acts, up to a maximum of three. We can think of each performer (group) as having three available slots for acts:

$$\frac{\rule{1cm}{0.4pt}\ \rule{1cm}{0.4pt}\ \rule{1cm}{0.4pt}\ \rule{1cm}{0.4pt}\ \rule{1cm}{0.4pt}\ \rule{1cm}{0.4pt}}{Q\quad R\quad T\quad V\quad W\quad X}$$

Note, however, the key phrase "one or more" (sometimes expressed on the LSAT as "at least one"). This means that any particular performer could be assigned one, two, or all three acts. Say, for example, that performer Q performs only as a juggler; two of Q's slots would remain empty. Just because we have three available slots for each performer doesn't mean that all slots will be filled. When the number of slots in each group is not clearly defined up front, and may in fact change from one question to the next, we call this situation Open Grouping.

MANHATTAN
PREP

So, how can we quickly determine whether we're dealing with an Open or Basic (Closed) Grouping game? Open situations will usually be cued by one of the following phrases:

1. **"One or more"**:

Exactly six performers—Q, R, T, V, W, and X—will perform at the county fair. Each performer will perform **one or more** of the following three acts: juggling, sword swallowing, unicycle riding.

2. **"At least one"**:

At a hospital, each of exactly five doctors—J, K, M, N, and O—will be on call on **at least one** of the following three days: Monday, Tuesday, Wednesday.

The Open Board

Let's use our Getting Familiar game to apply and build on the framework we introduced earlier:

> The Mizotron Corporation has exactly six managers: Holmes, Jin, Kaufman, Lu, Orr, and Pearson. Each manager has expertise in one or more of the following three areas: finance, marketing, technology. None of the managers has expertise in any other area. The following conditions apply:
>
>> Jin does not share any area of expertise with Orr.
>> Holmes has fewer areas of expertise than Lu.
>> Jin, Kaufman, and Pearson all have expertise in
>>   finance.
>> Holmes and Pearson have exactly two areas of
>>   expertise in common.
>> Orr does not have expertise in marketing.

This is a classic grouping situation. In this case we have two sets of elements: managers—H, J, K, L, O, and P—and areas of expertise—F, M, and T. The areas of expertise will be assigned to the managers, thus forming groups.

Is this an Open or Closed situation? Note the key phrase: "Each manager has expertise in **one or more** of the following three areas." This phrasing indicates that each of the managers will have three available slots.

However, some of these slots may be left empty. Thus, this is an Open Grouping game.

$$\text{F M T}\quad \underline{}\ \underline{}\ \underline{}\ \underline{}\ \underline{}\ \underline{}$$
$$\underline{}\ \underline{}\ \underline{}\ \underline{}\ \underline{}\ \underline{}$$
$$\text{H J K L O P}$$

Notice that we have *not* named the rows. For the purposes of the Open Board, there is no finance row, or marketing row, or technology row. You'll see the benefit of this setup momentarily.

Defining the Symbols

The Open Board uses three basic symbols. Let's define them here before we apply them to our game:

— **The Slot.** An element may or may not be assigned to this position.

☐ **The Box.** An element *must* be assigned to this position.

╱ **The Slash.** An element *must not* be assigned to this position.

Setting Up the Board

We'll start by identifying and marking all the slots that we know must be filled. We know from the scenario that each manager has expertise in at least one area. Thus, we know that one slot for each manager must be filled. Which slot? It doesn't really matter. For the purposes of simplicity, we'll put a box in the first slot for each manager:

F M T
```
—  —  —  —  —  —
—  —  —  —  —  —
☐  ☐  ☐  ☐  ☐  ☐
H  J  K  L  O  P
```

Now, it's time for the rules:

> *Jin does not share any area of expertise with Orr.*

In any other system, this rule would be difficult to diagram. After all, we can't really use this to place any letters in the slots, right? But what does this rule tell us about the *number* of slots that will be filled for Jin and Orr? If Jin does not share any area of expertise with Orr, then neither can have expertise in all three areas! We can slash one of Jin's slots and one of Orr's slots:

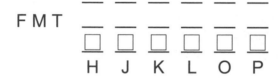

F M T
```
—  ╱  —  —  ╱  —
—  —  —  —  —  —
☐  ☐  ☐  ☐  ☐  ☐
H  J  K  L  O  P
```

It feels like we should also write out this rule in some more explicit way, but trust us, we'll do that later (if it turns out we need to).

> *Holmes has fewer areas of expertise than Lu.*

Again, we can't use this to place any letters on the board, but we *can* use this to discover more about the *number* of slots that will be filled for Holmes and Lu. If Holmes has fewer areas of expertise than Lu, there are three possibilities: 1) Lu has three areas and Holmes has two, 2) Lu has three areas and Holmes has one, or 3) Lu has two areas and Holmes has one. Regardless, Holmes has at most two areas of expertise and Lu has at least two areas of expertise. Thus, we can slash one of Holmes's slots and we can add a box to one of Lu's slots:

MANHATTAN
PREP

```
          ╱   ╱   __  __  ╱   __
  F M T   __  __  __  □   __  __
          □   F   F   □   □   F
          H   J   K   L   O   P
```

We can read the Board as follows: Holmes has at least one, and possibly two, areas of expertise. Lu has at least two, and possibly three, areas of expertise.

Jin, Kaufman, and Pearson all have expertise in finance.

This is a rare rule in that it gives us direct information about a particular placement of a letter. We can immediately add finance (F) to Jin's, Kaufman's, and Pearson's columns:

```
          ╱   ╱   __  __  ╱   __
  F M T   __  __  __  □   __  __
          □   F   F   □   □   F
          H   J   K   L   O   P
```

Holmes and Pearson have exactly two areas of expertise in common.

This tells us that Holmes has exactly two areas of expertise (since we know Holmes can't have three) and that Pearson has at least two areas of expertise. We can thus add a box to Holmes's remaining slot and we can add one more box to Pearson's column:

```
          ╱   ╱   __  __  ╱   __
  F M T   □   __  __  □   __  □
          □   F   F   □   □   F
          H   J   K   L   O   P
```

Note that we don't know yet if F is in the Holmes group, since Pearson could have all three areas of expertise.

Orr does not have expertise in marketing.

We can indicate this by putting a exclusion underneath Orr's column:

```
          ╱   ╱   __  __  ╱   __
  F M T   □   __  __  □   __  □
          □   F   F   □   □   F
          H   J   K   L   O   P
                              ̸M
```

Can we slash a second slot in Orr's column? We slashed the first one because J and O don't share any areas of expertise, but since we don't know which areas J has, we're not sure which element that slash is preventing from landing in Orr's column. We cannot put in a second slash at this point.

Cycling Through a Second Time

Now, here's a key step in setting up the Open Board. We need to go back through the rules one more time to see if any further inferences can be made. Sometimes a rule won't give us a whole lot of information the first time, but it becomes more valuable after we've added other information to the diagram. For example, let's look at the first rule again:

> *Jin does not share any area of expertise with Orr.*

If Jin does not share any area of expertise with Orr, then Orr cannot have expertise in finance. After marking this with a exclusion underneath Orr's column, we see that Orr must have just one area of expertise: technology. Thus, Jin cannot have technology:

Remember, we said we'd get to writing out this rule if we needed to? Do we need to?

No! We've been able to write under J and O the actual restrictions that this rule requires. There is no need to write anything else. In some situations, we will still need to notate this sort of rule; later in the chapter, we will discuss how to do this.

Let's look at the second rule one more time:

> *Holmes has fewer areas of expertise than Lu.*

We now know that Holmes has exactly two areas of expertise. Thus, Lu must have expertise in all three areas!

Upon reviewing the remaining rules a second time, we see that no further inferences can be made. This is our final Open Board diagram.

MANHATTAN
PREP

The Key to the Open Board

The biggest mistake that test-takers make on Open Grouping games is misunderstanding the goal of the game. Your job is *not* necessarily to place letters on the diagram. Rather, your job is to track to the best of your ability *how many* elements can end up in each group. The slash and box method allows us to track *number* very effectively, while also tracking any assignments that we can make.

Drill It: Open Grouping Setups

Work through the Open Board setup for each of the exercises below. Remember that you can often make additional inferences by cycling through the rules a second time. Be sure to check your solution before moving on to the next exercise.

1. YourHome Realty has exactly five condominiums on the market: P, Q, S, T, and V. Each of the condominiums has at least one of the following three features: fireplace, hardwood floors, modern appliances. The condominiums have no other features. The following conditions apply:

   Q has fewer features than S.
   P and T have exactly one feature in common.
   Both Q and V have hardwood floors.
   P has more features than any other condominium.

2. Each of exactly five radio stations—F, J, K, L, and M—plays one or more of the following four types of music: new age, oldies, rock, soul. None of the stations plays any other type of music. The following conditions apply:

   F plays more types of music than any other station.
   K plays new age and oldies, but no other type of music.
   Exactly three of the five stations play rock.
   L does not play new age or rock.
   M plays more types of music than K.

3. The town of Holden has exactly three movie theaters: J, K, and L. Each of the three theaters shows one or more of the following movies: *Rung, Stilted, Trouble*. None of the three theaters shows any other movie. The following rules apply:

   Any theater that shows *Rung* also shows *Trouble*.
   Exactly two of the theaters show *Stilted*.

4. At Riverside High School, six student athletes—Mitembe, Nathan, Paula, Raul, Victoria, and Yolanda—were chosen as Athletes of the Year. Each of the six athletes plays one or more of the following three sports: hockey, soccer, tennis. None of the athletes plays any other sport. The following must be true:

   Nathan plays exactly two of the sports.
   Yolanda plays more of the sports than Victoria.
   Raul and exactly three other student athletes play hockey.
   Victoria plays both soccer and tennis.
   Mitembe does not play any sport that Victoria plays.
   Paula does not play any sport that Mitembe plays.

11

Solutions: Open Grouping Setups

1. YourHome Realty has exactly five condominiums on the market: P, Q, S, T, and V. Each of the condominiums has at least one of the following three features: fireplace, hardwood floors, modern appliances. The condominiums have no other features. The following conditions apply:

    Q has fewer features than S.
    P and T have exactly one feature in common.
    Both Q and V have hardwood floors.
    P has more features than any other condominium.

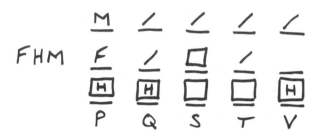

2. Each of exactly five radio stations—F, J, K, L, and M— plays one or more of the following four types of music: new age, oldies, rock, soul. None of the stations plays any other type of music. The following conditions apply:

    F plays more types of music than any other station.
    K plays new age and oldies, but no other type of music.
    Exactly three of the five stations play rock.
    L does not play new age or rock.
    M plays more types of music than K.

3. The town of Holden has exactly three movie theaters: J, K, and L. Each of the three theaters shows one or more of the following movies: *Rung, Stilted, Trouble.* None of the three theaters shows any other movie. The following rules apply:

> Any theater that shows *Rung* also shows *Trouble.*
> Exactly two of the theaters show *Stilted.*

Note: These rules don't give us very much information. All we can do is set up the Open Board and symbolize the rules to the right.

4. At Riverside High School, six student athletes—Mitembe, Nathan, Paula, Raul, Victoria, and Yolanda—were chosen as Athletes of the Year. Each of the six athletes plays one or more of the following three sports: hockey, soccer, tennis. None of the athletes plays any other sport. The following must be true:

> Nathan plays exactly two of the sports.
> Yolanda plays more of the sports than Victoria.
> Raul and exactly three other student athletes play hockey.
> Victoria plays both soccer and tennis.
> Mitembe does not play any sport that Victoria plays.
> Paula does not play any sport that Mitembe plays.

Try It Again

Now that you've learned how to set up the Open Board, it's time to put your skills to good use. Let's revisit the Getting Familiar game. Try developing the Open Board from scratch and then use it to tackle the questions. We'll work through the solutions together on the pages to come.

The Mizotron Corporation has exactly six managers: Holmes, Jin, Kaufman, Lu, Orr, and Pearson. Each manager has expertise in one or more of the following three areas: finance, marketing, technology. None of the managers has expertise in any other area. The following conditions apply:

> Jin does not share any area of expertise with Orr.
> Holmes has fewer areas of expertise than Lu.
> Jin, Kaufman, and Pearson all have expertise in finance.
> Holmes and Pearson have exactly two areas of expertise in common.
> Orr does not have expertise in marketing.

1. Which one of the following pairs of managers must have at least one area of expertise in common?

    (A) Holmes and Kaufman

    (B) Kaufman and Orr

    (C) Lu and Orr

    (D) Holmes and Jin

    (E) Jin and Orr

2. For how many of the six managers is it possible to determine exactly which of the three areas of expertise they have?

    (A) one

    (B) two

    (C) three

    (D) four

    (E) five

3. Which of the following must be false?

   (A) Exactly four of the six managers have exactly two areas of expertise.

   (B) Exactly one of the six managers has exactly two areas of expertise.

   (C) Exactly one of the six managers has exactly one area of expertise.

   (D) Exactly three of the six managers have exactly one area of expertise.

   (E) Exactly four of the six managers have exactly one area of expertise.

4. Which one of the following is a complete and accurate list of the managers who could have exactly three areas of expertise?

   (A) Holmes, Kaufman, Lu, Pearson

   (B) Kaufman, Lu, Pearson

   (C) Holmes, Lu

   (D) Kaufman, Lu

   (E) Pearson

5. Which of the following must be false?

   (A) Both Jin and Pearson have expertise in marketing.

   (B) Both Lu and Orr have expertise in technology.

   (C) Both Holmes and Lu have expertise in marketing.

   (D) Both Holmes and Orr have expertise in finance.

   (E) Both Kaufman and Pearson have expertise in technology.

6. Exactly how many of the managers could have expertise in both marketing and technology?

   (A) two

   (B) three

   (C) four

   (D) five

   (E) six

Answer Key

1. C   4. B
2. B   5. D
3. E   6. C

How Did You Do?

Earlier in the chapter, we discussed how to picture Open Grouping games and we've already worked through notating the rules and making inferences for this game. We make our inferences on the Open Board while going through the rules a second time, so The Big Pause gets wrapped into that step. Let's jump to the questions!

Step 4: Attack the Questions

1. Which one of the following pairs of managers must have at least one area of expertise in common?

    (A) Holmes and Kaufman

    (B) Kaufman and Orr

    (C) Lu and Orr

    (D) Holmes and Jin

    (E) Jin and Orr

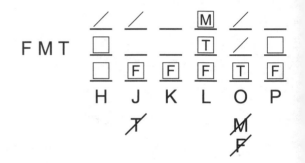

Answer choice (C) is correct.

K definitely has an F, but all we know about H's assignments is that there are two of them. H could have an M and a T, while K could have nothing more than an F. Eliminate (A).

O has exactly one assignment: T. Again, it's possible that K has nothing more than an F. Eliminate (B).

We can immediately see that L and O both have a T. Thus, L and O must have at least one area of expertise in common. Answer choice (C) is correct.

Under actual test conditions, we would choose answer (C) and move on. However, take the time now to disprove answers (D) and (E).

Before even looking at the answer choices, highly sophisticated game players might notice that L will share an area with every other group, because it has all three. In this case, simply looking for an answer that includes L does the trick!

2. For how many of the six managers is it possible to determine exactly which of the three areas of expertise they have?

    (A) one

    (B) two

    (C) three

    (D) four

    (E) five

Answer choice (B) is correct.

While we know that H has exactly two assignments, we don't know which ones. J and K both have an F, but they could potentially have more. L is completely defined. Similarly, we can see that O has one and only one assignment: T. On the other hand, P may have two or three assignments. Thus, only L and O are completely defined.

3. Which of the following must be false?

    (A) Exactly four of the six managers have exactly two areas of expertise.

    (B) Exactly one of the six managers has exactly two areas of expertise.

    (C) Exactly one of the six managers has exactly one area of expertise.

    (D) Exactly three of the six managers have exactly one area of expertise.

    (E) Exactly four of the six managers have exactly one area of expertise.

Answer choice (E) is correct.

It's simple enough to show that answers (A) through (D) all could be true:

    (A) H, J, K, and P could each have exactly two areas of expertise.
    (B) H could be the only manager to have exactly two areas of expertise.
    (C) O could be the only manager to have just one area of expertise.
    (D) J, K, and O could each have exactly one area of expertise.
    (E) This is impossible since the only managers who could have one area of expertise are J, K, and O.

11

4. Which one of the following is a complete and accurate list of the managers who could have exactly three areas of expertise?

    (A) Holmes, Kaufman, Lu, Pearson
    (B) Kaufman, Lu, Pearson
    (C) Holmes, Lu
    (D) Kaufman, Lu
    (E) Pearson

Answer choice (B) is correct.

Our diagram makes it clear that H, J, and O cannot have three assignments. That leaves K, L, and P.

5. Which of the following must be false?

    (A) Both Jin and Pearson have expertise in marketing.
    (B) Both Lu and Orr have expertise in technology.
    (C) Both Holmes and Lu have expertise in marketing.
    (D) Both Holmes and Orr have expertise in finance.
    (E) Both Kaufman and Pearson have expertise in technology.

Answer choice (D) is correct.

It is certainly possible that both Jin and Pearson have expertise in marketing. Eliminate (A).

We can quickly see that both Lu and Orr indeed do have expertise in technology. Eliminate (B).

Holmes could have expertise in marketing, and Lu definitely has expertise in marketing. Eliminate (C).

While Holmes could have expertise in finance, we can see that Orr has expertise only in technology. Therefore, (D) is correct.

Take a moment to verify that answer (E) could be true.

6. Exactly how many of the managers could have expertise in both marketing and technology?

    (A) two
    (B) three
    (C) four
    (D) five
    (E) six

Answer choice (C) is correct.

MANHATTAN
PREP

Four of the six managers—H, K, L, and P—could potentially have expertise in both marketing and technology. J can't have a T, and O is limited to only one element: T.

Choosing Your Base

With most Open Grouping games, it will be quite intuitive which set of elements you should use to form the base of our diagram and which set you should be assigning to those groups. But, consider this scenario:

> Four experimental drugs—M, O, P, and R—will be administered to four different patients—W, X, Y, and Z. No other drugs will be administered. Each drug will be used at least once and each patient will receive at least one drug.

This scenario has all the indications of an Open Grouping game. However, notice that both the number of drugs given to patients and the number of patients receiving each drug are open. We could conceivably create either of these Open Boards:

How will we know which one to use? For some games, one arrangement will be much more advantageous than the other, while for other games, either will be fine. There are two key ideas to consider when choosing your base:

> 1. **Which set of items is listed as being assigned "at least one" or "one or more?"** Usually that set should become the base of the board. Think of those letters as "receiving" the other ones.
> 2. **When looking at the rules, which arrangement will allow you to make more numerical inferences (slashes and boxes)?**

These two ideas should be enough to help you decide the base for most any Open Grouping game. If you start to diagram and realize you've chosen the wrong base, it's generally best to start over. As you've seen in this chapter, using the Open Board correctly can help uncover many inferences that will make answering questions much more efficient.

As we mentioned earlier, for most Open Grouping games, the base decision is an easy one. The few fuzzier situations tend to fall into two groups. Either it does not matter which base you use—either one can work fine—or you'll quickly see that you've chosen the wrong base as you start to diagram. As a brain-stretcher, in your review, try replaying Open Grouping games with the "wrong" base. You'll generally see that the diagramming phase quickly fizzles out. However, keep pushing through with the "wrong" diagram—solving games with a suboptimal diagram is a great way to practice your back-end game skills.

11

Back-End vs. Front-End Open Grouping Games

The games you've seen in this chapter have been decidedly front-end games. There have been cascades of numerical inferences to uncover. In some cases, it feels as if the test writers decided that typical questions would be too easy to anyone who "cracked the code," and so they had to create questions with especially complex wording just to keep things interesting!

However, in the past few years, we've seen more back-end Open Grouping games than we did in the previous five or so years. Do not be surprised if your diagramming process quickly peters out and the bulk of the work is found in the questions. The skills you developed in Basic Grouping games will prove handy with these games.

Elements Often Repeat

Let's return to the Getting Familiar game. In this scenario, notice that repeating elements are part of the game's organization. What does this mean? Let's look at our Open Board one more time:

The rules of the game were such that we were allowed to assign more than one F, more than one T, and more than one M. For example, all six managers might have had expertise in technology. This is an example of an Open Grouping game *with* repeating elements. Now consider the following scenario:

> Exactly five job applicants—J, K, M, N, and O—apply for jobs at exactly three companies—T, U, and V. Each applicant accepts a job with exactly one of the three companies, and each company hires at least one applicant.

In this case, the five job applicants—J, K, M, N, and O—will be assigned to the three companies: T, U, and V. The important thing to notice is that the job applicants *cannot* be repeated. In other words, once J, for example, is assigned to a company, J cannot then be assigned to another company (*each applicant accepts a job with exactly one of three companies*). So, this is an example of an Open Grouping game *without* repeating elements.

This has implications for our setup. First, we want to establish our base. In an Open Grouping game with non-repeating elements, always use the other element set as the base. In this case, since the job applicants will be assigned to the companies, we'll put the companies along the bottom:

$$\underline{} \quad \underline{} \quad \underline{}$$
$$\text{T} \quad \text{U} \quad \text{V}$$

The challenge comes in setting the slots. What is the maximum number of job applicants that any one company could hire? Well, we know that each company must be assigned at least one job applicant. We also know that all five applicants must be assigned. There are two possible scenarios:

Scenario 1: One company hires three applicants while the other two companies hire one applicant each (3, 1, 1).

Scenario 2: Two companies hire two applicants each while the other company hires one applicant (2, 2, 1).

It is important to note that any one of the three companies could potentially hire three applicants. Therefore, when we set up the slots, we will give each company three slots and we will put a box around one of the slots for each:

$$\text{J K M N O} \quad \begin{matrix} \underline{} & \underline{} & \underline{} \\ \underline{} & \underline{} & \underline{} \\ \square & \square & \square \\ \text{T} & \text{U} & \text{V} \end{matrix}$$

(By the way, it would be worthwhile to note these options next to our diagram with a simple "3, 1, 1 or 2, 2, 1.")

So, we must always set up our slots based on the maximum possible number of assignments. If at any point during the setup we discovered that one of the companies hired *exactly* two applicants, we would know that we were dealing with a 2, 2, 1 arrangement, and we could slash the third slot for each of the companies.

Also keep in mind that this is still an Open Grouping situation. We have exactly five applicants to be assigned to nine possible slots. We know ahead of time that exactly four slots will be left empty. While this doesn't allow us to add any slashes or boxes, it is a very important numerical restriction to keep in mind.

In "repeat" situations, you might find it hard to conceive of your task in terms of grouping. After all, we typically think of grouping as taking a collection of items and putting each item into one of the available groups. For instance, if you are getting ready for a move, you might sort your possessions into three groups: things to keep, things to give away, and things to throw out. If you are going to keep your old teddy bear, you're not also going to throw it out! However, there are certainly real-world cases of repeat grouping. For instance, one person might be a customer at multiple stores or a member of multiple organizations. Still, repeat grouping might feel strange to you at first. Make sure you always take note of whether elements can be repeated (or not).

11

Dotting Your Board

Before we move to a pair of practice games, let's look at one last issue. Go ahead and diagram the game you saw earlier (and be sure to look over the rules to decide which base to use):

> Four experimental drugs—M, O, P, and R—will be administered to four different patients—W, X, Y, and Z. No other drugs will be administered. Each drug will be used at least once and each patient will receive at least one drug. The following conditions apply:
>
> Any drug administered to W cannot be administered to Y.
> More drugs are administered to X than to any other patient.
> Fewer drugs are administered to W than to Y.
> M is not administered to X.

This is a front-end game. You can eliminate almost all uncertainty about the number of drugs each patient receives. Check your diagram against the one below and replay the setup until you can arrive at ours. Note how we chose to represent the rule about each drug being used at least once:

It's a great-looking diagram, but it's actually incomplete! We drew numerical inferences from the first rule, but our diagram does not tell us that W and Y can't share an element. There are a few ways we can do this:

1. **Write out the rule to the side of the diagram.** This is simple, but slightly dangerous if you tend to forget to look to the side when solving questions.
2. **Draw in some sort of arrow or line notation.** Perhaps it would look like this:

This sort of approach is fine as long as it's meaningful to you. It can become a bit messy if you're not careful or if there are several such rules that need to be notated that way.

3. **Use dots inside the boxes to show the relationships between the elements.** This is our recommended approach. Take a look at what we mean, and see if you can figure out the system before reading on:

Perhaps you've figured it out already: Each number of dots represents a different element, though we're not sure which one. However, we do know that the mystery element associated with one dot is assigned to W but not to Y, which is assigned two different elements.

To challenge you a bit, how would you add the following rules to the diagram?

> *Exactly two drugs are administered to Z.*
> *No drug is administed to both Y and Z.*

Clearly, you need to add a second box to Z, but since it can't share any elements with Y, which dots should it receive? If you're thinking that it should have four and five dots, you're close! However, there are only four element choices, so five dots—a fifth drug—is not possible. Instead, Z will receive the element associated with one dot and the element associated with four dots.

This is a slightly extreme version of the use of dots, but it's also a great example of how using the dots can lead to some otherwise hard to uncover inferences.

Use that diagram to consider this question:

Which of the following could be true?

(A) R is administered only to X.

(B) P is administered only to X.

(C) O is administered only to Y.

(D) M is administered only to W.

(E) M is administered only to Z.

Because we see all four elements represented by dots—W has one of the elements, Y has the second and third, and Z has the fourth—we know that between W, Y, and Z, each of the four drugs will be administered once, and one will be administered twice (to W and Z). With that in mind, we can evaluate the answer choices:

(A) is impossible—R must show up at least once between W, Y, and Z.

(B) is impossible—P must show up at least once between W, Y, and Z.

(C) is impossible—O is also administered to X!

(D) is impossible. Whatever is administered to W is also administered to Z.

(E) is possible—M could be the drug represented by the four dots, which is administered only to Z.

It's worth adding dots to your notation toolkit not only for Open Grouping games, but also for other game types.

To Redraw or Not to Redraw

Here's the situation: It's the fourth question of a game that has a rather involved diagram. The question is a conditional one and you don't want to bother writing out the entirety of the diagram; instead you just sketch the important parts, fill in your new condition, and start making inferences.

If that sounds familiar, great. You already figured out that redrawing the entirety of your master diagram is often unnecessary and inefficient. For Open Grouping games, this is a particularly important issue, since the diagrams can be rather involved. By all means, use your discretion on how much to sketch. For example, in some moments, just sketching the bases is enough:

$$\overline{}\quad\overline{}\quad\overline{}$$
$$X \quad\; Y \quad\; Z$$

Simply establishing the groups like that is particularly useful with no-repeat games, since there are usually fewer numerical issues in those. Furthermore, when you're several questions into a game, you might feel comfortable with an even sparser diagram: If the group headings are ingrained in your head, you can even skip writing those out.

11

At other times, particularly when the question is hinging on numerical issues that are hard for you to hold in your head, you may find you want to include the numerical restrictions and possibilities. You can adapt your system on the fly to skip using slashes, only putting slots when an assignment is possible:

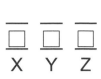

With all of these diagramming options, what is most important is that you refer to the master diagram when making inferences so that you don't miss anything.

Conclusion

What's the key to Open Grouping games? As much as possible, focus on the numbers! Let's look back at what we've discussed:

1. **Thorough setups**

   - When setting up the Open Board, remember to cycle through the rules until there are no more inferences to be made. Many numerical inferences result from the combination of several rules.

2. **Variation**

   - It's becoming increasingly common to see Open Grouping games with fewer numerical inferences. Don't panic if your Open Board is extremely open! Often, we'll see fewer numerical inferences when the game does not include repeats.

3. **Choosing your base**

   - The base for these games isn't always what your intuition tells you, so it's important to use the rules to determine which arrangement will lead to the most inferences. It's worth spending some time thinking about this, and if you realize that you've chosen the less ideal base, redo the diagram.

Practice Game 1: PT12, S2, G3

Here's your chance to put all the pieces together on some new games. We'll work through the setup and solutions together on the pages to come.

Lara, Mendel, and Nastassia each buy at least one kind of food from a street vendor who sells only fruit cups, hot dogs, pretzels, and shish kebabs. They make their selections in accordance with the following restrictions:

> None of the three buys more than one portion of each kind of food.
> If any of the three buys a hot dog, that person does not also buy a shish kebab.
> At least one of the three buys a hot dog, and at least one buys a pretzel.
> Mendel buys a shish kebab.
> Nastassia buys a fruit cup.
> Neither Lara nor Nastassia buys a pretzel.
> Mendel does not buy any kind of food that Nastassia buys.

12. Which one of the following statements must be true?

    (A) Lara buys a hot dog.
    (B) Lara buys a shish kebab.
    (C) Mendel buys a hot dog.
    (D) Mendel buys a pretzel.
    (E) Nastassia buys a hot dog.

13. If the vendor charges $1 for each portion of food, what is the minimum amount the three people could spend?

    (A) $3
    (B) $4
    (C) $5
    (D) $6
    (E) $7

MANHATTAN
PREP

14. If the vendor charges $1 for each portion of food,
    what is the greatest amount the three people could
    spend?

    (A) $5
    (B) $6
    (C) $7
    (D) $8
    (E) $9

15. If Lara and Mendel buy exactly two kinds of food
    each, which one of the following statements must be
    true?

    (A) Lara buys a fruit cup.
    (B) Lara buys a hot dog.
    (C) Mendel buys a fruit cup.
    (D) There is exactly one kind of food that Lara and
        Mendel both buy.
    (E) There is exactly one kind of food that Lara and
        Nastassia both buy.

16. If Lara buys a shish kebab, which one of the
    following statements must be true?

    (A) Lara buys a fruit cup.
    (B) Mendel buys a fruit cup.
    (C) Nastassia buys a hot dog.
    (D) Nastassia buys exactly one kind of food.
    (E) Exactly one person buys a fruit cup.

17. Assume that the condition is removed that prevents a
    customer who buys a hot dog from buying a shish
    kebab but all other conditions remain the same. If
    the vendor charges $1 for each portion of food, what
    is the maximum amount the three people could
    spend?

    (A) $5
    (B) $6
    (C) $7
    (D) $8
    (E) $9

11

Solutions: PT12, S2, G3

Answer Key

12. D   15. A

13. B   16. C

14. B   17. C

Step 1: Picture the Game

In this case, we have a cross between two sets of elements: people (Lara, Mendel, Nastassia) and food products (fruit cups, hot dogs, pretzels, shish kebabs). We need to assign one set to the other to form groups, but how do we know which set will be assigned and which will be the base?

In order to make this decision, we can start by looking at which set of items is being assigned one or more of the others. In this case, the scenario reads *Lara, Mendel, and Nastassia each buy at least one kind of food*. It looks like food items are being assigned to people, so we would use the people as the base. Each person can be assigned a maximum of four different kinds of food, and each person buys at least one kind of food. We should notice that repeats are allowed.

In this game, our second tool for deciding on the base—looking at the rules to see which arrangement will garner more numerical inferences—is not very useful. If we were to use the foods as the base, many of the rules would lead to numerical inferences. In fact, it's not that hard to play this game with the food choices as the base. However, since most people probably used the people as the base, and that arrangement is somewhat easier to use, we'll explain the game that way.

If you didn't play the game with the people as the base, go ahead and do so now before reading on. If you did use the people, when you're done reading this solution try playing the game with the food options as the base to stretch the old brain.

Step 2: Notate the Rules and Make Inferences

> *None of the three buys more than one portion of each kind of food.*

This rule may seem confusing, but it's basically telling us that we can't assign two or more fruit cups, for example, to any one of the people. In other words, each person can be assigned at most one F, one H, one P, and one S. Notice that we have not been told that every food is placed in a group.

> *If any of the three buys a hot dog, that person does not also buy a shish kebab.*

Remember, always think about what the rule tells us about the *number* of elements that can be assigned. Any person assigned an H cannot also be assigned an S. This means that no person can have all four foods! We can slash out one slot for each person.

> *At least one of the three buys a hot dog, and at least one buys a pretzel.*

This doesn't give us any further information about the number of filled vs. unfilled slots, but we can keep track of this rule by making a note to the side. So far we have the following:

> *Mendel buys a shish kebab.*
> *Nastassia buys a fruit cup.*

These are direct rules. We'll plug this information right into the board. Notice that if Mendel buys a shish kebab, he can't possibly buy a hot dog as well (the contrapositive of H ➞ –S is S ➞ –H). Also, we now know that every food is used in this game.

> *Neither Lara nor Nastassia buys a pretzel.*

We can symbolize this with exclusions underneath Lara and Nastassia. Also remember that we must have at least one pretzel. If neither Lara nor Nastassia buys a pretzel, Mendel must buy a pretzel.

> *Mendel does not buy any kind of food that Nastassia buys.*

We already know that Mendel has at least two types of food: pretzel and shish kebab. We also know that Mendel can't get a hot dog. Well, if Mendel can't share any food with Nastassia, Mendel can't get a fruit cup either. Thus, Mendel is limited to a pretzel and a shish kebab. Furthermore, if Mendel and Nastassia can't share any food, Nastassia can't get a pretzel or a shish kebab. Thus, the most that Nastassia can get is two foods:

Cycle Through a Second Time

Remember, we must go back through the rules one more time to see if any of them might offer new information after we've filled in our diagram. The second rule proves useful the second time through:

> *If any of the three buys a hot dog, that person does not also buy a shish kebab.*

In the diagram above, Lara is limited to three foods (she can't get a pretzel). However, if she gets the three remaining foods (fruit cup, hot dog, shish kebab), she'll break the H ➡ –S rule. Thus, she can't be assigned all three of the remaining foods. At most she can get two foods:

Upon further review, none of the other rules provide any additional information. So this is our completed diagram.

MANHATTAN
PREP

Step 3: The Big Pause

If you cycled through the rules twice, you should already have made all the inferences available, but it's still worth a moment to notice which rules are big players. The H ➔ –S rule will clearly come into play, and we'll have to remember to place an H somewhere. In fact, we could write in that H will be assigned to either L or N (or both).

Step 4: Attack the Questions

Let's use our diagram to tackle the questions:

12. Which one of the following statements must be true?

   (A) Lara buys a hot dog.
   (B) Lara buys a shish kebab.
   (C) Mendel buys a hot dog.
   (D) Mendel buys a pretzel.
   (E) Nastassia buys a hot dog.

Answer choice (D) is correct.

With the inferences, this is a 10-second question!

13. If the vendor charges $1 for each portion of food, what is the minimum amount the three people could spend?

   (A) $3
   (B) $4
   (C) $5
   (D) $6
   (E) $7

Answer choice (B) is correct.

The question is essentially asking about the minimum number of possible assignments. We already have three assignments, and if we place H in L, we don't need to make any other assignments. Thus, at a minimum, we'll have four elements assigned, which translates to $4. We could have just counted up the boxes here!

14. If the vendor charges $1 for each portion of food, what is the greatest amount the three people could spend?

   (A) $5
   (B) $6
   (C) $7
   (D) $8
   (E) $9

Answer choice (B) is correct.

This is essentially the same question, but instead of asking about the minimum number of assignments, it's asking about the maximum number of assignments. Again, we know that Mendel has exactly two. We also know that both Lara and Nastassia could have at most two assignments. Thus, it seems we have a maximum of six total assignments. A quick check tells us that no rules would be violated, so the answer is $6. Again, we could have found the answer by counting the slots not crossed out.

15. If Lara and Mendel buy exactly two kinds of food each, which one of the following statements must be true?

   (A) Lara buys a fruit cup.
   (B) Lara buys a hot dog.
   (C) Mendel buys a fruit cup.
   (D) There is exactly one kind of food that Lara and Mendel both buy.
   (E) There is exactly one kind of food that Lara and Nastassia both buy.

Answer choice (A) is correct.

If Lara buys exactly two kinds of food, we know for certain that these two foods can't be H and S (remember, H $\rightarrow$ –S). We also know that Lara can't buy a pretzel. Thus, Lara must buy a fruit cup and either a hot dog or a shish kebab.

16. If Lara buys a shish kebab, which one of the following statements must be true?

   (A) Lara buys a fruit cup.
   (B) Mendel buys a fruit cup.
   (C) Nastassia buys a hot dog.
   (D) Nastassia buys exactly one kind of food.
   (E) Exactly one person buys a fruit cup.

Answer choice (C) is correct.

If Lara buys a shish kebab, she can't buy a hot dog. So neither Lara nor Mendel buys a hot dog. But remember that we must assign at least one hot dog. This means that Nastassia must buy a hot dog in addition to her fruit cup.

Notice that we *didn't* examine each answer choice through trial and error. Rather, we started with the new rule given in the question ("Lara buys a shish kebab") and we traced this rule through a chain of inferences. "Lara buys a shish kebab" leads to the inference that she doesn't buy a hot dog, which means that Nastassia must buy a hot dog. We arrived a distance of two inferences away from where we started, and this turned out to be one of the answer choices. *Always* follow the inference chain as far as you can before implementing a trial-and-error approach.

17. Assume that the condition is removed that prevents a customer who buys a hot dog from buying a shish kebab but all other conditions remain the same. If the vendor charges $1 for each portion of food, what is the maximum amount the three people could spend?

(A) $5

(B) $6

(C) $7

(D) $8

(E) $9

Answer choice (C) is correct.

This is the toughest question of the bunch, and one that is designed to take up a lot of our time, as most Rule Substitution questions are. If we remove the second rule from consideration (H $\longrightarrow$ –S), how does this impact our diagram? The bad news is that we have to start from scratch. The good news—we should be able to draw a new diagram in about 30 seconds or so. If you didn't redraw the diagram to solve this question, do so before reading on.

Here's what we get:

If we count our available slots, it looks like we can have a total of eight assignments. But wait a moment—there's a rule we're overlooking! When we drew our original diagram, we didn't need to notate the rule that Mendel does not buy any kind of food that Nastassia buys. All of the needed inferences from that rule were built into our diagram. However, now that one of the other rules has been removed, and Mendel is free to buy a hot dog, we need to consider this rule again. The fact that M and N can't share any assignments means that at most one of the two could get a hot dog. If we gave the hot dog to Mendel, he would have three assignments and Nastassia would have one. If we gave the hot dog to Nastassia, she would have two assignments and Mendel would have two. Either way, we'd have four total assignments between Mendel and Nastassia. There's nothing stopping Lara from getting everything but the pretzel, so we can add three for Lara to reach a maximum total of seven.

Practice Game 2: PT18, S1, G1

Each of five students—Hubert, Lori, Paul, Regina, and Sharon—will visit exactly one of three cities—Montreal, Toronto, or Vancouver—for the month of March, according to the following conditions:

> Sharon visits a different city than Paul.
> Hubert visits the same city as Regina.
> Lori visits Montreal or else Toronto.
> If Paul visits Vancouver, Hubert visits Vancouver with him.
> Each student visits one of the cities with at least one of the other four students.

1. Which one of the following could be true for March?

   (A) Hubert, Lori, and Paul visit Toronto, and Regina and Sharon visit Vancouver.

   (B) Hubert, Lori, Paul, and Regina visit Montreal, and Sharon visits Vancouver.

   (C) Hubert, Paul, and Regina visit Toronto, and Lori and Sharon visit Montreal.

   (D) Hubert, Regina, and Sharon visit Montreal, and Lori and Paul visit Vancouver.

   (E) Lori, Paul, and Sharon visit Montreal, and Hubert and Regina visit Toronto.

2. If Hubert and Sharon visit a city together, which one of the following could be true in March?

   (A) Hubert visits the same city as Paul.

   (B) Lori visits the same city as Regina.

   (C) Paul visits the same city as Regina.

   (D) Paul visits Toronto.

   (E) Paul visits Vancouver.

3. If Sharon visits Vancouver, which one of the following must be true for March?

   (A) Hubert visits Montreal.
   (B) Lori visits Montreal.
   (C) Paul visits Toronto.
   (D) Lori visits the same city as Paul.
   (E) Lori visits the same city as Regina.

4. Which one of the following could be false in March?

   (A) Sharon must visit Montreal if Paul visits Vancouver.
   (B) Regina must visit Vancouver if Paul visits Vancouver.
   (C) Regina visits a city with exactly two of the other four students.
   (D) Lori visits a city with exactly one of the other four students.
   (E) Lori visits a city with Paul or else with Sharon.

5. If Regina visits Toronto, which one of the following could be true in March?

   (A) Lori visits Toronto.
   (B) Lori visits Vancouver.
   (C) Paul visits Toronto.
   (D) Paul visits Vancouver.
   (E) Sharon visits Vancouver.

6. Which one of the following must be true for March?

   (A) If any of the students visits Montreal, Lori visits Montreal.
   (B) If any of the students visits Montreal, exactly two of them do.
   (C) If any of the students visits Toronto, exactly three of them do.
   (D) If any of the students visits Vancouver, Paul visits Vancouver.
   (E) If any of the students visits Vancouver, exactly three of them do.

Solutions: PT18, S1, G1

Answer Key

1. C   4. A
2. D   5. C
3. D   6. E

Step 1: Picture the Game

It's Spring Break! We have five students and three Canadian cities. Each student visits exactly one city (no repeats), so we should use the students as elements and cities as the base:

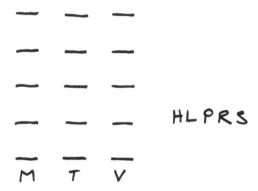

The lack of an "at least one" rule means that we can't be sure each city will be visited. We should not put boxes in—perhaps one column will remain empty.

Step 2: Notate the Rules and Make Inferences

Sharon visits a different city than Paul.
Hubert visits the same city as Regina.

These rules are easy to notate as a chunk and an anti-chunk. From the first rule, we can also infer that at least two cities will be visited. Since we can't have all five students in one city, we can limit each column to four slots.

Lori visits Montreal or else Toronto.
If Paul visits Vancouver, Hubert visits Vancouver with him.

MANHATTAN
PREP

The next two rules are easy to notate as well. We used an option for the Lori rule, but we could also have used a exclusion under V. So far there is nothing significant to infer, but we have the following:

$$
\begin{array}{ccc}
\underline{\diagup} & \underline{\diagup} & \underline{\diagup} \\
\underline{} & \underline{} & \underline{} \\
\underline{} & \underline{} & \underline{} \\
\underline{} & \underline{} & \underline{} \quad \text{HLPRS} \\
\underline{\text{L}\diagup} & \underline{\diagup\text{L}} & \underline{} \\
\text{M} & \text{T} & \text{V}
\end{array}
$$

$$\boxed{\begin{smallmatrix}S\\A\end{smallmatrix}} \quad \boxed{\begin{smallmatrix}H\\R\end{smallmatrix}} \qquad P_v \rightarrow H_v$$

Since H is in a chunk, we could also incorporate that chunk into the conditional rule:

$$P_v \rightarrow \boxed{\begin{smallmatrix}R\\H\end{smallmatrix}}_v$$

Each student visits one of the cities with at least one of the other four students.

Our final rule is a bit juicier! Another way of stating this rule is that there cannot be a group with just one student in it. What does this mean in terms of how the game might play out?

With only five elements, there is only one basic arrangement of numbers that works: two will go to one city and three will go to another (remember, because of the first rule, we can't have all the students go to one city). Thus, one sad city will go visitorless. We should notate this numerical inference somehow!

The first thing we can do is limit the slots in each city to a maximum of three, and then we can write the rest of the inference to the side:

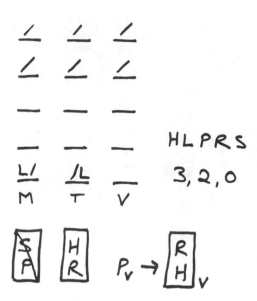

We now should take another spin through the rules. However, there seems to be nothing more to infer in terms of slashes and boxes. Let's take a moment to gather our thoughts about this game.

Step 3: The Big Pause

This is a different flavor of Open Grouping game than we've tasted so far. There are far fewer slashing inferences and no boxes! But there is a significant numerical inference nonetheless. We know we'll have two groups, one with three and one with two, and we know that one group has S and one group has P. We could represent this like so:

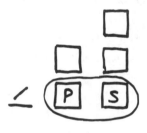

There's more we can infer, though! Where will the HR chunk go? Clearly, it will go in the group of three. That leaves L to fill in the remaining position in the group of two. So far, we have this:

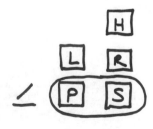

MANHATTAN
PREP

There are two things we have not noted so far: which city goes with which group and which group will have no elements. We could notate all of these undetermined issues like so:

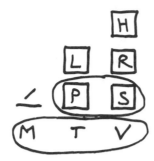

This diagram is far from the standard, but it's pure MacGyver and it represents a lot about this game! Except that we've lost a couple rules. Can you see which ones?

This new diagram no longer notes that L cannot be grouped with V. Nor do we have the $P_V \rightarrow H_V$ rule. We would need to notate these to the side or perhaps refer to the original diagram.

We could successfully tackle the game with either of these diagrams:

Option 1   Option 2

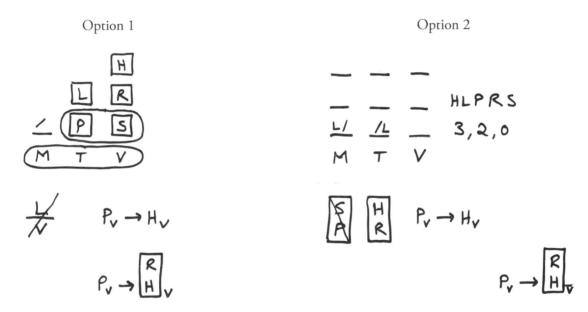

The fact that we've suggested the "radical" diagram on the left might seem troubling to you if you didn't come up with anything like that. However, instead of troubling you, this should confirm that we don't need to have the "right" diagram to solve a game. Is the diagram on the left a bit more thought out? Yes. But the truth is that when most of our teachers first solved the game, they used something similar to the one on the right and they did just fine. In fact, we've intentionally left out some of the cool numerical inferences from the diagram on the right because we don't want to leave you thinking that it's essential to figure out every little nook and cranny of every game.

In terms of rule prioritization, clearly, we'll always need to apply the SP and HR rules, but since there are so few options for how this game can play out, we love all these rules equally. Every element is involved in some rule; there's nothing to circle. Enough planning; time to attack!

Step 4: Attack the Questions

1. Which one of the following could be true for March?

    (A) Hubert, Lori, and Paul visit Toronto, and Regina and Sharon visit Vancouver.

    (B) Hubert, Lori, Paul, and Regina visit Montreal, and Sharon visits Vancouver.

    (C) Hubert, Paul, and Regina visit Toronto, and Lori and Sharon visit Montreal.

    (D) Hubert, Regina, and Sharon visit Montreal, and Lori and Paul visit Vancouver.

    (E) Lori, Paul, and Sharon visit Montreal, and Hubert and Regina visit Toronto.

Answer choice (C) is correct.

It's not a traditional question stem, but a quick glance at the answers shows us this is an Orientation question. Let's use the rules.

> Rule 1 eliminates (E).
> Rule 2 eliminates (A).
> Rule 3 eliminates (D).
> Rule 4 eliminates nothing that is left.
> Rule 5 eliminates (B).

2. If Hubert and Sharon visit a city together, which one of the following could be true in March?

    (A) Hubert visits the same city as Paul.

    (B) Lori visits the same city as Regina.

    (C) Paul visits the same city as Regina.

    (D) Paul visits Toronto.

    (E) Paul visits Vancouver.

Answer choice (D) is correct.

MANHATTAN
PREP

From the new condition, we can infer that the two groups are SHR and LP. To which cities could these groups be assigned? There are two rules to keep in mind: L can't be assigned to V, and if P is assigned to V, it would need to be with H. Since P and H are separate, we know that P is not assigned to V. Thus, the students must be assigned to either M or T:

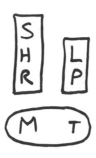

(A) through (C) and (E) can't be true, while (D) can.

3. If Sharon visits Vancouver, which one of the following must be true for March?

   (A) Hubert visits Montreal.
   (B) Lori visits Montreal.
   (C) Paul visits Toronto.
   (D) Lori visits the same city as Paul.
   (E) Lori visits the same city as Regina.

Answer choice (D) is correct.

What do we know if S goes to Vancouver? Well, we know P can't go with her, and L isn't welcome there. That means H and R go to Vancouver, too:

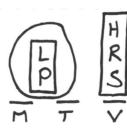

Here's what the answer choice vetting process might look like in real time:

   (A) must be false. Eliminate.
   (B) could be true, but we could also have L and P in T.
   (C) is another could be true. Hopefully, there's an easy answer ahead!
   (D) is true, so this is it.

11

4. Which one of the following could be false in March?

   (A) Sharon must visit Montreal if Paul visits Vancouver.
   (B) Regina must visit Vancouver if Paul visits Vancouver.
   (C) Regina visits a city with exactly two of the other four students.
   (D) Lori visits a city with exactly one of the other four students.
   (E) Lori visits a city with Paul or else with Sharon.

Answer choice (A) is correct.

No condition to work from. Let's dive in and remember that the wrong answers must be true!

(A) looks time-consuming to think about, but, scanning the rest of the answers, they all do! Let's dig in. If P is assigned to V, we know that the HR chunk must follow. Can we place the SL chunk in T, and thereby prove that this answer could be false? Yes, we can!

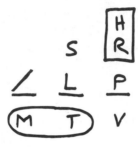

Go ahead and confirm that every other answer must be true. Don't be lazy—do it.

5. If Regina visits Toronto, which one of the following could be true in March?

   (A) Lori visits Toronto.
   (B) Lori visits Vancouver.
   (C) Paul visits Toronto.
   (D) Paul visits Vancouver.
   (E) Sharon visits Vancouver.

Answer choice (C) is correct.

With R assigned to T, we know H is there as well, along with either P or S. That leaves L for the other group. Since L can't be assigned to V, we know it's assigned to M, along with P or S. If we couldn't hold this in our head—it is a lot—we could write it out like this:

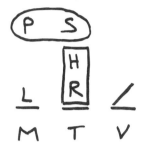

We can quickly eliminate any answer that references a visit to Vancouver, and after checking (A), (C) is clearly the only answer that could be true.

6. Which one of the following must be true for March?

    (A) If any of the students visits Montreal, Lori visits Montreal.
    (B) If any of the students visits Montreal, exactly two of them do.
    (C) If any of the students visits Toronto, exactly three of them do.
    (D) If any of the students visits Vancouver, Paul visits Vancouver.
    (E) If any of the students visits Vancouver, exactly three of them do.

Answer choice (E) is correct.

Tough question! For a change, let's begin by discussing the correct answer. Why is (E) correct? To start, who can visit Vancouver of the P/S option? It looks like either one. And who could accompany P or S there? We definitely can't have L, so we're stuck placing the HR chunk there, which brings us to three. We don't even need to think about the $P_V \longrightarrow H_V$ rule to confirm (E).

It's clear now that answer (E) is correct, but how could we have efficiently moved through answers (A) through (D)? The ideal process would have been to give each of those answers a short consideration and either eliminate it or defer judgment on it. But, at this point in the game, you should be able to quickly work through the wrong answers by using previous work and/or deftly moving elements around the diagram. The process might have looked like this in real time:

We want to "break" answer (A). Can we swing H, R, and S over to M, leaving L and P to T? Sure. Eliminate. We also could have used our hypothetical from question 2 to do this.

We can eliminate answer (B) with the scenario that just disproved (A)!

Once again, we can use our (A)-disproving scenario to eliminate answer (C)! If we weren't so lucky as to have done the above to disprove (A), we could eliminate (C) by quickly thinking out a scenario with two elements assigned to T. That's not too hard to do, especially using the diagram from question 2.

Can we have students visit V without P? Sure! H, R, and S visit V, while L and P visit T. Our diagram from question 3 could help us think this through. Eliminate answer (D).

LG Mixed Practice

Set 3

In This Practice Set...

Mixed Practice: Set 3

The games you'll see on your test will be a mix of front- and back-end games. Some people spend too much time on The Big Pause, which pays off in front-end games but is a waste in back-end games. Others don't spend enough time on The Big Pause, missing key inferences and frames that would help them fly through a game.

This mixed practice set is truly mixed: ordering and grouping; front-end and back-end games. For your first pass, we don't want you to time yourself overall. Instead, start the timer when you take The Big Pause. If, after 20 seconds, you don't see anything, move on. But force yourself to look for 20 seconds.

After completing the set and checking your work, replay the games with our strategies in mind. During The Big Pause, walk yourself through the decision to either spend time making inferences/building frames or to head quickly into the questions.

Practice Game 1: PT19, S1, G1

During a period of six consecutive days—day 1 through day 6—each of exactly six factories—F, G, H, J, Q, and R—will be inspected. During this period, each of the factories will be inspected exactly once, one factory per day. The schedule for the inspections must conform to the following conditions:

F is inspected on either day 1 or day 6.
J is inspected on an earlier day than Q is inspected.
Q is inspected on the day immediately before R is inspected.
If G is inspected on day 3, Q is inspected on day 5.

1. Which one of the following could be a list of the factories in the order of their scheduled inspections, from day 1 through day 6?

    (A) F, Q, R, H, J, G
    (B) G, H, J, Q, R, F
    (C) G, J, Q, H, R, F
    (D) G, J, Q, R, F, H
    (E) J, H, G, Q, R, F

2. Which one of the following must be false?

    (A) The inspection of G is scheduled for day 4.
    (B) The inspection of H is scheduled for day 6.
    (C) The inspection of J is scheduled for day 4.
    (D) The inspection of Q is scheduled for day 3.
    (E) The inspection of R is scheduled for day 2.

3. The inspection of which one of the following CANNOT be scheduled for day 5?

    (A) G
    (B) H
    (C) J
    (D) Q
    (E) R

4. The inspections scheduled for day 3 and day 5, respectively, could be those of

    (A) G and H
    (B) G and R
    (C) H and G
    (D) R and J
    (E) R and H

5. If the inspection of R is scheduled for the day immediately before the inspection of F, which one of the following must be true about the schedule?

    (A) The inspection of either G or H is scheduled for day 1.
    (B) The inspection of either G or J is scheduled for day 1.
    (C) The inspection of either G or J is scheduled for day 2.
    (D) The inspection of either H or J is scheduled for day 3.
    (E) The inspection of either H or J is scheduled for day 4.

6. If the inspections of G and of H are scheduled, not necessarily in that order, for days as far apart as possible, which one of the following is a complete and accurate list of the factories any one of which could be scheduled for inspection for day 1?

    (A) F, J
    (B) G, H
    (C) G, H, J
    (D) F, G, H
    (E) F, G, H, J

7. If the inspection of G is scheduled for the day immediately before the inspection of Q, which one of the following could be true?

    (A) The inspection of G is scheduled for day 5.
    (B) The inspection of H is scheduled for day 6.
    (C) The inspection of J is scheduled for day 2.
    (D) The inspection of Q is scheduled for day 4.
    (E) The inspection of R is scheduled for day 3.

MANHATTAN
PREP

Practice Game 2: PT30, S1, G3

Exactly five cars—Frank's, Marquitta's, Orlando's, Taishah's, and Vinquetta's—are washed, each exactly once. The cars are washed one at a time, with each receiving exactly one kind of wash: regular, super, or premium. The following conditions must apply:

The first car washed does not receive a super wash, though at least one car does.
Exactly one car receives a premium wash.
The second and third cars washed receive the same kind of wash as each other.
Neither Orlando's nor Taishah's is washed before Vinquetta's.
Marquitta's is washed before Frank's, but after Orlando's.
Marquitta's and the car washed immediately before Marquitta's receive regular washes.

11. Which one of the following could be an accurate list of the cars in the order in which they are washed, matched with type of wash received?

    (A) Orlando's: premium; Vinquetta's: regular; Taishah's: regular; Marquitta's: regular; Frank's: super

    (B) Vinquetta's: premium; Orlando's: regular; Taishah's: regular; Marquitta's: regular; Frank's: super

    (C) Vinquetta's: regular; Marquitta's: regular; Taishah's: regular; Orlando's: super; Frank's: super

    (D) Vinquetta's: super; Orlando's: regular; Marquitta's: regular; Frank's: regular; Taishah's: super

    (E) Vinquetta's: premium; Orlando's: regular; Marquitta's: regular; Frank's: regular; Taishah's: regular

12. If Vinquetta's car does not receive a premium wash, which one of the following must be true?

    (A) Orlando's and Vinquetta's cars receive the same kind of wash as each other.

    (B) Marquitta's and Taishah's cars receive the same kind of wash as each other.

    (C) The fourth car washed receives a premium wash.

    (D) Orlando's car is washed third.

    (E) Marquitta's car is washed fourth.

13. If the last two cars washed receive the same kind of wash as each other, then which one of the following could be true?

    (A) Orlando's car is washed third.

    (B) Taishah's car is washed fifth.

    (C) Taishah's car is washed before Marquitta's car.

    (D) Vinquetta's car receives a regular wash.

    (E) Exactly one car receives a super wash.

14. Which one of the following must be true?

    (A) Vinquetta's car receives a premium wash.

    (B) Exactly two cars receive a super wash.

    (C) The fifth car washed receives a super wash.

    (D) The fourth car washed receives a super wash.

    (E) The second car washed receives a regular wash.

15. Which one of the following is a complete and accurate list of the cars that must receive a regular wash?

    (A) Frank's, Marquitta's

    (B) Marquitta's, Orlando's

    (C) Marquitta's, Orlando's, Taishah's

    (D) Marquitta's, Taishah's

    (E) Marquitta's, Vinquetta's

16. Suppose that in addition to the original five cars Jabrohn's car is also washed. If all the other conditions hold as given, which one of the following CANNOT be true?

    (A) Orlando's car receives a premium wash.

    (B) Vinquetta's car receives a super wash.

    (C) Four cars receive a regular wash.

    (D) Only the second and third cars washed receive a regular wash.

    (E) Jabrohn's car is washed after Frank's car.

Practice Game 3: PT18, S1, G1

Each of five students—Hubert, Lori, Paul, Regina, and Sharon—will visit exactly one of three cities—Montreal, Toronto, or Vancouver—for the month of March, according to the following conditions:

Sharon visits a different city than Paul.
Hubert visits the same city as Regina.
Lori visits Montreal or else Toronto.
If Paul visits Vancouver, Hubert visits Vancouver with him.
Each student visits one of the cities with at least one of the other four students.

1. Which one of the following could be true for March?

   (A) Hubert, Lori, and Paul visit Toronto, and Regina and Sharon visit Vancouver.
   (B) Hubert, Lori, Paul, and Regina visit Montreal, and Sharon visits Vancouver.
   (C) Hubert, Paul, and Regina visit Toronto, and Lori and Sharon visit Montreal.
   (D) Hubert, Regina, and Sharon visit Montreal, and Lori and Paul visit Vancouver.
   (E) Lori, Paul, and Sharon visit Montreal, and Hubert and Regina visit Toronto.

2. If Hubert and Sharon visit a city together, which one of the following could be true in March?

   (A) Hubert visits the same city as Paul.
   (B) Lori visits the same city as Regina.
   (C) Paul visits the same city as Regina.
   (D) Paul visits Toronto.
   (E) Paul visits Vancouver.

3. If Sharon visits Vancouver, which one of the following must be true for March?

   (A) Hubert visits Montreal.
   (B) Lori visits Montreal.
   (C) Paul visits Toronto.
   (D) Lori visits the same city as Paul.
   (E) Lori visits the same city as Regina.

4. Which one of the following could be false in March?

   (A) Sharon must visit Montreal if Paul visits Vancouver.
   (B) Regina must visit Vancouver if Paul visits Vancouver.
   (C) Regina visits a city with exactly two of the other four students.
   (D) Lori visits a city with exactly one of the other four students.
   (E) Lori visits a city with Paul or else with Sharon.

5. If Regina visits Toronto, which one of the following could be true in March?

   (A) Lori visits Toronto.
   (B) Lori visits Vancouver.
   (C) Paul visits Toronto.
   (D) Paul visits Vancouver.
   (E) Sharon visits Vancouver.

6. Which one of the following must be true for March?

   (A) If any of the students visits Montreal, Lori visits Montreal.
   (B) If any of the students visits Montreal, exactly two of them do.
   (C) If any of the students visits Toronto, exactly three of them do.
   (D) If any of the students visits Vancouver, Paul visits Vancouver.
   (E) If any of the students visits Vancouver, exactly three of them do.

Practice Game 4: PT52, S2, G2

On a field trip to the Museum of Natural History, each of six children—Juana, Kyle, Lucita, Salim, Thanh, and Veronica—is accompanied by one of three adults—Ms. Margoles, Mr. O'Connell, and Ms. Podorski. Each adult accompanies exactly two of the children, consistent with the following conditions:

> If Ms. Margoles accompanies Juana, then Ms. Podorski accompanies Lucita.
> If Kyle is not accompanied by Ms. Margoles, then Veronica is accompanied by Mr. O'Connell.
> Either Ms. Margoles or Mr. O'Connell accompanies Thanh.
> Juana is not accompanied by the same adult as Kyle; nor is Lucita accompanied by the same adult as Salim; nor is Thanh accompanied by the same adult as Veronica.

8. Which one of the following could be an accurate matching of the adults to the children they accompany?

   (A) Ms. Margoles: Juana, Thanh; Mr. O'Connell: Lucita, Veronica; Ms. Podorski: Kyle, Salim
   (B) Ms. Margoles: Kyle, Thanh; Mr. O'Connell: Juana, Salim; Ms. Podorski: Lucita, Veronica
   (C) Ms. Margoles: Lucita, Thanh; Mr. O'Connell: Juana, Salim; Ms. Podorski: Kyle, Veronica
   (D) Ms. Margoles: Kyle, Veronica; Mr. O'Connell: Juana, Thanh; Ms. Podorski: Lucita, Salim
   (E) Ms. Margoles: Salim, Veronica; Mr. O'Connell: Kyle, Lucita; Ms. Podorski: Juana, Thanh

9. If Ms. Margoles accompanies Lucita and Thanh, then which one of the following must be true?

   (A) Juana is accompanied by the same adult as Veronica.
   (B) Kyle is accompanied by the same adult as Salim.
   (C) Juana is accompanied by Mr. O'Connell.
   (D) Kyle is accompanied by Ms. Podorski.
   (E) Salim is accompanied by Ms. Podorski.

10. If Ms. Podorski accompanies Juana and Veronica, then Ms. Margoles could accompany which one of the following pairs of children?

    (A) Kyle and Salim
    (B) Kyle and Thanh
    (C) Lucita and Salim
    (D) Lucita and Thanh
    (E) Salim and Thanh

11. Ms. Podorski CANNOT accompany which one of the following pairs of children?

    (A) Juana and Lucita
    (B) Juana and Salim
    (C) Kyle and Salim
    (D) Salim and Thanh
    (E) Salim and Veronica

12. Mr. O'Connell CANNOT accompany which one of the following pairs of children?

    (A) Juana and Lucita
    (B) Juana and Veronica
    (C) Kyle and Thanh
    (D) Lucita and Thanh
    (E) Salim and Veronica

QuickCheck: PT19, S1, G1

F G (H) J Q R

$\frac{F/}{1}$ $\frac{}{2}$ $\frac{}{3}$ $\frac{}{4}$ $\frac{}{5}$ $\frac{/F}{6}$

Ⓧ Ⓡ   Ⓙ Ⓙ
Ⓡ   Ⓠ

J – $\boxed{Q R}$

$G_3 \rightarrow Q_5$

$\cancel{Q}_5 \rightarrow \cancel{G}_3$

The Big Pause

- H is a stray.
- Q shows up more than once.
- Remember G3—this is the type of rule the LSAT likes to make you forget until a later question!

Frames?

There aren't consequences around F, so we won't be framing here.

---

1. (Ⓧ) 2
   (B) Ⓑ
   (Ⓒ) 3
   (Ⓓ) 1
   (Ⓔ) 4

2. (A)
   (B)
   (C)
   (D)
   Ⓔ

3. (A)
   (B)
   Ⓒ
   (D)
   (E)

4. (Ⓧ) 4
   (Ⓑ) 4
   (C) ~~Q R H ___ G~~
   (Ⓓ) Inference (J)
   Ⓔ

5. J – $\boxed{Q R F}$

   $\frac{\boxed{J-H,G}}{1}$ $\frac{}{2}$ $\frac{}{3}$ $\frac{Q}{4}$ $\frac{R}{5}$ $\frac{F}{6}$

   Ⓖ

   (Ⓧ)
   (Ⓑ)
   (Ⓒ)
   Ⓓ
   (E)

---

6. $\frac{F}{1}$ $\frac{G}{2}$ $\frac{J}{3}$ $\frac{Q}{4}$ $\frac{R}{5}$ $\frac{H}{6}$

   $\frac{G}{1}$ $\frac{J}{2}$ $\frac{Q}{3}$ $\frac{R}{4}$ $\frac{H}{5}$ $\frac{F}{6}$

   ⟨F G H⟩

   (A)
   (B)
   (C)
   Ⓓ
   (E)

7. J – $\boxed{G Q R}$

   F (J H) G Q R
   ~~G Q R~~ ___ 4

   $\frac{J}{1}$ $\frac{G}{2}$ $\frac{Q}{3}$ $\frac{R}{4}$ $\frac{H}{5}$ $\frac{F}{6}$

   (Ⓧ)
   (Ⓑ)
   Ⓒ
   (D)
   (E)

QuickCheck: PT30, S1, G3

C: FMOTV
W: r s p

W: ~~s~~ ~~p~~ ~~p~~ ___ ___ ___ ___ s=1+; p=1
C: V ___ ___ ___ ___
   1 2 3 4 5

V < O — [r r / M] — F
    T

The Big Pause
- 2 and 3 can't be premium.
- V must be first (everything after it).

Frames?
With a strong Tree, and a lot of information around M, we could make frames around the two places it can go.

Frame 1
~~s~~
___ r=r ___ ___
V   O   M (T F)
1   2   3   4 5

Frame 2
p r=r r   s
V (O T) M   F
1   2   3   4 5

11. (A) 4
    (B) ⓑ
    (C) 2
    (D) 1
    (E) 1

12. Frame 1
    r r=r (P S)
    V O M (T F)
    1 2 3   4 5
    Ⓐ
    (B)
    (C)
    (D)
    (E)

13. Frame 1
    p r=r s s
    V O M (T F)
    1 2 3   4 5
    (A)
    ⓑ
    (C)
    (D)
    (E)

14. (A)
    (B)
    (C)
    (D)
    Ⓔ

15. Frame 1: O M
    Frame 2: O T M
    O M
                fyi—or use
                prior work
    (A)
    ⓑ
    (C)
    (D)
    (E)

16. ~~p~~ ~~p~~ ~~p~~
    ___ ___ ___ ___ ___ ___
              (M)
    1   2   3   4   5   6

    V < O — [r r / M] — F ⓢ
        T

    Frame around M if no apparent answer

    Ⓐ   O in 2, 3, 4
    (B)
    (C)
    (D)
    (E)

QuickCheck: PT18, S1, G1

H L P R S (no repeat)

```
 __  __  __
 __  __  __
 __  __  __
 M   T   V
         L
```

```
┌───┐  ┌───┐
│ S/│  │ R │
│ P │  │ H │
└───┘  └───┘
```

$P_v \rightarrow H_v \rightarrow R_v$

No one goes solo

The Big Pause

- Last rule suggests we should figure out the distributions.
- Only way to split up is 3-2! (1-1-3 or 1-4 both leave someone solo.)

Frames?

We shouldn't make traditional frames. Instead, we should figure out how to split up the elements into groups. S/P each take up a slot in a group, and the HR chunk falls into places, separate from L.

Groups

```
┌───┐  ┌───┐
│ L │  │ R │
│S/P│  │ H │
└───┘  │P/S│
       └───┘
 M/T   M/T/V
```

1. Orientation!
   - (A) 2
   - (B) 5
   - (C) Ⓒ
   - (D) 3
   - (E) 1

2.
   ```
   ┌───┐  ┌───┐
   │ L │  │ R │
   │ P │  │ H │
   └───┘  │ S │
    M/T   └───┘
   ```
   - (A)
   - (B)
   - (C)
   - Ⓓ
   - (E)

3.
   ```
    R     L
    H     P
    S     M/T
    V
   ```
   - (A)
   - (B)
   - (C)
   - Ⓓ
   - (E)

4.
   - Ⓐ
   - (B) $P_v \rightarrow H_v \rightarrow R_v$
   - (C)
   - (D)
   - (E)

5.
   ```
    L     R
   S/P    H
    M    P/S
          T
   ```
   - (A)
   - (B)
   - Ⓒ
   - (D)
   - (E)

6.
   - (A)
   - (B)
   - (C)
   - (D)
   - Ⓔ

QuickCheck: PT52, S2, G2

J K L S T V

$$J_M \rightarrow L_P$$
$$K_P \rightarrow \cancel{J}_M$$
$$K_M \rightarrow V_O$$
$$\cancel{V}_O \rightarrow \cancel{K}_M$$

The Big Pause
- Those anti-chunks seem like they'll be important.
- The second rule tells us at least one of those two things must happen (K in M or V in O).

Frames?
There isn't a strong division in this game, and no single element seems to dominate the rules.

8. (A) 1
   (B) Ⓑ
   (C) 2
   (D) 4
   (E) 3

9.
   (A)
   (B)
   (C)
   (D)
   Ⓔ

10.
    KS or KL
    Ⓐ
    (B)
    (C)
    (D)
    (E)

11. Look for T
    (A)
    (B)
    (C)
    Ⓓ
    (E)

12. Look to Rule 2
    (A)
    (B) prev work (9)
    Ⓒ $K_O \rightarrow \cancel{K}_M \rightarrow V_O$
    (D)
    (E) prev work (10)

Chapter 12

3D Grouping

In This Chapter...

Getting Familiar

Do your best to complete the following game. Use whatever approach you see fit. Give yourself **10 minutes.**

Eight students—R, S, T, V, W, X, Y, and Z—are paired up into four teams—the Green team, the Indigo team, the Jade team, and the Purple team. Each team will have one leader and one assistant. A student's position is defined by both team and assigned role. The following conditions apply:

V is assigned to the Jade team, but R is not.
W and Y are assigned to the same team.
If S is an assistant, S is teamed with T.
If S is a leader, S is teamed with X.
R is not assigned to be a leader.

1. Which of the following could be a list of the leaders for the four teams?

    (A) Green team: W; Indigo team: S;
        Jade team: V; Purple team: R

    (B) Green team: W; Indigo team: S;
        Jade team: V; Purple team: X

    (C) Green team: V; Indigo team: S;
        Jade team: T; Purple team: Z

    (D) Green team: S; Indigo team: T;
        Jade team: V; Purple team: Z

    (E) Green team: W; Indigo team: S;
        Jade team: V; Purple team: T

2. If X is assigned to be an assistant for the Jade team, which one of the following can be determined?

    (A) the students assigned to the Green team

    (B) the students assigned to the Indigo team

    (C) the students assigned to the Purple team

    (D) which student each student is paired with

    (E) the role—either leader or assistant—that each student is assigned to

3. Which of the following must be false?

    (A) W is assigned to be a leader.

    (B) Y is assigned to be a leader.

    (C) X is assigned to be a leader.

    (D) T and Z are teamed together.

    (E) V and Z are teamed together.

4. Which of the following, if true, determines the pairings, though not necessarily the assigned positions, for each team?

    (A) S is teamed with T.

    (B) S is teamed with X.

    (C) V is teamed with Z.

    (D) R is teamed with Z.

    (E) R is teamed with X.

5. If either S or V, but not both, is assigned a leadership role, which of the following must be false?

    (A) Neither W nor Z is assigned a leadership role.

    (B) Neither X nor Y is assigned a leadership role.

    (C) Neither T nor Z is assigned a leadership role

    (D) Neither S nor Z is assigned an assistant role.

    (E) Neither T nor W is assigned an assistant role.

6. If neither T nor X nor Y is assigned to a leadership position, how many different pairs of students can be assigned to the Indigo team?

    (A) one

    (B) two

    (C) three

    (D) four

    (E) five

12

3D Grouping

Thus far, we've discussed a couple of different Grouping game types, with the emphasis on whether the number of elements within a group is defined. In this chapter, we will discuss another type of grouping scenario: Grouping games for which the positions within these individual groups are more specifically defined. We call these 3D Grouping games.

There are a variety of twists we might see in 3D Grouping games, and we'll discuss a few different strategies for dealing with the various issues that can arise. While we'll spell out our suggestions, this is a game type in which your flexibility and control of the rules will prove far more important than having the "right" diagram.

The primary diagram that we suggest for 3D Grouping games is one we call the 3D Board. The 3D Board allows us to use columns to organize information about groups, and rows to organize information about characteristics.

Let's go ahead and use a simple game scenario to discuss how we set up the 3D Board and how we can use it to effectively deal with a variety of rules:

> Six people—F, G, H, K, L, and N—will ride in three different types of automobiles—a minivan, a roadster, and an SUV—two people per car. In each car there will be one driver and one passenger. The following conditions apply:

Given this scenario, it would be a good idea to set up a board that looks something like this:

$$
\begin{array}{l}
\text{D} \; \underline{\quad} \; \underline{\quad} \; \underline{\quad} \quad \text{F G H K L N} \\
\text{P} \; \underline{\quad} \; \underline{\quad} \; \underline{\quad} \\
\phantom{\text{P}} \; \text{M} \quad \text{R} \quad \text{S}
\end{array}
$$

We are using the vertical orientation to represent groups and the horizontal orientation to represent characteristics. Let's take a look at a variety of rules that we might expect for a game such as this one and discuss the ways in which we would notate these rules.

Assignment Rules

As with all games, we will get rules that pertain to the assignment of specific elements to specific positions. Here are some examples:

> *K is not the driver of the minivan.*
> *N is a passenger in the SUV.*

If both of these rules appeared in the same game, we could notate them in this way:

$$\overset{\displaystyle \cancel{K}_D}{\underset{\underset{\text{M} \quad \text{R} \quad \text{S}}{\text{P} \; \underline{\quad} \; \underline{\quad} \; \underset{}{\overset{N}{\underline{\quad}}}}}{\text{D} \; \underline{\quad} \; \underline{\quad} \; \underline{\quad}}} \quad \text{F G H K L N}$$

Note that we've written the exclusion above the driver line so that we can see the rule a bit more directly as it relates to the position. You might find the subscript to be overkill, and in some instances it can seem unnecessary, but we suggest you use it in order to differentiate slot-specific exclusion rules from group-specific ones. To see what we mean, think about how you might notate *K is not the passenger in the minivan* and *K is not in the minivan*. If you avoid using subscript, those two could end up looking exactly the same.

Grouping Rules

By and large, the manner in which you deal with grouping rules will be largely the same as for other Grouping games, but keep in mind that we are now using the rows to differentiate characteristics, and this requires us to be a bit more specific in our diagramming.

For example, imagine we were given the rule:

F and L ride in the same car.

For other Grouping games, we would notate like this:

And that representation would be complete and sufficient. However, for a 3D Grouping game, that notation could be confusing.

To see why, think about how you would notate the following rule:

L is a passenger in the car that F drives.

The very same notation could be an accurate portrayal of this rule, and that's why we run into some trouble here. In order to combat the issue, we have two suggestions:

12

1. The Double Arrow

The double arrow is something you should be comfortable with by this point, and you can apply it to this situation to mean the same thing it does in other games. The notation would mean that we know F and L ride together, but we don't know which one drives.

2. The Vertical Cloud

We already know the cloud well and we can put it to use here vertically:

Once you've become comfortable with either of the above, be consistent so that you know that such notation means that F and L go in a column together, but we don't know the exact order.

Characteristics Rules

The most basic and common characteristics rules are those that tell us that an element has a certain characteristic, or doesn't have a certain characteristic.

Imagine we had the following two rules for our hypothetical game:

> *N drives one of the cars.*
> *H is not a passenger in one of the cars.*

We could represent these two rules in this way:

N   Drivers   —   —   —   F G H K L N

H   Passengers   —   —   —
                      M   R   S

Keep in mind that we could have just as well notated either of these rules based on the flip side of the information given—that is, for the first rule about N, we could have crossed out N from the Passenger's row, and for the second rule about H, we could have put H into the Drivers row. So if you prefer one type of representation, by all means go with that. Of course, if there were three or more characteristics rows, we'd have to be more careful about the "flip side."

More complex characteristics rules relate elements to one another. Here are some examples:

> *K drives if and only if N does not drive.*
> *Both G and H drive, or neither of them do.*
> *If K drives one of the cars, G will be a passenger in one of the cars.*
> *If G drives the SUV, F will be a passenger in the minivan.*

Let's discuss how we can notate each of these rules:

> *K drives if and only if N does not drive.*

This rule gives us two possibilities—K drives one of the cars and N doesn't, or N drives one of the cars and K doesn't. Essentially, what that means is that K and N will be in different rows. We can represent it this way:

You may also be tempted to notate it like this:

```
┌───┐  ↰
│ K │ ←┘
│ N │ ←┐
└───┘  ↲
```

But, keep in mind that we use that notation to mean that elements are in the same column.

> *Both G and H drive, or neither of them do.*

Take a moment to think about how G and H can be placed in the diagram.

This rule essentially means that G and H are in the same row—either both are in the Driver's row or both are in the Passenger's row. We can go ahead and notate this rule as follows:

Again, what the cloud means is that we know G and H go in a row together, but we do not know more about the arrangement.

> *If K drives one of the cars, G will be a passenger in one of the cars.*

Note that this is a conditional rule, and like other conditional rules, we want to go ahead and notate it next to our diagram, as opposed to *in* our diagram. Subscript is very effective for rules such as this one.

$$K_D \rightarrow G_P$$

Note that we can't use the cloud here because we don't have a biconditional. If G is a passenger, K might be a passenger also.

12

If G drives the SUV, F will be a passenger in the minivan.

This is another conditional rule, but this time there's even more to track. You could use a second set of subscript notes here, but keep in mind that when you go to extremes such as a second subscript, don't do so hastily; give yourself ample time to absorb exactly what the rule implies.

$$_S G_D \rightarrow \ _M F_P$$

Or you could avoid using subscripts by referencing how the diagram is arranged:

$$\frac{G_D}{S} \rightarrow \frac{F_P}{M}$$

Some people might want to go even further with this idea:

The point is to find a notation style that is meaningful to you under pressure.

3D Grouping & Frames

Like other games that throw a variety of rules and information at us, 3D Grouping games have a tendency to be back-end games.

Very commonly, 3D Grouping games will be limited to six elements and six positions. This type of scenario virtually guarantees a back-end game. With the positions so constrained, if there were significant up-front inferences, we would know too much about the game for the questions themselves to pose enough of a challenge.

As with other back-end games, the key to success for these games will be a clear, defined, and usable understanding of the rules. 3D Grouping games are particularly dangerous in that they often have rules that can easily be confused for one another. When you play 3D Grouping games in real time, make sure that you understand your notations completely and correctly before moving on to the questions. Be mindful of ways in which you can misunderstand your own notations; review them and work to remove ambiguity from your notations.

3D Grouping games rarely require framing. We often don't know even one actual assignment, so we have a board with mostly blank slots (never too inviting). As mentioned before, 3D Grouping games generally are designed so that once a little bit of information is uncovered (say, the positions of three of six elements), the options become very limited and manageable. Therefore, frames can be useful for these games, but you're more likely to employ frames to follow the inference chain as you work through a conditional question than when setting up the game in advance of the questions.

MANHATTAN
PREP

Try It Again

Now that you've learned how to notate the rules you'll meet in 3D Grouping games, let's return to the Getting Familiar game. If you'd like, give it one more shot before we work through it together.

Eight students—R, S, T, V, W, X, Y, and Z—are paired up into four teams—the Green team, the Indigo team, the Jade team, and the Purple team. Each team will have one leader and one assistant. A student's position is defined by both team and assigned role. The following conditions apply:

V is assigned to the Jade team, but R is not.
W and Y are assigned to the same team.
If S is an assistant, S is teamed with T.
If S is a leader, S is teamed with X.
R is not assigned to be a leader.

1. Which of the following could be a list of the leaders for the four teams?

(A) Green team: W; Indigo team: S;
    Jade team: V; Purple team: R

(B) Green team: W; Indigo team: S;
    Jade team: V; Purple team: X

(C) Green team: V; Indigo team: S;
    Jade team: T; Purple team: Z

(D) Green team: S; Indigo team: T;
    Jade team: V; Purple team: Z

(E) Green team: W; Indigo team: S;
    Jade team: V; Purple team: T

2. If X is assigned to be an assistant for the Jade team, which one of the following can be determined?

(A) the students assigned to the Green team

(B) the students assigned to the Indigo team

(C) the students assigned to the Purple team

(D) which student each student is paired with

(E) the role—either leader or assistant—that each student is assigned to

3. Which of the following must be false?

(A) W is assigned to be a leader.

(B) Y is assigned to be a leader.

(C) X is assigned to be a leader.

(D) T and Z are teamed together.

(E) V and Z are teamed together.

4. Which of the following, if true, determines the pairings, though not necessarily the assigned positions, for each team?

(A) S is teamed with T.

(B) S is teamed with X.

(C) V is teamed with Z.

(D) R is teamed with Z.

(E) R is teamed with X.

5. If either S or V, but not both, is assigned a leadership role, which of the following must be false?

(A) Neither W nor Z is assigned a leadership role.

(B) Neither X nor Y is assigned a leadership role.

(C) Neither T nor Z is assigned a leadership role

(D) Neither S nor Z is assigned an assistant role.

(E) Neither T nor W is assigned an assistant role.

6. If neither T nor X nor Y is assigned to a leadership position, how many different pairs of students can be assigned to the Indigo team?

(A) one

(B) two

(C) three

(D) four

(E) five

Answer Key

1. E   4. E
2. D   5. C
3. D   6. C

How Did You Do?

Step 1: Picture the Game

The eight students are to be put into four groups of exactly two each, so we'll use the four teams as our base. It's clearly a 3D Grouping game, because the group positions have characteristics: leaders and assistants. We have three dimensions to pay attention to: groups, characteristics, and elements.

We'll start by laying out our 3D Board:

Step 2: Notate the Rules and Make Inferences

The rules for this game are not easy to control. There are a lot of them, and they span all three dimensions of the game. However, we have the tools to represent them; we just need to be careful. Compare your diagram against ours (we haven't put in any inferences yet—and separating notation and making inferences might be helpful with such complex rules):

It's likely that you notated the third and fourth rules like this:

MANHATTAN
PREP

That's perfect, and it would be the ideal if there were any possibility of S not being selected. However, since every element in this game is used, the two-chunk notation we showed in the diagram encapsulates the situation a bit more succinctly.

Let's make some inferences!

We'll start with our grouping chunks. Since the J team already has one slot filled, the WY chunk can't go there.

And while we don't know which of the S chunks is going to be used in any given scenario, we know that neither one could fit on the J team. Be careful not to over apply this inference to T and X! They *can* go in the J group, just not as part of a chunk with S.

No other obvious inferences come to mind. Here's what we have so far:

R̶   A _ _ ⊘(V) _   R S T V W X Y Z
      L _ _ _ _
        G   I   J   P
                              (W/Y)   S_A → [S / T]
            R̶
            W̶   S_L → [X / S]
            X̶
            S̶

Step 3: The Big Pause

It's tough to say which rules will be most important in this game. It seems like all might play a big role in working through the questions. We'll be sure to keep an eye on our chunks, as those will force around the largest number of elements.

There aren't any obvious opportunities to frame this game in a formal sense. However, with so many restrictions on pairings, it's worth outlining the pairs in broad strokes. For starters, we know we have a WY pair. We'll also have S pairing with either X or T. And since neither V nor R will be with S or with each other, they each can start a pair (with R represented by a chunk since we know he's an assistant). That leaves T, X, and Z to place. We can represent our thinking as follows:

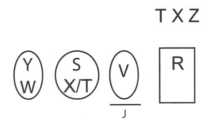

Other than for V, we don't yet know which team each element or group is assigned to, but with this formulation of the game, we've gained a handle on a lot of the moving parts. Similarly, other than for R, we don't know whether each element is assisting or leading.

We can circle Z, as it's the only element that has no rules attached.

Step 4: Attack the Questions

1. Which of the following could be a list of the leaders for the four teams?

    (A) Green team: W; Indigo team: S; Jade team: V; Purple team: R
    (B) Green team: W; Indigo team: S; Jade team: V; Purple team: X
    (C) Green team: V; Indigo team: S; Jade team: T; Purple team: Z
    (D) Green team: S; Indigo team: T; Jade team: V; Purple team: Z
    (E) Green team: W; Indigo team: S; Jade team: V; Purple team: T

Answer choice (E) is correct.

The first rule eliminates answer (C).

The second rule eliminates (D). Since W and Y must be on the same team, one of them must be a leader in any scenario.

The third and the fourth rules work together, and, like the second rule, require a bit of thought to use here. We're either going to have S assisting T or S leading X. That means that if we see S in the list, we can't see X, but if we don't see S, we must see T. This allows us to eliminate answer (B).

The fifth rule allows us to eliminate answer (A).

2. If X is assigned to be an assistant for the Jade team, which one of the following can be determined?

    (A) the students assigned to the Green team
    (B) the students assigned to the Indigo team
    (C) the students assigned to the Purple team
    (D) which student each student is paired with
    (E) the role—either leader or assistant—that each student is assigned to

Answer choice (D) is correct.

Let's work the new condition. If X is the assistant for the Jade team, V must lead. Since S is not with X, S will assist T.

MANHATTAN
PREP

This is where many students will stop making inferences; instead, ask yourself, "Who's left?" In this case, we've paired X with V (in J) and S with T. That leaves us R, W, Y, and Z. W and Y must always go together, so that leaves R and Z to be a pair. Finally, R must assist. Let's sketch out the groups:

There are no other rules about the teams, so it seems we've hit the end of the inference chain. Let's see if we've done enough to spot the right answer.

Other than the J team, we have no rules telling us about which team the elements are assigned to, so (A) through (C) are almost certainly all wrong.

(D) is what we figured out!

(E) is almost true, except for the WY group.

3. Which of the following must be false?

    (A) W is assigned to be a leader.
    (B) Y is assigned to be a leader.
    (C) X is assigned to be a leader.
    (D) T and Z are teamed together.
    (E) V and Z are teamed together.

Answer choice (D) is correct.

This is a tough question! Let's first work through the answer choices as if we had not broadly sketched the pairs during The Big Pause:

(A) can be eliminated based on our answer to the first question.

(B) is the flip side of (A). We don't have any information about who leads the WY pair.

(C) doesn't appear to trigger any rules, so let's defer.

(D) seems more promising. There are two elements referenced, so there's more opportunity to violate rules. If T and Z are paired, who's left to pair? W and Y are paired, leaving R, S, V, and X. Since R and S can't be grouped with V, X must be. That leaves S and R, which is not a viable pair according to the two S rules.

It's likely that we would have skipped thinking this deeply about (D) and instead deferred. That would have been a reasonable move. Let's examine (E).

(E) is another answer that's tough to work through quickly, especially if you don't employ the "Who's left?" question. If V and Z are together, and so are W and Y, we have R, S, T, and X to pair up. S could go with X and R could go with T. This could be true, so we can eliminate.

This was undoubtedly a time-consuming question for most people. However, anyone who did the work we did in The Big Pause saw the investment pay dividends here. T, X, and Z can never be grouped together since they were the elements left to fill in the S, V, and R groups!

4. Which of the following, if true, determines the pairings, though not necessarily the assigned positions, for each team?

   (A) S is teamed with T.
   (B) S is teamed with X.
   (C) V is teamed with Z.
   (D) R is teamed with Z.
   (E) R is teamed with X.

Answer choice (E) is correct.

After our work on the last question, it's somewhat easier to see what this question is asking. What will tell us who the four pairs are? We can dive into the answer choices, but let's take a moment to consider what must be done to find our four pairs.

We'll need to have the S choice settled, which will give us two pairs (since the W and Y pair is established). And then we'll need something that will determine the pairs among the remaining four.

For this question, it might be useful to rewrite the roster next to the question, crossing out or omitting W and Y since they are determined.

(A) seems unlikely. It settles the S issue, but we don't know about the four remaining elements (R, V, X, and Z).

(B) also settles only the S question. What about R, T, V, and Z? V can be paired with either T or Z.

(C) looks promising at first. We have settled V and Z, as well as W and Y, but we don't know whether S will be paired with T or X.

(D) leaves us not knowing about the S pair again.

(E) pairs R with X. We have W and Y already, leaving S, T, V, and Z. Of this group, S can be paired only with T, leaving V and Z to form the final pair.

Notice how (E) works: It settles the "S question" by using one of the possibilities for a different pair. This leaves S with only one pairing option. This is the same little trick that we saw in the second question!

12

5. If either S or V, but not both, is assigned a leadership role, which of the following must be false?

   (A) Neither W nor Z is assigned a leadership role.
   (B) Neither X nor Y is assigned a leadership role.
   (C) Neither T nor Z is assigned a leadership role
   (D) Neither S nor Z is assigned an assistant role.
   (E) Neither T nor W is assigned an assistant role.

Answer choice (C) is correct.

We'll sketch out the two possible arrangements. Noting that all the answer choices are about roles, we're not particularly concerned with the teams to which each pair is assigned.

If S leads and V assists, we know that S will be paired with X. We can use the four groups we identified in The Big Pause to help us determine who's left:

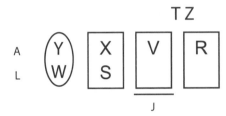

Before reading on, quickly sketch out what the other option—V leading but not S—would look like.

If S is assisting, we know it's paired with T. That leaves V leading and R, X, and Z to place. R must assist, so the other leader will be either X or Z.

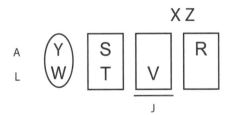

With these two hypotheticals in place, let's dive into the answer choices, remembering that every wrong answer will be something that could be true. Our focus should be on looking for something that must be false; the "could be true" answers will take up precious time. However, with such involved answer choices, that kind of savvy game playing might be impossible. Thankfully, we have two well-developed hypotheticals to rely upon.

Looking at the choices, each one presents a neither/nor situation in which two elements are restricted. Do we need both restrictions to be false for an answer to be false? No. If just one of the restrictions is impossible, the answer is false. Analogously, if someone states that she isn't human and can't be exposed to sunlight, we only have to prove that she can be exposed to sunlight (or that she is indeed human) to prove that her statement is false. Unfortunately, we have more work to do if we want to prove that a choice could be true. In this case, we will need to show that both restrictions could work at the same time.

(A) W can be assigned either role and thus it's possible that W isn't assigned a leadership role. The remaining question is whether Z is prohibited from assisting under the new condition. In the V-leading frame, Z can assist. Thus, this is a "could be true/false" answer, not something that must be false. Eliminate.

(B) We can ignore Y (like W in the last answer choice) and focus on X. Can X assist? Yes—in either hypothetical.

(C) Can T assist? No. In both hypotheticals it must lead. Can Z assist? Yes, but it doesn't matter! We've already proven that this answer must be false. It can't be true that neither T nor Z leads, since T must always lead in this scenario.

Take a moment to work through answers (D) and (E) to hone your ability to wrestle with these complex answer choices.

6. If neither T nor X nor Y is assigned to a leadership position, how many different pairs of students can be assigned to the Indigo team?

    (A) one
    (B) two
    (C) three
    (D) four
    (E) five

Answer choice (C) is correct.

This is a big condition! If T, X, and Y are assisting, what do we know? We already know that R must assist, so that leaves S, V, W, and Z to lead. We know W and Y are paired, and if S leads, S and X are grouped together. So we have all the pairs again!

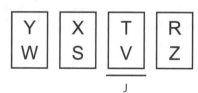

Let's return to the question stem: "How many different pairs can be assigned to the Indigo team?" The only restriction we have is that V cannot be. At this point, it's just a matter of counting: 1) YW, 2) XS, 3) RZ.

Confronting Subgroups

The 3D Board is very effective for the majority of Grouping games involving subsets, and it's what we recommend you think of first. Having said that, not all 3D Grouping games are created alike, and there are situations for which other notations may be more effective or efficient. Let's further discuss some additional tools that are useful to have in your belt.

Subscript and Cases

Subscript is also an effective way to deal with subgroups, and we've been using subscript throughout the book for a variety of issues. For 3D Grouping games, using subscript instead of a 3D Board makes sense when the subgroups are more about the elements themselves than about the positions or when the subgroups related to the positions have been left undefined.

Here is an example of a 3D Grouping game that involves subgroups but that may not require the 3D Board:

> Two Russian novels—G and H—two French novels—J and K—and two Italian
> novels—M and N—are placed in three different bins, numbered 1, 2, and 3.
> Two books will be placed in each bin.

Note that in this case the elements to be placed, the novels, have been defined in terms of subgroups, but the positions themselves have not been. We could get a rule or two relating subgroups to positions (e.g., one French novel is placed in the first bin), but not much more. Therefore, it would be difficult to put together a 3D Board. Instead, it would make sense to use something like this:

$$\underline{}\ \ \underline{}\ \ \underline{} \qquad \begin{array}{cc} G_R & H_R \\ J_F & K_F \\ M_I & N_I \end{array}$$
$$1\ \ \ \ 2\ \ \ \ 3$$

Here's a different type of 3D Grouping game that also involves subgroups, but may not fit into a 3D Board:

> Five veterans—K, L, M, N, and O—and four rookies—S, T, W, and Y—are to
> be grouped into three teams of three. Each team will have at least one veteran.

Note that in this case we can't use the 3D Board as we have before, because we don't know the exact subgroup for each of the positions (though we do know the subgroup for a few of the positions). Therefore, it would be effective to set up our diagram like this:

$$\underline{}\ \ \underline{}\ \ \underline{} \qquad S_R\ T_R\ W_R\ Y_R$$
$$\underline{_V}\ \ \underline{_V}\ \ \underline{_V} \qquad K_V\ L_V\ M_V\ N_V\ O_V$$

Or, if we'd like to avoid subscripts, we can quickly distinguish our elements by using uppercase for one set and lower-case for the other:

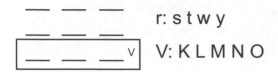

An Additional Layer of Slots

Grouping games can also define entire groups through the use of a subgroup (instead of defining the members within a group, such as assistant vs. leader). For these situations, we can borrow some of the strategies we used for 3D Ordering and add an additional layer of slots to represent the subgroup, or characteristic, of the group as a whole.

Consider this example:

> Four different bands—M, P, R, and T—will play on four different stages—the North Stage, the South Stage, the West Stage, and the East Stage—during a music festival. Each band consists of two of the following eight people—F, G, H, I, J, K, L, and O—and no person is in two different bands. The following conditions apply:
>
> > Band R will play on the West Stage.
> > F and H are in the same band.
> > K plays on the East Stage.

We've included some rules to give a better sense of what this type of game might be about. We have two separate but related mysteries in terms of positioning elements: which band plays on which stage and which people play on which stage. We can set up a board like this:

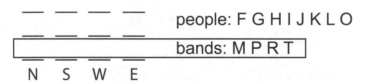

The different "layers" of positions help us to track band information and people information. Notice that we "locked in" the four stage positions. We also could have left the stages subgroup "floating," on a fourth row, but except in rare situations, it's advantageous to have at least one set of elements in fixed positions to allow easier conceptualization of the game.

Drill It: Confronting Subgroups

Let's get some practice in diagramming 3D Grouping games. More than in any other drill, you'll likely find that your diagram will look different from what we've written. 3D Grouping is one game type for which it's tough to argue that a certain diagram is the ideal. It's most important that you develop your own style and adapt that style to fit the game. That said, you do want to make sure that you haven't made any mistakes, so check every difference between our diagrams to make sure it's simply one of style, and hold yourself to a high standard for correct notation.

1. Four different bomb-detection units must be assembled from five police officers—M, N, Q, R, and S—and five bomb-sniffing dogs—G, H, J, K, and L. No police officer or dog is assigned to more than one unit, and each unit includes exactly one officer and one dog. The assignments must meet the following restrictions:

> Neither N nor M can be assigned to a unit with K.
> Any unit that includes J must also include R.
> L can be assigned only to units with either Q or R.
> S and H form one unit.

2. Four different bomb-detection units—W, X, Y, and Z—must be assembled from six police officers—M, N, Q, R, S, and T—and six bomb-sniffing dogs—F, G, H, J, K, and L. No police officer or dog is assigned to more than one unit, and each unit must have exactly three members. The assignments must adhere to the following conditions:

> Each unit must include at least one officer and at least one dog.
> Q must be in the same unit as K.
> T and M are assigned to Y.
> F must be assigned to Z with one other dog.
> Both G and H must be the only dogs in their respective units.
> Neither R nor S can be in the same unit as F.

3. As part of an unusual three-course meal, a restaurant serves exactly six different dishes—fried banana, green eggs, ham pudding, ice cream, jambalaya, and kiwi soup. Two dishes are served during the appetizer course, two are served during the main course, and two are served during the dessert course. Exactly one dish in each course is considered low-fat. The arrangement of dishes must comply with the following conditions:

> Ham pudding cannot be a low-fat dish.
>
> Ice cream must be served during the dessert course.
>
> Green eggs cannot be served with ham pudding or fried banana.
>
> Kiwi soup can be served as a main course only if fried banana is not.

4. As part of an unusual three-course meal, a restaurant offers six different dishes—fried banana, green eggs, ham pudding, ice cream, jambalaya, and kiwi soup. Two dishes are served during the appetizer course, two are served during the main course, and two are served during the dessert course. Exactly one dish in each course is considered low-fat. Each course is accompanied by exactly one type of wine—Pinot Noir, Riesling, or Shiraz—and each type of wine accompanies only one course. The arrangement of dishes must comply with the following conditions:

> Riesling must accompany green eggs.
>
> Ham pudding cannot be a low-fat dish.
>
> Green eggs cannot be served for dessert, but ice cream must be.
>
> If Shiraz accompanies the appetizer course, it accompanies kiwi soup.
>
> If Shiraz does not accompany the appetizer course, it accompanies the course in which jambalaya is served.

12

MANHATTAN
PREP

Solutions: Confronting Subgroups

1.

p.o. — — — $\underline{s}$ | — MNQR$\not{S}$

dog — — — $\underline{h}$ | — $\textcircled{g}\not{h}\,jkl$

$\not{N}\!\!/\!k$ $\not{M}\!\!/\!k$ $j \rightarrow \boxed{\begin{array}{c}R\\ \cdot\\ j\end{array}}$

$l \rightarrow \boxed{\begin{array}{c}Q\\ l\end{array}}$ or $\boxed{\begin{array}{c}R\\ l\end{array}}$

2.

$\not{R}$
$\not{S}$

p.o. $\underline{\textcircled{RS}}$ $\underline{T}$ $\underline{N/Q}$ $\not{M}\textcircled{N}Q\,RS\not{T}$

?   — — $\underline{M}$ $\underline{\quad}$dog

dog $\overline{}$ $\overline{}$ $\overline{}$ $\overline{\underset{z}{f}}$ $\not{f}\,g\,h\,\textcircled{j}\,k\,\textcircled{l}$
      w x y
              $\not{x}$ $\underset{\not{h}}{\overset{g}{}}$

$\boxed{\begin{array}{c}Q\\ \\ k\end{array}}$ g,h = only dog

$\underset{\not{h}}{\overset{g}{}}$

Note that g and h cannot be grouped with the Qk chunk because that chunk already includes a dog, and neither g nor h can be grouped with another dog.

12

3.

H̶ low   _ _ Ⓘ   F G H I Ⓙ K
       ‾A ‾M ‾D

              ⊓H⊓
              ⌷G⌷   ⊘F̶⊘
                         ⌷G⌷

         $K_M \rightarrow F̶_M$

4.

                    к
    wine   _ _ _   prs

           _ _ ⊓‾⊐
    H̶ low   ⎜ I ⎜   F G H I J K
           ‾A ‾M ‾D
                  &

                         ⊓r⊓
                         ⌷G⌷

         $S_A \rightarrow K_A$

         $S̶_A \rightarrow \boxed{\begin{array}{c} s \\ J \end{array}}$ $K̶_A \rightarrow S̶_A \rightarrow \boxed{\begin{array}{c} s \\ J \end{array}}$

Conclusion

At this point in the book, we're looking at variations on standard game types, so you're mostly working with tools you've already developed. However, we've tried to highlight two important skills here:

1. **Flexibility**
   - There are many ways to notate the various rules you'll encounter in 3D Grouping games. By test day, you should have established a standard notation system that encompasses most of the rules you'll encounter, but you should also be comfortable making minor changes if a rule doesn't fit your system.

2. **Rule mastery**
   - Usually, 3D Grouping games are back-end games. This means that your ability to control the rules is crucial. Success is not just about coming up with a great initial diagram; it's about quickly and accurately applying each rule in question after question. If you're stuck on a question, remember to scan your rules.

12

Practice Game 1: PT36, S4, G3

Gutierrez, Hoffman, Imamura, Kelly, Lapas, and Moore ride a bus together. Each sits facing forward in a different one of the six seats on the left side of the bus. The seats are in consecutive rows that are numbered 1, 2, and 3 from front to back. Each row has exactly two seats: a window seat and an aisle seat. The following conditions must apply:

> Hoffman occupies the aisle seat immediately behind Gutierrez's aisle seat.
> If Moore occupies an aisle seat, Hoffman sits in the same row as Lapas.
> If Gutierrez sits in the same row as Kelly, Moore occupies the seat immediately and directly behind Imamura's seat.
> If Kelly occupies a window seat, Moore sits in row 3.
> If Kelly sits in row 3, Imamura sits in row 1.

14. Which one of the following could be true?

    (A) Imamura sits in row 2, whereas Kelly sits in row 3.

    (B) Gutierrez sits in the same row as Kelly, immediately and directly behind Moore.

    (C) Gutierrez occupies a window seat in the same row as Lapas.

    (D) Moore occupies an aisle seat in the same row as Lapas.

    (E) Kelly and Moore both sit in row 3.

15. If Lapas and Kelly each occupy a window seat, then which one of the following could be true?

    (A) Moore occupies the aisle seat in row 3.

    (B) Imamura occupies the window seat in row 3.

    (C) Gutierrez sits in the same row as Kelly.

    (D) Gutierrez sits in the same row as Moore.

    (E) Moore sits in the same row as Lapas.

16. If Moore sits in row 1, then which one of the following must be true?

    (A) Hoffman sits in row 2.
    (B) Imamura sits in row 2.
    (C) Imamura sits in row 3.
    (D) Kelly sits in row 1.
    (E) Lapas sits in row 3.

17. If Kelly occupies the aisle seat in row 3, then each of the following must be true EXCEPT:

    (A) Gutierrez sits in the same row as Imamura.
    (B) Hoffman sits in the same row as Lapas.
    (C) Lapas occupies a window seat.
    (D) Moore occupies a window seat.
    (E) Gutierrez sits in row 1.

18. If neither Gutierrez nor Imamura sits in row 1, then which one of the following could be true?

    (A) Hoffman sits in row 2.
    (B) Kelly sits in row 2.
    (C) Moore sits in row 2.
    (D) Imamura occupies an aisle seat.
    (E) Moore occupies an aisle seat.

12

Solutions: PT36, S4, G3

Answer Key

14.	E	17.	B
15.	A	18.	C
16.	D		

Step 1: Picture the Game

This game requires a slow and steady hand to picture correctly.

We have six elements to place in a bus. The seats are arranged in two columns, with three rows. It's difficult to conceive of either the rows or the columns as the groups. This is not atypical for 3D Grouping—admittedly, the term "grouping" is getting stretched to its limit in this game! Regardless, we'll need to track both. We also must closely identify which column is the window and which is the aisle.

Let's set up our 3D Board:

MANHATTAN
PREP

Step 2: Notate the Rules and Make Inferences

These rules are all similar to ones we've seen before. The important issue for many of them is to link them to the first rule, which establishes that the GH chunk is in the aisle column. Here's how you could have notated all the rules:

$$
\begin{array}{cc}
 & \boxed{\begin{array}{c}G\\H\end{array}} \\
1\ \underline{\ \ } & \underline{\ \ \ } \\
2\ \underline{\ \ } & \underline{\ \ \ } \quad \text{G H I K L M}\\
3\ \underline{\ \ } & \underline{\ \ \ } \\
\ \ \ \ W & A
\end{array}
$$

$$M_A \rightarrow \boxed{L\,H}$$

$$\boxed{K\,G} \rightarrow \boxed{\begin{array}{c}I\\M\end{array}}$$

$$K_W \rightarrow M_3$$

$$K_3 \rightarrow I_1$$

We've notated the rules, but what connections between them can we make? Many people would move on to the questions at this point, but taking some time to dig for inferences is what separates the above-average test-taker from the pack. Even if there isn't a lot to figure out, considering the game will help you to master the rules rather than to simply notate them.

The last three rules seem connected. They all share K, and I and M both show up twice. If K is in the same row as G, it must be in a window seat, since G is stuck in the aisle in a chunk with H. This triggers our next conditional—if K is in a window seat, then M is in row 3. Since we must have H behind G in the aisle, the only place for our IM chunk is behind K in window seats 2 and 3.

It turns out that *if K and G are in the same row*, we can infer everyone's position!

$$\boxed{K\,G} \rightarrow \boxed{\begin{array}{cc}K & G\\I & H\\M & L\end{array}}$$

The above inference about the KG rule is probably one most people did not make when they played the game, and for the sake of showing a realistic solution, we'll pretend we did not figure all of that out as we explain the rest of the game. However, we know that you could have figured that out—did you?—if you gave the rules a serious review. To be clear, this chain of inferences doesn't "crack" the game, since it only applies when K is in the same row as G. (If you ever find yourself arriving at a setup that is completely filled in, something has gone wrong! LSAT games are never designed to work that way.)

Step 3: The Big Pause

There are so many rules in this game! Thankfully, the GH chunk takes up two of the six slots. Other than that chunk, it's difficult to prioritize any of the rules, as each of them is triggered in a very specific situation. It seems the trick to this game will be deft management of the rules.

Step 4: Attack the Questions

14. Which one of the following could be true?

  (A) Imamura sits in row 2, whereas Kelly sits in row 3.
  (B) Gutierrez sits in the same row as Kelly, immediately and directly behind Moore.
  (C) Gutierrez occupies a window seat in the same row as Lapas.
  (D) Moore occupies an aisle seat in the same row as Lapas.
  (E) Kelly and Moore both sit in row 3.

Answer choice (E) is correct.

This is a tough first question! It's hard to call this an Orientation question, since we have to do some serious work with the rules to eliminate these wordy answer choices. As we've said before, checking each answer is usually the slower route, but it's understandable here. For unconditional, "could be true" questions, checking each answer to see which rule it violates is a viable (if slow) strategy. The correct answer will be the only one that doesn't violate a rule.

> Rule 1, requiring the GH chunk in the aisle, eliminates (C).
> Rule 2 eliminates (D), since M in the aisle requires that H and L sit in the same row.
> Rule 3, with some consideration, eliminates (B). As we figured out above, if G and K are in the same row, we will have M behind I, in rows 2 and 3. Nothing could come behind M in this situation.
> Rule 5 eliminates (A).

How annoying that answer (E) is the correct answer! It took a while to get here (and perhaps we'd spend a few more seconds proving that (E) is valid to make sure the slog through the other four answer choices didn't mean we missed something about this game). On the bright side, this question—as first questions almost always do—provided a chance to warm up with the rules.

15. If Lapas and Kelly each occupy a window seat, then which one of the following could be true?

  (A) Moore occupies the aisle seat in row 3.
  (B) Imamura occupies the window seat in row 3.
  (C) Gutierrez sits in the same row as Kelly.
  (D) Gutierrez sits in the same row as Moore.
  (E) Moore sits in the same row as Lapas.

Answer choice (A) is correct.

If L and K are in the window column, what do we know? We know from the fourth rule that M will be in the third row. It's hard to figure out much more, so let's sketch out what we know and who's left:

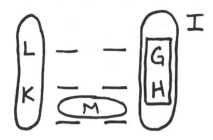

Let's roll into the answer choices:

(A) seems fine (and is). Since this is our first answer, we'd probably choose to confirm it rather than eliminate four other answers. But let's play out how deferring might look.

(B) seems okay. Defer.

(C) triggers the KG rule. As we discussed earlier, that requires IM in the window column. This all seems fine if you forget that the question's condition is that K and L are in the window column!

(D) can't be true since M must be in row 3 and G cannot be there.

(E) seems like it would work. We'd need to bring L into the third row with M. Check the rules. Ah! If M is in the aisle, L must be in the same row as H. Eliminate.

We're down to answers (A) and (B). We can simply try out one to see if it works, since this is a "could be true" question. (A) indeed works and (B) doesn't.

For review's sake, let's figure out what is wrong with answer (B). If I is in the window seat of row 3, M is forced into the aisle seat, which requires that L be next to H. That leaves K and G to sit next to each other, which would require the vertical IM chunk. Since M is next to I, that's impossible.

16. If Moore sits in row 1, then which one of the following must be true?

   (A) Hoffman sits in row 2.
   (B) Imamura sits in row 2.
   (C) Imamura sits in row 3.
   (D) Kelly sits in row 1.
   (E) Lapas sits in row 3.

Answer choice (D) is correct.

With M in row 1, what do we know? This triggers the contrapositives of the KW and KG rules. Thus, we know that K is in the aisle (where it clearly cannot be next to G). So far, we know this:

If we move into the answer choices with just that, we'll find that every answer seems like it could be true. There's more to figure out! Scan the rules once more, looking for triggers.

We have triggered the contrapositive of the K_3 rule, since I cannot be in the first row. Thus, K must be in front of the GH chunk, which is why answer (D) is correct.

17. If Kelly occupies the aisle seat in row 3, then each of the following must be true EXCEPT:

    (A) Gutierrez sits in the same row as Imamura.

    (B) Hoffman sits in the same row as Lapas.

    (C) Lapas occupies a window seat.

    (D) Moore occupies a window seat.

    (E) Gutierrez sits in row 1.

Answer choice (B) is correct.

With K in the aisle seat in row 3, what do we know? We know that the GH chunk is in rows 1 and 2. I, L, and M must go in the window column, and since K is in row 3, I must be in row 1. That leaves L and M's positioning slightly undetermined:

$$
\begin{array}{cc}
\underline{\text{I}} & \underline{\text{G}} \\
\begin{array}{c} \underline{\text{L}} \\ \underline{\text{M}} \end{array} & \begin{array}{c} \underline{\text{H}} \\ \underline{\text{K}} \end{array}
\end{array}
$$

It's tempting to keep pushing this inference chain further. However, notice that this is a "must be true EXCEPT" question, meaning that the correct answer doesn't have to be true. There must be some uncertainty left in this diagram! Let's leave our diagram as is and go look for answers that include L or M.

Answer choice (B) proves to be something that could be true or false.

18. If neither Gutierrez nor Imamura sits in row 1, then which one of the following could be true?

    (A) Hoffman sits in row 2.

    (B) Kelly sits in row 2.

    (C) Moore sits in row 2.

    (D) Imamura occupies an aisle seat.

    (E) Moore occupies an aisle seat.

Answer choice (C) is correct.

Let's follow the old inference chain one last time! If G isn't in row 1, we know that the GH chunk is in rows 2 and 3. We'll have to place I floating in those rows on the window side. Who's left? K, L, and M. So far we have this:

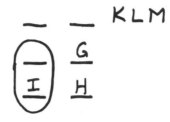

Scanning the rules—which we seem to have to do over and over in this game—we can infer that since we can't have I in the first row, we have triggered the contrapositive of the K_3 rule. Thus, K must be in row 1 or 2.

Let's keep thinking. The element that has the most rules attached to it is K. Is K really free to go anywhere other than the third row?

If we put K next to G in the second row, we'd need to have M behind I. But there'd be no room for that, so K cannot go next to G. Thus, K must go in the first row.

We end up with this diagram:

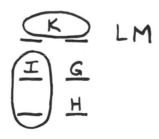

(A) and (B) are clearly impossible.

(C) seems doable, but it'd be smart to defer and see if (D) and (E) can be eliminated as easily as (A) and (B).

(D) is a clear elimination.

(E) seems fine. Let's check! The only available aisle seat is in the first row. That would force K into the window seat, which would require that M be in the last row! Therefore, (E) is impossible—M cannot be in an aisle seat with the new condition.

Practice Game 2: PTB, S2, G4

Zeno's Unfinished Furniture sells exactly five types of furniture—footstools, hutches, sideboards, tables, and vanities. Irene buys just four items, each of a different type, and each made entirely of one kind of wood—maple, oak, pine, or rosewood. The following conditions govern Irene's purchases:

> Any vanity she buys is maple.
> Any rosewood item she buys is a sideboard.
> If she buys a vanity, she does not buy a footstool.
> If Irene buys a footstool, she also buys a table made of the same wood.
> Irene does not buy an oak table.
> Exactly two of the items she buys are made of the same kind of wood as each other.

19. Which one of the following could be an accurate list of the items Irene buys?

    (A) maple footstool, maple hutch, rosewood sideboard, maple table

    (B) oak hutch, rosewood sideboard, pine table, oak vanity

    (C) rosewood hutch, maple sideboard, oak table, maple vanity

    (D) pine footstool, rosewood sideboard, pine table, maple vanity

    (E) maple footstool, pine hutch, oak sideboard, maple table

20. If Irene buys one item made of rosewood and two items made of maple, then which one of the following pairs could be two of the items she buys?

    (A) a rosewood sideboard and an oak footstool

    (B) an oak hutch and a pine sideboard

    (C) an oak hutch and a maple table

    (D) a maple sideboard and a maple vanity

    (E) a maple hutch and a maple table

21. Which one of the following is a complete and accurate list of all the woods any footstool that Irene buys could be made of?

    (A) maple, oak
    (B) maple, pine
    (C) maple, rosewood
    (D) maple, oak, pine
    (E) maple, oak, pine, rosewood

22. Suppose Irene buys a footstool. Then which one of the following is a complete and accurate list of items any one of which she could buy in maple?

    (A) footstool, hutch, sideboard, table, vanity
    (B) footstool, hutch, sideboard, table
    (C) footstool, hutch, sideboard
    (D) footstool, hutch
    (E) footstool

23. Which one of the following CANNOT be the two items Irene buys that are made of the same wood as each other?

    (A) footstool, hutch
    (B) hutch, sideboard
    (C) hutch, table
    (D) sideboard, vanity
    (E) table, vanity

24. If Irene does not buy an item made of maple, then each of the following must be true EXCEPT:

    (A) Irene buys a footstool.
    (B) Irene buys a pine hutch.
    (C) Irene buys a rosewood sideboard.
    (D) Irene buys exactly one item made of oak.
    (E) Irene buys exactly two items made of pine.

12

Solutions: PTB, S2, G4

Answer Key

19.	E	22.	B
20.	C	23.	A
21.	B	24.	B

Step 1: Picture the Game

We have to pay a little attention to the vocabulary here. Zeno's stocks five "types" of furniture, and Irene buys four items, each of a different type. So four of the types will be bought (in) and one type will not (out). Normally, we'd be starting our Logic Chain. However, there's an additional piece of information: Each item that Irene buys will be made of a certain kind of wood. We won't be able to incorporate that into our Logic Chain, so we have to find another way to tackle this game. What does this twist remind you of? Yes! 3D! We already know how to accommodate this kind of information in a diagram:

Step 2: Notate the Rules and Make Inferences

The first two rules can notated like this:

Any vanity she buys is maple.
Any rosewood items she buys is a sideboard.

MANHATTAN
PREP

Here, it isn't necessary to write the contrapositives, because these rules kick in only if the vanity or rosewood item is actually bought. The contrapositive would just tell us *If there is no maple vanity, Irene does not buy a vanity*. This is unlikely to be of use to us. Take a look at the remaining rules and consider which ones have useful contrapositives and which ones do not.

The third rule can be notated like this:

$$V \longrightarrow \cancel{F}$$
$$F \longrightarrow \cancel{V}$$

The fourth rule can be notated like this:

$$F_x \longrightarrow T_x$$

We use an "x" to designate the type of wood. If she buys a footstool made of x, she must also buy a table made of x.

The fifth rule may simply be best notated as a visual anti-chunk:

With rules similar to the sixth one on this game, it's usually easiest to write it out in a few words—possibly on or near the game board. What's most important is that you get something down quickly without agonizing over the perfect way to represent it:

$$\underline{\text{In}} \qquad \underline{\text{Out}}$$

Furniture: FHSTV _ _ _ _ _ | F/V

Wood: MOPR _ _ _ _ _ |
(2 the same)

So what inferences can we make? Let's focus on the most restrictive rule, the one regarding V and F. When one of them is in, the other must be out. You might remember this as a common placeholder type of rule. They cannot both be in. Therefore, one must always be out!

12

                                    In   Out

Furniture: FHSTV ___ ___ ___ ___ | F/V

Wood: MOPR ___ ___ ___ ___

There are only two possibilities for the game, then, and this is likely to have an impact on other rules. By now you know what to do. Frame!

Step 3: The Big Pause

Here's how we started our frames:

                                    In   Out

Furniture: FHSTV   F   H   S   T | V

Wood: MOPR
(2 the same) ___ ___ ___ ___ |

FHSTV   V   H   S   T | F

MOPR
(2 the same) ___ ___ ___ ___ |

How did we fill in all the items? Well, if the only out position has been filled, all of the other elements must be in!

12 Now let's apply the other rules. The first rule applies only to the second frame, and the second rule tells us which pieces of furniture are *not* made of rosewood. We'll write those in as exclusions. The third rule can be represented in a number of ways, so take a look at our method and steal it if you like our style. As long as you did something to show that those two slots in the first frame are the same, though, you're good to go.

		In			Out
Furniture: FHSTV	F̲	H̲	S̲	T̲	V̲
Wood: MOPR (2 the same)	O̲ (R̸)	̲ (R̸)	_	O̲ (R̸)	
FHSTV	V̲	H̲	S̲	T̲	F̲
MOPR (2 the same)	M̲	̲ (R̸)	_	̲ (R̸)	

The fifth rule provides that the table is *not* made of oak. Note the first frame has a table and a footstool made of the same wood. And since the table is *not* made of oak, neither is the footstool, leaving them both to be made of maple or else pine.

		In			Out
Furniture: FHSTV	F̲	H̲	S̲	T̲	V̲
Wood: MOPR (2 the same)	(M/P) R̸ Ø	̲ (R̸)	_	(M/P) R̸ Ø	
FHSTV	V̲	H̲	S̲	T̲	F̲
MOPR (2 the same)	M̲	̲ (R̸)	_	M/P R̸ Ø	

The final rule doesn't yield any inferences that are easy to write out. What it does tell us is that in the first frame, T and F are the two that will have the same wood, and therefore H and S must be made of different woods. That could be tricky to diagram, so we may be better off highlighting the fifth rule and promising ourselves to return to it again and again as we play the game.

Step 4: Attack the Questions

19. Which one of the following could be an accurate list of the items Irene buys?

    (A) maple footstool, maple hutch, rosewood sideboard, maple table

    (B) oak hutch, rosewood sideboard, pine table, oak vanity

    (C) rosewood hutch, maple sideboard, oak table, maple vanity

    (D) pine footstool, rosewood sideboard, pine table, maple vanity

    (E) maple footstool, pine hutch, oak sideboard, maple table

Answer choice (E) is correct.

Nothing like a good, ol'-fashioned Orientation question! Rule-by-rule will do the trick:

> Rule 1 eliminates (B).
> Rule 2 eliminates (C).
> Rule 3 eliminates (D).
> Rule 6 eliminates (A).

That leaves answer choice (E) as possible.

20. If Irene buys one item made of rosewood and two items made of maple, then which one of the following pairs could be two of the items she buys?

    (A) a rosewood sideboard and an oak footstool

    (B) an oak hutch and a pine sideboard

    (C) an oak hutch and a maple table

    (D) a maple sideboard and a maple vanity

    (E) a maple hutch and a maple table

Answer choice (C) is correct.

MANHATTAN
PREP

This new condition works in both frames, so we should draw out two hypotheticals:

In both frames, the rosewood item must be the sideboard. In the first frame, the two maples must be T and F. But in the second frame, we can't be sure whether the two maples are H and V or T and V.

Answer (A) is wrong because the footstool is either made of maple or the item in the out group. Answers (B) and (D) must be wrong because the sideboard has to be rosewood. Finally, answer (E) is out because having both a maple hutch and maple table results in three maple items in both frames.

21. Which one of the following is a complete and accurate list of all the woods any footstool that Irene buys could be made of?

    (A) maple, oak
    (B) maple, pine
    (C) maple, rosewood
    (D) maple, oak, pine
    (E) maple, oak, pine, rosewood

Answer choice (B) is correct.

These are the moments when we really, really love frames. The first frame tells us that the footstool must be made of either maple or pine.

22. Suppose Irene buys a footstool. Then which one of the following is a complete and accurate list of items any one of which she could buy in maple?

(A) footstool, hutch, sideboard, table, vanity

(B) footstool, hutch, sideboard, table

(C) footstool, hutch, sideboard

(D) footstool, hutch

(E) footstool

Answer choice (B) is correct.

Let's head to our first frame:

The footstool and table can both be maple. However, if they're both pine, that leaves open the possibility for either the hutch or the sideboard (but not both—don't forget the fifth rule!) to be maple. Remember, if there's a rosewood item, it's the sideboard; this doesn't mean the sideboard has to be made of rosewood.

23. Which one of the following CANNOT be the two items Irene buys that are made of the same wood as each other?

(A) footstool, hutch

(B) hutch, sideboard

(C) hutch, table

(D) sideboard, vanity

(E) table, vanity

Answer choice (A) is correct.

Like many unconditional questions, this one is best approached by evaluating the answer choices one at a time. Starting with answer (A), we should head to our first frame. Can F and H have the same wood there? No! F must have the same wood as T, and our fifth rule (singing "Don't You...Forget About Me") prevents a third item from being made of the same wood.

On the test, we're probably pretty short on time by question 23, so we'd move on. But this isn't the test, so get some practice in by seeing why each of the other answer choices is possible.

24. If Irene does not buy an item made of maple, then each of the following must be true EXCEPT:

    (A) Irene buys a footstool.
    (B) Irene buys a pine hutch.
    (C) Irene buys a rosewood sideboard.
    (D) Irene buys exactly one item made of oak.
    (E) Irene buys exactly two items made of pine.

Answer choice (B) is correct.

If Irene buys no item made of maple, we're working with the first frame. The table and and the footstool must be made of pine. That leaves only oak and rosewood for the hutch and sideboard. The hutch cannot be made of rosewood and so must be made of oak. The last rule further requires that in frame 1, the hutch and sideboard must be made of different wood. So the sideboard must be rosewood.

Answers (A), (C), (D), and (E) all must be true.

Chapter 13

Grouping Twists

In This Chapter. . .

Grouping Twists

Feeling comfortable with Grouping games? Excellent! It's time to look at some common grouping twists. The good news is that we've already seen each of the twists the LSAT uses to increase a game's difficulty—they're based on the same concepts from our chapter on ordering twists. Let's look at how subgroups, mismatches, special connections, and special positions affect logic games in the context of grouping.

Subgroups

Subgroups are the most common grouping twist, and the increased difficulty associated with them can vary significantly. Sometimes the setup and questions hardly make use of the subgroups at all, much like a dog that is all bark and no bite. On other games, the impact of subgroups will play a major role in setting up the game, and inferences will relate to the subgroups as much as the elements.

Since you've already completed the chapter on ordering twists, you should have a sense of whether you prefer to use subscripts to track each element's subgroup or to keep a list of the subgroups handy and refer back to it throughout the game:

$$F_m \quad G_m$$
$$M_n \quad O_n$$
$$Q_t \quad R_t \quad S_t$$

or

Mysteries:	F G
Novels:	M O
Textbooks:	Q R S

How could the rules make use of the subgroups? Sometimes the rules require that each group contain a minimum (or specified) number of elements from a subgroup:

Each team must have at least one geologist.

Each committee has exactly one graphic designer.

No more than two skinks are placed in any one of the terrariums.

Sometimes elements from one subgroup must be (or cannot be) placed in groups with elements from other subgroups:

Any team with an engineer must also have a computer scientist.

No animator is on a committee with a producer.

A terrarium cannot include any newts if it includes more than one skink.

13

Some rules reference both individual elements and subgroups:

> Jones must be on a team with a computer scientist.

> Gina cannot be on any committee with a set designer.

> W must not be in a terrarium with a frog.

And finally, conditional rules might reference specific subgroups:

> If a chemist is on team 2, then team 3 must have a biologist.

> If the committee to which Nolan is assigned lacks a producer, then it must have a cinematographer.

> If any terrarium contains both a frog and a newt, it is the only terrarium to do so.

Some of this probably seems very familiar from the chapter on ordering twists, and it should! The basic ideas are essentially the same—only the context has changed.

In the next few pages, we're going to dive into games with subgroups. We'll highlight the impact subgroups have on setting up the game, making inferences, and attacking the questions. Afterward, we'll revisit In/Out Grouping and that game type's special relationship with subgroups. Ready for your first drill?

13

MANHATTAN
PREP

Drill It: Grouping with Subgroups

Eight players from a local game club are pairing up for an upcoming dominos tournament. Each player will be placed at exactly one of four tables, and each table will feature a single pair of players. There are three experts—Grace, Harry, and Janice—and five novices—Val, Warren, Xavier, Yates, and Zoella. The following rules apply:

Grace is paired with neither Xavier nor either of the other experts.

If Yates is paired with an expert, so is Xavier.

1. If two of the tables feature only novices, which one of the following must be true?

    (A) Yates is paired with Xavier.

    (B) Yates is paired with Val.

    (C) Grace is paired with Zoella.

    (D) Grace is paired with Warren.

    (E) Janice is paired with Harry.

2. If Val is paired with Warren, and no experts are paired with each other, which of the following must be true?

    (A) Either Harry or Janice is paired with Yates.

    (B) Either Zoella or Yates is paired with Harry.

    (C) Either Xavier or Zoella is paired with Janice.

    (D) Either Harry or Janice is paired with Xavier.

    (E) Either Grace or Harry is paired with Zoella.

13

Solutions: Grouping with Subgroups

Answer Key

1. E
2. D

Step 1: Picture the Game

The scenario of this game gives us all of the information we need to start our diagram. We have eight players sitting at four tables with two players at each table. We're placing eight elements in eight spaces. A Closed Board appears appropriate for organizing our work.

The players are divided into two subgroups: experts and novices.

Experts   Novices

G H J   V W X Y Z

—   —   —   —

—   —   —   —

1   2   3   4

We've labeled these tables 1–4, but that's just so we can reference them. There's not actually a table 1 or table 2, just four pairs.

Step 2: Notate the Rules and Make Inferences

We can represent the first rule with three anti-chunks. The second rule is conditional, but it talks about both elements and subgroups. Check out how we represented it below, but if your diagram captures the same information, it doesn't have to be exactly the same.

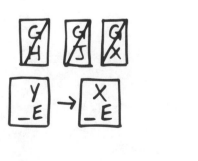

Experts   Novices

G H J   V W X Y Z

—   —   —   —

1   2   3   4

Step 3: The Big Pause

What inferences can we make? There are only three experts, and G cannot be paired with either of the other two experts. If two experts are paired up, they will be H and J. Also, since G cannot be paired with X, if X is with an expert, it will be either H or J (this plays into our conditional rule). Since there are five novices and four tables, we must have at least one pair of novices.

Although we might not add these inferences to our diagram, your understanding of the game increases as you explore the rules and the connections between the elements or subgroups.

There isn't a clear fork in this game to use as the basis for frames. Remember, it's generally not a good idea to base frames on a conditional rule.

Since we don't have significant inferences or frames, we should think about important elements and rules. Here, it looks like G is the most restricted, so let's keep our eyes on her.

Step 4: Attack the Questions

1. If two of the tables feature only novices, which one of the following must be true?

    (A) Yates is paired with Xavier.
    (B) Yates is paired with Val.
    (C) Grace is paired with Zoella.
    (D) Grace is paired with Warren.
    (E) Janice is paired with Harry.

Answer choice (E) is correct.

What do we know if two of the tables feature only novices? As usual, let's track our work in a diagram:

$$\frac{\quad N \quad}{\quad} \; \frac{\quad N \quad}{\quad} \; \frac{\quad}{\quad} \; \frac{\quad}{\quad}$$

$$\frac{\quad N \quad}{1} \; \frac{\quad N \quad}{2} \; \frac{\quad}{3} \; \frac{\quad}{4}$$

While the question is initially about the novices, we should quickly turn our attention to the experts. We have to assign all three of them to tables other than those with our two pairs of novices:

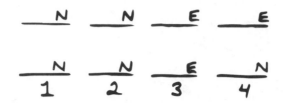

We've also placed that last novice, who must play with an expert. We know that G cannot be paired with another expert, so H and J must form a pair. Since the only expert left open is G, and X can't play against G, we know that Y also can't play with an expert.

V, W, or Z must pair with G, but this is a "must be true" question and we're at the end of our inference chain—let's check whether we've done enough work to answer the question. Scanning through the answer choices, (E) stands out as something we know must be true.

2. If Val is paired with Warren, and no experts are paired with each other, which of the following must be true?

   (A) Either Harry or Janice is paired with Yates.
   (B) Either Zoella or Yates is paired with Harry.
   (C) Either Xavier or Zoella is paired with Janice.
   (D) Either Harry or Janice is paired with Xavier.
   (E) Either Grace or Harry is paired with Zoella.

Answer choice (D) is correct.

The new condition in this question pairs V and W, and it separates G, H, and J across different tables. Who's left? Our three remaining novices—X, Y, and Z. Since X cannot be paired with G, either Y or Z will have to be, and X will be paired with either H or J. That leaves the novice who isn't paired with G to be paired with the expert not paired with X.

MANHATTAN
PREP

$$\underline{\text{V}} \quad \underline{\text{G}} \quad \underline{\text{H}} \quad \underline{\text{J}}$$

$$\underline{\text{W}} \quad \underline{\text{Y/z}} \quad \boxed{\text{z/y , X}}$$
$$\text{1} \qquad \text{2} \qquad \text{3} \qquad \text{4}$$
$$\qquad \ast$$

Let's see if we have enough information yet to find an answer that must be true. Skimming through the answer choices, (D) must be true.

    (A) could be false. G could be paired with Y.
    (B) could be false. X could be paired with H.
    (C) could be false. Y could be paired with J.
    (E) could be false. J could be paired with Z.

13

Practice Game 1: PT37, S3, G3

A total of six books occupies three small shelves—one on the first shelf, two on the second shelf, and three on the third shelf. Two of the books are grammars—one of Farsi, the other of Hausa. Two others are linguistics monographs—one on phonology, the other on semantics. The remaining two books are novels—one by Vonnegut, the other by Woolf. The books' arrangement is consistent with the following:

> There is at least one novel on the same shelf as the Farsi grammar.
> The monographs are not both on the same shelf.
> The Vonnegut novel is not on the same shelf as either monograph.

12. Which one of the following could be an accurate matching of the bookshelves to the books on each of them?

(A) first shelf: Hausa grammar
    second shelf: semantics monograph, Vonnegut novel
    third shelf: Farsi grammar, phonology monograph, Woolf novel

(B) first shelf: semantics monograph
    second shelf: Farsi grammar, Vonnegut novel
    third shelf: Hausa grammar, phonology monograph, Woolf novel

(C) first shelf: Vonnegut novel
    second shelf: phonology monograph, Farsi grammar
    third shelf: Hausa grammar, semantics monograph, Woolf novel

(D) first shelf: Woolf novel
    second shelf: phonology and semantics monographs
    third shelf: Farsi and Hausa grammars, Vonnegut novel

(E) first shelf: Woolf novel
    second shelf: Farsi grammar, Vonnegut novel
    third shelf: Hausa grammar, phonology and semantics monographs

13. Which one of the following CANNOT be true?

   (A) A grammar is on the first shelf.
   (B) A linguistics monograph is on the same shelf as the Hausa grammar.
   (C) A novel is on the first shelf.
   (D) The novels are on the same shelf as each other.
   (E) Neither linguistics monograph is on the first shelf.

14. Which one of the following must be true?

   (A) A linguistics monograph and a grammar are on the second shelf.
   (B) A novel and a grammar are on the second shelf.
   (C) At least one linguistics monograph and at least one grammar are on the third shelf.
   (D) At least one novel and at least one grammar are on the third shelf.
   (E) At least one novel and at least one linguistics monograph are on the third shelf.

15. If both grammars are on the same shelf, which one of the following could be true?

   (A) The phonology monograph is on the third shelf.
   (B) A novel is on the first shelf.
   (C) Both novels are on the second shelf.
   (D) The Farsi grammar is on the second shelf.
   (E) The phonology monograph is on the first shelf.

16. Which one of the following must be true?

   (A) A linguistics monograph is on the first shelf.
   (B) No more than one novel is on each shelf.
   (C) The Farsi grammar is not on the same shelf as the Hausa grammar.
   (D) The semantics monograph is not on the same shelf as the Woolf novel.
   (E) The Woolf novel is not on the first shelf.

17. If the Farsi grammar is not on the third shelf, which one of the following could be true?

   (A) The phonology monograph is on the second shelf.
   (B) The Hausa grammar is on the second shelf.
   (C) The semantics monograph is on the third shelf.
   (D) The Vonnegut novel is on the third shelf.
   (E) The Woolf novel is on the second shelf.

18. If the Hausa grammar and the phonology monograph are on the same shelf, which one of the following must be true?

   (A) The phonology monograph is on the third shelf.
   (B) The Vonnegut novel is on the second shelf.
   (C) The semantics monograph is on the second shelf.
   (D) The semantics monograph is on the first shelf.
   (E) The Woolf novel is on the third shelf.

13

Solutions: PT37, S3, G3

Answer Key

12. B   16. E

13. A   17. C

14. D   18. E

15. E

Step 1: Picture the Game

We know what you're thinking—could there be a more random selection of books on a shelf? And what kind of bookshelf has only six books on it? Nonetheless, beyond the real-world unlikelihood, the setup for this game is straightforward: a Closed Board and elements within subgroups.

The first time you wrote those subgroups, you likely focused on the first word of "linguistic monographs" and then were possibly tripped up as you read the second rule. If you hesitated to change your roster from "linguistic" to "monographs," remember that your diagramming needs to be flexible and you want to maintain a nimble approach.

You may have oriented your game board differently, like this:

MANHATTAN
PREP

Or even this:

3 __ __ __

2 __ __

1 __

Totally fine, as long as it was intuitive for you and your notations align with the diagram visually. In some games, an adjusted organizational layout can improve your process. For example, if there had been a rule *A novel is on the shelf above the Farsi grammar,* a diagram containing shelves stacked vertically would be very helpful indeed. As it is, this game lacks such a dynamic, so we opted to draw the diagram from left to right.

Step 2: Notate the Rules and Make Inferences

The three rules are short, sweet, and to the point:

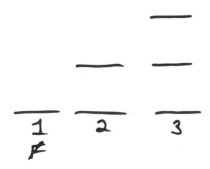

Beyond eliminating F from shelf one, it's hard to find any concrete inferences we can place on the diagram. You also might have written that first rule as a chunk with F and an empty slot with a small *n* in it, to represent *novel*. That works, too!

13

Step 3: The Big Pause

The rules that stand out most are the three anti-chunks because there's so much overlap between the elements included there. Between the three anti-chunks, V, P, and S must each be on a different shelf. Since we have three shelves, we can create a cloud spanning the shelves for these three elements:

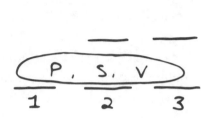

Of the three, V stands out as different from P and S (both monographs) in that it's a novel. Also, V connects to the first rule—it's one of the two elements that can go with F. V can go in three places, and there will be consequences in each one, so let's build three frames:

Take a minute and complete these frames on your own. And then check your work against ours.

In frame 1, F cannot be on the same shelf as V, so F and W must be on the same shelf, and the only shelf with room for both is shelf 3. That forces H onto shelf 2.

In frame 2, while F could go with V on shelf 2 or with W on shelf 3, W must be on shelf 3 either way. That leaves F and H to split between shelves 2 and 3.

In frame 3, F is either with W on shelf 3, or with V on shelf 3. Either way, F is on shelf 3, leaving W and H to split between the remaining slots.

	F	
H	W	
V	P/S	S/P
1	2	3
F		

Frame 1

	H/F	
F/H	W	
P/S	V	S/P
1	2	3
F		

Frame 2

	W/H	
H/W	F	
P/S	S/P	V
1	2	3
F		

Frame 3

It's one thing to follow our lead through the process of creating these frames; it's another to create them on your own. If you didn't build these frames when you were first attempting this game, head back to the beginning of this section and replay the game—this time framing it. You may also be wondering whether these frames are worth the time invested to create them. We suggest you rework these questions again, this time with the frames, and make your own assessment.

Step 4: Attack the Questions

12. Which one of the following could be an accurate matching of the bookshelves to the books on each of them?

    (A) first shelf: Hausa grammar

    second shelf: semantics monograph, Vonnegut novel

    third shelf: Farsi grammar, phonology monograph, Woolf novel

    (B) first shelf: semantics monograph

    second shelf: Farsi grammar, Vonnegut novel

    third shelf: Hausa grammar, phonology monograph, Woolf novel

    (C) first shelf: Vonnegut novel

    second shelf: phonology monograph, Farsi grammar

    third shelf: Hausa grammar, semantics monograph, Woolf novel

    (D) first shelf: Woolf novel

    second shelf: phonology and semantics monographs

    third shelf: Farsi and Hausa grammars, Vonnegut novel

    (E) first shelf: Woolf novel

    second shelf: Farsi grammar, Vonnegut novel

    third shelf: Hausa grammar, phonology and semantics monographs

Answer choice (B) is correct.

Even with frames, Orientation questions are typically best approached rule by rule:

> Rule 1 eliminates (C).
> Rule 2 eliminates (D) and (E).
> Rule 3 eliminates (A).

13. Which one of the following CANNOT be true?

    (A) A grammar is on the first shelf.
    (B) A linguistics monograph is on the same shelf as the Hausa grammar.
    (C) A novel is on the first shelf.
    (D) The novels are on the same shelf as each other.
    (E) Neither linguistics monograph is on the first shelf.

Answer choice (A) is correct.

Our P, S, V inference saves the day! None of those three are grammar books.

14. Which one of the following must be true?

    (A) A linguistics monograph and a grammar are on the second shelf.

    (B) A novel and a grammar are on the second shelf.

    (C) At least one linguistics monograph and at least one grammar are on the third shelf.

    (D) At least one novel and at least one grammar are on the third shelf.

    (E) At least one novel and at least one linguistics monograph are on the third shelf.

Answer choice (D) is correct.

With frames, this question shouldn't be too bad. Let's see which answer shows up in each frame:

        (A) doesn't show up in frame 3.
        (B) doesn't show up in frame 1.
        (C) doesn't show up in frame 3.
        (E) doesn't show up in frame 3.

Answer choice (D) shows up in each frame, so it must be true.

15. If both grammars are on the same shelf, which one of the following could be true?

    (A) The phonology monograph is on the third shelf.

    (B) A novel is on the first shelf.

    (C) Both novels are on the second shelf.

    (D) The Farsi grammar is on the second shelf.

    (E) The phonology monograph is on the first shelf.

Answer choice (E) is correct.

F and H can be on the same shelf only in frame 3.

$$
\begin{array}{ccc}
 & & \underline{H} \\
 & \underline{W} & \underline{F} \\
\underline{P/S} & \underline{S/P} & \underline{V} \\
1 & 2 & 3 \\
\not{F} & &
\end{array}
$$

Frame 3

Only P and S are left undetermined, so we should look for them in the answers. (A) isn't possible, but (E) is.

16. Which one of the following must be true?

(A) A linguistics monograph is on the first shelf.

(B) No more than one novel is on each shelf.

(C) The Farsi grammar is not on the same shelf as the Hausa grammar.

(D) The semantics monograph is not on the same shelf as the Woolf novel.

(E) The Woolf novel is not on the first shelf.

Answer choice (E) is correct.

Another question where we should consult our frames. The correct answer must show up in all three frames:

Frame 1 | Frame 2 | Frame 3

(A) could be false—frame 1.

(B) could be false—frame 3.

(C) could be false—frame 3.

(D) could be false—all three frames!

17. If the Farsi grammar is not on the third shelf, which one of the following could be true?

(A) The phonology monograph is on the second shelf.

(B) The Hausa grammar is on the second shelf.

(C) The semantics monograph is on the third shelf.

(D) The Vonnegut novel is on the third shelf.

(E) The Woolf novel is on the second shelf.

Answer choice (C) is correct.

The only frame where this is possible is frame 2. We could draw it out, but when there isn't much change in the frame, you can save time by checking the answers without drawing it out. In frame 2, with H and F set, we should expect the answer to involve S or P.

18. If the Hausa grammar and the phonology monograph are on the same shelf, which one of the following must be true?

(A) The phonology monograph is on the third shelf.

(B) The Vonnegut novel is on the second shelf.

(C) The semantics monograph is on the second shelf.

(D) The semantics monograph is on the first shelf.

(E) The Woolf novel is on the third shelf.

Answer choice (E) is correct.

Notice that H and P could be on the same shelf in each of our three frames. Drawing each one out would take a lot of time. But what choice do we have?

Well, we could take a second to scan the answers and frames. We need something that must be true, and it looks like V, P, and S shift around quite a bit. (A) through (D) address these elements, so let's defer on those and start with answer choice (E). In frames 1 and 2, W is always on the third shelf. In frame 3, when H and P are on the same shelf, W is once again on the third shelf.

In/Out Grouping & Subgroups

The overwhelming majority of In/Out Grouping games are open—the type we've been looking at so far—but occasionally we'll see a Closed In/Out Grouping game. Since this type of game *also* tends to throw in another twist, let's take a look at how we should adapt our Logic Chain and our process.

The Characteristics of Closed In/Out Grouping Games

In many ways, Closed In/Out Grouping games are very similar to Open In/Out Grouping games: Our job is to split the elements into two groups by utilizing a series of conditional rules. These games are closed, however, meaning that we know how many elements are in each group! Sounds nice, right?

If that was the only difference, it would be easier. But a few other characteristics tend to show up in these games:

1. **Subgroups.** In most *open* scenarios, the pool of elements is *not* broken down into subgroups. By contrast, *closed* games will almost always define subgroups (usually three) from the main pool. (In the example to follow, the subgroups are 1960s songs, 1970s songs, and 1980s songs.)

2. **Number rules.** *Closed* In/Out Grouping games almost always introduce number rules in addition to conditional rules. These generally limit the number of selections made from one of the three specific subgroups. This information can lead to some very important inferences. Take the following hypothetical example:

> A journalist reads exactly six books out of a pool of nine total books. Of the nine, three are fiction, three are nonfiction, and three are poetry. The journalist reads exactly one poetry book.

Putting together the rule that exactly six books are read and the rule that exactly one of those must be a poetry book, we can draw some very important inferences. We will need either three fiction and two nonfiction books or three nonfiction and two fiction books. Regardless, we will need all three of either the fiction or the nonfiction books.

These **numerical distributions** will very often let us quickly evaluate tricky answers.

3. **Fewer links.** The diagrams for Closed In/Out Grouping games usually have fewer arrows (conditional rules) in them than in open games. With so much of the game hinging on subgroups and number rules, it would be unfair for the LSAT to also expect us to track a large number of conditional rules.

We'll need to adapt our Logic Chain and process to account for these twists, but we're going to give you one piece of advice before throwing you into one of these games. When writing out your Logic Chain, instead of filling in the elements as they come up in the rules, start by listing them in order, based on their subgroups.

But that's all you're going to get from us—we don't want to make it too easy! Now, try this game on your own.

Practice Game 2: Authored by Manhattan Prep

A filmmaker will choose exactly five songs to use in a film project. Of the nine songs that she will choose from, three songs—F, G, and H—were written in the 1960s, three songs—J, K, and M—were written in the 1970s, and three songs—O, P, and Q—were written in the 1980s. The following conditions apply:

Exactly two songs from the 1980s are selected for the project.

G and J cannot both be selected.

H and O cannot both be selected.

If Q is selected, both G and H are selected.

1. Which one of the following is an acceptable selection of songs for the film project?

   (A) F, G, K, P, Q
   (B) G, J, K, O, P
   (C) G, K, M, O, P
   (D) G, H, K, M, Q
   (E) F, G, H, O, P

2. If Q is selected for the film project, each of the following could be true EXCEPT:

   (A) F is selected for the film project.
   (B) J is selected for the film project.
   (C) G is selected for the film project.
   (D) K is selected for the film project.
   (E) M is selected for the film project.

3. If neither K nor M is selected for the film project, how many of the five song selections are known with certainty?

   (A) one
   (B) two
   (C) three
   (D) four
   (E) five

4. If K is the only song from the 1970s selected for the film project, then which one of the following CANNOT be true?

   (A) O is not selected but F is selected.
   (B) Q is not selected but G is selected.
   (C) F is not selected but P is selected.
   (D) H is not selected but G is selected.
   (E) O is not selected but H is selected.

5. Which one of the following is a song that must be selected for the film project?

   (A) H
   (B) Q
   (C) F
   (D) P
   (E) G

6. If the condition that exactly two songs from the 1980s are selected for the project is replaced with the condition that at least one song from each time period must be selected, and if all other rules remain in effect, each of the following could be true EXCEPT:

   (A) Both O and P are selected.
   (B) Both G and H are selected.
   (C) Both P and Q are selected.
   (D) J, K, and M are selected.
   (E) F, P, and Q are selected.

Solutions: Practice Game 2

Answer Key

1. C   4. A
2. B   5. D
3. E   6. E

Step 1: Picture the Game

We've got a bunch of songs, and we're trying to figure out which are in the soundtrack, so this is In/Out Grouping. We also know that exactly five songs are in, so it's a closed game. Those parts of the game should have felt somewhat familiar.

The elements being broken up into subgroups, however, is a new twist. As if this game type wasn't hard enough already!

As we did for the open games discussed earlier in the chapter, we'll use a Logic Chain diagram to notate the conditional rules. As we discussed earlier, the only thing we'll do differently this time is to make certain that we arrange the letters by subgroup. So instead of placing the letters on the diagram according to which rule we're working on, we'll place all the letters on the diagram before notating the rules. Keeping subgroups together will make it easier for us to keep track of rules like that first one.

(Note: We think the Logic Chain is, without a doubt, better for In/Out games with subgroups than the Rule Chart. We're going to approach this game solely from that angle.)

Step 2: Notate the Rules and Make Inferences

Here is a completed diagram for this game:

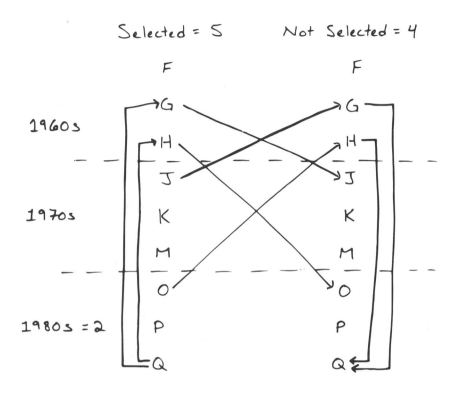

Notice the clear separation of subgroups and the way we've notated the number of songs from the 1980s.

Step 3: The Big Pause

Numerical Distributions

If you remember back to our discussion of frames and inferences in In/Out Grouping games, we didn't have many. We almost never make frames, and our inferences were mostly limited to our placeholders—elements that either couldn't both be in or out.

When we have subgroups—particularly when there are rules that limit how many of a subgroup can be in—we can often infer a limited set **numerical distributions,** which often play a critical role in following the inference chain when answering the questions. Take a second and run through a few scenarios in your mind. This quick little exercise will certainly come in handy as you consider the questions, so it's worth sketching out the possibilities on your paper:

We can see that there are four possible distributions. Some game players might want to explore a bit deeper to see if any of those distributions have specific inferences, but we find that they're usually not worth the investment of time. Feel free to try it out, though, to see if you find them useful.

Mutually Exclusive Pairs

It can also be very helpful to identify any mutually exclusive pairs that exist in the diagram. We already know that O and H are mutually exclusive (when O is in, H is out, and vice versa), as well as G and J.

In the chapter on In/Out Grouping, this is the point where we stopped looking for inferences. However, now that we're a little more experienced, let's dig a little deeper!

Since the Logic Chain does a great job of letting us see second-level inferences, let's move past those first-level mutually exclusive pairs. Two of our elements—J and O—start a chain. After J forces G out, G forces Q out; after O forces H out, H forces Q out. It seems as if we have a couple other mutually exclusive pairs—J and O are each mutually exclusive of Q!

Think we're done? Not even close. Since O and Q are mutually exclusive and they're both from the 80s *and* we have a number rule about songs from that decade, we should explore a bit further.

We need to have two songs from the 80s, and, if we set up a placeholder, we'd reserve a slot in the out group for either O or Q. But we know that there's only one slot for 80s in the out group, which means that O or Q is out, the other (that is P) *must be in*.

If you didn't see this before starting the questions, it's not the end of the world. We've said before that you won't always get all the important inferences up front, and that you don't need to. Many test-takers would not spot this inference until a specific question (such as question 5) prompted them to consider it. That said, often you'll be able to spot a big inference on a closed In/Out Grouping game by looking for mutually exclusive pairs, so be on the lookout and give yourself a bit more time up front to poke around.

Finally, who are the important elements? Undoubtedly, Q is the song of the hour since it being in affects four different elements.

Step 4: Attack the Questions

1. Which one of the following is an acceptable selection of songs for the film project?

    (A) F, G, K, P, Q
    (B) G, J, K, O, P
    (C) G, K, M, O, P
    (D) G, H, K, M, Q
    (E) F, G, H, O, P

Answer choice (C) is correct.

MANHATTAN
PREP

While you probably didn't have much of a problem using rules 2 through 4 to eliminate answers, that first rule was probably more difficult to check. Luckily, we've got a way to handle that! When dealing with games featuring sub-groups, draw lines separating the subgroups. The LSAT has always given the answers in order, and we don't expect that to change.

F, G, K, P, Q
G, J, K, O, P
G, K, M, O, P
G, H, K, M, Q
F, G, H, O, P

With these lines drawn in, it's easier to see that rule 1 eliminates (D).
Rule 2 eliminates (B).
Rule 3 eliminates (E).
Rule 4 eliminates (A).

2. If Q is selected for the film project, each of the following could be true EXCEPT:

(A) F is selected for the film project.

(B) J is selected for the film project.

(C) G is selected for the film project.

(D) K is selected for the film project.

(E) M is selected for the film project.

Answer choice (B) is correct.

It's time for a t-chart to play out any inferences from the new information. However, with our traditional t-chart, we wouldn't be able to track which elements are from which subgroup. You could use subscripts, but we find it easier to split our t-chart into three rows so that we can track the selection of songs from the 60s, 70s, and 80s separately. We also added in two boxes to the 1980s in column and one box to the 1980s out column. These boxes, shown below, indicate that two songs from the 80s must be chosen and one song must be left out.

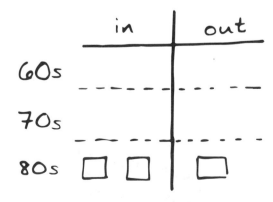

Now that we have our t-chart, let's put Q in. If we follow the arrows from Q in, we get G and H in, and J and O out. With O out, there are no more out slots for the 80s, so P must be in. But if we made that inference up front, then of course, that wouldn't be big news!

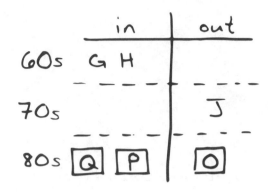

Now that we've followed the chain of inferences as far as we can take it, it's time to answer the question. A quick scan of the answers for what must be false—it's an EXCEPT question!—leads us to (B).

3. If neither K nor M is selected for the film project, how many of the five song selections are known with certainty?

   (A) one
   (B) two
   (C) three
   (D) four
   (E) five

Answer choice (E) is correct.

Tough question! There's a good chance you created your t-chart, filled in the new info, and then checked your Logic Chain for inferences. And…there were none. K and M have no rules associated with them. Easy enough, let's pick whichever answer says zero.

Which doesn't exist. It's easy to freak out at this point, but this is where pros separate themselves from everyone else. Instead of giving up, LSAT pros realize that they now have new information—there definitely is an inference yet to be made.

In a case like this, when the Logic Chain arrows don't lead to anything concrete, it's a good idea to consider the numerical distributions. We know that exactly two songs from the 80s must be selected. Therefore, one isn't selected. Added to K and M out, three of the four out slots are accounted for.

$$
\begin{array}{ccc}
60s: & 1 & 3 \\
70s: & 2 & 0 \\
80s: & 2 & 2
\end{array}
$$

MANHATTAN
PREP

From our numerical distributions we know that either three songs from the 60s and none from the 70s are in or that two songs from the 60s and one song from the 70s are in. Let's consider both of these hypotheticals.

With all three songs from the 60s in, we end up with the following:

Alternatively, when the distribution is two 60s/one 70s, since K and M are already out, J must be the 70s song. That forces G and Q out and, since there are now four elements out, the remaining songs must all be in:

When inferring which songs are in based on which songs are out, we should confirm that none of the rules are violated as a result. Scanning this hypothetical, we see that O and H can't be in together! Thus, this hypothetical doesn't work! We should cross it out so we don't accidentally use it in future questions, but now we know for sure that the first hypothetical is the only possibility when K and M are out. In it, we know which five elements are in and which four are out, so (E) is correct.

The key to answering this question was to focus on the numerical distributions.

4. If K is the only song from the 1970s selected for the film project, then which one of the following CANNOT be true?

   (A) O is not selected but F is selected.

   (B) Q is not selected but G is selected.

   (C) F is not selected but P is selected.

   (D) H is not selected but G is selected.

   (E) O is not selected but H is selected.

Answer choice (A) is correct.

If K is the only 70s song selected, J and M are not selected. Since we need exactly two 80s songs, this means we'll have exactly two 60s songs to get to five total songs.

We aren't able to infer much about which songs are selected—odd for a "must be false" question. What we do know, however, regards the number of songs from each subgroup, so we should expect the right answer to contradict the number of each subgroup selected: two 60s songs, one 70s song, and two 80s songs.

At this point, since we have a strong idea of what the correct answer is going to do, we should hop in and start looking.

In (A), O is out and F is in. Comparing that to our distributions, we don't know what the other 60s song is, but we do know that to have two 80s songs P and Q must both be selected. With Q in, G and H must also be selected. But that makes all three 60s songs selected.

(A) cannot be true since it violates the numerical distribution we inferred.

5. Which one of the following is a song that must be selected for the film project?

    (A) H
    (B) Q
    (C) F
    (D) P
    (E) G

Answer choice (D) is correct.

If you made this inference up front (like we did during The Big Pause), you could have answered this question very quickly.

Alternatively, if you had not made this inference, you could eliminate (A), (B), and (C) by looking back at the correct answer to question 1: G K M O P. Left with only (D) and (E), you could then test them to find that P must be selected.

6. If the condition that exactly two songs from the 1980s are selected for the project is replaced with the condition that at least one song from each time period must be selected, and if all other rules remain in effect, each of the following could be true EXCEPT:

    (A) Both O and P are selected.
    (B) Both G and H are selected.
    (C) Both P and Q are selected.
    (D) J, K, and M are selected.
    (E) F, P, and Q are selected.

Answer choice (E) is correct.

MANHATTAN
PREP

In this Rule Substitution question we need to include at least one song from each of the three subgroups. Since this is a "could be true EXCEPT" question, we're looking for the one answer choice that must be false.

We should look for an answer that will force a violation of the new rule—in other words, the right answer will prevent the selection of each element from at least one of the subgroups. We know that Q is our heavy hitter when it comes to forcing elements in and out, so let's first evaluate answers (C) and (E).

With answer (C), we can infer that along with P and Q, we'll need G and H, which forces out J and O, but we'll still be able to squeeze in a 70s song. Looks good, so let's move on to (E).

If F, P, and Q are all selected, then G and H must be selected as well. This brings the total to five, so no other songs are selected, and therefore all of the songs from the 70s are left out. This violates the new rule, so (E) must be false. While you may have simply started from answer (A) and worked your way down, notice how strategically choosing which answers to evaluate first can save you a lot of time.

Mismatch

The return of the mismatch! This twist showed up in our chapter on ordering twists.

As a refresher, there are two types of mismatch: 1) more elements than positions, or 2) more positions than elements.

In games where there are more elements than positions, either some elements will be left out or some positions will have more than one element.

In games where there are more positions than elements, either some positions will remain empty or some elements will show up more than once.

Here is a set of drills to bring this twist back into focus.

Drill It: Grouping with Mismatch

Vladimir is baking two kinds of cookies. Each cookie must have exactly three spices. He has eight spices to choose from—K, L, M, N, O, P, S, T—and each spice can only be used in one cookie. His spice selection adheres to the following conditions:

> M cannot be used in the same cookie with either O or T.
> If P is used in either cookie, then T is also used in the same cookie.
> If K is used in either cookie, then N is also used in the same cookie.
> Unless O is used in the same cookie as K, it is used in the same cookie as L.

1. Which of the following must be true?

   (A) M is not used in either cookie.

   (B) K is not used in either cookie.

   (C) S and P cannot be used in the same cookie.

   (D) N and P cannot be used in the same cookie.

   (E) M and P cannot be used in the same cookie.

2. Which of the following must be true?

   (A) Either N or K must be selected for one of the cookies.

   (B) Either M or S must be selected for one of the cookies.

   (C) Either K or P must be selected for one of the cookies.

   (D) Either L or M must be selected for one of the cookies.

   (E) Either P or T must be selected for one of the cookies.

Solutions: Grouping with Mismatch

Answer Key

1. E
2. A

Step 1: Picture the Game

Two groups and conditional rules? We should use the Logic Chain, right?

Wrong! There's a mismatch here between the number of slots (six) and the number of elements (eight). Two spices won't be used in these cookies (we're hoping they're Paprika and Turmeric), so we have three groups: Cookie 1, Cookie 2, and out. We should use our Closed Grouping Board: There are eight spices in this game, but we're using only six of them. We need two spaces in our diagram for the unused spices:

KLMNOPST

Step 2: Notate the Rules and Make Inferences

The first rule can be notated using two anti-chunks. The second rule applies whenever P is selected, so we should notate it as a conditional rule. The same applies to the third rule. The fourth rule is also a conditional rule: If O is not in a cookie with K, it is in one with L. And by contrapositive, if O is not in a cookie with L, it is in one with K.

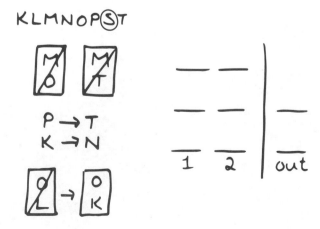

Step 3: The Big Pause

What can we infer? Let's look for rules that have elements in common. Our MT anti-chunk combined with the P rule tells us that M and P cannot be in the same cookie. O shows up in two rules, but no inferences surrounding them jump out.

Our last rule guarantees that O must be used in a cookie and must either be with K or L. If this is hard to see, consider where O would be if it isn't in a cookie with K. It would then need to be in a cookie with L.

Such rules—ones that force you to select one of two options—are great for building frames, so long as consequences follow from those selections. And since O is also in the first rule, we ought to look for additional consequences.

Since the rules and questions don't mention specific cookies, we can just pick whichever one to put our options of O together with K or L. Hence, in Frame 1 we'll put O and K together in a cookie and in Frame 2 we'll put O and L together in a cookie.

In Frame 1, we know that N will follow K into the first cookie, which is now full. And in Frame 2, M, P, and K are all excluded from the first cookie with O and L (M because of the OM anti-chunk; P and K because they each bring along another element for which there isn't room). In both frames, since M and P are mutually exclusive, at least one of them must not be in either cookie.

Step 4: Attack the Questions

1. Which of the following must be true?

    (A) M is not used in either cookie.

    (B) K is not used in either cookie.

    (C) S and P cannot be used in the same cookie.

    (D) N and P cannot be used in the same cookie.

    (E) M and P cannot be used in the same cookie.

Answer choice (E) is correct.

With frames, we should analyze the answers by seeing which one definitely shows up in both.

(A) and (B) are, generally, unlikely to be correct. While there are games where an element must be out, they're rare. Also, checking our frames, we know K can be in a cookie and there's an option for M.

(C) doesn't show up in our frames. Also, S is a floater. Let's defer, but we're not feeling good about this answer.

(D) pans out in Frame 1, but in Frame 2, there's no reason to believe that N and P couldn't be together in a cookie.

Down to the wire...and we're in luck! (E) restates an inference we made earlier.

2. Which of the following must be true?

    (A) Either N or K must be selected for one of the cookies.

    (B) Either M or S must be selected for one of the cookies.

    (C) Either K or P must be selected for one of the cookies.

    (D) Either L or M must be selected for one of the cookies.

    (E) Either P or T must be selected for one of the cookies.

Answer choice (A) is correct.

Here come those frames!

Frame 1

N __
O __
K __
1   2 | P/M
            Out

Frame 2

__ __
O __
L __
1   2 | P/M
            Out
M̸
P̸
K̸

While each answer names a pair of spices, the correct answer will name a pair that cannot both be out.

In neither frame is there enough room to put both N and K out. This means at least one of those spices is in, and so (A) is correct. Checking the other answers (not necessary, but often a confidence booster); each one includes either M or P. The reserved slot for M/P in the out group is what guaranteed that at least one of N or K must be in. Answers (B) through (E) don't have the same issue, since each includes M or P.

13

Practice Game 3: PT46, S4, G4

A reporter is trying to uncover the workings of a secret committee. The committee has six members—French, Ghauri, Hsia, Irving, Magnus, and Pinsky—each of whom serves on at least one subcommittee. There are three subcommittees, each having three members, about which the following is known:

> One of the committee members serves on all three subcommittees.
> French does not serve on any subcommittee with Ghauri.
> Hsia does not serve on any subcommittee with Irving.

17. If French does not serve on any subcommittee with Magnus, which one of the following must be true?

    (A) French serves on a subcommittee with Hsia.

    (B) French serves on a subcommittee with Irving.

    (C) Irving serves on a subcommittee with Pinsky.

    (D) Magnus serves on a subcommittee with Ghauri.

    (E) Magnus serves on a subcommittee with Irving.

18. If Pinsky serves on every subcommittee on which French serves and every subcommittee on which Ghauri serves, then which one of the following could be true?

    (A) Magnus serves on every subcommittee on which French serves and every subcommittee on which Ghauri serves.

    (B) Magnus serves on every subcommittee on which Hsia serves and every subcommittee on which Irving serves.

    (C) Hsia serves on every subcommittee on which French serves and every subcommittee on which Ghauri serves.

    (D) French serves on every subcommittee on which Pinsky serves.

    (E) Hsia serves on every subcommittee on which Pinsky serves.

19. If Irving serves on every subcommittee on which Magnus serves, which one of the following could be true?

    (A) Magnus serves on all of the subcommittees.
    (B) Irving serves on more than one subcommittee.
    (C) Irving serves on every subcommittee on which Pinsky serves.
    (D) French serves on a subcommittee with Magnus.
    (E) Ghauri serves on a subcommittee with Magnus.

20. Which one of the following could be true?

    (A) French serves on all three subcommittees.
    (B) Hsia serves on all three subcommittees.
    (C) Ghauri serves on every subcommittee on which Magnus serves and every subcommittee on which Pinsky serves.
    (D) Pinsky serves on every subcommittee on which Irving serves and every subcommittee on which Magnus serves.
    (E) Magnus serves on every subcommittee on which Pinsky serves, and Pinsky serves on every subcommittee on which Magnus serves.

21. Which one of the following must be true?

    (A) Ghauri serves on at least two subcommittees.
    (B) Irving serves on only one subcommittee.
    (C) French serves on a subcommittee with Hsia.
    (D) Ghauri serves on a subcommittee with Irving.
    (E) Magnus serves on a subcommittee with Pinsky.

22. Which one of the following must be true?

    (A) Every subcommittee has either French or Ghauri as a member.
    (B) Every subcommittee has either Hsia or Irving as a member.
    (C) No subcommittee consists of French, Magnus, and Pinsky.
    (D) Some committee member serves on exactly two subcommittees.
    (E) Either Magnus or Pinsky serves on only one subcommittee.

Solutions: PT46, S4, G4

Answer Key

17. C   20. D

18. C   21. E

19. B   22. D

Step 1: Picture the Game

We have three subcommittees, each with exactly three members, so let's set this up with a Closed Grouping Board. This is another game where the groups aren't labeled, but we're going to call them 1, 2, and 3, respectively, so it's easier to discuss!

Step 2: Notate the Rules and Make Inferences

It's important to note that "The committee has six members … each of whom serves on at least one subcommittee." It's also important to notice that there is a mismatch. There are nine positions and only six elements. Since we know that these secret subcommittees have three committee members each, we know some members must sit on more than one subcommittee.

The first rule controls the numerical distributions (i.e., how often the elements are going to repeat). If one member is assigned to all three subcommittees (the top spy? 007?), that leaves six spots left to fill with only five remaining members. If each of those remaining five members are assigned to only one subcommittee, there'd be one remaining spot left to fill. So, one of the committee members must be assigned to two subcommittees.

The next two rules create anti-chunks. More importantly, these limit which members can be assigned to all three subcommittees.

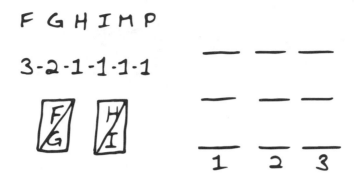

Let's consider which member could be our 007. As with Open Grouping games, anti-chunks affect the count. F has to go somewhere—"each of whom serves on at least one committee"—but if G were on all three subcommittees, F would have nowhere to go (and vice versa). Same goes for H and I. Therefore, none of F, G, H, or I can be the top spy, the one that shows up in all three groups. Who's left? Only M or P could be the member on all three subcommittees. Let's add that inference to our rules:

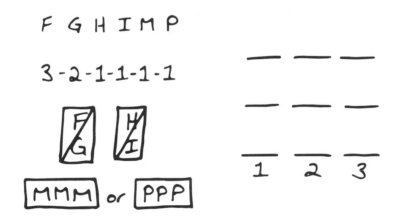

Step 3: The Big Pause

With our top spy limited to M or P, frames are worth exploring:

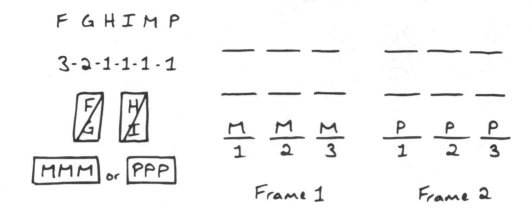

Since we know that F and G will be placed on different subcommittees, we can add them to the diagram. Be careful here! Once F and G are added to the diagram, we cannot place H and I with any confidence:

Note that we could have placed H and I into our diagram instead of F and G. That choice was arbitrary. The point is just that we cannot place both the FG anti-chunk and the HI anti-chunk. We have to choose.

Step 4: Attack the Questions

17. If French does not serve on any subcommittee with Magnus, which one of the following must be true?

   (A) French serves on a subcommittee with Hsia.
   (B) French serves on a subcommittee with Irving.
   (C) Irving serves on a subcommittee with Pinsky.
   (D) Magnus serves on a subcommittee with Ghauri.
   (E) Magnus serves on a subcommittee with Irving.

Answer choice (C) is correct.

MANHATTAN
PREP

This means that M cannot serve on all three subcommittees, and therefore P must do so. Since these answers all deal with people serving on the same subcommittee, and we know P is on each one, we should scan the answers to find the one with P, which is choice (C).

18. If Pinsky serves on every subcommittee on which French serves and every subcommittee on which Ghauri serves, then which one of the following could be true?

    (A) Magnus serves on every subcommittee on which French serves and every subcommittee on which Ghauri serves.
    (B) Magnus serves on every subcommittee on which Hsia serves and every subcommittee on which Irving serves.
    (C) Hsia serves on every subcommittee on which French serves and every subcommittee on which Ghauri serves.
    (D) French serves on every subcommittee on which Pinsky serves.
    (E) Hsia serves on every subcommittee on which Pinsky serves.

Answer choice (C) is correct.

The new condition indicates that P goes at least twice. We can narrow this down to two scenarios: P is on either two subcommittees or is on all three.

If P is on only the two subcommittees with F and G, though, then M is on all three. And that leaves only two spots for H and I to occupy, breaking our HI anti-chunk. Therefore, P must be the three-peater in this question and we're in the second frame:

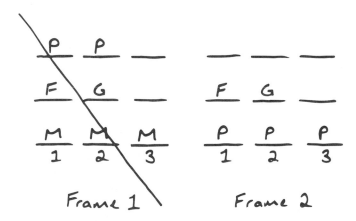

Comparing the answers to the frame, (C) is the only one that could work.

19. If Irving serves on every subcommittee on which Magnus serves, which one of the following could be true?

    (A) Magnus serves on all of the subcommittees.
    (B) Irving serves on more than one subcommittee.
    (C) Irving serves on every subcommittee on which Pinsky serves.
    (D) French serves on a subcommittee with Magnus.
    (E) Ghauri serves on a subcommittee with Magnus.

Answer choice (B) is correct.

The new condition precludes M from being the three-peater, since that would force I to also go three times. Filling the new information into Frame 2, we get:

Frame 2

With this information filled in, we have everything we need to get our answer.

20. Which one of the following could be true?

   (A) French serves on all three subcommittees.

   (B) Hsia serves on all three subcommittees.

   (C) Ghauri serves on every subcommittee on which Magnus serves and every subcommittee on which Pinsky serves.

   (D) Pinsky serves on every subcommittee on which Irving serves and every subcommittee on which Magnus serves.

   (E) Magnus serves on every subcommittee on which Pinsky serves, and Pinsky serves on every subcommittee on which Magnus serves.

Answer choice (D) is correct.

Let's tackle this question by eliminating the wrong answers and deferring on any answer choice we suspect is possible:

   (A), (B), and (C) all suggest that someone other than M or P is our three-peater.

   (D) is definitely possible—consider that P could three-peat!

   (E) suggests that both M and P three-peat, which wouldn't leave enough positions for our four remaining members.

21. Which one of the following must be true?

   (A) Ghauri serves on at least two subcommittees.

   (B) Irving serves on only one subcommittee.

   (C) French serves on a subcommittee with Hsia.

   (D) Ghauri serves on a subcommittee with Irving.

   (E) Magnus serves on a subcommittee with Pinsky.

Answer choice (E) is correct.

MANHATTAN
PREP

The key here is to defer on the first four choices, waiting until you have a home run choice—one that you know is definitely true. (E) must be true since either M or P is on all three subcommittees. This game is all about M and P!

22. Which one of the following must be true?

   (A) Every subcommittee has either French or Ghauri as a member.

   (B) Every subcommittee has either Hsia or Irving as a member.

   (C) No subcommittee consists of French, Magnus, and Pinsky.

   (D) Some committee member serves on exactly two subcommittees.

   (E) Either Magnus or Pinsky serves on only one subcommittee.

Answer choice (D) is correct.

Easy peasy! Since we figured out the numerical distribution in the very beginning, we already have the answer! Again, as on all unconditional "must be true" questions, defer on choices that seem less than certain and knock out the ones you know are wrong. Before running a scenario for each choice, keep moving until you've seen all the choices. Chances are that with a solid understanding of the game, one of them will stand out by referencing the inferences you make up front.

Special Positions & Special Connections

These two twists are rare and exotic, just as they are in Ordering games. With a special position, a game might require us to identify an individual team member as the "captain" or to label one of a group of projects as the "top priority." We can use a star or a simple abbreviation ("c" for captain) to notate the position and any rules associated with it.

A special connection will add a rule that connects a position or element in each group. For example, it might say that the captain of the football team must also be on the baseball team.

> Eight students applied to be one of four students chosen to compete on the spelling bee team in 2012, and the same eight applied again in 2013. In 2012, one member of the team won a gold medal at the regional competition. The gold-medal winner was automatically placed on the team again in 2013.

In this example, we have both a special position and a special connection. The special position is that of the gold-medal winner. The special connection is that a slot on the 2013 team is reserved for the gold-medal winner of 2012.

Practice Game 4: PT26, S1, G4

In each of two years exactly two of four lawmakers—Feld, Gibson, Hsu, and Ivins—and exactly two of three scientists—Vega, Young, and Zapora—will serve as members of a four-person panel. In each year, one of the members will be chairperson. The chairperson in the first year cannot serve on the panel in the second year. The chairperson in the second year must have served on the panel in the first year. Service on the panel must obey the following conditions:

> Gibson and Vega do not serve on the panel in the same year as each other.
> Hsu and Young do not serve on the panel in the same year as each other.
> Each year, either Ivins or Vega, but not both, serves on the panel.

19. Which one of the following could be the list of the people who serve on the panel in the first year?

    (A) Feld, Gibson, Vega, Zapora
    (B) Feld, Hsu, Vega, Zapora
    (C) Feld, Ivins, Vega, Zapora
    (D) Gibson, Hsu, Ivins, Zapora
    (E) Hsu, Ivins, Young, Zapora

20. If Vega is the chairperson in the first year, which one of the following is a pair of people who must serve on the panel in the second year?

    (A) Gibson and Young
    (B) Gibson and Zapora
    (C) Hsu and Ivins
    (D) Ivins and Young
    (E) Vega and Young

MANHATTAN
PREP

21. If Hsu is the chairperson in the first year, which one
    of the following could be the chairperson in the
    second year?

    (A) Feld
    (B) Gibson
    (C) Hsu
    (D) Ivins
    (E) Young

22. If Feld serves on the panel in a given year, any one of
    the following could serve on the panel that year
    EXCEPT:

    (A) Gibson
    (B) Hsu
    (C) Ivins
    (D) Vega
    (E) Young

23. If Ivins is the chairperson in the first year, which one
    of the following could be the chairperson in the
    second year?

    (A) Feld
    (B) Gibson
    (C) Hsu
    (D) Vega
    (E) Young

24. Which one of the following must be true?

    (A) Feld is on the panel in the second year.
    (B) Hsu is on the panel in the first year.
    (C) Ivins is on the panel in both years.
    (D) Young is on the panel in both years.
    (E) Zapora is on the panel in the second year.

Solutions: PT26, S1, G4

Answer Key

19. B	22. A
20. D	23. A
21. A	24. E

Step 1: Picture the Game

This game is a real doozy! The test writers reached deep into their well of twists to create this intimidating game. As this game contains subgroups, a special position, and a special connection, it'll serve as a nice capstone for the chapter.

Let's start by focusing on our task. We're asked to choose two of four lawmakers and two of three scientists to comprise a four-person panel in each of two years. At it's core, this is an In/Out Grouping game. However, with all these twists, we're better off using a modified Grouping Board. The Logic Chain would have difficulty tracking the chairperson, though we could probably rig something up, but trying to then also move between the two years would be too much.

But let's not throw out what we did for In/Out Grouping entirely—let's modify our Grouping Board to look more like a t-chart. Four are in and three are out. Adding a second row for year two simply acknowledges that we'll have to select both for Year 1 and Year 2.

We could reserve one slot for the chairperson, but that might create problems as we make inferences and hypotheticals. Let's leave it off the diagram and wait until we know who it is (or isn't) before writing it in:

Step 2: Notate the Rules and Make Inferences

Now that we're done with what's familiar, it's time to move on to figuring out how to notate the rules about the chairperson.

HINT: The key with oddball games and twists is to be creative and flexible. Don't put too much emphasis on the "perfect" way to notate a novel rule. Use your intuition and the skills you've developed and do something that makes sense to you in the moment. When the clock is running, a diagram that works and comes to you quickly is better than a "perfect" diagram that takes a while for you to develop.

MANHATTAN
PREP

So what do we need to know? First, there's a chairperson each year. Second, the chairperson in Year 1 is not on the panel in Year 2. Third, the chairperson for Year 2 is on the panel in Year 1.

I or V, but not both

Step 3: The Big Pause

Looking for rules that create divisions, the I/V exclusive option seems like a great place to build some frames. If we worry about Years 1 and 2, it'd quickly grow out of control. However, it's time to think like a pro—let's ignore the years for a moment. Instead, let's build frames around the potential panels that could be formed.

So, we'll start with a panel featuring I and another featuring V:

Lawmakers	Scientists				In		Out		
F G H I	V Y Z	—	—	—	—	I	V	—	—
(exactly 2)	(exactly 2)	—	—	—	—	V	I	—	—

G̶V̶

H̶Y̶

I or V, but not both

In Frame 1, with I selected and V not selected, the rules dictate that both Y and Z are selected. With Y selected, H is not selected, and so either F or G represents the final member of the panel.

In Frame 2, with V selected, neither I nor G is selected. Therefore, we know that both F and H must be selected. With H selected, Y is not selected, and that leaves Z for the final member of our four-person panel.

Our completed frames:

$$\begin{array}{cccc|ccc}
 & \text{In} & & & & \text{Out} & \\
 Y & Z & F/G & I & V & H & G/F \\
 F & H & Z & V & I & G & Y
\end{array}$$

These represent the only four-member panel combinations that satisfy the rules. But now that we have some control over the fundamental task, it's time to address the fact that this game involves two years of panel selection and a chairperson to be assigned.

If we extend our frames from one year to two, we find that the rule requiring that the chairperson in Year 1 not serve on the panel in Year 2 is actually quite helpful, since we cannot have the exact same four-member panel both years.

Our frames below take the panel selections above, assign them each to Year 1, and then consider which panel selections could occur in Year 2:

Frame 1

Year 1					Year 2		
F	H	Z	V	Y	Z	F/G	I

Frame 2

Year 1					Year 2		
Y	Z	F/G	I	Y	Z	G/F	I
				F	H	Z	V

While we haven't determined who the chairperson is in either frame, we know that the chairperson in Year 1 must be someone who does not serve on the panel in Year 2 and that the chairperson in Year 2 must be someone who served on the panel in Year 1. How fitting it is that while this game appeared very complex at the start, at this point, very few things are up in the air.

MANHATTAN
PREP

Step 4: Attack the Questions

19. Which one of the following could be the list of the people who serve on the panel in the first year?

    (A) Feld, Gibson, Vega, Zapora
    (B) Feld, Hsu, Vega, Zapora
    (C) Feld, Ivins, Vega, Zapora
    (D) Gibson, Hsu, Ivins, Zapora
    (E) Hsu, Ivins, Young, Zapora

Answer choice (B) is correct.

Frame 1! Simple as that.

20. If Vega is the chairperson in the first year, which one of the following is a pair of people who must serve on the panel in the second year?

    (A) Gibson and Young
    (B) Gibson and Zapora
    (C) Hsu and Ivins
    (D) Ivins and Young
    (E) Vega and Young

Answer choice (D) is correct.

Frame 1 again! Who must be on the panel in Year 2? Y, Z, and I must be on the panel in Year 2. Any combination of them would be correct, and answer choice (D) is the only answer choice with such a combination.

13

21. If Hsu is the chairperson in the first year, which one of the following could be the chairperson in the second year?

  (A) Feld
  (B) Gibson
  (C) Hsu
  (D) Ivins
  (E) Young

Answer choice (A) is correct

Wow! Frame 1 again. Who could serve on the panel in both years? F and Z.

22. If Feld serves on the panel in a given year, any one of the following could serve on the panel that year EXCEPT:

  (A) Gibson
  (B) Hsu
  (C) Ivins
  (D) Vega
  (E) Young

Answer choice (A) is correct.

In neither frame does F serve on a panel with G.

23. If Ivins is the chairperson in the first year, which one of the following could be the chairperson in the second year?

  (A) Feld
  (B) Gibson
  (C) Hsu
  (D) Vega
  (E) Young

Answer choice (A) is correct.

Frame 2 applies! Of the two possibilities for Year 2, the top row doesn't work because I serves in Year 2.

Frame 2

Year 1   Year 2

Y   Z   F/G   I | ~~Y~~   ~~Z~~   ~~G/F~~   ~~I~~

F   H   Z   V

Again, F and Z are the only two who can serve in both years and so could be the chairperson in Year 2. And, again, only one of them appears amongst the answer choices.

24. Which one of the following must be true?

  (A) Feld is on the panel in the second year.
  (B) Hsu is on the panel in the first year.
  (C) Ivins is on the panel in both years.
  (D) Young is on the panel in both years.
  (E) Zapora is on the panel in the second year.

Answer choice (E) is correct.

Both frames this time!

Frame 1

Year 1   Year 2

F   H   Z   V | Y   Z   F/G   I

Frame 2

Year 1   Year 2

Y   Z   F/G   I | Y   Z   G/F   I

F   H   Z   V

13

Conclusion

Another tough lesson. It seems like the LSAC has a room of people who just sit around all day, dreaming up ways to make logic games more complicated! However, if you look back at the chapter on ordering twists, you'll see that the twists almost completely overlap. In short, the LSAT really only has a handful of methods to bump up the difficulty on games. It's also important to recognize that our methods for handling the twists are largely the same across game types.

A quick review of what we've covered:

1. **Subgroups**
   - In In/Out Grouping games, we adapted our Logic Chain to keep the subgroups together. We also thought about numerical distributions—how many of each subgroup could be selected. For other Grouping games, we used subscripts if we found it difficult to keep track of our elements. We also used subgroups to help identify chunks and anti-chunks.

2. **Mismatch**
   - When there were more elements than positions, we kept track of the unselected elements in an out group or considered how many elements could be assigned to a position. When there were more positions than elements, we used numerical distributions to figure out how many repeaters there would be and how often they would go.

3. **Special positions/connections**
   - We notated any rules that dealt with the special positions/connections, and rephrased rules into more traditional types (such as a "can't be together" rule). For these, it was often helpful to defer identifying the special position/connection until after a hypothetical had been established.

A quick word of warning—the next Mixed Practice set is a doozy. We'd recommend putting this book down until at least tomorrow. Let this lesson sink in before moving on!

Set 4

In This Practice Set...

Mixed Practice: Set 4

Are you ready for this? Because we think you are.

The games in this Mixed Practice set are all hard. Some feature twists, while others don't. For those that don't, see if you can identify what makes these so challenging.

On this practice set, make sure to fully apply The Big Pause. We're not saying that each game will feature frames or game-breaking inferences, but there are a few in there.

For this reason, we recommend that, on your first play through this set, you take your time. Spend as long as you need to get through the game, and don't rush The Big Pause. Afterwards, compare your work against our QuickCheck. Review until you're sure that you could re-create our process on your own.

In a few days, revisit this Mixed Practice set and redo the games with the clock running. If you can finish these four games in under 35 minutes, nothing can stop you on test day!

Practice Game 1: PT36, S4, G4

An airline has four flights from New York to Sarasota—flights 1, 2, 3, and 4. On each flight there is exactly one pilot and exactly one co-pilot. The pilots are Fazio, Germond, Kyle, and Lopez; the co-pilots are Reich, Simon, Taylor, and Umlas. Each pilot and co-pilot is assigned to exactly one flight.

> The flights take off in numerical order.
> Fazio's flight takes off before Germond's, and at least one other flight takes off between their flights.
> Kyle is assigned to flight 2.
> Lopez is assigned to the same flight as Umlas.

19. Which one of the following pilot and co-pilot teams could be assigned to flight 1?

    (A) Fazio and Reich
    (B) Fazio and Umlas
    (C) Germond and Reich
    (D) Germond and Umlas
    (E) Lopez and Taylor

20. If Reich's flight is later than Umlas's, which one of the following statements cannot be true?

    (A) Fazio's flight is earlier than Simon's.
    (B) Kyle's flight is earlier than Reich's.
    (C) Kyle's flight is earlier than Taylor's.
    (D) Simon's flight is earlier than Reich's.
    (E) Taylor's flight is earlier than Kyle's.

21. If Lopez's flight is earlier than Germond's, which one of the following statements could be false?

    (A) Fazio's flight is earlier than Umlas's.
    (B) Germond is assigned to flight 4.
    (C) Either Reich's or Taylor's flight is earlier than Umlas's.
    (D) Simon's flight is earlier than Umlas's.
    (E) Umlas is assigned to flight 3.

22. What is the maximum possible number of different pilot and co-pilot teams, any one of which could be assigned to flight 4?

    (A) 2
    (B) 3
    (C) 4
    (D) 5
    (E) 6

23. If Simon's flight is later than Lopez's, then which one of the following statements could be false?

    (A) Germond's flight is later than Reich's.
    (B) Germond's flight is later than Taylor's.
    (C) Lopez's flight is later than Taylor's.
    (D) Taylor's flight is later than Reich's.
    (E) Umlas's flight is later than Reich's.

Practice Game 2: PT31, S1, G3

During a single week, from Monday through Friday, tours will be conducted of a company's three divisions— Operations, Production, and Sales. Exactly five tours will be conducted that week, one each day. The schedule of tours for the week must conform to the following restrictions:

> Each division is toured at least once.
> The Operations division is not toured on Monday.
> The Production division is not toured on Wednesday.
> The Sales division is toured on two consecutive days, and on no other days.
> If the Operations division is toured on Thursday, then the Production division is toured on Friday.

14. Which one of the following CANNOT be true of the week's tour schedule?

    (A) The division that is toured on Monday is also toured on Tuesday.
    (B) The division that is toured on Monday is also toured on Friday.
    (C) The division that is toured on Tuesday is also toured on Thursday.
    (D) The division that is toured on Wednesday is also toured on Friday.
    (E) The division that is toured on Thursday is also toured on Friday.

15. If in addition to the Sales division one other division is toured on two consecutive days, then it could be true of the week's tour schedule both that the

    (A) Production division is toured on Monday and that the Operations division is toured on Thursday
    (B) Production division is toured on Tuesday and that the Sales division is toured on Wednesday
    (C) Operations division is toured on Tuesday and that the Production division is toured on Friday
    (D) Sales division is toured on Monday and that the Operations division is toured on Friday
    (E) Sales division is toured on Wednesday and that the Production division is toured on Friday

16. If in the week's tour schedule the division that is toured on Tuesday is also toured on Friday, then for which one of the following days must a tour of the Production division be scheduled?

    (A) Monday
    (B) Tuesday
    (C) Wednesday
    (D) Thursday
    (E) Friday

17. If in the week's tour schedule the division that is toured on Monday is not the division that is toured on Tuesday, then which one of the following could be true of the week's schedule?

    (A) A tour of the Sales division is scheduled for some day earlier in the week than is any tour of the Production division.
    (B) A tour of the Operations division is scheduled for some day earlier in the week than is any tour of the Production division.
    (C) The Sales division is toured on Monday.
    (D) The Production division is toured on Tuesday.
    (E) The Operations division is toured on Wednesday.

18. If in the week's tour schedule the division that is toured on Tuesday is also toured on Wednesday, then which one of the following must be true of the week's tour schedule?

    (A) The Production division is toured on Monday.
    (B) The Operations division is toured on Tuesday.
    (C) The Sales division is toured on Wednesday.
    (D) The Sales division is toured on Thursday.
    (E) The Production division is toured on Friday.

Practice Game 3: PT12, S2, G3

Lara, Mendel, and Nastassia each buy at least one kind of food from a street vendor who sells only fruit cups, hot dogs, pretzels, and shish kebabs. They make their selections in accordance with the following restrictions:

> None of the three buys more than one portion of each kind of food.
> If any of the three buys a hot dog, that person does not also buy a shish kebab.
> At least one of the three buys a hot dog, and at least one buys a pretzel.
> Mendel buys a shish kebab.
> Nastassia buys a fruit cup.
> Neither Lara nor Nastassia buys a pretzel.
> Mendel does not buy any kind of food that Nastassia buys.

12. Which one of the following statements must be true?

    (A) Lara buys a hot dog.
    (B) Lara buys a shish kebab.
    (C) Mendel buys a hot dog.
    (D) Mendel buys a pretzel.
    (E) Nastassia buys a hot dog.

13. If the vendor charges $1 for each portion of food, what is the minimum amount the three people could spend?

    (A) $3
    (B) $4
    (C) $5
    (D) $6
    (E) $7

14. If the vendor charges $1 for each portion of food, what is the greatest amount the three people could spend?

    (A) $5
    (B) $6
    (C) $7
    (D) $8
    (E) $9

15. If Lara and Mendel buy exactly two kinds of food each, which one of the following statements must be true?

    (A) Lara buys a fruit cup.
    (B) Lara buys a hot dog.
    (C) Mendel buys a fruit cup.
    (D) There is exactly one kind of food that Lara and Mendel both buy.
    (E) There is exactly one kind of food that Lara and Nastassia both buy.

16. If Lara buys a shish kebab, which one of the following statements must be true?

    (A) Lara buys a fruit cup.
    (B) Mendel buys a fruit cup.
    (C) Nastassia buys a hot dog.
    (D) Nastassia buys exactly one kind of food.
    (E) Exactly one person buys a fruit cup.

17. Assume that the condition is removed that prevents a customer who buys a hot dog from buying a shish kebab but all other conditions remain the same. If the vendor charges $1 for each portion of food, what is the maximum amount the three people could spend?

    (A) $5
    (B) $6
    (C) $7
    (D) $8
    (E) $9

MANHATTAN
PREP

Practice Game 4: PT26, S1, G4

In each of two years exactly two of four lawmakers—Feld, Gibson, Hsu, and Ivins—and exactly two of three scientists—Vega, Young, and Zapora—will serve as members of a four-person panel. In each year, one of the members will be chairperson. The chairperson in the first year cannot serve on the panel in the second year. The chairperson in the second year must have served on the panel in the first year. Service on the panel must obey the following conditions:

> Gibson and Vega do not serve on the panel in the same year as each other.
> Hsu and Young do not serve on the panel in the same year as each other.
> Each year, either Ivins or Vega, but not both, serves on the panel.

19. Which one of the following could be the list of the people who serve on the panel in the first year?

    (A) Feld, Gibson, Vega, Zapora
    (B) Feld, Hsu, Vega, Zapora
    (C) Feld, Ivins, Vega, Zapora
    (D) Gibson, Hsu, Ivins, Zapora
    (E) Hsu, Ivins, Young, Zapora

20. If Vega is the chairperson in the first year, which one of the following is a pair of people who must serve on the panel in the second year?

    (A) Gibson and Young
    (B) Gibson and Zapora
    (C) Hsu and Ivins
    (D) Ivins and Young
    (E) Vega and Young

21. If Hsu is the chairperson in the first year, which one of the following could be the chairperson in the second year?

    (A) Feld
    (B) Gibson
    (C) Hsu
    (D) Ivins
    (E) Young

22. If Feld serves on the panel in a given year, any one of the following could serve on the panel that year EXCEPT:

    (A) Gibson
    (B) Hsu
    (C) Ivins
    (D) Vega
    (E) Young

23. If Ivins is the chairperson in the first year, which one of the following could be the chairperson in the second year?

    (A) Feld
    (B) Gibson
    (C) Hsu
    (D) Vega
    (E) Young

24. Which one of the following must be true?

    (A) Feld is on the panel in the second year.
    (B) Hsu is on the panel in the first year.
    (C) Ivins is on the panel in both years.
    (D) Young is on the panel in both years.
    (E) Zapora is on the panel in the second year.

QuickCheck: PT36, S4, G4

```
__  __  __  __   rstu
 1   K   3   4   FGKL
     2
```

```
┌─────┐
│ F __│ — G
└─────┘
```

```
┌───┐
│ u │
│ L │
└───┘
```

The Big Pause
- Hybrid game with 2 element sets that have their own rows.
- Both chunks are very limited.

Frames?
That FG rule takes up a lot of space. Thinking about it for a few seconds shows that there are only two possible splits for it, both which impact the uL chunk. It's ~~clobbering~~ framing time!

Frame 1
```
C  __ __ __ __ u
P   F  K  G  L
```

Frame 2
```
C  __ __ u __
P   F  K  L  G
```

19. (A)
    (B̶)
    (C̶)
    (D̶)
    (E̶)

20. Frame 2
```
   ( s + )  u   r
    F   K   L   G
```
    (A̶)
    (B̶)
    Ⓒ
    (D)
    (E)

21. Frame 2
    (A̶)
    (B̶)
    (C̶)
    Ⓓ
    (E̶)

22. Frame 1: │u/L│
    Frame 2: │r/s/t / G│ $\frac{1}{+3} = 4$
    (A)
    (B)
    Ⓒ
    (D)
    (E)

23. Frame 2
```
   ( r t )  u   s
    F   K   L   G
```
    (A̶)
    (B̶)
    (C̶)
    Ⓓ
    (E)

QuickCheck: PT31, S1, G3

O P S (min. 1)

$\overline{M}$ $\overline{T}$ $\overline{W}$ $\overline{Th}$ $\overline{F}$
Ø   P

S = 2, [SS]
$O_M \rightarrow P_F$
$P_F \rightarrow O_M$

The Big Pause
- Mismatch ordering with repeats
- S is most limited.
- Don't forget the conditional rule!

Frames?
We can build frames around the SS chunk since it removes that element from consideration. There are also consequences because of the exclusions.

Frames

1	S	S	O	P	O/P
2	P	S	S	O	O/P
3	P	O/P	S	S	O
4	P	O/P	O	S	S
	M	T	W	Th	F
	Ø		P		

14. (A) Frame 1
(B) Frame 2
(C)
(D)
(E)

15.
1	S	S	O	O/P	P	
2	P	S	S	O	O	Rule 4
3	P	P	S	S	O	
4	P	O/P	O	S	S	
	M	T	W	Th	F	

(A)
(B)
(C)
(D)
(E)

16. 3 | P | O | S | S | O |
| M | T | W | Th | F |

(A)
(B)
(C)
(D)
(E)

17.
2	P	S	S	O	
3	P	O	S	S	O/P
4	P	O	O	S	S
	M	T	W	Th	F

(A)
(B)
(C)
(D)
(E)

18.
2	P	S	S	O	
4	P	O	O	S	S

(A)
(B)
(C)
(D)
(E)

QuickCheck: PT12, S2, G3

F H P S

H = 1+
P = 1+

The Big Pause

- After cycling through rules twice, we should have most of the inferences.

Frames?

There's not a clear division here. We could frame around where the H goes, but there don't seem to enough consequences to make that worthwhile.

12. (A̶)
 (B̶)
 (C̶)
 Ⓓ
 (E)

13.
 (A)
 Ⓑ
 (C)
 (D)
 (E)

14.
 (A)
 Ⓑ
 (C)
 (D)
 (E)

15.
 Ⓐ
 (B)
 (C)
 (D)
 (E)

16.
 (A)
 (B)
 Ⓒ
 (D)
 (E)

17.
 H = 1+
 P = 1+

 max 4 b/w them from Rule 7

 L - 3 M - 3 N - 2
 3 + 4 = 7

 (A)
 (B)
 Ⓒ
 (D)
 (E)

MANHATTAN
PREP

QuickCheck: PT26, S1, G4

2/4 L: Ⓕ G H I
2/3 S: V Y Ⓩ

I				O		
L	L	S	S	L	L	S

Chairperson
$C_1 \rightarrow Out_2$
$C_2 \rightarrow In_1$

I or V, not both

The Big Pause

- Weird In/Out game with subgroups, but they tell us up front the distribution.
- Also weird because we have 2 years.
- Since this game is weird, we should move away from a Logic Chain.
- Watch out for special position & connection (chairperson rule).

Frames?

Yes, that I/V (but not both) rule creates a clear division. V also shows up in other rules, so there will be consequences. However, we're going to make frames around possible panels, not around complete, 2-year situations. We'll deal with those in the questions.

Frames

	I				O			
F/G	I	Y	Z	F/G	H	V	Year 1
L	L	S	S	L	L	S	
F	H	Z	V	I	G	Y	
L	L	S	S	L	L	S	
L	L	S	S	L	L	S	Year 2 Same options as above

19. (A̶) 1
    (B) Ⓑ
    (C̶) 3
    (D̶) scen (2L, 2S)
    (E̶) 2

20. Y1 F H Z Ⓥ | I G Y
    Y2 G/F I Z Y | F/G H V
    I Z Y
    (A)
    (B)
    (C)
    Ⓓ
    (E)

21. Y1 F Ⓗ Z V | I G Y
    Y2 F/G I Y Z | G/F H V
    F, Z
    Ⓐ
    (B)
    (C)
    (D)
    (E)

22. Frame 1: I Y Z
    Frame 2: H Z V   missing? G
    Ⓐ
    (B)
    (C)
    (D)
    (E)

23. Y1 F/G Ⓘ Y Z | G/F H V
    Y2 F H Z V | I G Y
    For Z
    Ⓐ
    (B)
    (C)
    (D)
    (E)

24. (A̶) prev work (20) | fyi - If we
    (B̶) prev work (23) | deferred on
    (C̶) prev work (20) | (A)-(D), (E)
    (D̶) prev work (20) | would have
    Ⓔ | jumped out
                         | of our frames

Chapter 14

Hybrid Games

In This Chapter...

Getting Familiar

Give yourself **10 minutes** to complete this game.

A photographer will take three photographs of a high school math team. The seven members of the team—P, R, S, T, V, W, and X—will each appear in exactly one of the photographs. There will be exactly one member in the first photograph, three members in the second photograph, and three members in the third photograph. The following conditions apply:

P does not appear in a later photo than does T or X.
R and S will appear in the same photograph together.
V and X will not be photographed together.

1. Which of the following could be the assignment of members to photographs?

   (A) Photo 1: V
       Photo 2: T, R, S
       Photo 3: P, W, X
   (B) Photo 1: V
       Photo 2: R, S
       Photo 3: P, T, W, X
   (C) Photo 1: V
       Photo 2: P, R, S
       Photo 3: T, W, X
   (D) Photo 1: P
       Photo 2: S, T, X
       Photo 3: R, V, W
   (E) Photo 1: P
       Photo 2: T, V, X
       Photo 3: R, S, W

2. Which of the following must be false?

   (A) W appears in photo 2.
   (B) T appears in photo 1.
   (C) P appears in photo 3.
   (D) V appears after X.
   (E) X appears after V.

3. If P is photographed with S, in how many different ways can all seven members be assigned to photographs?

   (A) one
   (B) two
   (C) three
   (D) four
   (E) five

4. If R is in an earlier photograph than X, how many different team members could be in the first photograph?

   (A) one
   (B) two
   (C) three
   (D) four
   (E) five

5. Which of the following pairs of assignments would determine the team members for each photograph?

   (A) V is in photo 1 and R is in photo 2.
   (B) V is in photo 1 and R is in photo 3.
   (C) P is in photo 1 and R is in photo 2.
   (D) P is in photo 1 and V is in photo 3.
   (E) W is in photo 1 and R is in photo 2.

6. If the rule that V and X will not be photographed together is replaced with a rule that V and X must be photographed together, each of the following could be true EXCEPT:

   (A) W appears in photo 1.
   (B) W appears in photo 2.
   (C) W appears in photo 3.
   (D) P appears in photo 2.
   (E) P appears in photo 3.

Hybrid Games

We are almost at the end of our journey through Logic Games, and, if we do say so ourselves, we've reached an impressive depth of understanding.

Let's go back to basics for a minute.

All games involve assigning elements to positions. Games are further defined by having these positions be in **order,** or by having these positions be in **groups** with one another.

Hybrid games are games that involve both ordering and grouping.

About 6% of games are Hybrids, and on average Hybrid games tend to fall on the higher end of the difficulty scale.

Why are Hybrid games more difficult? In general, it's not because they require more complicated inferences or because the problems require more layers of work out of us. It's typically because it's just more difficult for us to work with a variety of information than it is for us to work with a lot of the same type of information. An analogy can be made to juggling (we've moved on from spinning plates). Hybrid games are typically difficult in the same way that juggling tennis balls and bowling balls is more difficult than juggling just one or the other.

If you are nervous about juggling bowling balls and tennis balls, keep in mind that there is also a lot of good news to report about Hybrid games. Hybrid games don't tend to require the long chains of inferences that some other games do, such as Relative Ordering and In/Out Grouping games. For most games, if you can simply understand the rules clearly and use them efficiently, you will be fine.

Furthermore, you should feel like you are coming into this with a full head of steam, because you actually already know *everything* you need to know about Hybrid games. You know how to deal with all ordering and grouping issues that may come up. The key to Hybrid games success is going to be how you bring these various skills together.

We'll now look at how we'll bring things together in a bit more detail.

Order × Group (+ Assignment)

As mentioned above, the challenge of Hybrid games is that of bringing together, and organizing, a varied set of restrictions. Let's quickly look at the three primary issues for all Hybrid games.

Issue 1: Assignment

Rules of assignment describe a relationship between a specific element and a specific position (e.g., *X is assigned to the second group*). Every game involves assignment at some point.

Issue 2: Order

Rules of order relate elements to each other or to positions.

In general, we've been diagramming ordering rules in a horizontal plane, with earlier to the left and later to the right. We want to continue that habit for Hybrid games.

Issue 3: Group

Grouping rules relate elements to each other in terms of groups (e.g., *M and O are in different departments*).

We have diagrammed most every grouping rule on a vertical plane, and we want to continue that habit for Hybrid games.

Notating Hybrid Rules (You already know this.)

Let's use a very basic Hybrid game scenario to confirm our understanding of how we'd deal with these various types of rules. Imagine we were given the following:

> Eight people—M, N, O, P, Q, R, S, and T—will play in a total of four different tennis matches. The four matches will take place in order, and exactly two players will play in each match.

We have the order of the matches, and we are also grouping elements into pairs that will play together. For this basic scenario, we'd probably want to begin with a diagram that looks something like the framework we've used for some other Grouping games:

$$\begin{array}{cccc} \underline{\quad} & \underline{\quad} & \underline{\quad} & \underline{\quad} \\ \underline{\quad} & \underline{\quad} & \underline{\quad} & \underline{\quad} \\ 1 & 2 & 3 & 4 \end{array} \qquad \text{M N O P Q R S T}$$

We'll use the horizontal orientation to represent ordering rules and the vertical orientation to represent grouping rules.

Here are some common rules that may appear in a game like this one. These are all rules you've seen before, so you should be able to quickly picture how you would notate each of them. Check the notations on the next page (note that we didn't put any inferences in), marking any rules that might give you some trouble to remind yourself to review them later. Each set is to be diagrammed separately.

Sample Assignment Rules

M plays in the second game.
T does not play in the fourth game.
If P plays in the third game, R will not play in the first game.

Sample Grouping Rules

O plays against T.
P plays neither Q nor R.
If S plays M, N will play R.

Sample Ordering Rules

S plays at some point after N plays.
M plays before, but not immediately before, R does.
Q does not play before T.
P plays after N but before Q, or before N but after Q.

Rules That Combine Assignment, Ordering, and/or Grouping

If N is second, M must play later than N does.
If M does not play against T, M must play first.
T does not play last, nor does T play against P.

Suggested Notations

Assignment Rules

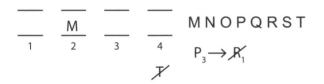

Grouping Rules

Ordering Rules

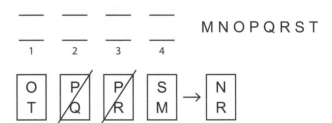

Combination Rules

Keep in mind that our diagrams above are only suggestions; depending on the game, writing some of those rules differently might be wise. We strongly encourage you to remain flexible. There is a subtle but significant difference between those who try to fit what they see on test day into what they are already comfortable with and those who are able to adapt their skills to the unique situations the exam provides. You will be in much better shape if you are in the latter category.

14

Let's look at the scenario for a slightly different Hybrid game:

> A building has three floors, numbered 1 to 3 from bottom to top. Six different companies—F, G, H, J,
> K, and L—are to occupy the building, and exactly two companies will go on each floor. The following
> conditions apply:
>
> G must be on a higher floor than K.
> H and F cannot be on the same floor.

Note that in this case it would make a lot more sense to think about the order vertically and the group horizontally.
We would then write out ordering rules in a vertical fashion and grouping rules in a horizontal fashion. An effective
diagram might look something like this:

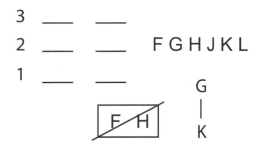

Even though this doesn't match what is typical, hopefully, you feel comfortable enough with your skills that you can
adapt your systems to match the unique characteristics of any game.

Hybrid Twists

Just like non-Hybrid Ordering and Grouping games, Hybrid games can be made more complicated through the
introduction of other game characteristics. You should already be familiar with each of these.

Subgroups

Subgroups are the most significant and challenging of the possible complications. The manner in which you deal with
them is going to be dependent primarily on how much information about them you are given. You want to think
about these subgroups as presenting two often overlapping but different challenges: Are the subgroups there to give
you additional information to juggle, or are they central to the inferences that you'll be expected to make by bringing
rules together?

Whenever possible, you want to represent subgroups in Hybrid games by using subscript. That way, the primary forms
of organization on your diagram—vertical and horizontal organization—are devoted to the two fundamental issues—
ordering and grouping. However, when the subgroups themselves are at the heart of the inferences to be made, you
may need to add another layer to show them more explicitly in the diagram.

14

To understand the difference between the situations that require these strategies, take a look at these two similar mini-game situations:

Six students—M and N from school X, O and P from school Y, and R and S from school Z—will appear in three dance routines. The routines will take place one at a time and in order. Each routine will involve two students, and each student will dance exactly once. The following conditions apply:

At least one student from school Y dances in the first routine.

No one from school Z performs in the third routine.

Two-person dance teams from three different schools—X, Y, and Z—will perform one at a time and in order during a recital. Six students—M, N, O, P, Q, and R—will perform. The following conditions apply:

The team from Z will not perform after the team from X performs.

O dances in the second performance.

P is from school Y.

Note that both mini games involve similar situations. We have six students performing in pairs in three different routines. However, in the first game, we know which school each student is from, but the students don't have to perform with their schoolmates. In the second game, the students perform in school teams, but we don't know which students are on which team, and the order of team performance is a primary issue.

For the first game, the subgroups are more clearly defined, and though they present challenges, they are not central to the inferences we're expected to make. Therefore, it will most likely be best to handle these subgroups using subscript. Here's a sample of how we could have laid out the diagram for the first game:

$$
\begin{array}{ccc}
\underline{} & \underline{} & \underline{} \\
\underline{Y} & \underline{} & \underline{} \\
1 & 2 & 3
\end{array}
\qquad
\begin{array}{l}
M_X\,N_X \\
O_Y\,P_Y \\
R_Z\,S_Z
\end{array}
$$

$$\require{cancel}\cancel{R}$$
$$\cancel{S}$$

We could also have written O/P in the bottom slot for group 1, since those are the only two students from school Y.

For the second game, both the order and the assignment of the teams are central to what we are expected to infer about the game. Furthermore, we don't have the benefit of knowing who is from each school ahead of time. Therefore, we want to integrate the subgroups into the base of our diagram. We can do this the same way that we did for 3D Ordering games: by adding an additional level to our diagram:

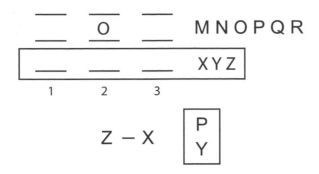

Mismatches

Like non-Hybrid games, Hybrid games can have the number of elements not equal the number of positions. All of the strategies you have learned for mismatch issues that appear in Ordering and Grouping games will serve you well.

Open Numbering

While many Hybrid games establish how many elements should go in each group, others are open. Apply the techniques and notations you learned with Open Grouping games.

Diagram Ambiguity

Because Hybrid games use ingredients from many other game types, at times your diagram for these games will be quite unusual. Don't be surprised if, for example, a large number of Relative Ordering rules leads you to a Tree diagram with grouped positions.

Hybrid games are the hardest games to fit into a category. Our teachers often disagree about whether a certain game is best categorized, for example, as a Hybrid game or as an Ordering game with a mismatch twist. Similarly, a 3D Grouping game may add in a small dash of order, making us wonder if it's a Hybrid game, even though the ordering of the elements may be almost irrelevant to how the game is played. This slipperiness is not important, since our goal is to picture the game and create a diagram that is useful; we're not scored on whether we can accurately categorize the game.

It is in these ambiguous moments that you must call upon your inner MacGyver!

Try It Again

Give yourself **10 minutes** to complete this game.

A photographer will take three photographs of a high school math team. The seven members of the team—P, R, S, T, V, W, and X—will each appear in exactly one of the photographs. There will be exactly one member in the first photograph, three members in the second photograph, and three members in the third photograph. The following conditions apply:

P does not appear in a later photo than does T or X.
R and S will appear in the same photograph together.
V and X will not be photographed together.

1. Which of the following could be the assignment of members to photographs?

    (A) Photo 1: V
        Photo 2: T, R, S
        Photo 3: P, W, X
    (B) Photo 1: V
        Photo 2: R, S
        Photo 3: P, T, W, X
    (C) Photo 1: V
        Photo 2: P, R, S
        Photo 3: T, W, X
    (D) Photo 1: P
        Photo 2: S, T, X
        Photo 3: R, V, W
    (E) Photo 1: P
        Photo 2: T, V, X
        Photo 3: R, S, W

2. Which of the following must be false?

    (A) W appears in photo 2.
    (B) T appears in photo 1.
    (C) P appears in photo 3.
    (D) V appears after X.
    (E) X appears after V.

3. If P is photographed with S, in how many different
   ways can all seven members be assigned to photographs?

   (A) one
   (B) two
   (C) three
   (D) four
   (E) five

4. If R is in an earlier photograph than X, how
   many different team members could be in the first
   photograph?

   (A) one
   (B) two
   (C) three
   (D) four
   (E) five

5. Which of the following pairs of assignments would
   determine the team members for each photograph?

   (A) V is in photo 1 and R is in photo 2.
   (B) V is in photo 1 and R is in photo 3.
   (C) P is in photo 1 and R is in photo 2.
   (D) P is in photo 1 and V is in photo 3.
   (E) W is in photo 1 and R is in photo 2.

6. If the rule that V and X will not be photographed
   together is replaced with a rule that V and X must be
   photographed together, each of the following could be
   true EXCEPT:

   (A) W appears in photo 1.
   (B) W appears in photo 2.
   (C) W appears in photo 3.
   (D) P appears in photo 2.
   (E) P appears in photo 3.

How Did You Do?

Answer Key

1. C	4. C
2. B	5. E
3. A	6. E

Step 1: Picture the Game

We have three groups in which to place seven members. A bit unusually, the groups are not of equal size.

Scanning the scenario and rules, we see references to group—*R and S will appear in the same photograph*—as well as one to order—*P does not appear in a later photo than does T or X.*

We'll set up a board with the right number of slots for each group.

Step 2: Notate the Rules and Make Inferences

The first rule is the most difficult to master. Be careful not to assume that this rule means—as it would in a standard Relative Ordering game—that P comes before T and X. In this game, P, T, and X could all be in the same group!

However, since photo 1 has only one slot, T or X in that group would require P to come after. Thus, we can restrict T and X from photo 1. Similarly, since R and S must be together, they cannot be in photo 1's single slot.

Compare your work to our diagram:

Step 3: The Big Pause

While we have not inferred a great deal, it's clear that this game will involve a lot of work with all three rules. The relative rule involves almost half of the elements, the chunk fills up most of either photo 2 or 3, and any time we place either member of the VX anti-chunk, we'll know the other member is not in that group.

We should remind ourselves of what the Relative Ordering rule really means. In our own words, the rule means that P can come at the same time as, or earlier than, T and X. It can't come after either of them.

There's no strong reason to consider framing this game. The only candidate for a division is the placement of the RS chunk. However, there are no significant consequences.

Finally, the only element not mentioned in a rule is W—circle it!

Step 4: Attack the Questions

1. Which of the following could be the assignment of members to photographs?

    (A) Photo 1: V
        Photo 2: T, R, S
        Photo 3: P, W, X
    (B) Photo 1: V
        Photo 2: R, S
        Photo 3: P, T, W, X
    (C) Photo 1: V
        Photo 2: P, R, S
        Photo 3: T, W, X
    (D) Photo 1: P
        Photo 2: S, T, X
        Photo 3: R, V, W
    (E) Photo 1: P
        Photo 2: T, V, X
        Photo 3: R, S, W

Answer choice (C) is correct.

Rule 1 eliminates answer (A).
Rule 2 eliminates answer (D).
Rule 3 eliminates answer (E).

We're done with rules, but we have two answers left! We could spin through the rules one more time to see if a rule is used twice—sometimes rules are used more than once—but that will lead nowhere in this case, so let's review the scenario to look for rules embedded there. It turns out that answer (B) violates the numerical arrangement of the groups.

2. Which of the following must be false?

    (A) W appears in photo 2.

    (B) T appears in photo 1.

    (C) P appears in photo 3.

    (D) V appears after X.

    (E) X appears after V.

Answer choice (B) is correct.

Can W appear in group 2? There seems to be plenty of room to place the chunk and the anti-chunk, as well as to make sure that P doesn't fall after either T or X.

Can T appear in group 1? No! We already figured that out. Answer choice (B) is our answer.

3. If P is photographed with S, in how many different ways can all seven members be assigned to photographs?

    (A) one

    (B) two

    (C) three

    (D) four

    (E) five

Answer choice (A) is correct.

If P is with S, we have a super chunk: PRS! Since P can't come after T and X, the chunk must be placed in photo 2 to leave room for T and X in photo 3. That means that V must be in photo 1 to avoid violating the VX anti-chunk. W clearly goes in the remaining slot in photo 3. Every element is placed—how satisfying!—and the answer is (A).

4. If R is in an earlier photograph than X, how many different team members could be in the first photograph?

    (A) one

    (B) two

    (C) three

    (D) four

    (E) five

Answer choice (C) is correct.

If R is earlier than X, we know that the RS chunk must be in photo 2 and X must be in photo 3. Let's write out the remaining elements to the side: P T V W. We'll use that to organize our thinking. Hopefully, our control of the rules is strong enough that we can visualize the rest:

$$
\begin{array}{ccc}
 & \underline{\text{R}} & \underline{} \qquad \text{P T V W} \\
\underline{} & \underline{\text{S}} & \underline{\text{X}} \\
1 & 2 & 3
\end{array}
$$

We can eliminate answer (E) since there are only four elements left to place.

Let's next figure out how many of the four we can place in photo 1: Can P go in photo 1? Sure! T and X would come after it and there's room for V in photo 2.

Can T? No! We can never place T in 1.

Can V? There's no problem with that. We can fit P into photo 2 and T into photo 3. The anti-chunk is safe as well.

Can W? Yes! P and T can go in photo 3 along with X, leaving the last slot in photo 2 for V.

5. Which of the following pairs of assignments would determine the team members for each photograph?

    (A) V is in photo 1 and R is in photo 2.
    (B) V is in photo 1 and R is in photo 3.
    (C) P is in photo 1 and R is in photo 2.
    (D) P is in photo 1 and V is in photo 3.
    (E) W is in photo 1 and R is in photo 2.

Answer choice (E) is correct.

In questions that ask you to **determines positions,** we recommend an answer that sets a nonconstrained element and also triggers a rule. W is our stray, so let's start there.

(E) is the only answer with W, and W in photo 1 fills up that group. R in photo 2 brings S along, which leaves P for either that last slot in 2 or to go into 3 (we're focusing on P because it's restricted). If P is in the second photo, though, V and X end up together in photo 3, which violates a rule. Therefore, PTX must make up photo 3, with V in photo 2. We have our answer!

6. If the rule that V and X will not be photographed together is replaced with a rule that V and X must be photographed together, each of the following could be true EXCEPT:

(A) W appears in photo 1.

(B) W appears in photo 2.

(C) W appears in photo 3.

(D) P appears in photo 2.

(E) P appears in photo 3.

Answer choice (E) is correct.

If V and X must be photographed together, we have two chunks. Let's sketch out what we have, along with the remaining elements and relationships, remembering that these are not yet in an established order:

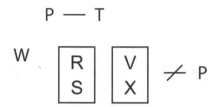

Why have we notated P before T? Well, remember that originally we had to leave open the possibility that P would appear together with both T and X. Now that we have V and X together, this is no longer a possibility. While P and X could be together, P cannot appear together with T, because the chunks leave only one empty spot left for each photo. Thus, P must precede T.

With this sketched out, we can see that (A) through (D) are all possibilities, while (E) is not.

Drill It: Hybrid Setups

Diagram each of the following scenarios to stretch your brain, then answer the question that follows. Be warned, these are extremely difficult. Check your diagram and answer against the solutions after each one.

1. As part of a simulation, the MPrep volunteer firefighter battalion is planning its response to a hypothetical fire that has spread to all floors of a four-story building, the floors of which are labeled 1–4, from bottom to top. There are exactly eight firefighters in the battalion—Farber, Gilad, Jorgeson, Mary, Nielsen, Palomba, Shinners, and Tyrrell. Each firefighter is assigned to exactly one floor, and each floor is assigned at least one firefighter, in accordance with the following requirements:

> Two floors are assigned exactly one firefighter.
> The first floor has more firefighters assigned to it than any other floor.
> Gilad and Mary are assigned to the same floor.
> Tyrrell, who is the sole firefighter assigned to his floor, is assigned to a higher floor than both Jorgeson and Palomba.
> At most one firefighter is assigned to a higher floor than Farber.

If Nielsen is assigned to the same floor as Shinners, and Jorgeson is assigned to the same floor as Mary, which of the following is a complete and accurate list of the floors to which Tyrrell can be assigned?

(A) 2

(B) 2, 4

(C) 3, 4

(D) 2, 3, 4

(E) 1, 2, 3, 4

2. Bettelheim Motors will produce three differently priced models of a certain car. Each model will come with two of the following options—Q, R, S, T, U, and W—and each model will come in only one of three colors—green, hot red, or indigo. The options and colors of all the cars must adhere to the following rules:

> No color or option is used on more than one car model.
> W and R are used on the same model.
> The green model is more expensive than the hot red one.
> T is not used on the least expensive model.
> The indigo car is more expensive than the car that includes R.

If the car that has S is more expensive than the one that has T, how many different arrangements of colors and options are possible?

(A) one

(B) two

(C) three

(D) four

(E) five

3. The Geekettes are planning a series of four consecutive concerts in exactly four states—Maryland, Nebraska, Oregon, and Pennsylvania. One concert will be played in each state. The Geekettes will invite three opening bands—R, S, and T—each of which will play at exactly one concert. Three special guests—F, G, and H—will also be invited, and each will also appear at exactly one concert. Either an opening band or a special guest must appear at each concert. The following rules apply to the concert schedule:

> At most, one opening band will appear at any concert.
> No more than one special guest will appear at any concert.
> S will play either in Maryland or Pennsylvania.
> The third concert is in Oregon.
> R will not play at a concert after the one that H plays at.
> No opening act will play between the concerts at which R and T play.
> There will be no opening act at the concert immediately following the concert at which F plays.

If T plays in Pennsylvania at the Geekettes's last concert of the tour, each of the following cannot be true EXCEPT:

(A) G plays at the second concert, held in Maryland, with no opening band.

(B) G plays at the third concert, held in Oregon, with S as the opening band.

(C) G plays at the first concert, held in Maryland, with S as the opening band.

(D) G plays at the second concert, held in Nebraska, with R as the opening band.

(E) G plays at the first concert, held in Oregon, with R as the opening band.

Solutions: Hybrid Setups

Answer Key

1. D
2. D
3. C

Diagrams

Note that your diagram might look somewhat different from ours. Keep an eye out for differences that indicate that you made a mistake. If you like how we notated a rule, then steal our style!

1. As part of a simulation, the MPrep volunteer firefighter battalion is planning its response to a hypothetical fire that has spread to all floors of a four-story building, the floors of which are labeled 1–4, from bottom to top. There are exactly eight firefighters in the battalion—Farber, Gilad, Jorgeson, Mary, Nielsen, Palomba, Shinners, and Tyrrell. Each firefighter is assigned to exactly one floor, and each floor is assigned at least one firefighter, in accordance with the following requirements:

> Two floors are assigned exactly one firefighter.
> The first floor has more firefighters assigned to it than any other floor.
> Gilad and Mary are assigned to the same floor.
> Tyrrell, who is the sole firefighter assigned to his floor, is assigned to a higher floor than both Jorgeson and Palomba.

At most one firefighter is assigned to a higher floor than Farber.

Answer choice (D) is correct.

MANHATTAN
PREP

If M and J are together, we have a GMJ chunk, which must go on 1. P must join them because all the other elements—T, F, and the NS chunk—have some restriction that keeps them from going to the first floor. This is the situation:

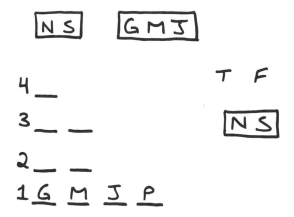

T can go on 4, with F on 3 and the NS chunk on 2. T can go on 3 with F above on 4 and NS on 2. T can go on 2, with F on 4 and NS on 3.

2. Bettelheim Motors will produce three differently priced models of a certain car. Each model will come with two of the following options—Q, R, S, T, U, and W—and each model will come in only one of three colors—green, hot red, or indigo. The options and colors of all the cars must adhere to the following rules:

> No color or option is used on more than one car model.
> W and R are used on the same model.
> The green model is more expensive than the hot red one.
> T is not used on the least expensive model.
> The indigo car is more expensive than the car that includes R.

If the car that has S is more expensive than the one that has T, how many different arrangements of colors and options are possible?

(A) one

(B) two

(C) three

(D) four

(E) five

Answer choice (D) is correct.

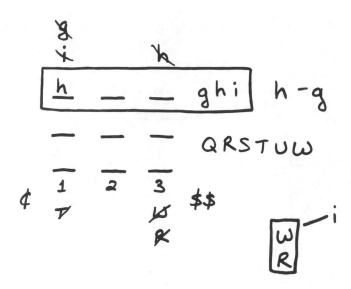

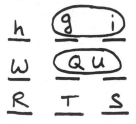

We've used the relative price as the base, with model 1 being the least expensive and model 3 being the most expensive.

If T must come before S, they must go in models 2 and 3, respectively. The WR chunk must go in model 1. All that's left are Q and U, which are floating between models 2 and 3. From the rules, model 1 will always have to be H, since both I and G have to come after something. So G and I are also floating between slots 2 and 3. Thus, we have this:

There are four ways to arrange what's still undetermined:

    1) GI & QU
    2) IG & QU
    3) GI & UQ
    4) IG & UQ

3. The Geekettes are planning a series of four consecutive concerts in exactly four states—Maryland, Nebraska, Oregon, and Pennsylvania. One concert will be played in each state. The Geekettes will invite three opening bands—R, S, and T—each of which will play at exactly one concert. Three special guests—F, G, and H—will also be invited, and each will also appear at exactly one concert. Either an opening band or a special guest must appear at each concert. The following rules apply to the concert schedule:

> At most, one opening band will appear at any concert.
> No more than one special guest will appear at any concert.
> S will play either in Maryland or Pennsylvania.
> The third concert is in Oregon.
> R will not play at a concert after the one that H plays at.
> No opening act will play between the concerts at which R and T play.
> There will be no opening act at the concert immediately following the concert at which F plays.

If T plays in Pennsylvania at the Geekettes's last concert of the tour, each of the following cannot be true EXCEPT:

(A) G plays at the second concert, held in Maryland, with no opening band.
(B) G plays at the third concert, held in Oregon, with S as the opening band.
(C) G plays at the first concert, held in Maryland, with S as the opening band.
(D) G plays at the second concert, held in Nebraska, with R as the opening band.
(E) G plays at the first concert, held in Oregon, with R as the opening band.

Answer choice (C) is correct.

If T and P go in slot 4, there are two options for R. Either we can place it in slot 2, with no opening act in 3 (thus, an "X"), or we can place R in slot 3. This is a particularly tough question, since it requires some time-consuming framing. If you didn't frame this, try it now before looking at the diagram below.

In the rxt frame, s must go in 1 with m, leaving n for 2. And with no opening act in 3, F must go in 2 as well. We cannot have another x in slot 3 and H cannot go in 1 since it would be ahead of r.

In the rt frame, there must be no opening act in slot 2 in order to fit in F (into slot 1). s is forced into 1, with m; n is left to be the location for 2. We cannot have two x's in slot 2, so we need to place G there. (H cannot go in 2, since it would be ahead of R.) This leaves X and H to fill slots 3 and 4 in some order.

The frames look like this:

Armed with those, it's easy to eliminate answers. Tough question!

Conclusion

On Hybrid games, we once again see these two themes:

1. Flexibility

- There are many ways that ordering and grouping rules can be combined. Set up your board, but be ready to adapt.

2. Rule mastery

- If you don't own the rules, they will own you!

MANHATTAN
PREP

Practice Game 1: PT36, S4, G4

Give yourself **17 minutes** for both of these games (or, if you're feeling confident, just 16).

An airline has four flights from New York to Sarasota—flights 1, 2, 3, and 4. On each flight there is exactly one pilot and exactly one co-pilot. The pilots are Fazio, Germond, Kyle, and Lopez; the co-pilots are Reich, Simon, Taylor, and Umlas. Each pilot and co-pilot is assigned to exactly one flight.

> The flights take off in numerical order.
> Fazio's flight takes off before Germond's, and at least one other flight takes off between their flights.
> Kyle is assigned to flight 2.
> Lopez is assigned to the same flight as Umlas.

19. Which one of the following pilot and co-pilot teams could be assigned to flight 1?

    (A) Fazio and Reich
    (B) Fazio and Umlas
    (C) Germond and Reich
    (D) Germond and Umlas
    (E) Lopez and Taylor

20. If Reich's flight is later than Umlas's, which one of the following statements cannot be true?

    (A) Fazio's flight is earlier than Simon's.
    (B) Kyle's flight is earlier than Reich's.
    (C) Kyle's flight is earlier than Taylor's.
    (D) Simon's flight is earlier than Reich's.
    (E) Taylor's flight is earlier than Kyle's.

21. If Lopez's flight is earlier than Germond's, which one of the following statements could be false?

    (A) Fazio's flight is earlier than Umlas's.
    (B) Germond is assigned to flight 4.
    (C) Either Reich's or Taylor's flight is earlier than Umlas's.
    (D) Simon's flight is earlier than Umlas's.
    (E) Umlas is assigned to flight 3.

22. What is the maximum possible number of different pilot and co-pilot teams, any one of which could be assigned to flight 4?

    (A) 2
    (B) 3
    (C) 4
    (D) 5
    (E) 6

23. If Simon's flight is later than Lopez's, then which one of the following statements could be false?

    (A) Germond's flight is later than Reich's.
    (B) Germond's flight is later than Taylor's.
    (C) Lopez's flight is later than Taylor's.
    (D) Taylor's flight is later than Reich's.
    (E) Umlas's flight is later than Reich's.

Here's a devilish one that we've written for this game:

24. Each of the following, if substituted for the rule that Fazio's flight takes off before Germond's, and at least one other flight takes off between their flights, would have the same effect on the assignment of pilots and co-pilots EXCEPT:

    (A) Fazio's flight takes off first.
    (B) Fazio's flight takes off before Kyle's.
    (C) Fazio's and Germond's flights do not take off consecutively, but Fazio's and Kyle's do.
    (D) Lopez's flight takes off immediately before or immediately after Germond's.
    (E) Lopez's flight takes off after Fazio's, and at least one other flight takes off between their flights.

14

Solutions: PT36, S4, G4

Answer Key

19. A	22. C
20. C	23. D
21. D	24. C

Step 1: Picture the Game

We have to place each pilot and co-pilot into one of four ordered groups. Classic Hybrid! To keep the pilots and co-pilots differentiated, we have several options. Perhaps the cleanest is to assign each subgroup its own row, and, for added clarity, use lower- and uppercase. However, using subscripts would also work.

Step2: Notate the Rules and Make Inferences

Compare your diagram against ours. It is crucial to infer the position of F! Once that's done, we actually don't need to refer to the FG chunk rule.

Step 3: The Big Pause

The bottom row of this diagram is well-developed, and there's actually only one rule—the uL chunk—that we still can put to use during the questions.

The questions will surely play on the top row and the G/L uncertainty.

We could circle all the co-pilots other than u.

Step 4: Attack the Questions

19. Which one of the following pilot and co-pilot teams could be assigned to flight 1?

    (A) Fazio and Reich
    (B) Fazio and Umlas
    (C) Germond and Reich
    (D) Germond and Umlas
    (E) Lopez and Taylor

Answer choice (A) is correct.

It's rare to start a game without an Orientation question. Rare, but not unheard of.

Our inferences tell us that F must be assigned to flight 1, and between the two answers with F, only (A) is possible. Umlas must fly with Taylor, ruling (B) out.

20. If Reich's flight is later than Umlas's, which one of the following statements cannot be true?

    (A) Fazio's flight is earlier than Simon's.
    (B) Kyle's flight is earlier than Reich's.
    (C) Kyle's flight is earlier than Taylor's.
    (D) Simon's flight is earlier than Reich's.
    (E) Taylor's flight is earlier than Kyle's.

Answer choice (C) is correct.

If r flies after u, we know that u must be in 3 with L, and r must be in 4 with G. The two remaining co-pilots—s and t—come in some order in the first two groups.

(C) is impossible since K is second, and that is the latest that t could go.

21. If Lopez's flight is earlier than Germond's, which one of the following statements could be false?

    (A) Fazio's flight is earlier than Umlas's.
    (B) Germond is assigned to flight 4.
    (C) Either Reich's or Taylor's flight is earlier than Umlas's.
    (D) Simon's flight is earlier than Umlas's.
    (E) Umlas is assigned to flight 3.

Answer choice (D) is correct.

L must come third, along with u; G must be in the fourth group. Since we're looking for what could be false, we'll keep our eyes out for answers referring to the elements that are left: r, s, and t.

Answers (A) through (C) must be true. (D) could be false, since s could be in 4.

22. What is the maximum possible number of different pilot and co-pilot teams, any one of which could be assigned to flight 4?

    (A) 2
    (B) 3
    (C) 4
    (D) 5
    (E) 6

Answer choice (C) is correct.

It's best just to count them out. L can be last, and only with u. G can be last with any co-pilot but u. Lu, Gr, Gs, and Gt = four groups.

23. If Simon's flight is later than Lopez's, then which one of the following statements could be false?

    (A) Germond's flight is later than Reich's.
    (B) Germond's flight is later than Taylor's.
    (C) Lopez's flight is later than Taylor's.
    (D) Taylor's flight is later than Reich's.
    (E) Umlas's flight is later than Reich's.

Answer choice (D) is correct.

This new condition forces L and u into group 3, and s and G into group 4. We're unsure where r and t will go between groups 1 and 2, thus (D) could be false.

And finally, the devilish one that we've written for this game:

24. Each of the following, if substituted for the rule that Fazio's flight takes off before Germond's, and at least one other flight takes off between their flights, would have the same effect on the assignment of pilots and co-pilots EXCEPT:

    (A) Fazio's flight takes off first.
    (B) Fazio's flight takes off before Kyle's.
    (C) Fazio's and Germond's flights do not take off consecutively, but Fazio's and Kyle's do.
    (D) Lopez's flight takes off immediately before or immediately after Germond's.
    (E) Lopez's flight takes off after Fazio's, and at least one other flight takes off between their flights.

Answer choice (C) is correct.

MANHATTAN
PREP

There's never been an EXCEPT Equivalent Rule question on the LSAT, but we figured we should keep you on your toes! Remember to start by identifying the effects of the original rule.

F having to come at least two spots before G is what forced F into group 1. With K taking up the pilot group in group 2, there was no choice but to have F in group 1 and G and L floating between groups 3 and 4.

Keep in mind that the four wrong answers will be valid equivalents:

(A) forces F into group 1; thus G and L will have to take the last two pilot groups. Eliminate.

(B) accomplishes the same thing as (A).

(C) looks good, but this rule would allow an otherwise prohibited arrangement: G K F L! We have our answer.

For review's sake, let's look at the rest:

(D) requires that the only two consecutive pilot groups—3 and 4—be occupied by G and L, leaving F to take group 1.

(E) is tricky. Just as the original rule pulled L into either group 3 or 4 even though it wasn't explicitly mentioned, this rule pulls G back there by forcing F into the first position.

Practice Game 2: PT29, S3, G4

Exactly six piano classes are given sequentially on Monday: two with more than one student and four with exactly one student. Exactly four females—Gimena, Holly, Iyanna, and Kate—and five males—Leung, Nate, Oscar, Pedro, and Saul—attend these classes. Each student attends exactly one class. The following must obtain:

Iyanna and Leung together constitute one class.
Pedro and exactly two others together constitute one class.
Kate is the first female, but not the first student, to attend a class.
Gimena's class is at some time after Iyanna's but at sometime before Pedro's.
Oscar's class is at some time after Gimena's.

20. Which one of the following students could attend the first class?

(A) Holly
(B) Leung
(C) Oscar
(D) Pedro
(E) Saul

21. Which one of the following is a complete and accurate list of classes any one of which could be the class Gimena attends?

(A) the fourth, the fifth
(B) the fourth, the sixth
(C) the second, the fourth, the fifth
(D) the third, the fifth, the sixth
(E) the second, the third, the fourth

22. Which one of the following pairs of students could be in the class with Pedro?

    (A) Gimena and Holly
    (B) Holly and Saul
    (C) Kate and Nate
    (D) Leung and Oscar
    (E) Nate and Saul

23. If Oscar and Pedro do not attend the same class as each other, then which one of the following could be true?

    (A) Gimena attends the fifth class.
    (B) Holly attends the third class.
    (C) Iyanna attends the fourth class.
    (D) Nate attends the fifth class.
    (E) Saul attends the second class.

24. Suppose the condition that Oscar attends a class after Gimena is replaced with the condition that Oscar attends a class before Gimena and after Kate. If all the other conditions remain the same, then which class must Holly attend?

    (A) the second
    (B) the third
    (C) the fourth
    (D) the fifth
    (E) the sixth

Solutions: PT29, S3, G4

Answer Key

20. E   23. D

21. A   24. E

22. B

Step 1: Picture the Game

This is not an easy game to picture. We have six groups, four of which are "groups" of one. We can't easily set up a Closed Board, as we don't know which groups have only one member.

When you're unsure of how to arrange a game, be sure you've scanned the rules. The final three rules are all Relative Ordering ones, so we can actually set this game up as a Tree! This is particularly possible because we know one of the two groups that has more than one member, but even if that were not so, we could still work with a Tree arrangement and keep in mind that some elements will be grouped together.

We have six groups and nine elements. Since four groups will have only one member, that leaves five elements to fill the two other groups. There's only one way to break five into two groups that each have at least two members: 2 and 3.

Step 2: Notate the Rules and Make Inferences

> *Iyanna and Leung together constitute one class.*
> *Pedro and exactly two others together constitute one class.*

The first rule settles who forms one of the two groups. We'll chunk them together. And the second rule gives us the other group! We'll notate these like so:

> *Kate is the first female, but not the first student, to attend a class.*

That's a rather complex rule, and it's unclear how it fits into what we have so far. Let's skip it for a moment and see if it's easier to incorporate later. Since we're building a Tree, it makes sense to reorder the rules.

> *Gimena's class is at some time after Iyanna's but at sometime before Pedro's.*
> *Oscar's class is at some time after Gimena's.*

The last two rules fit in nicely with what we've learned so far. It's important not to assume that O is necessarily part of the P group.

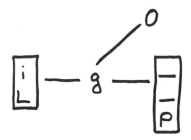

Let's swing back to the third rule about K. She's the first female, but not the first student. This means that she's before the IL chunk, and that a male must come before her. We can notate that like this:

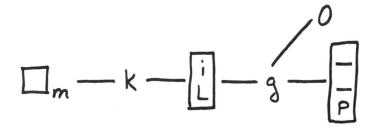

This leaves us with a lot of uncertainty. Let's try to reduce that uncertainty by identifying who's left. We haven't yet placed H, N, or S. We have three open slots, so it seems like a good fit. Right?

Watch out! We don't have to put O in the P group, but we can. Thus, while we'll need to use H, N, or S to complete that group, we may end up using only one of them. With regard to the first empty position, we'll need a male, meaning it's either N or S.

And, since H is a female, we know that she comes at some point after K. Our final diagram looks like this:

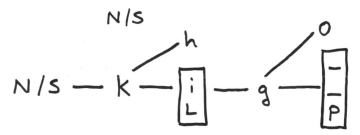

The N/S that is floating above the diagram is to remind us that whichever one of the pair that is not placed first will need to be placed somewhere—possibly in the P group, though not necessarily.

Step 3: The Big Pause

As is often the case with Tree diagrams, a lot of the game's original uncertainty is settled. We still don't know who will fill the P group, and the positions of N and S are still in the air (although we know that one will be filling the mandatory male slot before K).

It seems that a lot will ride on the P group's membership. Let's keep an eye on that.

Step 4: Attack the Questions

20. Which one of the following students could attend the first class?

   (A) Holly
   (B) Leung
   (C) Oscar
   (D) Pedro
   (E) Saul

Answer choice (E) is correct.

Everyone but N or S must come after someone.

21. Which one of the following is a complete and accurate list of classes any one of which could be the class Gimena attends?

   (A) the fourth, the fifth
   (B) the fourth, the sixth
   (C) the second, the fourth, the fifth
   (D) the third, the fifth, the sixth
   (E) the second, the third, the fourth

Answer choice (A) is correct.

At least three groups (N/S, K, IL) must precede G, so the earliest it could go is fourth. P's class must follow G, so G can't go last.

22. Which one of the following pairs of students could be in the class with Pedro?

   (A) Gimena and Holly
   (B) Holly and Saul
   (C) Kate and Nate
   (D) Leung and Oscar
   (E) Nate and Saul

Answer choice (B) is correct.

MANHATTAN
PREP

We know that the membership must be drawn from the three strays N/S, O, and H (we can consider N/S one element in this case, since one has to come first). We can thus eliminate any answer that has any element outside those. We're down to (B) and (E). (E) illegally puts both N and S into the P class, leaving no male student to attend class before K.

23. If Oscar and Pedro do not attend the same class as each other, then which one of the following could be true?

    (A) Gimena attends the fifth class.

    (B) Holly attends the third class.

    (C) Iyanna attends the fourth class.

    (D) Nate attends the fifth class.

    (E) Saul attends the second class.

Answer choice (D) is correct.

The new condition tells us that O is not in the P group, meaning that N/S and H must be. If we need to, we can sketch out the situation:

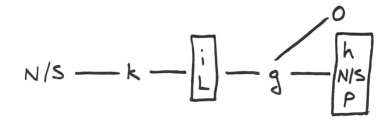

Since this is a "could be true" question, we can expect that the answer will play on the uncertainty around the order of the final two classes.

Answers (A) through (C) must be false. (D) puts N in the P class, which definitely could come before O's class.

24. Suppose the condition that Oscar attends a class after Gimena is replaced with the condition that Oscar attends a class before Gimena and after Kate. If all the other conditions remain the same, then which class must Holly attend?

    (A) the second

    (B) the third

    (C) the fourth

    (D) the fifth

    (E) the sixth

Answer choice (E) is correct.

We have to switch the order of O and G. It shouldn't take long to sketch this out:

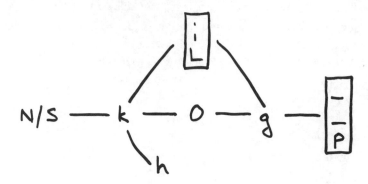

But now we've placed O out of the running for filling P's group. That means that H and the other of N/S must go there, leaving H to attend the final class.

MANHATTAN
PREP

Mini Sets
5.1 & 5.2

In This Practice Set...

Mixed Practice: Mini Sets 5.1 & 5.2

Let's bring together all of the strategies, insight, and experience you've now accumulated. Somewhere between framing, utilizing previous work, dealing with twists, and your freshly upgraded instincts, you'll find an approach uniquely adapted to solving each of the following games.

We've created two mini sets to give you an opportunity to consider pacing under some very challenging circumstances. The games are tough, so this is an opportunity to make tough decisions. Do not give yourself more than the suggested time. Cut bait when you need to and aim to get to the last question.

Mini Set 5.1

On this mini-set, give yourself **20 minutes to complete both games.**

Practice Game 1: PT37, S3, G3

A total of six books occupies three small shelves—one on the first shelf, two on the second shelf, and three on the third shelf. Two of the books are grammars—one of Farsi, the other of Hausa. Two others are linguistics monographs—one on phonology, the other on semantics. The remaining two books are novels—one by Vonnegut, the other by Woolf. The books' arrangement is consistent with the following:

There is at least one novel on the same shelf as the Farsi grammar.
The monographs are not both on the same shelf.
The Vonnegut novel is not on the same shelf as either monograph.

12. Which one of the following could be an accurate matching of the bookshelves to the books on each of them?

(A) first shelf: Hausa grammar
second shelf: semantics monograph, Vonnegut novel
third shelf: Farsi grammar, phonology monograph, Woolf novel

(B) first shelf: semantics monograph
second shelf: Farsi grammar, Vonnegut novel
third shelf: Hausa grammar, phonology monograph, Woolf novel

(C) first shelf: Vonnegut novel
second shelf: phonology monograph, Farsi grammar
third shelf: Hausa grammar, semantics monograph, Woolf novel

(D) first shelf: Woolf novel
second shelf: phonology and semantics monographs
third shelf: Farsi and Hausa grammars, Vonnegut novel

(E) first shelf: Woolf novel
second shelf: Farsi grammar, Vonnegut novel
third shelf: Hausa grammar, phonology and semantics monographs

13. Which one of the following CANNOT be true?

    (A) A grammar is on the first shelf.
    (B) A linguistics monograph is on the same shelf as the Hausa grammar.
    (C) A novel is on the first shelf.
    (D) The novels are on the same shelf as each other.
    (E) Neither linguistics monograph is on the first shelf.

14. Which one of the following must be true?

    (A) A linguistics monograph and a grammar are on the second shelf.
    (B) A novel and a grammar are on the second shelf.
    (C) At least one linguistics monograph and at least one grammar are on the third shelf.
    (D) At least one novel and at least one grammar are on the third shelf.
    (E) At least one novel and at least one linguistics monograph are on the third shelf.

15. If both grammars are on the same shelf, which one of the following could be true?

    (A) The phonology monograph is on the third shelf.
    (B) A novel is on the first shelf.
    (C) Both novels are on the second shelf.
    (D) The Farsi grammar is on the second shelf.
    (E) The phonology monograph is on the first shelf.

16. Which one of the following must be true?

    (A) A linguistics monograph is on the first shelf.
    (B) No more than one novel is on each shelf.
    (C) The Farsi grammar is not on the same shelf as the Hausa grammar.
    (D) The semantics monograph is not on the same shelf as the Woolf novel.
    (E) The Woolf novel is not on the first shelf.

17. If the Farsi grammar is not on the third shelf, which one of the following could be true?

    (A) The phonology monograph is on the second shelf.
    (B) The Hausa grammar is on the second shelf.
    (C) The semantics monograph is on the third shelf.
    (D) The Vonnegut novel is on the third shelf.
    (E) The Woolf novel is on the second shelf.

18. If the Hausa grammar and the phonology monograph are on the same shelf, which one of the following must be true?

    (A) The phonology monograph is on the third shelf.
    (B) The Vonnegut novel is on the second shelf.
    (C) The semantics monograph is on the second shelf.
    (D) The semantics monograph is on the first shelf.
    (E) The Woolf novel is on the third shelf.

Practice Game 2: PTB, S2, G4

Zeno's Unfinished Furniture sells exactly five types of furniture—footstools, hutches, sideboards, tables, and vanities. Irene buys just four items, each of a different type, and each made entirely of one kind of wood—maple, oak, pine, or rosewood. The following conditions govern Irene's purchases:

Any vanity she buys is maple.
Any rosewood item she buys is a sideboard.
If she buys a vanity, she does not buy a footstool.
If Irene buys a footstool, she also buys a table made of the same wood.
Irene does not buy an oak table.
Exactly two of the items she buys are made of the same kind of wood as each other.

19. Which one of the following could be an accurate list of the items Irene buys?

    (A) maple footstool, maple hutch, rosewood sideboard, maple table
    (B) oak hutch, rosewood sideboard, pine table, oak vanity
    (C) rosewood hutch, maple sideboard, oak table, maple vanity
    (D) pine footstool, rosewood sideboard, pine table, maple vanity
    (E) maple footstool, pine hutch, oak sideboard, maple table

20. If Irene buys one item made of rosewood and two items made of maple, then which one of the following pairs could be two of the items she buys?

    (A) a rosewood sideboard and an oak footstool
    (B) an oak hutch and a pine sideboard
    (C) an oak hutch and a maple table
    (D) a maple sideboard and a maple vanity
    (E) a maple hutch and a maple table

21. Which one of the following is a complete and accurate list of all the woods any footstool that Irene buys could be made of?

    (A) maple, oak
    (B) maple, pine
    (C) maple, rosewood
    (D) maple, oak, pine
    (E) maple, oak, pine, rosewood

22. Suppose Irene buys a footstool. Then which one of the following is a complete and accurate list of items any one of which she could buy in maple?

    (A) footstool, hutch, sideboard, table, vanity
    (B) footstool, hutch, sideboard, table
    (C) footstool, hutch, sideboard
    (D) footstool, hutch
    (E) footstool

23. Which one of the following CANNOT be the two items Irene buys that are made of the same wood as each other?

    (A) footstool, hutch
    (B) hutch, sideboard
    (C) hutch, table
    (D) sideboard, vanity
    (E) table, vanity

24. If Irene does not buy an item made of maple, then each of the following must be true EXCEPT:

    (A) Irene buys a footstool.
    (B) Irene buys a pine hutch.
    (C) Irene buys a rosewood sideboard.
    (D) Irene buys exactly one item made of oak.
    (E) Irene buys exactly two items made of pine.

Mini Set 5.2

Before taking on this mini set, consider what went well—and what didn't—in Mini Set 5.1. On this next set, give yourself **20 minutes to complete both games.**

Practice Game 1: PT36, S4, G3

Gutierrez, Hoffman, Imamura, Kelly, Lapas, and Moore ride a bus together. Each sits facing forward in a different one of the six seats on the left side of the bus. The seats are in consecutive rows that are numbered 1, 2, and 3 from front to back. Each row has exactly two seats: a window seat and an aisle seat. The following conditions must apply:

> Hoffman occupies the aisle seat immediately behind Gutierrez's aisle seat.
> If Moore occupies an aisle seat, Hoffman sits in the same row as Lapas.
> If Gutierrez sits in the same row as Kelly, Moore occupies the seat immediately and directly behind Imamura's seat.
> If Kelly occupies a window seat, Moore sits in row 3.
> If Kelly sits in row 3, Imamura sits in row 1.

14. Which one of the following could be true?

 (A) Imamura sits in row 2, whereas Kelly sits in row 3.
 (B) Gutierrez sits in the same row as Kelly, immediately and directly behind Moore.
 (C) Gutierrez occupies a window seat in the same row as Lapas.
 (D) Moore occupies an aisle seat in the same row as Lapas.
 (E) Kelly and Moore both sit in row 3.

15. If Lapas and Kelly each occupy a window seat, then which one of the following could be true?

 (A) Moore occupies the aisle seat in row 3.
 (B) Imamura occupies the window seat in row 3.
 (C) Gutierrez sits in the same row as Kelly.
 (D) Gutierrez sits in the same row as Moore.
 (E) Moore sits in the same row as Lapas.

16. If Moore sits in row 1, then which one of the following must be true?

 (A) Hoffman sits in row 2.
 (B) Imamura sits in row 2.
 (C) Imamura sits in row 3.
 (D) Kelly sits in row 1.
 (E) Lapas sits in row 3.

17. If Kelly occupies the aisle seat in row 3, then each of the following must be true EXCEPT:

 (A) Gutierrez sits in the same row as Imamura.
 (B) Hoffman sits in the same row as Lapas.
 (C) Lapas occupies a window seat.
 (D) Moore occupies a window seat.
 (E) Gutierrez sits in row 1.

18. If neither Gutierrez nor Imamura sits in row 1, then which one of the following could be true?

 (A) Hoffman sits in row 2.
 (B) Kelly sits in row 2.
 (C) Moore sits in row 2.
 (D) Imamura occupies an aisle seat.
 (E) Moore occupies an aisle seat.

Practice Game 2: PT29, S3, G4

Exactly six piano classes are given sequentially on Monday: two with more than one student and four with exactly one student. Exactly four females—Gimena, Holly, Iyanna, and Kate—and five males—Leung, Nate, Oscar, Pedro, and Saul—attend these classes. Each student attends exactly one class. The following must obtain:

Iyanna and Leung together constitute one class.
Pedro and exactly two others together constitute one class.
Kate is the first female, but not the first student, to attend a class.
Gimena's class is at some time after Iyanna's but at sometime before Pedro's.
Oscar's class is at some time after Gimena's.

20. Which one of the following students could attend the first class?

    (A) Holly
    (B) Leung
    (C) Oscar
    (D) Pedro
    (E) Saul

21. Which one of the following is a complete and accurate list of classes any one of which could be the class Gimena attends?

    (A) the fourth, the fifth
    (B) the fourth, the sixth
    (C) the second, the fourth, the fifth
    (D) the third, the fifth, the sixth
    (E) the second, the third, the fourth

22. Which one of the following pairs of students could be in the class with Pedro?

    (A) Gimena and Holly
    (B) Holly and Saul
    (C) Kate and Nate
    (D) Leung and Oscar
    (E) Nate and Saul

23. If Oscar and Pedro do not attend the same class as each other, then which one of the following could be true?

    (A) Gimena attends the fifth class.
    (B) Holly attends the third class.
    (C) Iyanna attends the fourth class.
    (D) Nate attends the fifth class.
    (E) Saul attends the second class.

24. Suppose the condition that Oscar attends a class after Gimena is replaced with the condition that Oscar attends a class before Gimena and after Kate. If all the other conditions remain the same, then which class must Holly attend?

    (A) the second
    (B) the third
    (C) the fourth
    (D) the fifth
    (E) the sixth

QuickCheck: PT37, S3, G3

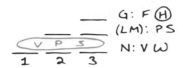

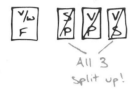

G: F (H)
(LM): PS
N: V W

All 3
split up!

The Big Pause

- The last two rules overlap in talking about monographs.
- H is a stray.

Frames?

V, P, and S all have to be split up, taking up one slot in each group. Since this fills up one group and half of another, there will be consequences, so we should build frames around these three!

Frames

①
W
H F
V (PS)
1 2 3

②
W
(F H)
P/S V S/P
1 2 3

③
H W
P S F V
P S V
1 2 3

12. (A) 3
(B) (B)
(C) 1
(D) 2
(E) 2

13. (A) frames!
(B)
(C)
(D)
(E)

14. (A) Frame 1
(B) Frame 1
(C) Frame 3
(D)
(E) Frame 3

15. Frame 3
H
W F
(P S) V
1 2 3
(A)
(B)
(C)
(D)
(E)

16. (A) Frame 1
(B) Frame 3
(C) Frame 3
(D) Frame 3
(E)

17. Frame 2
W
F H
P/S V S/P
1 2 3
(A)
(B)
(C)
(D)
(E)

18. Frame 1 or 2
W
H F
V P S
1 2 3 ①
W
F H
S V P
1 2 3 ②
(A)
(B)
(C)
(D)
(E)

QuickCheck: PTB, S2, G4

I: F Ⓗ S T V
w: m o p r

m o p r _ _ _ _ _ |unbought
F Ⓗ S T V _ _ _ _ _ |

V → $\boxed{\underset{V}{m}}$

r → $\boxed{\underline{S}}$

V → F̷

F → V

F_w → T_w

T → $\boxed{\not{P̸}}$

Ex 2 same w

The Big Pause

- An In/Out game with characteristics, so we can't use a Logic Chain.
- There's a lot going on with the rules.
- Better notice the difference between first and second rules.

Frames?

The third rule creates a division. Since putting a single item out results in the rest being in, we should build two frames around V/F being in, and the other being out.

Frames

① $\quad$ ø̸ $\quad$ ϕ̸
$\quad \underset{V}{m} \ \underline{H} \ \underline{S} \ \underline{T} \ | \ F$

② $\quad$ ø̸ø̸ $\quad$ ϕ̸
$\quad \boxed{\overset{m/p}{} \ne \overset{m/p}{}}$
$\quad \underline{F} \ \underline{H} \ \underline{S} \ \underline{T} \ | \ \underline{V}$

---

19. (A) 6
    (B) 1
    (C) 2
    (D) 3
    (E) Ⓔ

20. F1 $\ \underset{V}{m} \ \overset{m/p}{H} \ \underset{S}{r} \ \overset{m/p}{T} \ \Big| \ F$
    F2 $\ \underset{F}{m} \ \overset{m/p}{H} \ \underset{S}{r} \ \overset{m}{T} \ \Big| \ \underline{V}$

    (A)
    (B)
    Ⓒ
    (D)
    (E)

21. Frame 2 – m/p
    (A)
    Ⓑ
    (C)
    (D)
    (E)

22. Frame 2
    F, T, H, S
    (A)
    Ⓑ
    (C)
    (D)
    (E)

23. Ⓐ
    (B)
    (C) ⎫
    (D) ⎬ fyi–all others work
    (E) ⎭ $\quad$ in Frame 1

24. Frame 2
    $\ \underset{F}{p} \ \overset{o \ne r}{H} \ \underset{S}{r} \ \overset{p}{T} \ \Big| \ \underline{V}$

    (A)
    Ⓑ
    (C)
    (D)
    (E)

QuickCheck: PT36, S4, G3

G H I K L M

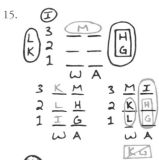

```
      ┌───┐
      │ H │
      │ G │
      └───┘
3  ___ ___   G̶
2  ___ ___
1  ___ ___   H̶
    W   A
```

$M_A \rightarrow \boxed{L\ H}$

$\boxed{K\ G} \rightarrow \boxed{\begin{matrix} M \\ I \end{matrix}}$

$K_W \rightarrow M_3$

$K_3 \rightarrow I_1$

The Big Pause

- There are a lot of moving pieces in this game, so a clear diagram is important.
- K shows up in a lot of rules.

Frames?

The HG chunk only has two possible positions, but there won't be many consequences. The other rules are all conditional, so it looks like this is a back-end game.

---

14. (A̶) 5
(B̶) 1 + 3
(C̶) 1
(D̶) 2
Ⓔ

15.
```
        ⎛ I ⎞                        ┌───┐
   ⎛L⎞  ⎝   ⎠  ⟨  M  ⟩               │ H │
   ⎝K⎠ 3 ___  ___                    │ G │
       2 ___  ___                    └───┘
       1 ___  ___
          W    A
```

```
3  K   M      3  M   I
2  L   H      2  K   H
1  I   G      1  L   G
   W   A         W   A
                 ┌─────┐
                 │ K G │
                 └─────┘
```

Ⓐ
(B)
(C)
(D)
(E)

16.
```
        ┌───┐
        │ H │
        │ G │
        └───┘
3  ⟨L⟩   H      K̶
2  ⟨I⟩   G
1   M    K      M
    W    A
```

(A̶)
(B̶)
(C̶)
Ⓓ
(E)

17.
```
3  ⟨L⟩   K
2  ⟨M⟩   H
1   I    G
    W    A
```
Look for LM answers

(A)
Ⓑ
(C)
(D)
(E)

18.
```
            ⎛M⎞  ┌───┐  ⟨L?⟩
            ⎝I⎠  │ H │
                 │ G │
                 └───┘
 K̶       3  ___   H     K̶ (Rule 5)
⎛M⎞  2  ___   G
⎝I⎠impossible  1  ⟨  K  ⟩  G̶  I̶
            W    A
```

(A̶)
(B̶)
Ⓒ
(D)
(E)

QuickCheck: PT29, S3, G4

F: G H I K
m: l n o p s

‾ ‾ ‾ ‾ ‾ ‾   4-1 student ✓
1 2 3 4 5 6   2-2+ students ✓

[l/I] [=/P] — 2 w/2+

1+
(lnops) — K< G
          H
          I

n/s — K< H (s/n)
        [l/I] — G < [=/P]
                    O

The Big Pause

- Mismatch Ordering that ends up being a Relative Ordering game.
- Subgroups seem to just matter for the third rule; with that in the Tree, we can more or less forget about it.

Frames?

We'll rarely make frames in a Relative Ordering game, and this is no exception.

20. n or s
   (A)
   (B)
   (C)
   (D)
   Ⓔ

21. Before: 3 must
   After: 1 must
      ↳ O could be with P
      4th or 5th

   Ⓐ
   (B)
   (C)
   (D)
   (E)

22. O, H, N, S
   (A̶)
   Ⓑ
   (C)
   (D)
   (E)

23.

n/s-K—[l/I]-G< [n/s H P]
                O

   (A̶)
   (B̶)
   (C̶)
   Ⓓ
   (E)

24.

n/s—K—O—G—[l/I] [n/s H P]
1   2   5   6

   (A)
   (B)
   (C)
   (D)
   Ⓔ

LG Chapter 15

Conclusion

In This Chapter...

Conclusion

You've made it! You've put in countless hours studying hypothetical scenarios about cat washings and toy trucks, figuring out better ways to notate conditional rules, and generally drawing your way into becoming a better lawyer. So…

What can possibly go wrong?

Professional athletes talk about the importance of a positive mind-set, the importance of being able to "picture" victory or success. That's all well and good, and envisioning success is very helpful, but we at Manhattan Prep find it more comforting to go into the exam with a positive attitude *and* with eyes wide open to everything that could possibly go wrong. With that said, let's start this chapter by running through a list of…

The Five Most Common Pitfalls to Avoid on Test Day

5. You forget that each question is worth only one point.

For all but a handful of us, missing a few questions will not make or break our games section. However, it's easy to spend three minutes on one question, miss it (or not), and allow it to distract you from the rest of the section, and thus cause you to score significantly worse than you otherwise would have.

Make sure that you don't overinvest time or energy in any one question. Develop guidelines for when you will force yourself to move on. For many students, a useful gauge is two attempts. If, after two different approaches, you are still unable to unlock a question, you should take an educated guess and move on. This should work out to you moving on at about 1:20 (none of your approaches should be such that, when they do work, they take any more than a minute). If you're short on time, skip questions that will probably be time-consuming. You know the usual suspects: Equivalent Rule questions or unconditional "could be true" questions with dense answer choices.

Overinvesting time on difficult questions is one of the most common mistakes that test-takers make, and nearly everyone who doesn't prepare for this issue will suffer from it at some point during the exam. The bad news is that you can't just tell yourself not to overinvest time and expect that to work. We all have a tendency to get lost in our work, especially when we are engrossed in games, and you only need to get lost once or twice to significantly and negatively impact your overall performance.

The good news is that this is a fairly easy issue to remedy with training and practice. Make sure that you take your practice exams (especially those final ones) as realistically as possible and that you develop habits for moving on. If you get in the habit of giving yourself extra time in your practice, it increases the likelihood that you will waste time on the real exam. If you can make moving on a habitual decision, rather than a conscious one, your chances of going astray on the real exam will be minimized. If this is a significant issue for you, it may be worth your while to time individual questions for a while. Monitoring your activity for the final few exams will be helpful in setting your internal clock.

Now, let's move on to the next common issue…

4. You have made a mistake or failed to understand something important about the game.

Oh, each element can be used more than once! Oh, there may be slots that are not used! Oh, I misconstrued that conditional statement! Oh, I misread what my notation was meant to stand for!

The vast majority of test-takers will make mistakes or miss significant characteristics for at least one of the four games that they see. Even though the design of the exam tempts us into thinking that it is the fastest and most clever test-takers who perform the best, in reality we know that those top scorers are also deliberate and accurate. If you can avoid making significant mistakes or omissions on test day, you will have an advantage over other test-takers.

These significant mistakes and omissions commonly occur in the first three minutes of the game. Unfortunately, often you won't realize you have any issues until you are two or three problems in—until you get an unconditional "could be true" question, say, and not only can you not figure out what could be true, you have significant trouble seeing that many of the answers must be false. Or, you get a conditional question, run through your chain of inferences, arrive at an answer, don't see it among the answer choices, and at that point realize you made a mistake in how you read one of the rules.

We've all been there. And we've all made such mistakes. The plan, of course, is to not let them hurt you when it actually counts on test day.

Slipups commonly occur because we are nervous, which makes us rush our work and be overly eager to take control of the situation. Timing restrictions are not meant to gauge how fast you can think. They are gauging your ability to prioritize—to focus on what is most important. Take time to set games up correctly; there is nothing more important than that. If making a quick but flawed diagram takes you 1 minute and 30 seconds, and doing it accurately takes a minute more, that extra minute is worth it.

In addition, if you do run into the unfortunate situation where you realize you've made a mistake or omission two or three questions in, we recommend that you stop and address the issue completely before moving forward. You may have a desire to quickly semi-correct your mistake and forge ahead, but this will often lead to you spinning your wheels and not having much success on subsequent problems.

If two or three questions in, you get the sense that something is not right, we recommend the following steps:

1. Stop what you are doing and take a look at your diagram. Look at each notation on it, and say to yourself what it means. Then check each notation against the original rules, to make sure that they either a) match the original rule correctly or b) can be inferred by bringing rules together.

2. If you find an error, redraw your diagram correctly and pay extra careful attention to inferences you may have made due to a misunderstanding. Students often feel that they won't have time for this, but drawing a second diagram takes far less time than drawing the first one, and generally, the time invested will be worth it. Practice this and you won't be as nervous about sometimes having to redraw.

3. After you've checked for errors, give yourself a good five seconds to become comfortable with your diagram—The Big Pause! Again, we know it's going to feel like you don't have enough time to do this,

but without a big-picture understanding, the questions will take much longer. Look for connections and prioritize what you know about a game.

If your goal is to get a perfect score, or a near perfect score, on the games section, it is important that you build in extra time so you can recover from a serious diagramming error on test day. If you design a timing strategy that accounts for no errors, you won't be able to recover when issues arise. To complete the games section perfectly, you should feel that, on a really good day, you can get through all four games in 32–33 minutes.

3. You haven't correctly prioritized the most important issues.

Issues 4 and 5 are black-and-white concerns that all test-takers, experienced and novice, can understand. Our top three issues become more obviously important once you have a secure footing in games, and especially if you are seeking a top games score.

Prioritizing the most important issues is more of an art than a science, and often you won't know whether you did this correctly until after the fact. If you have a correct sense of priorities, questions will often "flow," because you will be thinking about them in the same ways the test writers did. Even if you have a correct diagram, if you have no sense (or an incorrect sense) of a game's priorities, the questions will feel like a grind. They may seem to require unexpected, or unfair, leaps of thought from you.

Reviewing past work can be a great way to fine-tune your instincts in this area. Go back to games you have solved, set them up again, and decide on the priorities—which rules or inferences are most significant for understanding the game and answering the questions. Then go through the questions to see if your understanding of priorities was indeed correct, or if there was something else you should have focused on. You should find that you are able to prioritize just fine in most situations, and you may find commonalities in the situations where you have trouble prioritizing.

Finally, we want to mention that confidence tends to play a significant role in terms of prioritizing correctly. When we are uncertain or nervous, many of us have a natural tendency to prioritize that which is most difficult to understand or handle, assuming that the "secret" must be locked inside. For example, when we read challenging text, we tend to focus most on words that we don't know the meanings of. On games, while we do need to understand each rule, our prioritization of rules should be based on an understanding of which ones have the greatest effect, not on a fixation on those with the trickiest wording. Being confident in your abilities, and being in control of your task, can help you to prioritize with a clearer eye.

2. You can't picture the situation.

As learners, we tend to prioritize the conscious mind, the "front room," and this is with good reason: The front room is the one we understand better, and it's the one we can most directly control. However, the reality is that some of the work you do during a standardized exam takes place in the unconscious mind, the "back room." We're not talking about your deep, dark, animal instincts or childhood fears; your standardized test prep back room is where you somehow sense which answers are worth examining first and when a game or question is clicking. The back room is much harder to control and manipulate. However, what this back room thrives on is big-picture understanding. If you are able to visualize the situation, it makes it much easier for your brain to organize and relate the rules. If you can't visualize, you can't conceptualize. And if you can't conceptualize, you're dead in the water.

15

Burdening yourself with a lack of big-picture understanding is another common consequence of rushing and of lacking confidence. Expect to be able to understand the general parameters of a game, and know not to let yourself go forward into the questions without such an understanding.

The good news when it comes to picturing these games is that they are all variations on a theme. You will not face a situation on the exam that is disconnected from what we've discussed. If you can picture the games you've done for practice, you can picture the games that will appear on your official exam.

A good exercise for preparing for this challenge is to go through all of the games that you have done, hopefully mixed up in some fashion, and try to picture how you would set up each game. Don't solve the entire game—just walk through the setup in your mind. Then you can match up what you envisioned with how you actually solved the game, to reflect on how effectively you imagined the situation. Ideally, you want to get to a point where very few games seem unusual in their basic construction, and where—for the vast majority of games—you can quickly understand how to draw the base, and what the relationship will be between the base and the elements.

And now, what we've all been waiting for. The number one reason games cause trouble during the exam is…

1. You don't have control over the rules.

Control. It's a subjective gauge.

But think back to when you started learning games. Maybe you felt in control of rules from the get-go ("Sure, I know what *M is delivered before N* means!"), or maybe you felt in control of the rules once you became comfortable with all the notations, but we hope that as you've studied, the level of control that you *desire* to have, and *expect* to have, has risen correspondingly. You should feel far more in control now than you did before and you should have a much better understanding of what it *feels* like when you are in control—when the process of answering questions feels like it should.

Control over the rules will play a fundamental role in your success. Control does not mean that you solve a game during the setup, and it certainly doesn't mean that every question can be answered quickly. Control does not mean games are going to be easy. Control *does* mean that you understand exactly what each rule means. We expect that you can translate these rules into notations and that, by the time you go into the questions, you are very comfortable thinking about how these rules relate to the rest of your diagram and to one another. Control is not about knowing everything. It's about knowing what you know—and what you *don't* know—in a correct and usable way.

In your final few weeks of review, renew your focus on controlling the rules. Make sure you have confidence in your ability to accurately notate and understand rules, to see how rules relate to a game's big picture, to gauge their importance, to relate them to one another, and finally, to use the rules to perform the various tasks that different questions will present.

For different students, the order of dangers will be different, and we are sure that you know of a couple of elements on the above list that are of particular relevance to you, as well as perhaps a few challenges that are no longer issues for you. We do feel that everyone should agree with the following: If you can avoid these five pitfalls on test day, it is highly likely that you will end up very happy with your games score.

From Now until Test Day

Let's end this book by discussing what your focus should be for your final few weeks of study. At this point, your goal should not be to gather more information or to learn new strategies. Rather, your priority should be to organize and contextualize what you have learned already so that you can best apply the skills you have developed when it counts. Here are three general areas for you to address:

1. Review and organize what you have learned.

2. Set realistic goals and finalize timing strategies.

3. Immerse yourself in real games played in real time.

Let's touch on each of these briefly:

1. Review and organize what you have learned.

This is the time to take one final comprehensive look at every rare twist and turn that a game might take. More importantly, this is the time to organize and prioritize what is most important to remember about games, and in what order. You might find that in going back and reviewing, you will feel more comfortable with certain games than you did before, and that's a very common and natural consequence of developing a stronger big-picture understanding. You might also find that you are rusty when it comes to making certain types of inferences for certain types of games. A great way to knock that rust off is to replay games (and then replay them again).

2. Set realistic goals and finalize timing strategies.

At this point, you should have a pretty good sense of how comfortable you feel with logic games. You may be at a point where you are consistently able to get through three games well, but commonly run out of time for the fourth. Maybe you get through all four games, but in order to do so, you have to make educated guesses on certain questions. Or, maybe you are at a point where you are *expecting* to get a perfect score, or something close to that, on the Logic Games section.

One thing we strongly recommend is that you try to avoid a Clark Kent/Superman mentality; don't try to perform differently on the real exam than how you perform in your practice. If you consistently miss 5–8 questions in the games section, it's very unlikely that you will score −0 or −1 on test day, and altering your strategies can lead to unpleasant consequences. If you set out to miss your usual 5–8 questions, it's actually more likely that you'll beat your usual performance, as you'll be in a better position to capitalize on your strengths and minimize the amount of time you waste on your weaknesses.

Practice your timing strategies enough that they become internalized and require very little energy on test day.

Back in Chapter 8, we laid out a basic timing strategy based on allocating eight minutes to each game, along with three minutes in a "Time Bank." We also discussed the idea of adapting this strategy to match your own specific strengths, weaknesses, and goals. Use your next two practice tests to get a realistic sense of where you are on a good day or on a bad day. Develop your strategies accordingly. Just as importantly, make these plans with plenty of time to spare, so that you can practice applying them on several more practice tests.

Take a look at a few hypothetical game players and the strategies that would work well for each one. Note that the timing goals are written assuming an ascending order of game difficulty, though in practice, the easiest game might be the second one, and thus it would be treated as game 1 in terms of how much time it "deserves." Don't read these with an eye towards choosing the goal score you'd like; instead, look for ideas that ring true about your own strengths and weaknesses.

Jorgé
Goal: 175–180 overall, −0 or −1 on games

Characteristics: Generally strong at games, and extremely strong and fast with certain games, but very concerned about running into a game that is unusual, or turns into a slog.

Timing Goals
Game 1: 6
Game 2: 7
Game 3: 9
Game 4: 9
Bank: 4 minutes

Notes: Setting such tight goals for games 1 and 2 should help Jorgé push the pace, and it's likely that if he does run into an unusual and hard game, it will be game 3 or 4. Having an extra four minutes for that particular game can take a huge load off of his shoulders.

Karen

Goal: 172–176, –1 or –2 on games

Characteristics: Feels very comfortable with games and doesn't worry about running into a game that feels particularly different from others. What she does fear is making some silly mistake somewhere or getting stuck on one or two particular problems and being forced to move on. She knows her margin of error is small.

Timing Goals

Game 1: 7

Game 2: 8

Game 3: 9

Game 4: 10

Bank: 1 minute

Notes: She doesn't need the tight goals Jorgé does, because she's less afraid of the rogue game. One minute in the bank is not much, but giving herself more time for each game allows her to be more careful and spend a bit of extra time on any particularly tough questions.

Luna

Goal: 168, –3 to –4 on games

Characteristics: Feels comfortable with most games, but is usually stumped by one or two really tough questions, spends too much time on them, and ends up having to rush on the last game.

Timing Goals

Game 1: 7:30

Game 2: 8

Game 3: 8:30

Game 4: 10

Bank: 1 minute

Notes: Luna has to be realistic that she won't have a lot of time to waste. Thus, she must expect to skip a couple of questions during earlier games to give herself time for every game.

> **Jonah**
>
> Goal: 162, −5 to −7 on games
>
> Characteristics: Feels comfortable with simpler games, but has often found himself struggling in a significant way with one game per test.
>
> <u>Timing Goals</u>
> Game 1: 7
> Game 2: 7
> Game 3: 8
> Game 4: 10
> Bank: 3 minutes
>
> Notes: Jonah needs to focus on hitting his timing goals on the simpler games. To have a good chance of getting most of the questions right on the toughest game, he needs time to "play around," perhaps making a mistake in laying out the framework of the game and then starting again.

3. Immerse yourself in real games played in real time.

Play games you've already played, and then play them over again. More importantly, practice full sets just as if it were test day. Set goals to get even faster at games you are already good at, and practice "surviving" games that are tough for you. Focus on retaining your mental discipline and not making mistakes while reading or notating. You should play enough to be thoroughly engrossed in games, and you should use these final games to make your processes more automatic and to explore and shore up the final holes in your understanding.

Final Thoughts

What makes for a great surgeon? We don't mean some surgeon that shows up on a list of "Atlanta's Fifty Best" in some airline magazine—we're talking a surgeon whom you would trust with your life.

Sure, that person has to go to school for a long time, and has to know a lot of stuff, the right sort of stuff, but…is this knowledge what makes for a good surgeon? Is the surgeon who knows the most the one who is best in the operating room?

If so, it's only by coincidence.

Surgery is about **performance.** The knowledge in the surgeon's brain does not have a direct impact on the patient—certainly not as direct an impact as the actions of that surgeon's hand. Surgeons are experts, but expertise is only a necessary condition, rather than a sufficient one, for being a great surgeon.

The good news is that no matter how stressful the LSAT may seem, nobody's life is on the line! The bad news (or the other good news, depending on your perspective), the part that you will likely remember on test day, is that the LSAT is the primary factor driving your law school options.

In the pages of this book, you have been exposed to everything you could possibly need to know to deal with any game that the LSAT will throw in your direction. So, if you've been paying attention, you've got the knowledge part down. It's all in there somewhere. Your performance is what will dictate your score.

A great surgeon has the talent to be both disciplined and flexible. Something that is meant to be routine will stay routine and will be handled with absolute precision. At the same time, when challenges arise, as they often do, great surgeons must have the willingness and confidence to make decisions and alter the course.

In your final few weeks, we suggest that you do what you can to get into the mind-set of a great surgeon. Don't add another thing to learn on top of the pile. A surgeon does not try to learn new techniques a week before a tough surgery. Use this time to reflect on what you know, to organize what you know, and to figure out how best to utilize it. To mix in another analogy, don't work on your half-court shots; instead, work on making sure that all of your fundamentals are sound. Studying that extremely unusual game from 15 years ago won't help you now. Instead, you might try making sure you know exactly how to recognize when Ordering games have mismatches, and how to deal with these situations. Focusing on the central issues that will most likely define your performance will be a far better use of your final study hours.

Happy studying!

Coached Replays

Coached Replays

Replaying games is an essential part of your LSAT prep. When first learning about each game type and optimal diagram, replaying games is an efficient way to master the basic moves. But now that you know the basics—and more—replaying games is a great way to further develop your more subtle skills, which will also enhance your ability to adapt to twists.

In this section, we've reprinted some of the logic games you've met along your way through this book (actually, we're showing you just a few—you can find more in your online resources). You'll notice that these are not simply reprints of the games you've already seen. We've added suggestions at many points in each game. Think of it as having a coach yelling out pointers as you work through your training exercises. As with a good coach, some of the suggestions are meant to keep you in proper form, while others add an extra challenge because your coach suspects the game might be too easy for you. (We will warn you if we're adding an extra challenge.)

Of course, there are many ways to tackle a game, question, or answer choice, and different coaches will naturally offer different suggestions. We don't want you to get the impression that any one approach is the only effective one (to that end, you may find that some of the suggestions that follow differ from what you read earlier).

We have grouped the games into four-game sections to mimic an actual LSAT. Since you have seen these games before, you might want to consider giving yourself less than 35 minutes per section.

Note that in the answer key we put an asterisk next to any of the questions that we wrote and added to official games, so you don't call LSAC to complain about how hard a game is.

SET 1

To start, we'll just give you a three-game section. Give yourself **26 minutes** to complete them.

PT7, S2, G2

Doctor Yamata works only on Mondays, Tuesdays, Wednesdays, Fridays, and Saturdays. She performs four different activities—lecturing, operating, treating patients, and conducting research. Each working day she performs exactly one activity in the morning and exactly one activity in the afternoon. During each week her work schedule must satisfy the following restrictions:

> She performs operations on exactly three mornings.
> If she operates on Monday, she does not operate on Tuesday.
> She lectures in the afternoon on exactly two consecutive calendar days.
> She treats patients on exactly one morning and exactly three afternoons.
> She conducts research on exactly one morning.
> On Saturday she neither lectures nor performs operations.

Don't forget The Big Pause!

If this is not obvious, it's a sign you need to work on your setup.

8. Which one of the following must be a day on which Doctor Yamata lectures?

    (A) Monday
    (B) Tuesday
    (C) Wednesday
    (D) Friday
    (E) Saturday

Predict the element at play to speed things up even more.

9. On Wednesday Doctor Yamata could be scheduled to

    (A) conduct research in the morning and operate in the afternoon
    (B) lecture in the morning and treat patients in the afternoon
    (C) operate in the morning and lecture in the afternoon
    (D) operate in the morning and conduct research in the afternoons
    (E) treat patients in the morning and treat patients in the afternoon

10. Which one of the following statements must be true?

    (A) There is one day on which the doctor treats patients both in the morning and in the afternoon.
    (B) The doctor conducts research on one of the days on which she lectures.
    (C) The doctor conducts research on one of the days on which she treats patients.
    (D) The doctor lectures on one of the days on which she treats patients.
    (E) The doctor lectures on one of the days on which she operates.

Look for wrong answers! Figure out when treating patients must occur (this will sound like both "on __" and "on __ or ___") and then eliminate.

11. If Doctor Yamata operates on Tuesday, then her schedule for treating patients could be

    (A) Monday morning, Monday afternoon, Friday morning, Friday afternoon
    (B) Monday morning, Friday afternoon, Saturday morning, Saturday afternoon
    (C) Monday afternoon, Wednesday morning, Wednesday afternoon, Saturday afternoon
    (D) Wednesday morning, Wednesday afternoon, Friday afternoon, Saturday afternoon
    (E) Wednesday afternoon, Friday afternoon, Saturday morning, Saturday afternoon

If it's easy and you know it, clap your hands.

12. Which one of the following is a pair of days on both of which Doctor Yamata must treat patients?

    (A) Monday and Tuesday
    (B) Monday and Saturday
    (C) Tuesday and Friday
    (D) Tuesday and Saturday
    (E) Friday and Saturday

MPrep

Six doctors—Haddad, Johnson, Kwong, Lester, Murray, and Nelson—are assigned to the following three training rotations: orthopedics, pediatrics, surgery. Each doctor is assigned to exactly one rotation, and each rotation is assigned exactly two doctors. No other doctors are assigned.

The following conditions must be met:

Kwong is not assigned to the same rotation as Lester.
Murray is not assigned to surgery.
If Lester is assigned to orthopedics, then Haddad is assigned to surgery.
Johnson is assigned to surgery.

1. Which one of the following could be an accurate assignment of doctors to rotations?

    (A) orthopedics: Kwong, Haddad
        pediatrics: Lester, Nelson
        surgery: Johnson, Murray

    (B) orthopedics: Lester, Nelson
        pediatrics: Johnson, Murray
        surgery: Haddad, Kwong

    (C) orthopedics: Kwong, Nelson
        pediatrics: Lester, Murray
        surgery: Haddad, Johnson

    (D) orthopedics: Murray, Nelson
        pediatrics: Kwong, Lester
        surgery: Haddad, Johnson

    (E) orthopedics: Lester, Murray
        pediatrics: Haddad, Kwong
        surgery: Johnson, Nelson

The answer is obvious if you follow the chain!

2. If Kwong is assigned to surgery, each of the following could be true EXCEPT:

    (A) Murray is assigned to pediatrics.
    (B) Haddad is assigned to orthopedics.
    (C) Lester is assigned to orthopedics.
    (D) Nelson is assigned to pediatrics.
    (E) Nelson is assigned to orthopedics.

Scan the rules before looking at the answer choices to anticipate elements at play.

3. It can be determined to which rotation each of the six doctors is assigned if which one of the following statements is true?

    (A) Both Murray and Kwong are assigned to orthopedics.
    (B) Both Kwong and Nelson are assigned to pediatrics.
    (C) Both Haddad and Johnson are assigned to surgery.
    (D) Both Johnson and Lester are assigned to surgery.
    (E) Both Haddad and Nelson are assigned to pediatrics.

Write out who's left to make it easier to evaluate the answers.

4. If Murray and Lester are assigned to the same rotation, for how many of the six doctors is it known to which rotation each is assigned?

    (A) one
    (B) two
    (C) three
    (D) four
    (E) six

You should know the answer before looking at the answer choices.

5. If Nelson is assigned to surgery, which of the following is a complete and accurate list of doctors who could be assigned to the same rotation as Murray?

    (A) Kwong
    (B) Kwong, Lester
    (C) Haddad, Lester
    (D) Haddad, Kwong, Lester
    (E) Haddad, Johnson, Kwong, Lester

MANHATTAN
PREP

MPrep

One or more of six violinists—Greene, Holiday, Liu, Mann, Underwood, and Wilson—will be selected to perform at the year-end concert. No other violinists will be selected. The following conditions apply:

Challenge: Try playing this game WITHOUT using the Logic Chain. Instead, just write out the rules. Can you make it work?

If Holiday is selected, then Mann is not selected.
If Liu is selected, then both Mann and Wilson are selected.
If Underwood is not selected, then Holiday is selected.
Wilson is not selected unless Greene is selected.

Notice the mutually exclusive pairs.

1. Which of the following could be a complete and accurate list of the violinists selected for the concert?

   (A) Holiday, Liu, Wilson, Underwood
   (B) Liu, Mann, Wilson
   (C) Holiday, Liu, Mann
   (D) Liu, Mann, Wilson, Underwood
   (E) Mann, Underwood

2. Which of the following must be false?

   (A) Liu is selected but Underwood is not.
   (B) Neither Underwood nor Liu is selected.
   (C) Holiday is selected but Liu is not.
   (D) Both Greene and Underwood are selected.
   (E) Holiday is selected but Mann is not.

Predict the answer: notice the elements that, when out, force someone else in.

3. Which of the following could be the only violinist selected for the concert?

   (A) Liu
   (B) Mann
   (C) Greene
   (D) Wilson
   (E) Underwood

4. If Underwood is not selected, then which of the following must be true?

   (A) Wilson is not selected.
   (B) Greene is selected.
   (C) At least two violinists are selected.
   (D) At most three violinists are selected.
   (E) Neither Liu nor Holiday is selected.

5. If Greene is not selected, then each of the following could be true EXCEPT:

   (A) Exactly two violinists are selected.
   (B) Exactly one violinist is selected.
   (C) Mann is selected.
   (D) Holiday is selected.
   (E) Liu is selected.

Treat this like an Orientation question, and remember what it means if something is not listed.

6. Which of the following CANNOT be a complete and accurate list of the violinists who are selected for the concert?

   (A) Greene, Liu, Mann, Underwood, Wilson
   (B) Greene, Mann, Underwood
   (C) Greene, Mann, Wilson
   (D) Greene, Underwood
   (E) Holiday

This is designed to take time. First understand the original rule, then work from wrong to right.

7. Which of the following, if substituted for the condition that if Liu is selected then both Mann and Wilson are selected, would have the same effect in determining the violinists who are selected to perform?

   (A) If Liu is selected, then exactly two other violinists are selected.
   (B) If Liu is selected, then both Greene and Underwood are selected but Holiday is not.
   (C) If Mann and Wilson are selected, then Liu is selected.
   (D) If Liu is selected, then Mann is one of exactly five violinists selected.
   (E) If Liu is not selected, then neither Mann nor Wilson is selected.

SET 2

Allow yourself only **35 minutes** (or less) for these four games.

PT1, S2, G1

Exactly six trade representatives negotiate a treaty: Klosnik, Londi, Manley, Neri, Osata, Poirier. There are exactly six chairs evenly spaced around a circular table. The chairs are numbered 1 through 6, with successively numbered chairs next to each other and chair number 1 next to chair number 6. Each chair is occupied by exactly one of the representatives. The following conditions apply:

> Poirier sits immediately next to Neri.
> Londi sits immediately next to Manley, Neri, or both.
> Klosnik does not sit immediately next to Manley.
> If Osata sits immediately next to Poirier, Osata does not sit immediately next to Manley.

Simplify this to what situation cannot occur.

1. Which one of the following seating arrangements of the six representatives in chairs 1 through 6 would NOT violate the stated conditions?

    (A) Klosnik, Poirier, Neri, Manley, Osata, Londi
    (B) Klosnik, Londi, Manley, Poirier, Neri, Osatas
    (C) Klosnik, Londi, Manley, Osata, Poirier, Neri
    (D) Klosnik, Osata, Poirier, Neri, Londi, Manley
    (E) Klosnik, Neri, Londi, Osata, Manley, Poirier

Follow the chain and identify who's left.

2. If Londi sits immediately next to Poirier, which one of the following is a pair of representatives who must sit immediately next to each other?

    (A) Klosnik and Osata
    (B) Londi and Neri
    (C) Londi and Osata
    (D) Manley and Neri
    (E) Manley and Poirier

You should know the answer before looking at the answer choices.

3. If Klosnik sits directly between Londi and Poirier, then Manley must sit directly between

    (A) Londi and Neri
    (B) Londi and Osata
    (C) Neri and Osata
    (D) Neri and Poirier
    (E) Osata and Poirier

Follow the chain and identify who's left.

4. If Neri sits immediately next to Manley, then Klosnik can sit directly between

    (A) Londi and Manley
    (B) Londi and Poirier
    (C) Neri and Osata
    (D) Neri and Poirier
    (E) Poirier and Osata

Sketch out the condition and who's left to anchor your thinking.

5. If Londi sits immediately next to Manley, then which one of the following is a complete and accurate list of representatives any one of whom could also sit immediately next to Londi?

    (A) Klosnik
    (B) Klosnik, Neri
    (C) Neri, Poirier
    (D) Klosnik, Osata, Poirier
    (E) Klosnik, Neri, Osata, Poirier

With who's left, consider which rules apply.

6. If Londi sits immediately next to Neri, which one of the following statements must be false?

    (A) Klosnik sits immediately next to Osata.
    (B) Londi sits immediately next to Manley.
    (C) Osata sits immediately next to Poirier.
    (D) Neri sits directly between Londi and Poirier.
    (E) Osata sits directly between Klosnik and Manley.

Sketch out all the elements, consider what rule the right answer will predictably violate, and figure out the two possible answers.

7. If Klosnik sits immediately next to Osata, then Londi CANNOT sit directly between

    (A) Klosnik and Manley
    (B) Klosnik and Neri
    (C) Manley and Neri
    (D) Manley and Poirier
    (E) Neri and Osata

PT16, S1, G1

Eight new students—R, S, T, V, W, X, Y, Z—are being divided among exactly three classes—class 1, class 2, and class 3. Classes 1 and 2 will gain three new students each; class 3 will gain two new students. The following restrictions apply:

R must be added to class 1.
S must be added to class 3.
Neither S nor W can be added to the same class as Y.
V cannot be added to the same class as Z.
If T is added to class 1, Z must also be added to class 1.

1. Which one of the following is an acceptable assignment of students to the three classes?

	1	2	3
(A)	R, T, Y	V, W, X	S, Z
(B)	R, T, Z	S, V, Y	W, X
(C)	R, W, X	V, Y, Z	S, T
(D)	R, X, Z	T, V, Y	S, W
(E)	R, X, Z	V, W, Y	S, T

If you're not sure, leave this question for later.

2. Which one of the following is a complete and accurate list of classes any one of which could be the class to which V is added?

(A) class 1
(B) class 3
(C) class 1, class 3
(D) class 2, class 3
(E) class 1, class 2, class 3

Keep an eye on those anti-chunks.

3. If X is added to class 1, which one of the following is a student who must be added to class 2?

(A) T
(B) V
(C) W
(D) Y
(E) Z

Use what you just figured out.

4. If X is added to class 3, each of the following is a pair of students who can be added to class 1 EXCEPT

(A) Y and Z
(B) W and Z
(C) V and Y
(D) V and W
(E) T and Z

You should know the answer before looking at the answer choices.

5. If T is added to class 3, which one of the following is a student who must be added to class 2?

(A) V
(B) W
(C) X
(D) Y
(E) Z

For an added challenge, try not drawing out anything. Instead, use your master diagram, cover up the elements you've used with your fingers, and think!

6. Which one of the following must be true?

(A) If T and X are added to class 2, V is added to class 3.
(B) If V and W are added to class 1, T is added to class 3.
(C) If V and W are added to class 1, Z is added to class 3.
(D) If V and X are added to class 1, W is added to class 3.
(E) If Y and Z are added to class 2, X is added to class 2.

PT30, S1, G3

Exactly five cars—Frank's, Marquitta's, Orlando's, Taishah's, and Vinquetta's—are washed, each exactly once. The cars are washed one at a time, with each receiving exactly one kind of wash: regular, super, or premium. The following conditions must apply:

The first car washed does not receive a super wash, though at least one car does.
Exactly one car receives a premium wash.
The second and third cars washed receive the same kind of wash as each other.
Neither Orlando's nor Taishah's is washed before Vinquetta's.
Marquitta's is washed before Frank's, but after Orlando's.
Marquitta's and the car washed immediately before Marquitta's receive regular washes.

It's definitely possible to frame this game. This time around, try without. Optionally, play the game first without frames, and then with.

11. Which one of the following could be an accurate list of the cars in the order in which they are washed, matched with type of wash received?

   (A) Orlando's: premium; Vinquetta's: regular; Taishah's: regular; Marquitta's: regular; Frank's: super
   (B) Vinquetta's: premium; Orlando's: regular; Taishah's: regular; Marquitta's: regular; Frank's: super
   (C) Vinquetta's: regular; Marquitta's: regular; Taishah's: regular; Orlando's: super; Frank's: super
   (D) Vinquetta's: super; Orlando's: regular; Marquitta's: regular; Frank's: regular; Taishah's: super
   (E) Vinquetta's: premium; Orlando's: regular; Marquitta's: regular; Frank's: regular; Taishah's: regular

Get scrappy: Make the one "must be" inference and then scan the answers.

12. If Vinquetta's car does not receive a premium wash, which one of the following must be true?

   (A) Orlando's and Vinquetta's cars receive the same kind of wash as each other.
   (B) Marquitta's and Taishah's cars receive the same kind of wash as each other.
   (C) The fourth car washed receives a premium wash.
   (D) Orlando's car is washed third.
   (E) Marquitta's car is washed fourth.

What kind of wash must the last two get? Follow the chain, then predict the elements at play.

13. If the last two cars washed receive the same kind of wash as each other, then which one of the following could be true?

   (A) Orlando's car is washed third.
   (B) Taishah's car is washed fifth.
   (C) Taishah's car is washed before Marquitta's car.
   (D) Vinquetta's car receives a regular wash.
   (E) Exactly one car receives a super wash.

A sound setup pays off here. Defer judgment!

14. Which one of the following must be true?

   (A) Vinquetta's car receives a premium wash
   (B) Exactly two cars receive a super wash.
   (C) The fifth car washed receives a super wash.
   (D) The fourth car washed receives a super wash.
   (E) The second car washed receives a regular wash.

Consider who must have a regular wash, then try using previous work to eliminate the last incorrect choice.

15. Which one of the following is a complete and accurate list of the cars that must receive a regular wash?

   (A) Frank's, Marquitta's
   (B) Marquitta's, Orlando's
   (C) Marquitta's, Orlando's, Taishah's
   (D) Marquitta's, Taishah's
   (E) Marquitta's, Vinquetta's

It's possible to solve this by adding to your original diagram, but this time around, practice going back to square one and see how quickly you can redraw.

16. Suppose that in addition to the original five cars Jabrohn's car is also washed. If all the other conditions hold as given, which one of the following CANNOT be true?

   (A) Orlando's car receives a premium wash.

   (B) Vinquetta's car receives a super wash.

   (C) Four cars receive a regular wash.

   (D) Only the second and third cars washed receive a regular wash.

   (E) Jabrohn's car is washed after Frank's car.

Start by considering the implications of the rule in question—BOTH of them!

Try a question that we wrote for this game (assume that the rule change in question 16 is not applicable):

17. Which of the following, if substituted for the rule that the first car washed does not receive a super wash, though at least one car does, would have the same effect in determining the order of car washes and the type of each?

   (A) Vinquetta's car can receive only a regular or premium wash.

   (B) No more than three cars receive a regular wash.

   (C) Frank's car receives a super wash if, and only if, Taishah's car receives a regular or premium wash.

   (D) All cars except Frank's and Taishah's must receive either a regular or premium wash.

   (E) Either Frank's or Taishah's car receives a super wash, and no other car can receive that type of wash.

MPrep

A filmmaker will choose exactly five songs to use in a film project. Of the nine songs that she will choose from, three songs—F, G, and H—were written in the 1960s, three songs—J, K, and M—were written in the 1970s, and three songs—O, P, and Q—were written in the 1980s. The following conditions apply:

> Exactly two songs from the 1980s are selected for the project.
> G and J cannot both be selected.
> H and O cannot both be selected.
> If Q is selected, both G and H are selected.

Identify mutually exclusive pairs, and don't forget to note both the total number in and out.

Leave the first rule for last.

1. Which one of the following is an acceptable selection of songs for the film project?

   (A) F, G, K, P, Q
   (B) G, J, K, O, P
   (C) G, K, M, O, P
   (D) G, H, K, M, Q
   (E) F, G, H, O, P

Remember to add horizontal lines to your t-charts to help you track the different categories.

2. If Q is selected for the film project, each of the following could be true EXCEPT:

   (A) F is selected for the film project.
   (B) J is selected for the film project.
   (C) G is selected for the film project.
   (D) K is selected for the film project.
   (E) M is selected for the film project.

Don't waste too much time on this question.

3. If neither K nor M is selected for the film project, how many of the five song selections are known with certainty?

   (A) one
   (B) two
   (C) three
   (D) four
   (E) five

MANHATTAN
PREP

Frame this on the O/Q division.

4. If K is the only song from the 1970s selected for the film project, then which one of the following CANNOT be true?

    (A) O is not selected but F is selected.
    (B) Q is not selected but G is selected.
    (C) F is not selected but P is selected.
    (D) H is not selected but G is selected.
    (E) O is not selected but H is selected.

5. Which one of the following is a song that must be selected for the film project?

    (A) H
    (B) Q
    (C) F
    (D) P
    (E) G

Predict how the correct answer will violate the game.

6. If the condition that exactly two songs from the 1980s are selected for the project is replaced with the condition that at least one song from each time period must be selected, and if all other rules remain in effect, each of the following could be true EXCEPT:

    (A) Both O and P are selected.
    (B) Both G and H are selected.
    (C) Both P and Q are selected.
    (D) J, K, and M are selected.
    (E) F, P, and Q are selected.

Coached Replays Answer Key

Set 1

PT7, S2, G2	**Manhattan Prep – Doctor Rotations**	**Manhattan Prep – Violin Concert**	
8. B	1. C	1. E	7. D
9. C	2. C	2. A	
10. E	3. E	3. E	
11. E	4. A	4. D	
12. E	5. B	5. E	
		6. C	

Set 2

PT1, S2, G1		**PT16, S1, G1**	**PT30, S1, G3**		**Manhattan Prep – Filmmaker's Songs**
1. B	7. E	1. D	11. B	*17. E	1. C
2. A		2. E	12. A		2. B
3. B		3. A	13. B		3. E
4. E		4. E	14. E		4. A
5. E		5. C	15. B		5. D
6. C		6. D	16. A		6. E

Want More?

This book is already pretty big, so we've put the rest of the coached replays online.

Turn to page 7, the unnumbered page before the Table of Contents, for instructions on how to find that. We'll see you there!

MANHATTAN
PREP

LG

Appendix B

Logic Game Solutions

PrepTests 40–42

Logic Game Solutions

On the following pages you will find solutions to all the logic games from PrepTests 40 through 42. Manhattan Prep's online learning platform includes many more. They are done in a coded shorthand, the same one used for the Quick-Check solutions shown for the mixed sets in the book. We reprinted the code below for convenience. In writing these solutions, we initially hoped to authentically show you the work an expert would do to solve these games in real time. However, it soon became apparent that such solutions may not be particularly enlightening, since top test-takers often do a substantial amount of work in their heads. Thus, we have tried to show a sophisticated approach to each game while at the same time explaining the games clearly. Some solutions lean more one way or the other.

As we've stressed throughout this book, there is rarely (never?) one right way to solve a game. Do not despair if you find that you solved the game in a totally different manner than we have shown. Furthermore, these solutions were written and edited by a specific pair of teachers. If you were to ask another pair to draw up solutions to these same games, they would invariably approach some of the games quite differently. This variation would probably be most acute in *The Big Pause* and *To Frame or Not to Frame?* discussions for each game.

Key to the Code:

Darker shade = information provided explicitly by the game's rules, by a specific question stem, or by the information in a given answer choice

Lighter shade = inferences made on the basis of that provided information

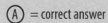 = answer eliminated

Ⓐ = correct answer

"Prev. work" = an answer choice was eliminated/selected based on a consideration of scenarios that were written for previous problems. The problem # used is listed in parentheses.

MANHATTAN
PREP

A

(B)

C

D

E

When only the correct answer is circled, this means that the test-taker actively looked for the correct answer and found it, without pausing to specifically eliminate wrong answers.

If a hypothetical scenario is written out to test an answer choice and the scenario turns out to be invalid, there will be an "X" beside it.

A̶

B̶

C   (C)

D̶

E̶

When the correct answer is written to the side of the answer choices, rather than just being circled, this indicates that the correct answer was chosen because the other four answers were found to be wrong. The correct answer itself was not evaluated.

A̶

B̶

C̲

D̶

E̲

When two or three answer choices are underlined, this indicates that some eliminations were easy (the crossed-out answers that are not underlined), while the underlined choices needed careful consideration. Here, it would be an arbitrary choice whether we started by testing (C) or (E).

A̶ 3

B̶ 2

C   (C)

D̶ 1

E̶ 4

On Orientation questions, the number next to the eliminated answer choice indicates which rule the answer choice breaks (some answers break more than one rule, but only one is listed).

in   out

T / V   V / (T)

The placeholder indicates that early in the deduction process, the test-taker split up these two elements. The circled letter shows that ultimately the test-taker realized that only one of those choices works.

Want More?

 As we mentioned earlier, this book is already pretty big, so we've put solutions for more PrepTests online. Turn to page 7, the unnumbered page before the Table of Contents, for instructions on how to find that. We'll see you there!

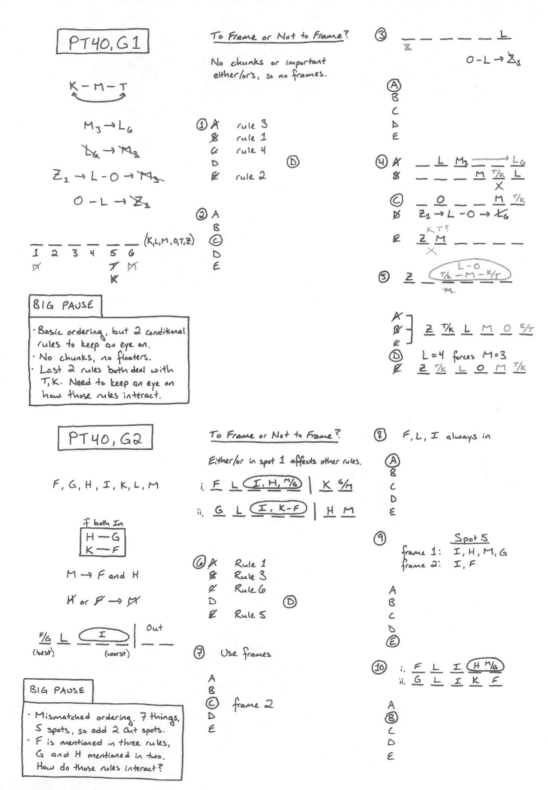

MANHATTAN
PREP

PT40, G3

H, M, P, T, V

```
/  /  /  /  _
/  _  /  /
   _
□  □  □  □  □
H  M  P  T  V
⸝  ⩍     ⩍
⸜⩍
```

H → T   ⸝ → ⩍
       (T ≥ H)

$P_T \rightarrow R_X$ $P_V \rightarrow R_T$

BIG PAUSE
- Weird game! Using open board helps to record quantity inferences, but each connection will have to be written twice (i.e. if P and T are connected, a 'T' goes in P's column and a 'P' goes in T's column).
- Montreal is most limited, Vancouver is least limited.
- H → T rule could be important.

To Frame or Not to Frame?

No chunks or either/or's.

(11)   Ⓐ
- A
- B̶   Rule 1
- C̶   Rule 3
- D̶   Rule 4
- E̶   Rule 2

(12)
```
    /     /  H      /
    P     P  M  ⓊV  P    V
    ─     ─  ─  ─   ─    ─
    H     M  P  T   M    V
    ⩍     ⩍          ⩍   ⸝
                          ⸝
```

- A
- B
- C
- D̶
- E̶
     Ⓑ

(13) Ⓐ   if M connects w/ H, it must also
- B   connect w/ T, but M
- C   only has 1 connection
- D
- E

(14)
```
        /  /  /
      V P M V T
   →  H M P T V      works
  Ⓐ     ⩍  ⩍  ⩍
   B
   C
   D  → Leaves nothing for H to connect with
   E  → Someone must connect w/ H,
        + that city will also connect w/ T
```

(15)
```
            /  /|T  Ⓜ
          V V|T M  T
          H  P  T  M
          ⩍  ⩍  T  P
          T  ⩍  H  P
          ⩍
```
- A̶
- B̶
- C̶
- Ⓓ
- E̶

(16)   13 open spots, so max 6 pairs.
      But can almost all spots be filled?
```
          /  /  M  P  /  /
          V  V  T  V  T
          P  P  H  H  H    maxed
          V  P  P  V  V    out
          H  M  T  H  T
          T  T     T  P
```
- A
- Ⓑ
- C
- D̶
- E̶

(17)   Only city that can have 4
     is Vancouver, so all cities
     are connected to V.
- A
- B
- Ⓒ
- D
- E

PT40, G4

in = 6   out = 3

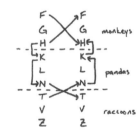

```
  in        out
─────────┬─────────
         │ F/H  N/T
─ ─ ─ ─ ─┤
         │  M
```

BIG PAUSE
- Not too bad. Logic chain has some decent connections.
- OUT column more limited than IN.
- Max 2 monkeys in, but it seems like all 3 P's and all 3 R's could be IN (though not at the same time).

To Frame or Not to Frame?

Conditional grouping almost never benefits from frames.

(18) A   Rule 2
- B̶   Rule 1
- C̶   Rule 4
- D   Ⓓ
- E̶   Rule 3

(19)
```
    H │ F
    K │
    N │L
  ────┼────
      │  T
```
- A̶
- B̶
- C   Ⓒ
- D̶
- E̶

(20)   Use logic chain
- A
- B
- C   K → N → T̶
- D
- E

(21)
```
   F G │ H
   L   │ N K
  ─────┼──────
   T   │
   Z   │ V
```
- A
- Ⓑ
- C̶
- D̶
- E̶

Once HNK are out, that's 3 out, so all others must be in.

(22)   Same diagram as 21!
- Ⓐ
- B̶
- C̶
- D̶
- E̶

(23) A̶   prev work (21)
- Ⓑ   or, from initial inferences, 3 P's + 3 R's imposs b/c N + T can't both be IN.
- C̶   prev work (21)
- D̶   (19) 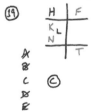 H L K N V Z │ F T G
          m p p p r r │ m   m
- E̶   prev work (21)

PT 41, G1

G, L, P, R, S, W

G - P   [SL]

R/		w/s			/R
1	2	3	4	5	6
R	S				G
L					S

BIG PAUSE
- [SL] chunk = high priority
- R only has two options
- Spot 3 only has two options
- G - P = last priority (No Floaters)

To Frame or Not To Frame?

[SL] chunk has 4 options. Probably should just go to questions.

① A
  B̶   3
  C̶   Rule 1
  D̶   4
  E̶   2

② A̶
  Ⓑ   G = odd / S = odd
  C   G can only be 1 or 5.
  D
  E   G _ _ S L _ R
       R W S L _ G P

③ A
  B
  C   S can only = 4, so W = 3
  D
  Ⓔ   _ _ _ W S L _
      (CBT quest. with a MBT ans.)

④ A
  B
  C   G P _ _ _ _ R
  D
  Ⓔ

⑤ A
  Ⓑ→   Can't happen when R is 1 or 6
  C
  D   Note: You can elim. the other
  E   four from previous work in #2

⑥ A   Can't happen when
  B→   R is 1 or 6
  C
  Ⓓ   Note: You can elim.
  E   E from #2, and C from #1

⑦ A   _ _ S W _ _
  B   _ S W _ _ _
  C   1 2 3 4 5 6
  Ⓓ   [SW]   G - P
  E
     Only 2 options for [SW] chunk

PT 41, G2

Songs - N Q R S

Instrum - f g h k

S → R   Q → N
k   h   k   f

R		N
	k	

S _ _ _ _
I _ _ _ _
  1 2 3 4
  ̶8̶

BIG PAUSE
- Rule 4 is a great chunk; it only has two options. Probably worth framing.

To Frame or Not To Frame?

Definitely frame Rule 4's two options:

S R q/s N s/q   S q/s R s/q N
I _ k _ _   I _ _ k _

Either S or Q will always be with k, so Rule 2 or 3 will always be in effect. 4 frames would cover everything:

① S R Q N S   ② S S R Q N
  I g/h k f h/g   I (g h) k f

③ S R S N Q   ④ S Q R S N
  I h k (g f)   I g h k f

⑧ A̶   3
  B   Ⓑ
  C̶   1
  D̶   3
  E̶   4

⑨ A̶
  B̶
  C̶
  D̶
  Ⓔ   frame 2 + 3

⑩ A̶   frame 3
  B̶   frame 1
  Ⓒ
  D
  E

⑪ A̶
  B   Frames 2 and 4
  C̶
  D
  Ⓔ

⑫ Ⓐ
  B   Frame 2
  C
  D
  E

MANHATTAN PREP

PT41, G3

Fin   Inc

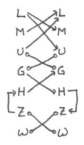

Fin	Inc
Z/W	W/Z
U/G	G/U

BIG PAUSE

· Chain looks pretty readable, just need to be aware of the UG and WZ double-headed arrows.

<u>To Frame or Not to Frame?</u>

Conditional rules (and Conditional Grouping games) almost never lend themselves to frames.

(13) A̶   1
   B̶   5
   C̶   4
   D̶   3
   E   (E)

(14) [Use chain to see if 1ˢᵗ guy in Inc forces 2ⁿᵈ guy to Fin]

A
B
(C)
D
E

$$H_I \rightarrow Z_I \rightarrow W_F$$

---

(15)

F	I
(U)	(G)
(W)	(Z)
(M)	(L)
H	

[M, H, L left
at most 2
can be F]

A
B
(C)
D
E

(16)

F	I
M	L
W	Z
(U)	(G)

A̶
B̶
C̶
(D)
E̶

(17)

F	I
U	G
	L

A
(B)
C
D
E

PT41, G4

F, G, H, I, K, (M), O, (P)

"Across" = 3 in between

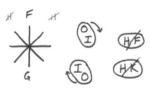

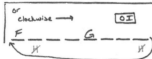

BIG PAUSE

· Yikes! Circular seating is a big curveball. We can use an unconventional circular diagram or use a conventional number line (but remind ourselves that 8 is next to 1).
· [OI] chunk seems most useful and it will be tricky to place.
· M + P are floaters.

<u>To Frame or Not to Frame?</u>

Chunk seems to have 4 options. Normally that's too many to frame, but weirdness of game may incline some to sketch these out just to have a better grasp.

(18) A̶   1
   B   1
   C   (C)
   D̶   3
   E̶   2

(19) [HGOI]

A̶
B̶
C̶
(D) FKPH
E

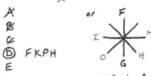

(20) (G4)̶

(A)
B
C
D
E

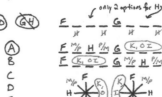

---

(21) [MOI]

A
B
(C)
D
E

(22) prev work (19), FKPHGOIM was pos.

(A)
B
C
D
E

(23) [OI___K] or [K___OI]
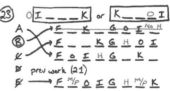

A
(B)
K̶
D̶ prev work (21)
E̶

(24)
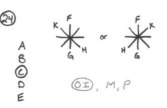

A
B
(C)
D
E

(OI), M, P

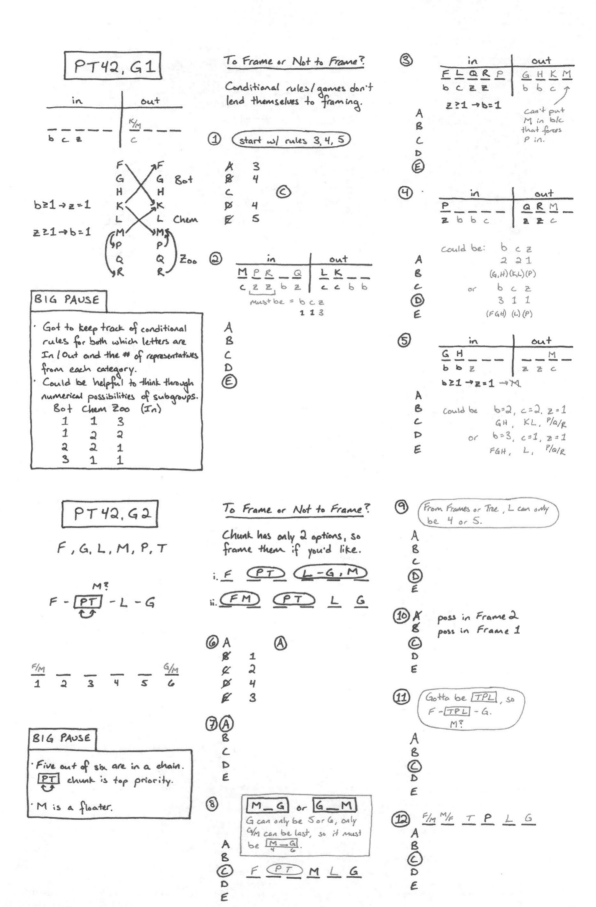

To Frame or Not to Frame?

Conditional rules/games don't lend themselves to framing.

① start w/ rules 3, 4, 5

A. ~~3~~
B. ~~4~~   Ⓒ
C.
D. ~~4~~
E. ~~5~~

②

in				out		
M	P	R	~~Q~~	L	K	
c	z	z	b z	c	c b	

must be = b c z
          1 1 3

A
B
C
D
Ⓔ

BIG PAUSE

· Got to keep track of conditional rules for both which letters are In/Out and the # of representatives from each category.
· Could be helpful to think through numerical possibilities of subgroups.

Bot	Chem	Zoo	(In)
1	1	3	
1	2	2	
2	2	1	
3	1	1	

③

in					out			
F	L	Q	R	P	G	H	K	M
b	c	z	z		b	b	c	↗

$z \geq 1 \to b = 1$

A
B
C
D
Ⓔ

Can't put M in b/c that forces P in.

④

in				out			
P				Q	R	M	
z	b	b	c	z	z	c	

Could be: b c z
           2 2 1
           (G,H)(K,L)(P)

or   b c z
     3 1 1
     (FGH) (L) (P)

A
B
C
Ⓓ
E

⑤

in			out			
G	H					M
b	b	z	z	z	c	

$b \geq 1 \to z = 1 \to$ ~~M~~

A
B   Could be   b=2, c=2, z=1
C   GH, KL, P/Q/R
D   or   b=3, c=1, z=1
E   FGH, L, P/Q/R

⑨ From Frames or True, L can only be 4 or 5.

A
B
C
Ⓓ
E

⑩ ~~A~~   poss in Frame 2
  ~~B~~   poss in Frame 1
  Ⓒ
  D
  E

⑪ Gotta be [TPL], so
  F - [TPL] - G.
  M?

A
B
Ⓒ
D
E

⑫ F/M M/F T P L G

A
B
Ⓒ
D
E

PT 42, G2

F, G, L, M, P, T

M?
F - [PT] - L - G

F/M ___ ___ ___ ___ G/M
 1   2   3   4   5   6

BIG PAUSE

· Five out of six are in a chain. [PT] chunk is top priority.

· M is a floater.

To Frame or Not to Frame?

Chunk has only 2 options, so frame them if you'd like.

i. F ⟮PT⟯ ⟮L - G, M⟯

ii. ⟮FM⟯ ⟮PT⟯ L G

⑥ A
  ~~B~~ 1
  ~~C~~ 2   Ⓐ
  ~~D~~ 4
  ~~E~~ 3

⑦ Ⓐ
  B
  C
  D
  E

⑧ [M _ G] or [G _ M]
  G can only be 5 or 6, only
  G/M can be last, so it must
  be [M _ G].
       4   5

A
B   F ⟮PT⟯ M L G
Ⓒ
D
E

MANHATTAN
PREP

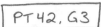

PT42, G3

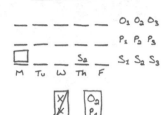

O_1 O_2 O_3
P_1 P_2 P_3
S_1 S_2 S_3

M   Tu   W   Th   F

To Frame or Not to Frame?

Frame! Chunk only has 2 options.

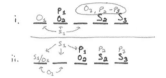

i.
O_1 P_1 $\boxed{O_2, P_2 - P_3}$ S_2 S_3
       O_2

ii.
S_1/O_2 P_1 P_2 P_3
           O_2 S_2 S_3

BIG PAUSE

· 9 things, 15 potential spots. It never says at least one batch per day, so a day could be empty.

· $O_2 P_1$ chunk is highest priority. Its earliest is Tues (forcing O_1 on Mon), and its latest is Wed (forcing $P_2 + P_3$ on Thu + Fri).

---

⑬ A ̶B̶ 4 ̶C̶ 2 ̶D̶ 3 ̶E̶ 3   (A)

⑭ frame 1: Tues, Thu, Fri could have 3
frame 2: Wed, Thu, Fri
Only Mon ≠ 3

(A)
B
C
D
E

---

⑮ ̶A̶ ̶B̶ (C) D E

Frame 1
O_1 S_1
P_1 S_1

⑯ A B C D E

Frame 1
O_1 P_1 ✗ P_2 P_3
O_2 S_2 S_3
  S_1 O_3

(D)

⑰ (A) B C D E

Frame 1
O_1 P_1 O_3 /
O_2 P_2 P_3 S_2 S_3
  S_1

⑱ 1 + 3 could only be together on Wed, so Frame 1

A B C D (E)

O_1 P_1 S_1 $\boxed{P_2 - P_3}$
O_2 O_3 S_2 S_3

PT42, G4

S, T, U

K < M
L < M
L ≠ J
M ≠ J

Exactly 2 columns match.

/   /   /   /   /
‾   ‾T‾ ‾   ☐   ‾T‾
J   K   L   M   O

BIG PAUSE

· O is the "floater" column. We could leave as is, or have 2, or have all 3.

· Interplay between J and M is most important — Whichever of S/T/U J has, M will have the other two.

To Frame or Not to Frame?

Diagram is already very limited (and bulky to re-write). There aren't any chunks or crucial either/or's. Don't frame.

⑲ We know K + O can't be in answer choice, since they have T. M can't be because it reviews 2 plays.

(A)
̶B̶ ∅
̶C̶ J ≠ L
̶D̶ K, ∅
̶E̶ M

⑳ A J, L = 1
(B) M = 2, J = 1
C
D
E

㉑ 3 U's → must go to L, M, O. If J got U, L + M couldn't have U.

/   /   /   /   /
‾   ‾T‾ ‾U‾ ☐   ‾U‾
S/T   ‾T‾
J   K   L   M   O

̶A̶
̶B̶
̶C̶
̶D̶
(E)

㉒ Everyone who has T must include K and O.
̶A̶ O?
̶B̶] either M or J must have T
̶C̶
(D)
̶E̶ K?

㉓ Using inference from Q22, either M or J must have T, so if J ≠ T → M = T.

A
B
̶C̶
(D)
̶E̶

Go beyond books. Try us for free.

In Person

Find an LSAT course near you and attend the first session free, no strings attached.

Find your city at manhattanprep.com/lsat/classes

Online

Enjoy the flexibility of prepping from home or the office with our online course.

See the full schedule at manhattanprep.com/lsat/classes

On Demand

Prep where you are, when you want with LSAT Interact™— our on-demand course.

Try multiple full lessons for free at manhattanprep.com/lsat/interact

Not sure which is right for you? Try all three! Or, give us a call, and we'll help you figure out which program fits you best.

Toll-Free U.S. Number 800.576.4628 | International 001 212.721.7400 | Email lsat@manhattanprep.com